Introduction to
Health Care
Management

Edited by

Sharon B. Buchbinder, RN, PhD
Professor and Program Coordinator
MS in Healthcare Management Program
School of Graduate and Professional Studies
Stevenson University
Owings Mills, Maryland

Nancy H. Shanks, PhD
Professor Emeritus
Department of Health Professions
Health Care Management Program
Metropolitan State University of Denver
Denver, Colorado

JONES & BARTLETT
LEARNING

World Headquarters
Jones & Bartlett Learning
5 Wall Street
Burlington, MA 01803
978-443-5000
info@jblearning.com
www.jblearning.com

Jones & Bartlett Learning books and products are available through most bookstores and online booksellers. To contact Jones & Bartlett Learning directly, call 800-832-0034, fax 978-443-8000, or visit our website, www.jblearning.com.

Substantial discounts on bulk quantities of Jones & Bartlett Learning publications are available to corporations, professional associations, and other qualified organizations. For details and specific discount information, contact the special sales department at Jones & Bartlett Learning via the above contact information or send an email to specialsales@jblearning.com.

Production Credits

VP, Executive Publisher: David D. Cella
Publisher: Michael Brown
Associate Editor: Lindsey Mawhiney Sousa
Associate Editor: Nicholas Alakel
Associate Production Editor: Rebekah Linga
Senior Marketing Manager: Sophie Fleck Teague
Manufacturing and Inventory Control Supervisor: Amy Bacus

Composition: Integra Software Services Pvt. Ltd.
Cover Design: Kristin E. Parker
Rights & Media Specialist: Merideth Tumasz
Media Development Editor: Shannon Sheehan
Cover and Title Page Image:
   © Yegor Korzh/ShutterStock, Inc.
Printing and Binding: LSC Communications
Cover Printing: LSC Communications

10950-4

Library of Congress Cataloging-in-Publication Data
Names: Buchbinder, Sharon Bell, editor. | Shanks, Nancy H., editor.
Title: Introduction to health care management / [edited by] Sharon B.
   Buchbinder and Nancy H. Shanks.
Description: Third edition. | Burlington, Massachusetts : Jones & Bartlett
   Learning, [2015] | Includes bibliographical references and index.
Identifiers: LCCN 2015040132 | ISBN 9781284081015 (paper)
Subjects: | MESH: Health Services Administration. | Efficiency,
   Organizational. | Health Care Costs. | Leadership.
Classification: LCC RA971 | NLM W 84.1 | DDC 362.1–dc23 LC record available at http://lccn.loc.gov/2015040132

6048

Printed in the United States of America
21 20 19   10 9 8 7 6

We dedicate this book to our loving husbands,
Dale Buchbinder and Rick Shanks—
Who coached, collaborated, and coerced us to
"FINISH THE THIRD EDITION!"

Contents

CHAPTER 13 Teamwork. 363

Sharon B. Buchbinder and Jon M. Thompson

CHAPTER 14 Addressing Health Disparities: Cultural
Proficiency 397

Nancy K. Sayre

Foreword

In the U.S., health care is the largest industry and the second-largest employer, with more than 11 million jobs. This continuous growth trend is a result of many consequences, including: the large, aging Baby Boomer population, whose members are remaining active later in life, contributing to an increase in the demand for medical services; the rapidly changing financial structure and increasingly complex regulatory environment of health care; the integration of health care delivery systems, restructuring of work, and an increased focus on preventive care; and the ubiquitous technological innovations, requiring unceasing educational training and monitoring.

Given this tremendous growth and the aforementioned causes of it, it is not surprising that among the fastest-growing disciplines, according to federal statistics, is health care management, which is projected to grow 23% in the next decade. Supporting this growth are the increasing numbers of undergraduate programs in health care management, health services administration, and health planning and policy—with over 300 programs in operation nationwide today.

The health care manager's job description is constantly evolving to adapt to this hyper-turbulent environment. Health care managers will be called on to improve efficiency in health care facilities and the quality of the care provided; to manage, direct, and coordinate health services in a variety of settings, from long-term care facilities and hospitals to medical group practices; and to minimize costs and maximize efficiencies, while also ensuring that the services provided are the best possible.

As the person in charge of a health care facility, a health care administrator's duties can be varied and complex. Handling such responsibilities requires a mix of business administration skills and knowledge of health services, as well as the federal and state laws and regulations that govern the industry.

Written by leading scholars in the field, this compendium provides future and current health care managers with the foundational knowledge needed to succeed. Drs. Buchbinder and Shanks, with their many years of clinical, practitioner, administration, and academic experience, have assembled experts in all aspects of health care management to share their knowledge and experiences. These unique viewpoints, shared in both the content and case studies accompanying each chapter, provide valuable insight into the health care industry and delve into the core competencies required of today's health care managers: leadership, critical thinking, strategic planning, finance and accounting, managing human resources and professionals, ethical and legal concerns, and information and technology management. Contributing authors include clinicians, administrators, professors, and students, allowing for a variety of perspectives.

Faculty will also benefit from the depth and breadth of content coverage spanning all classes in an undergraduate health care management curriculum. Its most appropriate utility may be found in introductory management courses; however, the vast array of cases would bring value to courses in health care ethics, managerial finance, quality management, and organizational behavior.

This text will serve as a cornerstone document for students in health management educational programs and provide them with the insight necessary to be effective health care managers. Students will find this textbook an indispensable resource to utilize both during their academic programs, as well as when they enter the field of health care management. It is already on its way to becoming one of the "classics" in the field!

Dawn Oetjen, PhD
Associate Dean, Administration and Faculty Affairs
College of Health and Public Affairs
University of Central Florida
Orlando, FL

Preface

The third edition of *Introduction to Health Care Management* is driven by our continuing desire to have an excellent textbook that meets the needs of the health care management field, health care management educators, and students enrolled in health care management programs around the world. The inspiration for the first edition of this book came over a good cup of coffee and a deep-seated unhappiness with the texts available in 2004. This edition builds on the strengths of the first two editions and is based on an ongoing conversation with end users—instructors and students—from all types of higher education institutions and all types of delivery modalities. Whether your institution is a traditional "bricks and mortar" school or a fully online one, this book and its ancillary materials are formatted for your ease of use and adoption.

For this edition, many of the same master teachers and researchers with expertise in each topic revised and updated their chapters. Several new contributors stepped forward and wrote completely new cases for this text because we listened to you, our readers and users. With a track record of more than eight years in the field, we learned exactly what did or did not work in the classrooms and online, so we further enhanced and refined our student- and professor-friendly textbook. We are grateful to all our authors for their insightful, well-written chapters and our abundant, realistic case studies.

As before, this textbook will be useful to a wide variety of students and programs. Undergraduate students in health care management, nursing, public health, nutrition, athletic training, and allied health programs will find the writing to be engaging. In addition, students in graduate programs in discipline-specific areas, such as business administration, nursing, pharmacy, occupational therapy, public administration, and public health, will find the materials both theory-based and readily applicable to real-world settings. With four decades of experience in higher education, we know first and foremost that teaching and learning are *not* solo sports, but a team effort—a *contact* sport. There must be a give-and-take between the students and the instructors for deep learning to take place. This text uses active learning methods to achieve this goal. Along with lively writing and content critical for a foundation in health care management, this third edition continues to provide realistic information that can be applied immediately to the real world of health care management. In addition to revised and updated chapters from the second edition, there are learning objectives, discussion questions, and case studies included for each chapter, with additional instructors' resources online and Instructor's

Guides for all of the case studies. PowerPoint slides, Test Bank items, and research sources are also included for each chapter, as well as a glossary. A sample syllabus is also provided. Specifically, the third edition contains:

- Significantly revised chapters on organizational behavior and management thinking, quality improvement, and information technology.
- Revisions and updates to all chapters, including current data and recent additions to the literature.
- A new emphasis on research that is ongoing in each of the areas of health care.
- A new chapter on a diverse group of emerging issues in health care management including: re-emerging outbreaks, vaccine-preventable diseases, and deaths; bioterrorism in health care settings; human trafficking; violence in health care settings; medical tourism; and consumer-directed health care.
- Forty cases in the last chapter, 26 of which are new or totally revised for this edition. They cover a wide variety of settings and an assortment of health care management topics. At the end of each chapter, at least one specific case study is identified and linked to the content of that chapter. Many chapters have multiple cases.
- Guides for all 40 cases provided with online materials. These will be beneficial to instructors as they evaluate student performance and will enable professors at every level of experience to hit the ground running on that first day of classes.
- Totally revised test banks for each chapter, providing larger pools of questions and addressing our concerns that answers to the previous test banks could be purchased online.

Never underestimate the power of a good cup of joe. We hope you enjoy this book as much as we enjoyed revising it. May your classroom and online discussions be filled with active learning experiences, may your teaching be filled with good humor and fun, and may your coffee cup always be full.

Sharon B. Buchbinder, RN, PhD
Stevenson University

Nancy H. Shanks, PhD
Metropolitan State University of Denver

Acknowledgments

This third edition is the result of what has now been a 10-year process involving many of the leaders in excellence in undergraduate health care management education. We continue to be deeply grateful to the Association of University Programs in Health Administration (AUPHA) faculty, members, and staff for all the support, both in time and expertise, in developing the proposal for this textbook and for providing us with excellent feedback for each edition.

More than 20 authors have made this contributed text a one-of-a-kind book. Not only are our authors expert teachers and practitioners in their disciplines and research niches, they are also practiced teachers and mentors. As we read each chapter and case study, we could hear the voices of each author. It has been a privilege and honor to work with each and every one of them: Mohamad Ali, Dale Buchbinder, Susan Casciani, Donna Cox, Amy Dore, Brenda Freshman, Callie Heyne, Ritamarie Little, Sheila McGinnis, Mike Moran, Patricia Patrician, Lou Rubino, Sharon Saracino, Grant Savage, Nancy Sayre, Windsor Sherrill, Jon Thompson, Eric Williams, and Kevin Zeiler.

And, finally, and never too often, we thank our husbands, Dale Buchbinder and Rick Shanks, who listened to long telephone conversations about the book's revisions, trailed us to meetings and dinners, and served us wine with our whines. We love you and could not have done this without you.

About the Editors

Sharon B. Buchbinder, RN, PhD, is currently Professor and Program Coordinator of the MS in Healthcare Management Program at Stevenson University in Owings Mills, Maryland. Prior to this, she was Professor and Chair of the Department of Health Science at Towson University and President of the American Hospital Management Group Corporation, MASA Healthcare Co., a health care management education and health care delivery organization based in Owings Mills, Maryland. For more than four decades, Dr. Buchbinder has worked in many aspects of health care as a clinician, researcher, association executive, and academic. With a PhD in public health from the University of Illinois School of Public Health, she brings this blend of real-world experience and theoretical constructs to undergraduate and graduate face-to-face and online classrooms, where she is constantly reminded of how important good teaching really is. She is past chair of the Board of the Association of University Programs in Health Administration (AUPHA) and coauthor of the Bugbee Falk Award–winning *Career Opportunities in Health Care Management: Perspectives from the Field.* Dr. Buchbinder also coauthors *Cases in Health Care Management* with Nancy Shanks and Dale Buchbinder.

Nancy H. Shanks, PhD, has extensive experience in the health care field. For 12 years, she worked as a health services researcher and health policy analyst and later served as the executive director of a grant-making, fund-raising foundation that was associated with a large multihospital system in Denver. During the last 20 years, Dr. Shanks has been a health care administration educator at Metropolitan State University of Denver, where she has taught a variety of undergraduate courses in health services management, organization, research, human resources management, strategic management, and law. She is currently an Emeritus Professor of Health Care Management and an affiliate faculty member, after having served as Chair of the Department of Health Professions for seven years. Dr. Shanks's research interests have focused on health policy issues, such as providing access to health care for the uninsured.

Contributors

Mohamad A. Ali, MBA, MHA, CBM
Healthcare Strategy Consultant
MASA Healthcare, LLC
Washington, DC

Dale Buchbinder, MD, FACS
Chairman, Department of Surgery
   and Clinical Professor of Surgery
The University of Maryland Medical School
Good Samaritan Hospital
Baltimore, MD

Susan Casciani, MSHA, MBA, FACHE
Adjunct Professor
Stevenson University
Owings Mills, MD

Donna M. Cox, PhD
Professor and Director
Alcohol, Tobacco, and Other Drugs Prevention Center
Department of Health Science
Towson University
Towson, MD

Amy Dore, DHA
Associate Professor, Health Care Management Program
Department of Health Professions
Metropolitan State University of Denver
Denver, CO

Brenda Freshman, PhD
Associate Professor
Health Administration Program
California State University, Long Beach
Long Beach, CA

Callie E. Heyne, BS
Research Associate
Clemson University
Clemson, SC

Ritamarie Little, MS, RD
Associate Director
Marilyn Magaram Center for Food Science,
    Nutrition, & Dietetics
California State University, Northridge
Northridge, CA

Sheila K. McGinnis, PhD
Healthcare Transformation Director
City College
Montana State University, Billings
Billings, MT

Michael Moran, DHA
Adjunct Faculty
School of Business
University of Colorado, Denver
Denver, CO

Patricia A. Patrician, PhD, RN, FAAN
Colonel, U.S. Army (Retired)
Donna Brown Banton Endowed Professor
School of Nursing
University of Alabama, Birmingham
Birmingham, AL

Louis Rubino, PhD, FACHE
Professor & Program Director
Health Administration Program
Health Sciences Department
California State University, Northridge
Northridge, CA

Sharon Saracino, RN, CRRN
Patient Safety Officer
Nursing Department
Allied Services Integrated Health Care
    System–Heinz Rehab
Wilkes-Barre, PA

Grant T. Savage, PhD
Professor of Management
Management, Information Systems, & Quantitative
    Methods Department
University of Alabama, Birmingham
Birmingham, AL

Nancy K. Sayre, DHEd, PA, MHS
Department Chair
Department of Health Professions
Coordinator, Health Care Management Program
Assistant Professor, Health Care Management
    Program
Metropolitan State University of Denver
Denver, CO

Windsor Westbrook Sherrill, PhD
Professor of Public Health Sciences
Associate Vice President for Health Research
Clemson University
Clemson, SC

Jon M. Thompson, PhD
Professor, Health Services Administration
Director, Health Services Administration Program
James Madison University
Harrisonburg, VA

Eric S. Williams, PhD
Associate Dean of Assessment and Continuous Improvement
Professor of Health Care Management
Minnie Miles Research Professor
Culverhouse College of Commerce
University of Alabama
Tuscaloosa, AL

Kevin D. Zeiler, JD, MBA, EMT-P
Associate Professor, Health Care Management Program
Department of Health Professions
Metropolitan State University of Denver
Denver, CO

CHAPTER 1

An Overview of Health Care Management

Jon M. Thompson, Sharon B. Buchbinder, and Nancy H. Shanks

LEARNING OBJECTIVES

By the end of this chapter, the student will be able to:

- Define healthcare management and the role of the health care manager;
- Differentiate among the functions, roles, and responsibilities of health care managers;
- Compare and contrast the key competencies of health care managers; and
- Identify current areas of research in health care management.

INTRODUCTION

Any introductory text in health care management must clearly define the profession of health care management and discuss the major functions, roles, responsibilities, and competencies for health care managers. These topics are the focus of this chapter. Health care management is a growing profession with increasing opportunities in both direct care and non–direct care settings. As defined by Buchbinder and Thompson (2010, pp. 33–34), **direct care settings** are "those organizations that provide care directly to a patient, resident or client who seeks services from the organization." **Non–direct care settings** are not directly involved in providing care to persons needing health services, but rather support the care of individuals through products and services made available to direct care settings. The Bureau of Labor Statistics (BLS, 2014) indicates health care management is one of the fastest-growing occupations, due to the expansion and diversification of the health care industry. The BLS projects that employment of medical and health services managers is expected to grow 23% from 2012 to 2022, faster than the average for all occupations (see Figure 1-1).

These managers are expected to be needed in both inpatient and outpatient care facilities, with the greatest growth in managerial positions occurring in outpatient centers, clinics, and physician practices. Hospitals, too, will experience a large number of managerial jobs because of the hospital sector's large size. Moreover, these estimates do not reflect the significant growth in managerial positions in non–direct care settings, such as consulting firms, pharmaceutical companies, associations, and medical equipment companies. These non–direct care settings provide significant assistance to direct care organizations, and since the number of direct care managerial positions is expected to increase significantly, it is expected that growth will also occur in managerial positions in non–direct care settings.

Health care management is the profession that provides leadership and direction to organizations that deliver personal health services and to divisions, departments, units, or services within those organizations. Health care management provides significant rewards

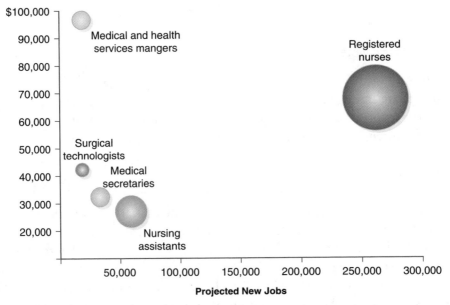

FIGURE 1-1 Occupations with the Most New Jobs in Hospitals, Projected 2012–2022. Employment and Median Annual Wages, May 2013

Source: U.S. Bureau of Labor Statistics, Employment Projections program (projected new jobs, 2012–2022) and Occupational Employment Statistics Survey (employment and median annual wages, May 2013).

and personal satisfaction for those who want to make a difference in the lives of others. This chapter gives a comprehensive overview of health care management as a profession. Understanding the roles, responsibilities, and functions carried out by health care managers is important for those individuals considering the field to make informed decisions about the "fit." This chapter provides a discussion of key management roles, responsibilities, and functions, as well as management positions at different levels within health care organizations. In addition, descriptions of supervisory level, mid-level, and senior management positions within different organizations are provided.

THE NEED FOR MANAGERS AND THEIR PERSPECTIVES

Health care organizations are complex and dynamic. The nature of organizations requires that managers provide leadership, as well as the supervision and coordination of employees. Organizations were created to achieve goals beyond the capacity of any single individual. In health care organizations, the scope and complexity of tasks carried out in provision of services are so great that individual staff operating on their own could not get the job done. Moreover, the necessary tasks in producing services in health care organizations require the coordination of many highly specialized disciplines that must work together seamlessly. Managers are needed to ensure organizational tasks are carried out in the best way possible to achieve organizational goals and that appropriate resources, including financial and human resources, are adequate to support the organization.

Health care managers are appointed to positions of authority, where they shape the organization by making important decisions. Such decisions relate, for example, to recruitment and development of staff, acquisition of technology, service additions and reductions, and allocation and spending of financial resources. Decisions made by health care managers not only focus on ensuring that the patient receives the most appropriate, timely, and effective services possible, but also address achievement of performance targets that are desired by the manager. Ultimately, decisions made by an individual manager impact the organization's overall performance.

Managers must consider two domains as they carry out various tasks and make decisions (Thompson, 2007). These domains are termed external and internal domains (see Table 1-1). The **external domain** refers to the influences, resources, and activities that exist outside the boundary of the organization but that significantly affect the organization. These factors include community needs, population characteristics, and reimbursement from commercial insurers, as well as government plans, such as the Children's Health Insurance Plans (CHIP), Medicare, and Medicaid. The **internal domain** refers to those

---

TABLE 1-1 Domains of Health Services Administration

External	Internal
Community demographics/need	Staffing
Licensure	Budgeting
Accreditation	Quality services
Regulations	Patient satisfaction
Stakeholder demands	Physician relations
Competitors	Financial performance
Medicare and Medicaid	Technology acquisition
Managed care organizations/insurers	New service development

Source: Thompson, 2007.

---

areas of focus that managers need to address on a daily basis, such as ensuring the appropriate number and types of staff, financial performance, and quality of care. These internal areas reflect the operation of the organization where the manager has the most control. Keeping the dual perspective requires significant balance and effort on the part of management in order to make good decisions.

MANAGEMENT: DEFINITION, FUNCTIONS, AND COMPETENCIES

As discussed earlier, management is needed to support and coordinate the services provided within health care organizations. **Management** has been defined as the process, comprised of social and technical functions and activities, occurring within organizations for the purpose of accomplishing predetermined objectives through human and other resources (Longest, Rakich, & Darr, 2000). Implicit in the definition is that managers work through and with other people, carrying out technical and interpersonal activities to achieve the desired objectives of the organization. Others have stated that a manager is anyone in the organization who supports and is responsible for the work performance of one or more other persons (Lombardi & Schermerhorn, 2007).

While most beginning students of health care management tend to focus on the role of the senior manager or lead administrator of an organization, it should be realized that management occurs through many others who may not have "manager" in their position title. Examples of some of these managerial positions in health care organizations include supervisor, coordinator, and director, among others (see Table 1-2). These levels of managerial control are discussed in more detail in the next section.

TABLE 1-2 Managerial Positions, by Organizational Setting

Organizational Setting	Examples of Managerial Positions
Physician practice	Practice Manager
	Director of Medical Records
	Supervisor, Billing Office
Nursing home	Administrator
	Manager, Business Office
	Director, Food Services
	Admissions Coordinator
	Supervisor, Environmental Services
Hospital	Chief Executive Officer
	Vice President, Marketing
	Clinical Nurse Manager
	Director, Revenue Management
	Supervisor, Maintenance

Managers implement six management functions as they carry out the process of management (Longest et al., 2000):

Planning: This function requires the manager to set a direction and determine what needs to be accomplished. It means setting priorities and determining performance targets.

Organizing: This management function refers to the overall design of the organization or the specific division, unit, or service for which the manager is responsible. Furthermore, it means designating reporting relationships and intentional patterns of interaction. Determining positions, teamwork assignments, and distribution of authority and responsibility are critical components of this function.

Staffing: This function refers to acquiring and retaining human resources. It also refers to developing and maintaining the workforce through various strategies and tactics.

Controlling: This function refers to monitoring staff activities and performance and taking the appropriate actions for corrective action to increase performance.

Directing: The focus in this function is on initiating action in the organization through effective leadership and motivation of, and communication with, subordinates.

Decision making: This function is critical to all of the aforementioned management functions and means making effective decisions based on consideration of benefits and the drawbacks of alternatives.

In order to effectively carry out these functions, the manager needs to possess several key competencies. Katz (1974) identified key competencies of the effective manager, including conceptual, technical, and interpersonal skills. The term **competency** refers to a state in which an individual has the requisite or adequate ability or qualities to perform certain functions (Ross, Wenzel, & Mitlyng, 2002). These are defined as follows:

Conceptual skills are those skills that involve the ability to critically analyze and solve complex problems. Examples: a manager conducts an analysis of the best way to provide a service or determines a strategy to reduce patient complaints regarding food service.

Technical skills are those skills that reflect expertise or ability to perform a specific work task. Examples: a manager develops and implements a new incentive compensation program for staff or designs and implements modifications to a computer-based staffing model.

Interpersonal skills are those skills that enable a manager to communicate with and work well with other individuals, regardless of whether they are peers, supervisors, or subordinates. Examples: a manager counsels an employee whose performance is below expectation or communicates to subordinates the desired performance level for a service for the next fiscal year.

MANAGEMENT POSITIONS: THE CONTROL IN THE ORGANIZATIONAL HEIRARCHY

Management positions within health care organizations are not confined to the top level; because of the size and complexity of many health care organizations, management positions are found throughout the organization. Management positions exist at the lower, middle, and upper levels; the upper level is referred to as senior management. The hierarchy of management means that authority, or power, is delegated downward in the organization, and lower-level managers have less authority than higher-level managers, whose scope of responsibility is much greater. For example, a vice president of Patient Care Services in a hospital may be in charge of several different functional areas, such as nursing, diagnostic imaging services, and laboratory services; in contrast, a director of Medical Records—a lower-level position—has responsibility only for the function of patient medical records. Furthermore, a supervisor within the Environmental Services department may have responsibility for only a small housekeeping staff, whose work is critical, but confined to a defined area of the organization. Some managerial positions, such as those discussed previously, are **line manager** positions because the manager supervises other employees; other managerial positions are **staff manager** positions because they carry out work and advise their bosses, but they do not routinely supervise others. Managerial positions also vary in terms of required expertise or experience. Some positions require extensive knowledge of many substantive areas and significant working experience, and other positions are more appropriate for entry-level managers who have limited or no experience.

The most common organizational structure for health care organizations is a **functional organizational structure**, whose key characteristic is a pyramid-shaped hierarchy that defines the functions carried out and the key management positions assigned to those functions (see Figure 1-2). The size and complexity of the specific health services organization will dictate the particular structure. For example, larger organizations—such as large community hospitals, hospital systems, and academic medical centers—will likely have deep vertical structures reflecting varying levels of administrative control for the organization. This structure is necessary due to the large scope of services provided and the corresponding vast array of administrative and support services that are needed to enable the delivery of clinical services. Other characteristics associated with this functional structure include a strict chain of command and line of reporting, which ensure communication and assignment and evaluation of tasks are carried out in a linear command and control environment. This structure offers key advantages, such as specific divisions of labor and clear lines of reporting and accountability.

Other administrative structures have been adopted by health care organizations, usually in combination with a functional structure. These include matrix, or team-based, models and service line management models. The **matrix model** recognizes that a strict functional structure may limit the organization's flexibility to carry out the work, and that the expertise of other disciplines is needed on a continuous basis. An example of the matrix method is when functional staff, such as nursing and rehabilitation personnel, are assigned to a specific program, such as geriatrics, and they report for programmatic purposes to the program director of the geriatrics department. Another example is when clinical and administrative staff are assigned to a team investigating new services that is headed by a marketing or business development manager. In both of these examples, management would lead staff who traditionally are not under their direct administrative control. Advantages of this structure include improved lateral communication and coordination of services, as well as pooled knowledge.

In **service line management**, a manager is appointed to head a specific clinical service line and has responsibility and accountability for staffing, resource acquisition, budget, and financial control associated with the array of services provided under that service line. Typical examples of service lines include cardiology, oncology (cancer), women's services, physical rehabilitation, and behavioral health (mental health). Service lines can be established within a single organization or may cut across affiliated organizations, such as within a hospital system where services are provided at several different affiliated facilities (Boblitz

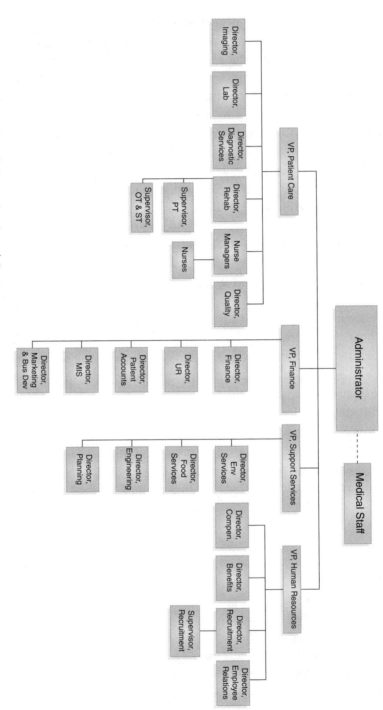

FIGURE 1-2 Functional Organizational Structure

& Thompson, 2005). Some facilities have found that the service line management model for selected clinical services has resulted in many benefits, such as lower costs, higher quality of care, and greater patient satisfaction, compared to other management models (Duffy & Lemieux, 1995). The service line management model is usually implemented within an organization in conjunction with a functional structure, as the organization may choose to give special emphasis and additional resources to one or a few services lines.

FOCUS OF MANAGEMENT: SELF, UNIT/TEAM, AND ORGANIZATION

Effective health care management involves exercising professional judgment and skills and carrying out the aforementioned managerial functions at three levels: self, unit/team, and organization wide. First and foremost, the individual manager must be able to effectively manage himself or herself. This means managing time, information, space, and materials; being responsive and following through with peers, supervisors, and clients; maintaining a positive attitude and high motivation; and keeping a current understanding of management techniques and substantive issues of health care management. Drucker (2005) suggests that managing yourself also involves knowing your strengths, how you perform, your values, where you belong, and what you can contribute, as well as taking responsibility for your relationships. Managing yourself also means developing and applying appropriate technical, interpersonal, and conceptual skills and competencies and being comfortable with them, in order to be able to effectively move to the next level—that of supervising others.

The second focus of management is the unit/team level. The expertise of the manager at this level involves managing others in terms of effectively completing the work. Regardless of whether you are a senior manager, mid-level manager, or supervisor, you will be "supervising" others as expected in your assigned role. This responsibility includes assigning work tasks, review and modification of assignments, monitoring and review of individual performance, and carrying out the management functions described earlier to ensure excellent delivery of services. This focal area is where the actual work gets done. Performance reflects the interaction of the manager and the employee, and it is incumbent on the manager to do what is needed to shape the performance of individual employees. The focus of management at this echelon recognizes the task interdependencies among staff and the close coordination that is needed to ensure that work gets completed efficiently and effectively.

The third management focus is at the organizational level. This focal area reflects the fact that managers must work together as part of the larger organization to ensure organization-wide performance and organizational viability. In other words, the success of the organization depends upon the success of its individual parts, and effective collaboration is needed to ensure that this occurs. The range of clinical and nonclinical activities that occur within a health care organization requires that managers who head individual units work closely with other unit managers to provide services. Sharing of information, collaboration, and communication are essential for success. The hierarchy looks to the contribution of each supervised unit as it pertains to the whole. Individual managers' contributions to the overall performance of the organization—in terms of various performance measures such as cost, quality, satisfaction, and access—are important and measured.

ROLE OF THE MANAGER IN ESTABLISHING AND MAINTAINING ORGANIZATIONAL CULTURE

Every organization has a distinct culture, known as the beliefs, attitudes, and behavior that are shared among organizational members. **Organizational culture** is commonly defined as the character, personality, and experience of organizational life i.e., what the organization really "is" (Scott, Mannion, Davies, & Marshall, 2003). Culture prescribes the way things are done, and is defined, shaped, and reinforced by the management team. All managers play a role in establishing the culture of a health care organization, and in taking the necessary leadership action to sustain, and in some cases change, the culture. Culture is shaped by the values, mission, and vision for the organization. **Values** are principles the organization believes in and shape the organization's purpose, goals, and day-to-day behaviors. Adopted values provide the foundation for the organization's activities and include such principles as respect, quality service, and innovation. The **mission** of the organization is its fundamental purpose, or what the organization seeks to achieve. The **vision** of the organization specifies the desired future state for the organization and reflects what the organization wants to be known and recognized for in the future. Statements of values, mission, and vision result from the organizational strategic planning process. These statements are communicated widely throughout the organization and to the community and shape organizational strategic and operational actions. Increasingly, organizations are establishing codes of conduct or **standards of behavior** that all employees must follow (Studer, 2003). These standards of behavior align with the values, mission, and vision. The role of managers in the oversight of standards of behavior is critical in several respects: for setting expectations for staff behavior, modelling the behavior, measuring staff performance, and improving staff performance. Mid-level and lower-level managers are instrumental to organization-wide adoption and embracing of the culture as they communicate desired behaviors and reinforce culture through modelling expectations through their own behaviors. For example, a value of customer service or patient focus requires that managers ensure proper levels of service by their employees via clarifying expectations and providing internal customer service to their own staff and other managers. Furthermore, managers can measure and evaluate employee compliance with organizational values and standards of behavior by reviewing employee performance and working with staff to improve performance. Performance evaluation will be explored in a later chapter in this text.

ROLE OF THE MANAGER IN TALENT MANAGEMENT

In order to effectively master the focal areas of management and carry out the required management functions, management must have the requisite number and types of highly motivated employees. From a strategic perspective, health care organizations compete for labor, and it is commonly accepted today that high-performing health care organizations are dependent upon individual human performance, as discussed further in Chapter 12. Many observers have advocated for health care organizations to view their employees as strategic assets who can create a competitive advantage (Becker, Huselid, & Ulrich, 2001). Therefore, human resources management has been replaced in many health care organizations with **talent management**. The focus has shifted to securing and retaining the talent needed to do the job in the best way, rather than simply filling a role (Huselid, Beatty, & Becker, 2005). As a result, managers are now focusing on effectively managing talent and workforce issues because of the link to organizational performance (Griffith, 2009).

Beyond recruitment, managers are concerned about developing and retaining those staff who are excellent performers. Many health care organizations are creating high-involvement organizations that identify and meet employee needs through their jobs and the larger organizational work setting (Becker et al., 2001). One of the critical responsibilities of managers in talent management is promoting **employee engagement**, which describes the motivation and commitment of staff to contribute to the organization. There are several strategies used by managers to develop and sustain employee engagement, as well as to develop and maintain excellent performers. These include formal methods such as offering training programs; providing leadership development programs; identifying employee needs and measuring employee satisfaction through engagement surveys; providing continuing education, especially for clinical and technical fields; and enabling job enrichment. In addition, managers use informal methods such as conducting periodic employee reviews, soliciting employee feedback, conducting rounds and employee huddles, offering employee suggestion programs, and other methods of managing employee relations and engagement. These topics are explored in more detail in a later chapter in this book.

ROLE OF THE MANAGER IN ENSURING HIGH PERFORMANCE

At the end of the day, the role of the manager is to ensure that the unit, service, division, or organization he or she leads achieves high performance. What exactly is meant by high performance? To understand performance, one has to appreciate the value of setting and meeting goals and objectives for the unit/service and organization as a whole, in terms of the work that is being carried out. Goals and objectives are desired end points for activity and reflect strategic and operational directions for the organization. They are specific, measurable, meaningful, and time oriented. Goals and objectives for individual units should reflect the overarching needs and expectations of the organization as a whole because, as the reader will recall, all entities are working together to achieve high levels of overall organizational performance. Studer (2003) views the organization as needing to be results oriented, with identified pillars of excellence as a framework for the specific goals of the organization. These pillars are people (employees, patients, and physicians), service, quality, finance, and growth. Griffith (2000) refers to high-performing organizations as being championship organizations—that is, they expect to perform well on different yet meaningful measures of performance. Griffith further defines the "championship processes" and the need to develop performance measures in each of the following: governance and strategic management; clinical quality, including customer satisfaction; clinical organization (caregivers); financial planning; planning and marketing; information services; human resources; and plant and supplies. For each championship process, the organization should establish measures of desired performance that will guide the organization. Examples of measures include medication errors, surgical complications, patient satisfaction, staff turnover rates, employee satisfaction, market share, profit margin, and revenue growth, among others. In turn, respective divisions, units, and services will set targets and carry out activities to address key performance processes. The manager's job, ultimately, is to ensure these targets are met by carrying out the previously discussed management functions. A control process for managers has been advanced by Ginter, Swayne, and Duncan (2002) that describes five key steps in the performance management process: set objectives, measure performance, compare performance with objectives, determine reasons for deviation, and take corrective action. Management's job is to ensure that performance is maintained or, if below expectations, improved.

Stakeholders, including insurers, state and federal governments, and consumer advocacy groups, are expecting, and in many cases demanding, acceptable levels of performance in health care organizations. These groups want to make sure that services are provided in a safe, convenient, low-cost, and high-quality environment. For example, The Joint Commission (formerly JCAHO) has set minimum standards for health care facilities operations that ensure quality, the National Committee for Quality Assurance (NCQA) has set standards for measuring performance of health plans, and the Centers for Medicare and Medicaid Services (CMS) has established a website that compares hospital performance along a number of critical dimensions. In addition, CMS has provided incentives to health care organizations by paying for performance on measures of clinical care and not paying for care resulting from **never events** i.e., shocking health outcomes that should never occur in a health care setting such as wrong site surgery (e.g., the wrong leg) or hospital-acquired infections (Agency for Healthcare Research and Quality, n.d.). Health insurers also have implemented pay-for-performance programs for health care organizations based on various quality and customer service measures.

In addition to meeting the reporting requirements of the aforementioned organizations, many health care organizations today use varying methods of measuring and reporting the performance measurement process. Common methods include developing and using dashboards or balanced scorecards that allow for a quick interpretation of organizational performance across a number of key measures (Curtright, Stolp-Smith, & Edell, 2000; Pieper, 2005). Senior administration uses these methods to measure and communicate performance on the total organization to the governing board and other critical constituents. Other managers use these methods at the division, unit, or service level to profile its performance. In turn, these measures are also used to evaluate managers' performance and are considered in decisions by the manager's boss regarding compensation adjustments, promotions, increased or reduced responsibility, training and development, and, if necessary, termination or reassignment.

ROLE OF THE MANAGER IN LEADERSHIP DEVELOPMENT AND SUCCESSION PLANNING

Because health care organizations are complex and experience challenges from internal and external environments, the need for leadership skills of managers at all levels of the organization has become paramount. Successful organizations that demonstrate high operational performance depend on strong leaders (Squazzo, 2009). Senior executives have a primary role in ensuring managers throughout the organization have the knowledge and skills to provide effective leadership to achieve desired levels of organizational performance. Senior management also plays a key role in succession planning to ensure vacancies at mid- and upper levels of the organization due to retirements, departures, and promotions are filled with capable leaders. Therefore, key responsibilities of managers are to develop future leaders through leadership development initiatives and to engage in succession planning.

Leadership development programs are broadly comprised of several specific organizational services that are offered to enhance leadership competencies and skills of managerial staff in health care organizations. **Leadership development** is defined as educational interventions and skill-building activities designed to improve the leadership capabilities of individuals (Kim & Thompson, 2012; McAlearney, 2005). Such initiatives not only serve to increase leadership skills and behaviors, but also ensure stability within organizational talent and culture through career advancement and succession planning (Burt, 2005). In order to embrace leadership development, managers provide technical and psychological support to the staff through a range of leadership development activities:

Leadership development program: Training and leadership development on a variety of required topics, through a formally designated program, using structured learning and competency-based assessment using various formats, media, and locations (Kim & Thompson, 2012)

Courses on leadership and management: Didactic training through specific courses offered face-to-face, online, or in hybrid form (Garman, 2010; Kim & Thompson, 2012)

Mentoring: Formal methods used by the organization for matching aspiring leaders with mid-level and senior executives to assist in their learning and personal growth (Garman, 2010; Landry & Bewley, 2010)

Personal development coaching: Usually reserved for upper-level executives; these formal organizational efforts assist in improving performance by shaping attitudes and behavior and focusing on personal skills development (Garman, 2010; Scott, 2009)

Job enlargement: The offering of expanded responsibilities, developmental assignments, and special projects to individuals to cultivate leadership skills for advancement advance within the organization (Fernandez-Aaroz, 2014; Garman, 2010; Landry & Bewley, 2010)

360-degree performance feedback: Expensive, labor-intensive, and usually reserved for upper-level executives; a multisource feedback approach where an individual staff member or manager receives an assessment of performance from several key individuals (e.g., peers, superiors, other managers, and subordinates) regarding performance and opportunities for improvement (Garman, 2010; Landry & Bewley, 2010)

Leadership development programs have shown positive results. For example, health systems report benefits such as improvement of skills and quality of the workforce, enhancing organizational efficiency in educational activities, and reducing staff turnover and related expenses when leadership training is tied to organization-wide strategic priorities (McAlearney, 2005). In addition, hospitals with leadership development programs have been found to have higher volumes of patients, higher occupancy, higher net patient revenue, and higher total profit margin when compared to hospitals without these programs (Thompson & Kim, 2013). Studies have also shown that leadership development programs in health systems are related to greater focus on employee growth and development, improved employee retention, and greater focus on organizational strategic priorities (McAlearney, 2010). Finally, within a single health system, a leadership development program led to greater market share, reduced employee turnover, and improved core quality measures (Ogden, 2007). However, one of the key drawbacks to leadership development programs is the cost of developing and operating the programs (Squazzo, 2009).

Due to the competitive nature of health care organizations and the need for highly motivated and skilled employees, managers are faced with the challenge of succession planning for their organizations. **Succession planning** refers to the concept of taking actions to ensure staff can move up in management roles within the organization to replace those managers who retire or move to other opportunities in other organizations. Succession planning has most recently been emphasized at the senior level of organizations, in part due to the large number of retirements that are anticipated from Baby Boomer chief executive officers (CEOs) (Burt, 2005). To continue the emphasis on high performance within health care organizations, CEOs and other senior managers are interested in finding and nurturing leadership talent within their organizations who can assume the responsibility and carry forward the important work of these organizations.

Health care organizations are currently engaged in several practices to address leadership succession needs. First, mentoring programs for junior management that includes the participation of senior management have been advocated as a good way to prepare future health care leaders (Rollins, 2003). Mentoring studies show that mentors view their efforts as helpful to the organization (Finley, Ivanitskaya, & Kennedy, 2007). Some observers suggest having many mentors is essential to capturing the necessary scope of expertise, experience, interest, and contacts to maximize professional growth (Broscio & Scherer, 2003). Mentoring middle-level managers for success as they transition to their current positions is also helpful in preparing those managers for future executive leadership roles (Kubica, 2008).

A second method of succession planning is through formal leadership development programs. These programs are intended to identify management potential throughout an organization by targeting specific skill sets of individuals and assessing their match to specific jobs, such as vice president or chief operating officer (COO). One way to implement this is through talent reviews, which, when done annually, help create a pool of existing staff who may be excellent candidates for further leadership development and skill strengthening through the establishment of development plans. Formal programs that are being established by many health care organizations focus on high-potential people (Burt, 2005). Thompson and Kim (2013) found that 48% of community hospitals offered a leadership development program, and McAlearney (2010) reported that about 50% of hospital systems nationwide had an executive-level leadership development program.

However, many health care organizations have developed programs that address leadership development at all levels of the organization, not just the executive level, and require all managers to participate in these programs to strengthen their managerial and leadership skills and to contribute to organizational performance.

ROLE OF THE MANAGER IN INNOVATION AND CHANGE MANAGEMENT

Due to the pace of change in the health services industry and the complexity of health services organizations, the manager plays a significant role in leading innovation and spearheading change management. Health services organizations cannot remain static. The environmental forces discussed earlier in this chapter strongly point to the need for organizations to respond and adapt to these external influences. In addition, achieving and maintaining high performance outcomes or results is dependent on making improvements to the organizational structure and processes. Moreover, managers are encouraged to embrace innovation to identify creative ways to improve service and provide care effectively and efficiently.

Innovation and change management are intricately related, but different, competencies. Hamel (2007) describes management innovation and operational innovation. **Management innovation** addresses the organization's management processes as the practices and routines that determine how the work of management gets conducted on a daily basis. These include such practices as internal communications, employment assessment, project management, and training and development. In contrast, **operational innovation** addresses the organization's business processes. In the health care setting, these include processes such as customer service, procurement of supplies and supply chain changes, care coordination across staff, and development and use of clinical procedures and practices. Some operational innovation is structural in nature and involves acquisition of information and clinical products, such as electronic medical/health records, or a new device or procedure, such as robotic surgery or new medications (Staren, Braun, & Denny, 2010). There are specific skills needed by managers to be innovators in management. These skills include thinking creatively about ways to proactively change management and operational practices to improve the organization. It also involves a willingness to test these innovative practices and assess their impact. Also, a manager must facilitate recruitment and development of employees who embrace creativity and innovation. Having innovative clinical and administrative staff is critical to implementing operational innovation. A culture of innovation depends upon staff who are generating ideas for operational innovation, and the manager is a linchpin in establishing a culture of innovation that supports idea generation. Recent studies of innovative and creative companies found that leaders should rely on all staff collaborating by helping one another and engaging in a dynamic process of seeking and giving feedback, ideas, and assistance (Amabile, Fisher, & Pillemer, 2014). Several barriers to innovation have been identified. These barriers include lack of an innovation culture that supports idea generation, lack of leadership in innovation efforts, and high costs of making innovative changes (Harrington & Voehl, 2010). In addition, formal rules and regulations, professional standards, and administrative policies may all work against innovation (Dhar, Griffin, Hollin, & Kachnowski, 2012). Finally, daily priorities and inertia reflecting the status quo that cause managers to focus on routines and day-to-day tasks limit staff ability to be creative, engage in discovery, and generate ideas (Dhar et al., 2012).

Organizational change, or **change management**, is related to but different from innovation. Organizational change is a structured management approach to improving the organization and its performance. Knowledge of performance gaps is a necessary prerequisite to change management, and managers must routinely assess their operational activities and performance and make adjustments in the work structure and processes to improve performance (Thompson, 2010). Managing organizational change has become a significant responsibility of managers and a key competency for health care managers (Buchbinder & Thompson, 2010). Managing the change process within health care organizations is critical because appropriately and systematically managing change can result in improved organizational performance. However, change is difficult and the change process creates both staff resistance and support for a change.

A process model of change management has been suggested by Longest et al. (2000). This rational, problem-based model identifies four key steps in systematically understanding and managing the change process: (1) identification of the need for change, (2) planning for implementing the change, (3) implementing the change, and (4) evaluating the change.

There are several key management competencies that health care managers need to possess to effectively manage change within their organizations. Thompson (2010) suggests that managers:

- —Embrace change and be a change agent;
- —Employ a change management process;
- —Effectively address support and resistance to change;
- —Use change management to make the organization innovative and successful in the future; and,
- —Recruit staff and succession plan with change management in mind.

ROLE OF THE MANAGER IN HEALTH CARE POLICY

As noted earlier in this chapter, managers must consider both their external and internal domains as they carry out management functions and tasks. One of the critical areas for managing the external world is to be knowledgeable about health policy matters under consideration at the state and federal levels that affect health services organizations and health care delivery. This is particularly true for senior-level managers. This awareness is necessary to influence policy in positive ways that will help the organization and limit any adverse impacts. Staying current with health care policy discussions, participating in deliberations of health policy, and providing input where possible will allow health care management voices to be heard. Because health care is such a popular yet controversial topic in the U.S. today, continuing changes in health care delivery are likely to emanate from the legislative and policy processes at the state and federal levels. For example, the Patient Protection and Affordable Care Act, signed into law in 2010 as a major health care reform initiative, has had significant implications for health care organizations in terms of patient volumes, reimbursement for previously uninsured patients, and the movement to improve population health and develop value-based purchasing. Other recent federal policy changes include cuts in Medicare reimbursement and increases in reporting require-ments. State legislative changes across the country affect reimbursement under Medicaid and the Children's Health Insurance Program, licensure of facilities and staff, certificate of need rules for capital expenditures and facility and service expansions, and state require-ments on mandated health benefits and modified reimbursements for insured individuals that affect services offered by health care organizations.

In order to understand and influence health policy, managers must strive to keep their knowledge current. This can be accomplished through targeted personal learning, net-working with colleagues within and outside of their organizations, and participating in professional associations, such as the American College of Healthcare Executives and the Medical Group Management Association. These organizations, and many others, monitor health policy discussions and advocate for their associations' interests at the state and fed-eral levels. Knowledge gained through these efforts can be helpful in shaping health policy in accordance with the desires of health care managers.

RESEARCH IN HEALTH CARE MANAGEMENT

Current research in management focuses on best practices. For example, the best practices of managers and leaders in ensuring organizational performance has been the focus of work by McAlearney, Robbins, Garman, and Song (2013) and Garman, McAlearney, Harrison, Song, and McHugh (2011). The best practices identified by these researchers include staff engagement, staff acquisition and development, staff frontline empowerment, and leadership alignment and development. Understanding what leaders do to develop their staff and prepare lower-level managers for leadership roles has been a common research focus as well. Leadership development programs have been examined in terms of their structure and impact. McAlearney (2008) surveyed health care organizations and key informants to determine the availability of leadership development programs and their role in improving quality and efficiency, and found these programs enhanced the skills and quality of the workforce, improved efficiency in educational development, and reduced staff turnover. A study of high-performing health organizations found various practices are used to develop leaders internally, including talent reviews to identify candidates for upward movement, career development planning, job rotations, and developmental assignments (McHugh, Garman, McAlearney, Song, & Harrison, 2010). In addition, a 2010 study examined leadership development in health and non-health care organizations and found best practices included 360-degree performance evaluation, mentoring, coaching, and experiential learning (National Center for Healthcare Leadership, 2010). A study of U.S. health systems found about half of health systems offered a leadership development program and also found that leadership development initiatives helped the systems focus on employee growth and development and improved employee retention (McAlearney, 2010). As noted earlier in this chapter, some recent studies have examined the characteristics of leadership development programs in hospitals, finding correlations of programs with size, urban location, and not-for-profit ownership status (Kim and Thompson, 2012; Thompson and Kim, 2013). A new area of management research is the participation of early careerists in leadership development programs, and recent evidence shows that some leadership development activities are of more interest to staff than others (Thompson and Temple, 2015). A number of important areas of management research exist today, and include looking at the effect of leadership development training on specific decision-making by managers, career progression due to participation in leadership development, and the impact of collaboration among staff on firm innovation and performance (Amabile, Fisher, & Pillemer, 2014).

CHAPTER SUMMARY

The profession of health care management is challenging yet rewarding, and requires persons in managerial positions at all levels of the organization to possess sound conceptual, technical, and interpersonal skills to carry out the necessary managerial functions of planning, organizing, staffing, directing, controlling, and decision making. In addition, managers must maintain a dual perspective where they understand the external and internal domains of their organization and the need for development at the self, unit/team, and organization levels. Opportunities exist for managerial talent at all levels of a health care organization, including supervisory, middle-management, and senior-management levels. The role of manager is critical to ensuring a high level of organizational performance, and managers are also instrumental in establishing and maintaining organizational culture, talent recruitment and retention, leadership development and succession planning, innovation and change management, and shaping health care policy.

Note: Portions of this chapter were originally published as "Understanding Health Care Management" in *Career Opportunities in Healthcare Management: Perspectives from the Field*, by Sharon B. Buchbinder and Jon M. Thompson, and an adapted version of this chapter is reprinted here with permission of the publisher.

DISCUSSION QUESTIONS

1. Define health care management and health care managers.

2. Delineate the functions carried out by health care managers and give an example of a task in each function.

3. Explain why interpersonal skills are important in health care management.

4. Compare and contrast three models of organizational design.

5. Why is the health care manager's role in ensuring high performance so critical? Explain.

6. Characterize the health care manager's role in change management and assess the extent to which this has an impact on the success of the change process.

REFERENCES

Agency for Healthcare Research and Quality (AHRQ). (n.d.). Never events. Retrieved from http://www.psnet.ahrq.gov/primer.aspx?primerID=3

Amabile, T., Fisher, C. M., & Pillemer, J. (2014). IDEO's culture of helping. *Harvard Business Review*, *92*, 54–61.

Becker, B. E., Huselid, M. A., & Ulrich, D. (2001). *The HR scorecard: Linking people, strategy, and performance.* Boston, MA: Harvard Business School Press.

Boblitz, M., & Thompson, J. M. (2005). Assessing the feasibility of developing centers of excellence: Six initial steps. *Healthcare Financial Management*, *59*, 72–84.

Broscio, M., & Scherer, J. (2003). Building job security: Strategies for becoming a highly valued contributor. *Journal of Healthcare Management, 48*, 147–151.

Buchbinder, S. B., & Thompson, J. M. (2010). *Career opportunities in health care management: Perspectives from the field.* Sudbury, MA: Jones and Bartlett.

Bureau of Labor Statistics (BLS). (2014). *Occupational outlook handbook 2014 edition.* Retrieved from www.bls.gov/oco/ocos014.htm

Burt, T. (2005). Leadership development as a corporate strategy: Using talent reviews to improve senior management. *Healthcare Executive, 20*, 14–18.

Curtright, J. W., Stolp-Smith, S. C., & Edell, E. S. (2000). Strategic management: Development of a performance measurement system at the Mayo Clinic. *Journal of Healthcare Management, 45*, 58–68.

Dhar, M., Griffin, M., Hollin, I., & Kachnowski, S. (2012). Innovation spaces: Six strategies to inform health care. *The Health Care Manager, 31*, 166–177.

Drucker, P. F. (2005). Managing oneself. *Harvard Business Review, 83*(1), 100–109.

Duffy, J. R., & Lemieux, K. G. (1995, Fall). A cardiac service line approach to patient-centered care. *Nursing Administration Quarterly, 20*, 12–23.

Fernandez-Araoz, C. (2014). 21st century talent spotting. *Harvard Business Review, 92*(6), 46–56.

Finley, F. R., Ivanitskaya, L. V., & Kennedy, M. H. (2007). Mentoring junior healthcare administrators: A description of mentoring practices in 127 U.S. hospitals. *Journal of Healthcare Management, 52*, 260–270.

Garman, A. N. (2010). *Leadership development in the interdisciplinary context.* In B. Freshman, L. Rubino, and Y. R. Chassiakos, (Eds.), *Collaboration across the disciplines in health care* (pp. 43–63). Sudbury, MA: Jones and Bartlett.

Garman, A. N., McAlearney, A. S., Harrison, M. I., Song, P. H., & McHugh, M. (2011). High-performance work systems in health care management, Part 1: Development of an evidence-informed model. *Health Care Management Review, 36*(3), 201–213.

Ginter, P. M., Swayne, L. E., & Duncan, W. J. (2002). *Strategic management of healthcare organizations* (4th ed.). Malden, MA: Blackwell.

Griffith, J. R. (2000). Championship management for healthcare organizations. *Journal of Healthcare Management, 45*, 17–31.

Griffith, J. R. (2009). Finding the frontier of hospital management. *Journal of Healthcare Management, 54*(1), 57–73.

Hamel, G. (2007). *The future of management.* Boston, MA: Harvard Business School Press.

Harrington, H. J., & Voehl, F. (2010). Innovation in health care. *International Journal of Innovation Science, 2*, 13–27.

Huselid, M. A., Beatty, R. W., & Becker, B. E. (2005, December). "A players" or "A" positions? The strategic logic of workforce management. *Harvard Business Review, 83*, 100–117.

Katz, R. L. (1974). Skills of an effective administrator. *Harvard Business Review, 52*, 90–102.

Kim, T. H., & Thompson, J. M. (2012). Organizational and market factors associated with leadership development programs in hospitals: A national study. *Journal of Healthcare Management, 57*(2), 113–132.

Kubica, A. J. (2008). Transitioning middle managers. *Healthcare Executive, 23*, 58–60.

Landry, A. Y., & Bewley, L. W. (2010). Leadership development, succession planning and mentoring. In S. R. Hernandez & S. J. O'Connor (Eds.), *Strategic management of human resources in health services organizations* (3rd ed., pp. 133–146). Clifton Park, NY: Delmar.

Lombardi, D. M., & Schermerhorn, J. R. (2007). *Healthcare management*. Hoboken, NJ: John Wiley.

Longest, B. B., Rakich, J. S., & Darr, K. (2000). *Managing health services organizations and systems*. Baltimore, MD: Health Professions Press.

McAlearney, A. S. (2005). Exploring mentoring and leadership development in health care organizations: Experience and opportunities. *Career Development International, 10*(6/7), 493–511.

McAlearney, A. S. (2008). Using leadership development programs to improve quality and efficiency in healthcare. *Journal of Healthcare Management, 53*(5), 319–332.

McAlearney, A. S. (2010). Executive leadership development in U.S. health systems. *Journal of Healthcare Management, 55*(3), 206–224.

McAlearney, A. S., Robbins, J., Garman, A. N., & Song, P. H. (2013). Implementing high performance work practices in healthcare organizations: Qualitative and conceptual evidence. *Journal of Healthcare Management, 58*(6), 446–462.

McHugh, M., Garman, A., McAlearney, A., Song, P., & Harrison, M. (2010). *Using workforce practices to drive quality improvement: A guide for hospitals*. Rockville, MD: Agency for Healthcare Research and Quality. Retrieved from www.hret.org/workforce/resources/workforce-guide.pdf

National Center for Healthcare Leadership (NCHL). (2010). *Best practices in healthcare leadership academies*. Chicago, IL: Author. Retrieved from http://www.nchl.org/Documents/Ctrl_Hyperlink /doccopy5381_uid6102014456192.pdf

Ogden, G. (2010). Talent management in a time of cost management. *Healthcare Financial Management, 64*(3), 80–82, 84.

Pieper, S. K. (2005). Reading the right signals: How to strategically manage with scorecards. *Healthcare Executive, 20*, 9–14.

Rollins, G. (2003). Succession planning: Laying the foundation for smooth transitions and effective leaders. *Healthcare Executive, 18*, 14–18.

Ross, A., Wenzel, F. J., & Mitlyng, J. W. (2002). *Leadership for the future: Core competencies in health care*. Chicago, IL: Health Administration Press/AUPHA Press.

Scott, G. (2009). The leader as coach. *Healthcare Executive, 24*(4), 40–43.

Scott, T., Mannion, R., Davies, H. T. O., & Marshall, M. M. (2003). Implementing culture change in health care: Theory and practice. *International Journal for Quality in Health Care*. Retrieved from http://intqhc.oxfordjournals.org/content/15/2/111

Squazzo, J. D. (2009, November/December). Cultivating tomorrow's leaders: Comprehensive development strategies ensure continued success. *Healthcare Executive, 24*(6), 8–20.

Staren, E. D., Braun, D. P., & Denny, D. (2010). Optimizing innovation in health care organizations. *Physician Executive Journal*, March/April, 54–62.

Studer, Q. (2003). *Hardwiring excellence*. Gulf Breeze, FL: Fire Starter.

Thompson, J. M. (2007). Health services administration. In S. Chisolm (Ed.), *The health professions: Trends and opportunities in U.S. health care* (pp. 357–372). Sudbury, MA: Jones and Bartlett.

Thompson, J. M. (2010). Understanding and managing organizational change: Implications for public health management. *Journal of Public Health Management & Practice, 16*(20), 167–173.

Thompson, J. M., & Kim, T. H. (2013). A profile of hospitals with leadership development programs. *The Health Care Manager, 32*(2), 179–188.

Thompson, J. M., & Temple, A. (2015). Early careerist interest and participation in leadership development programs. *The Health Care Manager, 34*(4), 350–358.

Leadership

Louis Rubino

LEARNING OBJECTIVES

By the end of this chapter, the student will be able to:

- Distinguish between leadership and management;
- Summarize the history of leadership in the U.S. from the 1920s to current times;
- Compare and contrast leadership styles, competencies, and protocols;
- Summarize old and new governance trends;
- Analyze key barriers and challenges to successful leadership;
- Provide a rationale for why health care leaders have a greater need for ethical behavior;
- Explore important new initiatives requiring health care leaders' engagement; and
- Discuss special research issues related to leadership.

LEADERSHIP VS. MANAGEMENT

In any business setting, there must be **leaders** as well as **managers**. But are these the same people? Not necessarily. There are leaders who are good managers and there are managers who are good leaders, but usually neither case is the norm. In health care, this is especially important to recognize because of the need for both. Health care is unique in that it is a service industry that depends on a large number of highly trained personnel as well as trade workers. Whatever the setting, be it a hospital, a long-term care facility, an ambulatory care center, a medical device company, an insurance company, an accountable care organization, or some other health care entity, leaders as well as managers are needed to keep the organization moving in a forward direction and, at the same time, maintain current operations. This is done by leading and managing its people and assuring good business practices.

Leaders usually take a focus that is more external, whereas the focus of managers is more internal. Even though they need to be sure their health care facility is operating properly, leaders tend to spend the majority of their time communicating and aligning with outside groups that can benefit their organizations (partners, community, vendors) or influence them (government, public agencies, media). See Figure 2-1. There is crossover between leaders and managers across the various areas, though a distinction remains for certain duties and responsibilities.

Usually the top person in the organization (e.g., Chief Executive Officer, Administrator, Director) has full and ultimate accountability. This type of leader may be dictated by the current conditions faced by the organization. A more **strategic leader**, who defines purpose and vision and aligns people, processes, and values, may be needed. Or, a **network leader**, who could connect people across disciplines, organizational departments, and regions, may be essential. Whichever type surfaces, there will be several managers reporting to this person, all of whom have various **functional responsibilities**

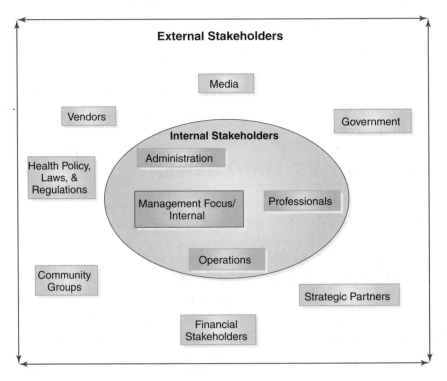

FIGURE 2-1 Leadership and Management Focus

for different areas of the organization (e.g., Chief Nursing Officer, Physician Director, Chief Information Officer). These managers can certainly be leaders in their own areas, but their focus will be more internal within the organization's operations. They are the **operational leaders** of the organization. Together, these three types of leaders/followers produce an interdependent leadership system, a team which will prove more high performing in the current health care field (Maccoby, Norman, Norman, & Margolies, 2013).

Leaders have a particular set of competencies that require more forward thinking than those of managers. Leaders need to set a **vision** or direction for the organization. They need to be able to motivate their employees, as well as other stakeholders, so the business continues to exist and, hopefully, thrive in periods of change. No industry is as dynamic as health care, with rapid change occurring due to the complexity of the system and government regulations. Leaders are needed to keep the entity on course and to maneuver around obstacles, like a captain commanding his ship at sea. Managers must tend to the business at hand and make sure the staff is following proper procedures and meeting established targets and goals. They need a different set of competencies. See Table 2-1.

HISTORY OF LEADERSHIP IN THE U.S.

Leaders have been around since the beginning of man. We think of the strongest male becoming the leader of a caveman clan. In Plato's time, the Greeks began to talk about the concept of leadership and acknowledged the political system as critical for leaders to emerge in a society. In Germany during the late 19th century, Sigmund Freud described leadership as unconscious exhibited behavior; later, Max Weber identified how leadership is present in a bureaucracy through assigned roles. Formal leadership studies in the U.S., though, have only been around for the last 100 years (Sibbet, 1997).

TABLE 2-1 Leadership vs. Management Competencies

Leadership Competencies	Management Competencies
Establishing mission	Staffing personnel
Setting vision/direction	Assuring patient-centered practices
Motivating stakeholders	Controlling resources
Being an effective spokesperson	Supervising the service provided
Determining strategies for the future	Overseeing adherence to regulations
Transforming the organization	Counseling/developing employees
Networking	Managing operations

We can look at the decades spanning the 20th century to see how leadership theories evolved, placing their center of attention on certain key components at different times (Northouse, 2016). These emphases often matched or were adapted from the changes occurring in society.

With the industrialization of the U.S. in the 1920s, productivity was of paramount importance. Scientific management was introduced, and researchers tried to determine which characteristics were identified with the most effective leaders based on their units having high productivity. The **Great Man Theory** was developed out of the idea that certain traits determined good leadership. The traits that were recognized as necessary for effective leaders were ones that were already inherent in the person, such as being male, being tall, being strong, and even being Caucasian. Even the idea that "you either got it or you don't" was supported by this theory, the notion being that a good leader had charisma. Behaviors were not considered important in determining what made a good leader. This theory discouraged anyone who did not have the specified traits from aspiring to a leadership position.

Fortunately, after two decades, businesses realized leadership could be enhanced through certain conscious acts, and researchers began to study which behaviors would produce better results. Resources were in short supply due to World War II, and leaders were needed who could truly produce good results. This was the beginning of the **Style Approach to Leadership**. Rather than looking at only the characteristics of the leader, researchers started to recognize the importance of two types of behaviors in successful leadership: completing tasks and creating good relationships. This theory states leaders have differing degrees of concern over each of these behaviors, and the best leaders would be fully attentive to both.

In the 1960s, American society had a renewed emphasis on helping all of its people and began a series of social programs that still remain today. The two that impact health care directly, by providing essential services, are Medicare for the elderly (age 65 and over) and the disabled and Medicaid for the indigent population. The **Situational Approach to Leadership** then came into prominence and supported this national concern. This set of theories focused on the leader changing his or her behavior in certain situations in order to meet the needs of subordinates. This would imply a very fluid leadership process whereby one can adapt one's actions to an employee's needs at any given time.

Not much later, researchers believed perhaps leaders should not have to change how they behaved in a work setting, but instead the appropriate leaders should be selected from the very beginning. This is the **Contingency Theory of Leadership** and was very popular in the 1970s. Under this theory, the focus was on both the leader's style as well as the situation in which the leader worked, thus building upon the two earlier theories. This approach was further developed by what is known as the **Path–Goal Theory of Leadership**. This theory still placed its attention on the leader's style and the work situation (subordinate characteristics and work task structure) but also recognized the importance of setting goals for employees. The leader was expected to remove any obstacles in order to provide the support necessary for them to achieve those goals.

In the later 1970s, the U.S. was coming out of the Vietnam War, in which many of its citizens did not think the country should have been involved. More concern was expressed over relationships as the society became more psychologically attuned to how people felt. The **Leader–Member Exchange Theory** evolved over the concern that leadership was being defined by the leader, the follower, and the context. This new way of looking at leadership focused on the interactions that occur between the leaders and the followers. This theory claimed leaders could be more effective if they developed better relationships with their subordinates through high-quality exchanges.

After Vietnam and a series of weak political leaders, Americans were looking for people to take charge who could really make a difference. Charismatic leaders came back into vogue, as demonstrated by the support shown to President Ronald Reagan, an actor turned politician. Unlike the Great Man Theory earlier in the century, this time the leader had to have certain skills to transform the organization through inspirational motivational efforts. Leadership was not centered upon transactional processes that tied rewards or corrective actions to performance. Rather, the **transformational leader** could significantly change an organization through its people by raising their consciousness, empowering them, and then providing the nurturing needed as they produced the results desired.

In the late 1980s, the U.S. started to look more globally for ways to have better production. Total Quality Management became a popular concept and arose from researchers studying Japanese principles of managing production lines. In the health care setting, this was embraced through a process still used today called Continuous Quality Improvement or Performance Improvement. In the decade to follow, leaders assigned subordinates to a series of work groups in order to focus on a particular area of production. Attention was placed on developing the team for higher level functioning and on how a leader could create a work environment that could improve the performance of the team. Individual team members were expendable, and the team entity was all important.

We have entered the 21st century with some of the greatest leadership challenges ever in the health care field. Critical personnel shortages, limited resources, and increased governmental regulations provide an environment that yearns for leaders who are attentive to the organization and its people, yet can still address the big picture. Several of today's leadership models relate well to the dynamism of the health care field and are presented here. Looking at these models, there seems to be a consistent pattern of self-aware leaders who are concerned for their employees and understand the importance of meaningful work. As we entered the 2000s, leaders needed to use **Adaptive Leadership** to create flexible organizations able to meet the relentless succession of challenges faced in health care and elsewhere (Heifetz, Grashow, & Linsky, 2009). Plus, today's astute health care leaders recognize the importance of considering the global environment, as health care wrestles with international issues that impact us locally, such as outsourcing services, medical tourism, and over-the-border drug purchases, giving rise to the **global leader**. See Table 2-2.

CONTEMPORARY MODELS

Today's health care industry does not prescribe any one type of leadership model. Many leaders are successful drawing from a variety of traditional and contemporary models. It is wise for the leadership student, as well as the practitioner, to become familiar with the various contemporary models so they can be utilized when appropriate. See Table 2-3.

TABLE 2-2 Leadership Theories in the U.S.

Period of Time	Leadership Theory	Leadership Focus
1920s and 1930s	Great Man	Having certain inherent traits
1940s and 1950s	Style Approach	Task completion and developing relationships
1960s	Situational Approach	Needs of the subordinates
Early 1970s	Contingency and Path–Goal	Both style and situation
Late 1970s	Leader–Member Exchange	Interactions between leader and subordinate
1980s	Transformational Approach	Raise consciousness and empower followers
1990s	Team Leadership	Team performance and development
2000s	Adaptive Leadership	Build capacity to thrive in a new reality
2010s	Global Leader	Recognizing the impact of globalization for their industry

TABLE 2-3 Contemporary Leadership Models

Model	Leadership Application
Emotional Intelligence	Tools to be well adjusted leader
Authentic Leadership	Follows internal compass of true purpose
Diversity Leadership	Culturally competent leader
Servant Leadership	Desire to serve others
Spirituality Leadership	Supports finding meaning
Resilient Leadership	Build inner strength and perseverance
Emerging Leadership	Continual learners and developers

Emotional Intelligence (EI)

Emotional Intelligence (EI) is a concept made famous by Daniel Goleman in the late 1990s. It suggests that there are certain skills (**intrapersonal and interpersonal**) that a person needs to be well adjusted in today's world. These skills include **self-awareness** (having a deep understanding of one's emotions, strengths, weaknesses, needs, and drives), **self-regulation** (a propensity for reflection, an ability to adapt to changes, the power to say no to impulsive urges), **motivation** (being driven to achieve, being passionate about one's profession, enjoying challenges), **empathy** (thoughtfully considering others' feelings when interacting), and **social skills** (moving people in the direction you desire by your ability to interact effectively) (Freshman & Rubino, 2002).

Since September 11, 2001, leaders have needed to be more understanding of their subordinates' world outside of the work environment. EI, when applied to leadership, suggests a more caring, confident, enthusiastic boss who can establish good relations with workers. Researchers have shown that EI can distinguish outstanding leaders and strong organizational performance (Goleman, 1998). For health care as an industry and for health care managers, this seems like a good fit, especially during this time of change (Delmatoff & Lazarus, 2014). See Table 2-4.

Authentic Leadership

The central focus of **authentic leadership** is that people will want to naturally associate with someone who is following their internal compass of true purpose (George & Sims, 2007). Leaders who follow this model are ones who know their authentic selves, define their values and leadership principles, understand what motivates them, build a strong support team, and stay grounded by integrating all aspects of their lives. Authentic leaders

TABLE 2-4 Emotional Intelligence's Application to Health Care Leadership

EI Dimension	Definition	Leadership Application
Self-Awareness	A deep understanding of one's emotions and drives	Knowing if your values are congruent with the organization's
Self-Regulation	Adaptability to changes and control over impulses	Considering ethics of giving bribes to doctors
Motivation	Ability to enjoy challenges and being passionate toward work	Being optimistic even when census is low
Empathy	Social awareness skill, putting yourself in another's shoes	Setting a patient-centered vision for the organization
Social Skills	Supportive communication skills, abilities to influence and inspire	Having an excellent rapport with the board

have attributes such as confidence, hope, optimism, resilience, high levels of integrity, and positive values (Brown & Gardner, 2007). Assessments given to leaders in a variety of international locations have provided the evidence-based knowledge that there is a correlation between authentic leadership and positive outcomes based on supervisor-rated performance (Walumbwa, Avolio, Gardner, Wernsing, & Peterson, 2008).

Diversity Leadership

Our new global society forces health care leaders to address matters of diversity, whether with their patient base or with their employees. This commitment to diversity is necessary for today's leader to be successful. The environment must be assessed so goals can be set that embrace the concept of diversity in matters such as employee hiring and promotional practices, patient communication, and governing board composition, to name a few. Strategies have to be developed to make diversity work for the organization. The leader who recognizes the importance of diversity and designs its acceptance into the organizational culture will be most successful (Warden, 1999). Health care leaders are called to be role models for **cultural competency** (see Chapter 14 for more on this important topic) and to be able to attract, mentor, and coach those of different, as well as similar, backgrounds (Dolan, 2009).

Servant Leadership

Many people view health care as a very special type of work. Individuals usually work in this setting because they want to help people. **Servant leadership** applies this concept to top administration's ability to lead, acknowledging that a health care leader is largely motivated by a desire to serve others. This leadership model breaks down the typical organizational hierarchy and professes the belief of building a community within an organization in which everyone contributes to the greater whole. A servant leader is highly collaborative and gives credit to others generously. This leader is sensitive to what motivates others and empowers all to win with shared goals and vision. Servant leaders use personal trust and respect to build bridges and use persuasion rather than positional authority to foster cooperation. This model works especially well in a not-for-profit setting, since it continues the mission of fulfilling the community's needs rather than the organization's (Swearingen & Liberman, 2004).

Spirituality Leadership

The U.S. has experienced some very serious misrepresentations and misreporting by major health care companies, as reported by U.S. governmental agencies (e.g., Columbia/ HCA, GlaxoSmithKline, HealthSouth). Trying to claim a renewed sense of confidence in the system, a model of leadership has emerged that focuses on spirituality. This **spiritual focus** does not imply a certain set of religious beliefs but emphasizes ethics, values, relationship skills, and the promotion of balance between work and self (Wolf, 2004). The goal under this model is to define our own uniqueness as human beings and to appreciate our spiritual depth. In this way, leaders can deepen their understanding and at the same time be more productive. These leaders have a positive impact on their workers and create a working environment that supports all individuals in finding meaning in what they do. They practice five common behaviors of effective leaders as described by Kouzes and Posner (1995): (1) Challenge the process, (2) Inspire a shared vision, (3) Enable others to act, (4) Model the way, and (5) Encourage the heart, thus taking leadership to a new level.

Resilient Leadership

Being a health care leader is an exciting yet challenging job. Much stress is placed on the executive and its takes a strong, **resilient leader** to overcome these pressures, bounce back, and keep the organization moving forward. Certain resilience-building practices can be used by the leader to build inner strength and perseverance (Wicks & Buck, 2013). A self-care protocol that includes self-awareness, alone time, mindfulness, and keeping a healthy perspective can be essential to not only the individual leader but also to coach his/her team members to avoid burnout and foster high staff morale.

The Emerging Health Care Leader

Students of health administration do not become successful leaders overnight. It usually takes years of study and experience to become comfortable and proficient in the role. A basic foundation is necessary before a leader can emerge and certain strategies can be applied to help an individual build and grow their career (Baedke & Lamberton, 2015). Some of these include paying attention to one's character, examining self-discipline, cultivating your personal brand, and to constantly network. The best leaders are ones who are continually learning and using this new knowledge to further their development as a leader in today's changing health care world.

LEADERSHIP STYLES

Models give us a broad understanding of someone's leadership philosophy. Styles demonstrate a particular type of leadership behavior that is consistently used. Various authors have attempted to explain different leadership styles (Northouse, 2015; Studer, 2008). Some styles are more appropriate to use with certain health care workers, depending on their education, training, competence, motivation, experience, and personal needs. The environment must also be considered when deciding which style is the best fit.

In a **coercive leadership style** power is used inappropriately to get a desired response from a follower. This very directive format should probably not be used unless the leader is dealing with a very problematic subordinate or is in an emergency situation and needs immediate action. In health care settings over longer periods of time, three other leadership styles could be used more effectively: **participative**, **pacesetting**, and **coaching**.

Many health care workers are highly trained, specialized individuals who know much more about their area of expertise than their supervisor. Take the generally trained chief operating officer of a hospital who has several department managers (e.g., Imaging, Health Information Systems, Engineering) reporting to him or her. These managers will respond better and be more productive if the leader is **participative** in his or her style. Asking these managers for their input and giving them a voice in making decisions will let them know they are respected and valued.

In a **pacesetting style**, a leader sets high performance standards for his or her followers. This is very effective when the employees are self-motivated and highly competent—e.g., research scientists or intensive care nurses. A **coaching style** is recommended for the very top personnel in an organization. With this style, the leader focuses on the personal development of his or her followers rather than the work tasks. This should be reserved for followers the leader can trust and those who have proven their competence. See Table 2-5.

LEADERSHIP COMPETENCIES

A leader needs certain skills, knowledge, and abilities to be successful. These are called **competencies**. The pressures of the health care industry have initiated the examination of a set of core competencies for a leader who works in a health care setting (Dye & Garman, 2015). Criticism has been directed at educational institutions for not producing administrators who can begin managing effectively right out of school. Educational programs in health administration are working with the national coalition groups (e.g., Health Leadership Council, National Center for Healthcare Leadership, and American College of Healthcare Executives) and health care administrative practitioners to come up with agreed upon competencies. Once identified, the programs can attempt to have their students learn how to develop these traits and behaviors.

TABLE 2-5 Leadership Styles for Health Care Personnel

Style	Definition	Application
Coercive	Demanding and power based	Problematic employees
Participative	Soliciting input and allowing decision making	Most followers
Pacesetting	Setting high performance standards	Highly competent
Coaching	Focus on personal development	Top level

Some of the competencies are technical—for example, having analytical skills, having a full understanding of the law, and being able to market and write. Some of the competencies are behavioral—for example, decisiveness, being entrepreneurial, and an ability to achieve a good work/life balance. As people move up in organizations, their behavioral competencies are a greater determinant of their success as leaders than their technical competencies (Hutton & Moulton, 2004). Another way to examine leadership competencies is under four main groupings or domains. The **Functional and Technical Domain** is necessary but not sufficient for a competent leader. Three other domains provide competencies that are behavioral and relate both to the individual (**Self-Development and Self-Understanding**) and to other people (**Interpersonal**). A fourth set of competencies falls under the heading **Organizational** and has a broader perspective. See Table 2-6 for a full listing of the leadership competencies under the four domains.

TABLE 2-6 Leadership Domains and Competencies

Domain: Functional and Technical
Competencies:
- Knowledge of business/business acumen
- Strategic vision
- Decision making and decision quality
- Managerial ethics and values
- Problem solving
- Change management/dealing with ambiguity
- Systems thinking
- Governance

Domain: Self-Development and Self-Understanding
Competencies:
- Self-awareness and self-confidence
- Self-regulation and personal responsibility
- Honesty and integrity
- Lifelong learning
- Motivation/drive to achieve
- Empathy and compassion
- Flexibility
- Perseverance
- Work/life balance

Domain: Interpersonal
Competencies:
- Communication
- Motivating
- Empowerment of subordinates
- Management of group process
- Conflict management and resolution
- Negotiation
- Formal presentations
- Social interaction

Domain: Organizational
Competencies:
- Organizational design
- Team building
- Priority setting
- Political savvy
- Managing and measuring performance
- Developing others
- Human resources
- Community and external resources
- Managing culture/diversity

Hilberman, D. (Ed.), The 2004 ACHE-AUPHA Pedagogy Enhancement Work Group. June 2005.

LEADERSHIP PROTOCOLS

Health care administrators are expected to act a certain way. Leaders are role models for their organizations' employees, and they need to be aware that their actions are being watched at all times. Sometimes people at the top of an organization get caught up in what they are doing and do not realize the message they are sending throughout the workplace by their inappropriate behavior. Specific ways of serving in the role of a health care leader can be demonstrated and can provide the exemplary model needed to send the correct message to employees. These appropriate ways in which a leader acts are called protocols.

There is no shortage of information on what protocols should be followed by today's health care leader. Each year, researchers, teachers of health administration, practicing administrators, and consultants write books filled with their suggestions on how to be a great leader (for some recent examples, see Dye, 2010; Ledlow & Coppola, 2011; and Rath and Conchie, 2008). There are some key ways a person serving in a leadership role should act. These are described here and summarized in Table 2-7.

Professionalism is essential to good leadership. This can be manifested not only in the way people act but also in their mannerisms and their dress. A leader who comes to work in sloppy attire or exhibits discourteous or obnoxious behavior will not gain respect from followers. Trust and respect are very important for a leader to acquire. Trust and respect must be a two-way exchange if a leader is to get followers to respond. Employees who do not trust their leader will consistently question certain aspects of their job. If they do not have respect for the leader, they will not care about doing a good job. This could lead to low productivity and bad service.

Even a leader's mood can affect workers. A boss who is confident, optimistic, and passionate about his or her work can instill the same qualities in the workers. Such enthusiasm is almost always infectious and is passed on to others within the organization. The

---

TABLE 2-7 Key Leadership Protocols

1. Professionalism
2. Reciprocal trust and respect
3. Confident, optimistic, and passionate
4. Being visible
5. Open communicator
6. Risk taker/entrepreneur
7. Admitting fault
8. Balancing being a motivator, vision-setter, analyzer, and task-master

same can be said of a leader who is weak, negative, and obviously unenthusiastic about his or her work—these poor qualities can be acquired by others.

Leaders must be very visible throughout the organization. Having a presence can assure workers that the top people are "at the helm" and give a sense of stability and confidence in the business. Quint Studer (2009), founder and CEO of Studer Group, states how **rounding** can help leaders meet certain standard goals: making sure staff know they are cared about, know what is going on (what is working well, who should be recognized, which systems need to work better, which tools and equipment need attention), and know that proper follow-up actions are taking place. Leaders must be open communicators. Holding back information that could have been shared with followers will cause ill feelings and a concern that other important matters are not being disclosed. Leaders also need to take calculated risks. They should be cautious, but not overly so, or they might lose an opportunity for the organization. And finally, leaders in today's world need to recognize that they are not perfect. Sometimes there will be errors in what is said or done. These must be acknowledged so they can be put aside and the leader can move on to more pressing current issues.

Health care leaders today need to balance many agendas. To do so, a set of protocols needs to be followed which allows a systems-thinking perspective. The **Master Leadership** framework takes into account these competing values and encourages the leader to shift to being a motivator, vision-setter, analyzer, and task-master depending upon the immediate concern (Belasen, Eisenberg, & Huppertz, 2016). All of these roles though must be followed, and it is the accomplished leader who can develop a sense of equilibrium when he/she acts between them.

GOVERNANCE

Individuals are not the only ones to consider in leadership roles. There can be a group of people who collectively assume the responsibility for strategic oversight of a health care organization. The term governance describes this important function. **Governing bodies** can be organized in a variety of forms. In a hospital, this top accountable body is called a board of trustees in a not-for-profit setting and a board of directors in a proprietary, or for-profit, setting. Since many physician offices, long-term care facilities, and other health care entities are set up as professional corporations, these organizations would also have boards of directors.

Governing boards are facing heightened scrutiny due to the failure of many large corporations in the last decade. The U.S. government recognizes the importance of a group of people who oversee corporate operations and give assurances for the fair and honest functioning of the business. **Sarbanes-Oxley** is a federal law enacted in 2002 that set new or enhanced standards for proprietary companies that are publicly traded. Financial records must be appropriately audited and signed off by top leaders. Operations need to be discussed more openly so as to remove any possibility of cover-up, fraud, or self-interest. Each governing board member has fiduciary responsibility to forgo his or her own personal interests and to make all decisions concerning the entity for the good of the organization. Many believe the not-for-profits should have the same requirements and are applying pressure for them to fall under similar rules of transparency.

Although health care boards are becoming smaller in size, they recognize the importance of the composition of their members. A selection of people from within the organization (e.g., system leaders, the management staff, physicians) should be balanced with outside members from the community who represent the populations served by the organization (see Table 2-8). The trend is to appoint members who have certain expertise to assist the board in carrying out its duties. Also, having governing board members who do not have ties to the health care operations will reduce the possibility of conflicts of interests. Board meetings have gone from ones in which a large volume of information is presented for a "rubber stamp" to meetings that are well prepared, purposeful, and focused on truly important issues. A self-assessment should be taken at least annually and any identified problem areas (including particular board members) addressed. This way, the governing board can review where it stands in its ability to give fair, open, and honest strategic oversight (Gautam, 2005). A new way of looking at governance goes beyond fiduciary and strategic responsibility, whereby the board serves as the generative source of leadership, espousing the

TABLE 2-8 Health Care Governance Trends

Function	Old Way	New Trend
Size of board	Larger	Smaller (average 13 people)
Membership	Many members from within the organization	More balance of members within and outside the organization
Conflicts of interest	Some present, not disclosed	Must be disclosed but prefer none
Meetings	Voluminous detailed information presented	Strategic information and trends presented
Evaluations	If done, not taken too seriously	Taken seriously to identify issues and correct
Focus	Competence of individual providers	Focus on functioning of the system
Leadership	Fiduciary and strategic responsibilities	Generative source of reframing priorities
Goal	Keep stable	Manage change

meaning for the organization's health care delivery and reframing the priorities (Chait, Ryan, & Taylor, 2005). The American Hospital Association Center for Healthcare Governance (2012) produced a Blue Ribbon Panel Report which identified recommendations for health care governance during this period of transformation. These included: strengthen the board and organizational capacity to manage change; encourage collaboration among providers; actively oversee physician alignment, integration, engagement and development; and create a compelling vision for the future.

BARRIERS AND CHALLENGES

Health care leaders are confronted with many situations that must be dealt with as they lead their organizations. Some can be considered barriers that, if not managed properly, will stymie the capacity to lead. Certain other areas are challenges that must be addressed if the leader is to be successful. A few of the more critical ones in today's health care world are presented here. See Table 2-9.

Due to the complex health care system in the U.S., many regulations and laws are in place that sometimes can inhibit innovative and creative business practices. Leaders must ensure the strategies developed for their entity comply with the current laws, or else they jeopardize its long-term survivability. Leaders are expected to sometimes think "outside the box," i.e., go beyond the usual responses to a situation, to provide new ideas for the development of their business. This can be challenging when many constraints must be considered. Some examples are the government's antitrust requirements, which can affect developing partners; federal privacy laws, which can prevent sharing patient information needed for collaboration; and safe harbor requirements, which can affect physician relations. These and other laws and regulations can affect a health care leader's ability to lead.

The health care industry is unique. Major players in the arena, physicians, are not always easily controlled by the medical organizations where they work (e.g., hospitals, medical groups, insurance companies). Yet this very influential group of stakeholders has

---

TABLE 2-9 Key Health Care Leadership Barriers and Challenges

1. Laws and regulations (Barrier)
2. Physicians (Challenge)
3. New technology (Barrier)
4. Culture of safety (Challenge)
5. Value-based purchasing (Challenge)
6. Women in top leadership positions (Barrier)

substantial input over the volume of patients that a health care facility receives and revenues produced. This necessitates that the health care leader find ways to include doctors in the process of setting a direction, monitoring the quality of care, and fulfilling other administrative functions. The wise health care leader will include physicians early on in any planning process. Doctors are usually busy with their own patients and practices, but if they are not looked to for their expertise and advice on certain important matters in the facilities where they work, they will become disengaged. Everybody would much rather work at a place where their opinions are requested and respected. Health care leaders must pay special attention to physicians during the current period to overcome any resistance to change as the health care system evolves (Kornacki & Silversin, 2012).

Technology is a costly requirement in any work setting. Information systems management and new medical equipment are especially expensive for the modern health care facility or practice due to the rapidly changing data collection requirements and medical advances in the field. Health care leaders must assess the capabilities of their entities for new technology and determine if their systems and equipment are a barrier to making future progress. The U.S. Department of Health and Human Services (2009) has provided incentives for health care organizations to promote the adoption and meaningful use of health information technology through the **HITECH Act** (Health Information Technology for Economic and Clinical Health Act) (U.S. Department of HHS, 2009). Health care leaders cannot be successful if their organizations have antiquated systems and out-of-date support devices in today's high-tech world. Computer hardware and clinical software must be integrated to provide the quality and cost information needed for an efficient medical organization. Electronic medical records, wireless devices, and computerized order entry systems, as well as advanced medical equipment and new pharmaceuticals, will be items the leader must have in place in order to lead his or her health care organization in the 21st century.

Safety concerns have traditionally been a management responsibility. However, safety has become such an important issue in today's health care world that leaders must be involved in its oversight. A top-down direction must be given throughout the organization that mistakes will not be tolerated. Coordinated efforts must shift from following up on errors to preventing their recurrence to developing systems and mechanisms to prevent them from ever occurring. The Joint Commission (TJC) has leadership standards for all sectors, calling for the leaders in the health care entity to accept the responsibility for fostering a culture of safety. The focus of attention is on the performance of systems and processes instead of the individual, although reckless behavior and blatant disregard for safety are not tolerated (The Joint Commission, 2010).

Value-based purchasing is quickly becoming the norm. The Centers for Medicare and Medicaid Services' game-changing initiative is being adopted by private payers. It provides reimbursement incentives to accountable providers who produce high-quality outcomes, and disincentives for the provision of poor-quality outcomes (i.e., readmissions within 30 days for some diagnoses). Health care leaders need to focus on demonstrating achievement of high-quality standards to ensure not only the operational excellence but also the fiscal stability of their organizations (Chan & Rubino, 2014).

Even though women make up the majority of the health care workforce, they are underrepresented in the top leadership positions. One recent study showed that only 24% of the senior health care executives were women and only 14% were members of boards of directors (Hauser, 2014). A call must be made to existing health care leaders to pave the way for women to be given the opportunity for these executive jobs by removing traditional barriers and providing active mentoring, introduction into the promotion pipeline, and leadership development programs.

ETHICAL RESPONSIBILITY

Ethics are principles determining behavior and conduct appropriate to a certain setting. It is a matter of doing right vs. wrong (see Chapter 15 for a detailed discussion of ethics and law). Ethics are especially important for health care leadership and require two areas of focus. One area is **biomedical ethics** and the actions a leader needs to consider as he or she relates to a patient. Another is **managerial ethics**. This involves business practices and doing things for the right reasons. A leader must ensure an environment in which good ethical behavior is followed.

The American College of Healthcare Executives (ACHE, 2014) does an excellent job in educating its professional membership as to the ethical responsibilities of health care leaders. Ethical responsibilities apply to several different constituencies: to the profession itself, to the patients and others served, to the organization, to the employees, and to the community and society at large (see Table 2-10). A health care leader who is concerned about an ethical workplace will not only model the appropriate behavior but will also have zero tolerance for any deviation by a member of the organization. A **Code of Ethics** gives specific guidelines to be followed by individual members. An **Integrity Agreement** would address a commitment to follow ethical behavior by the organization.

IMPORTANT NEW INITIATIVES

The world is constantly changing all around us and health care is no different. Several new initiatives are coming on to the scene in which a health care leader must demonstrate active engagement in order to have everyone in the organization recognize its importance.

With health care reform comes a need for a **population health** approach to health care education, delivery, and policy. The distribution of health outcomes within a specific

TABLE 2-10 American College of Healthcare Executives Code of Ethics

Responsible Area	Sample Guidelines
To the profession	Comply with laws Avoid any conflicts of interest Respect confidences
To the patients or others served	Prevent discrimination Safeguard patient confidentiality Have process to evaluate quality of care
To the organization	Proper resource allocation Improve standards of management Prevent fraud and abuse within
To the employees	Allow free expression Ensure a safe workplace environment Follow nondiscrimination policies
To the community and society	Work to meet the needs of the community Provide appropriate access to services Advocate for healthy society
To report violations of the code	Healthcare executive–supplier interactions Decisions near the end of life Impaired healthcare executives

population will be used to measure a health care organization's success and determine its reimbursement under new payment methods. A movement away from focusing on individualized care to group performance will require the health care leader to shift his/her team's attention to innovative strategies to promote wellness and coordination of care. Productive interactions are necessary if the organization is to be successful in the new health care environment (Nash, Reifsnyder, Fabius, & Pracilio, 2011).

Health care is moving away from a provider-centeredness to **patient-family centeredness**. An astute health care leader will recognize the importance in such a shift as consumers are making more direct health care decisions based on the information now readily available. All leaders of a health care organization, from the board level down, need to embrace this concept and be actively engaged in its roll-out, serving as a role model for others (Cliff, 2012).

LEADERS LOOKING TO THE FUTURE

Some people believe leaders are born and that one cannot be taught how to be a good leader. The growing trend, however, is that leaders can, in fact, be taught skills and behaviors that will help them to lead an organization effectively (Parks, 2005). In health care, many clinicians who do well at their jobs are promoted to supervisory positions. Yet they do not have the management training that would help them to be successful in their new roles. For example, physicians, laboratory technologists, physical therapists, and nurses are often pushed into management positions with no administrative training. We are doing a disservice to these clinicians and setting them up for failure.

Fortunately, this common occurrence has been recognized, and many new programs have sprouted to address this need. Universities have developed executive programs to attract medical personnel into a fast-track curriculum to attempt to give them the essential skills they need to be successful. Some schools have developed majors in health care leadership or created online programs for better accessibility, and some health care systems have started internal leadership training programs. This trend will continue into the future, since health care services are expected to grow due to the aging population, and thus there will be a need for more people to be in charge. In addition, leaders should continually be updated as to the qualities that make a good leader in the current environment, and therefore, professional development, provided through internal or external programs, should be encouraged.

The **Baldrige National Quality Program** recognizes in its most recent criteria for performance excellence the need for senior leaders to create a sustainable environment for their organizations through the continual development of future leaders by enhancing their personal leadership skills, such as communicating with the entire workforce and key customers and focusing on action that will achieve the organizations' mission (Baldrige Excellence Framework, 2015). Yet Garman and Dye (2009) caution us to distinguish **leader development** from **leadership development**. They call for the need to bind leadership development activities into a collective network of leaders who are linked to organizational level goals rather than each leader's individual performance. Further understanding of the difference can be explained through decision making. A leader collaborating with his or her superior would be considered leader development, but in leadership development, the process would be team based.

Each of the different sectors in health care has a professional association that will support many aspects of its particular career path. These groups provide ongoing educational efforts to help their members lead their organizations. Another benefit for leaders is that these groups provide up-to-date information about their particular field. Professional associations are a good way to network with people in similar roles, a highly desirable process for health care leaders. Also, ethnic professional associations link health care leaders from representative minority groups as they attempt to increase diversity in the health care profession and improve health status, economic opportunities, and educational advancement for their communities. Most of these various professional groups have student chapters, and early involvement in these organizations is highly recommended for any future health care leader. Table 2-11 lists some of these associations.

TABLE 2-11 Professional Associations

Name	Acronym	Targeted Career	Website
American College of Healthcare Executives	ACHE	Health administrators	www.ache.org
Healthcare Financial Management Association	HFMA	Health care chief financial officers	www.hfma.org
Association for University Programs in Health Administration	AUPHA	Health administration education program directors	www.aupha.org
Medical Group Management Association	MGMA	Medical group administrators	www.mgma.org
American College of Health Care Administrators	ACHCA	Long-term care administrators	www.achca.org
American Academy of Nursing	AAN	Nurse leaders	www.aannet.org
American College of Physician Executives	ACPE	Physician leaders	www.acpe.org
National Association of Health Services Executives	NAHSE	Black health care leaders	www.nahse.org
National Forum for Latino Healthcare Executives	NFLHE	Latino health care leaders	www.nflhe.org
Asian Health Care Leaders Association	AHCLA	Asian health care leaders	www.asianhealthcareleaders.org
Rainbow Healthcare Leaders Association	RHLA	LGBT (lesbian, gay, bi-sexual, transgender) health care leaders	www.RHLA.org

To prepare an organization for the future, its leader needs to be looking out for opportunities to partner with other entities. Health care in the U.S. is fragmented, and to be successful, different services need to be aligned and networks need to be created that will allow patients to flow easily through the continuum of care. Leaders must determine who are the best partners and negotiate a way to have a win–win situation. Of course, these efforts to develop partnerships must be in line with the organization's mission and vision, or the strategic direction will have to be reexamined. The health care leader who is concerned about the future, as well as today's business, must continuously reassess how he or she fits in the organization. Nothing could be worse than a disenchanted person trying to lead a group of followers without the motivation and enthusiasm needed by great leaders. A leader should consider his or her own **succession planning** so that the organization is not left at any time without a person to lead. Truly unselfish leaders think about their commitment to their followers and do their best to ensure that consistent formidable leadership will be in place in the event of their departure. This final act will allow adequate time for a smooth transition and ensure the passage of accountability so that the followers can realign themselves with the new leader.

SPECIAL RESEARCH ISSUES

A leader who is concerned about the future will stay on top of things in the health care industry. Reading newspapers, industry journals, and Web reports, as well as attending industry conferences, helps to keep leaders in the know and allows them to determine how changes in the field could impact their organization. Leaders who remain current will be better positioned to act proactively and to provide the best chance for their organizations to seize a fresh opportunity.

A new appreciation for **evidence-based management** commands today's health care leader go beyond the typical sources of current information and dive deeper into the latest peer-reviewed research articles on health administration. These secondary sources of information will review how to improve leadership capabilities, and thus organizational performance, based on demonstrated studies in the field. White papers prepared by government, as well as private agencies, are easily obtainable through the Internet and can provide important insight on how to address common industry issues.

An exciting opportunity is upon us to go beyond what has been analyzed before due to the emergence of **big data sets**. With electronic medical records, various information systems, and advanced biomedical devices, organizations have more data and information than ever before. The potential benefits of integrating and analyzing the abundance of cost and clinical information exist to support data driven decision making. Leaders must become executive champions in knowledge management and use technology to have their teams develop new projects which will reduce costs, optimize quality, and increase performance. Better strategic planning resource utilization, unit productivity, and insurance contract risk management are just a few of the areas which could be enhanced by leveraging new information technology and putting big data to good use (Hood, 2011). Some examples of big data sets available to the public are at the end of this chapter.

CONCLUSION

There has been a lot of struggle to roll out the **Patient Protection and Affordable Care Act**. This Act may not have provided the U.S. with full health care reform, but it has dramatically altered the way health insurance is administered and care is delivered. Millions of Americans have selected affordable health plans through insurance exchanges and many have qualified under Medicaid expansion. Yet, there will continue to be challenges to the Act in the years to come (Antos, 2014).

A call is made for a new breed of leaders at every level to tame the chaos associated with this dynamic industry (Lee, 2010). Johansen (2012) writes how leaders will make the future by continuously cycling through phases of foresight (seeing the big picture), insight (being able to sense what is important), and action (being able to decide on a strong path ahead). These will certainly be challenging times for health care leaders, and some of the key elements identified for success will be perspective, adaptability, and finding their inner passion as a personal driving force (Sukin, 2009). There is no doubt there will be opportunities for leaders in all disciplines to make a difference for their organizations and their communities as we enter this exciting new phase of American health care delivery.

DISCUSSION QUESTIONS

1. What are the key differences between leadership and management?

2. Are leaders born, or are they trained? How has the history of leadership in the U.S. evolved to reflect this question?

3. List and describe the contemporary models of leadership. What distinguishes them from past models?

4. What are the leadership domains and competencies? Can you be a good leader and not have all the competencies listed in this model?

5. Why do health care leaders have a higher need for ethical behavior than might be expected in other settings?

6. Do health care leaders have a responsibility to be culturally competent? Why or why not?

7. Why is emotional intelligence (EI) important for health care managers? Identify three ways someone who is new to the field can assess and develop his or her EI quotient.

8. What are some ways health care leaders can use research to improve their ability to lead?

Cases in Chapter 18 that are related to this chapter include:

- Metro Renal
- Sustaining an Academic Food Science and Nutrition Center Through Management Improvement
- Emotional Intelligence in Labor and Delivery
- Recruitment Challenge for the Middle Manager

Case study guides are available in the online Instructor's Materials.

REFERENCES

American College of Healthcare Executives. (2014). *Annual report and reference guide.* Chicago: IL: Author.

American Hospital Association Center for Healthcare Governance. (2012). *Governance practices in an era of health care transformation,* Chicago, IL: Author.

Antos, J. (2014). Health care reform after the ACA. *New England Journal of Medicine, 370,* 2259–2261. doi: 10.1056/NEJMp1404298

Baedke, L., & Lamberton, N. (2015). *The emerging healthcare leader.* Chicago, IL: Health Administration Press.

Baldrige Performance Excellence Program (2015). *2015–2016 Baldrige excellence framework.* Gaithersburg, MD: National Institute for Standards and Technology.

Belasen, A. T., Eisenberg, B., & Huppertz, J. W. (2016). *Mastering leadership: A vital resource for health care organizations.* Burlington, MA: Jones & Bartlett Learning.

Brown, J. A., & Gardner, W. L. (2007). Effective modeling of authentic leadership. *Academic Exchange Quarterly, 11*(2), 56–60.

Chait, R., Ryan, W., & Taylor, B. (2005). *Governance as leadership.* Hoboken, NJ: Wiley.

Chan, M., & Rubino, L. (2014). Leading quality initiatives. In *New leadership for today's health care professionals: Concepts and cases.* Burlington, MA: Jones & Bartlett Learning.

Cliff, B. (2012). Patient-centered care: The role of healthcare leadership. *Journal of Healthcare Management, 57*(6), 381–383.

Delmatoff, J., & Lazarus, I. R. (2014). The most effective leadership style for the new landscape of healthcare. *Journal of Healthcare Management, 59*(4), 245–249.

Dolan, T. C. (2009). Cultural competency and diversity. *Healthcare Executive, 24*(6), 6.

Dye, C. F. (2010). *Leadership in healthcare: Essential values and skills* (2nd ed.). Chicago, IL: Health Administration Press.

Dye, C. F., & Garman, A. N. (2015). *Exceptional leadership: 16 critical competencies for healthcare executives* (2nd ed.). Chicago, IL: Health Administration Press.

Freshman, B., & Rubino, L. (2002). Emotional intelligence: A core competency for health care administrators. *The Health Care Manager, 20,* 1–9.

Garman, A., & Dye, C. (2009). *The healthcare c-suite: Leadership development at the top.* Chicago, IL: Health Administration Press.

Gautam, K. (2005). Transforming hospital board meetings: Guidelines for comprehensive change. *Hospital Topics: Research and Perspectives on Healthcare, 83*(3), 25–31.

George, B., & Sims, P. (2007). *True north: Discover your authentic leadership.* San Francisco, CA: Jossey-Bass.

Goleman, D. (1998, December). What makes a leader? *Harvard Business Review, 76*(6), 93–102.

Hauser, M. C. (2014). Leveraging women's leadership talent in healthcare. *Journal of Healthcare Management, 59*(5), 318–322.

Heifetz, R., Grashow, A., & Linsky, M. (2009, July–August). Leadership in a (permanent) crisis. *Harvard Business Review.* Retrieved from http://hbr.org/2009/07/leadership-in-a-permanent-crisis/ar/1

Hilberman, D. (Ed.). (2005, June). *Final report: Pedagogy enhancement project on leadership skills for healthcare management.* The 2004 ACHE-AUPHA Pedagogy Enhancement Work Group. Washington, D.C.: Association of University Programs in Health Administration.

Hood, M. M. (2011). How CEOs drive the clinical transformation and information technology agenda, *Frontiers of Health Services Management, 28*(1), 15–23.

Hutton, D., & Moulton, S. (2004). Behavioral competencies for health care leaders. *Best of H&HN OnLine. American Hospital Association,* 15–18.

Johansen, B. (2012). *Leaders make the future: Ten new leadership skills for an uncertain world.* San Francisco; CA: Berrett-Koehler Publishers, Inc.

The Joint Commission. (2010). *Hospital accreditation standards.* Oakbrook Terrace, IL: Author.

Kornacki, M. J., & Silversin, J. (2012). *Leading physicians through change* (2nd ed). Tampa: FL: American College of Physician Executives.

Kouzes, J. M., & Posner, B. Z. (1995). *The leadership challenge: How to keep getting extraordinary things done in organizations.* San Francisco, CA: Jossey-Bass.

Ledlow, G. R., & Coppola, M. N. (2011). *Leadership for health professionals: Theories, skills, and applications.* Sudbury, MA: Jones and Bartlett.

Lee, T. H. (2010, April). Turning doctors into leaders. *Harvard Business Review, 88*(4), 50–58.

Maccoby, M., Norman, C. L., Norman, C. J., & Margolies, R. (2013). *Transforming health care leadership: A systems guide to improve patient care, decrease costs, and improve population health.* San Francisco: CA: Jossey-Bass.

Nash, D. B., Reifsnyder, J., Fabius, R. J., & Pracilio, V. P. (2011). *Population health: Creating a culture of wellness.* Sudbury, MA: Jones and Bartlett.

Northouse, P. (2015). *Introduction to leadership concepts and practice* (2nd ed.). Thousand Oaks, CA: Sage.

Northouse, P. (2016). *Leadership: Theory and practice* (7th ed.). Thousand Oaks, CA: Sage.

Parks, S. (2005). *Leadership can be taught: A bold approach for a complex world.* Boston, MA: Harvard Business School Press.

Rath, T., & Conchie, B. (2008). *Strengths-based leadership: Great leaders, teams, and why people follow.* New York, NY: Gallup Press.

Sibbet, D. (1997, September/October). 75 years of management ideas and practice 1922–1997. *Harvard Business Review Supplement.*

Studer, Q. (2008). *Results that last: Hardwiring behaviors that will take your company to the top.* Hoboken, NJ: Wiley.

Studer, Q. (2009). *Straight A leadership: Alignment, action, accountability.* Gulf Breeze, FL: Fire Starter Publishing.

Sukin, D. (2009). Leadership in challenging times: It starts with passion. *Frontiers of Health Services Management, 26*(2), 3–8.

Swearingen, S., & Liberman, A. (2004). Nursing leadership: Serving those who serve others. *The Health Care Manager, 23*(2), 100–109.

U.S. Department of Health & Human Services. (2009). *HITECH Act enforcement interim final rule.* Retrieved from http://www.hhs.gov/ocr/privacy/hipaa/administrative/enforcementrule/hitechenforcementifr.html

Walumbwa, F., Avolio, B., Gardner, W., Wernsing, T., & Peterson, S. (2008). Authentic leadership: Development and validation of a theory-based measure. *Journal of Management, 34*(1), 89–126.

Warden, G. (1999). Leadership diversity. *Journal of Healthcare Management, 44*(6), 421–422.

Wicks, R. J., & Buck, T. C. (2013). Riding the dragon: Enhancing resilient leadership and sensible self-care in the healthcare executive. *Frontiers of Health Services Management, 30*(2), 3–13.

Wolf, E. (2004). Spiritual leadership: A new model. *Healthcare Executive, 19*(2), 22–25.

Additional Websites to Explore

American College of Healthcare
    Executives   http://www.ache.org/
Center of Healthcare Governance   http://www.americangovernance.com/
Coach John Wooden's Pyramid
    of Success   http://www.coachwooden.com/
Healthcare Leadership Alliance
    Competency Directory   http://www.healthcareleadershipalliance.org/
Health Leadership Council   www.hlc.org
Institute for Diversity of Health
    Management   www.diversityconnection.org
National Center for Healthcare
    Leadership   www.nchl.org
National Quality Forum   http://www.qualityforum.org/Home.aspx
World Health Organization Leadership
    Service   http://www.who.int/hrh/education/en/

White Papers for Healthcare Leaders

American Hospital Association. (2004). *Strategies for leadership: Does your hospital reflect the community it serves? A diversity and cultural proficiency assessment tool for leaders.* Chicago, IL: Author. Retrieved from http://www.aha.org/content/00-10/diversitytool.pdf

Garman, A., & Carter, C. (2014, October 14). *Implications of health reform for healthcare executives positions: A national study of senior leadership teams in freestanding hospitals.* Chicago, IL: American College of Healthcare Executives. Retrieved from https://www.ache.org/pubs/research/Implications_of_Health_Reform_for_Healthcare_Executive_Positions.pdf

Swensen, S., Pugh, M., McMullan, C., & Kabcenell, A. (2013). *High-impact leadership: Improve care, improve the health of populations, and reduce costs.* IHI white paper. Cambridge, MA: Institute for Healthcare Improvement. Retrieved from http://www.ihi.org/resources/Pages/IHIWhitePapers/HighImpactLeadership.aspx

Management and Motivation

Nancy H. Shanks and Amy Dore

LEARNING OBJECTIVES

By the end of this chapter, the student will be able to:

- Conceptualize who and what motivates employees;
- Examine the relationship between engagement and motivation;
- Explain why motivation is important;
- Differentiate between the different theories of motivation;
- Compare and contrast extrinsic and intrinsic factors of motivation;
- Assess misconceptions about motivation;
- Analyze issues relating to motivating and managing across generations; and
- Critique strategies to enhance employee motivation.

INTRODUCTION

Managers are continually challenged to motivate a workforce to do two things. The first is to motivate employees to work toward helping the organization achieve its goals. The second is to motivate employees to work toward achieving their own personal goals.

Meeting the needs and achieving the goals of both the employer and the employee is often difficult for managers in all types of organizations. In health care, however, this is often more difficult, in part as a result of the complexity of health care organizations, but also as a function of the wide array of employees who are employed by or work collaboratively with health care providers in delivering and paying for care. Workers run the gamut from highly trained and highly skilled technical and clinical staff members, e.g., physicians and nurses, to relatively unskilled workers (see Chapter 11 for more on this topic). To be successful, health care managers need to be able to manage and motivate this wide array of employees.

MOTIVATION—THE CONCEPT

According to Webster's New Collegiate Dictionary, a **motive** is "something (a need or desire) that causes a person to act." Motivate, in turn, means "to provide with a motive," and **motivation** is defined as "the act or process of motivating." Thus, motivation is the act or process of providing a motive that causes a person to take some action. In most cases, motivation comes from some need that leads to behavior which, in turn, results in some type of reward when the need is fulfilled. This definition raises a couple of basic questions.

What Are Rewards?

Rewards can take two forms. They can be either intrinsic/internal rewards or extrinsic/external rewards. **Intrinsic rewards** are derived from within the individual. For a health care employee, this could mean taking pride and feeling good about a job well done (e.g., providing excellent patient care). **Extrinsic rewards** pertain to those reinforcements that are given by another person, such as a health care organization giving bonuses to teams of workers when quality and patient satisfaction are demonstrated to be exceptional.

Who Motivates Employees?

While rewards may serve as incentives and those who bestow rewards may seek to use them as motivators, the real motivation to act comes from within the individual. Managers do exert a significant amount of influence over employees, but they do not have the power to force a person to act. They can work to provide various types of **incentives** in an effort to influence an employee in any number of ways, such as by changing job descriptions, rearranging work schedules, improving working conditions, reconfiguring teams, and a host of other activities. While these may have an impact on an employee's level of motivation and willingness to act, when all is said and done, it is the employee's decision to take action or not. In discussing management and motivation, it is important to continually remember the roles of both managers and employees in the process of motivation.

Is Everybody Motivated?

As managers, we often assume that employees are motivated or will respond to inducements from managers. While this is perhaps a logical and rational approach from the manager's perspective, it is critical to understand this is not always the case. The majority of employees do, in fact, want to do a good job and are motivated by any number of factors.

Others, however, may not share that same drive or high level of motivation. Those people may merely be putting in time and may be more motivated by other things, such as family, school, hobbies, or other interests. Keeping this in mind is useful in helping health care managers understand employee behaviors that seem to be counterproductive.

HISTORY OF MOTIVATION

There is a plethora of research on the topic of motivation, particularly motivation in the workplace. The concepts of management and motivation often coincide when an organization is striving toward a goal. In order to fully understand the concept of motivation, a manager must understand its significance. Motivation is not a new concept. Approximately 2,500 years ago, Athens rose to unparalleled political and economic power and allowed the citizenry to become active in civic governance. Through an engaged and participative citizenry, the Athenian people helped produce the first great Greek empire, which allowed for better commerce and trade; increased wealth of its citizens; and a culture that spawned historically known philosophers, artists, and academics. To achieve this type of success, organizations must recognize the full power of their employees and motivate them to reach for the common good of the organization (Manville & Ober, 2003).

Fast forward to more recent times, and we can continue to identify the historical significance of motivation. In 1890, empirical psychologist William James identified aspects of motivation and its relationship with intrinsically motivated behavior. In 1943, psychologist Clark Hull published his now famous **drive theory**. Hull believed all behaviors to be connected to four primary drives: hunger, thirst, sex, and the avoidance of pain; according to this view, all drives provide the energy for behavior (Deci & Ryan, 1985). Research into human behavior started being recognized in the workplace in the 1940s. Researchers recognized people were motivated by several types of varying needs, not only in the workplace but also in their personal lives (Sperry, 2003). Workplace motivational theories continue to evolve, as is shown in the discussion concerning theories of motivation.

THEORIES OF MOTIVATION

Psychologists have studied human motivation extensively and have derived a variety of theories about what motivates people. This section briefly highlights the motivational theories that are widely known in the field of management. These include theories that focus on motivation being a function of (1) employee needs of various types, (2) extrinsic factors, and (3) intrinsic factors. Each set of theories follows.

Needs-Based Theories of Motivation
Maslow's Hierarchy of Needs

Maslow (1954) postulated a **hierarchy of needs** that progresses from the lowest, subsistence-level needs to the highest level of self-awareness and actualization. Once each level has been met, the theory is that an individual will be motivated by and strive to progress to satisfy the next higher level of need. The five levels in Maslow's hierarchy are:

- **Physiological needs**—including food, water, sexual drive, and other subsistence-related needs;
- **Safety needs**—including shelter, a safe home environment, employment, a healthy and safe work environment, access to health care, money, and other basic necessities;
- **Belonging needs**—including the desire for social contact and interaction, friendship, affection, and various types of support;
- **Esteem needs**—including status, recognition, and positive regard; and
- **Self-actualization needs**—including the desire for achievement, personal growth and development, and autonomy.

The movement from one level to the next was termed **satisfaction progression** by Maslow, and it was assumed that over time individuals were motivated to continually progress upward through these levels. While useful from a theoretical perspective, most individuals do not view their needs in this way, making this approach to motivation a bit unrealistic.

Alderfer's ERG Theory

The three components identified by Alderfer (1972) in his **ERG theory** drew upon Maslow's theory, but also suggested individuals were motivated to move forward and backward through the levels in terms of motivators. He reduced Maslow's levels from five to the following three:

- **Existence**—which related to Maslow's first two needs, thus combining the physiological and safety needs into one level;
- **Relatedness**—which addressed the belonging needs; and
- **Growth**—which pertained to the last two needs, thereby combining esteem and self-actualization.

Alderfer also added his **frustration–regression principle**, which postulated that individuals would move in and out of the various levels, depending upon the extent to which their needs were being met. This approach is deemed by students of management to be more logical and similar to many individuals' worldviews.

Herzberg's Two-Factor Theory

Herzberg (2003) further modified Maslow's needs theory and consolidated it down to two areas of needs that motivated employees. These were termed:

- **Hygienes**—lower-level motivators which included, for example, "company policy and administration, supervision, interpersonal relationships, working conditions, salary, status, and security" (p. 5).
- **Motivators**—higher-level factors which focused on aspects of work, such as "achievement, recognition for achievement, the work itself, responsibility, and growth or advancement" (p. 5).

Herzberg's is an easily understood approach that suggests that individuals have desires beyond the hygienes and that motivators are very important to them.

McClelland's Acquired Needs Theory

The idea here is that needs are acquired throughout life. That is, needs are not innate but are learned or developed as a result of one's life experiences (McClelland, 1985). This theory focuses on three types of needs:

- **Need for achievement**—which emphasizes the desires for success, for mastering tasks, and for attaining goals;
- **Need for affiliation**—which focuses on the desire for relationships and associations with others; and
- **Need for power**—which relates to the desires for responsibility for, control of, and authority over others.

All four of these theories approach needs from a somewhat different perspective and are helpful in understanding employee motivation on the basis of needs. However, other theories of motivation also have been posited and require consideration.

Extrinsic Factor Theories of Motivation

Another approach to understanding motivation focuses on external factors and their role in understanding employee motivation. The best known of these follow.

Reinforcement Theory

B. F. Skinner (1953) studied human behavior and proposed that individuals are motivated when their behaviors are reinforced. His theory is comprised of four types of reinforcement.

The first two are associated with achieving desirable behaviors, while the last two address undesirable behaviors:

- **Positive reinforcement**—relates to taking action that rewards positive behaviors;
- **Avoidance learning**—occurs when actions are taken to reward behaviors that avoid undesirable or negative behaviors. This is sometimes referred to as **negative reinforcement**;
- **Punishment**—includes actions designed to reduce undesirable behaviors by creating negative consequences for the individual; and
- **Extinction**—represents the removal of positive rewards for undesirable behaviors. Likewise, if the rewards for *desirable* behaviors cease, those actions can be impacted as well.

The primary criticism of the reinforcement approach is that it fails to account for employees' abilities to think critically and reason, both of which are important aspects of human motivation. While reinforcement theory may be applicable in animals, it doesn't account for the higher level of cognition that occurs in humans.

Intrinsic Factor Theories of Motivation

Theories that are based on **intrinsic or endogenous factors** focus on internal thought processes and perceptions about motivation. Several of these are highlighted:

- **Adams' Equity Theory**—proposes individuals are motivated when they perceive they are treated equitably in comparison to others within the organization (Adams, 1963);
- **Vroom's Expectancy Theory**—addresses the expectations of individuals and hypothesizes they are motivated by performance and the expected outcomes of their own behaviors (Vroom, 1964); and
- **Locke's Goal-Setting Theory**—hypothesizes establishing goals motivates individuals to take action to achieve those goals (Locke & Latham, 1990).

While each of these theories deals with a particular aspect of motivation, it seems unrealistic to address them in isolation, since these factors often do come into play in and are important to employee motivation at one time or another.

Management Theories of Motivation

Other approaches to motivation are driven by aspects of management, such as productivity, human resources, and other considerations. Most notable in this regard are the following:

- **Scientific Management Theory**—Frederick Taylor's ideas, put into practice by the Gilbreths in the film *Cheaper by the Dozen*, focused on studying job processes, determining the most efficient means of performing them, and in turn rewarding employees for their productivity and hard work. This theory assumes people are motivated and able to continually work harder and more efficiently and that employee pay should be based on the amount and quality of the work performed. Over time, this approach is limited by the capacity of employees to continue to increase the quantity of work produced without sacrificing the quality.

- **McGregor's Theory X and Theory Y**—draws upon the work of Herzberg and develops a human resources management approach to motivation. This theory first classifies managers into one of two groups. **Theory X** managers view employees as unmotivated and disliking work. Under the Theory X approach, the manager's role is to focus on the hygienes and to control and direct employees; it assumes employees are mainly concerned about safety. In contrast, **Theory Y** managers focus on Herzberg's motivators and work to assist employees in achieving these higher levels. In assessing this theory, researchers have found approaching motivation from this either/or perspective is short-sighted.
- **Ouchi's Theory Z**—is rooted in the idea that employees who are involved in and committed to an organization will be motivated to increase productivity. Based on the Japanese approach to management and motivation, **Theory Z** managers provide rewards, such as long-term employment, promotion from within, participatory management, and other techniques to engage and motivate employees (Ouchi, 1981). In fact, Theory Z can be considered an early form of engagement theory.

While all of these theories are helpful in understanding management and motivation from a conceptual perspective, it is important to recognize that most managers draw upon a combination of needs, extrinsic factors, and intrinsic factors in an effort to help motivate employees, to help employees meet their own personal needs and goals, and ultimately to engage employees in and to achieve effectiveness and balance within the organization. Managers typically take into account most of the aspects upon which these theories focus. That is, expectations, goal setting, performance, feedback, equity, satisfaction, commitment, and other characteristics are considered in the process of motivating employees.

A BIT MORE ABOUT INCENTIVES AND REWARDS

Throughout this chapter, we have discussed what motivates employees. As the previous discussion indicates, motivation for employees results from a combination of incentives that take the form of extrinsic and intrinsic rewards. These topics warrant a bit more discussion.

Extrinsic Rewards

There are a host of external things that managers can provide that may serve as incentives for employees to become more engaged in an organization and increase their productivity. These include tangible rewards, such as: money (pay, bonuses, stock options), benefits (health, dental, vision, paid time off, retirement accounts, etc.), flexible schedules, job responsibilities and duties, promotions, changes in status, supervision of others, praise, feedback and recognition, a good boss, a strong leader, other inspirational people, and a nurturing organizational culture.

As this list demonstrates, extrinsic rewards are all tangible types of rewards. Intrinsic rewards stand in marked contrast to these.

Intrinsic Rewards

Intrinsic rewards are internal to the individual and are in many ways less tangible. In fact, they are highly subjective in that they represent how the individual perceives and feels about work and its value. Five types of **intrinsic rewards** that have been summarized by Manion (2005) include:

- *Healthy relationships*—in which employees are able to develop a sense of connection with others in the workplace.
- *Meaningful work*—where employees feel they make a difference in people's lives. This is typically a motivator for people to enter and stay employed in the health care industry. This type of work is viewed as that in which the meaningful tasks outweigh the meaningless ones. This reinforces the mantra Herzberg first espoused in 1968 and revisited in a 2003 issue of the *Harvard Business Review*, in which he stated: "Forget praise. Forget punishment. Forget cash. You need to make their jobs more interesting" (Herzberg, 2003, p. 87). As documentation and the hassle factor of getting approvals and reimbursement in health care have increased, managers need to be aware that such tasks and hassles detract from the meaningfulness quotient.
- *Competence*—where employees are encouraged to develop skills that enable them to perform at or above standards, preferably the latter.
- *Choice*—where employees are encouraged to participate in the organization in various ways, such as by expressing their views and opinions, sharing in decision making, and finding other ways to facilitate participatory approaches to problem solving, goal setting, and the like.
- *Progress*—where managers find ways to hold employees accountable, facilitate their ability to make headway toward completing their assigned tasks, and celebrate when progress is made toward completing important milestones within a project.

Intrinsic rewards, coupled with extrinsic ones, lead to high personal satisfaction and serve as motivators for most employees.

WHY MOTIVATION MATTERS

Health care organizations face pressure externally and internally. Externally, the health care system must confront challenges such as the aging population, economic down-turns, reductions in reimbursements, increases in market competition, increases in the cost of providing care, and health care reform. Internally, our health care system faces pressure stemming from challenges such as shortages of certain types of health care workers, increasing accreditation requirements, increasing regulations, dealing with limited resources, increasing responsibilities connected with providing quality care, and ensuring patient safety. These pressures can lead to employees who feel burned out, frustrated, and overworked. As health care employees are continually being asked to increase their responsibilities with fewer resources, managers must create a work environment in which employees are engaged, happy at their job, inspired, and motivated.

People spend approximately one-third of their lives at work, and managers need to recognize the workplace is one of the most important aspects of a person's identity. In situations where people are not free to work at their maximum effectiveness and their self-esteem is constantly under attack, stress occurs, morale diminishes, illness prevails, and absenteeism goes up (Scott & Jaffe, 1991; Sherwood, 2013). As noted, motivated employees are fully engaged in their work and contribute at a much higher level than their counterparts who see their work as simply a job. Additional reasons why motivation matters include:

- Employees who are motivated feel invested in the organization, are happier, work harder, are more productive, and typically stay longer with an organization (Levoy, 2007, p. 70).
- Managers play important roles in the engagement process (O'Boyle & Harter, 2013), particularly with respect to providing recognition (Towers Watson, 2010a, 2010b).
- Managers who understand employees' job-related needs experience a higher level of motivated behavior from their employees (Levoy, 2007, p. 113).
- All behavior is needs oriented. Even irrational behavior stems from a motivator of some sort. Once a need is satisfied, its impact as a motivator lessens. This basic foundational understanding of motivation is essential to successful motivation and management of employees (Levoy, 2007, p. 118).
- Managers need to draw upon different strategies in order to engage different types of workers, such as Baby Boomers, Millennials, women, etc. (O'Boyle & Harter, 2013).
- Disengaged employees, as mentioned, have significant financial impacts on an organization's bottom line (O'Boyle & Harter, 2013). They can also act as "Debby Downers" who pull other employees down, decrease morale, and increase turnover.

- A motivated and engaged workforce experiences better outcomes and provides an organization with a competitive edge to successfully compete and be viewed as a dominant force in the market.

MOTIVATED VS. ENGAGED—ARE THE TERMS THE SAME?

Oftentimes when you read about motivation, the term *engaged* appears within the same context. In order to be motivated, employees must be engaged—and in order to be engaged, they must be motivated. Towers Watson's definition of **employee engagement** encompasses three dimensions:

- *Rational*—How well employees understand their roles and responsibilities;
- *Emotional*—How much passion they bring to their work and their organization; and,
- *Motivational*—How willing they are to invest discretionary effort to perform their roles well (Towers Watson, 2010a, p. 1).

This definition demonstrates the linkage between the two concepts and the importance of focusing on both of these areas by managers and leaders.

Why is this important in health care? The impacts can be significant. In fact, Cornerstone OnDemand reported, "recent research and practical in-the-field experience demonstrates that healthcare organizations can create the most profound improvements in patient care and satisfaction levels simply by improving employee engagement" (2014, p. 3). In particular, such engagement results in:

- Better quality;
- Increased patient safety;
- Higher patient satisfaction; and
- Stronger organization financial performance.

In addition, Gallup studies also show that engaged health care "employees are more:

- loyal to the organization
- willing to put forth discretionary effort
- willing to trust and cooperate with others
- willing to work through challenges
- willing to speak out about problems and offer constructive suggestions for improvements" (Kamins, 2015, p. 1).

The health policy changes to move reimbursement to a "value-based purchasing" system, where payments from Medicare and Medicaid are tied to quality and patient care outcomes, suggest additional focus needs to be paid to those who deliver care to patients, which in turn suggests the need to enhance employee motivation and engagement (Sherwood, 2013). While several recent articles have been critical of the benefits and costs of employee engagement, the relationship to organizational outcomes and improvement efforts, and the lack of a uniform definition of the concept, Leeds and Nierle (2014) conclude continued efforts to study the concept and to utilize employee engagement strategies have been deemed effective.

This is also supported by other recent studies that suggest disengaged employees bring morale down and impact the organization's bottom line. According to Gallup only 30% of U.S. full-time employees were highly engaged in their work; they estimated the cost of this at between $450 billion and $550 billion in lost productivity alone as a result of the 70% who are disengaged employees (O'Boyle & Harter, 2013). Towers Watson's (2014) *Global Workforce Study* found a slightly higher percentage (40%) of workers being highly engaged. While the percentage of the hospital workforce is even a bit higher, it is still estimated by Towers Watson to be only 44% (Sherwood, 2013). This suggests leaders and managers need to increase their attention to engagement and motivation of their workforces. Sherwood (2013) states, "when employees believe their organization truly values quality care – and also get the support they need on the job – their patients are more satisfied, they take less sick time and have fewer on-the-job accidents, and health outcomes are better" (p. 5). This, in turn, impacts the organization's bottom line.

MEASURING ENGAGEMENT

The issues of accurately measuring engagement have become front and center for employers. Recent backlash has taken different forms, including concerns with companies' abilities to define "fuzzy" concepts (like engagement), to separate the concept from other ideas (such as job satisfaction and commitment), to measure accurately, and/or to link engagement to performance, and has suggested that change is needed (Bersin, 2014a; Brown & Reilly, 2013; Ott, 2011; Saks & Gruman, 2014; Shuck, Ghosh, Zigarmi, & Nimon, 2012). While some have said to just not bother to worry about engagement (Keegan, 2014), others see opportunity in the world of **people analytics**. According to Fuller (2014b) "People analytics is the use of people-related data to optimize business outcomes (and solve business problems) at the individual, team or organizational levels" (p. 2). Several authors, including Bersin (2014b, 2015), Fuller (2014a), Housman (2015), and Mims (2015), suggest the future holds great promise for demonstrating the use of "big data" and analytics to improve measurement, data collection, and prediction in the human resources area. That is, an evidence-based approach will be used to assess organizational, team, and individual performance in an effort to better understand the relationships between motivation and engagement with rewards, as well as to address all types of business problems such as employee retention, turnover, fraud, customer satisfaction, absenteeism, patient safety, etc. Employee engagement will be an important area of investigation in the people analytics discussion.

MISCONCEPTIONS ABOUT MOTIVATION AND EMPLOYEE SATISFACTION

Managers tend to have many misconceptions about motivation. As health care managers, it is important to assess and understand such misconceptions in an effort to become more effective managers and to not perpetuate myths about motivation. For example, research indicates managers typically make incorrect assumptions about what motivates their employees. Morse (2003) states "managers are not as good at judging employee motivation as they think they are. In fact, people from all walks of life seem to consistently misunderstand what drives employee motivation" (p. 18). The following is an enumeration of many of these misconceptions.

- *Although I'm not motivated by extrinsic rewards, others are.* This idea is discussed by Morse (2003) in his review of Chip Heath's study of intrinsic and extrinsic rewards. The conclusion is an "extrinsic incentive bias" exists and is, in fact, widespread among managers and employees. That is, individuals assume others are driven more by extrinsic rewards than intrinsic ones. Some studies have shown this to be a false assumption. Recent research suggests, however, employee views about extrinsic rewards do differ across generations, with Baby Boomers ranking extrinsic rewards less highly than Gen Xers and Millennials (Schullery, 2013).
- *All motivation is intrinsic.* Managers need to remember that typically a combination of factors motivates employees, not just one type of extrinsic or intrinsic reward (Manion, 2005).
- *Some people just are not motivated.* Everyone is motivated by something; the problem for managers is that "that something" may not be directed toward the job. This creates challenges for managers who must try to redirect the employees' energies toward job-related behaviors (Manion, 2005).
- *People are motivated by money.* Compensation motivates only to a point; that is, when compensation isn't high enough or is considered to be inequitable, it's a de-motivator. In contrast, when it is too high, it also seems to be a de-motivator, what Atchison (2003) calls the "golden handcuffs," and results in individual performance being tempered to protect the higher compensation level. Santamour states, "Eighty-nine percent of managers believe that for their employees it is all about the money, but there is no research to support that" (2009b, p. 10). Generally, employees tend

to rank pay as less important than other motivators. This is supported by the 1999 Hay Group study, in which 500,000 employees ranked fair pay and benefits as the least important of 10 motivating factors that keep them committed to staying with their companies. Chamorro-Premuzic (2013) also reviewed numerous research studies that linked pay and motivation and concluded "if we want an engaged workforce, money is clearly not the answer.....money does not buy engagement" (p. 2). The bottom line from Atchison's (2003) perspective is that "as soon as money is predictable, it is an entitlement, not a motivator" (p. 21).

- *Motivation is manipulation.* Manipulation carries negative implications; in contrast, motivation is positive and benefits both management and the employee (Manion, 2005).
- *One-size-fits-all reward and recognition programs motivate staff.* People, being people, are different, act in different ways, and are motivated by different things. Tailoring rewards and recognition is viewed as a way to focus on and understand the individual and his/her unique qualities (Atchison, 2003).
- *Motivational people are born, not made.* Studies show that people aren't born to motivate. In fact, Manion states, "anyone can become an effective motivator. It simply takes an understanding of the theories and basic principles" (Manion, 2005, p. 284), as well as the desire to develop these skills.
- *There is one kind of employee satisfaction.* Atchison (2003) discusses the pros and cons of "egocentric and other-centered satisfaction" and suggests that in the short run, employees respond to specific rewards that they receive personally, but in the longer run, they respond to quality performance of the team and the organization. Thus, they migrate from being self-centered to being other-centered in terms of job satisfaction—from a "me" to a "we" mentality.
- *Motivation and engagement at work only relates to what happens at work.* Several authors have suggested employers need to take a more holistic approach to understand their employees (Bersin 2014a; Kilatalahti & Vittala, 2014; LaMotte, 2015). Doing this requires taking a broader view, asking questions about, and developing an understanding of employees' lives inside and outside the work environment.

MOTIVATIONAL AND ENGAGEMENT STRATEGIES

The literature provides an array of strategies for managers to use in seeking to help motivate and engage individuals. Some of these seem very obvious, while others represent the "tried-and-true" approaches to management. Still others represent innovations. No matter, they are worth enumerating here.

- *Expect the best.* People live up to the expectations they and others have of them. As stated best by Henry Ford: "Whether you think you can or you think you can't, you're right!" (Manion, 2005).
- *Communicate and address the big picture.* Employees are more engaged when their bosses communicate regularly, keep them apprised of what is happening, and what the collective purpose is of the organization. They also need to understand how what they are tasked with fits into the larger picture of the organization (Baldoni, 2008, 2013), as well as society as a whole (Kanter, 2013). The latter is particularly true in health care, whereas Herzer and Pronovost (2013) suggest "inspiring a collective purpose and vision" is an important motivator for physicians. This is also the case for other health care professions in both direct care and non-direct care settings.
- *Reward the desired behavior.* Make sure that rewards are not given for undesirable behaviors and be sure to use many different types of rewards to achieve the desired outcomes (Manion, 2005). Do something special to recognize desired behavior; examples suggested by Studer (2003, 2014) include sending a written thank you note to an employee's home or using a "WOW card." The latter is a simple card that can be filled out and sent to an employee, explaining that "Today you 'WOWed' me when you _____." Fill in the blank with an explanation of what that special something was.
- *Create a "FUN (Focused, Unpredictable, and Novel) approach."* Atchison (2003, p. 21) suggests using money for a variety of creative employee rewards, such as giving $50 gift certificates to a shopping center in recognition of employees' exceeding expected patient outcomes.
- *Celebration.* Baldoni (2008) suggests using celebration to communicate the importance of completed projects or progress made.
- *Reward employees in ways that enhance performance and motivate them.* Don't waste money on traditional types of recognition. Though these are viewed as being nice, they don't motivate (Atchison, 2003). Money is better spent on true rewards for specific types of performance and outcomes.
- *Tailor rewards.* As mentioned earlier, Atchison (2003) steers managers away from standard types of rewards, such as giving the obligatory Thanksgiving turkey—unless the employees look forward to those turkeys. Instead, he recommends finding more creative ways to spend the organization's money and reward employees.
- *Focus on revitalizing employees.* Research shows that, when employees are working on overloaded circuits, motivation is diminished and productivity declines. This is particularly true in health care organizations. Hallowell (2005) suggests managers can help to motivate employees by encouraging them to eat right, exercise regularly, take "real" vacations, get organized, and slow down.

- *Find creative ways to obtain information and recognize excellence in employees.* Studer (2003) suggests asking for feedback on service excellence when doing patient satisfaction surveys and hospital discharge phone calls. With data and information from these sources, recognition can be provided to individual employees, thereby motivating them to continue providing excellent customer service. This also communicates to the entire organization the importance of and commitment to a patient-centered and service-oriented culture.

- *Get subordinates to take responsibility for their own motivation.* This can be achieved by managers taking steps to deal with problem employees, to understand employees' needs, to determine what motivates their employees, to engage employees in the problem-solving process, and to really work hard at resolving, rather than ignoring, difficult employee problems (Nicholson, 2003).

- *"Do unto others as you would have done unto you."* It goes without saying that everyone wants to be treated well at work, making it important for managers to respect the employees they work with (Lipman, 2013).

- *Focus on collaboration instead of competition.* Health care is a team sport, where patient care is frequently provided by an array of employees. This is true of physicians collaborating with others to be patient-centered and work to enhance the quality of care (Herzer & Pronovost, 2013).

- *Play to employees' strengths, promote high performance, and focus on how they learn.* This requires managers to know what their employees' strengths and weaknesses are, to find out what will be required to get specific employees to perform, and to understand how to capitalize on the ways those employees learn as an alternative method of encouraging and motivating them (Buckingham, 2005).

- *Give employees "three compliments for every criticism."* Studer states: "I thought I heard that compliments and criticism were supposed to be balanced. But the truth is, if you give a staff member one compliment and one criticism, it equals a negative relationship. If you give a staff member two compliments to one criticism, it will equal a neutral relationship. If you give a staff three compliments to one criticism, it will equal a positive relationship" (2003, p. 232).

- *Acknowledge the importance of work-life balance and employee well-being.* Several studies, particularly those pertaining to younger generations, point out the importance of promoting well-being (Caver, Davenport, & Nyce, 2015; Gallup, 2014). A recent study of health care employees by Shuck and Reio (2014) states "high engagement group employees demonstrated higher psychological well-being and personal accomplishment, whereas low engagement group employees exhibited higher emotional exhaustion and depersonalization" (p. 43). Several other studies focus on balancing life at work with leisure activities (Kultalahti & Viitala, 2014;

O'Boyle & Harter, 2013; Zwilling, 2012). As managers, it is important to recognize this for all employees and respect their needs regarding leisure and other activities outside of work (Lipman, 2013).

MOTIVATING ACROSS GENERATIONS

The U.S. has experienced a health professions labor force shortage over the last decade. By the year 2020, a nationwide shortage is projected of approximately 100,000 physicians, one million nurses, and 250,000 public health professionals (Health Resources and Services Administration, n.d.). This shortage, along with the aging Baby Boomer population, means an intense focus is vital in order for health care organizations to successfully function over the next few decades. Total employment is estimated by the U.S. Bureau of Labor Statistics (BLS) to increase by 15.6 million, or 10.8%, during the period of 2012–2022. These projections include a changing labor force, specifically one that is older, more racially and ethnically diverse, as well as more demanding. More than 50% of new jobs are projected to be in professional and service-providing occupations. Of the four fastest growing occupations, three are in the health field, i.e., health care, health care support, personal care services—the fourth being the construction field. These four occupational fields are expected to comprise over 5.3 million new jobs, or one-third of total employment growth, by the year 2022 (BLS, 2009, 2013).

Health care managers need to embrace the challenges, opportunities, and new strategies when managing such a diverse labor force (American Hospital Association, 2010). This will require managers to evaluate their current management styles, especially when considering actively engaging and motivating a labor force across multiple generations. According to the American Hospital Association's (AHA) 2010 study, *Workforce 2015: Strategy Trumps Shortage*, social trends over the last several decades have been dominated by the values, preferences, and experiences of the Baby Boomer generation, which includes those born between 1946 and 1964. However, the **Baby Boomers** are only one of four generations that comprise today's labor force. A **generation** is a "group of individuals born and living contemporaneously who have common knowledge and experiences that affect their thoughts, attitudes, values, beliefs and behaviors" (Johnson & Johnson, 2010, p. 6). Members of the four main generations include **the traditionalists, the Baby Boomers, Generation X, and the Millennials (Generation Y)**. One consideration not previously addressed is that our workforce is experiencing history in the making as it is on the cusp of accommodating the newest generation, **Generation Z**, making five generations working alongside each other in the workplace. As pointed out by the AHA (2014) and Johnson and Johnson (2010), the intergenerational workforce reflects a continuum, with each generation moving along it and eventually leaving the workforce.

Each generation has unique characteristics and expectations and is motivated in different ways. Literature might vary slightly regarding the nicknames, birth date ranges, and cohort sizes, especially when considering the newest generations entering the workforce. The key points provided in Table 3-1 illustrate an overview of generational differences among workplace characteristics and motivational preferences.

What appeals to one generation more than likely will not appeal to another generation. Motivational techniques, such as rewards and incentives, vary widely across generations. One generation might prefer recognition based on proof of their time-tested work ethic, while another generation might expect instant gratification stemming from what they consider a job well done. Schullery (2013) found "Millennials are significantly more interested in extrinsic rewards than are Boomers, although Millennials are less interested than GenX" and that "each generation is increasingly less likely to value intrinsic rewards as highly as the previous generation" (p. 260). A caveat to this is that these results may change over time.

Different standards of motivation are required for each generation. In order for health care organizations to be successful in the future, the workplace needs to be one of coexistence of all generations, even when their workplace characteristics and motivational preferences are drastically different. Managers play a key role in how the generations will work together and what it takes to engage employees to be motivated workers.

MANAGING ACROSS GENERATIONS

Our current workforce is comprised of four predominant generations with the newest (and fifth) generation (Generation Z) just now entering the workforce in various positions such as part-time, summer, or college-type jobs. This multi-faceted workforce requires awareness from managers about how to manage across generations. A one-size-fits all management theory will not produce desired organizational outcomes. Additionally, encouraging employees to reach their optimal productivity while retaining valued employees during a labor workforce shortage will continue to be at the forefront of all organizational strategic plans.

Each person holds experiences that shape their lives, form their belief system and values, and contribute to their decision-making processes. Referred to as a **generational signpost**, each generation has experienced an event(s) or cultural phenomenon specific to one generation. Authors Johnson and Johnson (2010) theorize that these signposts "shape, influence, and drive expectations, actions, and mind-sets about the products we buy, the companies for which we work, and our expectations about life in general" (p. 4). Examples of these include questions like "Where were you the day Kennedy was shot?" or "Where were you when the Challenger blew up?" or "Where were you when the Twin Towers went down?" These signposts are important because they can help guide managers in managing their employees by recognizing how these signposts mold beliefs regarding company

TABLE 3-1 Generation Characteristics and Motivational Preferences

Generation	Traditionalist	Baby Boomers	Generation X	Generation Y	Generation Z
Born:	Before 1945	1946–1964	1965–1978	1979–1995	Born after 1995
Cohort size	27 million	76 million	60 million	88 million	20 million
Nickname	Silent Generation/ Matures	Boomers/ Woodstock Generation	Gen Xers	Millennials	Linksters/New Silent Generation
Workplace characteristics	Respectful of authority Value duty and sacrifice Value accountability and practical experience Strong work ethic with emphasis on timeliness and productivity Strong interpersonal skills Value academic credentials Accept limited resources Loyal to employer and expect loyalty in return	Individuality Driven by goals for success Measure work ethic in hours worked and financial rewards Believe in teamwork Emphasize relationship building Expect loyalty from coworkers Career equals identity A democratic approach Competitive	Self-reliant Highly educated Questioning Risk-averse Most loyal employees Want open communication Respect production over tenure Value control of their time Invest loyalty in a person, not in an organization	Image conscious Need constant feedback and reinforcement Idealist Team-oriented Want open communication Search for an individual who will help them achieve their goals Search for ways to shed stress Racial and ethnic identification of reduced importance Organized and prefer structure	Results-focused Tech savvy, yet struggle with face-to-face communications Value structure, routine, and predictability Prefer clear, direct job descriptions/ duties, and expectations Strong work ethic Leaders in online collaboration Strong ability to multitask High entrepreneurial attributes
Motivational preferences	Loyalty Hierarchical structure	Work for managers who treat them as equals	Genuine and informal managers	Value instant gratification	Search for and value ways to improve the world they live in (community service-oriented)

(continued)

TABLE 3-1 Generation Characteristics and Motivational Preferences (Continued)

Generation	Traditionalist	Baby Boomers	Generation X	Generation Y	Generation Z
	Status Rewards based on promotion and job tenure Recognition of hard work and work ethic	Assurance that they are making a difference Work–life balance	Training and growth opportunities Flexibility Work deadlines, but with freedom and flexibility on how to reach those deadlines Results-oriented	Collaborative and positive interactions Achievement-oriented Coaching and support focused Personal fulfillment in job	Prefer management practices and workspaces that best support their needs Appreciation of collaboration tools Regular and consistent feedback Rewards that are consistent and tied to specific performance goals

Adapted from AHA, 2010, 2014; Johnson & Johnson, 2010.

loyalty, work ethics, and creating shared values that serve as bonding mechanisms among individuals of a team (Johnson & Johnson, 2010).

Managing the Gap

Managing across generations is not as simple as recognizing the workplace characteristics and motivational preferences of each generation. Managers must also be able to manage the gap that comes with different generations working side-by-side. The American Hospital Association (AHA) Committee on Performance Improvement (CPI) report titled, *Managing an Intergenerational Workforce: Strategies for Health Care Transformation* (2014), discusses generational diversity and its impact that is quickly altering workforce dynamics. In addition to recognizing workplace characteristics and motivational preferences, managers must also acknowledge the different priorities, communication styles, and interaction preferences, all of which influence organizational culture and performance. Tension amongst employees from different generations becomes apparent when working together, and these tensions are a result of different historical experiences and attitudes (AHA, 2014). In a survey by Lee Hecht Harrison, referenced in the AHA CPI report, "more than 60 percent of employers are experiencing tension between employees from different generations. The survey found that more than 70 percent of older employees are dismissive of younger workers' abilities, and nearly 50 percent of younger employees are dismissive of their older colleagues' abilities" (AHA, 2014, p. 9). Additionally, a 2013 study by Ernst & Young surveyed 1,215 professionals evenly divided across three generations—Baby Boomers, Generation X, and Generation Y (Millennials)—to assess perceptions on a variety of topics. Some key findings include:

- Many Gen Y members (87%) had moved into management roles during 2008 and 2013, while most of the Gen Xers and Boomers had been in these roles prior to that time.
- Boomers were seen as being more cost-effective than Gen Xers and more than twice as cost-effective as members of Gen Y: 78% vs. 59% vs. 34%.
- Both Boomers and Gen Yers were viewed as being difficult to work with, while Gen Xers were less so, but these numbers were smaller: 29% vs. 16% vs. 36%.
- Of the respondents 73% saw Boomers as hardworking as compared to 69% of Gen Xers, but only 39% of Millennials.
- Millennials and Gen Xers were far more tech savvy than Boomers: 85%, 77%, and 27%, respectively.
- Not surprisingly, a similar finding showed these same groups as being social media opportunists as compared to Boomers.
- While there were differences across the groups, the majority saw all generations as problem solvers and collaborators.

These findings indicate that managers have some significant challenges when trying to get these generations to work well together. Capitalizing on strengths and commonalities of each generational cohort can assist managers in creating a dynamic and engaged workforce. Recommended strategies for organizations to create high-performing teams that are able to evolve alongside the demands of our ever-changing health care system include the following:

- Perform an intergenerational evaluation to ascertain the organization's workforce profile and create a comprehensive plan;
- Employ targeted recruitment, segmented retention, and succession planning strategies; and
- Develop customized communication strategies designed to foster generational understanding and sensitivity (AHA, 2014).

These recommendations are a starting point, but it takes extensive consideration of timely and appropriate strategies to move beyond the generational gaps and tensions in the workplace. Utilizing the generational differences to work for the common good of the organization is key. Focusing on singular strategies specific to each generation is important, but not always feasible when considering five generations that vary greatly in their characteristics and motivational preferences. Consideration of universal strategies to achieve maximum productivity and increased morale will help organizations thrive when it comes to supporting and communicating with employees. We know with certainty each generation sets similar expectations from their jobs, such as work-life balance, a good salary with benefits, flexible work hours, and interesting work. It is the micro-details of each of these aspects of work that need to be designed differently for each generation in order to be effective and meaningful (Saleh, n.d.). As an example, research shows that Generation Zers have experienced a protected upbringing with extremely high parental involvement and parental mediation on their behalf. As a result, they are not experienced in dealing with conflict as compared to other generations. On the other end, Generation Xers are highly independent and grew up as "latchkey" kids. How would a manager manage these two groups?

Managers must also consider cultural factors inherent to each employee such as where people are born or where they live. Additionally, these generations are also diverse on many other factors, including politics, religion, gender, race, ethnicity, educational level, environment, disability, and socioeconomic status, all of which managers must be cognizant and make efforts to understand as they develop their cultural competence. (See Chapter 14 for more on this topic.)

As mentioned earlier in this chapter, the health care system is moving from a volume-based payment model to a value-based payment model. This movement can be paradoxical to some as it is focused on improving quality of care while lowering costs—two strategies that seemingly are difficult to achieve simultaneously. Bottom line, managers must not only manage across generations, they must also manage within this new health care paradigm. With a goal to utilize generational commonalities and differences for favorable organizational outcomes, our intergenerational workforce just might be able to make this movement work. According to the AHA (2014), a competitive advantage amongst health care leaders involves creating a culture that supports and fosters intergenerational teams using three intergenerational management strategies:

- Create a strong generational foundation;
- Institute effective generational management practices; and,
- Develop generational competence.

Competence as a managing factor includes those organizational core competencies that stem from the organization's mission and vision statements. The AHA (2014) identified a total of 17 must-do strategies and core organizational competencies to help leaders achieve the Triple Aim of health care. Of the 17 items, six were identified to support building a strong organizational intergenerational workforce.

1. Align hospitals, physicians, and other providers across the continuum of care.
2. Instruct and engage employees and physicians to produce leaders.
3. Create and employ patient-centered, integrated care.
4. Initiate accountable governance and leadership.
5. Encourage internal and external collaboration.
6. Engage employees' full potential.

TEXTBOX 3-1. FAQ: WHAT IS THE TRIPLE AIM?

The Triple Aim is a health care initiative that focuses on enhancing the individual experience of care; improving the health of populations; and minimizing the per capita costs of care for populations.

Berwick, D.M., Nolan, T.W. and Whittington, J. (2008). The triple aim: Care, health, and cost. Health Affairs, *27*(3):759–769. Brown, D. & Reilly, P. (2013). Reward and engagement: The new realities. Compensation & Benefits Review, *45*(3), 145–157.

Along with the motivational strategies listed earlier in this chapter, in consideration of managing the gap and managing across generations, managers can institute the following universal strategies:

- Evaluate before implementing. Before implementing new workplace strategies, review where you are and plan where you want to go.
- Obtain regular feedback and demonstrate the ability to act on suggestions.
- Encourage communication, understanding, and respect for differences.
- Tailor your workplace strategies and avoid the temptation to use a one size fits all management model.
- Focus on results, rather than process.
- Understand what it means to have engaged employees and strive for this goal.
- Encourage formal mentorship programs within the organization.
- Learn to recognize when someone may need extra support.
- Regularly give praise, say thanks, and celebrate when an employee or team gets it right (Saleh, n.d.).

RESEARCH OPPORTUNITIES IN MANAGEMENT AND MOTIVATION

Thanks to over a century of psychological investigators' interest in management, motivation, and organizational behavior, an abundance of research on these topics and applications to health care settings await you. An organization such as the Society for Industrial-Organization Psychology (SIOP), a special interest group of the American Psychological Association (APA), is especially productive in these domains. Likewise, the Academy of Management (AOM) delves into these issues. In addition to SIOP and AOM, here are some other agencies and organizations ripe for your examination:

- Agency for Healthcare Research and Quality;
- American College of Healthcare Executives;
- Health Occupations Students of America (HOSA);
- Hospital Research and Educational Trust (HRET);
- Inter-university Consortium for Political and Social Research (ICPSR);
- Johari Window;
- MindTools;
- O*Net;
- Studer Group;
- SHRM Foundation; and,
- U.S. Department of Health and Human Services, Health Resources and Services Administration (HRSA).

CONCLUSION

Motivation of employees is a tricky business. Managers often do not understand the concepts, principles, and myths about motivation well enough to put them in practice. Greater awareness and better understanding of motivation will result in better management. Managers can improve their success rate by providing extrinsic rewards that will help their employees to be intrinsically motivated to become top performers. As Studer, Hagins, and Cochrane (2014) state "without exception, we find that organizations that consistently improve their performance also have workforces that are passionate, productive, and proactive in finding ways to better meet patient needs. In a word, they are engaged" (p. S79). Successful managers also are able to recognize the differences when managing, motivating, and engaging across varying generations.

DISCUSSION QUESTIONS

1. Motivation is not a new concept, so why is motivation important? Is it more important for an employee to be motivated or engaged?

2. Compare and contrast needs-based theories of motivation. Which offers the most value to health care managers?

3. Discuss any limitations of the management approaches to motivation.

4. Which types of rewards are more important: intrinsic or extrinsic?

5. Does the importance of different types of rewards change over time as one progresses through one's career? What are some examples of rewards tailored to different generations?

6. Which myth of motivation is the most important? Are there other myths you can identify?

7. What motivational strategy would you apply with an employee who you think is capable of doing the work but is underperforming?

8. What motivational strategy would you apply with a highly effective employee who you want to keep performing at a very high level?

9. Which generation resonates best with you? In your opinion, which generation do you feel would be the most difficult to manage or motivate? Why?

10. Grace Jones is a four-decade Billing department employee in Happy Hollow Hospital. A recent graduate of Whassamatter U, Lindsey Flohan is a new hire in the Billing department. Grace has been assigned to train Lindsey to do her new job. Using the generational framework provided above, what conflicts can you anticipate between Grace and Lindsey?

Cases in Chapter 18 that are related to management and motivation (or related to this chapter) include:

- The Magic Is Gone
- Set Up for Failure?

Case study guides are available in the online Instructor's Materials.

REFERENCES

Adams, J. S. (1963, November). Towards an understanding of inequity. *Journal of Abnormal and Social Psychology*, *67*(5), 422–436.

Alderfer, C. P. (1972). *Existence, relatedness and growth: Human needs in organizational settings*. New York, NY: Free Press.

American Hospital Association (AHA). (2010, January). *Workforce 2015: Strategy trumps shortage.* Retrieved from http://www.aha.org/content/00-10/workforce2015report.pdf

American Hospital Association (AHA). (2014, January). *Managing an intergenerational workforce: Strategies for health care transformation*. Chicago, IL: Health Research & Educational Trust.

Atchison, T. A. (2003). Exposing the myths of employee satisfaction. *Healthcare Executive*, *17*(3), 20.

Baldoni, J. (2008, March 26). The three rules of employee engagement. *Harvard Business Review*. Retrieved from https://hbr.org/2008/03/the-three-rules-of-employee-en

Baldoni, J. (2013, July 4). Employee engagement does more than boost productivity. *Harvard Business Review*. Retrieved from https://hbr.org/2013/07/employee-engagement-does-more/

Bersin, J. (2014a, April 10). It's time to rethink the 'employment engagement' issue. *Forbes*. Retrieved from http://www.forbes.com/sites/joshbersin/2014/04/10/its-time-to-rethink-the-employee-engagement-issue/

Bersin, J. (2014b, November 4). The people analytics market heats up with new cloud offerings, *Forbes*. Retrieved from http://www.forbes.com/sites/joshbersin/2014/11/04/the-talent-analytics-market-heats-up-with-new-cloud-offerings/

Bersin, J. (2015, February 1). The geeks arrive in HR: People analytics is here. *Forbes*. Retrieved from http://www.forbes.com/sites/joshbersin/2015/02/01/geeks-arrive-in-hr-people-analytics-is-here/

Berwick, D. M., Nolan, T. W., & Whittington, J. (2008). The triple aim: Care, health, and cost. *Health Affairs*, *27*(3), 759–769.

Brown, D., & Reilly, P. (2013). Reward and engagement: The new realities. *Compensation & Benefits Review*, *45*(3), 145–157.

Buckingham, M. (2005). What great managers do. *Harvard Business Review*, *3*(3), 70–79.

Bureau of Labor Statistics (BLS). (2009, December). *Employment projections: 2008–2018*. Retrieved from http://www.bls.gov/news.release/ecopro.toc.htm

Bureau of Labor Statistics (BLS). (2013, December). *Occupational employment projections to 2022*. Retrieved from http://www.bls.gov/opub/mlr/2013/article/occupational-employment-projections-to-2022.htm

Caver, K., Davenport, T. O., & Nyce, S. (2015, Winter). Capturing the value of health and productivity programs. *Organizational Health and Wellness*, *38*(1), 30–35.

Chamorro-Premuzic, T. (2013, April 10). Does money really affect motivation? A review of the research. *Harvard Business Review*. [Blog post]. Retrieved from https://hbr.org/2013/04/does-money-really-affect-motiv

Cornerstone OnDemand. (2014). *The challenging state of employee engagement in healthcare today—and strategies to improve it*. Retrieved from http://www.cornerstoneondemand.com/sites/default/files/whitepaper/csod-wp-healthcare-employee-engagement-012015.pdf

Deci, E., & Ryan, R. (1985). *Intrinsic motivation and self-determination in human behavior*. New York, NY: Plenum Press.

Ernst & Young. (2013). *Younger managers rise in the ranks: Survey quantifies management shift and reveals challenges, preferred workplace perks, and perceived generational strengths and weaknesses.* Retrieved from http://www.ey.com/Publication/vwLUAssets/EY-Survey_shows_younger_managers_rising_in_the_ranks/$FILE/Executive-Summary-Generations-Research.pdf

Fuller, R. (2014a, November 17). A primer on measuring employee engagement. *Harvard Business Review.* Retrieved from https://hbr.org/2014/11/a-primer-on-measuring-employee-engagement

Fuller, R. (2014b, February 18). *People analytics: Forever changing the way you manage your business.* [Blog post]. Retrieved from http://www.volometrix.com/blog/people-analytics-forever-changing-the-way-you-manage-your-business

Gallup. (2014). Memo to executives: Well-being boosts engagement. *Gallup Business Journal.* Retrieved from http://www.gallup.com/businessjournal/180146/memo-executives-boosts-employee-engagement.aspx?version=print

Hallowell, E. M. (2005). Overloaded circuits: Why smart people underperform. *Harvard Business Review, 83*(1), 54–62.

Hammill, G. (2005). Mixing and managing four generations of employees. *FDU Magazine Online.* Retrieved from http://www.fdu.edu/newspubs/magazine/05ws/generations.htm

Health Resources and Services Administration (HRSA). (n.d.). *Health workforce studies.* Retrieved from http://bhpr.hrsa.gov/healthworkforce/

Herzberg, F. (2003). One more time: How do you motivate employees? *Harvard Business Review, 81*(1), 86–96.

Herzer, K. R., & Pronovost, P. J. (2013). Motivating physicians to improve quality. *American Journal of Medical Quality, 29*(5), 452–453.

Housman, M. (2015). The next frontier for human resources? It's people analytics? *HR Insights.* Retrieved from http://www.eremedia.com/tlnt/the-next-frontier-for-human-resources-its-people-analytics/

Johnson, M., & Johnson, L. (2010). *Generations inc.* New York, NY: American Management Association.

Kamins, C. (2015, February 23). What too many hospitals are overlooking. *GALLUP Business Journal.* Retrieved from http://www.gallup.com/businessjournal/181658/hospitals-overlooking.aspx?utm_source=&utm_medium=&utm_campaign=tiles

Kanter, R. M. (2013, October 23). Three things that actually motivate employees. *Harvard Business Review.* Retrieved from https://hbr.org/2013/10/three-things-that-actually-motivate-employees/

Keegan, P. (2014). The five new rules of employee engagement. *Inc.* Retrieved from http://www.inc.com/magazine/201412/paul-keegan/the-new-rules-of-engagement.html

Kultalahti, S., & Viitala, R. L. (2014). Sufficient challenges and a weekend ahead—Generation Y describing motivation at work. *Journal of Organizational Change Management, 27*(4), 569–582.

LaMotte, S. (2015, January 13). Employee engagement depends on what happens outside of the office. *Harvard Business Review.* Retrieved from https://hbr.org/2015/01/employee-engagement-depends-on-what-happens-outside-of-the-office

Leeds, J. P., & Nierle, D. (2014, Winter). Engaging in healthy debate over employee engagement. *The Public Manager, 43*(4), 61.

Levoy, B. (2007). *222 secrets of hiring, managing, and retaining great employees in healthcare practices.* Sudbury, MA: Jones and Bartlett.

Lipman, V. (2013, March 18). 5 easy ways to motivate—and demotivate—employees. *Forbes*. Retrieved from http://www.forbes.com/sites/victorlipman/2013/03/18/5-easy-ways-to-motivate-and-demotivate-employees/

Locke, E. A., & Latham, G. P. (1990). *A theory of goal setting and task performance*. Englewood Cliffs, NJ: Prentice Hall.

Manion, J. (2005). *From management to leadership*. San Francisco, CA: Jossey-Bass.

Manion, J. (2009). *The engaged workforce: proven strategies to build a positive health care workplace*. Chicago, IL: Health Forum, Inc.

Manville, B., & Ober, J. (2003). Beyond empowerment: Building a company of citizens. *Harvard Business Review, 81*(1), 48–53.

Maslow, A. H. (1954). *Motivation and personality*. New York, NY: Harper & Row.

McClelland, D. C. (1985). *Human motivation*. Glenview, IL: Scott, Foresman.

Mims, C. (2015, February 16). In 'people analytics,' you're not a human, you're a data point. *Wall Street Journal*. Retrieved from http://www.wsj.com/articles/in-people-analytics-youre-not-a-human-youre-a-data-point-1424133771

Morse, G. (2003). Why we misread motives. *Harvard Business Review, 81*(1), 18.

Nicholson, N. (2003). How to motivate your problem people. *Harvard Business Review, 81*(1), 57–65.

O'Boyle, E., & Harter, J. (2013). *State of the American workplace: Employee engagement insights for U.S. business leaders*. Washington, DC: GALLUP.

Ott, A. C. (2011, July 12). Are scorecards and metrics killing employee engagement? *Harvard Business Review*. Retrieved from https://hbr.org/2011/07/are-scorecards-and-metrics-kil

Ouchi, W. G. (1981). *Theory Z*. Reading, MA: Addison-Wesley.

Saks, A. M., & Gruman, J. A. (2014). What do we really know about employee engagement? *Human Resource Development Quarterly, 25*(2), 155–182.

Saleh, K. (n.d.). *Managing to manage across generations at work*. Toronto, ON: The Psychology Foundation of Canada. Retrieved from http://www.psychologyfoundation.org/pdf/publications/GenerationsAtWork.pdf

Santamour, B. (2009). Inspired staff can see you through hard times. *Hospitals & Health Networks, 83*(3), 10.

Schullery, N. M. (2013). Workplace engagement and generational differences in values. *Business Communication Quarterly, 76*(2), 252–265.

Scott, C., & Jaffe, D. (1991). *Empowerment: A practical guide for success*. Los Altos, CA: Crisp.

Sherwood, R. (2013, October 30). Employee engagement drives health care quality and financial returns. *Harvard Business Review*. Retrieved from https://hbr.org/2013/10/employee-engagement-drives-health-care-quality-and-financial-returns/

Shuck, B., Ghosh, R., Zigarmi, D., & Nimon, K. (2012). The jingle jangle of employee engagement: Further exploration of the emerging construct and implications for workplace learning and performance. *Human Resources Development Review, 12*(1), 11–35.

Shuck, B., & Reio, T. G. (2014). Employee engagement and well-being: A moderation model and implications for practice. *Journal of Leadership & Organizational Studies, 21*(1), 43–58.

Skinner, B. F. (1953). *Science and human behavior*. New York, NY: Macmillan.

Sperry, L. (2003). *Becoming an effective health care manager*. Baltimore, MD: Health Professions Press.

Studer, Q. (2003). *Hardwiring excellence*. Gulf Stream, FL: Fire Starter Publishing.

Studer, Q. (2012, March 31). 10 free (or very inexpensive) ways to engage staff. *Becker's Hospital Review.* Retrieved from http://www.beckershospitalreview.com/hospital-management-administration/10-free-or-very-inexpensive-ways-to-engage-staff.html

Studer, Q, Hagins, M., & Cochrane, B. S. (2014). The power of engagement: Creating the culture that gets your staff aligned and invested. *Healthcare Management Forum, 27,* S79–S87.

Towers Watson (Originally published by Towers Perrin). (2010a). *Turbocharging employee engagement: The power of recognition from managers—Part 1.* Retrieved from http://www.towerswatson.com/en-US/Insights/IC-Types/Survey-Research-Results/2009/12/Turbocharging-Employee-Engagement-The-Power-of-Recognition-From-Managers-Part-1

Towers Watson (Originally published by Towers Perrin). (2010b). *Turbocharging employee engagement: The power of recognition from managers—Part 2.* Retrieved from http://www.towerswatson.com/en-US/Insights/IC-Types/Survey-Research-Results/2009/12/Turbocharging-Employee-Engagement-The-Power-of-Recognition-From-Managers-Part-2

Towers Watson. (2014). *Global workforce study at a glance.* Retrieved from http://www.towerswatson.com/en-US/Insights/IC-Types/Survey-Research-Results/2014/08/the-2014-global-workforce-study

Vroom, V. H. (1964). *Work and motivation.* New York, NY: Wiley.

Zwilling, M. (2012, January 10). 8 ways leaders can motivate employees beyond money. *Forbes.* Retrieved from http://www.forbes.com/sites/martinzwilling/2012/01/10/8-ways-leaders-can-motivate-employees-beyond-money/

Organizational Behavior and Management Thinking

Sheila K. McGinnis

LEARNING OBJECTIVES

By the end of this chapter, the student will be able to:

- Characterize organizational behavior and explain how thinking and soft skills relate to organizational behavior;
- Critique how three management roles relate to organizational behavior and thinking;
- Assess the importance of four key features of thinking;
- Distinguish between three types of mental structures and how they affect thinking;
- Differentiate between four information processing features and how they shape the way we think;
- Compare and contrast the differences in the two modes of thinking;
- Appraise three common distortions in decision making and how they can affect decisions in the workplace;
- Analyze four social cognition distortions and how they affect social interactions in the workplace;
- Apply techniques to counter negative self-talk and manage emotions;
- Assess how to develop empathy for others and how to manage social motivation in the workplace; and
- Demonstrate how to increase the use of deliberate thinking processes in decision-making and organization-wide.

INTRODUCTION

We all want to understand ourselves and others, especially in the workplace. The well-known Shakespearean quote from *Julius Caesar* about our faults not lying in the stars reminds us that many thorny issues we face do not originate "out there," caused by circumstances beyond our control. Instead they can be of our own making—or more specifically—be caused by our own thinking, much of which is beyond our awareness.

When we appreciate how we ourselves think, we will be prepared to understand the behavior of others in organizations. As an aspiring manager, you will be expected to think clearly and keep learning. Clear thinking means knowing why you think what you think, why you believe what you believe, and how you know what you know. Much of what you currently "know" is based on your prior life experiences, which most people seldom examine critically. In today's world, we all are called upon to think deeply. By examining your own thinking and letting go of past unexamined notions and habitual thought patterns, you can become more aware and deliberate in future thinking. You discover the world anew when you take charge of your own thinking.

Health care managers, like managers in other industries, are responsible for effectively using the informational, financial, physical, and human resources of their organizations to deliver patient services. As you can see from the topics presented in this textbook, the manager's role requires a wide range of interpersonal skills. Leadership (Chapter 2), motivation (Chapter 3), managing health care professionals (Chapter 11), and teamwork (Chapter 13) are some of the most important interpersonal skills examined at length in other chapters of this text. Organization behavior leverages these "soft skills"—arguably the hardest skills of all to master.

In today's job market, technical skills alone are not enough. Employers seek job candidates who also have well developed soft skills. **Soft skills** include both **thinking skills** (critical thinking, reasoning, problem-solving, decision making, and flexibility) and **socio-emotional skills** (interpersonal relations, teamwork, communication, empathy, self-awareness, and self-discipline). Soft skills are organizational behavior skills, and developing them is advantageous for initial hiring and future advancement in management. They can make the difference between being a manager and being a leader.

The purpose of this chapter is to see how managers think, especially the mental processes that short circuit quality thinking. As you read and participate in class discussion, *pay attention to how you think*. Knowledge of how your brain works gives you the ability to modify your own thinking and find ways to work more effectively with others—developing your organizational behavior skills.

THE FIELD OF ORGANIZATIONAL BEHAVIOR

Organizational behavior is a broad area of management that studies how people act in organizations. Managers can use theories and knowledge of organizational behavior to improve management practices for effectively working with and influencing employees to attain organization goals. The field of organizational behavior has evolved from the scientific study of management during the industrial era to administrative theories of the manager's role, principles of bureaucracy, human relations studies of employees' needs, and new insights from human cognition and complexity theory. Organizational behavior is an interdisciplinary field that draws on the ideas and research of many disciplines concerned with human behavior and interaction. These include psychology, social psychology, industrial psychology, sociology, communications, anthropology, and, increasingly, neuroscience, which reveals images of our neurological responses to cognitive, emotional, and social stimuli (Becker, Cropanzano, & Sanfey, 2011; Robbins, 2003). In this chapter, we will highlight ideas from cognitive psychology (the study of human thinking) and their application to organizational behavior.

ORGANIZATIONAL BEHAVIOR'S CONTRIBUTION TO MANAGEMENT

The most successful organizations make the best use of their employees' talents and energies (Heil, Bennis, & Stephens, 2000; Huselid, 1995). Firms that effectively manage employees have a competitive advantage in their field. Pfeffer (1998) estimates that organizations can reap a 40% gain by managing people in ways that build commitment, involvement, learning, and—ultimately—organizational competence and performance. In short, as noted previously, the so-called "soft skills" matter.

Because employees drive an organization's success, how well the manager interacts and works with a variety of individuals is key to the manager's success. The manager who is skilled in organizational behavior will be able to work effectively with employees and colleagues across the organization, assisting and influencing them to support and achieve organization goals.

KEY TOPICS IN ORGANIZATIONAL BEHAVIOR

Organizational behavior is a broad field comprised of many topics. Work behaviors are typically examined at different levels—individual behavior, group behavior, and collective behavior across the organization—with different topics prominent at each level. Studying individual behavior helps managers understand how assumptions, perceptions, and personality influence work behavior, motivation, and other important work outcomes like satisfaction, commitment, and learning. Examining interactions in the group setting provides insight into the challenges of leadership, teamwork, decision making, power, and conflict. Studying collective organization-wide behavior (sometimes referred to as organization theory) helps explain how to organize work, structure authority and power relationships, how to use systems for decision making and control, how to design human resource activities (staffing, training, appraisal, compensation), how organization culture affects behavior, how organizations learn, and how they adapt to changing competitive, economic, social, and political conditions.

ORGANIZATIONAL BEHAVIOR ISSUES IN HEALTH ORGANIZATIONS

Organizational behavior, whether in a health care organization or another type of organization, is concerned with behavior that occurs under the conditions found in an organizational setting. While a specific organization setting may create unique challenges or certain sets of problems, the behaviors of interest are similar to those of individuals, groups, and often organizations in other settings or industries (Weick, 1969). Thus, health care organizational behavior does not create unique management issues so much as certain issues are more prevalent in health care and can occur along with other challenges (Shortell & Kaluzny, 2000).

Many of these challenges directly or indirectly impact what is expected of health care workers and how they behave in health care organizations. Health organizations are staffed with a professional workforce and impose exacting requirements on how work is organized and accomplished. The complex work of health care has a high risk of serious or deadly error, which necessitates extremely reliable systems of practice at all organization levels. Complex technical and medical systems demand sophisticated technical expertise, which requires a highly educated, efficient, and well-coordinated workforce. Professional workers, especially physicians, work with a great deal of autonomy and control over the technical and clinical aspects of care delivery. As a result, health care managers are responsible for facilitating the delivery of complex medical services that must be carefully coordinated by autonomous professionals over whom the manager has little direct authority—all within an industry system that is facing extreme financial and policy challenges.

The work of health care is carried out against the backdrop of many complex demands. Yet every day, the health care manager must orchestrate the collective work of employees and colleagues to achieve organizational goals. Managers with organizational behavior skills can unleash the talents of others to help their organizations thrive in a demanding industry. In just one chapter we cannot examine the many interesting topics in organizational behavior such as personality, conflict, communication, or culture. Instead, this chapter starts at the very beginning, with management thinking—the "inner game" of organizational behavior.

THINKING: THE "INNER GAME" OF ORGANIZATIONAL BEHAVIOR

The purpose of thinking is to inform our actions—our choices, decisions, interactions, and behaviors. Organization science explanations of human behavior increasingly draw upon human thinking, especially cognitive psychology and social cognition. In the cognitive framework, all behavior is inextricably tied to thinking, social interactions, and emotions. However, how human thinking affects life in organizations often goes unnoticed because much thinking is unspoken or beyond one's own awareness—in our "hidden brain" (Vedantam, 2010). We cannot understand behavior—our own and others'—without understanding the thoughts, assumptions, and perceived attributes of a situation that precede behavior and its consequences. Collectively, cognitive psychology and social cognition principles demonstrate the power of thought, showing that how people view a situation has a strong effect on how they respond to and act upon that situation. They remind managers that much of organizational behavior is about each person's "inner game," which is often not known by the individuals themselves nor revealed during interpersonal interactions.

Cognition refers to the mental processes involved in thinking, including perceiving and attending to information, processing information, and ordering information to create meaning that is the basis for choosing, acting, learning, and other human activities. Cognitive sciences have taught us that information processing capacities and mental habits shape and govern one's perceptions, assumptions (what we take for granted), and ultimately one's behaviors. This focus on thinking highlights the importance of perceptions, assumptions, expectations, individual identity, and judgments. In addition, it calls attention to hidden thinking, biases in information processing, and barriers to creating common meaning during communication. Finally, thinking sets the stage for individual and organizational learning. The human capacity to adapt is rooted in learning new ways of thinking and acting, which depends upon how we perceive the facts of a situation, act upon them, and rewire our brains to retain new ways of doing things. Contrary to the idea that organizations are well-oiled machines that respond perfectly to every management command, studies of thinking teach managers that humans have a limited capacity to process information and organizations are relational enterprises. We learn humans simplify and take shortcuts, individuals' actions are largely determined by how they perceive the world, and humans engage in an ongoing construction of their world by using stored information structures to guide perception and interpretation of events and information (Fiske & Taylor, 1991).

Social cognition, a special branch of social psychology, provides insight into how we understand and process social situations. **Social cognition** "is the study of how people make sense of other people and themselves" (Fiske & Taylor, 2013, p. 1). In the social world of work, our thinking patterns affect how we perceive others and make judgements about them, and socio-emotional intelligence affects our relationships. Experts have identified predictable habits of the mind based on the power of our perceptions and patterns of thinking. Those with particular relevance for managers and organizations include schemas, mental models, mindsets, attention, perceptions, automatic processing, cognitive heuristics and biases, attributions, social biases, and social motivations.

Emotions, our feelings towards people, things, or events, are *not* separate from thinking. The relationship between emotions and cognitions is complex, and emotions are interwoven into our thinking in countless ways (Kahneman, 2011). Emotions can influence what we notice, perceive, and recall; how we make decisions; and distort our reasoning. Emotions can affect whether we think deliberately or reactively, and our moods can affect how we make judgments (i.e., positive moods foster positive judgments). Under stress, strong emotions can even "hijack" our reasoning brain (Goleman, 1995): the more emotionally charged a situation the harder it is to be rational. In fact, our emotions are a major reason why much of our thinking is non-rational and contribute to biases. So while this chapter only examines emotions in the final section on social thinking, keep in mind that emotions play an implicit role in nearly all aspects of thinking.

The Manager's Job and Thinking

Managers wear many hats at work. Their tasks can be divided into three main kinds of work, comprised of three key roles and ten areas within those roles. First is the informational role, where the manager acts as monitor, disseminator, and spokesperson. Second is the decisional role, where the manager acts as entrepreneur, disturbance handler, and resource allocator. Third is the interpersonal role where the manager acts as negotiator, leader, liaison, and figurehead (Mintzberg, 1973). A manager's day-to-day effectiveness in these informational, decisional, and interpersonal roles largely depends on human thinking processes and social interactions. Understanding the ways others think and applying cognition principles, especially to achieve group and collective understanding, is a challenging skill for managers to master.

THE FOUR KEY FEATURES OF THINKING

The cognitive sciences examine numerous areas where thinking and how we see our world play a prominent role in organizational life. Daniel Kahneman, winner of the 2002 Nobel prize in economics, is actually a leading psychologist. His work on human cognition and judgment has revolutionized our understanding of thinking. Kahneman laid much of the foundation to identify many distortions (biases and shortcuts) in human reasoning. He also challenged the longstanding social science premise that humans are inherently rational decision makers. As behavioral economist Dan Ariely (2008) says, we humans are "predictably irrational," i.e., there are patterns in our non-rationality that make it predictable. So while we like to assume thinking is a rational process, in reality, much thinking is non-rational. Non-rational does not mean erratic or illogical thinking, and it is not inherently "bad" thinking. **Non-rational thinking** simply means much of the time our brains do not engage in active, conscious deliberation. Non-rational thinking is normal, useful, and necessary to help us cope with the large volume of information streaming through our daily lives.

Four key areas of thinking in organizational life are most relevant to the manager's three roles noted above (Hodgkinson & Healey, 2008). The brain is like a muscle—you need to use it properly to gain strength. You can learn to be your own coach to train your brain the right way. Consider the four factors we review next as different types of muscles. The first two are the small, seemingly insignificant muscles that are often neglected when training. They provide crucial support for the large muscle groups that actually deliver the body's major physical movement. So you will need to learn to use all four factors, because the first two factors we discuss are like the small muscles that support the next two factors, which are like performing large physical tasks.

MENTAL REPRESENTATION: THE INFRASTUCTURE OF THINKING

We usually see thinking as a way to gain knowledge. Yet our knowledge—especially how we represent what we know and believe—is also the starting point for how we think. Our brains do not store knowledge and beliefs as facts, we store them in memory as simplified **mental representations** that only approximate the real world. These representations contain concepts (about objects, causal reasoning, our identity, and relationships) that translate into our knowledge and experience (Dweck & London, 2004). We construct these representations to classify and organize what we "know" and to create meaning as we interpret our world. **Schemas**, **mental models**, and **mindsets** are all forms of mental representation that organize our knowledge and experience and underlie our knowledge, beliefs, and assumptions. These mental representations share some similarities. The different terms reflect different ways they have been studied and used in research. Our mental representations serve as stored templates that automate much of our thinking. They are also the source of our preconceptions, beliefs, and assumptions about how we see the world, how the world works, and how we expect others to behave.

Schemas, mental models, and mindsets are networks of associated concepts that become more elaborate (though not necessarily more accurate) when we map new experience and learning onto our existing mental representations. Existing knowledge, attitudes, and beliefs are structures that both guide and filter how we perceive, interpret, and judge a situation, others, and even ourselves. Think of them as preconceptions—useful yet imperfect templates for taking in and integrating what we know and believe. As you already know from your own experience, everyone's knowledge stuctures are unique—we start at different points of 'knowing' and follow our own paths to greater understanding. So a critical workplace challenge is how to reconcile all our different ways of knowing and thinking.

Schemas—Individual and Organizational

Schemas are mental representations of one's general knowledge and expectations about a concept. They contain knowledge of the concept's attributes, connections among those attributes, and examples of the concept (Fiske & Taylor, 1991). Schemas are cognitive simplifications of what we know and believe. They are the scaffold that directs how we perceive, classify, store, and act upon schema-relevant information. They organize what we know and guide how we use our knowledge. However, because they are simplifications they are incomplete and may be inaccurate.

According to Fiske and Taylor (1991), people develop schemas for many different concepts and situations. **Person schemas** characterize a certain person's traits and actions (e.g., Dad will loan me his car if I mow the lawn); **role schemas** define appropriate behaviors and expectations for a social category (e.g., grandmothers bake cookies, professors should grade fairly); and **event schemas** dictate one's expected "scripts" for how certain events should unfold (e.g., taking final exams, interviewing for a job, conducting a performance evaluation). Schemas tell us what to do and expect in many situations without having to think deeply. In health care organizations, members may hold schemas about strategies to attract and retain nurses, the patient's role in deciding about treatment, or how to work with other health care organizations in the local market.

We know thinking is an individual process, and can also be a collective one. As collectives of individuals, organizations are often viewed as perceiving, thinking, and learning—though collective thinking operates differently than individual thinking (Mohammed, Ferzandi, & Hamilton, 2010). While an organization does not literally think, its capacity to take collective action depends upon the degree to which organization members share a common viewpoint or common way of thinking about a situation. **Organizational schemas** serve as a form of organizational thinking. For managers, schemas are one way to foster the collective thinking and common understanding needed to mobilize members and coordinate organization-wide action. **Interpretative schemas**—commonly called "frames" or "framing"—are a way to shape collective understanding. Frames guide our interpretation of information by focusing our attention on certain elements and organizing our understanding of the social world (Goffman, 1974). Frames act as filters by structuring how we see things. Frames make it easier to handle complex information, yet can restrict our capacity to understand something in a new way.

Shared organizational schemas support member collaboration on organizational goals and initiatives that are consistent with the schemas. Conversely, when members have conflicting schemas, collaboration on organizational goals and initiatives will be hindered. How managers frame or present important ideas and major changes to the organization can influence how the idea or change is interpreted and how well it is accepted. For example, when introducing a patient safety initiative, managers need to legitimatize key elements of the new schema (e.g., the safety initiative, its purpose, how it works, how it changes daily work, etc.) and reduce barriers posed by beliefs of the old schema (e.g., individuals are to blame for medical errors, it is not okay to challenge authority or question clinical experts, the work of independent units is more important than the work of the entire system).

Mental Models

Recent efforts to understand individual and group psychology has led to the study of individual and group "mental models" and "mind-sets," two popular terms that are often used interchangeably. **Mental models** are "deeply held internal images of how the world works" (Senge, 1990, p. 174). **Mind-sets** are assumptions about personal abilities and characteristics (Dweck, 1986). While schemas are concerned with how we take in and integrate information, mental models and mindsets are concerned with our "**worldview**"—how we see the world and act upon it. These beliefs and assumptions shape our attitudes, interpretations, and behaviors (Dweck, 2006).

Scholars call mind-sets "lay" theories or implicit (i.e., unconscious) theories. These **implicit theories**, thus, are unconscious perceptions about how people behave and how the world works (Plaks, Grant, & Dweck, 2005). Like schemas, these mindsets are the frameworks that guide how we understand and act upon our world. Like schemas, mental models are abstract representations of reality that define what we expect or perceive in a situation, and how we interpret our experience of it. Mental models are initially flexible and become resistant to change over time. People are usually unaware that "implicit" mental models guide their actions, so they also fail to see when mental models limit their point of view. Managers can change and improve organizations by discovering, sharing, challenging, and changing the mental models and mindsets—both their own and others'.

For example, a new long-term care center manager finds the facility's occupancy rate is too low, and the staff is convinced the center's location is undesirable. When the manager does a market analysis, she learns that client decisions are more influenced by the range of services available rather than location alone. The staff's mental model that location drives client choice of facility was incorrect. When they revised their shared mental model to address the variety of services offered, the center's occupancy rate improved.

The Power of Our Beliefs

Psychologist Carol Dweck (2006) popularized one specific set of mindsets. Her theory of growth mindsets and fixed mindsets demonstrates the power of our fundamental beliefs about our own and others' abilities and personality traits. People with a **growth mindset** believe their intelligence and abilities are malleable, that they can be developed through learning, practice, and hard work. On the other hand, people with a **fixed mindset** believe their intelligence and abilities are fixed traits that cannot be cultivated or increased. The growth mindset person is curious, values learning and striving to overcome challenges. The fixed mindset person fears failing and tries to avoid situations with the potential for failure, which undermines growth and achievement.

Mindset matters. Years of research show that this fundamental belief dramatically affects how hard we work, our drive for challenge, our resilience in the face of setbacks. Our ultimate success in our careers and happiness in life depends more upon the mindset we adopt—and how we apply it—than our natural abilities and intellect (Dweck, 2006).

Mindsets have been studied extensively in many settings, including education, athletics, business, and politics. Studies show developing a growth mindset improves outcomes in math, science, sports training, interpersonal relationships, and intergroup ethnic conflict. A growth mindset can also improve business outcomes from employee hiring, training, performance appraisal, and interpersonal relations, to business innovation, negotiation, and change management (Dweck, 2014).

You may find that sometimes you approach challenges with a fixed mindset. Just as personal traits really can be developed, a fixed mindset can also be changed. First notice your **self-talk**—that internal coach or critic in your head—and recognize when you are using the self-defeating fixed mindset. Then confront the fixed mindset messages with growth mindset arguments to find your inner potential to stretch and learn.

Just as individuals may see their own personality traits as either changable or fixed, they may also see others' traits as changable or fixed. Managers' mindsets towards employees have a major impact on how they manage. Believing others have the potential to grow is critical to success in coaching and performance appraisal. Managers who believe employees' traits are fixed do not value coaching, and they may not recognize when an employee's performance changes, for good or bad (Heslin, Latham, & VandeWalle, 2005, 2006). On the other hand, the growth mindset manager is more apt to offer fair appaisals and coaching, thus increasing employee performance and commitment (Heslin & VandeWalle, 2011).

The growth mindset manager believes all employees can succeed and helps all employees grow. The fixed mindset manager focuses attention and resouces on those employees believed to have talent, to the detriment of the total workforce.

In short, mental representations are the source of preconceptions and assumptions about how we see the world, how the world works and how we expect others to behave. Understanding schemas and mindsets leads to the important conclusion that a manager's assumptions and beliefs in the workplace are key determinants of how a manager behaves. Arguably the first step to managerial success begins with awareness of one's own ways of seeing the world and the ability to critically reassess our own views. Learn to recognize your personal beliefs and experiences and to think critically.

PROCESSING INFORMATION: FUNDAMENTAL THINKING HABITS

The second set of factors that affects thinking in organizations is how we actually process information and our thinking habits. The use of two different thinking speeds and the sequence of processing steps contribute to non-rational thinking in several ways. Daniel Kahneman's best-selling 2011 book, *Thinking, Fast and Slow*, popularized a well established principle in cognition, **dual mode thinking**. Human thinking occurs along a continuum of two modes or speeds—one mode is more automatic and one is more deliberate. The **automatic system** is fast, unconscious, effortless, and uses intuition; it includes both innate and learned skills. However, it is primed to jump to conclusions and to believe things we recall are likely to be true. The **deliberate system** is slow, conscious, controlled, effortful, and uses reasoning. However, it is "lazy" and often does not challenge automatic

---

TEXTBOX 4-1. CRITICAL THINKING: THE ANTIDOTE TO PRECONCEPTIONS

Critical thinking requires identifying and testing assumptions from multiple perspectives.

1. Identify the assumptions that frame our thinking and determine our actions;
2. Check out the degree to which these assumptions are accurate and valid;
3. Look at our ideas and decisions (intellectual, organizational, and personal) from several different perspectives; and
4. On the basis of these reflections, take informed actions.

Teaching for critical thinking: Tools and techniques to help students question their assumptions. San Francisco, CA: Jossey-Bass.

thinking patterns. These two modes jointly run our thought processes, directing what we perceive and pay attention to, and how we make decisions (Kahneman, 2011).

Much of our life is negotiated using the automatic, unconscious mode—it works continuously to sense what is happening around and to us, and often functions without conscious thought. The deliberate, conscious mode is reserved for the heavy lifting—understanding complex information or situations, solving problems, making thoughtful decisions. The automatic mode helps us move easily though the day to handle routine actions and choices quickly without consciously thinking—making breakfast, driving to work, or operating a computer. Automatic mode also includes instinctive reactions: hitting the brakes when a car runs a red light, grabbing the toddler when she crawls towards the fireplace, or halting the watercooler chat when the boss frowns your way. We could not function without the automatic mode to efficiently process information; our brains would be overwhelmed by the sheer volume of information and stimuli encountered daily. However, automatic mode is a form of habitual thinking that is good at making "snap judgments." Automatic mode can interfere with our ability to be rational, because it can fail to detect something unique in a familiar situation, it often relies on implicit assumptions and our mental representations, reacts to our emotions, and may stereotype others.

The conscious rationality of the deliberate mode is highly valued; we are urged to reason carefully. We need the deliberate mode to apply controlled, focused thinking to a situation or problem such as planning, accomplishing a goal, or making a decision—from getting directions or scheduling a vacation, to taking exams or buying a house. In deliberate mode, our intentions direct our thinking process and we are consciously aware of our thinking (Fiske & Taylor, 2008). However, the deliberate mode is slow, with limited processing capacity, and depends on attention—which is easily distracted by other stimuli. Deliberate processing requires effort and self-control to do its work.

One of the most important elements of automatic and deliberate processing is the interaction between the two modes. We want to believe the deliberate mode is the ultimate authority over how we think. In reality, unconscious automatic processing plays a prominent role in our decisions and reasoning (Kahneman, 2011). Our automatic system keeps tabs on our world so things run smoothly, and the deliberate system steps in to handle challenges and exceptions noticed by the automatic system. Brooks (2011, p. xi) called the conscious mind a "general" directing from afar and the unconscious mind "a million little scouts" reacting immediately and continuously feeding information to the conscious mind.

The net effect of interaction between the two systems is that automatic thinking occurs continuously, setting in motion preconscious forces (beliefs, preconceptions, and biases arising from our mental representation of knowledge). When our deliberate reasoning takes over, it is often unaware of prior automatic processes, so we never realize that our thinking begins with faulty information.

Attention, Perception, Cognitive Evaluation, and Cognitive Consistency—The Processing Steps

At its simplest, thinking can be depicted as processing information, much like a computer. Human thinking is really more complicated and iterative, and we don't simply record information. Keep in mind that we must deliberately *process* or "do" something with information to understand and retain it. Building on the foundation of mental representation (which informs all stages of thinking), the thinking process begins with attention (i.e., noticing) and perceptual selection. So much information is available in a situation that we cannot absorb it all. Instead, we automatically use attention processes to focus on information and selectively perceive a subset of informational cues. This **selective perception** is guided by our expectations, beliefs, existing knowledge, or striking cues in the situation itself. In **cognitive evaluation**, we categorize the new information by grouping it with similar concepts or knowledge based upon common characteristics. This sorting process of classifying and categorizing concepts and objects lies at the core of all thinking. Early on we learn to make automatic, yet meaningful, distinctions that become increasingly elaborate and abstract. The brain asks whether this is new information or is it related to something known or familiar (e.g., tables, horses, zebras, and chairs all have four legs in common, yet represent unique examples of specific categories that we developed over time).

Next we organize new information using the principle of **cognitive consistency** to compare it to prior knowledge (in the form of the mental representations described previously). Consistency means we integrate new information with existing information by subjectively deciding how well it fits our categories and existing knowledge and beliefs. The brain wants to know how it fits what is known, is it the same or does it add something new. In general, new information that conforms to existing beliefs is more readily integrated (and thus remembered), while information that does not fit our beliefs is harder to integrate and may not be stored in memory (and thus forgotten). Our brains naturally prefer ease of processing and agreement with what we already know. Finally, our behaviors occur as a result of perceiving, evaluating, and checking the consistency of information about the situation.

Attention, Perception, and Preconceptions in Thinking

The old adage "perception is reality" is true. Human understanding and the resulting organizational behavior are largely based upon how a person perceives and thinks about a situation (Elsbach, Barr, & Hargadon, 2005; Fiske & Taylor, 1991). Perceptions matter because how a person makes sense of a situation affects his or her attitudes, attributions, and behaviors. When we react to a situation, we are really reacting to our own unique perceptions of the situation; at the same time others are reacting to their own perceptions of the same situation.

Attention and **perception** are automatic processes to notice, select, and organize information in order to respond. People vary greatly in what they notice and what draws their focused attention. Their attention processes are filtered by their assumptions, expectations, values, knowledge, goals, past experiences, and other personal differences. As a result, they will only take in part of the information they are presented with and thus subsequently act upon partial information. In addition, the partial information taken in is subject to other mental processes that can create other distortions.

Attention and perception are guided by the stored mental representations or preconceptions discussed earlier. Because they are thinking templates, preconceptions signal the brain what to perceive or expect in a situation. For example, assumptions and beliefs ("my boss won't like my idea") or situational cues ("organic chemistry is a difficult course," or "that teacher is a tough grader") influence how we perceive, remember, judge, and act in certain situations and events (Bandura, 1977). In short, preconscious, automatic thoughts can focus attention and set perceptual expectations, creating a situation in which "believing is seeing" that again confounds deliberate processing and rational thinking.

In addition to individual expectations, expectations can also arise from social interactions between people. At an extreme, expectations about another's behavior can create a "self-fulfilling prophecy." For example, classroom teachers who expect students to perform a certain way may verbally and nonverbally transmit their expectations to students in a way that increases the likelihood that the expected effect will occur. A nurse who believes a dementia patient is aggressive may try to overcontrol the patient and increase the patient's agitation and resistance. Similarly, a manager who believes that a certain employee has an "attitude problem" may treat that person in a way that elicits the very behavior that is objectionable.

Scholars have found physician perception has important implications for health care quality and patient health outcomes. Researchers studying patient–physician communication have found perceptions influence a variety of patient–physician interactions and subsequent outcomes (Hall, Epstein, DeCiantis, & McNeil, 1993; Street, Gordon, & Haidet, 2007). For example, liking or disliking a patient may affect the quality of the physician–patient relationship and the patient's ultimate health outcome. Studies show healthier patients and male patients were liked better (i.e., perceived more positively) by physicians than sicker patients and female patients (Hall, Horgan, Stein, & Roter, 2002). In addition, most patients accurately perceived physicians' like or dislike for them. Physicians' positive perceptions of their patients are further associated with important behaviors such as providing and eliciting information, longer visits with patients, and positive support and expectations. These physician behaviors help build trust, respect, and rapport that can improve medical diagnosis, care management, and treatment compliance. As a result, physicians' positive perceptions of patients are associated with higher patient satisfaction with care and better patient health (Hall et al., 2002).

The bottom line in organizations is that we are working and communicating with others across our mutual yet individual preconceptions, assumptions, and thinking habits. A valuable management skill is the ability to elicit thoughts in a way that organization members can work with them and reduce differences in understanding. Preconceptions, distortions, and shortcuts are inherent to human thinking. Questions, discussion, and debate are the most effective antidote to implicit assumptions and faulty thinking habits (Heil et al., 2000). Instead of assuming that thinking and meaning are clear, effective managers check employees' mental models and assumptions and elicit their thinking processes to help organization members think critically together. Beware of snap judgments, they may actually signal the need for deliberate thinking processes. As the ideas in this chapter suggest, effective thinking is less about following step-by-step procedures and more about deliberately working through preconceptions, assumptions, and thinking habits to create common meaning.

DECISION MAKING, PROBLEM SOLVING, AND BIASED THINKING HABITS

Perhaps the most important work of a manager is to ensure decisions are made and problems are resolved. Decision-making illustrates some of the consequences of non-rational thinking. Experts identify multiple tasks in making decisions and resolving problems. The two main phases are (1) recognizing and understanding the decision situation, and (2) then choosing a course of action. The **recognition phase of decision making** involves recognizing and identifying the decision or problem and its causes, setting goals, and generating options. Defining the decision need or problem is considered the more important phase because it helps identify goals, underlying causes, barriers, and information needs. It is a learning process, and yet habitual thinking narrows our capacity for new information. The **choice phase of decision making** involves assessing options and choosing, implementing, and evaluating the chosen solution.

While it seems logical to follow these steps, actual problem solving and decision making in organizations can vary greatly from this ideal process. Decisions and problems pose challenges because managers may have incomplete information or may be unable to process all of the information related to the problem, goals and priorities may be unclear or in dispute, and results of alternatives may be uncertain.

Heuristics and Cognitive Biases

Not surprisingly, a third set of cognitive factors can sabotage the decision making and problem solving process, especially when we face ambiguous and complex information inherent in important decisions. Individuals compensate for their limited capacity to effectively process information with unconscious judgment shortcuts that simplify the decision process and create serious biases that distort their judgments (Bazerman, 1998; Tversky & Kahneman, 1974). Our brains simplify the difficult task of judging complex, uncertain, and numeric or probabilistic information by using **heuristics**—mental or cognitive shortcuts or "rules of thumb." Heuristics can be useful because they simplify assessing information and making judgements, often through automatic processing. Heuristic principles can often lead to incorrect conclusions, creating biases or systematic errors in thinking and judgment.

TEXTBOX 4-2. THE ATYPICAL HEART ATTACK

Dr. Pat Croskerry examined an apparently healthy forest ranger experiencing chest pain and failed to recognize coronary artery disease. The ranger appeared so healthy—athletic, fit, and trim without the typical warning signs that precede a heart attack—that Croskerry failed to consider possible heart disease. The next day, the ranger was admitted and successfully treated for acute myocardial infarction. Croskerry realized he had made the cognitive mistake of representiveness error. That is, perceiving that the ranger fit a very healthy stereotype (called a prototype), Croskerry's thinking was guided by this prototype, and he overlooked the true cause of the ranger's symptoms. Croskerry went on to research and teach medical students about cognitive error, identifying 30 heuristics (i.e., shortcuts) and biases that can lead to error in emergency medicine (2002).

Groopman, 2007.

The cognitive simplifications provided by judgment heuristics clearly streamline information processing. These shortcuts also make the complex processes of perceiving and judging vulnerable to the influence of prior beliefs, assumptions, and experiences that are readily recalled and guide what we perceive. A perceiver may notice and select only a subset of the information to which he is exposed because he is more apt to notice familiar cues or to arrange cues into interpretations based on his preconceptions and what he has learned from his own prior experiences and the experiences of others. For example, a mother can identify her child's cry in a noisy room, while a stargazer finds it easier to locate a constellation when she knows the pattern to expect. Similarly, a physician in the U.S. who does not expect to see an exotic condition like hantavirus or Ebola may fail to diagnose these relatively rare conditions.

Studies consistently document more than a dozen common **biases**, or systematic errors of perception and judgment, that, used inappropriately, diminish decision quality by limiting the amount and richness of information processing. Let's look at four important distortions: overconfidence, confirmation, and availability and familiarity heuristics.

Overconfidence bias is the widespread tendency to overestimate the accuracy of our own judgements (Kahneman, 2011), so we act upon opinion or intuition without searching for proven information. Across many decision settings and expertise levels, people are highly confident their conclusions are right when, in reality, they are wrong. Overconfidence occurs because automatic thinking quickly reaches plausible conclusions from available information, ignoring the reality of what is unknown about a complex issue or future state, or one's actual ability to make an accurate decision. Instead our automatic processes conveniently accept what makes sense and choose a plausible option, rather than engaging in the work of serious reflection and analysis (Kahneman, 2011). The following are a few examples of how people overestimate judgments of their own abilities:

- "94% of college professors consider themselves above-average teachers;
- 90% of entrepreneurs think their new business will be a success;
- 98% of students who take the SAT say they have average or above-average leadership skills" (Brooks, 2011, p. 218).

Confirmation bias means we unconsciously and selectively notice information that simply confirms our existing beliefs. It is easier to process information that fits our expectations, and the brain tends to avoid internal conflict by thinking recalled information is true (Kahneman, 2011). Noticing and accepting disconfirming information requires extra effort and deliberate reasoning to assess it. For example, during the 2014 Ebola outbreak in Africa, many Americans had a greater fear of contracting Ebola than contracting influenza, yet influenza was the greater threat within the U.S. However, our memory recalls the extensive news coverage of Ebola and our automatic thinking process exaggerates the remote possibility of Ebola exposure in the U.S. The so-called media "echo chamber" effect is related to confirmation bias—people follow media that align with their existing beliefs. In social situations, our initial assessment of someone ("first impressions") creates expectations that lead us to notice subsequent actions and behaviors that reinforce our initial judgment of that person.

Availability and familiarity heuristics are two heuristics that show how our brains take the easy route to a difficult decision (Kahneman, 2011). The **availability heuristic** refers to judging the importance of information because it is easy to recall examples. For example, travelers may worry more about an airplane crash than a car crash, because vivid reporting of airplane crashes make them easier to recall, yet travelers are much more likely to be involved in a car accident. The **familiarity heuristic** refers to judging an unknown quality of something simply because we are familiar with that thing. For example, when asked which one of two cities has the larger population, most people will choose the city with name recognition, even though they don't know the population of either. When asked to judge the probability of something without knowing its true probability, we simplify by substituting our judgment about a related dimension, such as feelings about the topic, familiarity with it, or our impressions about it. In these two heuristics, our automatic brain quickly forms the impression that recall and familiarity mean we have past experience with the thing, so we trust our intuition to make a judgment call (Kahneman, 2011).

TEXTBOX 4-3. THE WRONG DIAGNOSIS: A LESSON FOR MANAGERS?

Groopman (2007) examines physician thinking and medical reasoning, summarizing the extensive research on this subject. Experts estimate that 10–15% of all medical diagnoses are wrong and are learning that physician reasoning is a more likely culprit than lack of knowledge or technical error. Groopman explains that "cognitive traps" skew doctors' clinical reasoning and reinforce the negative effects of biases, heuristics, and intuition.

Managers face a parallel situation when facing a problem and making a decision on how to solve it. The act of medical diagnosis is similar to problem identification in management. Identifying and solving organizational problems is a process much different from clinical diagnosis and treatment. However, organizational problem solving is probably subject to even greater cognitive distortion because management information is more ambiguous and business knowledge is evolving. When solving problems, the skilled manager will beware of "gut feelings," question assumptions, search for best evidence and gaps in knowledge, and be open to many ideas and alternatives.

Groopman, 2007.

Decision-making is non-rational; even when we strive to be rational these non-rational habits substantially limit understanding and analysis. The management challenge is that information is naturally lost or distorted in this unconscious, complex process. As a result, the knowledge one acts upon may be incomplete or inaccurate, yet the manager assumes it is complete.

Every day, health care organizations face decisions related to treatment plans for patients, improving patient safety and quality of care, meeting patients' needs and expectations, determining the best mix of services to offer, and attracting and retaining the best workers. The successful manager is able to handle complex, ambiguous problems that are not clearly defined and for which opinions vary on the nature of the problem and possible solutions. Managers and clinicians use several strategies to increase deliberate processing and reduce the effects of bias, including wide participation in decision-making, evaluating multiple alternatives, decision protocols, evidence-based medicine, bias awareness and training, and use of cognitive aids and decision support systems (Croskerry, 2003). Managers who are aware of biases (including their own) can reduce bias and error through thoughtful reflection, open discussion, and appropriate use of information to significantly improve organizational decisions and actions (Bazerman, 1998).

SOCIAL COGNITION AND SOCIO-EMOTIONAL INTELLIGENCE

Humans are social beings who need to be connected to other people. Recent work in cognition, neuroscience, and management underscores the importance of understanding how we think in social situations, because it dramatically affects how we perceive, judge, and influence others. Many of the previously described distortions also arise when we interact with others (Fiske & Taylor, 2008). In social settings, we still rely on our automatic thinking mode, our perceptions are selectively filtered, and our judgments of others are guided by existing mental representations.

The fourth set of factors affecting thinking—social thinking—includes attributions, several common biases, and social categorization. While emotional factors affect our thinking in many ways, they are especially relevant to social thinking and are discussed in this section.

Types of Attribution

To attribute is to make an inference, or to explain what causes something. According to **attribution theory**, our brains intuitively seek to explain the causes of behavior and outcomes. **Attributions** are a specific form of social judgment in which the presumed cause of observed behavior is attributed to either a person's disposition and personality (internal factors), or to the situation (external factors) in which the behavior occurs.

Fundamental attribution error is a cognitive bias in which an observer makes incorrect causal attributions about the presumed cause of another's behavior. In **fundamental attribution error**, we erroneously attribute another's behavior to their internal disposition, rather than external circumstances. When we presume those dispositional factors are under the other's control, we hold them responsible for the behavior, when the behavior may really be due to situational factors beyond their control.

For instance, if a stranger cuts in line ahead of you at the movies or in traffic, you may conclude that the action is intentional and decide the person is rude, even though it could have occurred because directional signs were not clear to the person who went ahead of you. In health care, physicians who label a patient with a negative stereotype (e.g., smokers, obese, alcoholics, homeless) risk erroneously attributing the patient's health concerns to risky behavior brought upon themselves (Groopman, 2007). As a result, physicians may distance themselves from the patient and miss important information, resulting in poor patient compliance and low-quality care.

Managers are susceptible to fundamental attribution error when judging employee performance, sometimes blaming an employee for poor performance that may actually be caused by circumstances beyond the employee's control. For example, attribution error occurs when a manager decides an employee performing a task poorly is lazy or incompetent, rather than recognizing that the employee needs training, clear incentives, or improved work equipment. To avoid making an erroneous performance attribution the manager must understand how the work setting affects employee performance. We can't read the minds of others, so a manager should ask an employee how he or she sees the work setting and its effect on job performance before inferring reasons for poor performance.

Types of Biases

Our perceptions of others can be biased in multiple ways, including how we relate to them (affinity), belonging to the same social group (in-group), or through prior knowledge of someone (halo). We then make inferences about the qualities or traits they possess and make decisions that favor them instead of using concrete information to support our conclusions. It is well-documented that we often cannot recognize our own biases because they are unconscious (bias blindness), and we are better able to see others' biases.

Affinity biases are several related biases centered on preferring others because we see them as likeable, like us, or part of our social group. **Affinity bias** means favoring people we like. For example, an interviewer may spend more time with an applicant who is engaging, or we may gravitate towards outgoing personalities. **Similar-to-me bias** refers to favoring those we see as being most like ourselves. For example, we favor people or the opinions of others in our same college major or line of work. **In-group bias** (also called "us vs. them" or "in-group vs. out-group") means we make a positive judgment about someone when we both belong to the same social group, they are from "our side." For example, we may favor someone or value their opinion because we are both directors in our organization, went to the same school, or belong to the same race or church. We believe we share a common (and thus "correct") viewpoint. In contrast to these affinities, we may be less positive towards or discount the opinion of others simply because we don't share one of these affinities with them.

When we make such assumptions in the workplace, affinity biases can distort thinking. They may lead to poor decisions (e.g., decision participation, job assignments, staffing, performance ratings, etc.) or cause a failure to tap all employees' talents, thus diminishing organizational performance.

The **halo effect** occurs when positive or negative information about others on one dimension colors our judgment about them on a different dimension. For example, we may infer that an outgoing person will be a good leader or that a member of a chess club is good at math, when neither is necessarily true. We could also negatively infer that a quiet person will not be an effective team member, which is not necessarily true. Halo effect is of special concern in appraisals, because the reviewer may automatically rate an employee favorably or unfavorably simply on the basis of performance in just one category, rather than rate each performance dimension independent of other categories. For example, a supervisor rates the administrative staffer excellent in all categories when she is really great with people but neglects to maintain budget accounts.

Bias blind spot occurs when we believe others are more influenced by biases than we are (Pronin, Gilovich, & Ross, 2004). It is very difficult for individuals to correct for their own biases. When we believe our own view is objective, we may dismiss differing views because we think *they* are biased, not us. Describing this belief in our own objectivity as "I think, therefore it's true" mindset, researchers found managers who believed they were unbiased were more, rather than less, likely to be influenced by stereotypes in the hiring process (Uhlmann & Cohen, 2007).

Social Categorization and Biases

As mentioned earlier, categorization is central to the thinking process; objects are assigned to categories with an associated set of characteristics and expectations. Similarly, **social categorization** means we group people into social categories. We all automatically categorize people, and then implicitly stereotype, or assume individuals possess the traits of everyone in that category. Examples of some common social categorizations include gender, race, sexual orientation, age, religion, national origin, disability, physical characteristics (height, weight), personality (e.g., introversion, extroversion), accents, social status, etc. The process of cognitive categorization simplifies our ability to organize our social world. The process can also distort our judgments of others, leading to subconscious cognitive stereotypes, prejudicial attitudes, or discriminatory behaviors, which may result in poor organizational performance and even lawsuits.

Recent research makes distinctions among cognitive biases (stereotypes), emotional biases (prejudice), and behavioral biases (discrimination) (Talaska, Fiske, & Chaiken, 2008). **Stereotypes** are generalized beliefs about expected attributes of individuals who belong to a group. The cognitive error of stereotyping is that we overgeneralize, thinking an entire group has the same characteristics, rather than recognizing individual differences and the real person behind the stereotype. **Prejudice** is holding certain attitudes (whether positive or negative) toward members of a group. **Discrimination** is treating members of a group differently (which may also be illegal). Stereotypes, prejudice, and discrimination are manifested in different ways:

- Cognitive stereotype example: assuming women are not as strong as men;
- Emotional prejudice example: expressing negative attitudes about women employed in construction; and
- Discriminatory behavior example: actively discouraging women from employment in construction.

Explicit vs. Implicit Bias

Our understanding of social biases today is more sophisticated than when non-discrimination practices were codified in employment law. We now distinguish between explicit and implicit bias (Fiske, 2010). **Explicit bias**—traditional prejudice—is overt and the actor is consciously aware of stereotyping or discriminating. **Implicit bias**—today's 'hidden bias'—is subtle and unconscious, hidden from the actor's direct awareness, and seldom noticed in the decision process. Implicit bias has been documented in lab studies and organizational settings (schools, academia, medicine, law enforcement, courts, even politics), in a range of organizational (hiring, interviews, leadership, participation, performance evaluation), and social (policing, housing, and housing pricing) decisions, as well as across many social categories (Staats, 2014). In health care, implicit biases of physicians and other providers can affect treatment outcomes and contribute to health disparities (Sabin, Nosek, Greenwald, & Rivara, 2009).

Managers are increasingly concerned with implicit biases because these biases affect employees in social categories beyond the protected groups traditionally recognized by law. Implicit biases may hinder an organization's diversity efforts, leading to exclusion, isolation, reduced teamwork, low morale, and higher turnover (Jost et al., 2009). Training managers and strengthening human resource practices (hiring, promotion, training and development, appraisal, and compensation) can reduce implicit bias. By addressing implicit bias, employers can engage the talents of all workers, thereby improving business decisions and performance, workplace climate, and employee satisfaction and retention (Ernst & Young, 2013).

Empathy and Socio-Emotional Intelligence

In the last decade there has been a surge of interest in non-cognitive intelligences—both social intelligence and emotional intelligence. The two overlap and are jointly called "socio-emotional intelligence" here. **Socio-emotional intelligence** is the ability to sense, understand, and effectively respond to others' emotions (Zautra, Zautra, Rivers, & Rivers,

2012). **Emotional intelligence (EI)** is characterized as "the intelligent use of emotions" (Seal, Naumann, Scott, & Royce-Davis, 2011, p. 5). A socio-emotional intelligent person is self-aware, aware of other's emotions, and can establish meaningful relations with others. Studies find the various forms of socio-emotional intelligence benefit organizational collaboration, problem-solving, creativity, and innovation in organizations.

Perhaps most important of all, working with others is central to management. Socio-emotional intelligence smooths employee interactions; strengthens the manager–employee relationship; and builds a positive, supportive workplace climate. Daniel Goleman, who popularized emotional intelligence (1995), concludes that high perfoming managers are high in emotional intelligence, and that EI is a better predictor of a manager's performance than IQ (intelligence quotient).

Empathy is a fundamental skill identified by studies of socio-emotional intelligence that fosters reciprocity and connection in relationships. Empathy is being sensitive to the emotional state of others. Empathy takes three progressively more evolved forms.

- **Emotional empathy** is sharing another's feelings (emotional "contagion"),
- **Cognitive empathy** is knowing and understanding another's perspective, and
- **Empathic perspective-taking** is cognitive understanding plus shared emotions, which supports taking appropriate action in response to those emotions (de Waal, 2008).

The importance of empathy in health care and other organizations has prompted major efforts to teach and develop empathy in clinicians, managers, and employees.

RESEARCH OPPORTUNITIES IN ORGANIZATIONAL BEHAVIOR AND MANAGEMENT THINKING

Thanks to decades of psychological investigators' interest in organizational behavior, as noted in Chapter 3, an abundance of reseach on these topics and applications to health care settings await you. An organization such as the Society for Industrial-Organization Psychology (SIOP), a special interest group of the American Psychological Association (APA), is an especially productive organization in these domains. Likewise, the Academy of Management (AOM) delves into these issues. In addition to SIOP and AOM, here are some other agencies and organizations ripe for your examination:

- Agency for Healthcare Research and Quality;
- Center for Creative Leadership;
- Center for Evidence-Based Management;
- Consortium for Research on Emotional Intelligence in Organizations;
- Hospital Research and Educational Trust (HRET);

- Inter-university Consortium for Political and Social Research (ICPSR);
- The Robert Wood Johnson Foundation; and
- U.S. Department of Health and Human Services Health Resources and Services Administration (HRSA).

CONCLUSION

Thinking is a complex and non-rational process subject to powerful unconscious forces. The four central features of cognition—mental representation, information perception and processing, decision-making, and social cognition and emotions—each play a unique role in thinking and each also has characteristic habits that can distort thinking and lead to error or bias. Knowledge of our hidden brain can't handle every situation encountered in an organization. However, these ideas show that human and organizational behavior is best understood as driven by people's perceptions of their individual world. What one believes about a person or a situation, even if incomplete or inaccurate, will determine how one responds to that person or situation. The adage that "perception is reality" is true in organization behavior, so knowledge of cognitive principles helps the manager work with perceived realities. The manager who is blind to assumptions and perceptions—both her own and others'—is working from an incomplete and inaccurate knowledge base.

The implication for managers is that fundamental organizational activities depend less on following a certain procedure and more on the manager's efforts to bring employees together in defining a shared understanding that supports a focus on collective action. A critical management task is to remedy the limits of human cognition and organizational thinking to create common understanding among organization members. This is largely accomplished by sharing mental models and understandings with others through questioning, dialogue, and discussion. The process of sharing assumptions and perceived realities makes them available to others, encourages individuals to refashion their own mental constructs, and promotes elaboration of common mental frameworks. In short, the thinking manager who can work with perceptions and mental models contributes to creating a learning organization that generates common meaning and useful knowledge.

DISCUSSION QUESTIONS

1. Review the manager's three types of roles. Give examples you recall from work, school, or other settings of leaders who were especially effective or ineffective in one of the roles. What was the situation, what did the person do, and what effect did it have on others? Which were instrumental in his or her effectiveness?

2. Describe an incident from a past job where you would like to better understand how the organizational setting influenced employee behavior. What was the situation, and what happened? If you had been the manager in that situation, what would you have needed to understand to handle that situation?

3. Which of the four features of cognition—mental representation, processing speed and habits, decision-making and problem-solving, or socio-emotional intelligence—do you consider most important and why? Which one would you like to further develop?

4. Think of a recent situation in which you participated where you think it would have been helpful to surface underlying assumptions. Describe the situation, who was involved, their roles, what they were trying to accomplish, and what actually happened. What did you observe that leads you to believe assumptions played a role in this situation? What could you have done differently to change the situation? What will you do or say differently in similar situations in the future?

5. Compare automatic and deliberate thinking processes. Give examples of when it would be better to use automatic processing and when it would be better to use deliberate processing.

6. Have you heard the phrase "A solution in search of a problem?" The text asserts that the first phase of decision-making and problem-solving—specifying the correct decision to be made or problem to be solved—is the more important phase. Recall problems or decisions you have observed where the nature of the problem and appropriate solutions were not clear at the outset (i.e., an "ill-structured problem"). Discuss how well the problem was found and defined (including learning about factors contributing to the problem and agreeing upon goals) and how well the solution worked. To what extent do you think the problem definition process affected the adequacy of the solution chosen? In retrospect do you see how the quality of thinking affected the decision identification process?

7. Medical error is a serious and controversial problem for health care. Dr. Lucian Leape, a leading researcher on medical error, concludes "Errors result from faulty systems not from faulty people" (2000, p. 97). Discuss how Leape's view fits with attribution theory, and the implications for health care managers. What does the literature say about what managers believe about the causes of medical error? What messages do organizational practices send employees about the causes of medical error?

8. Implicit bias is unconscious bias, which makes it difficult to recognize and change. What can an individual employee do to reduce bias and discrimination in the workplace?

9. Why does empathy matter in the workplace, and how would it benefit the organization and its members?

10. How are emotions handled where you have worked? How does understanding your own emotions help you at work? Why is it important to understand someone else's emotions at work?

Cases in Chapter 18 that are related to organizational behavior and management thinking (or related to this chapter) include:

- How Do We Handle a Girl Like Maria?
- The Condescending Dental Hygenist
- Giving Feedback—Empathy or Attributions?
- Socio-Emotional Intelligence Exercise: Understanding and Anticipating Major Change

Case study guides are available in the online Instructor's Materials.

REFERENCES

Ariely, D. (2008). *Predictably irrational: The hidden forces that shape our decisions.* New York, NY: Harper Collins.

Arnsten, A., Mazure, C. M., & Sinha, R. (2012). This is your brain in meltdown. *Scientific American, 306,* 48–53.

Bandura, A. (1977). Self-efficacy: Toward a unifying theory of behavioral change. *Psychological Review, 84*(2), 191–215.

Barends, E., Rousseau, D. M., & Briner, R. B. (2014). *Evidence-based management: The basic principles.* Amsterdam, Netherlands: Center for Evidence-Based Management. Retrieved from http://www .cebma.org/wp-content/uploads/Evidence-Based-Practice-The-Basic-Principles.pdf

Bazerman, M. (1998). *Judgment in managerial decision-making* (4th ed.). New York, NY: Wiley.

Becker, W. J., Cropanzano, R., & Sanfey, A. G. (2011). Organizational neuroscience: Taking organizational theory inside the neural black box. *Journal of Management, 37*(4), 933–961.

Brookfield, S. D. (2011). *Teaching for critical thinking: Tools and techniques to help students question their assumptions.* San Francisco, CA: Jossey-Bass.

Brooks, D. (2011). *The social animal: The hidden sources of love, character, and achievement.* New York, NY: Random House.

Center for Evidence-Based Management. (2013). *A definition of evidence-based management.* Retrieved from http://www.cebma.org/a-definition-of-evidence-based-management/

Croskerry, P. (2002). Achieving quality in clinical decision making: Cognitive strategies and detection of bias. *Academic Emergency Medicine, 9*(11), 1184–1204.

Croskerry, P. (2003). The importance of cognitive errors in diagnosis and strategies to minimize them. *Academic Medicine, 78*(8), 775–780.

David, S., & Congleton, C. (2013). Emotional agility. *Harvard Business Review, 91*(11), 125–128.

de Waal, F. B. M. (2008). Putting the altruism back into altruism: The evolution of empathy. *Annual Review of Psychology, 59*, 279–300.

Dweck, C. S. (1986). Motivational processes affecting learning. *American Psychologist, 41*(10), 1040–1048.

Dweck, C. S. (2006). *Mindset: The new psychology of success.* New York, NY: Random House.

Dweck, C. S. (2014). How companies can profit from a "growth mindset." *Harvard Business Review, 92*(11), 28–29.

Dweck, C. S., & London, B. (2004). The role of mental respresentation in social development. *Merrill-Palmer Quarterly, 50*(4), 428–444.

Easterby-Smith, M., Crossan, M., & Nicolini, D. (2000). Organizational learning: Debates past, present and future. *Journal of Management Studies, 37*(6), 783–795.

Elsbach, K. D., Barr, P. S., & Hargadon, A. B. (2005). Identifying situated cognition in organizations. *Organization science, 16*(4), 422–433.

Ernst & Young. (2013). *Outsmarting our brains: Overcoming hidden biases to harness diversity's true potential.* Retrieved from http://www.ey.com/Publication/vwLUAssets/Outsmarting-our-brains/$FILE/EY-RBC-Overcoming-hidden-biaises-to-harness-diversity.pdf

Finkelstein, S., Whitehead, J., & Campbell, A. (2008). *Think again: Why good leaders make bad decisions and how to keep it from happening to ou.* Boston, MA: Harvard Business Press.

Fiske, S. T. (2010). Are we born racist? In J. Marsh, R. Mendoza-Denton, & J. A. Smith (Eds.), *Are we born racist?: New insights from neuroscience and positive psychology.* Boston, MA: Beacon Press.

Fiske, S. T., & Taylor, S. E. (1991). *Social cognition* (2nd ed.). New York, NY: McGraw Hill.

Fiske, S. T., & Taylor, S. E. (2008). *Social cognition: From brains to culture.* Boston, MA: McGraw-Hill Higher Education.

Fiske, S. T., & Taylor, S. E. (2013). *Social cognition: From brains to culture* (2nd ed.). Thousand Oaks, CA: Sage Publications.

Gentry, W. A., Weber, T. J., & Sadri, G. (2010). *Empathy in the workplace.* Greensboro, NC: The Center for Creative Leadership. Retrieved from http://www.ccl.org/leadership/pdf/research/EmpathyInTheWorkplace.pdf

Goffman, E. (1974). *Frame analysis: An essay on the organization of experience.* London, UK: Harper & Row.

Goleman, D. (1995). *Emotional intelligence: Why it can matter more than IQ.* New York, NY: Bantam Books.

Goleman, D. (2013). *Focus: The hidden driver of excellence.* New York, NY: HarperColllins.

Groopman, J. (2007). *How doctors think.* Boston, MA: Houghton Mifflin.

Hall, J. A., Epstein, A. M., DeCiantis, M. L., & McNeil, B. J. (1993). Physicians' liking for their patients: More evidence for the role of affect in medical care. *Health Psychology, 12*(2), 140–146.

Hall, J. A., Horgan, T. G., Stein, T. S., & Roter, D. L. (2002). Liking in the physician–patient relationship. *Patient Education and Counseling, 48*(1), 69–77.

Heil, G., Bennis, W., & Stephens, D. C. (2000). *Douglas McGregor, revisited.* New York, NY: Wiley.

Heslin, P. A., Latham, G. P., & VandeWalle, D. (2005). The effect of implicit person theory on performance appraisals. *Journal of Applied Psychology, 90*(5), 842–856.

Heslin, P. A., & VandeWalle, D. (2011). Performance appraisal procedural justice: The role of a manager's implicit person theory. *Journal of Management, 37*(6), 1694–1718.

Heslin, P. A., VandeWalle, D., & Latham, G. P. (2006). Keen to help? Managers' implicit person theories and their subsequent employee coaching. *Personnel Psychology, 59*(4), 871–902.

Hodgkinson, G. P., & Healey, M. P. (2008). Cognition in organizations. *Annual Review of Psychology, 59*, 387–417.

Huselid, M. A. (1995). The impact of human resources management practices on turnover, productivity, and corporate financial performance. *Academy of Management Journal, 38*(3), 645.

Jost, J. T., Rudman, L. A., Blair, I. V., Carney, D. R., Dasgupta, N., Glaser, J., & Hardin, C. D. (2009). The existence of implicit bias is beyond reasonable doubt: A refutation of ideological and methodological objections and executive summary of ten studies that no manager should ignore. *Research in Organizational Behavior, 29*, 39–69.

Kahneman, D. (2011). *Thinking, fast and slow.* New York, NY: Farrar, Straus & Giroux.

Kahneman, D., Lovallo, D., & Sibony, O. (2011). Before you make that big decision. *Harvard Business Review, 89*(6), 51–60.

Lai, C. K., Hoffman, K. M., & Nosek, B. A. (2013). Reducing implicit prejudice. *Social and Personality Psychology Compass, 7*(5), 315–330.

Leape, L. L. (2000). Institute of Medicine medical error figures are not exaggerated. *Journal of the American Medical Association, 284*(1), 95–97.

Lieberman, M. D., Eisenberger, N. I., Crockett, M. J., Tom, S. M., Pfeifer, J. H., & Way, B. M. (2007). Putting feelings into words: Affect labeling disrupts amygdala activity in response to affective stimuli. *Psychological Science, 18*(5), 421–428.

Mintzberg, H. (1973). *The nature of managerial work.* New York, NY: Harper & Row.

Mohammed, S., Ferzandi, L., & Hamilton, K. (2010). Metaphor no more: A 15-year review of the team mental model construct. *Journal of Management, 36*(4), 876.

Narayanan, J., & Prasad, S. (2015). Neurobiological systems: Implications for organizational behavior In S. M. Colarelli & R. D. Arvey (Eds.), *The biological foundations of organizational behavior.* Chicago, IL: University of Chicago Press.

Pfeffer, J. (1998). *The human equation.* Boston, MA: Harvard Business School Press.

Plaks, J. E, Grant, H., & Dweck, C. S. (2005). Violations of implicit theories and the sense of prediction and control: Implications for motivated person perception. *Journal of Personality and Social Psychology, 88*(2), 245–262.

Pronin E., Gilovich, T., & Ross L. (2004). Objectivity in the eye of the beholder: Divergent perceptions of bias in self versus others. *Psychological Review, 111*(3), 781–799.

Rajah, R., Song, Z., & Arvey, R. D. (2011). Emotionality and leadership: Taking stock of the past decade of research. *The Leadership Quarterly, 22*(6), 1107–1119.

Robbins, S. P. (2003). *Essentials of organizational behavior.* Upper Saddle River, NJ: Prentice Hall.

Sabin, J. A., Nosek, B. A., Greenwald, A. G., & Rivara, F. P. (2009). Physicians' implicit and explicit attitudes about race by md race, ethnicity, and gender. *Journal of Health Care for the Poor and Underserved, 20*(3), 896–913.

Scott, W. R. (1992). *Organizations: Rational, natural, and open systems* (3rd ed.). Englewood Cliffs, NJ: Prentice Hall.

Seal, C. R., Naumann, S. E., Scott, A., & Royce-Davis, J. (2011). Social emotional development: A new model of learning in higher education. *Research in Higher Education Journal, 10*, 1–13.

Senge, P. M. (1990). *The fifth discipline.* New York, NY: Currency-Doubleday.

Shortell, S. M., & Kaluzny, A. D. (2000). *Health care management* (4th ed.). New York, NY: Thomson Learning.

Staats, C. (2014). *State of the science: Implicit bias review 2014*. Columbus, OH: Kirwan Institute for the Study of Race and Ethnicity; Ohio State University. Retrieved from http://kirwaninstitute.osu.edu/wp-content/uploads/2014/03/2014-implicit-bias.pdf

Steers, R. M., Sanchez-Runde, C. J., & Nardon, L. (2012). Culture, cognition, and managerial leadership. *Asia Pacific Business Review. 18*(3),425–439.

Street, R. L., Gordon, H., & Haidet, P. (2007). Physicians' communication and perceptions of patients: Is it how they look, how they talk, or is it just the doctor? *Social Science & Medicine, 65*(3), 586–598.

Talaska, C. A., Fiske, S. T., & Chaiken, S. (2008). Legitimating racial discrimination: Emotions, not beliefs, best predict discrimination in a meta-analysis. *Social Justice Research, 21*(3), 263–296.

Tversky, A., & Kahneman, D. (1974). Judgment under uncertainty: Heuristics and biases. *Science, 185*(4157), 1124–1131.

Uhlmann, E. L., & Cohen, G. L. (2007). "I think it, therefore it's true": Effects of self-perceived objectivity on hiring discrimination. *Organizational Behavior and Human Decision Processes, 104*(2), 207–223.

Vedantam, S. (2010). *The hidden brain: How our unconscious minds elect presidents, control markets, wage wars, and save our lives*. New York, NY: Random House.

Weick, K. E. (1969). *The social psychology of organizing*. Reading, MA: Addison-Wesley.

Zautra, A. J., Zautra, E. K., Rivers, C., & Rivers, D. (2012). Foundations of social intelligence: A conceptual model with implications for business performance. *Current Topics in Management, 16*, 15–37.

Strategic Planning

Susan Casciani

LEARNING OBJECTIVES

By the end of this chapter, the student will be able to:

- Critique strategic planning and sketch the strategic planning process;
- Explain the importance of strategic planning as a dynamic process;
- Analyze health care market powers and trends, and their potential impact on health services;
- Conduct a SWOT analysis;
- Compare and contrast methods to monitor and control strategy execution; and
- Identify the role of the manager in the strategic planning process.

INTRODUCTION

Every organization needs to be successful over the long term to survive; a critical factor leading to that success lies in how well an organization can plan for the future and tap market opportunities. **Strategic planning** is the process of identifying a desired future state for an organization and a means to achieve it. Through an ongoing analysis of the organization's operating environment, matched against its own internal capabilities, an organization's leadership is able to identify strategies that will drive the organization from its present condition to that desired future state.

Strategic planning in health care has had a relatively short history. As recently as the 1970s, strategic planning in the health care industry mainly consisted of planning for new buildings and funding expanding services in response to population growth. With the introduction of the federal Prospective Payment System (PPS) in the 1980s, the field of health care strategic planning received a transforming jolt as organizations scrambled to compete in an increasingly demanding environment. The turbulent managed care era of the 1980s and 1990s only served to further fuel the growth of the field as the cost of health care continually rose faster than the gross domestic product (GDP) and competition among providers intensified. Today, hospitals and other health care organizations have come to embrace strategic planning as a valuable tool to evaluate alternative paths and help them prepare for the future. Health care managers at all levels need to understand the purpose of strategic planning, its benefits and challenges, the key factors for its success, and their vital role in the process.

PURPOSE AND IMPORTANCE OF STRATEGIC PLANNING

In any organization's operating environment there are market forces, both controllable and uncontrollable, that will undoubtedly influence the future success of that organization. Only by identifying these forces and planning for ways to adapt to them can an organization achieve the greatest success. At the extreme, completely ignoring these forces can most certainly lead to organizational death. Although no one can predict the future, one can systematically think about it; the purpose of strategic planning is to identify market forces and how they may affect the organization and to determine an appropriate strategic direction for the organization to take that will counteract those forces and/or tap their potential.

Furthermore, strategic planning serves to focus the organization and also its resource allocation. At any given point in time, there are multiple and often competing initiatives and projects to be undertaken in an organization. By understanding the organization's operating environment and identifying a strategy to reach a desired future state, resources can be allocated appropriately and effectively.

THE PLANNING PROCESS

The **strategic planning process** consists mainly of two interrelated activities: the development of the strategic plan and execution of the organization's strategy. The development of the plan is most often done with a multiyear time horizon (3, 5, or 10 years, for example) and updated annually. Strategy execution, on the other hand, is done on a continuous basis and is the critical factor in management of the organization's strategic intentions, optimally providing continual feedback for the development of any future plans.

Although strategic planning is a dynamic and not a linear process, Figure 5-1 attempts to depict a logical progression of the steps undertaken to develop a strategic plan. As shown in Figure 5-1, the **SWOT (Strengths, Weaknesses, Opportunities, Threats) Analysis** provides a foundation for strategy development. This analysis serves two important functions: to gather a snapshot of how the organization is currently interacting with the market in

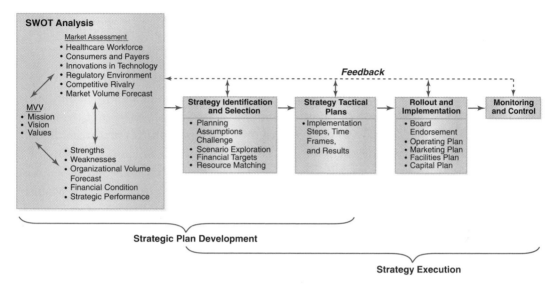

FIGURE 5-1 Strategic Planning Process

comparison to the internal capabilities and intended strategic direction of the organization, and to identify market opportunities and threats that the organization may want to address in future strategic efforts.

Through analysis of the SWOT, strategy identification can begin. In this stage, the organization's leadership team uses the information provided in the SWOT analysis to identify specific strategies that may be worthy of pursuit either to grow the organization or to protect current areas of strength. Once these strategies have been identified, they must be narrowed down to a manageable number through selection and prioritization, and tactical implementation plans must be created. With the strategic plan completed, operating, marketing, and other supporting plans are developed. Control and monitoring of the plan follows and is most effectively done on an ongoing basis throughout the year. We will look at each of these stages of strategic planning in more detail; however, it is important to again keep in mind that strategic planning is not a linear process. The feedback loop depicted in Figure 5-1 shows the critical nature of planning as an ongoing, dynamic, iterative process.

SWOT ANALYSIS

The initial planning phase is often referred to as a **SWOT analysis**, as it aims to identify the internal **strengths** and **weaknesses** of an organization, along with external market **opportunities** and **threats**. It includes three distinct but intricately related components: the

market assessment; the statement of the **mission, vision, and values** of the organization; and the **organizational assessment**.

Market Assessment

The development of the **market assessment** may be the most complex and time-consuming section of the strategic plan in that, in this component, virtually *all* aspects of the market must be examined to determine whether they represent **opportunities** or **threats** for the organization and to determine their future implications for the organization. Any of a number of market assessment models can be utilized for this analysis, but one of the most common is the **Five Forces Model** developed by Harvard University professor Michael Porter (1998). In this model, Porter identifies five market or industry forces that, when combined, determine the attractiveness of competing in a particular market. For health care, this model can be adapted to analyze the interactions between the power of the health care workforce, the power of consumers and payers, innovations in technology, the regulatory environment, and competitive rivalry, as depicted in Figure 5-2.

Power of the Health Care Workforce

The **power of the health care workforce** can have significant strategic implications for any health care organization, as the workforce is composed of the front line of caregivers and support staff in providing services. In the SWOT analysis, an organization should look at the availability of all subsets of health care providers that are critical to its success. As an example, if obstetrics is a major clinical program of the organization, the organization should closely consider the future anticipated supply and demand of obstetricians (OBs)

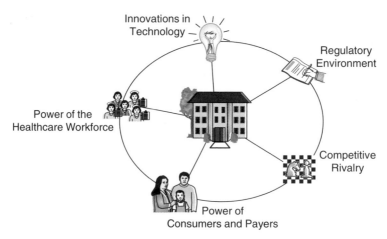

FIGURE 5-2 Market Assessment Model

in its market. With the significant increases in malpractice insurance targeted at obstetricians across the country, many OBs have elected to discontinue delivering babies and focus solely on gynecology, while others have opted to retire early. This has dramatically reduced the supply of obstetricians in many areas of the country and forced some hospitals to hire their affiliated obstetrical staff in an effort to cover their malpractice insurance premiums and keep them practicing. Other hospitals have developed "laborists"—OBs who are hired solely to work in the hospital and deliver babies. These moves are examples of strategies that could be adopted by organizations to either maintain or grow their obstetrical services and are in response to market trends.

Another example of the power of the health care workforce is the potential ramification of the specific personnel shortages (e.g., nursing). With a shortage of personnel, wage and hiring expenses increase, jeopardizing the ability to offer those specific services. A nursing shortage may affect a hospital's ability to add beds to meet growing demand for services. A shortage of radiology technicians may affect an organization's opportunity to offer new state-of-the-art technologies. The influence and availability of these and other health care personnel (and the organization's dependency on them) must be considered when developing future strategies.

Power of Consumers and Payers

At the other end of the spectrum, as the ultimate purchasers of health care, the power of consumers is becoming a more significant market force—and one that has required a dramatic shift in the way the industry offers services. Today's consumers are demanding more and more from their health care providers on all levels (e.g., physicians, payers, and hospitals), both in terms of the availability of specific service offerings and in the delivery of those services. Historically, health care organizations viewed physicians as the primary customers; without them, the organization could not provide services. However, in today's world, the *patient* is becoming the central focus of customer service. The potential impact of this shift to a **patient-centric model of care** needs to be considered when developing future strategies.

Consumers can influence the health care market in other ways as well. Different communities have different health care needs—one community may need increased access to primary care channels, while another may need better health education and screenings for chronic conditions. By identifying specific community needs, health care organizations can better target their services and potential growth opportunities. The best way to do this is to understand the consumers in a particular market, and determine in what ways they may need to access health care services.

In concert with consumers is the **power of payers**. Some markets have multiple payers of various sizes and strengths, while others have one or two major payers that dictate market payments. In either case, a health care organization that relies on these payers must stay abreast of their needs and demands and how each may affect future operations and strategies. A good example of this is a market with one or two powerful payers that prefer a "late adopter" stance for new medical technologies. In other words, they prefer not to pay for new technologies until the technologies have been proven either medically effective or financially efficient or both. This would be a significant threat to an organization that strives for a competitive advantage by being first to market with the adoption of new medical technologies. Alternately, the power of payers may also create opportunities for an organization. An example would be the general preference of payers for less costly outpatient services. Health care organizations that specialize in these types of service offerings (e.g., ambulatory surgery centers, diagnostic/imaging centers) have capitalized on this payer influence in many areas of the country.

Innovations in Technology

Another market force to be considered is **innovations in technology**. These innovations may represent the threat of substitute products, as new technologies often replace standard operations and services. A good example of this was the introduction of Picture Archive Communication Systems (PACS). This filmless imaging system significantly reduced the need for storage space for films and readers and the staff to maintain those areas, and allowed for remote electronic accessing of files, ultimately requiring a potentially smaller number of physicians necessary to interpret the images. Innovations in technology may also reduce the need for other types of clinical staff, as in the case of some surgical innovations (e.g., minimally invasive surgery, robotic technologies, drug advancements, etc.), and/or they may significantly increase the requirement of financial resources, as in the case of new radiology equipment (e.g., a new CT scanner, new fluoroscopy equipment, MRI, etc.) or new electronic health record systems (EHRs). As these and other new technologies become available, their potential impact on operations and systems needs to be considered in strategy development.

The Regulatory Environment

As a market force, the **regulatory environment**—on all levels, federal, state, and local—needs to be monitored for its effects on strategy development as well. Congress continually enacts influential legislation, such as the 1986 Emergency Medical Treatment and Active Labor Act (EMTALA), the 1996 Health Insurance Portability and Accountability Act (HIPAA), focus on mandatory error reporting and physician self-referrals, and of course the Affordable Care Act (ACA) or "Obamacare." Legislation at all government levels can have significant and rippling effects on all participants in the health care industry. Furthermore, the Centers for Medicare and Medicaid Services (CMS) often take the lead in changes in health care payment formulas that are frequently followed by payers at local levels. Other far-reaching issues such as liability reform and quality of care measures may be dealt with on local, state, and federal levels as well. All of these actions can influence a particular health care organization's strategy and need to be monitored and analyzed for their potential impacts.

Competitive Rivalry

Competitive rivalry, the last market force to be considered, is probably given the most significant attention in most organizations' strategy development. Whether an organization operates in a near monopoly or an oligopoly, strategically savvy organizations always track their competitors' moves and suspected intentions. Although it is unlikely that you will gain access to the actual strategy of your competitors, much information on their strategic intent can be gleaned from their market activities. Information on their service volumes, market share, and news coverage and press releases should be monitored. Ongoing discussions with your own physicians, staff, and suppliers will likely also yield valuable competitive intelligence. Compiling this information together to see a larger picture often leads to an indication of competitors' strategies. Once their strategic intent has been identified, market **opportunities** for and **threats** against your own organization can be further addressed.

Mission, Vision, Values

The information gleaned regarding the interaction of these five forces (health care workforce, consumers and payers, innovations in technology, regulatory environment, and competitive rivalry) in the market is matched against the organization's **Mission, Vision, and Value (MVV)** statements. As the driving purpose of the organization, the MVVs are reviewed as part of the strategic planning process to ensure they continue to be aligned with the organization's future market environment and to help identify future desired strategic directions. The **mission** of any organization is its enduring statement of purpose. It aims to identify what the organization does, whom it serves, and how it does it. For example, the mission statement for Genesis Healthcare, a skilled nursing and rehabilitation therapy provider, states "We improve the lives we touch…through the delivery of high quality healthcare and everyday compassion" (Genesis, 2014, para. 1). On the other hand, a **vision** statement strives to identify a specific future state of the organization, usually an inspiring goal for many years down the road. The vision of the American Hospital Association is "of a society of healthy communities, where all individuals reach their highest potential for health" (AHA, 2015, para. 1). The **values** statement should help define the organization's culture—what characteristics it wants employees to convey to customers. An example of one such value from Duke Medicine in North Carolina is: "We hold each other accountable to constantly improve a culture that ensures the safety and welfare of all patients, visitors, and staff" (DukeMedicine, 2015, para. 6).

Although the mission statement is generally the most enduring of the three, each of these statements may be altered over time to adapt to the environment. As an example, the increasing influence of consumerism in health care drove many an organization to revise its vision and value statements to become more customer service focused, which in turn (hopefully) helped to change the organization's culture. Reaffirming and/or adjusting these three statements in relation to market activity is a critical step in determining the desired future state of the organization.

Organizational Assessment

Now that we have an idea of what our market looks like and understand our desired intent from our (reaffirmed) MVV, it's time to take a hard, honest look at our own organization. In conducting an internal assessment, an organization turns the analytical lens inward to examine the areas in which it has **strengths** and **weaknesses**, as well as how it may build or sustain a competitive advantage in the market. Like the market assessment, the **organizational assessment** has both quantitative as well as qualitative components. The quantitative section of the internal assessment consists mainly of the organizational volume forecast and an assessment of the financial condition. The qualitative section focuses on past strategic performance and leadership's interpretation of the organization's core capabilities (or lack thereof). Each of these components is discussed further.

Organizational Volume Forecast

The **volume forecast** is initiated by identifying the organization's service area—usually a zip code–defined area where 70–80% of its patients are drawn from—and determining the population use rates for applicable service lines (e.g., cardiology, orthopedics, home care visits, CT scans, etc.). These data are usually collected for several historical time periods (e.g., the previous three years or twelve quarters) and can then be forecasted out several more time periods simply by using a mathematical trend formula, resulting in a **baseline scenario**. Historical market share information is then applied to each service line, therein highlighting some of an organization's strengths and weaknesses. By holding its market share growth trends constant, an organization can formulate a preliminary idea of how well it would fare if it were to stay its current course (and if its competitors do as well). Examining the forecast from the perspective of market share, contribution margin, and/or medical staff depth will also yield service lines or areas of strength that may need to be protected and service lines or areas that could be developed further.

Financial Condition

As with the volume forecast, several years' worth of key financial indicators should be analyzed to highlight additional strengths and weaknesses of the organization. These may include indicators such as operating margin, net income, gross and net revenues, bond ratings, fund-raising, key financial ratios, payer mix, pricing, and/or rate-setting arrangements. The organization's historical performance against budget is also helpful to analyze and should yield further insight into strengths and weaknesses. Any financial forecasts that are available should also be included, as well as any routine or planned capital spending and/or facility improvement plans. It is critical to tie the financial reserves and needs of the organization to the strategic planning process to ensure the resulting strategies can and will be funded appropriately. Tying the financial information to the volume forecast also serves to provide budget targets for the upcoming year(s).

Strategic Performance

It is important to remember strategic planning is a dynamic rather than linear process and, as such, there should optimally be no distinct beginning or end. Thus, a review of the organization's past strategic performance should be included as part of future strategy development. This review can be as simple as an assessment of whether past strategies accomplished their intended goals or as multifaceted as an ad hoc leadership meeting to discuss roadblocks that led to failure or factors that drove success. Either way, this review can and should provide valuable information for future strategy development and implementation.

Organizational Core Capabilities

In addition to the more quantitative **strengths** and **weaknesses** that can be outlined through the volume forecast and financial condition review, there are subjective strengths and weaknesses that need to be identified for strategy development as well. Identifying these capabilities can be quite challenging, as planners usually have to rely on surveys of and/or interviews with the leadership of the organization to gather this information. This can be both time-consuming and value laden, but this information will be critical input for the plan's overall success. With that said, Table 5-1 highlights some common methods of collecting this information and the benefits and limitations of each.

The key to gathering the most value from the leadership input is to challenge leaders (e.g., executives, physicians, managers, etc.) to think within a strategic context, as opposed to the operational mode they are involved in on a day-to-day basis. Merely asking leaders to identify an organization's weaknesses, for example, can result in responses such as poor parking or a lack of marketing, whereas framing the question to identify challenges to the organization in growing service volumes may better yield answers such as an aging medical staff, lack of capacity, etc. It is important to incorporate these identified strengths and weaknesses into the organizational assessment for further discussion.

TABLE 5-1 Data Collection Methods

	Pros	Cons
Interviews	■ opportunity to clarify responses ■ encourages free thinking ■ can ensure representative sample	■ time-consuming ■ potential for interviewer bias ■ open answers difficult to analyze
Focus Groups	■ opportunity to clarify responses ■ allows for relatively large sample ■ can be economically efficient	■ potential for groupthink ■ open answers difficult to analyze
Surveys	■ effective way to obtain large sample ■ standardized answers allow for easier analysis no interviewer bias	■ can be expensive ■ lag time for responses ■ potential for low response rate

STRATEGY IDENTIFICATION AND SELECTION

Throughout the development of the SWOT, the building blocks for strategy identification begin to emerge. If the organization is at the start of the development of a multiyear plan, it will usually conduct a rather thorough SWOT analysis. However, if the organization has an identified long-term strategic direction, the SWOT may selectively analyze only those areas that are relevant to the identified strategic direction. For example, if the organization has resolved to grow defined service lines, the analysis may focus more specifically on those areas of the market. Alternately, if the direction is diversification, the analysis may focus more on areas related to the organization's current strengths, whether they are related to service line or internal capability. Regardless of the depth of the SWOT, it serves as input for the next step in the process, strategy identification and selection.

Scenario Development

Strategy identification usually begins with the baseline scenario developed for the volume forecast. However, at this point, it is important to apply planning assumptions to the scenario and not simply accept the baseline. For example, will the organization plan to hold market share constant for a particular service, or will the organization hope to grow that market? Alternatively, the organization may decide to discontinue a specific service, perhaps due to predicted declining reimbursement or lack of physicians. By applying different planning assumptions, many different scenarios may result.

It is also critical that the information and data gathered in the market assessment, including the competitor assessment, be incorporated into this forecast in the form of further planning assumptions. For example, are there new technologies on the horizon that will affect service volumes? Or is there a dearth of providers that may counteract predicted increasing utilization of a particular service for a period of time? Desired financial targets also need to be incorporated here.

Overlaying these planning assumptions onto the baseline scenario can result in any number of future scenarios by adjusting their relative impacts. This is where strategic planning really becomes an art vs. a science, and it is often difficult to quantitatively determine the extent to which market forces may affect future market volumes. Because of this, the underlying planning assumptions should be debated extensively. To this end, there are several companies that provide assistance and/or models for quantifying market forces; a sampling of these companies is provided as additional resources at the end of this chapter.

From this scenario analysis, several potential strategic directions for the organization may emerge. The **strategic direction** is the goal that the organization desires to accomplish within the planning time frame. Generally, as each scenario may have different probabilities for success and may require different levels of resource investment, the specific scenario (and strategic direction) that will ultimately be chosen will often depend on an organization's tolerance for risk.

Outcomes

Once a strategic direction is chosen, specific desired outcomes should be targeted and strategies to accomplish this identified. As an example, if an organization concludes it will differentiate itself through its orthopedic services (strategic direction), the desired outcome may be to lead the market in orthopedic service volumes within two years. To accomplish this, the organization may identify strategies to increase its surgeon base, add rehabilitation services, or develop a center-of-excellence program. A **strategy** is a carefully designed plan to accomplish the desired outcomes.

Even the largest and most fiscally sound organization cannot successfully implement all the strategies it can conceive of, nor should it try to. A successful strategic plan is focused and, just as importantly, executable; too many strategies may render the plan ineffective simply because there is too much to do. Strategy is all about making choices. A clear and focused strategy will guide decision making, prioritize resource allocation, and keep the organization on its desired course; in choosing which strategies to pursue, an organization is also choosing which strategies *not* to pursue. At this stage in the planning process, the organization's leadership must determine its ability to successfully execute the strategies it has identified.

Factors to consider in making this determination are highlighted in Table 5-2 and include, for example, the degree to which the strategy has the ability to help the organization meet its financial targets. Alternatively, does the organization have the financial resources to fund the strategy appropriately in terms of operating and capital expense? Additionally, does the organization have the internal capabilities to successfully execute the strategy—does it have, or can it acquire, the necessary human resources? Is the strategy

TABLE 5-2 Successful Strategies

Successful Strategies

■ Are focused on the desired future state
■ Align internal capabilities with market opportunities and threats
■ Provide or sustain a competitive advantage for the organization
■ Are funded and resourced long term

transformational enough to bring about the desired change? Equally important, is there a champion to take ownership of the strategy's success? By going through the exercise of matching potential strategies to financial and other targets, and matching implementation requirements to resource availability, strategy selection is accomplished.

Strategy Tactical Plans

The final step in the actual development of the strategic plan is the creation of specific **tactical plans** for each strategy, which are necessary for translating the plan into action. Tactical plans answer the who, what, when, where, and how questions of strategy implementation. Table 5-3 shows an example of a basic template for a tactical plan that, when completed, will help drive implementation of the strategy.

ROLLOUT AND IMPLEMENTATION

With the development of the tactical plans, the strategic plan is complete. The plan is then presented to the board of directors for approval and endorsement and is then rolled out across the organization. Rollout of the plan has two main steps: first, the plan is

TABLE 5-3 Tactical Plan Template

Goal	Key Actions	Target Completion Date	Resources Required	Dependencies	Revenue Projection	Success Metric

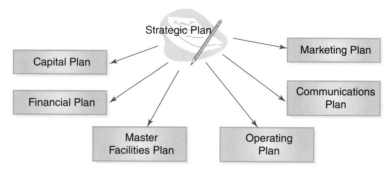

FIGURE 5-3 Supporting Plans

communicated at all levels of the organization; only by communicating the strategy to all necessary stakeholders can an organization gain the support necessary for successful execution of the strategy. Second, supporting plans such as the financial and budgeting, operating, marketing, capital, and master facilities plans are developed or updated with the intent and strategies developed in the strategic plan. Having all of the organization's supporting plans tied to the strategic plan is a critical factor in reinforcing its strategic direction. Figure 5-3 depicts some of the supporting plans that may be drawn from the strategic plan.

OUTCOMES MONITORING AND CONTROL

Monitoring and control of the strategic plan is most often accomplished through the use of an organizational dashboard, or scorecard. A **dashboard** is a visual reference used to monitor an organization's performance against targets over time. Its simplistic design should allow for quick assessment of areas that may need adjustment, similar to an automobile dashboard. Dashboards can depict strategic, operational, and/or financial outcome indicators, depending on the organization's needs, but care must be taken to highlight a *manageable* number of indicators, or the dashboard will lose its functionality. Figure 5-4 depicts an example of a dashboard, although templates abound in the industry.

Depending on the organization's needs and on the types of indicators management identifies, the dashboard should be monitored regularly (e.g., monthly or quarterly). At a minimum, as soon as an indicator highlights a variance from the desired target, managers must address the variance with tactics that correct or alter the results. Optimally, the dashboard should serve to facilitate ongoing management discussion regarding execution of the strategy. To help best ensure success of the strategic plan, dashboard indicators are aligned with operational plans and their associated identified goals.

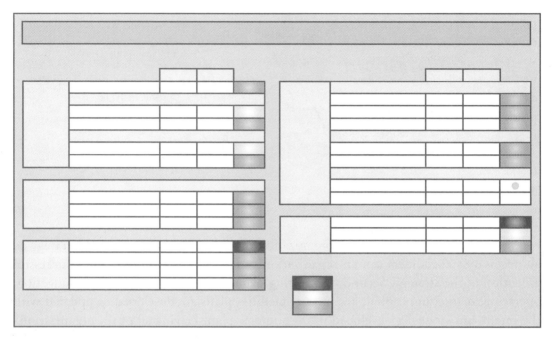

FIGURE 5-4 Dashboard

STRATEGY EXECUTION

Although the development of the actual strategic plan occurs in a logical progression, other than perhaps the creation of the SWOT, every stage of the plan's development should really be viewed as part of its execution. **Strategy execution** is crucial for organizational success and cannot be overstated in terms of importance; unfortunately, this is often an element of strategic planning that many organizations overlook. With the flurry of activity and intensity that usually surrounds the development of the strategic plan itself, there can be a collective sigh of relief following board approval of the plan, and leadership may be relieved to be able to return to their "real work" and the day-to-day operations. Yet successful organizations know that execution is much more important than the plan.

Barriers

Execution, however, isn't easy, and there are many roadblocks on the path to success. It has been said that "culture eats strategy for lunch." Even that may be an understatement. If an organization's stakeholders are not ready for the strategy, it will not be executed by even the most tenacious of leaders. With the heightened influence of consumerism, many health care organizations attempted strategies early on to shift the organization from a physician-centric to a more patient-centric focus, aiming to gain a competitive advantage on this emerging market trend. However, many of these organizations were faced with a strong undercurrent of resistance from an internal culture that was not prepared for this new paradigm, and the strategy failed. This example demonstrates the need for strategy execution to start early in the planning process, enabling the organization to either better prepare itself for implementation of the strategy or table the strategy until the organization is ready to implement it successfully.

Other barriers to successful strategy execution include a lack of focus of the strategy. Often, during the plan development phase, leadership will inevitably develop more strategies than it can successfully execute. If this list is not pared down to a reasonable number, or if the few strategies that are planned do not align appropriately, execution attempts will be futile. Additionally, as mentioned earlier, if the strategies are not appropriately funded and resourced, they cannot be executed, or if they result in competing priorities, the organization will likely be unsuccessful. All of these barriers can be overcome, however, in part by focusing on execution at the earliest stages of strategy development.

Strategy execution is also most successful with a combination of strong leadership and organizational buy-in. Although leadership will need to have flexibility to adjust strategies as market conditions and internal developments warrant, they must also have the consistency over time to stay the course. Too often, strategies have failed because the organization has fallen to the temptation of bright and shiny new priorities, or they simply fail to resource the strategy over multiple years or time periods. Strategy is not a quick fix or immediate turnaround, and strong leadership is needed to maintain a long-term focus. In addition, organizational buy-in at all levels is critical. As demonstrated earlier in the example regarding culture, strategy cannot be implemented solely in the top layers of an organization. All stakeholders must be aware of and buy in to the desired future state and the path that leads them there in order to ensure the momentum necessary to achieve results. Optimally, a successfully conducted strategic planning process will generate "strategy champions" at all levels of the organization.

Participants

All organizations generally involve key leadership in the strategic planning process, but the extent to which other stakeholders are involved varies considerably. There is no one best answer as to who should be involved in the planning process and how, because each organization and culture is different, but one caveat generally holds true: the more stakeholders that are aware of and own the strategy, the greater the chance of success. That said, the strategic planning process should involve representatives from the board of trustees, upper and middle management, the medical staff, general staff, and community leaders as much as possible to the extent appropriate throughout the process. When the plan is completed, it should be communicated to all stakeholders as discussed earlier.

STRATEGIC PLANNING AND EXECUTION: THE ROLE OF THE HEALTH CARE MANAGER

A good portion of this chapter has been dedicated to discussion of the content of the strategic plan, and with good reason: health care managers need to understand the types of information and intelligence gathered and analyzed for plan development, and how that information is interpreted and acted upon. However, it has often been said that "the plan is worthless but planning is priceless." The value of strategic planning lies not in the plan itself, but in the planning process. Properly conducted, the strategic planning process will challenge management to robustly confront the facts of its market and the organization, to persistently test planning assumptions, and to continually refine the organization's execution skills.

Health care managers at all levels have the responsibility to continually monitor their environment—both internal and external—and assess and act upon the possible implications of any trends or events that are of note. They have the responsibility to understand their local market on an ongoing basis and to know their organization's strategic direction and intent. They are responsible for identifying ways to support the organization's strategy and for ensuring that their subordinates have the knowledge and understanding of the strategy in order to do the same. Strategic planning may be driven by the planning or business development function of an organization, but it is the responsibility of leadership at all levels to help execute and manage the organization's strategy. Strategic plans may also be developed for departments and other levels within the organization and may be helpful to the manager in achieving the department's goals as well.

OPPORTUNITIES FOR RESEARCH IN STRATEGIC PLANNING

Opportunities for in-depth research on strategic planning in health care exist in a variety of venues, including your own health care organization. Many of the resources used in writing this chapter also include extensive research holdings and data sets, which are available to students and academic researchers to utilize. Herewith is a partial listing of some resources.

- American Hospital Association Data and Directories;
- Balanced Scorecard Institute;
- Center for Studying Health Systems Change (HSC): Health Care Markets;
- Centers for Disease Control and Prevention Community Health Status Indicator;

- Centers for Medicare and Medicaid Services Cost Reports;
- DataBay Resources;
- Esri;
- Hospital Consumer Assessment of Healthcare Providers and Systems;
- National Center for Policy Analysis;
- Press Ganey;
- Sg2 Healthcare Intelligence;
- Society for Healthcare Strategy and Market Development;
- The Dartmouth Atlas of Healthcare;
- The Henry J. Kaiser Family Foundation; and
- U.S. Department of Health and Human Services Health Resources and Services Administration.

As the need for improved strategic planning is demonstrated in every health care organization, you can be sure there will be many more research sources.

CONCLUSION

Effective strategic planning is a critical element in the success of today's health care organizations. Through understanding its competitive and other market environments, an organization can best identify a desired future state and a means to achieve it, but as discussed, the true value of strategic planning lies in the process, and less in the resulting plan (Blatstein, 2012). Strategic planning will most certainly continue to be a valued function in health care organizations in the future, and management at all levels needs to understand the process, and its purpose and their critical role in development and execution of the successful strategy.

DISCUSSION QUESTIONS

1. What are some of the health care market trends you can identify in your market? How might they affect your job as a manager, and how would you react to/prepare for them?

2. In what ways can you, as a manager, contribute to the management and execution of your organization's strategy?

3. Discuss how strategic planning is a dynamic, vs. linear, process. Why is this important?

4. Summarize the purpose of the SWOT analysis and how it is best used in the planning process.

5. Describe resources you could use as a manager to stay current in your field/area. Select one research source and describe how you might apply it in strategic planning.

Cases in Chapter 18 that are related to this chapter include:

- United Physician Group
- Last Chance Hospital
- Are We Culturally Aware or Not?
- Patients "Like" Social Media
- To Partner or Not to Partner with a Retail Company
- Wellness Tourism: An Option for Your Organization?

Case study guides are available in the online Instructor's Materials.

REFERENCES

American Hospital Association (AHA). (2015). *American Hospital Association.* Retrieved from http://www.aha.org

Blatstein, I. M. (2012). Strategic planning: Predicting or shaping the future? *Organization Development Journal, 30*(2), 31–38.

DukeMedicine. (2015). *About us.* Retrieved from http://corporate.dukemedicine.org/AboutUs

Genesis HealthCare. (2014). *Mission & core values.* Retrieved from http://www.genesishcc.com/about-us/company-profile/mission-core-values

Porter, M. (1998). *On competition.* Boston, MA: Harvard Business School Press.

Additional Readings

Bossidy, L., & Charan, R. (2004). Execution: The discipline of getting things done. *AFP Exchange, 24*(1), 26–30.

Collins, J. (2001). *Good to great: Why some companies make the leap… and others don't.* New York, NY: Harper Business.

Ginter, P., Duncan, W. J., & Swayne, L. (2013). *Strategic management of healthcare organizations* (7th ed.). San Francisco, CA: Jossey-Bass.

Kaplan, R., & Norton, D. (2005). The balanced scorecard: Measures that drive performance. *Harvard Business Review, 83*(7), 172.

Lenert, L. (2010). Transforming healthcare through patient empowerment. *Information Knowledge Systems Management, 8*(1–4), 159–175. doi:10.3233/IKS-2009-0158

Porter, M. E., & Lee, T. H. (2013). The strategy that will fix health care. *Harvard Business Review, 91*(10), 50–70.

Senge, P., Kleiner, A., Roberts, C., Ross, R. B., Roth, G., & Smith, B. J. (1994). *The fifth discipline fieldbook: Strategies and tools for building a learning organization.* New York, NY: Doubleday.

Zuckerman, A. M. (2014). Successful strategic planning for a reformed delivery system. *Journal of Healthcare Management, 59*(3), 168–172.

CHAPTER 6

Healthcare Marketing

Nancy K. Sayre

LEARNING OBJECTIVES

By the end of this chapter, the student will be able to:

- Assess marketing and the progression of becoming a market-oriented organization;
- Critique the critical link between strategic management and health care marketing;
- Differentiate among the major components that are part of the marketing management process;
- Compare and contrast several important marketing terms, including market segmentation, target markets, marketing mix, and positioning;
- Evaluate consumer behavior and the decision making process as it relates to health care offerings and distinguish between marketing approaches;
- Analyze how health care managers can integrate ethics and social responsibility into marketing strategy; and
- Create marketing tactics such as using social media related to the strategic goals of a health care organization.

INTRODUCTION

Today's practicing managers are being challenged to operate in increasingly complex, interdependent, financially-relevant, and dynamic health care markets. These same managers must understand essential principles and practices of marketing in order to support the organization's broader strategic goals and financial objectives, as identified in the previous chapter. The extent of marketing in the health care industry is enormous.

Health care marketing consists of the kinds of activities a firm uses to satisfy customer needs; the approaches managers pursue to create, communicate, and deliver value in selected markets; and the means of capturing value in return (Kotler, Shalowitz, & Stevens, 2008). A **customer** is the purchaser of products, services, and ideas (Pride & Ferrill, 2009). All marketing activities should focus on the customer. In this sense, the role of health care marketing must be understood as the process of creating long-term, mutually beneficial relationships between the organization and well-defined target customers. However, as discussed later in detail, the purchaser of products, services, or ideas may not necessarily be the decision-maker or ultimate health care consumer. Nonetheless, optimal integrated marketing practice will take into consideration the various roles in the health care purchasing process.

To quote Peter Drucker, seminal management thinker and sound practitioner, "There is only one valid definition of business purpose: to create a customer.... It is the customer who determines what the business is.... Because it is its purpose to create a customer, any business enterprise has two—and only these two—basic functions: marketing and innovation" (1954, p. 37). According to Drucker (1974), "Any organization in which marketing is either absent or incidental is not a business and should never be managed as if it were one" (p. 62). Although marketing is now widely accepted as a critical organizational function, from a historical perspective, when compared to other sectors, health care has lagged in the adoption of a customer orientation. Marketing as an organizational function did not generally exist in health care before the 1980s (Berkowitz, 2011; Kotler et al., 2008; Thomas, 2005). In 1975, the appointment of a vice president of marketing at Evanston Hospital in Evanston, Illinois (now NorthShore University Health System), was one notable exception. With the growing significance of consumer-driven health care, the use of the Internet on all frontiers, and increased demand for personalized services, understanding strategic marketing has become increasingly important.

WHAT IS MARKETING?

Many people mistakenly equate marketing with advertising, promotion, or selling. The American Marketing Association (2013) defines **marketing** as "the activity, set of institutions, and processes for creating, communicating, delivering, and exchanging offerings that have value for customers, clients, partners, and society at large" (para. 1). What can we learn from this definition? First, it places marketing in the central role of satisfying customer needs. Second, all marketing activities center on building a sustainable value-driven system for customers, stakeholders, and society. These customers can include individual health care consumers, physicians, insurers, or other organizations. Third, health care organizations and managers with a relentless focus on creating long-term customer relationships will generally achieve superior performance over those who only focus on short-term results.

Key Components of the Marketing Concept

The previous discussion introduces a managerial philosophy that suggests that *all* organizations, regardless of industry, must be in the business of satisfying customer needs. According to the **marketing concept**, an organization must create, communicate, and deliver customer value to selected target markets more effectively than its competition to achieve its goals and objectives (Kotler & Keller, 2009). **Customer value** is the difference between the benefits a consumer perceives from the purchase of a product, service, or idea and the cost to acquire those benefits. Through a coordinated set of well-defined activities, the marketing manager must do the right things at the right time to orchestrate individual strategies into a wholly integrated system. In general, an organization can be characterized as production oriented, sales oriented, or marketing oriented. Figure 6-1 depicts the sharp contrast between the three types of organizational orientations.

A BRIEF HISTORY OF MARKETING IN HEALTH CARE

Because the health care industry is a relative newcomer to marketing, it is useful to consider a historical perspective. Prior to the past few decades, marketing lacked widespread acceptance in the health care industry. During the 1970s and 1980s in particular, it was difficult for managers to agree on the role and value of marketing for health care organizations.

FIGURE 6-1 Production, Sales, and Marketing Orientation

As a result, most hospitals, insurers, managed care organizations, nursing homes, physician and dental practices, and other health care providers had limited use for marketing (Robinson & Cooper, 1980–1981). It is not surprising that books devoted to health care marketing did not appear until the late 1970s and the first formal conference on the topic did not take place until 1977 (Keith, 1985; MacStravic, 1990; Thomas, 2005). As late as 1990, the future of marketing in health care remained unclear. In reviewing the slow progression, MacStravic (1990) presented the following reasons:

- Some managers supported marketing, but chose not to disclose its success.
- Others were optimistic about marketing's potential, but were experimenting.
- In a number of health care organizations, managers were frustrated, but uncertain as to why marketing was not working.
- Other health care administrators and managers viewed marketing as a hoax.
- For the most part, organizations were only getting started in marketing.

Despite the differences in approach, early practitioners and scholars were asking precisely the same question we are asking today: "Why is marketing different in health care?" With roughly four decades of research into the nature and scope of marketing as it applies to health care, a number of issues are among the most mentioned. First, in the past (and in some cases today), health care professionals, especially physicians, scorned marketing activities based on the belief that, while suitable in non-health care entities, they were inappropriate and contemptible for health care organizations (Thomas, 2005). With respect to this issue, there was a time when even the American Medical Association declared such activities as unethical. Second, health care professionals raised considerable doubt that health care is a "market" comparable to other industries. A chorus of practitioners and scholars said health care was uniquely different from other industries. Thomas perhaps best describes this view: "Healthcare is different from other industries in terms of characteristics inherent in the industry and the attributes of its buyers and sellers" (2005, p. 47). Even the most casual observer would agree that health consumers typically have not been responsible for paying all the associated costs of medical treatment. Additionally, imperfect knowledge about costs and services constrains consumer decision making. For example, knee replacement surgery could cost anywhere between $17,000 and $61,000 depending upon where you live in the U.S. (Millman, 2015). A third major shortcoming is a weak consumer-driven health care system, where third-party payers (e.g., employers and health insurers) are in charge and neither consumers nor their providers have direct decision-making power (Herzlinger, 2002, 2004). While a totally consumer-driven health care system seems unreasonable, empowering consumers to have a greater voice and more accountability is certainly an attainable goal. A fourth issue is that the marketing function has been further constrained by the absence of value-based competition. As Porter and

Teisberg (2006) point out, there is dysfunctional competition in health care where participants drive not to create value for patients but to capture more revenue, shift costs, and restrict services. They state:

> Consumers will only be able to play a bigger role in their care, and make better choices if providers and health plans re-align competition around patient results and disseminate the relevant information and advice. Reform does not require consumers to become medical experts or to manage their own care; it requires providers and health plans to compete on value, which will allow and enable consumers to make better choices and be more responsible. (Porter & Teisberg, 2006, p. 8)

Taken together, these arguments explain some of the reasons why marketing as a management tool has been neglected in the past in the health care industry. Today, however, the extent of marketing in the health care industry is enormous. In 2013 in the U.S., hospitals, clinics, and medical centers spent about $1.8 billion on media, just one aspect of marketing, to attract revenue-generating patients (Rodriguez, 2014). Now, health care managers are making the strategic choice to enable internal collaboration and enterprise-wide knowledge sharing with nurses, physicians, and other clinicians in order to build a customer-driven health care organization. As a result, understanding and applying the essential elements of marketing falls squarely into the health care manager's domain of responsibility.

THE STRATEGIC MARKETING PROCESS

The emergence of a market orientation where sustainable distinctive advantage is based on the ability of an organization to create, communicate, and deliver customer lifetime value more effectively than its competitors is creating profound changes in the practice of health care marketing. The unforgiving global competitive environment is forcing organizations to derive value not just from the production of goods and services, but also from connecting with customers and patients. This may require conducting primary or secondary research. For example, NorthShore University Health System commissioned a market research study to understand consumer motivation. By listening to patients, they learned consumers were interested in talking about their medical conditions—not hospital services. They also learned patients identify with physicians and nurses—not hospitals. With such market insights, the hospital staff was better prepared to integrate more relevant and compelling messages throughout the NorthShore University delivery system (Bendycki, 2010).

In response to many of the same market forces, challenges, and opportunities discussed in Chapter 5, the role of marketing continues to evolve as a critical strategic management function. Uncontrollable forces, i.e., the dramatic pace of technology, continuous changes

Key Stakeholders
- Customers
- Board of Directors
- Suppliers
- Physicians
- Employers
- Society at Large

Controllable Variables
- Product
- Price
- Promotion
- Place

Organizations

Uncontrollable Environment
- Political
- Economic
- Social and Cultural
- Technological
- Regulatory
- Competitive

FIGURE 6-2 Components of Strategic Marketing

in U.S. health insurance reimbursement trends, and the prospect of more empowered consumers, have elevated marketing into the strategic realm (Berkowitz, 2011).

Although external uncontrollable (marketplace) and internal controllable (organizational) complexities present marketing issues, agile health care organizations can achieve extraordinary results by keeping the customer front and center as the focal point in all marketing activities. Figure 6-2 depicts the essential components of strategic marketing.

As shown in Figure 6-2, organizations can formulate an effective marketing strategy within the context of the organization's strategic plan and in concert with other functional areas (e.g., finance, human resources, operations, etc.). Once established, the mission, vision, and value statements dictate the broad direction for the organization (as noted in Chapter 5), including strategic marketing planning. Marketing, in this sense, relies on the strategic plan to deliver a sound and reasonable fit between the external environment and internal organizational capabilities. However, from a managerial perspective, it is important to keep in mind that formulating an effective marketing plan is not an easy task. Hence, organizations often assemble cross-functional teams (see Chapter 13 for more on teamwork) to provide input and insights throughout the strategic marketing process, as shown in Figure 6-3.

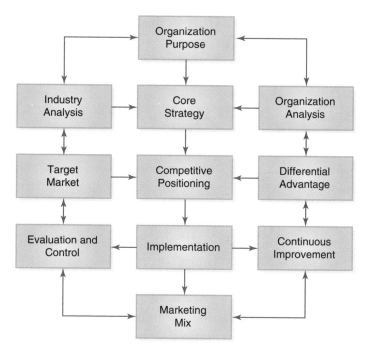

FIGURE 6-3 Strategic Marketing Process Framework

The development of a marketing strategy can be viewed at three main levels:

1. Establishment of a **core strategy**: As linked to the organization's strategic plan, an effective marketing strategy starts with a detailed and creative assessment of both the company's capabilities—its strengths and weaknesses relative to the competition—and the opportunities and threats posed by the environment. This may require conducting primary or secondary market research.

2. Creation of the company's **competitive positioning**: At the next level, target markets are selected, which determines who the competitors are. At the same time, the company's differential advantage, or competitive edge in serving the customer targets, is defined. Together the identification of targets and the definition of differential advantage constitute the creation of the competitive positioning of the organization and its offerings.

3. **Implementation of the strategy**: At the implementation level, a marketing-oriented organization must be capable of putting the strategy into practice. Implementation is also concerned with establishing the optimal marketing mix,

which will be discussed in detail later in the chapter. Control concerns both the efficiency with which the strategy is put into operation and the ultimate effectiveness of that strategy.

UNDERSTANDING MARKETING MANAGEMENT

Health care marketers must continually scan the external environment and conduct a situation assessment to determine the **strengths**, **weaknesses**, **opportunities**, and **threats (SWOT Analysis)** for a given offering, set of offerings, or an entire portfolio of products and services. As such, **health care marketing management** is the art and science of selecting target markets and creating, communicating, and delivering value to selected customers in a manner that is both sustainable and differentiated from the competition (Kotler et al., 2008; Kotler & Keller, 2009).

Segmentation, Targeting, and Positioning

A **market** is a diverse group of organizations or individuals who have disparate needs for products and services. **Market segmentation** is the process of dividing the total market into groups or segments that have relatively similar needs for products and services. Segmentation enables organizations to design marketing activities that will more precisely match the needs of the selected segments (Kotler et al., 2008). Using this method, segmentation is most useful when buyers in target segments have the budget, authority, need, and time with a propensity to purchase products and services. In other words, attractive health care market segments must also be measureable and actionable (Kotler et al., 2008). Again, it is important to note that since it is nearly impossible for a firm to serve an entire market; marketing managers often divide a diverse heterogeneous market into smaller homogenous segments. Hence, a **target market** consists of a more narrowly defined group of individuals or organizations with relatively similar wants and needs. Through segmentation, a health care organization seeks to match its offerings and services to the needs of the select segments.

Target Market Segment Selection

How do organizations choose some segments to serve and not others? The combination of target market needs and characteristics, the offering portfolio, and the organization's objectives and resources must be taken into consideration. Berkowitz (2011) distinguishes between the two categories of strategies as follows:

Concentration strategy: This approach targets a single market in order to specialize with the objective of gaining a large share of the market. An orthodontic practice choosing to focus solely on children and adolescents as a **niche market** is an example. An advantage of this strategy is that specialization enables the health care provider to focus all marketing activities on creating, delivering, and sustaining long-term value to a distinct set of customers. The disadvantage, of course, is that specialization may preclude the organization from entering other attractive markets, such as treating adults in the orthodontic practice.

Multisegment strategy: This approach targets several segments with differentiation among the selected group of customers. For example, a general dental practice might choose to serve both children and adults, but might also offer orthodontic services. Choosing this strategy extends the reach to a broader share of the total market. However, more organizational resources are required to satisfy the wants and needs of multiple customer segments.

To select target segments wisely, health care marketers need to determine whether the market is identifiable, divisible, and accessible, and has enough revenue potential to justify the allocation of organizational resources. After the organization identifies an appropriate marketing strategy, the next step in selecting a target market is determining which segmentation variables to use. The challenge of precisely meeting the needs of selected segments is addressed by dividing them into broad groups based on key distinguishing variables. As can be seen in Table 6-1, there are five broad groups of variables commonly used to segment health consumer markets.

Table 6-1 depicts the many layers of segmentation at the health care manager's disposal. Market segmentation based on demographic variables is a case in point. Perhaps the most widely used, demographic segmentation is a relatively easy way to estimate customer demand, i.e., wants and needs. Marketing in long-term care is a good example of the use of demographic segmentation. Consumers ranging from age 55 to 95+ represent a diverse range of people who are at various stages with respect to retirement, but at the same time, all have needs related to quality of life. In the U.S., there are approximately 12 million Americans who belong to the pre-Depression generation (individuals born before 1930); the Depression generation (born between 1930 and 1945) is composed of another estimated 28 million; and the Baby Boomer generation (born between 1946 and 1964 and rapidly approaching the retirement phase of life) accounts for 80 million (Hawkins & Mothersbaugh, 2010). Various types of long-term care facilities (e.g., independent living, assisted living, and skilled nursing) offer different levels of care. These different services suggest a need for long-term care facilities to market themselves in different ways to these demographic segments and to overcome the negative connotations associated with words like "nursing home" (Laurence & Kash, 2010).

TABLE 6-1 Segmentation Broad Categories, Variables, and Indicative Examples

Category	Variables	Example(s)
Demographic	Age; Gender; Ethnicity and race; Country of origin; Education; Occupation; Income; Generation; Life cycle stage	Changing U.S. demographics offer new opportunities to target retiring and aspiring retiree segments. A long-term care facility might develop a communications plan to reach seniors 55 and older.
Geographic	State; City; County; Urban; Rural	Marketing food products typically varies by region and geographic segmentation. Because tastes and preferences differ, recipes, packaging and promotion are different for many parts of the country.
Psychographic	Values; Lifestyle; Personality; Motivation; Self-efficacy; Attitudes	Four groups of distinct health information–seeking orientations were found to be significantly associated with certain prevention-related attitudes and behaviors. Using a research screening instrument, respondents were segmented into four psychographic consumer segments—*independent actives, doctor-dependent actives, independent passives*, and *doctor-dependent passives* (Wolff et al., 2010).
Situational	Life events	Health insurance firms use situational segmentation to reach employed and unemployed segments. Segment examples include: (1) employer-based health insurance coverage, (2) Consolidated Omnibus Budget Reconciliation Act (COBRA) coverage for 18 months after job termination, and (3) individual health plans beyond COBRA.
Behavioral	Usage rates; Tech-savvy users	In the midst of a recession and in a state with the highest unemployment rate in the nation in 2009, the Henry Ford Health System in Detroit led local competitors in inpatient growth, with a 7.4% increase in admissions over the previous year. Of the 8,201 new admissions, the seven-hospital system segmented the customer base to reach Internet users through social media and other online tools (Glenn, 2010).

Positioning

The **positioning** aspect of the strategic marketing process brings health care marketing closer to tactical implementation. Once an organization determines which portion of the larger market to serve, it then positions itself in the face of competition.

Hence, health care organizations and providers must deliberately position the brand image and offerings in the mind of the target market. Kotler et al. (2008) argue that "good brand positioning helps guide marketing strategy by clarifying the brand's essence, what goals it helps the consumer achieve.... The result of positioning is the successful creation of a customer-focused value proposition" (p. 235). To position products or services apart from the competition, managers must determine what makes them unique or differentiates them and focus on these features in the marketing strategy.

HEALTH CARE BUYER BEHAVIOR

In creating and executing marketing strategy, managers face the central question of how buyers make decisions. There are fundamental differences between organizational and consumer markets. Health care managers need to gain a deep understanding of consumer and business behavior in order to meet customer needs.

Organizational Buying Behavior

The **business market** has been defined as all organizations that acquire goods and services (Kotler et al., 2008). For the purposes of this discussion, both for-profit and non-profit organizations are considered business markets. **Business-to-business (B2B) marketing** concentrates on organizational buyers. Consider the following examples:

- Employers purchase health insurance coverage for employees.
- Local, state, and national governments hire health policy consultants.
- Physician practices contract with vendors of electronic health record software.
- Medical devices, pharmaceuticals, and medical surgical supplies comprise a large share of virtually every hospital's total expenditures.
- Group purchasing organizations facilitate the complex task of sourcing and contracting products and services for health care systems.

These illustrations are indicative of the degree of complexity associated with organizational purchase decisions as compared with consumer buyers. With respect to health care organizations, there are many people involved in the selling and buying process. Additionally, both buyers and sellers typically follow formal policies and procedures. **Derived demand** is the term given to indicate that the demand for goods, services, and ideas in organizations is derived from consumer demand. Health care managers are expected to work with various decision-making units to influence either buying or selling decisions on behalf of the organization.

Consumer Buying Behavior

Consumer behavior refers to the totality of consumers' decisions with respect to the acquisition, consumption, and disposition of goods, services, time, and ideas by humans over time (Hoyer & MacInnis, 2008). The study of consumer behavior seeks to understand how people select, secure, use, and dispose of products, services, experiences, or ideas to satisfy their needs (Hawkins & Mothersbaugh, 2010). To understand consumer behavior, health care managers must draw heavily from the field of psychology. A number of psychological theories have been used to explain the consumer decision-making process. By understanding how people make decisions and the associated internal and external influences on the consumer decision-making process, a health care manager can anticipate consumer needs and develop solutions for those needs.

Internal influences include consumers' motivation, attitudes, perceptions, learning, memory and retrieval, personality, values, emotions, and behavioral intentions. External influences include consumers' family and friends, reference groups, situational factors, culture and subculture, and marketing stimuli.

In addition to understanding the many influences, it is helpful to be aware of the consumer decision-making process as depicted in Table 6-2.

TABLE 6-2 Consumer Decision-Making Process

Stage	Definition
I. Problem Recognition	The health consumer recognizes a difference between an actual and desired state. The individual or group is motivated to reach the desired state. For example, a person may feel that he or she is overweight and wishes to reach a specific weight goal.
II. Internal Search	The consumer searches internal memory to find a solution to the problem. The person may remember a previous experience such as dieting that may or may not have led to solving the problem.
III. External Search	If the problem cannot be solved through an internal search, the health consumer is likely to seek external information that may lead to a solution. The health consumer might consult with family and friends, consult with a physician, or search the Internet or any number of external sources.
IV. Alternative Evaluation	In the fourth stage of the decision-making process, the consumer evaluates the various alternatives to arrive at a solution.
V. Purchase	The fifth stage involves the purchase by selecting the health product, service, or idea. For example, an individual might decide that gastric bypass surgery is the most viable solution.
VI. Post-Purchase Evaluation	In the final stage, the consumer evaluates his or her choice. Generally speaking, in a high-involvement purchase decision with several equally attractive alternatives, the consumer may experience cognitive dissonance, a state of anxiety where there is uncertainty about the selection.

It is fair to say health care providers will continue to have a prominent role in the decision-making process in the foreseeable future. At the same time, the growing availability of health care information due to the Internet, mobile computing, other unprecedented technological advancements, consumer empowerment (see Chapter 17 for more on this subject), personalized health care trends, and more sophisticated and socially responsible marketing practices is giving consumers a greater role in their health care decisions.

MARKETING MIX

Putting the marketing strategy into practice requires attending to the controllable variables for the organization presented earlier in Figure 6-2. The marketing mix consists of these **four controllable P's**: (1) **Product**—goods, services, or ideas; (2) **Price**—value placed on the product; (3) **Promotion**—marketing activities used to communicate to the target market, including public relations, advertising, personal selling, and integrated marketing campaigns; and (4) **Place**—the offering delivery route (e.g., a pediatric optometrist office). The promotional component of the marketing mix (e.g., advertising, sales promotion, events, etc.) is too often considered to be marketing (Clarke, 2010). Instead, the effective marketing mix considers all four factors and is closely aligned with the strategy.

MARKETING PLAN

The **marketing plan** is a written document that serves to guide marketing initiatives across the organization. It is typically a part of the broader strategic plan that has a long-term horizon. Once the organization's strategic plan has been written and adopted, the marketing plan is written containing specific tactical marketing activities, which are more short-term in nature. Promotional tactics such as community engagements, sponsorships, and social media are often included; but television and newspapers still comprise the largest portion of hospital advertising budgets. Digital strategies built around banner ads, wellness advice, and patient testimonials are growing in importance. Although the time frame varies, organizations usually develop tactical implementation plans on an annual or biannual basis.

Promotion via Social Media

One of the most common Internet activities is looking for health information. According to a September 2012 survey, 72% of Internet users say they looked online for health information within the past year. Most start at a search engine and the most commonly researched topics are diseases or conditions, treatments or procedures, and doctors or other health professionals. Given that 87% of U.S. adults use the Internet, this is a huge audience for health marketers to consider when planning promotional tactics. "Women are more likely than men to go online to figure out a possible diagnosis. Other groups that have a high likelihood of doing so include younger people, white adults, those who live in households earning $75,000 or more, and those with a college degree or advanced degrees" (Fox & Duggan, 2013, para. 5). Others who are high users of the Internet for health information include caregivers; those with chronic or disability conditions; those who track their nutrition, exercise, and health; and those with a recent change in health status. Given this compelling data, social media marketing experts in health care suggest producing webinars or YouTube videos on popular health topics; creating supporters by using blogs, Facebook, or on LinkedIn; using twitter.com for instant messages; or any one of the sites used particularly on mobile devices to establish a sense of community. Based on the ubiquity of email, patients also desire or expect their practitioners to communicate directly with them. Even organizations such as the American Medical Association, American Nurses Association, and Centers for Disease Control and Prevention have issued comprehensive social media tips and guidelines for their members. Given the pace of change in the social media space, managers may want to consult with experts or firms working in this arena to establish a successful social media promotional strategy.

Types of Marketing

Philip Kotler and numerous colleagues broadened the traditional marketing concept from the commercial for-profit sector to the not-for-profit realm (Cheng, Kotler, & Lee, 2011; Kotler & Andreasen, 1996; Kotler & Lee, 2008; Kotler & Levy, 1969; Kotler, Roberto, & Lee, 2002; Kotler & Zaltman, 1971). Kotler and Zaltman coined the term social marketing as "the design, implementation, and control of programs calculated to influence the acceptability of social ideas and involving consideration of product planning, pricing, communication, distribution, and marketing research" (Kotler & Zaltman, 1971, p. 5). In health care, **social marketing** is:

1. the application of commercial marketing principles and techniques;
2. used to influence behavioral change;
3. focused on a specific target audience;
4. used in order to promote public health; and
5. intended to benefit society as a whole (Andreasen, 1995; Evans, 2006; Kotler et al., 2002).

Consider the marketing efforts inspired by Susan G. Komen for the Cure. Figure 6-4 depicts the ribbon that has come to symbolize breast cancer awareness. In 1982,

Nancy Brinker, with the support of a handful of dedicated friends and a mere $200, founded the Susan G. Komen Breast Cancer Foundation in memory of her sister. According to the Komen website, the Susan G. Komen Race for the Cure series is today "the world's largest and most successful education and fund-raising event ever created" (Susan G. Komen for the Cure, n.d., para. 2). Since its inception, the non-profit has harnessed the power of social marketing principles and techniques to garner a vast array of strategic partners and sponsors that represent a global network for breast cancer awareness. Other non-profit organizations have followed and created their own ribbons in a variety of colors and patterns.

FIGURE 6-4 Ribbon Used for Social and Cause-Related Marketing

In contrast to social marketing, **cause-related marketing** links a for-profit company and its offerings to a societal issue, such as breast cancer, with the goal of building brand equity and increasing profits. In working with Komen, global networks of corporation partnerships have leveraged cause-related marketing techniques with significant benefits to both partners in the strategic alliance. For example, manufacturers of women's athletic clothing have aligned with the Komen Foundation to support research for breast cancer and are prominently listed on their web site.

In the past, the choice of drugs and procedures was made by physicians and insurers. Now, marketing directly to the end user of health care products and services has been recognized as extremely beneficial for pharmaceutical companies, medical device manufacturers, health plans, and certainly physicians and hospitals. Consequently, there has been tremendous growth in **direct-to-the-consumer advertising (DTCA)**. In 1991, $55 million was spent on DTCA and in 2003, $3.2 billion was spent (Adeoye & Bozic, 2007). This has sparked vigorous debate surrounding the benefits and drawbacks including the impact on the physician–patient relationship, inappropriate resource utilization, health care costs, and overall patient well-being. Once again, the role of marketing and advertising in health care is under scrutiny.

ETHICS AND SOCIAL RESPONSIBILITY

Any chapter on marketing would be incomplete without a discussion of ethics and social responsibility. At this mature stage, the marketing discipline must take into consideration the impact that marketing activities have on individual, group, organizational, and societal outcomes. There can be a dark side of marketing such as firms that market unhealthy products such as cigarettes or encourage behaviors such as alcohol consumption and video game addiction. In addition, there are ethical issues associated with advertising to children and vulnerable populations. Social responsibility and ethical approaches need to be learned and applied to marketing (Hoyer & MacInnis, 2008). Every day, consumers are affected directly and indirectly by marketing influences. These influences can be subtle or insidious, as in the case of the food industry and the epidemic of obesity in the U.S. (Kessler, 2009).

Health care leaders and their respective organizations should model ethically responsible marketing practices. Physicians also must avoid conflict of interest whenever possible in the delivery of health care, not seeking to induce demand for unnecessary procedures. Whether for-profit or not-for-profit, successful marketing practices should be developed to promote consumer well-being. Extending the reach through community-based intervention campaigns, influencing public policy, and emphasizing prevention are just some examples. There are huge implications. Future health care leaders have both the moral responsibility and the opportunity to leverage the power of marketing to improve society as a whole.

TEXTBOX 6-1. HAS HEALTH CARE MARKETING GONE TOO FAR?

An elderly man living in New York City went out to walk his dog one evening in April 2011, and was struck by a sanitation truck. Immediately, he was transported to the nearest hospital with life-threatening injuries. The emergency department physicians and nurses tried to revive him, but his blood pressure continued to drop, and despite cardioversion, he died. Sixteen months later, his wife is watching television in her apartment. She is startled to see her husband's ordeal on the show, *NY Med*, even though no one in the family ever gave permission to televise his situation in the emergency department. Ongoing litigation is occurring in this case.

Rules have been put in place to protect patients' privacy and confidentiality via the Health Insurance Portability and Accountability Act (HIPAA), but real life medical shows have proliferated nonetheless, even over the protests of patients' family members. Hospitals do not receive money for allowing reality shows to film. However, according to hospital marketing and public relations executives, "Advertising is just so saturated right now...you can't buy that kind of publicity." Television endorsements have been found to be beneficial to recruiting insured individuals to become hospital patients. Has health care marketing gone too far?

Ornstein, C. (2015, January 4). Dying in the E.R., and on TV. *The New York Times*, p. 22.

OPPORTUNITIES FOR RESEARCH IN HEALTH CARE MARKETING

Opportunities for in-depth research on health care marketing exist in a variety of venues, including your own health care organization. Many of the resources used in writing this chapter also include extensive research holdings and data sets, which are available to students and academic researchers to utilize (as noted in Chapter 5). Herewith is a partial listing of some resources.

- American Hospital Association Data and Directories;
- Balanced Scorecard Institute;
- Center for Studying Health Systems Change (HSC): Health Care Markets;
- Centers for Disease Control and Prevention Community Health Status Indicator;
- Centers for Medicare and Medicaid Services Cost Reports;
- DataBay Resources;
- Esri;
- Healthcare Marketing Association;
- Hospital Consumer Assessment of Healthcare Providers and Systems;
- Medical Marketing Association;
- National Center for Policy Analysis;
- Press Ganey;
- Sg2 Healthcare Intelligence;
- Society for Healthcare Strategy and Market Development;
- The Dartmouth Atlas of Healthcare;
- The Henry J. Kaiser Family Foundation; and
- U.S. Department of Health and Human Services Health Resources and Services Administration.

As the need for improved marketing practices grow, you can be sure there will be many more research sources.

CONCLUSION

There has never been a more exciting time for understanding the role of marketing in health care. Whereas this chapter places emphasis on the strategic view, health care marketing has many facets. Each health care organization, in its own way, leverages marketing to a greater or lesser extent in creative ways within budget constraints. As remarkable technological advancements reach more and more customers, prudent health care managers must ensure that marketing is not a random activity. Even the most attractive Internet social networking site means little without an orchestrated marketing plan built on the strategic goals of the organization.

Marketing is a management orientation centered on customer satisfaction and an organizational function that is integrally related to the entire organization's mission, objectives, and resources. Consistent with this view, the role of marketing in the health care organization is to create, communicate, and deliver value to customers through mutually beneficial relationships. At the same time, marketing is a discipline in itself. Health care managers should seek assistance from market researchers, strategic planners, advertising agencies, public relations firms, and other consultants.

DISCUSSION QUESTIONS

1. Define marketing and describe why it is important for all health care managers to understand the key components of the marketing concept.

2. A few decades ago, the idea of marketing in many health care organizations was almost unthinkable. Discuss why health care organizations of the past were slow to integrate marketing principles and practices as compared to other industries. Why has it come under scrutiny again?

3. Summarize how health care managers benefit from the study of marketing.

4. You have just inherited $1 million. After paying all your outstanding student loans, you decide to start a health care enterprise. What business are you in? Is it for-profit or not-for-profit? What segments would you choose to serve? Briefly describe the steps you would take to divide the broad market into your selected segments. Will you use a concentrated or differentiated targeting strategy? Refer to Table 6-1 in this chapter; identify the key segmentation variables that you would use, and explain why.

5. Locate an ad that seeks to influence the acquisition of a health care offering or service. Identify the specific consumer decision-making unit that might be affected by this ad. How do you think this ad will affect the consumer's behavior?

6. Differentiate between organizational and consumer buying behavior.

7. Use an example to compare and contrast social marketing and cause-related marketing. Why is cause-related marketing often successful?

8. Today, health care marketing is a pervasive reality. What is the role of marketing ethics and social responsibility in health care today?

Cases in Chapter 18 that are related to this chapter include:

- Last Chance Hospital
- Patients "Like" Social Media
- To Partner or Not to Partner With a Retail Company

Case study guides are available in the online Instructor's Materials.

REFERENCES

Adeoye, S., & Bozic, K. J. (2007). Direct to consumer advertising in healthcare: history, benefits, and concerns. *Clinical Orthopaedics and Related Research*, *457*, 95–104.

American Marketing Association (AMA). (2013). *About AMA*. Retrieved from https://www.ama.org/AboutAMA/Pages/Definition-of-Marketing.aspx

Andreasen, A. (1995). *Marketing social change: Changing behavior to promote health, social development and the environment*. San Francisco, CA: Jossey-Bass.

Bendycki, N. A. (2010). What do consumers want? *Journal of Health Care Marketing*, *30*(1), 3.

Berkowitz, E. (2011). *Essentials of health care marketing* (3rd ed.). Sudbury, MA: Jones and Bartlett.

Cheng, H., Kotler, P., & Lee, R. (2011). *Social marketing for public health: Global trends and success stories*. Sudbury, MA: Jones and Barlett.

Clarke, R. (2010). Marketing health care services. In L. Wolper, *Health care administration: Planning, implementing, and managing organized delivery systems* (4th ed.). Sudbury, MA: Jones and Bartlett.

Drucker, P. (1954). *The practice of management*. New York, NY: Harper & Row.

Drucker, P. (1974). *Management*. New York, NY: Harper & Row.

Evans, W. D. (2006). How social marketing works in health care. *British Medical Journal*, *332*(7551), 1207–1210.

Fox, S., & Duggan, M. (2013). Health Online 2013. *Pew Health Fact Sheet*. Retrieved from http://www.pewinternet.org/2013/01/15/health-online-2013/

Glenn, R. (2010). Growth in a parched economy: The Henry Ford system's success story. *Journal of Marketing*, *30*(2), 10–13.

Hawkins, D., & Mothersbaugh, D. (2010). *Consumer behavior: Building marketing strategy* (11th ed.). Boston, MA: McGraw-Hill/Irwin.

Herzlinger, R. (2002). Let's put consumers in charge of health care. *Harvard Business Review*, *80*(7), 44–55.

Herzlinger, R. (2004). *Consumer-driven health care: Implications for providers, payers, and policy makers*. San Francisco, CA: Jossey-Bass.

Hoyer, D., & MacInnis, D. (2008). *Consumer behavior* (5th ed.). Mason, OH: South-Western Cengage-Learning.

Keith, J. (1985). Marketing health care: What the recent literature is telling us. In P. D. Cooper, *Health care marketing: Issues and trends* (2nd ed., pp. 13–26). Rockville, MD: Aspen Systems Corporation.

Kessler, D. A. (2009). *The end of overeating: Taking control of the insatiable American appetite*. Emmaus, PA: Rodale Press.

Kotler, P., & Andreasen, A. (1996). *Strategic marketing for nonprofit marketing* (5th ed.). Englewood Cliffs, NJ: Prentice Hall.

Kotler, P., & Keller, K. (2009). *Marketing management.* Upper Saddle River, NJ: Pearson Prentice Hall.

Kotler, P., & Lee, N. (2008). *Social marketing: Influencing behaviors for good.* Thousand Oaks, CA: Sage.

Kotler, P., & Levy, J. J. (1969). Broadening the concept of marketing. *Journal of Marketing, 33*(1), 10–15.

Kotler, P., Roberto, N., & Lee, N. (2002). *Social marketing: Improving the quality of life.* Thousand Oaks, CA: Sage.

Kotler, P., & Zaltman, G. (1971). Social marketing: An approach to planned social change. *Journal of Marketing, 35*(3), 3–12.

Laurence, J. N., & Kash, B. A. (2010). Marketing in the long-term care continuum. *Health Marketing Quarterly, 27*(2), 145–154.

MacStravic, R. S. (1990). The end of health care marketing? *Health Marketing Quarterly, 7*(1–2), 3–12.

Millman, J. (2015). A knee replacement surgery could cost $17k or $61k. And that's in the same city. *The Washington Post.* Retrieved from http://www.washingtonpost.com/blogs/wonkblog/wp/2015/01/21/a-knee-replacement-surgery-could-cost-17k-or-61k-and-thats-in-the-same-city/

Ornstein, C. (2015, January 4). Dying in the E.R., and on TV. *The New York Times,* p. 22.

Porter, M., & Teisberg, E. (2006). *Redefining health care: Creating value-based competition on results.* Cambridge, MA: Harvard Business School Press.

Pride, W., & Ferrell, O. (2009). *Foundations of marketing.* Boston, MA: Houghton Mifflin.

Robinson, L. M., & Cooper, D. P. (1980–1981). Roadblocks to hospital marketing. *Journal of Health Care Marketing, 1*(1), 18–24.

Rodriguez, A. (2014, September 16). Why digital marketing has become the health care industry's Rx for revenue. *Advertising Age.* Retrieved from http://adage.com/article/digital/digital-health-care-industry-s-rx-revenue/294940/

Susan G. Komen for the Cure. (n.d.). *About us.* Retrieved from http://ww5.komen.org/AboutUs/AboutUs.html

Thomas, R. K. (2005). *Marketing health services.* Chicago, IL: Health Administration Press.

Wolff, L. S., Massett, H. A., Maibach, E. W., Weber, D., Hassmiller, S., & Mockenhaupt, R. E. (2010). Validating a health consumer segmentation model: Behavioral and attitudinal differences in disease prevention–related practices. *Journal of Health Communication, 15*(2), 167–188.

CHAPTER 7

Quality Improvement Basics

Eric S. Williams, Grant T. Savage, and Patricia A. Patrician

LEARNING OBJECTIVES

By the end of this chapter, the student should be able to:

- Contrast prior definitions of health care quality with current ones;
- Investigate the importance of quality in health care settings;
- Apply key quality concepts;
- Describe the Baldrige criteria;
- Assess the leading models of quality improvement; and
- Apply tools used in quality improvement.

INTRODUCTION

Health care quality gained significant public focus in the U.S. with two publications from the Institute of Medicine (IOM): *To Err Is Human* (Kohn, Corrigan, & Donaldson, 2000) and *Crossing the Quality Chasm* (IOM, 2001). *To Err Is Human* first brought public attention to the issue of medical errors, concluding that between 44,000 and 98,000 people die every year from medical mistakes. It also diagnosed the quality problem as not one of poorly performing people, but of people struggling to perform within a system that is riddled with opportunities for mistakes to happen. The second IOM report, *Crossing the Quality Chasm*, outlined a number of goals for improving the quality and performance of the U.S. health care system, as well as some of the methods for achieving those goals.

This chapter builds on these two significant reports. The first section presents several of the more common definitions of quality, discusses the importance of health care quality, delineates the impact of information technology on quality, and introduces key figures in quality improvement. The second section provides a strategic framework for improving quality and performance based on the Baldrige Award criteria. The third section expands on the common elements of quality improvement, while the fourth and fifth sections examine several approaches for implementing quality improvement as well as discussing many of the tools and techniques for improving health care quality.

DEFINING QUALITY IN HEALTH CARE

Health care quality may be defined in various ways, with differing implications for health care providers, patients, third-party payers, policy makers, and other stakeholders. The IOM provides the most widely accepted definition of health care quality as the "degree to which health services for individuals or populations increase the likelihood of desired health outcomes and are consistent with the current professional knowledge" (IOM, 1990). This definition highlights several aspects of quality. First, high quality health services should be effective, achieving desired health outcomes for individuals. Second, health care services should achieve desired health outcomes for populations, while matching the societal preferences of policy makers and third-party payers for efficiency. And third, health care providers should adhere to professional standards and base treatments on their efficacy, as determined by the best scientific evidence available.

Another way to define quality is the result of a system with interdependent parts that must work together to achieve outcomes such as those noted above. Using this system perspective, Avedis Donabedian defined quality in terms of **structures, processes, and outcomes** (Donabedian, 1966). The **structural elements** of quality involve the material and human resources of an organization and the facility itself. The quality of personnel is documented in their numbers (nurse staffing), skill level (e.g., certified nursing assistant), and various certifications (e.g., board-certified physician), while the quality of facilities lies in accreditation (in hospitals through The Joint Commission) and/or certification (e.g., Magnet Hospital certification). **Process** involves the actual delivery of care as well as its management (e.g., the quality of basic care including cleanliness, feeding, hydration, delivery of treatments, and keeping patients safe from falls and errors). **Outcomes** are the resulting health status of the patients (e.g., mortality, morbidity, length of stay, and functional status) and organizations (turnover of staff, cost outcomes). As a physician, Donabedian championed the development of

best practices, i.e., "the ideal to which organizations should aspire" to improve care (Cooper, 2004, p. 827), linking structures, processes, and outcomes with a feedback loop, that is, information given back to providers to achieve better care. Moreover, he defined quality as having at least four components (Donabedian, 1986):

1. The technical management of health and illness;
2. The management of the interpersonal relationship between the providers of care and their clients;
3. The amenities of care; and
4. The ethical principles that govern the conduct of affairs in general and the health care enterprise in particular.

The four parts of this definition highlight the need to incorporate multiple stakeholder perspectives to understand health care quality. On one hand, the **technical management** of health focuses on the clinical performance of health care providers; on the other hand, the **management of interpersonal relationships** underscores the coproduction of care by both providers and patients. In other words, at the patient–provider encounter level, health service quality is driven both by clinical and nonclinical processes (Marley, Collier, & Goldstein, 2004). The **amenities of care** speak to the patient's interest in being treated in comfortable, clean surroundings while the **ethical principles** speak to the provider's ethical conduct in delivering care and his/her interest in furthering societal and organizational well-being (or effectiveness).

A related, but more focused, view of quality represents two fundamental questions about any clinical service, procedure, or activity occurring in a health care setting: (1) "are the right things done?" and (2) "are things done right?" The first question assesses the effectiveness of clinical care; the second considers the efficiency of care services. Importantly, the performance of health care organizations depends on both its effectiveness and efficiency. Moreover, both are discussed in the IOM's *Crossing the Quality Chasm* as specific aims for quality improvement. **Effectiveness** is defined as "providing services based on scientific knowledge to all who could benefit and refraining from providing services to those not likely to benefit (avoiding underuse and overuse)"; **efficiency** is defined as "avoiding waste, in particular waste of equipment, supplies, ideas, and energy" (IOM, 2001, p. 6).

WHY IS QUALITY IMPORTANT?

One of the key issues in health care quality is the appropriate use of limited resources to improve the health of both individuals and the entire population. Problems in this domain can take three forms: **underuse**, **overuse**, and **misuse**. Chassin (1997) defines these terms as follows:

Underuse is the failure to provide a service whose benefit is greater than its risk. **Overuse** occurs when a health service is provided when its risk outweighs its benefits or it simply has no added benefit, as with overuse of certain diagnostic tests. **Misuse** occurs, for example, when the right service is provided badly and an avoidable complication reduces the benefit the patient receives.

Underuse is a problem since clinical research has produced a large number of effective treatments that are not widely used. One study found that it takes an average of 17 years for evidence-based practices to reach clinical practice (Balas & Boren, 2000). Even when these practices reach clinicians, evidence-based recommended treatments may not be consistently used. For example, McGlynn and colleagues (2003) found that 54.9% of participants in a nation-wide study received recommended care.

Overuse is also a quality problem, as certain treatments are provided despite evidence that the treatment is ineffective or even dangerous. Gonzales, Steiner, and Sande (1997) documented the overuse of antibiotics among their sample of adults. They found antibiotics were prescribed 51% of the time for common colds, 52% for upper respiratory infections, and 75% for bronchitis. The prescriptions were written even though these maladies are caused by viruses, not bacteria, rendering antibiotics useless in these cases. Furthermore, the indiscriminant use of antibiotics has fed the rise of multi-drug-resistant strains of bacteria (Arias & Murray, 2009).

Misuse caught the public's attention with the publication of the first IOM report on patient safety (Kohn et al., 2000), which examined the high rate of medical errors in hospitals, noting, as pointed out earlier, that thousands of patients die every year from preventable adverse events and another million are injured. One recent estimate suggested that at least 210,000 people die each year from medical errors in hospital settings. The cost of these errors has been estimated at $17.1 billion for 2008 (Van Den Bos et al., 2011).

The prevalence of overuse, underuse, and misuse is documented in *The Dartmouth Atlas of Health Care* (see www.dartmouthatlas.org). The atlas, created by John Wennberg and associates, shows wide variation in medical practice. The variation has been shown to result not from severity of illness or patient preferences, but from "idiosyncratic and unscientific" practice patterns and "local supply of resources" (Wennberg, 2002). For example, Boston and New Haven—demographically similar and geographically close—might be expected to be fairly similar in their utilization of surgical services. However, there are big differences in the use of surgical services (Wennberg, 2002). Wennberg (2002) stated "residents of New Haven were more than twice as likely to receive coronary bypass surgery and 50% more likely to undergo hysterectomy" than Bostonians, while Bostonians "were two times more likely to undergo carotid artery surgery and 50% more likely to have their hip joints replaced than the residents of New Haven" (p. 962).

THE RELEVANCE OF HEALTH INFORMATION TECHNOLOGY IN QUALITY IMPROVEMENT

Historically, the U.S. health care system has lagged far behind other industries in the use of information technology. For example, as noted in Chapter 8, one can use an ATM anywhere in the world—yet much health care information exists in a paper rather than electronic format. However, this is coming to an end. Clinics and hospitals spurred by The American Recovery and Reinvestment Act of 2009 have adopted electronic health records (EHR) and have begun to integrate them with previously stand-alone systems like those for medical imaging and pharmaceutical management, as well as new innovations such as web-based patient portals. Without a doubt, these systems will be a great boon to improving quality in our health care system. However, there still remains the issue of turning raw data into actionable information for improving quality. Health informatics, health analytics, and data mining are terms used in this conversation.

Health informatics is the multidisciplinary field in which information technology is brought to bear on our health care system with a goal to improve quality, raise efficiency, and lower costs. Cortada, Gordon, & Lenihan define **analytics** as "the systematic use of data and related business insights developed through applied analytical disciplines (e.g., statistical, contextual, quantitative, predictive, cognitive, other models) to drive fact-based decision making for planning, management, measurement, and learning" (2012, p. 2). These data come from a broad variety of sources including electronic medical records, medical claims data, pharmaceutical records, and medical imaging. There are a number of options including "small data" analytics, predictive modeling, and real-time analytics. For example, real-time analytics transforms various types of data, such as pharmaceutical, medical, or patient-specific morbidities, to create information for decision support at the bedside (Ozga, 2013). The information collected is integrated with an electronic medical record to show drug interactions, suggest different treatment methods, or provide alerts for patient complications (Taylor, 2010).

Related to health analytics is **data mining**, which uses what is commonly referred to as "big data." Using the same repositories of data mentioned above, analysts attempt to predict treatment outcomes or forecast future medical costs and utilization (Ingenix, 2006). For example, Mace (2012) discusses the predictive modeling that the Blue Cross Blue Shield of North Carolina uses to understand their enrolled patients. They found that 50% of its costs were being driven by 4% of its patients. Predictive models allowed them to implement new initiatives to improve health conditions among these costly patients.

The relevance of health informatics, health analytics, and data mining to quality improvement is that they provide a platform and set of tools that can be used to understand a population, to measure and compare responses to treatments, and to identify factors that contribute to health care errors. In fact, many of the quality improvement tools discussed in this chapter are also used in health analytics and data mining.

QUALITY IMPROVEMENT COMES (BACK) TO AMERICA

During the 1970s, oil shortages induced by the Organization of Petroleum Exporting Countries (OPEC) compelled many people in the U.S. to purchase fuel-efficient and inexpensive cars. Although U.S. automobile manufacturers tried to produce such cars, only the Japanese were manufacturing fuel-efficient, yet inexpensive automobiles that were reliable and durable. The quality of these small Japanese vehicles greatly surpassed those manufactured in the U.S. Newspapers, magazines, and television news asked the question, "Can America compete with Japan?" This rapid shift in the marketplace created a new awareness among U.S. industrial leaders that quality mattered.

To address the quality deficit, automobile and other manufacturers in the U.S. sought the help of quality improvement experts. The contributions ensured that **Total Quality Management (TQM)**—referred to as **Continuous Quality Improvement (CQI)** in health care—became the new paradigm for quality improvement within the U.S. during the 1980s and 1990s. The fundamental insight of this movement is that quality results from (continuously) upgrading the ability of the work processes to produce quality products. Put another way, when defects occur, it is more likely due to the operation of the work process rather than individual error. Thus, inspection, as a method of quality assurance, is considerably inferior to perfecting the work process through CQI (or other process-based methods).

LEADERS OF THE QUALITY MOVEMENT

Walter A. Shewhart, W. Edwards Deming, and Joseph M. Juran are generally recognized as key leaders of the quality movement. During the mid-1920s, Walter A. Shewhart, a physicist at Bell Laboratories, was asked to study the variations in Western Electric's production processes and formulate a means to ensure that products met specifications. Rather than inspecting each product for defects, Shewhart's practical perspective led him to try to control the source of quality variation in the entire production process (system). This led him to differentiate between **common-cause** and **special-cause variation**. He knew that common-cause variation in the production process—due to natural variations in raw materials, minor electrical voltage fluctuations, etc.—often was impractical to control. However, special-cause variation—due to operator behaviors, incorrectly calibrated machinery, the substituting of different types of raw materials, etc.—could be controlled (Kolesar, 1993). His book, *Economic Control of Quality of Manufactured Product* (Shewhart, 1931), articulated these principles of statistical process control (SPC) for reducing variation in production processes. With editorial assistance from his protégé, W. Edwards Deming, Shewhart also wrote a monograph on quality control, *Statistical Method from the Viewpoint of Quality Control*, which introduced the **Plan-Do-Check-Act (PDCA)** cycle model for improving production processes (Shewhart, 1939).

Known also as the **Shewhart cycle** in the U.S., the PDCA cycle was popularized by W. Edwards Deming, and it is called the **Deming cycle** in Japan. A statistician, Deming further developed the principles underlying TQM/CQI while working with the Japanese to reconstruct their industries after World War II. His approach with the Japanese was to help them fundamentally change work processes and systems to produce quality products. Deming developed a management philosophy that encouraged worker participation in process change, focused on data-based decision making, and embraced a standardized approach to quality improvement. This management philosophy was eventually codified into 14 points (Deming, 2000).

Joseph M. Juran was a contemporary and colleague of Deming's. An engineer at Western Electric's Hawthorne Works in 1925, he was one of the first engineers trained by Shewhart to apply the principles of SPC. While at Western Electric, Juran championed the **Pareto principle** from economics, focusing attention and resources on those important quality problems that are attributable to a small number of factors (e.g., the 80/20 rule, that 80% of quality problems result from 20% of the possible factors). During World War II, Juran worked as assistant to the administrator of the Foreign Economic Administration under the Office for Emergency Management. In this role, he oversaw the logistics for providing materials and supplies to allied governments and troops on both fronts. Building on this experience, another of Juran's important contributions was the "Juran Trilogy of quality planning, quality control, and quality improvement." All of these notions were first codified in the 1951 publication of the *Quality Control Handbook* (Juran, Gryna, & Bingham, 1974).

BALDRIGE AWARD CRITERIA: A STRATEGIC FRAMEWORK FOR QUALITY IMPROVEMENT

Effective quality improvement programs operate both at the top (strategic) level and at the operational (tactical) level of the organization. That is, quality improvement programs outline both an overall strategy (philosophy, framework) and a set of tactical processes and tools for quality improvement. Thus, prior to discussing the tactics of specific approaches to quality improvement, we present the **Baldrige Award** Criteria. These criteria are named after Malcolm Baldrige, who was President Reagan's Secretary of Commerce and died in office in 1987. In his honor, the Malcolm Baldrige National Quality Award was created in 1988 for companies that display excellent performance across seven dimensions (the Award Criteria). These dimensions of quality have been continually refined and expanded from their original manufacturing base to include health care organizations (see Figure 7-1). The Baldrige Award models excellence using a structure-process-results framework. At the left-hand side of the figure is a set of three structural variables: leadership; strategic planning; and focus on patient, other customers, and markets. This reflects the notion that integration of customer needs (broadly defined) within the organization's leadership and strategic planning process is necessary for creating the conditions for quality. The three process variables are performance analysis, staff focus, and process management, illustrating that quality improvement is recognized as an organization-wide responsibility. In other words, engaging staff in process management is another necessary condition for quality.

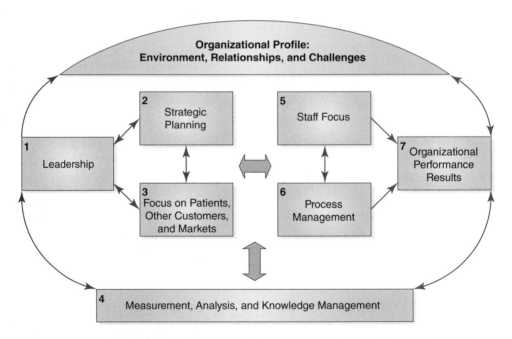

FIGURE 7-1 Baldrige Health Care Criteria for Performance Excellence Framework: A Systems Perspective

Reproduced from: Baldrige National Quality Award Brochure, National Institute of Standards and Technology. 2010.

Both structural and process variables interact to produce the organizational performance result variable, health care and process effectiveness. At the bottom of the figure is the diffuse influence of measurement, analysis, and knowledge management, important elements that influence the structure, process, and outcome variables.

The strength of the Baldrige criteria is that it encourages a systematic approach to each of the six categories and specifically links them to measureable business outcomes. These criteria provide the overall strategy and framework for success but are not prescriptive as to which approach (e.g., CQI, Six Sigma, TPS/Lean) should drive improvements in organizational performance. Instead, they leave the organization to determine which approach best fits the organization.

COMMON ELEMENTS OF QUALITY IMPROVEMENT

Before we consider **Continuous Quality Improvement**, **Six Sigma**, and **Toyota Production System/Lean** as methods to improve quality, we need to discuss several key concepts common to all quality improvement methods. These concepts are: **measurement, process variation**, and **statistical process control**.

Measurement

The most basic concept in quality improvement is that of **measurement** and the **metrics** associated with it. **Measurement** is the translation of observable events into quantitative terms, while **metrics** are the means actually used to record these observable events. All quality improvement efforts require numerical data because "you can't manage what you can't measure." In this way, quality improvement is driven by data-based evidence rather than subjective judgments or opinions.

Good measurement begins with the rigorous definition of the concept to be measured. It then requires the use of a measurement methodology that yields reliable (e.g., consistent) and valid (e.g., accurate) measures of the concept. Rigorous definition means that the concept to be measured (e.g., wait times) needs to be defined in very specific terms. This definition should be written and should include the unit of measure. For example, wait times could be defined as the time interval between the arrival of a patient at the office and the time he or she is first seen by the doctor. The unit of measure is time, but the start and end points are important for assessing the reliability and validity of the measure.

Once a good definition of the concept is developed, one challenge is to measure it reliably. If every recorded wait time starts with the arrival of the patient and ends with the patient's first encounter with the doctor, then the measure should be consistent, or reliable. **Measurement reliability** means that if a measure is taken at several points over time or by various people, the measure will generally be consistent (that is, not vary too much). For example, if a person takes his or her temperature each morning, it should be close to 98.6 degrees Fahrenheit each time, assuming that he or she is not ill. If it substantially deviates from 98.6, then that person is ill, the thermometer is broken and not giving consistent readings, or the way in which the thermometer is used varies from day to day (e.g., length of time). Another example of reliability is that of reliability among people. If two nurses in a practice are measuring wait times but use different definitions of waiting, then their measurement of waiting time will not be consistent (i.e., reliable).

Another challenge is to ensure that measurement of the concept is valid. Its validity depends on the accuracy of the measure. If two nurses use the same stopwatch to record waiting times, as long as the clock itself is accurate and the nurses adhere to the same definition of waiting, the wait times should be accurate. In other words, **validity** is the extent to which the measure used actually measures the concept. As with reliability, having a rigorous definition and method of data collection will yield a valid measure.

Process Variation and Statistical Process Control (SPC)

Process variation is the range of values that a quality metric can take as a result of different causes within the process. As Shewhart (1931) noted, these causes can take two forms: **special- and common-cause variation**. **Special-cause variation** is due to unusual, infrequent, or unique events that cause the quality metric to deviate from its average by a statistically significant degree. **Common-cause variation** is due to the usual or natural causes of variation within a process. Following Shewhart, quality improvement now involves (1) detecting and eliminating special-cause variation in a process; and (2) detecting and reducing, whenever feasible, common-cause variation within a process.

Statistical Process Control (SPC) is a method by which process variation is measured, tracked, and controlled in an effort to improve the quality of the process. SPC is a branch of statistics that involves time-series analysis with graphic data display. The advantage of this method lies in the use of a visual display, which is intuitive for most decision makers. In essence, it relies on the notion that "a picture is worth a thousand words" for its import. Quality data from a particular process are graphed across time. When enough data exist, the mean and standard deviation are derived and a control chart constructed. The construction begins with graphing the data across time. It continues with the calculation of upper and lower control limits. Think of these limits as similar to the tolerances for machined parts. Complex machinery, like aircraft, requires parts that are manufactured to very tight tolerances so that they will fit together well. The larger the tolerance, the greater the likelihood that a part will not fit the way it is supposed to fit and will fall apart. These limits show the range of variation where the process is thought to be "in control." Typically these limits are set at plus and minus three standard deviations from the mean. With these control limits in place, the data can be interpreted and times when the process was "out of control" investigated and remedied.

THREE APPROACHES TO QUALITY IMPROVEMENT

Three quality improvement approaches that have been widely used in health care are Continuous Quality Improvement, Six Sigma, and Toyota Production System /Lean. Each is discussed further below.

Continuous Quality Improvement

The concept of **Continuous Quality Improvement (CQI)** can be defined as an organizational process in which employee teams identify and address problems in their work processes. When applied across the organization, CQI creates a continuous flow of process improvements that meet or exceed customer—or patient—expectations. Inherent within this definition are five dimensions of CQI: (1) process focus, (2) customer focus, (3) data-based decision making, (4) employee empowerment, and (5) organization-wide impact.

CQI focuses on the process part of Donabedian's quality conception as key to developing high-quality health care. Specifically, CQI promotes the view that understanding and addressing the factors that create variation in an administrative or clinical process (e.g., long wait times, high hospital readmission rates) will produce superior patient care quality and organizational performance. Furthermore, quality improvement should not be a one-time activity; rather, it should be a normal activity, resulting in a continual flow of improvements.

Underpinning this approach are the concepts and tools of **statistical process control (SPC)** that Shewhart developed. For example, a manager of an ambulatory clinic tracked an increase in complaints about patient wait time from quarterly patient satisfaction surveys. For the next month, the wait time for each patient was collected, and the daily average was graphed. At the same time, data were collected about why waiting time increased, and the clinic manager found the special-cause variation was driven by (1) the number of medically complex, time-consuming patients each day; (2) the training needs of a new LPN and receptionist; and (3) the overscheduling of new patients. Armed with these findings, the manager was able to work with both clinical and administrative personnel to address these concerns and reduce the variability of the process, resulting in lower average wait time.

The second element in CQI is the focus on the customer. That is, every effort in the organization must be taken in order to "delight the customer." CQI defines a customer in broad terms. Normally, patients are thought of as the main customers in health care. CQI's view is that any person, group, or organization that is impacted by a process at any point is a customer. For example, a doctor ordering an MRI can be considered a customer because she receives the service of the radiology department. Thus, CQI takes the position that each process has a variety of both internal and external customers. The customer focus is best exemplified in the widespread use of patient satisfaction surveys by hospitals and physician groups.

The third element in CQI is an emphasis on using data to make all quality improvement decisions. The foundation of SPC, as discussed earlier, rests on the collection, analysis, and use of data to improve processes and monitor the success of process interventions. The use of carefully collected data reduces both uncertainty and the dependence on uninformed impressions or biases for improving an organizational process. It also provides good evidence to convince skeptics that a process problem exists. Returning to our earlier example, the collected data on waiting times enabled not only the clinic manager to understand the special-cause factors creating waiting times but also helped physicians, nurses, and front desk and other staff understand the sources of the problem.

The fourth element of CQI is employee empowerment. This empowerment is manifested by the widespread use of quality improvement teams composed of the individuals who have the most intimate knowledge of how the system works (the front line providers). Empowerment at its core suggests the individuals who do the work have a say in improving the work. The typical CQI team consists of employees whose day-to-day work gives them a unique perspective and detailed knowledge of patient care processes. Another important individual for a CQI team is the facilitator, who typically provides training on CQI tools and philosophy. Members of the CQI team are not only empowered to improve their work environment, but also can become advocates for change, overcoming resistance among other employees. In our prior example, the clinic manager worked with both clinical employees (e.g., RNs, LPNs, and the nurse manager) and administrative employees (e.g., receptionists, admission and billing clerks, and their supervisor) to decrease the wait times and improve patients' satisfaction with the clinic.

The final element in CQI is its strategic use across the organization, accomplished through the coordinated and continuous improvement of various operational processes across organizational levels. Quality must be recognized as a strategic priority requiring executive leadership. Supporting this priority requires substantial training in quality methods and tools as well as an organizational culture that values quality.

In order to make specific quality improvements, the Shewhart/Deming cycle of PDCA is generally used in manufacturing and other industries. However, during the early 1980s, the Hospital Corporation of America (HCA) modified the PDCA cycle to create the **FOCUS–PDCA framework**, which has become the most commonly used quality improvement framework in the health care industry. The addition of FOCUS clarifies the steps that need to be done prior to the implementation of any process change. The changes in the process will then be guided by the PDCA cycle.

FOCUS (Find, Organize, Clarify, Understand, and Select):

- Find means identifying a process problem, preferably a "high-pain" one, to address.
- Organize means to put together a team of people who work on the process. These people would then be trained on process improvement skills and tools.
- Clarify results in the team moving to clarify the process problem through some type of process mapping (flowcharting).
- Understanding the process problem comes next. It involves measurement and data collection of key metrics to document the dimensions of the process problem and to provide a benchmark for goal setting.
- Select means to identify a set of process improvements and then select from them for implementation.

PDCA (Plan, Do, Check, and Act):

- Plan means to take the process improvement from the S phase of FOCUS and create a plan for its implementation.
- Do, not surprisingly, means to actually implement the process improvement.
- Check means to study whether the process is improving, using the measures identified and measured in the U phase of FOCUS.
- Act means to determine whether the process improvement was successful.

If the process improvement was successful, the cycle terminates. If the process improvement was not successful, then the cycle continues back to the planning stage to identify and plan the implementation of another process improvement. It is important to emphasize the iterative nature of repeated PDCA cycles. That is, if something is not working, one does not wait for an extended period of time, rather another plan is formulated and the cycle repeats until the process is back in control.

Six Sigma

Six Sigma is an extension of Joseph Juran's approach to quality improvement and was developed by Motorola and popularized by Jack Welch at General Electric. It has been defined as a "data-driven quality methodology that seeks to eliminate variation from a process" (Scalise, 2001, p. 42). Six Sigma, like CQI, is a resource-intensive tool requiring substantial up-front training in quality improvement tools and concepts, time and personnel resources to carry out quality improvement projects, and long-term management commitment. For these reasons, Six Sigma is best applied to important, costly issues in key processes.

Six Sigma employs a structured process called **DMAIC (Define, Measure, Analyze, Improve, and Control)**:

- Define includes delimiting the scope of work, determining due dates, and mapping the future state of the process, including improvements.
- Measure encompasses both the creation of measures or metrics and their application to determine how well a process is performing.
- Analyze further breaks down the understanding of the process and often includes flowcharting the process.
- Improve specifies the steps that will be taken to meet the goals outlined during the define step.
- Control is about ensuring that the improvements are permanent rather than temporary.

While DMAIC guides the actual improvement project, Six Sigma also features major training and human resource components (Six Sigma Online, n.d.). Because of these components, many large hospitals and health systems have begun adopting Six Sigma as a way to change the organization and establish a culture of quality. Such change begins with a CEO who supports the method; without top management support, efforts like this generally flounder. A champion is a senior executive (generally VP level or above) who has full-time responsibility for quality improvement efforts. Beyond the champion are a number of experts in quality improvement generally classed into different "belts" based on their level of expertise and experience.

Toyota Production System/Lean

The **Toyota Production System** gained prominence as Americans demanded inexpensive, fuel-efficient, reliable cars during and after the oil shocks of the 1970s. Manufacturers from around the world flocked to Toyota plants to see what made Toyota cars so competitive in the world market. They saw assembly lines not unlike their own, but with a series of innovations that revolutionized car manufacturing (Womack, Jones, & Roos, 1990). Key among these innovations were the "just-in-time" delivery of parts to the assembly line and an obsession with reducing waste characterized by a relentless experimentation by line workers and management to continually improve the manufacturing process. All of these innovations were supported by a culture characterized by continuous improvement, experimentation, innovation, and teamwork. Together these became known as the **Toyota Production System (TPS)** and later as **Lean**.

Like other quality improvement systems, **Lean** features both strategic (culture) and tactical elements. What distinguishes Lean from other systems are its rigorous definition of value and its relentless pursuit of the elimination of non–value added activities (waste) in a process. **Lean** as applied to the health care industry views waste as coming in the following categories: overproduction, inventory, motion, transportation, overprocessing, defects, waiting, and underutilization of staff.

- **Overproduction** can be defined as production that is in excess, early, and faster than is needed. In health care, this can be seen in the overuse of pre-operative bloodwork which research suggests as not being medically necessary in most surgical situations (Pastides et al., 2012).
- **Motion** is wasted when patients, inventory, and personnel move inefficiently around a facility.
- **Overprocessing** results when the product provided to the customer is complex or confusing. For example, both hospitals and physicians bill for services that are presented to the patient and insurer at different times.
- **Defects** include medical mistakes and delays in treatment. Waiting is a feature of the U.S. health care system, from waiting for a doctor's appointment to waiting for the insurance company and hospital to settle a claim.
- **Underutilization of staff** is defined as not using staff time efficiently. Such inefficiency often means failing to use staff knowledge, skills, and abilities in an optimal fashion. For example, due to clinical policies and/or regulatory constraints, nurse practitioners and physician assistants are often underutilized in hospital and ambulatory settings.

Toussaint and Berry (2013) describe six principles of Lean in health care and they are summarized here:

- *Attitude of continuous improvement.* This can be seen on multiple levels from individuals' experimentation in reducing waste in their part of the work process, to the collaboration of a work team in a quality circle, to the overall culture of quality in an organization as reflected in its strategic plan and its everyday operations.
- *Value creation.* Value is defined in the customers' terms. Customers, like in other QI approaches, are broadly defined. Anyone downstream in the work process can be defined as a customer. Lean creates value by eliminating the forms of waste described above. A principal tool for this elimination of waste is the value stream map, which is a very detailed flowchart showing the material, people, and information flows for a particular process. From this map, opportunities for waste removal can be discerned and addressed.
- *Unity of purpose.* While a quality culture and strategic plan are necessary for Lean to have a significant effect, it is the unity of purpose across the organization that makes Lean truly effective. Lean thinking through value stream mapping clarifies priorities for improvement and focuses the attention of managers and workers. These priorities

must be clearly communicated up and down the organizational hierarchy so that everyone is "on the same page."

- *Respect for people who do the work.* Deming, in his 14 points, and the principles of CQI drill home the point that quality improvement is a team sport. Quality is very difficult to mandate from the top. In fact, Toussant and Berry (2013) make the point that Lean actually flips leadership to those doing the work. In many ways, this is simply the most radical type of worker empowerment. Workers are assumed to have the motivation and capability (which can be developed) to improve the work process using different QI tools. In such a system, leaders are called on to support, sustain, and train.

- *Visualization.* Visual media are necessary to communicate the Lean experience. One aspect of this is value stream mapping, which provides detailed visual representations of the people, material, and information flows in the organizations. Another aspect is the public and conspicuous display of key quality metrics (patient satisfaction, infection rate, etc.). These displays continually update workers and managers, as well as provide transparency about quality improvement goals and achievements.

- *Flexible regimentation.* This seeming contradiction in terms refers to the necessity of standardizing every part of the work process possible to remove waste (unnecessary variation that is not valued by customers) coupled with the ongoing experimentation and improvement of the work processes. Like the successful use of the FOCUS-PDCA cycle, Lean relies on intensive iterations of process mapping, data collection, and process analysis in order to improve work processes.

QUALITY IMPROVEMENT TOOLS

Both CQI and Six Sigma use a variety of tools to help improve quality. These can be divided into three categories: process mapping, data collection, and process analysis.

Mapping Processes

Flowcharting (also referred to as Process Mapping) is the main way that processes are mapped (Figure 7-2). A flowchart is a picture of the sequence of steps in a process. Various geometric shapes denote different action steps within the process. A basic flowchart outlines the major steps in a process. A detailed flowchart is often more useful in quality improvement. Developing a flowchart requires not only substantial investigation (e.g., asking front-line staff and professionals how work is carried out), but also direct observation of each aspect of the process to be flowcharted. Determining the level of detail to be used should be driven by its use within the quality improvement process. A top-down flowchart is often used for providing an overview of large or complex processes. It shows the major

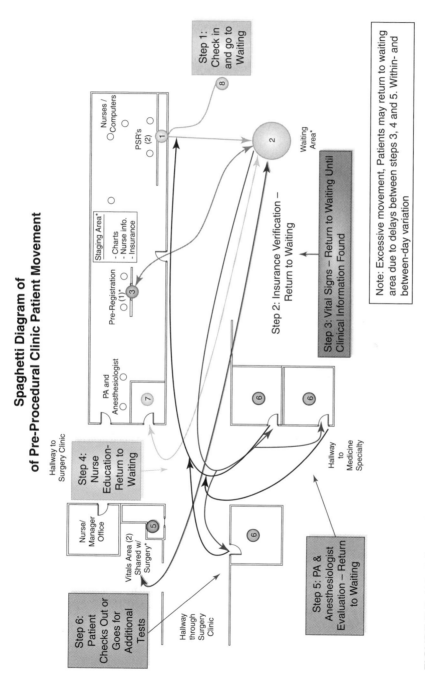

FIGURE 7-2 Workflow Diagram

Source: Wait time project, University of Missouri.

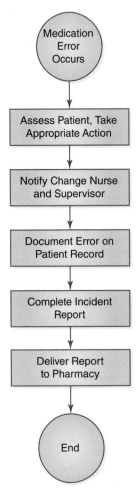

FIGURE 7-3 Medication Error Reporting Flowchart

steps in the process and lists, below each major step, the sub-steps. The development flowchart adds another dimension. Often it is useful for tracking the flow of information between people. That is, the development flowchart shows the steps of the process carried out by each person, unit, or group involved in a process. Since hand-offs are often where errors may occur, this flowchart provides a target for data collection efforts.

A marriage of geographic and processing mapping is the **workflow diagram** (Figure 7-3). Simply put, this reflects the movements of people, materials, documents, or information in a process. Plotting these movements on the floor plan of a building or around a paper document can present a very vivid picture of the inefficiency of a process. With the advancement of information technology, increasingly sophisticated geographic mapping and tracking programs have become available, making this complex task easier to do.

Value Stream Mapping is used to identify the seven types of waste or non–value added activities discussed in Lean. Material and information flow across the entire process of transforming raw materials into a finished product to delivery to the customer is mapped. These maps include both current value stream maps as well as future state value stream maps. Waste is documented in the gap between the current value stream map and the future stream map. These maps also provide the platform for quality improvement activities.

Data Collection

The **check sheet** is a simple data collection form in which occurrence of some event or behavior is tallied. At the end of the data collection period, they are added up. The best check sheets are those that are simple and have well-defined categories of what constitutes a particular event or behavior. For example, a doctor's office staff wanted to find out the reasons why patients showed up late. This is a "high pain" problem because no or late shows result in disruptions to the clinic's work schedule and extra work for staff. The staff asked late arrivers about the reasons for being late and after carefully defining each reason, they developed the check sheet. The check sheet was pilot tested, and several new reasons were added while other reasons were refined. The check sheet was then employed during a month-long data collection period. They found that transportation problems and babysitting problems jointly accounted for 63% of the late shows.

Another example is the use of **chart abstractions** or **chart audits**. In this process, a check sheet is used to collect information from a patient's medical record. Often this is a manual process that involves an individual looking at the medical record and finding the requested information and recording it on a check sheet. The use of electronic medical records may take some or all of the labor out of this process, as pertinent medical information can be collected and appropriate metrics reported.

Geographic mapping is a pictorial check sheet in which an event or problem is plotted on a map. This is often used in epidemiological studies to plot where victims of certain diseases live, work, play, etc. For example, the 2014 Ebola outbreak in Western Africa was traced to a single 2-year-old in Guinea. This finding was enabled by tracing the geographic dispersion of the Ebola infections back over time to the original patient. Importantly, such maps also are helpful in then estimating the future growth of an epidemic. Within the clinical setting, geographic mapping can help track infectious disease outbreaks within a hospital, as well as trace the origin of the outbreak to a particular ward, laboratory, or operating theater.

Analyzing Processes

The **cause-and-effect diagram** helps to identify and organize the possible cause for a problem in a structured format. It is commonly referred to as a **fishbone diagram** for its resemblance to a fish (see Figure 7-4). It is also called an **Ishikawa diagram**, in honor of Kaoru Ishikawa, who developed it. The diagram begins with the problem under investigation described in a box at the right side of the diagram. The fish's spine is represented by a long arrow within the box. The major possible causes of the problem are arrayed as large ribs along the spine. These are broad categories of causes to which smaller ribs are attached that identify specific causes of the problem.

A **Pareto chart** is a simple frequency chart. It takes advantage of the Pareto principle, or the 80/20 rule, that Juran applied to quality improvement, i.e., the observation that 80% of the problems with any process are due to 20% of the defects (Best & Neuhauser, 2006). Put another way, most of the problems in any process are due to a small number of defects in the procedure. The frequency of each problem, reason, etc. is listed on the x-axis, and the number or percentage of occurrences is listed on the y-axis. This analysis is most useful in identifying the major problems in a process and their frequency of occurrence. Another version of the frequency chart is the histogram, which shows the range and frequency of values for a measure. When complete,

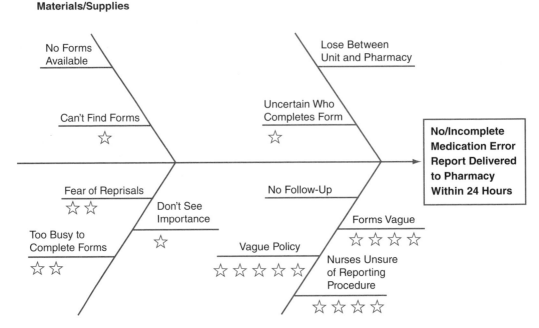

FIGURE 7-4 Fishbone Diagram

it shows the complete distribution of some variable. This is often useful in basic data analysis.

As mentioned earlier, quality improvement has its greatest impact if it becomes a part of the strategic mission of a health care organization. When that occurs, it is then possible to look beyond the boundaries of the organization and to consider ways in which the health care system at the local, regional, and national levels could be improved.

OPPORTUNITIES FOR RESEARCH IN HEALTH CARE QUALITY

Opportunities for in-depth research in health care quality exist in a variety of venues, including your own health care organization. Many of the resources used in writing this chapter also include extensive research holdings and data sets that are available to students and academic researchers to utilize. Herewith is a partial listing of resources.

- Accreditation Association for Ambulatory Health Care;
- Agency for Health Care Research and Quality;

- Agency for Health Care Research and Quality's Healthcare Cost and Utilization Project Databases;
- Agency for Health Care Research and Quality's National Guideline Clearinghouse;
- Agency for Health Care Research and Quality's United State Health Information Database;
- American College of Surgeons' Inspiring Quality Program;
- American Health Quality Association;
- American Healthcare Association;
- American Nurses Association's National Database of Quality Indicators;
- American Society for Quality;
- Baldrige National Quality Award;
- Center for Improvement in Healthcare Quality;
- Cochrane Collaboration's Evidence Based Medicine and Guidelines Database;
- Florida's Medical Quality Assurance Services;
- Healthcare Team Vitality Instrument;
- Health Resources and Services Administration's Quality Toolbox;
- Institute for Healthcare Improvement;
- Institute for Healthcare Improvement's Improvement Map;
- Institute for Healthcare Improvement's Outpatient Adverse Event Trigger Tool;
- Institute for Healthcare Improvement's Quality Improvement Measure Tracker;
- The Joint Commission;
- Maryland Health Services Cost Review Commission;
- MATCH Medication Reconciliation Toolkit;
- Medicare's Hospital Compare Database;
- Minnesota's All Payer Claims Database;
- National Committee for Quality Assurance (NCQA) HEDIS measures;
- National Library of Medicine's Health Services Research Information Central;
- National Quality Forum;
- New York's All Payer Claims Database;
- Organization for Economic Cooperation and Development's (OECD) Health Care Quality Indicators Program;
- Patient Safety Handling;
- Press Ganey's Hospital and Nursing Quality Database;
- Texas's Health Care Information Collection; and
- Understanding the Healthcare Database.

As you can see, quality is a rich area for research in health care. In the future, you can be certain this list will grow.

CONCLUSION

Quality, access, and cost are the three core policy issues facing every health care system. For the U.S., improving quality is a challenge in a health care system undergoing a vast expansion of access via health insurance reform along with continuous pressures to contain costs. A new brief from the Kaiser Family Foundation indicated that health care quality has improved in the U.S., but still lags on key measures when compared to peer countries (Claxton, Cox, Gonzales, Kamal, & Levitt, 2015). The models and tools presented earlier will be needed, along with new ones, to improve quality of care, even in a challenging environment.

DISCUSSION QUESTIONS

1. Compare and contrast the different stakeholders' views of health care quality.

2. Using a health care organization you are familiar with, analyze how structure, process, and outcomes interact.

3. Compare and contrast CQI (TQM) and Six Sigma (Lean) approaches to quality improvement. Provide a real world example in a health care organization of where you believe one would be preferable to another. What is your rationale for your choice?

4. Summarize the functions of the Baldrige criteria and their interaction with CQI or Six Sigma.

5. Provide three real world examples in a health care organization of underuse, overuse, and misuse for both quality and cost. What are the implications for effectiveness, efficiency, and patient for each of these examples?

Cases in Chapter 18 that are related to this chapter include:

- Madison Community Hospital Addresses Infection Prevention
- Trouble with the Pharmacy
- Communication of Patient Information During Transitions in Care
- Multidrug Resistant Organism (MDRO) in a Transitional Care Unit

Case study guides are available in the online Instructor's Materials.

REFERENCES

Arias, C. A., & Murray, B. E. (2009). Antibiotic-resistant bugs in the 21st century—A clinical super-challenge. *New England Journal of Medicine, 360*, 439–443.

Balas, E. A., & Boren, S. A. (2000). Managing clinical knowledge for health care improvement. In J. Bemmel & A. T. McCray (Eds), *Yearbook of medical informatics 2000: Patient-centered systems* (pp. 5–70). Stuttgart, Germany: Schattauer Verlagsgesellschaft mbH.

Baldrige National Quality Program at the National Institute of Standards and Technology. (2009–2010). Baldrige national quality program criteria for performance excellence. Retrieved from http://www.baldrige.nist.gov/PDF_files/2009_2010_Business_Nonprofit_Criteria.pdf

Best, M., & Neuhauser, D. (2006). Joseph Juran: Overcoming resistance to organizational change. *Quality and Safety in Health Care, 15*, 380–382.

Chassin, M. R. (1997). Assessing strategies for quality improvement. *Health Affairs, 16*(3), 151–161.

Claxton, G., Cox, C., Gonzales, S., Kamal, R., & Levitt, L. (2015). *Measuring the quality of healthcare in the U.S.* Kaiser Family Foundation. Retrieved from http://www.healthsystemtracker.org/insight/measuring-the-quality-of-healthcare-in-the-u-s/

Cooper, M. R. (2004). Quality assurance and improvement. In L. F. Wolper (Ed.), *Health care administration: Planning, implementing, and managing organized delivery systems* (4th ed., p. 827). Sudbury, MA: Jones and Bartlett.

Cortada, J. W., Gordon, D., & Lenihan, B. (2012). *The value of analytics in healthcare.* IBM Institute for Business Value. Retrieved from https://www.ibm.com/smarterplanet/global/files/the_value_of_analytics_in_healthcare.pdf

Deming, W. E. (2000). *Out of the crisis.* Cambridge, MA: MIT Press.

Donabedian, A. (1966). Evaluating the quality of medical care. *Milbank Memorial Fund Quarterly, 44*, 194–196.

Donabedian, A. (1986). Quality assurance in our health care system. *Quality Assurance, 1*(1), 6–12.

Gonzales, R., Steiner, J. F., & Sande, M. A. (1997). Antibiotic prescribing for adults with colds, upper respiratory tract infections and bronchitis by ambulatory care physicians. *Journal of the American Medical Association, 278*, 901–904.

Ingenix. (2006) *Five essentials for evaluating predictive modeling solutions.* Retrieved from https://etg.optum.com/~/media/Ingenix/Resources/White%20Papers/5EssentialsforEvaluatingPMSolutions.pdf

Institute of Medicine (IOM). (1990). *Medicare: A strategy for quality assurance.* Washington, DC: National Academies Press.

Institute of Medicine (IOM). (2001). *Crossing the quality chasm: A new health system for the 21st Century.* Washington, DC: National Academies Press.

Juran, J. M., Gryna, F. M., & Bingham, J. (1974). *Quality control handbook.* New York, NY: McGraw-Hill.

Kohn, J. T., Corrigan, J. M., & Donaldson, M. S. (Eds.). (2000). *To err is human: Building a safer health care system.* Washington, DC: National Academies Press.

Kolesar, P. J. (1993). The relevance of research on statistical process control to the total quality movement. *Journal of Engineering and Technology Management, 10*(4), 317–338.

Mace, S. (2012, June). *Payer analytics for the new consumer market.* Retrieved from http://content.hcpro.com/pdf/content/281331-5.pdf

Marley, K. A., Collier, D. A., & Goldstein, S. M. (2004). The role of clinical and process quality in achieving patient satisfaction in hospitals. *Decision Sciences, 35*(3), 349–369.

McGlynn, E. A., Asch, S. M., Adams, J., Kessey, J., Hicks, J., DeCristofaro, A., and Kerr, E. A. (2003). The quality of health care delivered to adults in the United States. *New England Journal of Medicine, 348*(26), 2635–2645.

Ozga, J. P. (2013). How analytics can help employers measure and manage risks. *Employee Benefit News.* Retrieved from http://ebn.benefitnews.com/news/how-analytics-help-employers-measure-manage -risks-2733568-1.html

Pastides, P., Tokarczyk, S., Ismail, L., Sarraf, K., & Ahearne, D. (2012). The use of routine preoperative blood tests: An overuse request. *Journal of Bone and Joint Surgery, 94*(Supp 34), 12.

Scalise, D. (2001). Six Sigma: The quest for quality. *Hospitals and Health Networks, 75*(12), 41–45.

Shewhart, W. A. (1931). *Economic control of quality of manufactured product.* New York, NY: Van Nostrand.

Shewhart, W. A. (1939). *Statistical method from the viewpoint of quality control.* Washington, DC: The Graduate School of the Department of Agriculture.

Six Sigma Online. (n.d.). Best self-paced Six Sigma certified training available online. Retrieved from http://www.sixsigmaonline.org/

Taylor, J. (2010). *Transforming healthcare delivery with analytics.* Retrieved from ftp://public.dhe.ibm .com/software/data/sw-library/infosphere/analyst-reports/Transforming_Healthcare_Delivery.pdf

Toussaint, J. S., & Berry, L. L. (2013). The promise of Lean in health care. *Mayo Clinic Proceedings, 88*(1), 74–82.

Van Den Bos, J., Rustagi, K., Gray, T., Halford, M., Ziemkiewicz, E., & Shreve, J. (2011). The $17.1 billion problem: The annual cost of measurable medical errors. *New England Journal of Medicine, 30*(4), 596–603.

Wennberg, J. E. (2002). Unwarranted variation in healthcare delivery: Implications for academic medical centres. *British Medical Journal, 325,* 961–964.

Womack, J. P., Jones, D.T., & Roos, D. (1990). *The machine that changed the world.* New York, NY: Free Press.

Information Technology

Nancy H. Shanks and Sharon B. Buchbinder

LEARNING OBJECTIVES

By the end of this chapter, the student will be able to:

- Distinguish between information systems common to all industries and those unique to health care;
- Appraise key systems used by health care managers;
- Differentiate between the electronic medical record (EMR) and the electronic health record (EHR);
- Analyze the challenges to clinical system adoption;
- Examine the concept of meaningful use and its implications for health care providers;
- Assess the future of health-care information technology (HIT) and the vision of an integrated U.S. health care system;
- Critique the impact of HIT on the health care manager;
- Examine the impacts of HIPAA and other regulations, laws, and policies regarding confidentiality of patient information; and
- Investigate sources of data for assessing the impact of electronic health record implementation.

INTRODUCTION

Have you ever considered why it is so easy to get your money almost anywhere in the world from an automated teller machine (ATM), but impossible to have easy access to your health and medical history—even during a medical emergency? Information technology has traditionally been relegated to the administrative functions of health care—in the back office with payroll and accounting. Today, as pressures mount for safer and more cost-effective care, and as software applications become easier to use, the introduction of information technology into the clinical setting has accelerated. While introducing a new complexity, this phenomenon also creates great opportunity for safer care, more standardized practice, greater accuracy and portability of data and information, and achieving the elusive vision of electronic health records for U.S. citizens. The purpose of this chapter is to explain the current state of information technology in health care and to discuss the impact the acceleration of its implementation will have on managing an already complex environment for the health care manager.

Health information systems (HIS) have been defined by Balgrosky (2015) "as including all computer systems (including hardware, software, operating systems, and end-user devices connecting people to the systems), networks (the electronic connectivity between systems, people, and organizations), and the data those systems create and capture through the use of software" (p. 13). These are the "building blocks" for all of the functions and applications that comprise the work of health care providers, organizations and professionals. It is from these basic building blocks that Balgrosky (2015) has developed the "HIS Scope Model," shown in Figure 8-1.

In this model, HIS are organized and managed to facilitate several higher level purposes. The main purposes of the clinical and other administrative systems are to provide the information and primary data needed to operate an efficient and effective health care organization; this occurs at the Systems and Management level of the model. Those data,

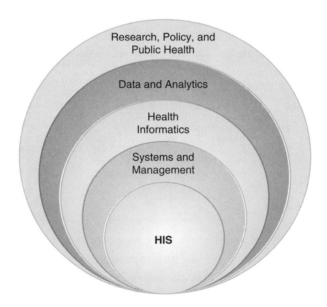

FIGURE 8-1 HIS Scope Model

in turn, provide the foundations for the other higher level purposes. That is, the data can be used in health informatics, analytics, research, and policy. The intent of this chapter is to focus primarily on HIS and the Systems and Management part of the model, but these other areas will also be defined and briefly discussed later in the chapter.

INFORMATION SYSTEMS USED BY MANAGERS

A Few Basics about System Technology

The foundation for all information systems applications is telecommunication, as well as a variety of types of networks and data storage capabilities. "Telecommunications is defined as the electrical transmission of data among systems, whether through analog, digital, or wireless media" (Balgrosky, 2015, p. 62). **Networks** can be categorized as Intranets, which are internal to an organization, or Extranets, which are external and allow users to share information. Networks also can be characterized as "local area networks (LANs), wireless LANs (WLANs), wide area networks (WANs), wireless WANs (WWANs), and storage area networks (SANs). The Internet is a well-known WAN" (Balgrosky, 2015, p. 81). As examples, when a medical assistant wheels a laptop computer into an exam room, she is using in WLAN to record vital signs and other information (Balgrosky, 2015); if you are connecting to the Internet at Starbucks, you are using a WWAN.

Data collected are stored either where the HIS are housed on a server or, increasingly, in some remote, virtual location. Specifically, "the sizes of health data centers are decreasing due to advances in server and storage consolidation, virtualization, and cloud computing" (Balgrosky, 2015, p. 81).

System Applications in Health Care

Similar to other industries, health care businesses, whether for-profit or not-for-profit, are supported by traditional software applications used to run the business. The key purpose of these systems is to manage the organization's expenses and revenues. For most health care entities, you'll also find more sophisticated systems to manage two of their most costly resources—staff and equipment. These common systems, some of which health care organizations widely implement, include:

- Standard office applications such as word processing, spreadsheet management, and e-mail and other administrative tools to enable collaboration;
- Budget systems to manage expenses and income;
- Cost accounting systems to model the profit (or loss) of key services/products;
- Enterprise resource planning (ERP) systems, which include human resource, payroll, accounts payable, materials management, and general ledger functions;

- Time and attendance, staffing and scheduling, and productivity systems to manage a diverse exempt and nonexempt, and in many health care organizations a 24/7, 365-days-a-year, workforce;
- Marketing systems including customer relationship management (CRM) and typically the organization's website, Facebook and other social media accounts;
- For those health care entities that are non-profit, fund-raising systems that play a key role in identifying and managing the contributions of donors; and
- Billing and accounts receivable systems used to bill clients and customers (e.g., patients and insurance companies) for the goods or services of the entity.

Prior to the 1990s, information technology found in most health-care organizations—hospitals, physician practices, nursing homes, etc.—supported mostly the administrative transactions unique to health care. More specifically, these were systems that either assisted in the billing and accounts receivable processes, such as patient scheduling and registration systems, or systems that assisted health care entities in meeting regulatory requirements, such as The Joint Commission (TJC), Centers for Medicare and Medicaid Services (CMS), the American Association of Blood Banks (AABB), the College of Pathologists (CAP), etc. For example, a clinical information system enables a hospital to document how they reconcile the medications a patient brings into the facility with those prescribed while visiting, as required by The Joint Commission. As technology has matured and its benefits around efficiency and patient safety have been identified, information technology has begun to be seen in more clinical areas. The delivery of health care includes many repetitive workflows, such as filling prescriptions, reporting results of laboratory tests, and completing radiology images, to name but a few. These workflows lend themselves to becoming more effective and efficient through automation. As a result, clinical systems that supported these areas and patient care processes came to the forefront (see Table 8-1). Nonetheless, many of these systems didn't effectively communicate with each other within a single organization, let alone as patients moved from one part of the industry to another. In addition, through the 1990s, systems remained so cumbersome that most direct care personnel (e.g., nurses, physicians, home health workers) were not asked to use them to support direct care processes. And if they had been asked, they probably would not have done so because of the amount of additional time it would have introduced into their workflow.

As efficiencies through automation were gained by these ancillary information systems, a parallel maturation of medical devices occurred. Many of these device types are oriented to enhancing workflow through increased throughput and reduced variation. Often they are physically connected to the ancillary system. These included robotic prescription dispensing services in the pharmacy, which pick, dispense, and label medications for delivery

TABLE 8-1 Examples of Typical Clinical Systems in Hospitals

Clinical System Name	Clinical System Function	Primary User(s)
Laboratory System	Tracks lab order and results	Laboratory department
Radiology System	Tracks radiology orders and results	Radiology department
Pharmacy System	Tracks medication orders including when dispensed	Pharmacy department
Clinical Data Repository (CDR)	Storage of all clinical data	Clinicians
Computerized Provider Order Entry (CPOE)	Electronic ordering of all orders for a patient by a provider such as a physician, pharmacist, or advanced practitioner	Providers
Nursing/Clinical Documentation	Online documentation of the care of patients by nursing, physical therapy, respiratory therapy, etc.	Nurses, therapists
Clinical Decision Support System (CDSS)	Alerts that indicate potentially harmful situations for patients	Physicians, pharmacists, nurses
Picture Archiving and Communications System (PACS)	System that stores actual digital imaging of radiology, cardiology, and other studies	Physicians

to patients, and analyzers in the laboratory, which afford high-speed and consistent processing of specimens. As more information about patients became available through the use of these systems, the promise of a complete and unified place to find patient information began to become reality. While traditional business systems have become standard and pervasive for effective daily management, the recent increase in the use of clinical systems presented and continues to present a unique challenge to those managing the impacted areas. In summary, health care managers must be comfortable and confident with information technology to manage their administrative responsibilities. Health care managers should anticipate the need to be flexible and to educate and train staff as new tools become more pervasive in the areas they manage.

THE ELECTRONIC MEDICAL RECORD (EMR)

In 1991, the Institute of Medicine (IOM) issued a report concluding that computer-based patient records are "an essential technology" for health care (IOM, 2001). Even so, adoption of these technologies continued to be low. Additional industry pressure came with another IOM report, *To Err Is Human* (Kohn, Corrigan, & Donaldson, 2000). This report highlighted the need to build a safer health care system and presented the astounding figure of 98,000 annual preventable deaths in the U.S. due to clinical quality issues.

Recommendations from the report suggested the establishment of a federal Center for Patient Safety. One of the initial areas of attention was to "increase understanding of the use of information technology to improve patient safety (e.g., automated drug order entry systems, reminder systems that prompt nurses and other care providers when a patient's medication or other treatments are due)" (Kohn et al., 2000, p. 80). As clinicians began to realize the value of information technology, adoption of **electronic medical records (EMRs)** for patients accelerated.

In the mid-2000s, HIMSS Analytics characterized an **EMR** as an application environment composed of the clinical data repository, clinical decision support, controlled medical vocabulary, order entry, computerized provider order entry, pharmacy, and clinical documentation applications. This environment supports the patient's electronic medical record across inpatient and outpatient environments, and is used by health care practitioners to document, monitor, and manage health care delivery within a care delivery organization (CDO). The data in the EMR are legal records of what occurred during patient encounters at the CDO and are owned by the CDO (Garets & Davis, 2006, p. 2). More recently the federal Office of the National Coordinator for Health Information Technology (ONC) has defined "electronic medical records (EMRs) [as] a digital version of the paper charts in the clinicians office" (Garrett & Seidman, 2011, p. 1).

Adoption of Clinical Systems by Hospitals

The **Healthcare Information and Management Systems Society (HIMSS)** is a professional organization made up of members committed to leveraging information technology to better serve the health care industry. These are people who primarily have information technology jobs in hospitals, physician practices, pharmaceutical companies, insurance companies, software vendors, and so on (HIMSS, n.d.). HIMSS supports the educational and networking needs of information technology (IT) professionals who have chosen health care as their industry of focus. By 2000, HIMSS Analytics had designed a model to track EMR progress at hospitals and health systems in the U.S. called the **Electronic Medical Record Analytical Model (EMRAM)**. See Figure 8-2. The EMRAM scores hospitals in the HIMSS Analytics database on their progress in implementing progressively more complicated clinical systems from stage 0 to stage 7, ultimately resulting in the ability to exchange their clinical information with external partners (such as labs or physician offices) (HIMSS Analytics, 2015a).

The foundational implementation of an EMR is a hospital's ability to first automate data in individual areas within the hospital, as represented by stages 0 and 1. Next is the ability to bring this data together for clinical decision making, stage 2. Stages 3–6 include the implementation of advanced clinical systems primarily used by direct care personnel such as nurses and physicians. In a hospital where all key clinical processes

EMR Adoption Model^SM	
Stage	Cumulative Capabilities
Stage 7	Complete EMR; CCD transactions to share data; Data warehousing; Data continuity with ED, ambulatory, OP
Stage 6	Physician documentation (structured templates), full CDSS (variance & compliance), full R-PACS
Stage 5	Closed loop medication administration
Stage 4	CPOE, Clinical Decision Support (clinical protocols)
Stage 3	Nursing/clinical documentation (flow sheets), CDSS (error checking), PACS available outside Radiology
Stage 2	CDR, Controlled Medical Vocabulary, CDS, may have Document Imaging; HIE capable
Stage 1	Ancillaries—Lab, Rad, Pharmacy—All Installed
Stage 0	All Three Ancillaries Not Installed

FIGURE 8-2 EMRAM model
Courtesy of HIMSS ANALYTICS

are fully automated, stage 7 represents the ability of that organization to then share or exchange data with external entities. It is at the achievement of this stage where real impacts on safety and efficiencies can be realized. Consider the impact of having all hospital-based information from a recent surgery available to your physician at your next follow-up appointment and/or the availability of your medication history and recent lab and X-ray results to a hospital's emergency room (ER) when an unintended visit occurs. The physician can immediately identify any allergies you may have, understand what medications you are already on, and potentially avoid ordering duplicate tests and services.

As shown in Table 8-2, while the EMRAM scores from 2008 compared to the first quarter of 2015 reflect an increase of hospitals that have moved from lower to higher stages in the model, 56% of all hospitals in the U.S. had progressed past stage 4 as of the beginning of 2015. And while we see movement to stage 7, this represents only 3.7% of all hospitals: a meager 197 of 5,467 U.S. hospitals. High cost and user "unfriendliness," combined with slow progress in developing standards for defining complex clinical information, have contributed to such slow movement to stage 7. Organizations like Kaiser Permanente currently are truly exceptions given the size of the challenges to clinical system adoption.

TABLE 8-2 Comparison of 2008 to 2015 EMRAM Scores for American Hospitals

EMRAM Stage	2008 Q4	2010 Q4	2014 Q4	2015 Q1
Stage 7	0.3%	1.0%	3.6%	3.7%
Stage 6	0.5%	3.2%	17.9%	22.2%
Stage 5	2.5%	4.5%	32.8%	30.8%
Stage 4	2.5%	10.5%	14.0%	13.6%
Stage 3	35.7%	49.0%	21.0%	19.7%
Stage 2	31.4%	7.1%	5.1%	4.3%
Stage 1	11.5%	7.1%	2.0%	2.2%
Stage 0	15.6%	11.5%	3.7%	3.5%
Total hospitals	5,168	5,281	5,467	5,462

Courtesy of HIMSS ANALYTICS

This slow progress is further complicated by the highly sensitive and confidential nature of patients' clinical data. Americans are fiercely protective of patient rights, including control over access to medical information. This lack of trust that electronic clinical information will remain secure, underscored by high profile hacking of health insurance databases, has also had an impact on slow clinical system adoption; the primary stakeholder—the patient—isn't demanding it (Vijavan, 2015). In addition to the risk of identity theft, other risks include use of medical and financial information to obtain drugs, commit health care fraud, or reveal medical conditions and sensitive lab results such as a positive HIV or pregnancy test. As much as we love our technology and convenience of having information at our fingertips, this same ease of use can be turned against us by those who want it for darker purposes. Security of health care data is crucial to ensure movement from Level 0 to Level 7.

From EMR to EHR

Many people use the terms electronic medical record and **electronic health record** interchangeably. There is, however, a distinction beyond the mere one word difference. Garrett and Seidman (2011) point out that "EHRs focus on the total health of the patient—going beyond standard clinical data collected in the provider's office and inclusive of a broader view on a patient's care....[and] are built to share information with other health care providers" (p. 2). That means EHR is a broader term than EMR. The data in the EHR are accessible to many different entities, particularly the patient, and the information goes with the patient to various health care settings, making test results, allergy information, medications, and other health care information available to other providers.

Reaching EHR status has been elusive for many hospitals. In recent years, the federal government has made a significant effort to facilitate the utilization of EHRs in all types of hospitals. Despite these efforts, adoption of EHRs by certain types of hospitals has been a challenge. This is particularly true for "small and rural hospitals [that] continue to lag behind their better resourced counterparts" (Adler-Milstein et al., 2014, p. 1670). The specific challenges for rural hospitals "include resource constraints and EHR implementation costs, availability of grants and loans to support EHR implementation, and workflow challenges" (ONC, 2014c, p. 17).

Adoption of EMRs and EHRs by Physician Practices and Other Providers

Adoption rates have not just been low in hospitals, but have been even lower in the setting where Americans receive most of their health care: physician offices. Think about your own experience: unless you've dealt with serious or chronic health issues, the times in which you sought care in the health care industry are largely identified through visits to your physician's office. In short, the setting where we receive most of our health care is the setting with lower levels of technology adoption, unless one is enrolled in a large managed care organization, such as Kaiser Permanente.

Currently, while 96.4% of hospitals have some semblance of an EMR (HIMSS Analytics, 2015a), 62.8% of physician offices do as of January 2015 (SK&A, 2015). The cost of purchasing and implementing EMR systems is the single greatest barrier (Runy, 2009). The larger the physician practice, the higher degree of administrative complexity, and the higher the rate of EMR adoption—77.2% of practices with more than 26 physicians have adopted EMR (SK&A, 2015). While seemingly positive, more than 40% of physician practices in the U.S. had between 1 and 5 physicians (Liebhaber & Grossman, 2007). Although there has been a shift toward hospital employment, 60.1% of physicians still work in practices that are wholly owned by physicians and 40% are still small in size (Kane & Emmons, 2013). In these smaller practices, the adoption rate has been much lower than larger practices (S&K, 2015). In the past, physicians have had neither a compelling business reason nor the requisite resources to buy these systems, although this began to change with the federal push toward use of EHR as discussed in the next section.

There continue to be many barriers for both EHR adopters and non-adopters. In a 2014 survey conducted by the ONC and the Centers for Disease Control and Prevention (CDC), both groups reported the following "top 5 'major barriers' to EHR adoption:

- Cost of purchasing a system;
- Loss of productivity;
- Annual maintenance costs;

- Adequacy of training; and
- Finding EHR to meet practice needs" (ONC, 2014c, p. 15).

In addition, physician practices often have not had the depth of staffing to adequately select, implement, and support an EMR. To the extent the patient record in the physician practice has remained on paper, physicians' notes, prescriptions, and lab and X-ray results have also remained in a format prohibitive to sharing. As mentioned earlier, there are certainly exceptions to this. Kaiser Permanente has demonstrated it is possible to have physicians practicing in an entirely automated environment with both efficiency and patient safety gains (McGee, 2010). It is important to realize Kaiser Permanente is a massive health care system with "38 hospitals, 618 medical offices, 17,425 physicians, 48,285 nurses, and 174,415 employees" as of December 31, 2013, with "$56.4 billion in annual operating revenue" for 2014 (Kaiser Permanente, 2015).

Not only has the implementation of EHRs been difficult for physicians, it has been equally, if not more difficult, in other sectors of the health care industry. Mohamoud, Byrne, and Samarth (2009) reported that long-term care settings face great challenges, including "regulatory and legal concerns, insufficient funding, technology fears, staff turnover, lack of interoperable standards and discontinuity of care" (pp. 21–22).

THE CHALLENGES TO CLINICAL SYSTEM ADOPTION

The barriers to adoption of clinical systems go back many years. The IOM report *Crossing the Quality Chasm* detailed numerous obstacles (IOM, 2001). Patient privacy and a

---

TEXTBOX 8-1. PHYSICIAN RANK EHRs ON QUALITY OF CARE

- SOAPWare
- MEDENT
- Healthfusion
- e-MDs
- Epic
- Amazing Charts
- Advanced MD
- Practice Fusion
- Modernizing Medicine
- athenahealth

Data from: Medical Economics, 2014. Quality of care: http://medicaleconomics.modernmedicine.com /medical-economics/content/tags/2014-ehr-scorecard/best-ehr-systems-2014-physicians-rank-five-key-per

TEXTBOX 8-2. TOP FIVE VENDORS OF EHRs

Large Hospitals and Academic Medical Centers
- Allscripts Healthcare Solutions
- Epic Systems
- Cerner
- McKesson
- Quadramed

Community Hospitals (with 100–299 beds)
- Siemens
- McKesson
- Epic
- Allscripts Healthcare Solutions

Small Hospitals (under 100 beds)
- CPSI
- Cerner
- Healthland
- Health Management Systems
- Razorinsights

Data from: McCann, 2014; The Advisory Board Company, 2014.

patient's desire to ensure that others could not see their health information was a primary concern. Sharing of information is all the more challenging in health care because a "standard vocabulary" doesn't exist as it does in other industries such as banking, where information about your bank account can electronically move all over the world. This lack of one system being able to speak to another (e.g., physician's system to insurer's system) not only slows down productivity, but also can contribute to delays in health care delivery. As noted previously, the cost to purchase, implement, and support these systems is a core barrier in an industry where recent and extreme focus on cost exists. Finally, but not least, the majority of the health care industry–specific software applications were not developed in a manner in which the user interfaces were intuitive or easy to use, making the user, at least initially, frustrated and slower in implementing it. Based upon recent hospital EMR adoption numbers, these same barriers continue to remain relevant (IOM, 2001).

Governmental Involvement in EHR

Concerns about the Baby Boomers' impact on Medicare and the percentage of the gross domestic product (GDP) going to the cost of health care have been raised by the IOM and other authors (Chiplin & Lilly, 2013). Projections suggested that, within

10 years, Americans would spend one of every five dollars on health care. The Obama administration recognized the potential to reduce health care expenses through standards and automation and made the decision to jumpstart health information technology (HIT) investments. Understanding that an electronic health record would provide organization to the complex and vast amount of clinical information on patients, thus leading to better clinical decisions, a higher quality of care, and a reduction in overutilization, aggressive measures were put forward in the American Recovery and Reinvestment Act (ARRA) in 2009 around EMR adoption (CMS, 2009). Under the Health Information Technology for Economic and Clinical Health Act (HITECH) portion of the ARRA, hospitals and physicians in the U.S. were to receive funding incentives to adopt and implement clinical health care information technology. By 2015, organizations that failed to do so were to be unable to participate in the Medicare program and were to be subjected to fines and penalties. The HITECH provisions don't sound like much, but they provided the foundation and funneled billions of dollars into the development of HIS. This, in turn, laid the foundation for achieving the health care reform goals (improved quality, reduced cost, and improved access) of the Patient Protection and Affordable Care Act (ACA) and reforming the health care system. The achievement of those goals "require[s] better methods of storing, analyzing, and sharing health information.... HITECH builds this infrastructure through incentive payments of meaningful use to doctors and hospitals, and through programs that address specific obstacles to health IT adoption and exchange" (Buntin, Jain, & Blumenthal, 2010, p. 1219).

In moving this process forward, CMS, in conjunction with ONC, developed what have become known as the **meaningful use** criteria for EHR. This involved defining the goals/priorities and setting a schedule for the attainment of them. "The concept of meaningful use rested on the '5 pillars' of health outcomes policy priorities, namely:

1. Improve quality, safety, efficiency, and reduce health disparities
2. Engage patients and families in their health
3. Improve care coordination
4. Improve population and public health
5. Ensure adequate privacy and security for patient health information" (CDC, 2012, para. 2).

To achieve meaningful use, providers were expected to progress through three stages of development, over the following five-year period:

1. "2011–2012 – Stage 1 – Data capture and sharing
2. 2014 – Stage 2 – Advance clinical processes
3. 2016 – Stage 3 – Improved outcomes" (HealthIT, 2015, para. 4).

Additionally, HealthIT (2013) established the Medicare and Medicaid EHR Incentive Programs for eligible professionals (EPs) and eligible hospitals "to provide financial incentives for the adoption and meaningful use of certified EHR technology to improve patient care" (ONC, 2014c, p. 13). In addition, the Regional Extension Center (REC) program was created to provide technical assistance in achieving meaningful use to "providers that historically have lower rates of EHR adoption, such as small practices, community health centers, and rural and public hospitals" (ONC, 2014c, p. 16).

One issue related to this discussion is how the meaningful use stages equate to the EMRAM stages. A comparison of the two by Murphy (2013) indicates that Stage 4 on the EMRAM model equates to Stage 1 of meaningful use in terms of data collection and using electronic means to share it. Murphy (2013) goes on to indicate "that Stage 2 Meaningful Use correlates most closely with Stage 6 of the EMR Adoption Model" (p. 3), while Stage 3 Meaningful Use correlates with Stage 7 of the EMRAM. It should be noted that the Meaningful Use Stage 3 criteria and implementation timeline were only released on March 29, 2015 (HIMSS, 2015), so this process is just beginning for providers.

"As of September 2014, only 93 hospitals and 2,282 doctors had successfully progressed to Stage 2 meaningful use" (OIG, 2014, p. 2). This fact indicates that, despite considerable effort on the part of providers and significant financial contributions by the federal government, there is a long way to go before EHR adoption reaches its potential and fulfills the federal goals.

Part of the slow progress can be attributed to push back from physicians. Some of the push back is coming from concerns physicians are attending more to computers than to patients (Patel, 2015). Additionally, as alluded to earlier in this chapter, there has been considerable criticism of the process to move toward EHRs and meaningful use. Physicians have complained that software vendors have not kept up with the demands of the conversion, nor have the designers of the systems always listened to the end users. One example of this is not attending to the needs of different specialties. Unlike internists or primary care physicians (PCPs), surgeons do not prescribe a lot of different drugs. Yet, when a patient arrives at a surgeon's office the EHR may report that the surgeon has ordered a laundry list of medications, when in fact he hasn't. This raises significant liability issues for the surgeon who should not be held responsible for the PCPs prescribing practices. In situations such as this, a quick fix would be to insert a disclaimer on the screen that the surgeon is not responsible for these prescriptions. However, not all systems permit an easy or a quick fix. Some require expensive and major reprogramming, which is completed only when a critical threshold of "bugs" has been met to reduce costs.

The quality of shared medical images has been identified as a significant issue with some EHRs (Rosenfeld, 2013; Tieche, FitzGerald, & Martin, 2014). In its 2013 electronic health record study, Black Book Rankings found that "nearly one in five physician users indicated the high likelihood of shifting systems after disappointing first vendor results" (PRWeb, 2013, p. 1). A major study of physician professional satisfaction funded by the American Medical Association (AMA) and conducted by the RAND Corporation found "the current state of EHR technology significantly worsened professional satisfaction in multiple ways" and "aspects of current EHRs that were particularly common sources of dissatisfaction included poor usability, time-consuming data entry, interference with face-to-face patient care, inefficient and less fulfilling work content, inability to exchange health information, and degradation of clinical documentation" (Friedberg et al., 2013, p. xvi). Several articles also reported the dissatisfaction and concerns of physicians that EHRs were developed to facilitate reimbursement and not to collect data about patients (American College of Physicians, 2013; Chuang, 2014; Fallows, 2014; May, 2013; Modernizing Medicine, 2014). Both the AMA and the American Hospital Association (AHA) have expressed strong opinions about the timing of issuing the meaningful use criteria for the various stages, the short timeframes for achieving various stages, the potential penalties that providers face for not meeting timeframes, and the absence of flexibility and willingness to make modifications on the part of and the heavy handedness of regulators (AHA, 2015; AMA, 2014; Fishman, 2015; Stack, 2014). As of July 2015, the President of the AMA has declared "EHR meaningful use isn't meaningful" and called on physicians to petition Congress "to halt Stage 3 meaningful use until the program is fixed" (Stack, 2015b, para. 14).

The 2013 IOM report, *Best Care at Lower Cost: The Path to Continuously Learning Health Care in America*, tackled the issue of EHRs and low utilization in health care head on with the following analogy: "If banking were like health care, automated teller machine (ATM) transactions would take not seconds but perhaps days or longer as a result of unavailable or misplaced records" (IOM, 2013a, p. 5). A companion infographic called "What's Possible for Healthcare?" provides a visual overview of how our health care system compares to other industries (IOM, 2013b). In online banking, we can have access to our financial data in seconds. In health care, 50% of patients indicated information necessary for their health care was not *available*, and 25% of patients reported their health care providers had to *re-order* tests for needed information. This loss of critical information contributes to delay of care and costs of care. Likewise, in manufacturing, companies can respond to changes in demand and track a complex network of suppliers. In health care, we have an equally complex network of supply and demand, yet one provider often cannot speak to another via an EHR. Over 200 other physicians are involved in treating the average primary care physician's Medicare patient and over 180 tasks are managed by physicians in intensive care units. In the absence of a good health information management system to juggle all these balls, it's a wonder more mistakes don't occur in health care.

The complexity and cost of health care means we must have improved computing power, connectivity, organizational capabilities, and teamwork between clinicians and patients. Health care organizations must reduce financial waste and human suffering by improving the quality and quantity of information sharing. The IOM report concluded:

> Advances in computing, information science, and connectivity can improve patient-clinician communication, point-of-care guidance, the capture of experience, population surveillance, planning and evaluation, and the generation of real-time knowledge—features of a continuously learning health care system. (IOM, 2013a, p. 16)

Recommendations included improvements to the digital infrastructure to "[i]mprove the capacity to capture clinical, delivery process, and financial data for better care, system improvement, and creating new knowledge" as well as "improved data utility by streamlining and revising research regulations to improve care, promote the capture of clinical data, and generate knowledge" (IOM, 2013a, p. 29).

The bottom line is that, while the barriers appear to have been lessened somewhat due to governmental involvement, many issues still remain to be resolved. The process of adopting EHRs in physician practices and hospitals will continue. However, as both the 2013 IOM and RAND Corporation reports underscore, many challenges remain to get to the point where clinical information is stored in systems that use a standard vocabulary, can communicate with each other, contain data that can be shared with patients and other providers, and include data and information to be used for a variety of purposes.

Government Involvement in Protecting Health Information

In 1996, Congress passed the **Health Insurance Portability and Accountability Act (HIPAA)** with the intent of developing standards for health care data and their exchange and regulations on privacy protections (CMS, 2013). The concept of **Protected Health Information (PHI)** is to protect all

> "individually identifiable health information" held or transmitted by a covered entity or its business associate, in any form or media, whether electronic, paper, or oral. The HIPAA Privacy Rule calls this information "protected health information (PHI)."
>
> "Individually identifiable health information" is information, including demographic data, that relates to:
>
> - the individual's past, present, or future physical or mental health or condition;
> - the provision of health care to the individual, or,
> - the past, present, or future payment for the provision of health care to the individual; and
> - that identifies the individual or for which there is a reasonable basis to believe it can be used to identify the individual.

Individually identifiable health information includes many common identifiers (e.g., name, address, birth date, Social Security Number). The Privacy Rule excludes from protected health information employment records that a covered entity maintains in its capacity as an employer and education and certain other records subject to, or defined in, the Family Educational Rights and Privacy Act, 20 U.S.C. §1232g (U.S. Department of Health and Human Services [DHHS], 2003, pp. 3–4).

In 2013, several changes were made to the HIPAA regulations. "The Final Rule enhances patient privacy protection, provides individuals with new rights to their health information and strengthens the government's enforcement of and penalties under the law" (APA Practice Organization, 2013). These actions address the following:

- **Notice of privacy**: the revisions now require patient consent for the use of PHI in marketing, the sale of PHI, and "the use and disclosures of psychotherapy notes."
- **Breach notification rules and enforcement**: a risk assessment of any PHI breach must now be carried out and must consider "the following factors:
  1. Nature and extent of PHI involved;
  2. To whom the PHI may have been disclosed;
  3. Whether that PHI was actually acquired or viewed; and
  4. The extent to which the risk to the PHI has been mitigated (for example, assurances from recipient that information has been destroyed or will not be further used or disclosed)" (APA Practice Organization, 2013, para. 11).
- **Business associate agreements**: the requirements of the law are extended to include all groups that hospitals or other covered entities do business with, as well as to the subcontractors with whom those associates do business. Contracts with business associates and subcontractors now need to address HIPAA requirements.

In addition, the fines for breaches have been increased and now "range from $100 to $50,000 per violation with a cap of $1.5 million on violations of identical provisions happening within the same calendar year" (APA Practice Organization, 2013, para. 16). The HIPAA Security Rule focuses on protecting PHI in all patient medical records, be they in paper or electronic form. Enforcement of these rules now rests with the Office of Civil Rights (OCR), which is the agency to which any HIPAA security breach is reported (DHHS, 2015).

It is critical that today's health care manager be aware of the impact of these laws on health care workers, as well as informed about the more significant concepts of HIPAA, such as the **Notice of Privacy Practice (NOPP)** and these Final Rule changes, and ensure that employees only have access to patients' PHI on a need-to-know basis.

THE FUTURE OF HEALTH CARE INFORMATION TECHNOLOGY

The era of carrying your personal EHR on a card in your purse, wallet, or embedded under your skin in a microchip with every conceivable piece of medical information about you is on the horizon (Jones, 2015). The ability to have a new physician evaluate your medical history without ever physically seeing you, and the ability to diagnose and treat you without you having to visit a doctor's office or clinic, is definitely in the offing. A new mobile application for smartphones enables patients to track cold, flu, allergy, and other symptoms and maps them by automatically scanning social networks and media for symptoms of emerging outbreaks. This McNeil Consumer Healthcare app provides alerts and maps of sick zones on specific illnesses based on the consumer's concerns (Barris, 2015). With re-emerging outbreaks of vaccine-preventable and other diseases, such as we discuss in Chapter 17, there will be even more of these apps for your phone. With our information becoming more mobile, we don't need to be in the physician's office or in the hospital to be "seen."

This mobility, driven by a wireless world, is creating the ability for virtual care. In 2013, there were 7.1 billion people worldwide and more than 6.8 billion had cell phones—more than "ever [the number who] had land-lines" (Fernholz, 2014, para. 1). Some of the possibilities of this wired and mobile world that already exist include medications with embedded microchips that, after being ingested, send information to either the patient or the physician (Mathews, 2010); capsule endoscopy where the patient swallows a tiny wireless camera that films the digestive track (Mayo Clinic, 2012); using 3-D printers to make artificial body parts like ears or hands (Rieland, 2014); and a plethora of wearable devises including electrocardiogram (EKG) patches, heart monitors, and breathing devices, etc. The list continues to grow, limited only by one's imagination. There are also wearable headsets that monitor brain waves and wearable clothing, like the vest that sends physiological values (blood pressure, sugar levels, cardiac monitoring, etc.) to a remote location where nurses are monitoring the vests without the patient ever having to leave home. This boom in "wearable wireless medical devices sales will reach more than 100 million devices annually....and is projected to exceed $2.9 billion in 2016" (McNickle, 2012, p. 1). Somehow, all of this data will need to be captured in EHRs.

Some of the areas that will likely confound this process include:

- **Optimizing existing vs. replacing EHRs**: The trend of physician practices changing their EHRs, mentioned above, has continued. "Nearly 60% of providers are unsatisfied with their EHR system due to usability and work flow issues....this growing unrest is driving some practices to consider EHR replacement—with several reports from 2013 indicating that between 17% and 31% of physician practices were planning to replace their existing systems" (ECG Management Consultants, 2014, p. 3). Health care managers will need to make careful and difficult decisions about whether it makes sense to optimize an existing system or take on the challenge of converting to a different system.

- **Data integrity**: The old saying "**garbage in, garbage out**" or **GIGO** is applicable to EHRs. As Chuang (2014) has pointed out, "data is king…if data is not good, the technology is meaningless" (p. 2). This is a call for data integrity and accuracy (White, 2014). Data entry and correct coding are clearly integral to the integrity of the data.

- **Promoting safety**: A safety concerns study conducted by ECRI Institute pointed out the link between data integrity and patient safety. In fact, for 2014 information technology was the number one concern on ECRI's list (Rice, 2014), and for 2015 it came in second. Data integrity problems relating to missing data, erroneous data, data coded to the incorrect record, and other inconsistencies were among the problems noted in 2015 (ECRI Institute, 2015). Textbox 8-3 provides an example a potential patient safety issue that resulted from EHR miscommunication.

- **Interoperability**: This refers to the "ability of different information technology systems and software applications to communicate, exchange data, and use the information that has been exchanged" (HIMSS, 2013, para. 2). This means providers will need to have progressed through Stage 1 and be in Stage 2 of meaningful use. As pointed out above, very few hospitals and physician practices have reached these milestones. To keep moving toward the goal of an interoperable health care system, ONC has developed "A 10-Year Vison" and a draft "Roadmap" for implementing the former (ONC, 2014a; ONC, 2014b).

- **Cybersecurity**: The issues of security of patient data have come to the fore in recent years, as significant security breaches, data spills, and data hacking threats have been prominent in the media. Incidents have included the 2011 case "where medical files belonging to nearly 300,000 Californians sat unsecure on the Internet for the entire world to

---

TEXTBOX 8-3. PATIENT SAFETY CONCERNS

"The patient's peanut allergy was listed in the EHR but the information did not cross over to the dietary department's system. The patient questioned whether the food allergy information had been received by the dietary department after receiving a food tray that was not identified as free of peanut products."
Source: ECRI Institute, 2015, p. 10.

see" (Robertson, 2011, para. 1), and the 2015 hack of Anthem's data bases, exposing all types of personal data (names, addresses, birth dates, Social Security numbers, etc.) for 80 million employees and insureds (Chuang, 2015). To address these types of problems, managers need "to make sure the equipment your hospital uses has the most recent security updates installed. Any device used to store or access PHI should be encrypted, and network access should be limited only to those who need it" (White, 2014, para. 12). Jenkins (2013) lists "The 'Dirty Dozen' Healthcare IT Issues," as shown in Textbox 8-4, are issues that health care executives need to address to secure data, manage risk, and prevent HIPAA violations. To address this problem, most states have now passed laws requiring companies to inform consumers about data breaches (NCSL, 2015). President Obama urged Congress to pass cybersecurity legislation, and on February 13, 2015, President Obama signed an Executive Order—Promoting Private Sector Cybersecurity Information Sharing to address some of these problems and to encourage sharing of information about cyber threats (The White House, 2015). Finally, the Office of the Inspector General (OIG) has warned efforts must be taken by providers to protect EHRs from being used for fraudulent purposes (OIG, 2014).

- A new twist to cybersecurity will require health care managers to consider the new **BYOD** (Bring Your Own Device) to work movement and the extent to which this approach may compromise EHRs and health data systems. BYOD companies are requiring their employees to provide their own computer equipment. It is important

---

TEXTBOX 8-4. "THE DIRTY DOZEN" HEALTHCARE IT ISSUES

1. Unsupported, unpatched operating systems
2. Antivirus/antimalware issues
3. Poor security authentication
4. Unsecured wireless networks
5. No data redundancy, backups
6. Portable media and laptop security
7. Poor user training
8. Old, out-of-date, out-of-warranty systems
9. Lack of employee computer use policies
10. E-mail scams, hoaxes, phishing
11. Inept/untrained IT support resources
12. Data on workstations, laptops

Excerpted with permission from Jenkins, M. K. The Dirty Dozen Healthcare IT Issues, in S. T. Canale (ed): *AAOS Now*. Rosemont, IL, American Academy of Orthopaedic Surgeons, November 2013.

to note that companies requiring BYOD are forecasted to reach 38% in 2016 and 50% in 2017 (Bolgar, 2014), although it is not clear whether health care organizations will be among them.

- **Capturing Socioeconomic Data in EHRs** became increasingly important with the passage of the ACA and its emphasis on increasing prevention and reducing health disparities. This led the IOM to convene a Committee to study and make recommendations on this topic (IOM, 2014a). The Committee found that "despite strong evidence of the influence of social and behavioral factors on health, these factors have not been well addressed in clinical care" (IOM, 2014b, p. 1). Charged with recommending specific measures to be added to EHRs, the committee narrowed these down to address the following:

  - "psychosocial vital signs include four measures that are already widely collected (race/ethnicity, tobacco use, alcohol use, and residential address), and
  - eight additional measures (education, financial resource strain, stress, depression, physical activity, social isolation, intimate partner violence, and neighborhood median household income)" (IOM, 2014b, p. 1).

  Additionally, the IOM Committee recommended the inclusion of these measures in the ONC/CMS meaningful use criteria, that standardized measures be specified, that a plan be developed to conduct research using these measures from EHRs, and that the results of the Committee's recommendations be reviewed for progress made. These future changes will clearly have an impact on all health care providers and require yet another set of criteria to be met by EHRs.

- **ICD-10 Adoption**: The U.S. has continued to utilize the International Classification of Diseases ICD-9 codes to classify diagnoses and diseases since the late-1970s. The ICD-9 codes have been criticized for being "too outdated and no longer workable for treatment, reporting, and payment processes" and no longer "reflect all advances in medical technology and knowledge" (AMA, n.d., p. 3). In fact, "most other countries moved to the more granular and therefore more data-rich ICD-10 when it was released in the 1990s, leaving the U.S. behind as far as research capabilities are concerned" (SearchHealthIT, n.d., para. 4). The conversion to the more specific ICD-10 codes has been delayed several times over the last several years. It was originally mandated by the CMS in 2009, but the conversion date was moved to October 1, 2015. This is a huge undertaking in terms of health system and software upgrades; training of clinical, coding, and billing staff, as well as management; and increased expenditures for HIS. This is yet another activity that must be achieved concurrently with EHR implementation and meeting meaningful use criteria. That said, "standardizing codes improves consistency among physicians in recording patient symptoms and diagnoses for the purposes of payer claims research and clinical research" (SearchHealthIT, n.d., para. 1), as well as for the accuracy of EHRs. In July 2015, the CMS announced that efforts will be made to ease the changeover to ICD-10 for physicians, taking steps to not deny Medicare claim payments because of coding errors and other actions to avoid disruption in payments because of transition issues during the first year of ICD-10 implementation (Stack, 2015a).

The future of information technology in health care encompasses a number of additional areas that managers need to be aware of and potentially involved in, including:

- "**e-health** is the transfer of health resources and health care by electronic means. It encompasses three main areas:

  - The delivery of health information, for health professionals and health consumers, through the Internet and telecommunications.
  - Using the power of IT and e-commerce to improve public health services, e.g. through the education and training of health workers.
  - The use of e-commerce and e-business practices in health systems management" (World Health Organization, n.d., p. 1).

- "**mHealth** is the use of mobile technologies for the purposes of health care, public health, and health-related activities at the individual level" (Balgrosky, 2015, p. 243). These technologies include all types of mobile devices, such as laptops, tablets, smartphones, mobile medical devices, apps, and other wearables. In its 2014 Mobile Devices Study, HIMSS Analytics provided data on the rapid increased use of devices and specifically "reported that smartphones and tablet computers greatly enhance [clinicians'] ability to communicate with other clinicians and healthcare providers... and that use of [these devices] will positively impact the delivery of patient care" (HIMAA Analytics, 2014, p. 4). Additionally, patients have begun to embrace what has been termed "do-it-yourself [DIY] health care," such as mobile devices used to "monitor vital signs, analyze blood and urine, track medication adherence and more" (PwC Health Research Institute, 2014, p. 2). Some of these devices may require regulatory approval from the Food and Drug Administration (FDA) to assure patient safety. There are also concerns about how data from wearables will become part of EHRs, consistency of reported data, and data privacy and security issues (Ranney, 2015).

- **Telemedicine** has been available for a while and relates to the use of technology to deliver clinical care to outlying and inaccessible areas. This allows for the use of sophisticated technologies and access to health care professionals and specialists in rural areas. An example of this is teledermatology, which has been used and studied as a means of bringing dermatological care to underserved populations

(Armstrong, Kwong, Ledo, Nesbitt, & Shewry, 2011). If you've seen the commercial where the middle-aged couple re-enacts a dance scene from a popular film and crashes onto their dining room table, then have a video consultation with a puzzled physician, you are familiar with the concept of telemedicine. In the past there have been many barriers to the use of telemedicine, but as LeRoughe and Garfield (2013) point out, considerable progress has been made to address these by expanding broadband coverage to rural areas, changing licensure to allow physicians to practice outside their own states, enabling the reimbursement by Medicare and Medicaid for telemedicine services, researching and documenting the cost-effectiveness of these services, and incorporating telemedicine into organizational business strategies. That said, in April 2015 the Texas Medical Board took steps to limit the use of telemedicine in the state (Goodnough, 2015), and in May 2015 the U.S. House of Representatives passed a bill that would prohibit the obtaining of "telemed" abortion drugs (Andres, 2015). There is also pressure coming from the American Academy of Family Physicians, AMA, AHA, American Association of Retired Persons (AARP), Anthem Blue Cross Blue Shield, and other organizations to get Congress to pass legislation to make telemedicine more accessible and convenient for Medicare patients and in turn to decrease costs and improve quality (Galewitz, 2015).

- **Telehealth** is a related term but refers to the slightly different idea of providing "the remote delivery of health-related information from one site to another via electronic communications to improve a person's health awareness and access to health-related information" (Balgrosky, 2015, p. 269). That is, telehealth pertains to providing a variety of non-clinical services. The **Telehealth Enhancement Act of 2013** was introduced to the 113th Congress (i.e., in 2014) in an effort to focus on reimbursement and coverage issues under Medicare and Medicaid (HIMSS, 2014). This was not enacted before Congress adjourned in December 2014, and it remains to be seen if new bills will be introduced in a later legislative session. Despite the absence of legislation, the CMS did release a "Telehealth Services" fact sheet for "physicians or practitioners at the distant site" who provide services to Medicare recipients enrolled under fee-for-service plans (CMS, 2014).

- **Health informatics**: Informatics relates to "the use of information systems and technology to redesign, improve, and create the ways disciplines such as the practice of medicine, nursing, medical imaging, and public health do their work" (Balgrosky, 2015, p. 264). That is, by aggregating and evaluating EHR data from health information systems, results can be used to make better decisions about improving the delivery of care. With the proliferation of EHRs, this will become increasingly possible and health care managers may find this a useful tool.

- **Analytics/Big Data**: This refers to "the process of inspecting aggregated data, looking for patterns and statistics to help improve processes and creating information ultimately leading to new knowledge that helps improve efficiency and effectiveness in health care, and other goals of health and public health" (Balgrosky, 2015, p. 260). When we think of our individual health records and how complex those data are, consider having the ability to use millions of peoples' data to analyze, predict, create policy, and recommend changes to improve population-based health care. Every year, public health officials promote influenza vaccines to increase the "herd immunity." That means if the majority of the population is immunized and protected from the disease, we are less likely to see epidemics or worse yet, pandemics such as the influenza pandemic of 1918 that killed 50 million people (DHHS, n.d.). Big data, in turn, relates to the massive data bases that are becoming available in health care, as well as in other industries, to which investigators can apply analytics for a multitude of purposes, including predicting and preventing pandemics.
- **Research and Policy**: Big data and analytics enhance the capacity to conduct research and utilize research findings in making policy. For example, the Agency for Healthcare Research and Quality (AHRQ) anticipates the use of "big data analytics" to develop new research methodologies, to offer many new sources of data, "to incorporate new information flows into clinical workflows" (Dimitropoulos, 2014, p. 4), and to develop a research agenda assessing new topics and care models. In addition, numerous apps are being developed for smartphones to facilitate medical research data collection. "More than 75,000 people have enrolled in health studies that use specialized iPhone apps…to submit data daily by answering survey questions or using the iPhone's built-in sensors to measure their symptoms" (Bailey, 2015, para. 5). These include, for example, an Asthma Health app, a Parkinson's disease app, and others. These developments clearly open new, deep reservoirs of data for researchers and organizations.

As advances occur in information systems, a parallel and equally accelerated process has been and will continue to occur in medical devices and technology. Advanced genetics will become a predictive part of our health record, indicating potential treatments to avoid, or at least proactively manage the expression of later-onset inherited illnesses. A large number of clinical decisions can be made by a computer programmed to respond to an X-ray or lab result rather than a physician—involving the specialist only when a set of conditions is unknown to the knowledge base. Admittedly, some of these possibilities may seem straight out of science fiction and perhaps as silly as the idea that a telephone would not have to be plugged into the wall in our home or place of business might have been in 1985, or that you could talk to someone on that unplugged device and see them at the same time!

The availability of health information, combined with its ability to be mobile and shared, has the potential to transform the workplace of the future. The health care manager must be aware of and understand the impact of HIT to ensure that workers are productive, sensitive data is protected, and patients remain safe.

THE IMPACT OF INFORMATION TECHNOLOGY ON THE HEALTH CARE MANAGER

More than ever before, the health care work environment requires comfort with and knowledge of information systems. This means managers need to have the competencies to effectively evaluate the experience of their staff in the use of required systems as well as their own ability to quickly adapt to new tools to manage their own workload. The nurse or medical coder who will not or cannot adapt to new tools will be unable to perform his or her job. Technology has also given rise to new types of employees, such as medical scribes who assist physicians with entry of data into EHRs (Gellert, Ramirez, & Webster, 2015). Health care managers will need to evaluate whether utilizing this type of employee would be beneficial for their organizations.

This increasing dependency on computers and mobile devices creates new workplace challenges when those technologies are not available or are not working optimally. Downtime and upgrades that add extra steps for the workforce will create new situations to be effectively managed. And while clinical care cannot stop merely because a system is down, the gap in information during that downtime must be filled so a break in the documented care of the patient is addressed. The health care manager of the future must be able to navigate technology used by his or her team and understand the barriers to be addressed to increase productivity and enhance job satisfaction. Take, for example, a manager's commitment to ensure that health care employees are only accessing patient information on a need-to-know basis. Historically, this meant ensuring that charts were locked away when not used and not even accessible to those not physically in receipt of them. Today, with patient records online and able to be accessed by many simultaneously, the ability to uphold this obligation requires monitoring audit files to ensure that electronic "straying" doesn't happen, and if it does occur, it is addressed immediately. There is a human side of computing and IT: for every system created to ensure the security of health data and information, there is someone who can find a way around it and break into the system. New laws and policies regarding insurance and the confidentiality of patient information, such as the HIPAA, create new challenges for the use, maintenance, and sharing of privileged health information. For an industry that is steeped in the creation and use of paper documentation and medical records, it continues to be a difficult leap into the virtual world of EHRs. Textbox 8-5 provides an example of a breach of privacy and the consequences.

TEXTBOX 8-5. BREACH OF PATIENT PRIVACY

In August 2014, Dr. Rick Sacra, a physician from Boston, contracted Ebola while volunteering to provide aid and medical care during the Ebola outbreak in Liberia. He was brought back to the U.S. for treatment at Omaha's Nebraska Medical Center in early September and subsequently recovered (Pollack, 2014). During a routine patient privacy audit, the hospital concluded that two employees had inappropriately accessed his medical records. The hospital released a statement which read, in part and was reported by a local television station:

"…we discovered that two med center employees inappropriately accessed the record of Ebola patient Dr. Rick Sacra. This is a violation of HIPAA regulations… Based on the results of the investigation conducted, two employees no longer work for the organization and other corrective action has been taken. In accordance with HIPAA regulations, Dr. Sacra was notified in person and in writing before his departure from the hospital."

Source: WOWT NBC Omaha, 2014.

In cases like this, these individuals did not hold a job or perform a role in which they had any legitimate need to know the clinical information that they had accessed about Dr. Sacra. It is not clear what other action has been taken against these two individuals. As a HIPAA privacy rule violation, complaints are reported to the OCR in the DHHS, and under the new security rules the risk assessment had to be undertaken. It is not yet clear, however, what action the OCR has or will take in this case. Additional action may be taken on the basis of their findings.

HIPAA privacy rules violations are considered misdemeanors, if there was no "evidence of malicious intent [and]…are punishable by a maximum fine of $50,000 and/or imprisonment for up to 1 year. But defendants who harbored ill will or used false pretense in obtaining or disclosing individually identifiable health information may face felony charges instead, which are punishable with a maximum fine of $100,000 and 5-year prison terms" (Seitz, 2010, p. 746).

As this demonstrates, easy access to medical records information often creates a situation where the curiosity of individuals clouds their judgment, resulting in very real punishments.

OPPORTUNITIES FOR RESEARCH ON HEALTH CARE PROFESSIONALS

Technological advances in U.S. health care will continue to be spurred by the HITECH Act and consumer demands for increased transparency and transferability of data across the spectrum of care. In addition, big data, data mining, and analytics will become increasingly important in policy development, and planning, organizing, and evaluating delivery of care. Many of the resources used in writing this chapter also include extensive research holdings and data sets that are available to students and academic researchers. Herewith is a partial listing of these resources.

- Agency for Healthcare Research and Quality Health Information Tools and Resources;
- American Hospital Association;
- Centers for Medicare and Medicaid Electronic Health Records Incentive Programs;
- ECRI Institute; and,
- U.S. Department of Health and Human Services Health Resources and Services Administration (HRSA) Health Information Technology.

You will have an abundance of information at your fingertips at any one of these websites.

CONCLUSION

Health care information technology (HIT) is having an increasingly large impact on the health care industry and therefore on the health care manager. Health care costs in the U.S. have risen, while quality has not. This situation within the global economy is unsatisfactory to both the public and private sectors. In what has traditionally been seen as a high-touch industry, the promise of increased clinical quality and cost-effectiveness through the use of high tech health information systems has become a significant and urgent goal. As the adoption of clinical systems increases, so does the need for more sophisticated knowledge about them. Effectively operating in this new environment will require the successful manager to be comfortable with using and taking advantage of the benefits of the use of HIT and carefully manage its risks. Above all, the successful manager must always remember that the focus of HIT cannot be only about the gadgets and high tech toys, but on improving the health care of patients and populations served by the health care organization.

This chapter has provided the basics around the key health information systems used by health care managers and the significance of and challenges to adoption of the electronic health record (EHR). The future of HIT creates a vision of seamless movement of clinical information to wherever and whenever it is needed for patient care. While achieving this vision once seemed almost impossible, recent quality and cost concerns, as well as the impetus provided by the federal government and other influential bodies, suggest that it is essential and inevitable. This inevitability will require new skills of and offer new opportunities for health care managers.

DISCUSSION QUESTIONS

1. Explain how the delivery of health care services can benefit from health information systems, and provide two examples.

2. What two pressures on the health care industry, the first in the 1990s and the second in the 2000s, conclude that electronic medical records are essential?

3. Jefferson Hospital has recently implemented computerized provider order entry (CPOE). What EMRAM stage are they in, and what projects might Jefferson undertake next to progress its EMR implementation?

4. Identify and describe the four primary barriers to health care information systems adoption.

5. As a health care manager, it is critical that your employees value and preserve the privacy of patient information. What measures might you put into place to encourage and monitor this?

6. What are the differences between EMRs and EHRs? What challenges have they presented for health care managers? And, what challenges does the future proffer?

7. What are the implications of the recent changes to HIPAA with regard to protecting PHI?

8. Using one of the data resources provided by your instructor, identify what stage of EMRAM U.S. hospitals are in for 2015 Q4. What suggestions for improvement can you make based on this information?

9. A large (100) physician cardiology group has decided it is time to move to a new EHR. As the practice manager, what key features should you be looking for and how will you integrate this into the practice? Keeping in mind the objections the physicians might throw at you during the monthly practice meeting, create a pitch to the managing partners for the system you think would work best for the practice. Assuming the partners approve, what is your plan to implement the new system? Provide timelines, deliverables, who is responsible for what step, as well as a staff training plan.

Cases in Chapter 18 that are related to this chapter include:

- Building a Better MIS-Trap
- The "Easy" Software Upgrade at Delmar Ortho

Case study guides are available in the online Instructor's Materials.

REFERENCES

Adler-Milstein, J., DesRoches, C. M., Furukawa, M. F., Worzala, C., Charles, D., Kralovec, P.,... & Jha, A. K. (2014). More than half of US hospitals have at least a basic EHR, but Stage 2 criteria remain challenging for most. *Health Affairs, 33*(9), 1664–1671.

The Advisory Board Company. (2014, March 14). Hospitals rank their favorite EHR systems. *The Daily Briefing: News for Health Care Executives.* Retrieved from http://www.advisory.com/daily -briefing/2014/03/14/hospitals-rank-their-favorite-ehr-systems

American College of Physicians (ACP). (2013, March 5). *Survey of clinicians: User satisfaction with electronic health records has decreased since 2010.* Retrieved from https://www.acponline.org /newsroom/ehrs_survey.htm

American Hospital Association (AHA). (2015, February 11). *Getting meaningful use right.* Retrieved from http://www.aha.org/content/14/fs-meaningfuluse.pdf

American Medical Association (AMA). (n.d.). *Preparing for conversion from ICD-9 to ICD-10: What you need to be doing today.* Retrieved from http://www.sccma-mcms.org/Portals/19/assets/docs /ICD10PreparingForConversion.pdf

American Medical Association (AMA). (2014, October 14). *AMA provides blueprint to improve the meaningful use program.* Retrieved from http://www.ama-assn.org/ama/pub/news /news/2014/2014-10-14-ama-blueprint-improve-meaningful-use.page

Andres, M. (2015, May 19). Telemedicine under attack as abortion rights supporters seek more options for women. *Kaiser Health News.* Retrieved from http://khn.org/news/telemedicine-under-attack -as-abortion-rights-supporters-seek-more-options-for-women/

APA Practice Organization. (2013, March 14). *HIPAA Final Rule highlights for practitioners.* Retrieved from http://www.apapracticecentral.org/update/2013/03-14/final-rule.aspx

Armstrong, A. W., Kwong, M. W., Ledo, L., Nesbitt, T. S., & Shewry, S. L. (2011, December). Practice models and challenges in teledermatology: A study of collective experiences from teledermatologists. *PLoS One, 6*(12), 1–6.

Bailey, B. (2015, August 3). Software turns smartphones into tools for medical research. *Denver Post.* Retrieved from http://www.denverpost.com/business/ci_28568871/software-turns-smartphones-into-tools-medical-research

Balgrosky, J. A. (2015). *Essentials of health information systems and technology.* Burlington, MA: Jones & Bartlett Learning.

Barris, M. (2015, June 12). McNeil Consumer Healthcare's app helps users manage cold symptoms. *Mobile Marketer.* Retrieved from http://www.mobilemarketer.com/cms/news/software -technology/20647.html?utm_content=buffer77092&utm_medium=social&utm _source=linkedin.com&utm_campaign=buffer

Bolgar, C. (2014, October 20). *Work practice on the move.* Retrieved from http://knowledge.zurich.com/ risk-interconnectivity/work-practices-on-the-move/

Buntin, M. B., Jain, S. H., & Blumenthal, D. (2010). Health information technology: Laying the infrastructure for national health reform. *Health Affairs, 29*(6), 1214–1219.

Centers for Disease Control and Prevention (CDC). (2012, October 11). *Meaningful use.* Retrieved from http://www.cdc.gov/ehrmeaningfuluse/introduction.html

Centers for Medicare and Medicaid Services (CMS). (2009). *American Recovery and Reinvestment Act of 2009, HITECH.* Retrieved from http://www.cms.gov/Recovery/Downloads/CMS-2009-0117 -0002.pdf

Centers for Medicare and Medicaid Services (CMS). (2013). *HIPAA – general information.* Retrieved from http://www.cms.gov/Regulations-and-Guidance/HIPAA-Administrative-Simplification/HIPAAGenInfo/index.html?redirect=/HIPAAGenInfo/01_Overview.asp

Centers for Medicare and Medicaid Services (CMS). (2014, December). *Telehealth services.* Retrieved from http://www.cms.gov/Outreach-and-Education/Medicare-Learning-Network-MLN/MLNProducts/downloads/TelehealthSrvcsfctsht.pdf

Chiplin, A. J., & Lilly, B. J. (2013, Spring). Medicare's future: Letting the Affordable Care Act work, while learning from the past. *NAELA Journal 9*(1), 25–66.

Chuang, I. (2014, July). Transforming the EHR into a knowledge platform to ensure improved health and healthcare. *Netsmart.* Retrieved from http://www.ntst.com/demos_white-papers_seminars/white_papers_live/WP_Ian_Chuang_Knowledge_Flow-Whitepaper_080714.pdf

Chuang, T. (2015, February 5). Anthem breach a wake-up call to health care industry. *The Denver Post.* Retrieved from http://www.denverpost.com/business/ci_27469493/anthem-breach-wake-up-call-health-care-industry

Dimitropoulos, L. (2014, October 19). *Health IT research priorities to support the health care delivery system of the future.* Rockville, MD: Agency for Healthcare Research and Quality. Retrieved from https://healthit.ahrq.gov/sites/default/files/docs/citation/health-it-research-priorities-to-support-health-care-delivery-system-of-future.pdf

ECG Management Consultants. (2014). *The EHR replacement dilemma.* Retrieved from http://s3.amazonaws.com/rdcms-himss/files/production/public/FileDownloads/2014-04-09%20ECG%20Managment%20Consultants%20EHR_System_Replacement.pdf

ECRI Institute. (2015, April). *Top 10 patient safety concerns for healthcare organizations.* Retrieved from https://www.ecri.org/components/hrc/pages/RMRep0414_Focus.aspx

Fallows, J. (2014, March 24). The use and misuse of information technology in health care: Several doctors reply. *The Atlantic.* Retrieved from http://www.theatlantic.com/health/archive/2014/03/the-use-and-misuse-of-information-technology-in-health-care-several-doctors-reply/284601/

Fernholz, T. (2014, February 25). More people around the world have cell phones than ever had land lines. *Quartz.* Retrieved from http://qz.com/179897/more-people-around-the-world-have-cell-phones-than-ever-had-land-lines/

Fishman, L. E. (2015, March 20). *Statement on meaningful use.* [Press release, American Hospital Association]. Retrieved from http://www.aha.org/presscenter/pressrel/2015/150320-pr-meaningfuluse.shtml

Friedberg, M. W., Chen, P. G., Van Busum, K. R., Aunon, F., Pham, C., Caloyeras, J.,… & Tutty, M. (2013). *Factors affecting physician professional satisfaction and their implications for patient care, health systems, and health policy.* Santa Monica, CA: RAND Corporation. Retrieved from http://www.rand.org/content/dam/rand/pubs/research_reports/RR400/RR439/RAND_RR439.sum.pdf

Galewitz, P. (2015, June 23). Medicare slow to adopt telemedicine due to cost concerns. *Kaiser Health News.* Retrieved from http://khn.org/news/medicare-slow-to-adopt-telemedicine-due-to-cost-concerns/

Garets, D., & Davis, M. (2006). *Electronic medical records vs. electronic health records: Yes, there is a difference.* A HIMSS Analytics white paper. Retrieved from http://s3.amazonaws.com/rdcms-himss/files/production/public/HIMSSorg/Content/files/WP_EMR_EHR.pdf

Garrett, P., & Seidman, J. (2011, January 4). *EMR vs EHR—what is the difference?* Retrieved from http://www.healthit.gov/buzz-blog/electronic-health-and-medical-records/emr-vs-ehr-difference/

Gellert, G. A., Ramirez, R., & Webster, S. L. (2015). The rise of the medical scribe industry: Implications for the advancement of electronic health records. *Journal of the American Medical Association, 313*(13), 1315–1316.

Goodnough, A. (2015, April 11). Texas medical panel votes to limit telemedicine practices in the state. *New York Times.* Retrieved from http://www.nytimes.com/2015/04/11/us/texas-medical-panel-votes-to-limit-telemedicine-practices-in-state.html?_r=0

Healthcare Information and Management Systems Society (HIMSS). (n.d.). *About HIMSS.* Retrieved from http://www.himss.org/ASP/aboutHIMSSHOme.asp

Healthcare Information and Management Systems Society (HIMSS). (2013, April 5). *What is interoperability?* Retrieved from http://www.himss.org/library/interoperability-standards/what-is-interoperability

Healthcare Information and Management Systems Society (HIMSS). (2014, October 10). *Pending telehealth bills in the 113th Congress.* Retrieved from http://www.himss.org/News/NewsDetail.aspx?ItemNumber=33937

Healthcare Information and Management Systems Society (HIMSS). (2015, March 2015). *Meaningful use stage 3 released.* Retrieved from http://www.himss.org/News/NewsDetail.aspx?ItemNumber=41038

Healthcare Information and Management Systems Society (HIMSS) and HIMSS Analytics. (2013). *2013 annual report of the U.S. hospital IT market.* Chicago, IL: HIMSS.

HealthIT. (2013, January 15). *EHR incentive programs.* Retrieved from http://www.healthit.gov/providers-professionals/ehr-incentive-programs

HealthIT. (2015, February 6). *Meaningful use definition & objectives.* Retrieved from http://www.healthit.gov/providers-professionals/meaningful-use-definition-objectives

HIMSS Analytics. (2014, December). *2014 mobile devices study.* Retrieved from http://www.himssanalytics.org/research/essentials-brief-mobile-devices-study

HIMSS Analytics. (2015a). *Current EMRAM scores.* Retrieved from https://app.himssanalytics.org/emram/scoreTrends.aspx

HIMSS Analytics. (2015b). *HIMSS Analytic EMR Adoption Model^{SM} (EMRAM).* Retrieved from http://www.himssanalytics.org/research/emram-stage-criteria

Institute of Medicine (IOM). (2001). *Crossing the quality chasm: A new health system for the 21st century.* Washington, DC: National Academies Press.

Institute of Medicine (IOM). (2013a). *Best care at lower cost: The path to continuously learning health care in America.* Washington, DC: National Academies Press.

Institute of Medicine (IOM). (2013b). *What's possible for health care?* [Infographic.] Retrieved from http://www.iom.edu/~/media/Files/Report%20Files/2012/Best-Care/bestcare_infographic.png

Institute of Medicine (IOM). (2014a). *Capturing social and behavioral domains in electronic health records. Phase 1.* Washington, DC: National Academies Press.

Institute of Medicine (IOM). (2014b). *Capturing social and behavioral domains in electronic health records. Phase 2.* Washington, DC: National Academies Press.

Jenkins, M. K. (2013, November). "The dirty dozen" healthcare IT issues. *AAOS Now.* Retrieved from http://www.aaos.org/news/aaosnow/nov13/managing9.asp

Jones, R-C. (2015, January 29). Office puts chips under staff's skin. *BBC.* Retrieved from http://www.bbc.com/news/technology-31042477

Kaiser Permanente. (2015). *Fast facts about Kaiser Permanente*. Retrieved from http://share.kaiserpermanente.org/article/fast-facts-about-kaiser-permanente/

Kane, C. K., & Emmons, D. W. (2013). *New data on physician practice arrangements: private practice remains strong despite shifts toward hospital employment*. Chicago, IL: American Medical Association. Retrieved from http://www.nmms.org/sites/default/files/images/2013_9_23_ama_survey_prp-physician-practice-arrangements.pdf

Kohn, J. T., Corrigan, J. M., & Donaldson, M. S. (Eds.). (2000). *To err is human: Building a safer health system*. Washington, DC: National Academies Press.

LeRouge, C., & Garfield, M. J. (2013). Crossing the telemedicine chasm: Have the U.S. barriers to widespread adoption to telemedicine been significantly reduced? *International Journal of Environmental Research and Public Health, 10*, 6472–6484.

Liebhaber, A., & Grossman, J. M. (2007, August). *Physicians moving to mid-sized, single-specialty practices*. Center for Studying Health System Change, Tracking Report No. 18. Retrieved from http://www.hschange.com/CONTENT/941/#ib1

Mathews, A. W. (2010, March 2). Beep! It's your medicine nagging you. *Wall Street Journal*, p. D1. Retrieved from http://www.wsj.com/articles/SB10001424052748703431604575095771390040944

May, H. (2013, May 10). Why electronic medical records are failing to meet expectations. [Blog post]. Retrieved from http://rockhealth.com/2013/05/why-electronic-medical-records-are-failing-to-meet-expectations/

Mayo Clinic. (September 27, 2012). Capsule endoscopy. Retrieved from http://www.mayoclinic.org/tests-procedures/capsule-endoscopy/basics/definition/prc-20012773

McCann, E. (2014, February 28). Blackbook names best of the best EHRs. *Healthcare IT News*. Retrieved from http://www.healthcareitnews.com/news/black-book-names-best-best-ehrs

McGee, M. K. (2010, March 10). Kaiser Permanente finishes EMR rollout. *Information Week*. Retrieved from http://www.informationweek.com/healthcare/electronic-health-records/kaiser-permanente-finishes-emr-rollout/d/d-id/1087491?

McNickle, M. (2012, October 31). 10 wearable health tech devices to watch. *Information Week*. Retrieved from http://www.informationweek.com/mobile/10-wearable-health-tech-devices-to-watch/d/d-id/1107148?print=yes

Medical Economics. (2014, October 9). Best EHR systems of 2014: Physicians rank five key performance areas. *Medical Economics*. Retrieved from http://medicaleconomics.modernmedicine.com/medical-economics/content/tags/2014-ehr-scorecard/best-ehr-systems-2014-physicians-rank-five-key-per?page=full

Modernizing Medicine. (2014, April). *Should you switch to a new electronic medical record (EMR) system?* Retrieved from https://www.modmed.com/whitepaper-should-you-switch-to-a-new-electronic-medical-record-emr-system/

Mohamoud, S., Byrne, C., & Samarth, A. (2009, October). *Implementation of health information technology in long-term care settings: Finding from the AHRQ health IT portfolio*. Rockville MD: Agency for Healthcare Research and Quality. Retrieved from http://library.ahima.org/xpedio/groups/public/documents/government/bok1_045572.pdf

Murphy, K. (2013, January 29). Stages of meaningful use, EMR adoption: HIMSS Analytics Q&A. *EHR Intelligence*. Retrieved from https://ehrintelligence.com/2013/01/29/stages-of-meaningful-use-emr-adoption-himss-analytics-qa/

National Conference of State Legislatures (NCSL). (2015, April 23). *2015 security breach legislation.* Retrieved from http://www.ncsl.org/research/telecommunications-and-information-technology/2015 -security-breach-legislation.aspx

Office of the Inspector General (OIG). (2014). *Challenge 6: The meaningful and secure exchange and use of electronic health information.* Retrieved from http://oig.hhs.gov/reports-and-publications/top -challenges/2014/challenge06.asp

Office of the National Coordinator for Health Information Technology (ONC). (2014a). *Connecting health and care for the nation: A 10-year vision to achieve an interoperable health IT infrastructure.* Retrieved from http://healthit.gov/sites/default/files/ONC10yearInteroperabilityConceptPaper.pdf

Office of the National Coordinator for Health Information Technology (ONC). (2014b). *Connecting health and care for the nation: A shared nationwide interoperability roadmap. Draft version 1.0.* Retrieved from http://www.healthit.gov/sites/default/files/nationwide-interoperability-roadmap -draft-version-1.0.pdf

Office of the National Coordinator for Health Information Technology (ONC). (2014c). *Report to Congress: Update on the adoption of health information technology and related efforts to facilitate the electronic use and exchange of health information.* Retrieved from http://www.healthit.gov /sites/default/files/rtc_adoption_and_exchange9302014.pdf

Patel, J. J. (2015). Writing the wrong. *JAMA, 314*(7), 671–672.

Pollack, A. (2014, September 11). Aid worker recovering from Ebola. *New York Times.* Retrieved from http://www.nytimes.com/2014/09/12/us/aid-worker-recovering-from-ebola.html

PRWeb. (2013, May 30). "The year of the big EHR switch" confirms physicians favor iPad and mobile applications. *PRWeb.* Retrieved from http://www.prweb.com/releases/2013/5/prweb10553455 .htm

PwC Health Research Institute. (2014, December). *Top health industry issues of 2015: Outlines of a market emerge.* Retrieved from http://www.pwc.com/en_US/us/health-industries/top-health -industry-issues/assets/pwc-hri-top-healthcare-issues-2015.pdf

Ranney, M. (2015, February 9). *mhealth and wearables: Is the info getting to the right place?* Retrieved from http://www.himss.org/News/NewsDetail.aspx?ItemNumber=38691

Rice, S. (2014, April 22). Health IT issues, care-coordination worries top new ECRI safety list. *Modern Healthcare.* Retrieved from http://www.modernhealthcare.com/article/20140422 /NEWS/304229954

Rieland, R. (2014, January 6). 7 medical advances to watch in 2014. *Smithsonian Magazine.* Retrieved from http://www.smithsonianmag.com/innovation/7-medical-advances-to-watch-in -2014-180948286/?no-ist

Robertson, J. (2011, August 21). New data spill shows risk of online health records. *Yahoo News.* Retrieved from http://news.yahoo.com/data-spill-shows-risk-online-health-records-120743449 .html

Rosenfeld, K. H. (2013). *Streamlining medical image access and sharing: Integrating image workflow and patient referrals.* An eHealth Technologies white paper. Retrieved from http://www.interoperabilityshowcase .org/himssme14/documents/eHealthTechnologiesWhitePaperforInteropShowcase.pdf

Runy, L. A. (2009, November). IT challenges in physician practice management. *H&HN: Hospitals & Health Networks, 83*(11), 37–43.

SearchHealthIT. (n.d.). *ICD-9-CM (International Classification of Diseases, Ninth Revision, Clinical Modification) definition*. Retrieved from http://searchhealthit.techtarget.com/definition/ICD-9-CM

Seitz, E. (2010). Privacy (or piracy) of medical records: HIPAA and its enforcement. *Journal of the National Medical Association, 102*(8), 745–748.

SK&A. (2015). *Physician office usage of electronic medical records software*. Irvine, CA: Author. Retrieved from http://www.skainfo.com/health_care_market_reports/EMR_Electronic_Medical_Records.pdf

Stack, S. J. (2014, December 17). *AMA responds to CMS regarding meaningful use penalties for eligible professionals*. [Press release, American Medical Association]. Retrieved from http://www.ama-assn.org/ama/pub/news/news/2014/2014-12-17-cms-meaningful-use-penalties.page

Stack, S. J. (2015a, July 6). CMS to make ICD-10 transition less disruptive for physicians. *AMA Wire*. Retrieved from http://www.ama-assn.org/ama/ama-wire/post/cms-icd-10-transition-less-disruptive-physicians

Stack, S. J. (2015b, July 21). Physicians, we hear you: EHR meaningful use isn't meaningful. *AMA Wire*. Retrieved from http://www.ama-assn.org/ama/ama-wire/post/physicians-hear-ehr-meaningful-use-isnt-meaningful

Tieche, M., FitzGerald, B., & Martin, T. (2014, December). *2014 imaging technology study*. Chicago, IL: HIMSS Analytics.

U.S. Department of Health and Human Services (DHHS). (n.d.) The great pandemic: The United States in 1918–1919. Retrieved from http://www.flu.gov/pandemic/history/1918/

U.S. Department of Health and Human Services (DHHS). (2003). *Summary of the HIPAA privacy rule*. Office for Civil Rights Privacy Brief. Retrieved from http://www.hhs.gov/ocr/privacy/hipaa/understanding/summary/privacysummary.pdf

U.S. Department of Health and Human Services (DHHS). (2015, April 14). *Health information privacy: Enforcement highlights*. Retrieved from http://www.hhs.gov/ocr/privacy/hipaa/enforcement/highlights/

Vijavan, J. (2015, March 20). Premera hack: What criminals can do with your healthcare data. *The Christian Science Monitor*. Retrieved from http://www.csmonitor.com/World/Passcode/2015/0320/Premera-hack-What-criminals-can-do-with-your-healthcare-data

The White House, Office of the Press Secretary. (2015, February 13). *Executive order—promoting private sector cybersecurity information sharing*. [Press release]. Retrieved from https://www.whitehouse.gov/the-press-office/2015/02/13/executive-order-promoting-private-sector-cybersecurity-information-shari

White, J. (2014, December 9). 10 healthcare technology hazards for 2015. *Healthcare News & Insights*. Retrieved from http://www.healthcarebusinesstech.com/2015-healthcare-technology/

World Health Organization (WHO). (n.d.) *E-health*. Retrieved from http://www.who.int/trade/glossary/story021/en/

WOWT NBC Omaha. (2014, September 26). Hospital employees fired for accessing Sacra's medical record. Retrieved from http://www.wowt.com/home/headlines/Two-Med-Center-Employees-Fired-For-Accessing-Dr-Sacras-File-277242411.html

Financing Health Care and Health Insurance

Nancy H. Shanks

LEARNING OBJECTIVES

By the end of this chapter, the student will be able to:

- Analyze health care spending, how it has grown, and whether it is expected to continue to grow;
- Critique the concepts of health care financing and payment for health care;
- Provide an overview of how health insurance works;
- Outline a brief history of how health insurance has evolved;
- Assess the terms and characteristics of health insurance;
- Compare and contrast the different types of private health insurance;
- Differentiate the types of social insurance;
- Evaluate data on health insurance coverage and lack thereof;
- Characterize the uninsured;
- Assess health care reform and changes to insurance resulting from it;
- Explain the implications of health care financing and health insurance for management; and
- Investigate sources of research on finance and health insurance.

INTRODUCTION

As health care managers, there are a number of concerns relating to the overall costs of health care, how it is financed, how health insurance works, and where the gaps in insurance are. It is critical for managers to understand these issues and learn how to better manage these areas.

National Health Spending

Health care spending in the U.S. has grown over the last 50 years at what has been characterized as an alarming rate. While the increases have not returned to the double-digit levels that existed in the 1980s and early 1990s, the Centers for Medicare and Medicaid Services (CMS) are predicting the expansion in national health care spending will continue. "During 2009–11 per capita national health spending grew about 3 percent annually, compared to an average of 5.9 percent annually during the previous ten years" (Ryu, Gibson, McKellar, & Chernew, 2013, p. 835). The reduction in the rate of growth has been attributed to several factors, including a slowing of the economic recovery, private sector benefit changes that increased cost sharing by employees, and the "effects of sequestration" (Ryu et al., 2013; Sisko et al., 2014). Even with this slackening, health care expenditures in the U.S. were $2.9 trillion in 2013 (Hartman, Martin, Lassman, Catlin, & the National Health Expenditure Accounts Team, 2015). National Health Expenditures (NHE) for 2015 were projected to reach $3.2 trillion and to account for 17.6% of gross domestic product (GDP), or $9,983 per capita (Sisko et al., 2014).

Expenditures for health care were directed to a variety of services, as shown in Table 9-1. Five areas accounted for more than three-quarters of those expenditures in 2013. Hospital care accounted for 32.1%; physician and clinical services represented another

TABLE 9-1 2013 National Health Spending by Type of Expenditure

Expenditure Type	Amount (in billions)
Hospital care	936.9
Physician and clinical services	586.7
Other professional, dental, and personal care services	191.2
Other health, residential and personal care*	148.2
Prescription drugs	271.1
Durable medical equipment and other nondurable medical products	98.9
Nursing home and home health care	235.6
Government administration	37.0
Net cost of health insurance	173.6
Public health activities	75.4
Research	43.6
Structures and equipment	117.9
TOTAL	$2,919.1

Source: CMS, 2014a.

*Includes health-related spending for Children's Health Insurance Program (CHIP) Titles XIX and XXI, Department of Defense, and Department of Veterans Affairs.

20.1%; other professional, dental, and personal care services costs were 6.5%; prescription drug costs made up 9.3%; and nursing home and home health care comprised 8.1% (CMS, 2014a).

In addition, CMS has also projected health care spending will reach $5.2 trillion and will account for 19.3% of GDP by 2023 (Sisko et al., 2014); this increase is projected "at an average rate of 5.8 percent per year" for 2014–2024 (CMS, 2015b, para. 1). This will equate to an estimated $14,944 per capita by 2023. In sharp contrast, national health expenditures were $247.3 billion in 1980 and accounted for only 8.9% of GDP (Levit et al., 1997). Chernew, Hirth, and Cutler (2009) argue that the continued growth in health care spending crowds out other areas and limits the resources available for other non-health-related types of goods and services, and efforts are needed to slow the rate of health care spending. Whether the slowing of national health expenditures will continue is up for debate. In fact, Dranove, Garthwaite, and Ody (2014) state

> the economic slowdown explained approximately 70 percent of the slowdown in health spending growth for the people in our sample. This suggests that the recent decline is not primarily the result of structural changes in the health sector or of components of the Affordable Care Act, and that—absent other changes in the health care system—an economic recovery will result in increased health spending. (p. 1399)

The most recent data from the U.S. Census Bureau Quarterly Services Survey seem to indicate this has begun to happen, as "health spending was 7.3% higher in the first quarter of 2015 than in the first quarter of last year. Hospital spending increased 9.2%" (Altman, 2015d, para. 2). This was attributed to more people having coverage and utilizing more services.

Paying for Health Care

Payments to cover these health care expenditures are derived from a variety of sources. These include individuals who pay out of pocket, private health insurance of a variety of types, other private funds, and public insurance programs. These categories are described below.

- **Out-of-pocket payments** include payments by individuals who buy individual insurance policies, pay for services themselves, and/or pay for part of those services through copayments and/or deductibles.
- **Private health insurance** includes payments made by individuals and/or their employers for health insurance premiums, which in turn cover the costs of payments made by various health plans, including indemnity plans, preferred provider organization plans (PPOs), point-of-service plans (POSs), health maintenance

organizations (HMOs), and catastrophic plans, such as high-deductible health plans (HDHPs).

- **Public health insurance** sources include funding from federal, state, and local government programs, including, among others, Medicare, Medicaid, the Children's Health Insurance Program (CHIP), and the Military Health System.
- Investment includes funding for research, as well as structures and equipment.

The breakdown of expenditures by these sources of funding for 2013 is shown in Figure 9-1. These data show the close to 50% of expenditures are derived from public sources.

INTRODUCTION TO HEALTH INSURANCE

As with other types of insurance, the intent of health insurance is to provide protection should a covered individual experience a health event, adverse or otherwise, that requires treatment. **Risk** is the money that might be lost due to insuring people who utilize health care services. Insurance transfers the risk from one person to many people by pooling the risk across a large number of subscribers or members. When individuals purchase coverage, they join with others and pool their resources to protect against losses. In so doing, they pool the potential risk for losses that might be experienced and the cost of risk is shared among the many. This is called **cost-sharing**. The larger number of healthy people in the pool, the lower the risk. The greater number of sick people in the pool, the greater the risk. Thus, two key concepts in insurance are:

- **risk** is transferred from the individual to the group,
- with **cost sharing** of any covered losses incurred by the group members.

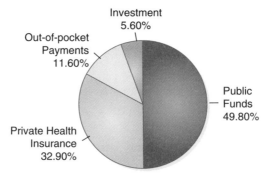

FIGURE 9-1 National Health Expenditures by Source of Funds, 2013
CMS, 2014a.

Fifty years ago, health insurance coverage was typically purchased on an individual basis, much like car insurance. Individuals bought policies to protect themselves and their families against catastrophic illness. This was at a time when health care was not as expensive as it is today and individuals paid for routine types of care out of pocket, thereby using health insurance to cover catastrophic expenditures and to protect against income loss. The latter, while technically a form of health insurance, is what we now think of as disability income insurance coverage.

During the second half of the 20th century, the demand for and use of health insurance changed in significant ways. Health insurance products have also changed in response to that demand. Of particular importance were the following:

- Most health insurance coverage included a comprehensive set of health care benefits, most frequently including hospital stays and physician care, as well as other types of services and benefits;
- Both the public and private sectors began to have expanded and increasingly important roles in the provision of health insurance coverage;
- Group health insurance policies began to be offered as an employee benefit, with the purchasing of coverage being handled by companies and fewer people taking out individual insurance policies;
- Mechanisms for reimbursing health care providers have expanded from solely paying on the basis of costs to reimbursing on a prepaid basis; and
- The cost of health care began to rise.

BRIEF HISTORY OF HEALTH INSURANCE

During the Great Depression of the 1930s, there were discussions about creating a national health insurance policy that would provide a system of universal health insurance coverage in the United States. While the proposal had some proponents, the American Medical Association (AMA) and others opposed the move. With the subsequent U.S. involvement in World War II, the funding required for such a system was not available. While there continued to be interest in national health insurance after the war, the concept of a universal health insurance mechanism eventually became synonymous with "socialized medicine" and all the negative associations with Communism during the cold war of the 1950s. The end result was a health insurance system rooted in the private sector (Starr, 1982).

Although the expansionist social policies of President Lyndon B. Johnson's Great Society in the 1960s are credited with development of the largest social health insurance programs this country has ever known, now known as Medicare and Medicaid, the seeds of these programs were actually sown by Congress during the Eisenhower administration in the 1950s. At a time when private health insurance coverage was increasingly being provided for workers by their employers, the elderly had virtually no such coverage and yet were the group in society with the largest health costs and often the most limited financial resources. The ultimate passage of the Kerr-Mills Act by Congress in 1960 provided for federal matching grants to the states for a new category of "medically indigent" individuals, but still did not cover elders other than those who had become poor. However, this piece of legislation played a pivotal role as the precursor to Medicaid.

It was actually President John F. Kennedy, backed by senior interest groups and supported by labor unions and nurses, who proposed the first Medicare bill to Congress in 1962 in keeping with his strong belief in the need for federal health care for the elderly. Although this measure was defeated by legislative opponents in the Senate, it did serve to raise public awareness and support and set the stage for President Johnson to utilize his considerable political popularity, legislative liaisons, and persuasiveness in small groups (such as the leadership of the AMA) to lead the charge for passage of the Medicare and Medicaid legislation in 1965.

Over time, these public programs have been expanded to bring more eligible individuals into coverage, have added types of benefits, and have changed in a variety of other ways. One such major expansion took place with the creation of the Children's Health Insurance Program in 1997, which provides health insurance coverage to children in low-income families. The most recent, and some would argue the second most historic, change in health insurance occurred in March 2010 with the enactment of the **Patient Protection and Affordable Care Act**, commonly referred to as the **Affordable Care Act, ACA** or Obamacare. The primary intent of this health care reform legislation was to expand access to care by providing increased health insurance coverage and bringing the uninsured into coverage. This was to be achieved via an "individual mandate" that by 2014 required "most legal residents of the United States to obtain health insurance." The law also mandated significant changes in health insurance practices for both the public and private sectors (Iglehart, 2010a, 2010b). The ACA is described in greater depth later in the chapter.

The federal government also has an extensive program for providing health care to active-duty military personnel, veterans, and their dependents. The military medical system is one of the most advanced in the world and has come to serve as a model in many ways.

Private health care coverage has evolved significantly in the last 60 to 70 years, as well. Employers began to provide health insurance as an employee benefit, electing to offer the benefit in lieu of providing wage increases to employees. This was primarily the result of collective bargaining agreements, where unions negotiated increased benefits for workers and their families. Over time, private health insurance has evolved from being primarily conventional indemnity insurance to various types of prepaid and managed care plans. Today, a variety of different types of coverage are used in the industry.

CHARACTERISTICS OF HEALTH INSURANCE

This section discusses some important aspects of health insurance, including how health care is financed, how costs are controlled, and the types of benefits offered.

Forms of Payment

Two forms of payment provide the basis for all types of health insurance coverage. These are:

- **Fee-for-service**—This approach was developed by Blue Cross Blue Shield plans and is based on the idea of an insured individual purchasing coverage of a set of benefits, utilizing individual medical services, and paying the health care provider for the services rendered. The provider is paid either by the insurer or out of pocket by the insured, who, in turn, is reimbursed by the insurer. Typically, the insured must meet deductibles and make copayments for their care.
- **Prepayment**—In this approach, an insured individual pays a fixed, prespecified amount in exchange for services. Routine types of care are typically covered in full, with small copayments for selected services (e.g., prescriptions).

Cost Sharing

Most insurance policies require insured individuals to bear some of the cost of care out of pocket. Cost sharing may take different forms but may include some or all of the following:

- **Copayments**—are costs that are borne by the insured individual at the time of service. For example, a prescription medication or a physician office visit may require a $15 or $20 copay. Copayments are used in both fee-for-service and prepaid plans.
- **Deductibles**—are required levels of payments that the insured individual/family must meet before the insurer begins making its payments for care in a fee-for-service plan. Deductibles are regularly met at the beginning of each year and vary by policy type. They can range from relatively small amounts for traditional types of insurance to quite substantial amounts under high-deductible, catastrophic coverage plans.
- **Coinsurance**—Under a fee-for-service policy, insured individuals pay a portion of the cost of their care, while the insurer is responsible for the remaining costs. For example, the insured's coinsurance is often 20%, while the insurer pays 80%.

Policy Limitations

Often the insurance policy has various types of limitations—some that limit payments by the policy holder and some that limit how much total coverage the insurer will provide.

- **Maximum out-of-pocket expenditure**—This is an amount where the insured individual's cost sharing is capped. After reaching this point, the insurer will pick up 100% of the tab.
- **Lifetime limit**—This is the maximum amount that the policy will pay out over the lifetime of the insured individual. This type of limit usually only comes into play when there are catastrophic types of illnesses requiring very costly care. For example, in various types of transplants or spinal cord injuries, the treatment costs can escalate to hundreds of thousands of dollars. The limit can be $1 million or higher.

Types of Benefits

Different types of benefit packages can be purchased that offer varying types of coverage for individuals and families. These include:

- **Comprehensive policies**—These policies provide benefits that typically include physician and other types of outpatient visits, inpatient hospitals stays, outpatient surgery, medical testing and ancillary services, medical equipment, therapies, and other types of services. Prescription drugs are sometimes covered, as are rehabilitation services, hospice, and mental health care. Despite the name "comprehensive," most policies do not cover everything and thus have exclusions; in particular, most types of experimental treatments and long-term care are excluded.
- **Basic, major medical, or hospital-surgical policies**—Referred to by several different names, the benefits provided by these policies are limited to types of illness that require hospitalization. Benefits include inpatient hospital stays, surgery, associated tests and treatments, related physician services, and other expenses incurred during an illness. There usually are limits on hospital stays and caps on expenditures.
- **Catastrophic coverage policies**—Benefits under these policies are intended to cover extraordinary types of illness; policies typically carry very sizable deductibles ($15,000 or higher) and lifetime limits on coverage.
- **Disease-specific policies**—In these policies, the benefits cover only the specific disease(s) covered (e.g., a cancer care policy).

- **Medigap policies**—These policies provide supplemental coverage of certain benefits that are excluded from other types of policies (e.g., prescription drugs).
- **Long-term care insurance**—Coverage under these policies typically includes various types of assistance for in-home care, assisted living, skilled nursing, home, and other specialized care, such as in an Alzheimer's unit.

Other Concerns Regarding Health Insurance

There are a number of issues that are important when managers and/or individuals are making decisions about health care coverage. These include the following:

- **Access to vs. restrictions on care**—This pertains to whether access to care is limited or controlled for the insured individual. Under some insurance policies, there is unlimited access, while under others, access is restricted by a gatekeeper.
- **Moral hazard**—This concept refers to the idea that existence of insurance coverage provides an incentive for insured individuals to secure and use coverage. For example, a woman who knows she is going to become pregnant may be more likely to opt into coverage than a woman who is not expecting to have a need for this type of care.
- **Pre-existing conditions**—These are medical conditions that make a person a risk to an insurer, as the pre-existing condition may result in high expenditures. In the past, those who have had these types of conditions (e.g., cancer) have found it difficult or impossible to obtain coverage.
- **Buy-downs**—This is a situation that occurs with individual policies. "When insurers inform members of large premium hikes, they commonly suggest that the increase can be mitigated (or sometimes even eliminated) by switching to a lower-cost policy (which means a policy with higher deductibles and/or greater limits on benefits)" (Altman, 2010, para. 2).
- **Coordination of benefits (COB)** —This is important when someone has two insurance plans: for example, a husband and wife both have coverage at work *and* have a family insurance plan. Each company seeks to ensure it pays only that which it is obligated to pay.

The remaining sections of this chapter explore the different types of insurance coverage in greater depth. The chapter includes a discussion of the numbers and demographics of specific segments of the population who do and do not have health insurance coverage. Finally, the chapter concludes with a discussion of the implications for health care managers.

PRIVATE HEALTH INSURANCE COVERAGE

Each type of private health insurance is described briefly below. Additionally, consideration is given to the pluses and minuses of the type of insurance with respect to access to care, choice of providers, and cost.

Conventional Indemnity Insurance

Most indemnity insurance products are based on the fee-for-service model. When the insured individuals utilize health care services, they pay for those services and seek reimbursement from the insurer. Care is rendered by independent health care providers, without gatekeeping or other restrictions. Management of care only comes into play in elective admissions, which may require preauthorization. While this type of coverage used to be predominant in the health insurance industry, as shown in Table 9-2 later in this section, it now represents only a very small segment of the market. Additionally, Table 9-3 compares indemnity and other types of health plan coverages on a variety of characteristics which help to explain the loss of dominance of this type of coverage.

Managed Care Plans

Unlike indemnity plans, these health plans seek to manage cost, quality, and access to health services through control mechanisms on both patients and providers. These delivery systems attempt to integrate both the financing and provision of health care into one organization. The primary types include HMOs, PPOs, and POS plans and are described further below.

Health Maintenance Organizations (HMOs)

Individuals become members of the organization by paying a fixed prepayment amount. Once they become members, they are enrolled in the HMO. Enrollees are eligible to get care from the providers and facilities that are aligned with the HMO. Services are used at no charge, although minor copays are often required for prescription medications. Administration is centralized, with providers typically being reimbursed under a capitated rate. This means that providers are paid a set amount no matter how much care they need to provide. As described by Kongstvedt (2007), various types of contracting arrangements exist with providers, which may take the form of:

- **Closed-Panel HMO**—physicians practice only with the HMO, frequently in an HMO-owned health center;
- **Open-Panel HMO**—physicians practice within and outside the HMO;

- **Group Model HMO**—the HMO contracts with a multispecialty group practice to care for its enrollees;
- **Staff Model HMO**—groups of physicians are either salaried employees of the HMO or salaried employees of a professional group practice contracting exclusively with the HMO;
- **Independent Practice Association, or IPA Model**—the HMO contracts with an association of physicians practicing independently in their own offices; and
- **Network Model HMO**—the HMO contracts with several groups of physicians or with individual physicians or multispecialty medical clinics (physicians and hospitals) to provide a full range of medical services.

Preferred Provider Organizations (PPOs)

These plans reflect a combination of indemnity insurance and managed care options. In PPOs, insured individuals purchase coverage on a fee-for-service basis, with deductibles, copays, and coinsurances to be met. Care is managed in the sense that insured individuals pay less if care is obtained from a network of preferred providers with which the insurer contracts for discounted rates. Preferred providers include physicians, hospitals, diagnostic facilities, and other service providers. If care is not provided by a preferred provider, the insured individual pays a higher undiscounted rate and must meet higher deductibles and coinsurances for these services.

Point-of-Service (POS) Plans

These plans provide some flexibility to the HMO model described above and are sometimes referred to as open-ended plans. Under a POS plan, an enrollee can use services that are out of plan, in exchange for deductibles and coinsurance payments. The plan tries to address some of the shortcomings of the pure HMO approach.

High-Deductible Health Plan with Savings Option (HDHP/SO)

A form of consumer-driven health plan, these types of plans offer the enrollee catastrophic coverage for a relatively low premium that is coupled with a high deductible. The savings option is typically a **Health Savings Account** (HSA) or some other type of vehicle. HSAs serve as a way to bank pretax dollars with an employer up to a certain amount to be used for medical expenses. If the consumer does not spend the HSA account down, the money will carry over to the next year. Among the many provisions of the Medicare Prescription Drug, Improvement, and Modernization Act (MMA) of 2003, HSAs were mandated to "pair high-deductible plans that meet certain requirements with fully portable, employee-owned, tax-advantaged accounts" (Wilensky, 2006, p. 175). The underlying ideas behind HSAs are that consumers will become more educated users of health care, be more likely to utilize preventive and chronic care services, become more cognizant of the costs of care, be less likely to make poor decisions about using care that is not necessary or not appropriate, and be more prudent when using an account that is seen as containing "their own funds."

In the mid-1990s, many people thought managed care was the solution to the rising health care cost problem. While initially there was tremendous growth in managed care, particularly in HMOs, that trend slowed in early part of the 21st century. Consumer perceptions indicated negative views of managed care plans, concerns about the restrictions imposed in the plans, and the quality of care provided.

Evidence and data suggest that PPOs have become the dominant form of coverage (Hurley, Strunk, & White, 2004). This represents a radical shift in choice of plan over time, as shown in Table 9-2. In 1988 the majority (73%) of covered workers were enrolled in conventional indemnity types of health insurance plans, 16% were in HMOs, 11% were in PPOs, and POS and HDHO/SO plans weren't even options. By 2014, 58% of workers enrolled in health plans opted for a PPO, while only 13% and 8% were in HMOs and POSs, respectively. The penetration of HDHP/SOs into the health insurance market increased from zero to 20% in less than 10 years. Less than 1% of workers were still covered by conventional indemnity health plans in 2014 (Kaiser Family Foundation and Health Research and Educational Trust, 2014).

The primary types of private health insurance coverage are compared across a number of important dimensions in Table 9-3. These include issues of access to care in general and to specialists, choice of providers, cost sharing, restrictions on utilization, administrative costs, paperwork, and several other dimensions. It is clear from reviewing this information that there are distinct tradeoffs between plans. For example, those that provide unlimited access tend to have difficulties controlling costs, but afford higher quality. Those that are able to manage and control costs do so by limiting access and utilization.

TABLE 9-2 Health Plan Enrollment by Type of Plan, 1988–2014

Type of Plan	1988	1993	1998	2003	2008	2013	2014
Conventional	73%	46%	14%	5%	2%	<1%	<1%
HMO	16%	21%	27%	24%	20%	14%	13%
PPO	11%	26%	35%	54%	58%	57%	58%
POS	0%	7%	24%	17%	12%	8%	8%
HDHP/SO	0%	0%	0%	0%	8%	20%	20%

Data from: Kaiser Family Foundation and Health Research and Educational Trust, 2014.

TABLE 9-3 Comparison of Insurance Plan Characteristics

	Indemnity Plans	Health Maintenance Organizations (HMOs)	Preferred Provider Organizations (PPOs)	Point-of-Service Plans (POSs)	High-Deductible Health Plans (HDHPs)
Access to Care	Unlimited	Limited and controlled; may require waiting for care	Unlimited	Unlimited	Unlimited
Geographic Limitations	None	Limited to geographic regions served by HMO, except in emergencies	Unlimited	Unlimited	Unlimited
Choice of Provider	Unlimited	Limited to in-network providers	Unlimited, but pay less when preferred (in-network) providers used	Can go out of network, but pay more	Unlimited
Access to Specialists	Unlimited	Limited; need referral from gatekeeper for some services	Unlimited; can self-refer	Unlimited; may self-refer out of plan at a higher cost	Unlimited
Utilization Restrictions	None	Limitations may be imposed on certain services	Mostly unlimited; plan may place annual dollar or visit limits	Mostly unlimited; plan may place annual dollar or visit limits	Unlimited
Deductibles/ Copayments	Both typically must be met	No deductibles/small copays	Deductibles and copays required	Deductibles and copays required	High deductibles required
Coinsurance	Required	None	Required	Required for services received out of plan	None
Quality Issues	Likely to be high	May be lower, if patients have to wait for care	Likely to be high	Likely to be high, if patient gets second opinions	Likely to be high
Paperwork	Insured must complete to get reimbursed	Minimal; billing only needed on a small number of procedures	Excessive	Moderate for out-of-plan services	Minimal, unless catastrophic incident occurs
Administrative Costs	Moderately high	Low; controlled by not having to bill for most services	High; uncontrolled	Moderate to high	Low
Management of Costs	Costs difficult to manage; plans are cost inducing	Costs are known and can be managed	Costs are difficult to manage; costs are based on utilization	Costs are partially known for in-plan care; out-of-plan care is less known	Patients manage expenditures, unless catastrophic incident occurs

THE EVOLUTION OF SOCIAL INSURANCE

As with private insurance, many changes have taken place in how individuals can access care via social insurance or federal entitlement programs. The changes in both areas are discussed below, along with key pieces of legislation that also relate to the private sector.

Major Legislation

The social health insurance programs of Medicare and Medicaid have continued to evolve over the past 50 years. The following discussion will address some of the major pieces of legislation shaping this evolution.

Social Security Act of 1965

The 1965 Amendments to the Social Security Act of 1935 established the two largest government-sponsored health insurance programs in the history of the U.S. Medicare, Title XVIII of the Act, entitled persons 65 and over to coverage of hospital care under Part A and physicians' and other outpatient health services under Part B. Eligibility for Medicare benefits has since been extended to younger people with permanent disabilities, individuals with end-stage renal disease (ESRD), and persons under hospice care. Medicaid, Title XIX, set up a joint federal–state program entitling financially qualified indigent and low-income persons to basic medical care. This program, too, has undergone numerous iterations at both the state and federal levels as these governments have attempted to strike a balance between equity in coverage for certain services (mandated at the federal level) and states' rights in controlling the use of public funds.

Employee Retirement and Income Security Act

"The Employee Retirement Income Security Act of 1974 (ERISA) protects the interests of participants and beneficiaries in private-sector employee benefit plans....An employee benefit plan may be either a pension plan (which provides retirement benefits) or a welfare benefit plan (which provides other kinds of employee benefits such as health and disability benefits" (Purcell & Staman, 2008, p. 1). This federal law allows private companies to provide health benefits to employees through their own self-funded health insurance plan. The plan must meet the legal requirements of ERISA but can be customized to include only the benefits the company defines. While the law has been periodically amended to require these plans to comply with other federal laws, such as the requirements of temporary coverage under the Consolidated Omnibus Budget Reconciliation Act (COBRA), the preexisting conditions provisions of the Health Insurance Portability and Accountability Act (HIPAA), the coverage requirements of the Mental Health Parity Act, and other specific coverage areas (Pozgar, 2007;

Purcell & Staman, 2008), there are no requirements for these plans in terms of specific covered benefits. Additionally, since federal law preempts state law, companies that opt for this type of health plan have in almost all instances been exempted from the requirements of state health insurance mandates and laws.

TEFRA 1982 and OBRA 1989

In response to rapidly rising health care costs, Congress passed the **Tax Equity and Fiscal Responsibility Act (TEFRA)** in 1982, with particular emphasis on Medicare cost controls. Among its key provisions were the following:

- a mandate for a prospective payment system (PPS) for hospital reimbursement, with payment rates established up front for conditions known as Diagnosis-Related Groups (DRGs);
- the option of providing managed care plans to Medicare beneficiaries; and
- the requirement that Medicare become the secondary payer when a beneficiary had other insurance.

Similar payment arrangements have been mandated for other types of providers, such as compensation for physician office services to Medicare beneficiaries using the **Resource-Based Relative Value System (RBRVS)**, mandated as part of the Omnibus Budget Reconciliation Act (OBRA) of 1989 and implemented in 1992. Under RBRVS, payments are determined by the costs of resources needed to provide each service, including physician work, practice expenses, and professional liability insurance.

Balanced Budget Act of 1997

Despite reductions in reimbursements for hospital admissions and physician visits, Medicare expenditures continued to soar throughout the 1990s. Congress passed the Balanced Budget Act (BBA) of 1997 in an attempt to control costs for other health care services, mandating some 200 changes (primarily restrictive) to Medicare alone, as well as changes to Medicaid. Medicare PPSs were phased in and implemented in other health care settings beginning in 1998 as follows:

- Skilled nursing facilities (SNFs), in 1998, with RUGs (Resource Utilization Groups);
- Home health agencies (HHAs), in 2000, with HHRGs (Home Health Resource Groups);
- Hospital outpatient department services, in 2002, with OPPS (Outpatient Prospective Payment System); and
- Payment reductions and prospective payment arrangements for hospice care, rehabilitation hospitals, ambulance services, and durable medical equipment.

Other key provisions of the BBA, providing for cost controls in some areas and expansion of coverage in others, were:

- the creation of Medicare Part C, originally known as Medicare+Choice and now referred to Medicare Advantage Plans, to move Medicare recipients into alternative forms of coverage, including HMOs and PPOs;
- provisions relating to fraud and abuse;
- improvements in protecting program integrity;
- restrictions on public benefits for illegal immigrants;
- addition of Medicare prevention initiatives (such as mammography, prostate cancer, and colorectal screenings);
- addition of rural initiatives; and
- establishment of the **Children's Health Insurance Program** (CHIP) to provide increased access to health care coverage for low-income children; this became Title XXI of the Social Security Act.

Medicare Prescription Drug, Improvement, and Modernization Act of 2003

Known as the Prescription Drug Benefit, Medicare Part D, and/or MMA, this produced the largest additions and changes to Medicare and was projected to cost $395 billion in its first decade alone. Effective January 1, 2006, this controversial entitlement to prescription drugs instigated a flurry of activities by individual states to mitigate uncertainties in its implementation and to temporarily provide prescription coverage for millions of seniors still in the process of meeting eligibility requirements. Tax breaks, subsidies, and other incentives to pharmaceutical companies and private, managed care insurers, along with significant pressure on seniors to enroll in Medicare Advantage Plans or risk significant out-of-pocket costs, were among the most contentious provisions of the drug benefit portion of this legislation.

With so much attention focused on the drug benefit, it has become easy for other provisions of this legislation to become lost in the discussion. Some of the more important ones include:

- increased prevention benefits;
- an extra $25 billion boost to often severely underfunded rural hospitals;
- a requirement for higher fees to be collected from wealthier seniors; and
- the addition of a pretax health savings account for working people.

Patient Protection and Affordable Care Act of 2010

President Obama signed Public Law 111-148 on March 23, 2010. This law called for sweeping changes in health insurance, including both individual and employer mandates, creation of health insurance exchanges to allow choice in purchasing coverage, subsidies for small businesses, changes to Medicare, expansion of Medicaid to provide coverage for more children and low-income adults, expansion of CHIP to provide additional federal funding, cost-containment efforts for both Medicare and Medicaid, provisions for improving quality of care and performance, expansion of prevention and wellness programs, and elimination of cost sharing for screening and prevention services, to name some of the key provisions (Iglehart, 2010b; Kaiser Commission on Medicaid and the Uninsured, 2010a; Kaiser Family Foundation, 2010c). Lifetime limits on health insurance coverage were eliminated as of 2014 (Iglehart, 2010b). The new health care reform legislation created the Pre-Existing Condition Insurance Plan (PCIP) to allow access to coverage for individuals in this group (Kaiser Family Foundation, 2010c). A website was created by the federal government to provide details about the new law, to link people to the health insurance marketplace in order to enroll for coverage through either the federal or state health care exchanges, to provide ready access to policies and regulations, to make data readily available for researchers, and a host of other uses (see http://www.healthcare.gov). The Kaiser Family Foundation published a summary of the law (2010c). A timeline for implementation of the ACA is also available for 2010 through 2022 (Obamacare Facts, 2015c).

There have been numerous problems with the rollout of the health exchanges, use of the federal website for enrolling, and other logistical issues, but these have for the most part been resolved. There have also been a large number of legal challenges to the ACA relating to whether the federal government has the authority to mandate health insurance coverage; taxing of health benefits; required coverage of certain benefits; and the impacts on businesses (particularly small businesses), the states, insurers, and health care providers (Abelson, 2010; Helms, 2009; Kaiser Commission on Medicaid and the Uninsured, 2010c; Luo, 2010; Miller, 2010; Sack, 2010; Schwartz, 2010). Several have been heard by the U.S. Supreme Court. The first case upheld most of the provisions of ACA, but did prohibit the federal government from cutting funding to states if they did not expand their Medicaid programs (Cauchi, 2015). The second case focused on benefit coverage and found that "closely held corporations cannot be required to provide contraception coverage under Obamacare if they had religious objections" (National Constitution Center Staff, 2015). The most recent challenge, known as *King v. Burwell* and heard by the Court in March 2015, questions the constitutionality of the verbiage in the ACA with regard to providing tax subsidies to individuals through the health care exchanges (Cauchi, 2015; National Constitution Center Staff, 2015).

These types of challenges to the health care reform legislation may continue, in part because there continues to be dissension about the value and provisions of the law. For example, a Kaiser Family Foundation Health Tracking Poll found that only 19% of people polled felt that the ACA has been beneficial for them or the families, while 22% indicated that it has hurt them and the remaining 56% saw no direct impact (Altman, 2015b), but the Foundation's March Health Tracking Poll also showed that Americans were almost evenly divided on whether they favor the ACA or oppose it (41% vs. 43%, respectively) (Altman, 2015a). There also continue to be misunderstandings about the law. For example, many individuals who change their status as a result of a "qualifying life event" may be eligible to apply for coverage outside the yearly "open enrollment periods" (Hartman, Espinoza, Fried, & Sonier, 2015). This suggests the need for better communication about the ACA.

Finally, it is also important to recognize who has benefited from the ACA. "The data shows that the law has done something rather unusual in the American economy of this century: It has pushed back against inequality, essentially redistributing income—in the form of health insurance or insurance subsidies—to many of the groups that have fared poorly over the last few decades" (Quealy & Sanger-Katz, 2014, para. 2). While that is true, the bottom line is that it will be many years before we know the true costs, long-term benefits and overall results of this legislative action.

Medicare Access and CHIP Reauthorization Act of 2015

This legislation, sometimes referred to as MACRA or the Medicare "Doc Fix" bill, included several important provisions. The first changed the formula for reimbursing physicians and prevented reductions in physician payments that were scheduled to take place in April 2015. The intent was to forestall physicians from not accepting Medicare patients and thereby increasing access for them. Another set of provisions reauthorized the Children's Health Insurance Program. Finally, several provisions authorized spending cuts to Medicare for supplemental Medigap plans and requiring "higher premiums for seniors who make more than $133,500.... starting in 2018" (Cubanski & Neuman, 2015; Obamacare Facts, 2015a, para. 7).

MAJOR "PLAYERS" IN THE SOCIAL INSURANCE ARENA

Medicare

As discussed previously, this federal program provides access to health care for the elderly over 65 years of age, for permanently disabled younger adults, and for those suffering from end-stage renal disease (ESRD). End-of-life "palliative" care (or comfort care) is also provided for terminally ill enrollees in their last six months of life. The primary benefits of this program, as delineated by the CMS (2015a) and Kaiser Family Foundation (2010b), can best be summarized through description of its four "parts":

- **Part A—Hospital Insurance (HI)**, allowing 90 days of inpatient hospital coverage per benefit period (with a 60-day lifetime inpatient hospital reserve), inpatient skilled nursing facility (SNF) coverage of up to 100 days per episode (with a 90-day lifetime SNF reserve), currently prequalified home health care services, and hospice care for the terminally ill.

- **Part B—Supplemental Medical Insurance (SMI)**, providing coverage for visits to physicians, outpatient treatments, and preventive services, including flu and hepatitis B vaccines, mammography, and Pap smears.
- **Part C—Medicare Advantage Plans (MAs)**, allowing beneficiaries to enroll in a variety of capitated health insurance plans, which are required to provide the same types of services covered under traditional Medicare plans and may offer the option of additional benefits such as prescription drugs.
- **Part D—The Prescription Drug Benefit**, with drug coverage being available through Prescription Drug Plans (PDPs), Medicare Advantage Drug Plans (MA PDs), or other Medicare-approved prescription plans.

Administered federally by the CMS, Medicare has been financed through three primary means. The first has been through assessments to employers and employees, contributing 2.9% of payroll (1.45% each), "along with an additional 0.9 percent paid by higher-income taxpayers (wages above $200,000/individual and $250,000/couple" (Cubanski et al., 2015, p. 2). This funding is dedicated entirely to paying Part A benefits. The second means of financing has involved increased cost sharing by beneficiaries, including premiums (financing 25% of all Part B benefits and 25.5% of Part D benefits, with wealthier beneficiaries again paying higher percentages, "ranging from 35 percent to 80 percent" (Cubanski et al., 2015, p. 32), deductibles, coinsurance, and balance billing. The third and largest financing source has increasingly been derived from allocations from general revenues (i.e., federal tax revenues). Total Medicare revenues from all sources were estimated at $575.8 billion in 2013 (Cubanski et al., 2015). Figure 9-2 summarizes the relative percentages from major Medicare revenue sources.

Public policy circles have become increasingly concerned about the growth in Medicare program enrollment and the concomitant rise in expenditures. According to CMS data, 19.1 million individuals were enrolled in Medicare at its inception in 1966; this number grew to 55 million in 2015 (Cubanski et al., 2015). With the influx of the huge Baby Boom generation (born between 1946 and 1964) that began to turn 65 in 2011, enrollment is projected to swell "to 93 million, while the ratio of workers per beneficiary is expected to decline from 3.2 to 2.3" by 2050 (Cubanski et al., 2015, p. 34), resulting in significantly fewer revenues being derived from payroll taxes. Medicare's share of the U.S. economy is also expected to increase from 3.5% (as a percentage of the GDP) in 2013 to 5.3% in 2035 "and will increase gradually thereafter to about 6.9 percent of GDP by 2088" (Social Security and Medicare Boards of Trustees, 2014, p. 5).

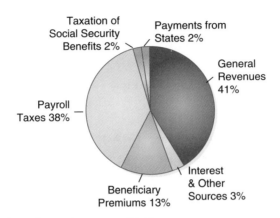

FIGURE 9-2 Estimated Medicare Revenues, 2013

Data from: Kaiser Family Foundation based on data from 2014 Annual Report of the Boards of Trustees of the Federal Hospital Insurance and Federal Supplementary Medical Insurance Trust Funds.

Another issue of concern surrounding Medicare expenditures is the distribution by percentages of dollars allocated to various sectors of the health care arena. Figure 9-3 summarizes this distribution. These numbers are partially indicative of the aging of the population, with increased life expectancy. Research has shown that health care services are used by those 65 and older at a much higher rate than other age groups, particularly by those who are very old. Yet these factors do not tell the entire story. Why else have Medicare expenditures grown so dramatically? The following are among the most frequent and significant factors:

- a shift from treatment of acute illnesses to more chronic care as society ages and lives longer, with more substantial outlays of money to treat the latter;
- tremendous growth in hospital expenditures;
- initial lack of cost-conscious Medicare reimbursement, using retrospective fee-for-service (payments based on charges) methods;
- huge growth in pharmaceutical costs and in technological innovations in the medical field;
- increased payments under Part C plans;
- the need for higher payments to rural health providers;
- rising medical malpractice premiums related to increasing litigation; and
- as shown in a recent study, "two-thirds of traditional Medicare beneficiaries older than 65 have multiple chronic conditions, according to a *USA Today* analysis of county-level Medicare data. More than 4 million—about 15%—have at least six long-term ailments. Those sickest seniors account for more than 41% of the $324 billion spent on traditional Medicare" (Hoyer, 2015, para. 5).

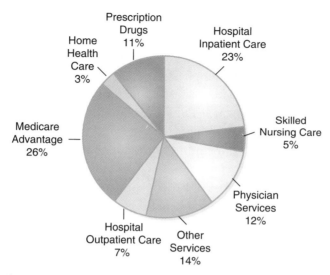

FIGURE 9-3 Distribution of Medicare Expenditures, 2014

Adapted from: Kaiser Family Foundation based on data from 2014 Annual Report of the Boards of Trustees of the Federal Hospital Insurance and Federal Supplementary Medical Insurance Trust Funds, p. 29 (Figure 24). Retrieved from http://files.kff.org/attachment/report-a-primer-on-medicare-key-facts-about-the-medicare-program-and-the-people-it-covers

During the early 1990s, federal policy makers were already alarmed by the dramatic rise in health care expenditures, particularly concerning Medicare. In fact, during the first Clinton administration in the early 1990s, there was a push toward legislation providing for a national health care system. Efforts to slow the rate of growth were mandated. The 2010 health care reform legislation included provisions for this, including changes to Medicare Advantage, reducing payments to hospitals for patient readmissions, changing premiums for Parts B and D, promoting preventive care, and working to reduce fraud (Kaiser Family Foundation, 2010c). Additionally, Medicare is currently testing new delivery mechanisms mandated by the ACA that are designed to reduce costs and improve quality, including creating Accountable Care Organizations (ACOs), bundling payments, and creating Medical Homes, as well as developing a "value-based purchasing program" for reimbursing hospitals. These reforms are discussed further in Chapter 10.

Medicaid

Medicaid, the second largest provider of socialized health insurance in the United States, provides health care coverage to the medically indigent (those below certain poverty-level determinations) and is jointly funded by state and federal governments. Mandatory services required by the federal government include: "physician, midwife and certified nurse practitioner services; inpatient and outpatient hospital services; laboratory and x-ray services; family planning services and supplies; rural health clinic/federally qualified health center services; nursing facility and home health care for adults over 21; and Early Periodic Screening, Diagnostic, and Treatment (EPSDT) services for children under age 21" (Center on Budget and Policy Priorities, 2013, para. 15). Beyond this, each state has authority in administering Medicaid programs, including the amount and scope of services and differences in eligibility requirements.

There is huge variation in the types of benefits provided by various states. For example, some states provide a wide array of dental benefits to beneficiaries. Others provide mental health benefits and/or drug and alcohol treatment. Similarly, there are significant variations in coverage of the poor. Some "bare bones" Medicaid programs cover only individuals mandated by the federal government, while other states cover individuals with higher incomes. These differences, as well as differences in ages of individuals covered, result in wide gaps in Medicaid coverage from state to state.

Despite the considerable discretion given to the states in terms of eligibility requirements in relation to income, the following categories of medically indigent and low-income individuals must be included in state Medicaid programs:

- The medically indigent, historically linked to two federal assistance programs: Temporary Aid to Needy Families (TANF), which replaced Aid to Families with Dependent Children (AFDC) in 1996, and Supplemental Security Income (SSI);
- Low-income pregnant women, children, and infants, as mandated through the Omnibus Budget Reconciliation Act (OBRA) of 1986; and
- Children whose parents have income too high for Medicaid but too low for private insurance, through CHIP.

The primary problems caused by allowing such liberal state discretion have been the huge inequities in the numbers and percentages of residents being served and the types of benefits being received. Part of these discrepancies may be related to the differences in how Medicaid is financed. The federal government finances 50% to 77% of Medicaid costs in any given state, depending on the state's poverty status (i.e., the number of individuals living below the federal poverty level). This leaves state contributions ranging from 23% to 50%, with the poorer states contributing the lowest percentages. Many "richer" states, often feeling the pinch of reduced state coffers related to factors other than income, feel it is unfair that they must shoulder 50% of the health insurance burden of their poorest members and thus often contribute a smaller proportion of their General Fund to the provision of Medicaid services.

The changes from the ACA have had a tremendous impact on Medicaid, as a result of the provisions calling on states to expand their coverage of the uninsured. "Specifically, the ACA expanded Medicaid eligibility to nearly all non-elderly adults with income at or below 138% of the federal poverty level—about $16,245 for an individual in 2015… [and] provided for 100% federal funding of the expansion through 2016, declining gradually to 90% in 2020 and future years" (Paradise, 2015, p. 1). This provision of the law was, however, challenged by several states and the U.S. Supreme Court ruled in 2012 that expansion would be optional for the states. The result is again significant variation in how the expansion has been handled. As of May 26, 2015, 30 states and DC had expanded their Medicaid programs, 3 states were considering it, and the remaining 18 states (mainly in the South and Midwest) were not adopting the provision (Kaiser Commission on Medicaid and the Uninsured, 2015). The states that do expand are also required to comply with the minimum coverage requirements of the law, thus bringing greater uniformity to benefits across the states (Mahan & Traver, 2013).

Between October 2013 and October 2014, Medicaid added 8.7 million people to the Program (Pear, 2014), bringing the total enrollment to approximately 70 million. These changes have brought many uninsured Americans into health care coverage. The groups covered by Medicaid have remained relatively stable and include low-income individuals (including the elderly), families, and children, as well as the disabled. What has changed radically over time, however, is the dollars consumed by these different groups. For example, the aged, blind, and disabled represented 24.0% of Medicaid beneficiaries, but accounted for 65.0% of Medicaid spending in 2012 (Truffer, Klemm, Wolfe, Rennie, & Shuff, 2013, p. 16). This radical difference can be seen graphically in Figure 9-4. This difference is likely to be accentuated with the influx of new enrollees who are mostly children and adults in low income families who use fewer resources, while the elder and disabled enrollees continue to be responsible for the majority of spending.

As with Medicare expenses, Medicaid expenditures have grown dramatically over the past couple of decades. In 1966, at the inception of Medicaid, there were only 10 million recipients of Medicaid, with total spending at only $1.7 billion (in 1966 dollars). While expenditures reached $431.9 billion in FY 2012, the rate of increase had slowed to some extent. In fact, "total Medicaid expenditures increased by 0.8 percent in 2012, which is the second-lowest rate of growth in the program's history, as States acted to limit the rate of growth of expenditures while the States' share of costs increased" (Truffer et al., 2013, p. iii). That said, the Office of the Actuary of CMS has estimated that "over the next 10 years, expenditures are projected to increase at an average annual rate of 7.1 percent and to reach $853.6 billion by 2022" (Truffer et al., 2013, p. iv). Thus, the slowdown appears to be temporary as "Medicaid spending grew 6.1% to $449.4 billion in 2013, or 15 percent of total NHE" (CMS, 2014b, para. 1).

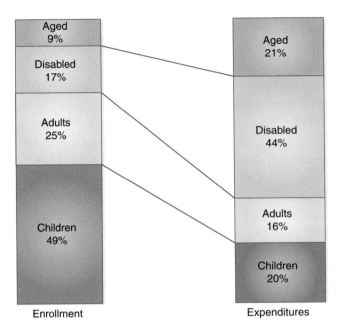

FIGURE 9-4 Estimated Medicaid Enrollment and Expenditures by Enrollment Group, as Share of Total, Fiscal Year 2012

CMS, 2013, Acturial Report on the Financial Outlook for Medicaid (Truffer, Klemm, Wolfe, Rennie, & Shuff, 2013, p. 16).

Medicaid is thus one of the primary funders of health care in the country. This includes the following:

- accounting for "35% of safety-net hospitals' revenues";
- providing "40% of health center revenues";
- paying for "one-quarter of all behavioral health care spending nationally";
- financing "nearly half of all births in the U.S."; and
- covering "half the national bill for long-term services and supports needed by people with disabilities and the elderly" (Paradise, Lyons, & Rowland, 2015, p. 19).

As previously asked regarding Medicare expenditures, why have Medicaid expenditures grown so dramatically? The following are illustrative of the most significant reasons given for growth in spending and numbers of Medicaid recipients:

- Changes in Medicaid policies, particularly expansion of eligibility requirements.
- Expansion of types of services provided, including dental care, rehabilitation, preventive services, mental health care, and drug and alcohol treatment, in more generous states.

- Downturns in the economy and rising unemployment rates that have resulted in increasing numbers of the poor and uninsured since 2001. For example, the 2008 recession led to one of the largest single-year enrollment increases since the program's inception between June 2008 and June 2009; 3.3 million people were added to the Medicaid rolls, an increase of 5.4% (Kaiser Commission on Medicaid and the Uninsured, 2010b, 2010c).
- The unexpected significant increases in Medicaid expenditures as a result of higher payment rates to providers and more spending on those who "deserve" public support, including the aged, blind, disabled, and children.
- There is an increasing number of elderly and disabled individuals who enter long-term care institutions as private pay and "spend down" their assets to become eligible for Medicaid.

As the federal government has been attempting to control escalating Medicare costs, the CMS and individual states alike have been active in implementing cost controls. At the federal level, one of the most important measures enacted was the provision in the Balanced Budget Act of 1997 allowing states to enroll Medicaid recipients in managed care health plans. "As of 2015, 38 states and DC have risk-contracting programs, and more than half of all Medicaid beneficiaries nationally are enrolled in comprehensive managed care plans, many on a mandatory basis" (Paradise et al., 2015, p. 16). Additionally, the Deficit Reduction Act of 2005 attempted to reduce expenditures even more dramatically by calling for net Medicaid "reductions of $4.8 billion over the next five years and $26.1 billion over the next 10 years" (Kaiser Commission on Medicaid and the Uninsured, 2006, p. 1). The Medicaid Integrity Program resulted from this and created new efforts to reduce Medicaid fraud and abuse (CMS, 2009; Wachino, 2007). Efforts to offset the 2009/2010 increases in spending benefitted from a temporary increase in the federal Medicaid match that was authorized as part of the American Recovery and Reinvestment Act (ARRA) (Kaiser Family Foundation, 2010a). One aim of the new health care reform legislation is to reduce costs. Thus, Medicaid is experimenting with ACOs, increasing efforts to help elderly enrollees remain in their homes under the home and community-based services programs, and undertaking other efforts to ensure access to quality care while undertaking payment reforms (Paradise, 2015). The growth in Medicaid spending has exacerbated state budgets deficits, led to cuts in other state programs, and resulted in other cost-containment efforts (Kaiser Commission on Medicaid and the Uninsured, 2010b; National Governors Association, 2010). The concerns of the states continue and are apparent with the changes brought about by the ACA. That said, the compact between the federal government and the states to provide care to low income Americans is clearly being fulfilled by the Medicaid Program.

The Children's Health Insurance Program

Originally called the State Children's Health Insurance Program, CHIP provides health care coverage for children in low-income families that do not qualify for Medicaid. CHIP, thus, picks up covering uninsured children where Medicaid leaves off, by covering children in families with slightly higher incomes with respect to the federal poverty level. Like Medicaid, CHIP is a joint federal/state programs, where states have the option of running the program as part of Medicaid, as a separate program, or as a combination of the two. Funding for CHIP also comes from both federal and state governments, but applies a matching rate that is 15% higher than Medicaid. The ACA increased the federal match, so that "beginning October 1, 2015 the already enhanced CHIP federal matching rate will increase by 23 percentage points, bringing the average federal match rate for CHIP to 93%...[and continuing it] until September 30, 2019" (CMS, n.d., para. 3). Given the relationship to Medicaid, children often move back and forth between the two programs. As of FY 2013, 8.1 million children were enrolled in CHIP (Kaiser Family Foundation, 2014).

Insuring Veterans, Active and Retired Military Personnel, and Their Families

The Military Health System covers federal health benefits for veterans, military personnel, and their family members under the Department of Defense's (DOD) medical facilities and TRICARE plan, the medical facilities of the Department of Veterans Affairs (VA) and the VA's Civilian Health and Medical Program (CHAMPVA), and other specialized programs (TRICARE, 2007, 2008, 2010a, 2010b). While everyone who served in the military is a veteran, only those who served for an extended period (normally 20 years) are retired. Health benefits described in this section are federal benefits or entitlements—technically, not insurance.

TRICARE and DOD

TRICARE is not an abbreviation; it is the title of the military health program. It covers active duty military personnel, retired military personnel, and their family members. DOD's medical facilities are considered part of TRICARE. "The Veterans Health Administration (VHA) is home to the United States' largest integrated health care system consisting of 150 medical centers, nearly 1,400 community-based outpatient clinics, community living centers, Vet Centers and Domicillaries. Together, these health care facilities and more than 53,000 independent licensed health care practitioners who work within them provide comprehensive care to more than 8.3 million Veterans each year" (VHA, n.d.). DOD has also contracted with various companies to provide health care in the private sector both in the U.S. and overseas.

TRICARE offers three separate programs: an HMO, a PPO, and a fee-for-service option. All active duty members are automatically enrolled at no cost in the HMO option called TRICARE Prime. Other categories must enroll. Retirees and their families pay an annual enrollment fee; active duty families do not. All enrollees (except active duty) have copays for office visits, prescription medication, diagnostic tests, and hospitalization. Most preventive services are free. Individuals who do not elect to enroll in TRICARE Prime pay an annual deductible and copays. Those who use the PPO (called TRICARE Extra) have a 15% or 20% copay; the former percentage applies to active duty family members, the latter to retirees. Those who use the fee-for-service option (called TRICARE Standard) are subject to higher copays of 20% and 25% for those same respective groups. Other special programs, including TRICARE Reserve Select and TRICARE Retired Reserve, provide coverage for reservists; TRICARE Young Adult allows unmarried children under age 26 to retain coverage; TRICARE for Life is for military retirees who are eligible for Medicare; and the Extended Care Health Option (ECHO) provides additional services "that are not covered by TRICARE, such as assistive services, equipment, in-home respite care services and special education for qualifying mental and physical conditions" (Jansen, 2014, p. 14). DOD offers all participants a mail-order pharmacy program. Dental services for active duty members are free; for others, there is an insurance plan where enrollees pay a monthly premium for covered services. There is no long-term care coverage under TRICARE.

The U.S. Army, Navy, and Air Force operate military medical facilities around the world and afloat. DOD (as opposed to the three military services organizations) manages the contracted arrangements, except in the limited case where contracts are issued by a medical facility—these are managed by the medical facility. Medical personnel from each of the three services provide staff to the DOD organizations that oversee the contracted arrangements.

Problems with TRICARE primarily focus on:

- the limited network of providers in rural areas;
- providing rehabilitative care to soldiers injured in 21st-century wars;
- in particular, treating veterans with traumatic brain injuries (TBIs) and mental health problems, e.g., post-traumatic stress disorder (PTSD);
- providing care to National Guard and Reserve personnel who alternate from active duty to inactive duty; and
- ensuring there are sufficient providers to meet the needs of the 9.2 million beneficiaries (Auerbach, Weeks, & Brantley, 2013; Office of the Secretary of Defense, n.d.).

These problems are normally addressed within DOD and the services, but veterans' organizations and Congress take an active role in helping to ensure that beneficiaries receive access to quality services at a reasonable cost.

Veterans Affairs

Operated through the **Veterans Health Administration (VHA)**, the VA manages the nation's largest health care delivery system with "152 medical centers, 800 community-based outpatient clinics, and 126 nursing homes, staffed by doctors and nurses who are VHA employees" (Auerbach et al., 2013, p. 1). Every VA medical center is affiliated with a national medical school. Unlike the DOD, the VA does not differentiate between veterans who retired from the military and those who did not. Virtually all veterans are eligible for care in the VA, although those receiving less than honorable discharges or who left the service before serving 180 days may have limited or no benefits. The VHA operates its medical facilities in 22 regions called Veteran Integrated Service Networks (VISN). VISN directors are responsible for providing or arranging care for enrolled veterans, as well as some who are not enrolled. Individuals who enroll are placed in one of eight categories based on disability or service, as shown in Table 9-4. The VHA also purchases care from private providers when the VA does not have the needed service. Veterans who are in categories 1 through 4 are provided virtually all their medical needs by the VA. Those in categories 5 through 8 are provided care primarily for conditions that the veteran incurred while in the military—called service-connected conditions.

Family members of selected veterans are provided care through the VA's special health benefits programs. If the veteran is not retired from the military and the military determines the veteran is permanently and totally disabled or has died from a condition related to military service, family members are eligible for the CHAMPVA program. CHAMPVA is a fee-for-service program patterned after the TRICARE fee-for-service option with an annual deductible and a 25% copay. Unlike TRICARE, CHAMPVA is operated completely by the VA and not through contractors. If a veteran is a Vietnam veteran or served in Korea between 1967

TABLE 9-4 VA Enrollment Categories (Abbreviated Explanation)

Category 1: Service-connected (SC) veterans—50% or more disabled

Category 2: SC veterans—30–40% disabled

Category 3: SC 10–20%; former prisoners of war; Purple Heart recipients

Category 4: Vets receiving aid and attendance allowance or catastrophically disabled

Category 5: Low-income SC veterans with 0% disability and non-SC vets; vets receiving VA pension; vets eligible for Medicaid

Category 6: WWI vets; Mexican Border War vets; compensable SC vets with 0% disability; vets seeking care for herbicide exposure (Vietnam); vets exposed to ionizing radiation; vets with Gulf War illness; vets who participated in Project SHAD

Category 7: Vets with income above a certain limit and below the HUD geographic index who agree to pay copays for services

Category 8: Same as Category 7 except above the HUD geographic index

Source: U.S. Department of Veterans Affairs, 2009b.

and 1971 near the Demilitarized Zone (DMZ) and his or her child has spina bifida, the VA provides 100% coverage of medical care and supplies for these children under the Spina Bifida Healthcare Program (U.S. Department of Veterans Affairs, Health Administration Center, 2009). For women Vietnam veterans who have children with certain birth defects, the VA provides 100% coverage for the related condition under the Children of Women Vietnam Veterans Healthcare Program. Both programs were established because of veterans' exposure to Agent Orange, a defoliant used extensively in Vietnam and near the DMZ in Korea.

Problems with VA health programs are addressed through typical patient advocate activities. As with the DOD, veteran organizations and Congress play very active roles in the oversight of the VA's health system. The VA has problems providing services in rural areas, much like the DOD. Also, the large number of Guard and Reserve members serving in Operation Iraqi Freedom and Operation Enduring Freedom, who continually change status from active to inactive, sometimes have problems with continuity of care issues, mental health, and treatment of other injuries resulting from service.

Financing for DOD and VA Health Programs

To obtain funds for their programs, the DOD and VA submit budgets to the Office of Management and Budget (OMB). The OMB validates the requests and includes them in the President's request to Congress, which appropriates funds for the operation of the health systems. The President's Budget for FY 2015 for the VA was $163.9 billion. Of that total, $56.0 billion was earmarked for VA health care, with an additional 4.7% increase in advance for the following year, bringing that advance appropriation for 2016 to $58.7 billion (U.S. Department of Veterans Affairs, 2015).

Operational Issues

The VA leads the nation in providing quality care to veterans. Researchers, including the Congressional Budget Office (2007), tout the quality provided by the VA, with one pointing out that "at least in terms of process quality…the VHA has improved substantially and now seems to be outperforming the rest of U.S. health care" (Oliver, 2007, pp. 11–12). The VA is also noted for being an early adopter of electronic health records, as well as dealing with crises. When New Orleans was devastated by hurricanes in late 2005, not one veteran's medical record was lost.

While positive, there have been several recent scandals confronting the VA. In particular, the VA Hospital in Phoenix came under fire in 2014 for manipulating wait lists, thereby delaying treatment for many veterans, some of whom subsequently died (Philipps, 2015), and has subsequently been criticized for its slow response in addressing these problems (Shear & Phillipps, 2015). There have also been significant delays and huge cost overruns with the construction of the new VA medical center in Aurora, Colorado, which requires

$830 million in additional funding to complete the $1.73 billion project (Armbrister, 2015). Congress and the VA are currently trying to resolve the funding issue.

Despite these problems, Krumholz (2014) cautioned about how the VA is judged and that focus should be on the following three positives; (1) "that the VA healthcare system has consistently out-performed the non-VA/private sector in quality of care and patient safety," (2) "that the VA health care system has been a model for account- ability," and (3) that the VA has typically adopted "a more contemporary and effec- tive approach…to understand the problem, embrace the opportunity to improve, and strengthen the systems" (paras. 2, 3, 6). He concludes his article by saying incidents such as those in Phoenix should be used as opportunities for problem solving that will result in system and quality improvements. To this end, the VHA developed its "Blueprint for Excellence" in fall 2014, which delineates its vision for the future and its plan for addressing the following themes of "improving performance, promoting a positive culture of service, advancing healthcare innovation for Veterans and the coun- try, and increasing operational effectiveness and accountability," as well as the strategies for achieving them (VHA, 2014, p. 4).

In sum, the Military Health System plays a large and critical role in providing care to veterans, active duty military personnel, and their families. It is, thus, a huge contributor to public sector health care coverage.

STATISTICS ON HEALTH INSURANCE COVERAGE AND COSTS

As a part of the U.S. Census Bureau's Current Population Survey, health insurance cover- age data are collected on an annual basis. The most recent data from 2012 indicated that 84.6% of the population had some type of coverage (U.S. Census Bureau, 2013). The data presented in Figure 9-5 show the breakdown of health insurance by type of coverage for those who were insured in 2012.

These data reflect only modest changes from previous years. The individuals covered by some form of insurance increased by 3.0 million between 2011 and 2012. Coverage of individuals increased slightly or remained the same in all categories (U.S. Census Bureau, 2013). Earlier changes were directly linked to the recession and job loss (Bernstein, 2009; Truffer et al., 2010), while more recent changes have resulted from the ACA.

At the outset of this chapter, there was a brief discussion of the increases in the expen- ditures for health care. While government programs are funded primarily from taxes, pay- ments to the Social Security Trust Fund, and cost sharing by recipients, private health insurance must be financed by employers and employees. "It appears that public programs control per capita spending somewhat more effectively than private coverage does. That

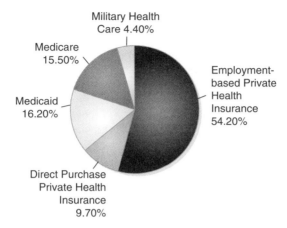

FIGURE 9-5 Health Insurance Coverage, 2012

U.S. Census, 2013.

may be just the opposite of what many would presume in a country where the private market is generally expected to outperform the public sector" (Altman, 2015e, para. 4).

The costs of premiums for different types of private health insurance, presented in Table 9-5, show the variation in the contributions toward premiums paid by employees and employers. Data are provided for individual policy holders, as well as for those opting for family coverage. These data also only reflect premiums and thus do not include deductibles, coinsurance, and/or copayments.

Premiums for family coverage increased 69% between 2004 and 2014. The split between employer and worker contributions was 65% for the former and 81% for the latter, which suggests companies are continuing to require greater cost sharing on the part of employees. While these increases seem substantial, they are slower than had been anticipated at the start of the period and are not huge on an annual basis. They also support the fact that the ACA has not had a major impact on employer-sponsored plans (Claxton et al., 2014). That said,

> the relatively quiet period in 2014 may give way to bigger changes in 2015 as the employer shared-responsibility provision in the ACA take effect for large employers. This provision requires firms with more than 100 full time equivalent employees (FTEs) in 2015 and more than 50 FTEs in 2016 to provide coverage to their full-time workers or possibly pay a penalty if workers seek subsidized coverage in health care exchanges....We expect some employers to revise eligibility and contributions for benefits in response to the new provisions. (Kaiser Family Foundation and the Health Research and Educational Trust, 2014, p. 7–8)

As an example showing this may have already begun, Japsen (2014) reported findings from the Mercer annual national survey of employer-sponsored health plans that in an

TABLE 9-5 Premiums Paid by Employees and Employers by Type of Plan, 2014

Type of Plan	Employee Contribution	Employer Contribution	Total Premium
Individual coverage			
All plans	$1,081	$4,944	$6,025
HMO	$1,182	$5,041	$6,223
PPO	$1,134	$5,082	$6,217
POS	$984	$5,182	$6,166
HDHP/SO	$905	$4,394	$5,299
Family coverage			
All plans	$4,823	$12,011	$16,834
HMO	$5,254	$12,129	$17,383
PPO	$4,877	$12,456	$17,333
POS	$4,849	$11,188	$16,037
HDHP/SO	$4,385	$11,016	$15,401

Data from: Kaiser Family Foundation and the Health Research and Educational Trust, 2014, p. 2.

effort to reduce employer expenses, increase employee cost sharing, and provide more consumer direction to health plan selection, employers are increasingly offering high deductible health plans. That said, despite many people purchasing these high deductible plans, Altman (2015f) reported that "they aren't all that happy about [them]" (para. 1). While changes to private health insurance coverage will no doubt continue, the early evidence of the impact of the ACA are that "it has had no impact on employer coverage" (Blavin, Shartzer, Long, & Holahan, 2015, p. 170). That may change in the future, as the ACA provision known as the 'Cadillac Tax' is slated to begin taxing high cost, employer-sponsored health plans in 2018 (Troy, 2015). Efforts may, however, be undertaken to amend this and other provisions of the law.

THOSE NOT COVERED—THE UNINSURED

There were 44.8 million people without insurance coverage in the U.S. in 2008, which represented 14.9% of the population. That number had increased 7.1% to 48.0 million or 15.4% of the 2012 population. Over the 14-year period 1999 to 2012, the percentage of uninsured increased 27% (U.S. Census Bureau, 2013).

A breakdown of the data, as shown in Figure 9-6, indicates differences in those who are uninsured by racial group. For example, while Blacks made up 14.0% of the population in 2012, they accounted for 16.9% of the uninsured, and while Hispanics comprised only

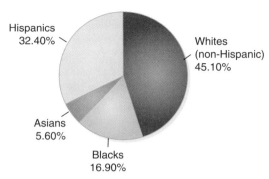

FIGURE 9-6 Distribution of Uninsured by Race, 2012

U.S. Census, 2013.

17.1% of the population, 32.4% of the uninsured were from this ethnic group. These disparities are a function of many things, among them differences in employment, eligibility for public programs, and income.

Additionally, when these numbers are broken down by age, the distribution shows that those without insurance coverage spanned all age groups in 2012. Figure 9-7 indicates that, while only a small number of those 65 and over were uninsured (as would be expected due to Medicare coverage), all other age groups included several million uninsured individuals, with more than four-fifths being adults. The majority of the uninsured were individuals under 35 years of age, but the largest single group was the 11.4 million people ages 25 to 34.

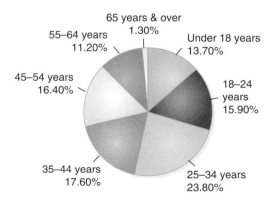

FIGURE 9-7 Distribution of the Uninsured by Age, 2012

U.S. Census, 2013.

Research about other characteristics of the uninsured also helps us to understand who this population includes (Abel, 1998; Rowland, Lyons, Salganicoff, & Long, 1994). The following are some of the key characteristics of these individuals.

- Approximately 25% were in families where income was below the poverty level.
- Most were individuals from families with incomes above the poverty level, but many had incomes below 300% of the poverty level.
- More than four-fifths were workers or dependents of workers who were employed in industries that do not typically provide health insurance coverage.
- The percentages of individuals without health insurance coverage vary across the states. More people in states in the South and the West tend be uninsured than those living in the Midwest and East.
- Those who are uninsured have been shown to use the health care delivery system in different ways. Without coverage and/or ability to pay, studies have shown that the uninsured:
  - do not typically have a primary care physician;
  - delay seeking care until they are sicker; and
  - utilize hospital emergency departments, the most expensive entry point to the health care system, to access the system and receive health care.
- The cost of insurance and job loss are also major contributors to being uninsured.

These characteristics of the uninsured continue to hold true for those who continue to be uninsured (Kaiser Commission on Medicaid and the Uninsured, 2014).

The ACA and the Uninsured

The ACA has had a significant impact on the number of uninsured. "National plan selection data show that as of the end of the second Open Enrollment period, nearly 11.7 million Americans selected or were automatically reenrolled into a 2015 health insurance plan through the Health Insurance Marketplaces" (U.S. Department of Health and Human Services, 2015, p. 4). While not all of these individuals were uninsured, Obamacare Facts (2015b) reported that 12.9% of Americans were still uninsured as of January 2015. According to Gallup, which conducted the poll, "this is down slightly from 13.4% in the third quarter of 2014 and down significantly from 17.1% a year ago" (Levy, 2015, para. 1). These numbers are mirrored by other polls conducted by the Urban Institute, the RAND Corporation, the Commonwealth Fund, and the Centers for Disease Control and Prevention (CDC); the consensus is the number of uninsured had decreased by 25% by 2014 (Sanger-Katz, 2014),

Several states (including Rhode Island, Oregon, West Virginia, Washington, Kentucky, Colorado, and Arkansas), all of which opted to expand their Medicaid programs, saw the largest decreases in the percentages of their population who were uninsured (Obamacare Facts, 2015b). The largest drop was in West Virginia, where the uninsured rate dropped from 17.34% of the population before the ACA to 6.59% afterwards; this represents a 62% change. Thus, the inclusion of the Medicaid expansion provisions has had a major impact on the uninsured rates (Sanger-Katz, 2014).

Additionally, the provision of the ACA that allows young adults, under age 26, to remain on their parents' health insurance policies has been instrumental in reducing the number of uninsured among those aged 19–25 (McMorrow, Kenney, Long, & Anderson, 2015). Research has also shown a reduction in the use of hospital emergency departments by this age group "of 2.7 ED visits per 1,000," when compared to those in the 26–31 year age group (Hernandez-Boussard, Burns, Wang, Baker, & Goldstein, 2014).

These data clearly support the fact that significant inroads have been made toward achieving the ACA goal of reducing the number of the uninsured. That said, however, as pointed out by Sanger-Katz (2014) "about 30 million people are expected to remain uninsured even after several years, according to the Congressional Budget Office" (para. 12).

Research has shown that several other problems persist. For example, Mitts and Fish-Parcham (2015) reported that despite having coverage, 25.2% of adults still have trouble paying for care, have gone without care, and are unable to make copays and or meet deductibles. This finding was also noted by Goodnough, Abelson, and Hartocollis (2014), who reported that high deductibles and copays restrict the use of coverage and that the Affordable Care Act is not necessarily "affordable." Altman (2015c) has pointed out that deductibles are a particular problem for many families with low or moderate incomes. This may be the result of the fact that deductibles have grown much more rapidly than wages. Between 2006 and 2014 wages increased 23%, as compared to deductibles, which increased 108% (Altman, 2015g).

Another concern is that many states have not opted into Medicaid expansion, resulting in a major coverage gap in 21 states as of April 2015 (Buettgens, Holahan, & Recht, 2015). It was estimated "nearly four million poor uninsured adults fall into the 'coverage gap' that results from state decisions," and thus are not eligible for other public coverage programs, do not get health benefits at work, and cannot afford to buy coverage outright (Garfield, Damico, Stephens, & Rouhani, 2015, p. 2). Pear (2014) reported almost 50% of these "coverage gap" adults are residents of just three states— Texas, Georgia, and Florida—with the majority being Black or Latino and younger adults.

Providing health care to the uninsured continues to fall primarily to hospitals, where much of it becomes uncompensated care. There are still some funds available to assist hospitals through the federal government's disproportionate-share program that provides some funding for providing large amounts of uncompensated care. Although the ACA called for funding reductions for the program, these will not be imposed until 2018 (Snyder & Rudowitz, 2015). There are also state and local programs that help to support these hospitals. The cost of care provided to the uninsured is borne by the taxpayers, as well as by insured patients, with those costs being passed along in the form of higher taxation and higher health insurance costs.

Great strides in addressing the problem of the uninsured have been made, but we still have a long way to go in resolving the problem. The long-term impact is at this point not known with respect to whether access to and outcomes of care have been achieved, whether the uninsured have been able to maintain coverage when premiums come due, and whether the cost of care will moderate or grow.

OPPORTUNITIES FOR RESEARCH ON EMERGING ISSUES

This chapter has discussed some of the research on financing and cost issues and health care management being conducted. While our nation continues to move toward insuring those previously un- or under-insured citizens, consumers, providers, payers, and other stakeholders press for evidence of improved access, reduced costs, and improved quality of health care. Opportunities for in-depth research on these emerging issues exist in a variety of venues, including your health care organization. Many of the resources we used in writing this chapter also include extensive research holdings and data bases available to citizens, students, and academic researchers. Herewith is a partial listing of these resources.

- Agency for Healthcare Research and Quality;
- Centers for Medicare and Medicaid Services;
- Centers for Disease Control and Prevention (CDC);
- Hospital Research and Educational Trust (HRET);
- Inter-university Consortium for Political and Social Research (ICPSR);
- Institute for Healthcare Improvement (IHI);
- Kaiser Family Foundation;
- National Center for Health Statistics (NCHS);
- Pew Charitable Trusts: Health;
- Robert Wood Johnson Foundation;
- Social Security Administration;
- U.S. Census Bureau; and
- U.S. Department of Veterans Affairs.

CONCLUSION

The changes that will occur over the next five years as health care reform continues to be implemented will bring new and different challenges for health care managers. While much will change, much will remain the same. There will still be two primary ways that health insurance issues will affect health care managers. The first relates to managing the health insurance benefit for employees and their dependents. In this regard, managers need to understand the options available to them in selecting plans that meet the needs of their employees, as well as the needs of the company. For small businesses, new opportunities to provide coverage to workers will be in the offing. The affordability of providing health benefits to employees will continue to be an increasingly difficult proposition for organizations, both large and small. Managers will be called upon to try to reduce the costs of coverage, to select cost-effective health plans, to understand the pros and cons of different types of coverage, to encourage employees to manage their care better, and to take steps to have employees bear more of the cost of coverage.

The second way that health insurance will be important for managers is related to patients—their insurance coverage and how they receive reimbursement from their insurers. Managing the patient health insurance function well will be critical to the financial success and viability of the organization. Issues relating to coding, billing, and other aspects of financing are discussed further in Chapter 10.

DISCUSSION QUESTIONS

1. Compare and contrast fee-for-service and prepaid health plans.

2. What types of cost sharing in health insurance are most effective? Provide a rationale for your response.

3. What are the pros and cons of the different types of health insurance benefit packages that someone might purchase?

4. Why have conventional indemnity policies been supplanted by other forms on health insurance coverage?

5. What is the best type of health insurance? Justify your answer.

6. Compare and contrast Medicare and Medicaid in terms of eligibility, benefit packages, access to care, and other key dimensions.

7. How does CHIP add to coverage provided under the Medicaid Program?

8. What issues and concerns have arisen relating to Medicare Part D? How can they be resolved?

9. Discuss the different types of health care coverage/health insurance that are provided to military personnel and their dependents.

10. What factors make it difficult to provide health care coverage for everyone in the U.S.?

11. How has the Affordable Care Act brought more people into coverage? Is this trend likely to continue? Explain why or why not?

Cases in Chapter 18 that are related to this chapter include:

- United Physician Group
- Piecework
- My Parents Are Turning 65 and Need Help Signing Up for Medicare
- Newby Health Systems Needs Health Insurance

Case study guides are available in the online Instructor's Materials.

REFERENCES

Abel, P. (1998, April). *1997 Colorado health source book: Insurance, access & expenditures.* Denver, CO: Colorado Coalition for Health Care Access and Coalition for the Medically Underserved.

Abelson, R. (2010, July 23). For insurers, fight is now over details. *New York Times.* Retrieved from http://www.nytimes.com/2010/07/24/business/24insure.html

Altman, D. (2010). When premiums go up 39%. *Kaiser Family Foundation.* Retrieved from http://www.kff.org/pullingittogether/031010_altman.cfm

Altman, D. (2015a, March 19). After five years, public opinion on health law remains divided. *Wall Street Journal.* [Blog post]. Retrieved from http://blogs.wsj.com/washwire/2015/03/19/after-five-years-public-opinion-on-health-law-remains-divided/

Altman, D. (2015b, May 20). Are more Americans benefiting from Obamacare than realize it? *Wall Street Journal.* [Blog post]. Retrieved from http://blogs.wsj.com/washwire/2015/05/20/are-more-americans-benefiting-from-obamacare-than-realize-it

Altman, D. (2015c, March 11). Health-care deductibles climbing out of reach. *Wall Street Journal.* [Blog post]. Retrieved from http://blogs.wsj.com/washwire/2015/03/11/health-care-deductibles-climbing-out-of-reach/

Altman, D. (2015d, June 11). New evidence health spending is growing faster again. *Wall Street Journal.* [Blog post]. Retrieved from http://blogs.wsj.com/washwire/2015/06/11/new-evidence-health-spending-is-growing-faster-again

Altman, D. (2015e, April 16). Public vs. private health insurance on controlling spending. *Wall Street Journal.* [Blog post]. Retrieved from http://blogs.wsj.com/washwire/2015/04/16/public-vs-private-health-insurance-on-controlling-spending/

Altman, D. (2015f, May 21). The 'value' trade-off in high-deductible health plans. *Wall Street Journal*. [Blog post]. Retrieved from http://blogs.wsj.com/washwire/2015/05/21/the-value-trade-off-in -high-deductible-health-plans/

Altman, D. (2015g, April 8). Why growth in health low costs still stings. [Blog post]. *Wall Street Journal*. Retrieved from http://blogs.wsj.com/washwire/2015/04/08/why-low-growth-in-health-costs -still-stings/

Armbrister, M. (2015, April 15). Congressional panel skeptical of VA's funding proposal for Aurora hospital. *Denver Business Journal*. Retrieved from http://www.bizjournals.com/denver/blog/real _deals/2015/04/house-committee-skeptical-of-vas-funding-proposal.html?s=print

Auerbach, D. I., Weeks, W. B., & Brantley, I. (2013). *Health care spending and efficiency in the U.S. Department of Veterans Affairs*. Santa Monica, CA: RAND Corporation. Retrieved from http ://www.rand.org/content/dam/rand/pubs/research_reports/RR200/RR285/RAND_RR285.pdf

Bernstein, J. (2009, August). *Impact of the economy on health care*. Retrieved from http://www.academyhealth .org/files/HCFO/findings0809.pdf

Blavin, F., Shartzer, A., Long, S. K., & Holahan, J. (2015). An early look at changes in employer-sponsored insurance under the Affordable Care Act. *Health Affairs, 34*(1), 170–177.

Buettgens, M., Holahan, J., & Recht, H. (2015, April). *Medicaid expansion, health coverage, and spending: An update for the 21 states that have not expanded eligibility*. Washington, DC: Kaiser Commission on Medicaid and the Uninsured. Retrieved from http://kff.org/medicaid/issue-brief /medicaid-expansion-health-coverage-and-spending-an-update-for-the-21-states-that-have-not -expanded-eligibility/

Cauchi, R. (2015, April 9). *State laws and actions challenging certain health reforms*. Washington, DC: National Conference of State Legislatures. Retrieved from http://www.ncsl.org/research/health /state-laws-and-actions-challenging-ppaca.aspx

Center on Budget and Policy Priorities. (2013, May 8). *Policy basics: Introduction to Medicaid*. Retrieved from http://www.cbpp.org/research/policy-basics-introduction-to-medicaid

Centers for Medicare & Medicaid Services (CMS). (n.d.). *Children's Health Insurance Program financing*. Retrieved from http://medicaid.gov/chip/financing/financing.html

Centers for Medicare & Medicaid Services (CMS). (2009). *CMS financial report*. Baltimore, MD: Author. Retrieved from http://www.cms.gov/CFOReport/Downloads/2009_CMS_Financial _Report.pdf

Centers for Medicare & Medicaid Services (CMS). (2014a). *Historical National Health Expenditures (NHE) tables*. Retrieved from http://www.cms.gov/Research-Statistics-Data-and-Systems/Statistics -Trends-and-Reports/NationalHealthExpendData/NationalHealthAccountsHistorical.html

Centers for Medicare & Medicaid Services (CMS). (2014b). *National Health Expenditures (NHE) fact sheet*. Retrieved from http://www.cms.gov/Research-Statistics-Data-and-Systems/Statistics-Trends -and-Reports/NationalHealthExpendData/NHE-Fact-Sheet.html

Centers for Medicare & Medicaid Services (CMS). (2015a). *Medicare & you*. Retrieved from http ://www.medicare.gov/publications/pubs/pdf/10050.pdf

Centers for Medicare & Medicaid Services CMS. (2015b). *National Health Expenditures (NHE) projections 2014–2024 tables*. Retrieved from https://www.cms.gov/research-statistics-data-and-systems /statistics-trends-and-reports/nationalhealthexpenddata/nationalhealthaccountsprojected.html

Chernew, M. E., Hirth R. A., & Cutler, D. M. (2009, September/October). Increased spending on health care: Long-term implications for the nation. *Health Affairs, 28*(5), 1253–1255.

Claxton, G., Rae, M., Panchal, N., Whitmore, H., Damico, A., & Kenward, K. (2014). Health benefits in 2014: Stability in premiums and coverage for employer-sponsored plans. *Health Affairs, 33*(10), 1851–1860.

Congressional Budget Office (CBO). (2007). *The health care system for veterans: An interim report.* Retrieved from http://www.cbo.gov/ftpdocs/88xx/doc8892/12-21-VA_Healthcare.pdf

Congressional Budget Office (CBO). (2009, March 24). *CBO's March 2009 baseline: MEDICARE.* Retrieved from https://www.cbo.gov/sites/default/files/cbofiles/attachments/medicare.pdf

Cubanski, J., & Neuman, T. (2015, June). *Medicare's income-related premiums: A data note.* Menlo Park, CA: Kaiser Family Foundation. Retrieved from http://files.kff.org/attachment/data-note -medicares-income-related-premiums-a-data-note

Cubanski, J., Swoope, C., Boccuti, C., Jacobson, G., Casillas, G., Griffin, S., & Neuman, T. (2015, March). *A primer on Medicare.* Menlo Park, CA: Kaiser Family Foundation. Retrieved from http ://files.kff.org/attachment/report-a-primer-on-medicare-key-facts-about-the-medicare-program -and-the-people-it-covers

Dranove, D., Garthwaite, C., & Ody, C. (2014). Health spending slowdown is mostly due to economic factors, not structural change in the health care sector. *Health Affairs, 33*(8), 1399–1406.

Garfield, R., Damico, A., Stephens, J., & Rouhani, S. (2015, April). *The coverage gap: Uninsured poor adults in states that do not expand Medicaid – An update.* Menlo Park, CA: Kaiser Family Foundation. Retrieved from http://files.kff.org/attachment/issue-brief-the-coverage-gap-uninsured-poor -adults-in-states-that-do-not-expand-medicaid-an-update

Goodnough, A., Abelson, R., & Hartocollis, A. (2014, October 26). Is the Affordable Care Act working?: 2. Has insurance under the law been affordable? *New York Times.* Retrieved from http://www .nytimes.com/interactive/2014/10/27/us/is-the-affordable-care-act-working.html?_r=0#affordability

Hartman, L., Espinoza, G. A., Fried, B., & Sonier, J. (2015). Millions of Americans may be eligible for marketplace coverage outside open enrollment as a result of qualifying life events. *Health Affairs, 34*(5), 857–863.

Hartman, M., Martin, A. B., Lassman, D., Catlin, A., & the National Health Expenditure Accounts Team. (2015). National health spending in 2013: Growth slows, remains in step with the overall economy. *Health Affairs, 34*(1), 150–160.

Helms, R. B. (2009, November). *Medicaid: The forgotten issue in health reform.* Washington, DC: American Enterprise Institute for Public Policy Research. Retrieved from http://www.aei.org/publication /medicaid-the-forgotten-issue-in-health-reform/

Hernandez-Boussard, T., Burns, C. S., Wang, N. E., Baker, L. C., & Goldstein, B. A. (2014). The Affordable Care Act reduces emergency department use by young adults: Evidence from three states. *Health Affairs, 33*(9), 1648–1654.

Hoyer, M. (2015, June 10). Nation's sickest seniors reshape health care. *USA Today.* Retrieved from http ://www.usatoday.com/story/news/2015/06/05/medicare-costs-seniors-sick-chronic-conditions /27390925/

Hurley, R. E., Strunk, B. C., & White, J. S. (2004, March/April). The puzzling popularity of the PPO. *Health Affairs, 23*(2), 56–68.

Iglehart, J. K. (2010a, February). Medicaid expansion offers solutions, challenges. *Health Affairs, 29*(2), 230–232.

Iglehart, J. K. (2010b, May). The end of the beginning: Enactment of health reform. *Health Affairs, 29*(5), 758–759.

Jansen, D. J. (2014, January 2). *Military medical care: Questions and answers*. Washington, DC: Congressional Research Service. Retrieved from https://www.fas.org/sgp/crs/misc/RL33537.pdf

Japsen, B. (2014, November 19). Half of employers pushing high deductible plans onto workers. *Forbes*. Retrieved from http://www.forbes.com/sites/brucejapsen/2014/11/19/half-of-employers-pushing -high-deductible-plans-onto-workers/

Kaiser Commission on Medicaid and the Uninsured. (2006, February). *Deficit Reduction Act of 2005: Implications for Medicaid*. Washington, DC: Author. Retrieved from http://www.kff.org/medicaid /upload/7465.pdf

Kaiser Commission on Medicaid and the Uninsured. (2010a, July). *Expanding Medicaid to low- income childless adults under health reform: Key lessons from state experiences*. Washington, DC: Author. Retrieved from http://www.kff.org/medicaid/upload/8087.pdf

Kaiser Commission on Medicaid and the Uninsured. (2010b). *Medicaid's continuing crunch in a recession: A mid-year update for state FY 2010 and preview for FY 2011*. Washington, DC: Author. Retrieved from http://www.kff.org/medicaid/upload/8049.pdf

Kaiser Commission on Medicaid and the Uninsured. (2010c). *State Medicaid agencies prepare for health care reform while continuing to face challenges from the recession*. Washington, DC: Author. Retrieved from https://kaiserfamilyfoundation.files.wordpress.com/2013/01/8091 .pdf

Kaiser Commission on Medicaid and the Uninsured. (2014, October). *Key facts about the uninsured population*. Washington, DC: Author. Retrieved from http://files.kff.org/attachment/key-facts -about-the-uninsured-population-fact-sheet

Kaiser Commission on Medicaid and the Uninsured. (2015). *Current status of state Medicaid expansion decisions*. Washington, DC: Author. Retrieved from http://kff.org/health-reform/slide/current -status-of-the-medicaid-expansion-decision/

Kaiser Family Foundation. (2010a). *Medicaid: A primer 2010*. Menlo Park, CA: Author. Retrieved from http://www.kff.org/medicaid/upload/7334-04.pdf

Kaiser Family Foundation. (2010b). *Medicare: A primer 2010*. Menlo Park, CA: Author. Retrieved from https://kaiserfamilyfoundation.files.wordpress.com/2013/01/7615-03.pdf

Kaiser Family Foundation. (2010c, June 18). *Summary of new health reform law*. Menlo Park, CA: Author. Retrieved from http://www.kff.org/healthreform/upload/8061.pdf

Kaiser Family Foundation. (2014). *Total number of children ever enrolled in CHIP annually*. Menlo Park, CA: Author. Retrieved from http://kff.org/other/state-indicator/annual-chip-enrollment

Kaiser Family Foundation and the Health Research and Educational Trust. (2014). *Employer health benefits 2014 summary of findings*. Menlo Park, CA: Author. Retrieved from http://files.kff.org /attachment/ehbs-2014-abstract-summary-of-findings

Kongstvedt, P. R. (2007). *Essentials of managed health care*. Sudbury, MA: Jones and Bartlett.

Krumholz, H. (2014, May 23). Three things to know before you judge VA health system. *Forbes*. Retrieved from http://www.forbes.com/sites/harlankrumholz/2014/05/23/3-things-to-know -before-you-rush-to-judgment-about-va-health-system/

Levit, K. R., Lazenby, H. C., Braden, B. R., Cowan, C. A., Sensenig, A. L., McDonnell, P. A., … & Stewart, M. W. (1997, Fall). National Health Expenditures, 1996. *Health Care Financing Review*, *19*, 161–200.

Levy, J. (2015, January 7). In U.S., uninsured rate sinks to 12.9%. *GALLUP Well-Being*. Retrieved from http://www.gallup.com/poll/180425/uninsured-rate-sinks.aspx

Luo, M. (2010, March 26). Some states find burdens in health law. *New York Times*. Retrieved from http://www.nytimes.com/2010/03/27/health/policy/27impact.html?scp=1&sq=states+find+burdens+in+health+law&st=nyt

Mahan, D. & Traver, A. (2013, September). *Medicaid Alternative Benefit Plans: What they are, what they cover, and states choices*. Washington, DC: Families USA. Retrieved from http://familiesusa.org/sites/default/files/product_documents/Alternative-Benefit-Plans.pdf

McMorrow, S., Kenney, G. M., Long, S. K., & Anderson, N. (2015). Uninsurance among young adults continues to decline, particularly in Medicaid expansion states. *Health Affairs, 34*(4), 616–620.

Miller, T. P. (2010, June). Health reform: Only a cease-fire in a political hundred years' war. *Health Affairs, 29*(6), 1101–1105.

Mitts, L., & Fish-Parcham, C. (2015, May). *Non-group health insurance: Many insured Americans with high out-of-pocket costs forgo needed health care*. Washington, DC: Families USA. Retrieved from http://familiesusa.org/product/non-group-health-insurance-many-insured-americans-high-out-pocket-costs-forgo-needed-health

National Constitution Center Staff. (2015, March 23). *How Obamacare has faced five years of constitutional challenges*. [Blog post]. Retrieved from http://blog.constitutioncenter.org/2015/03/how-obamacare-survived-five-years-of-constitutional-challenges/

National Governors Association and National Association of State Budget Officers. (2010, June). *The fiscal survey of states*. Washington, DC: National Association of State Budget Officers. Retrieved from http://www.nga.org/files/live/sites/NGA/files/pdf/FSS1006.PDF

Obamacare Facts. (2015a). *"Doc fix" Medicare Access and CHIP Reauthorization Act of 2015*. Retrieved from http://obamacarefacts.com/doc-fix-medicare-access-and-chip-reauthorization-act-of-2015/

Obamacare Facts. (2015b). *Let's take a look at the uninsured and how the Affordable Care Act has changed things*. Retrieved from http://obamacarefacts.com/uninsured-rates/

Obamacare Facts. (2015c). *A timeline of health care reforms 2010–2022*. Retrieved from http://obamacarefacts.com/health-care-reform-timeline/

Office of the Secretary of Defense. (n.d.). *Health affairs senior leaders briefing*.

Oliver, A. (2007). The Veterans Health Administration: An American success story. *The Milbank Quarterly, 85*(1), 5–35.

Paradise, J. (2015, March). *Medicaid moving forward*. Washington, DC: Kaiser Commission on Medicaid and the Uninsured. Retrieved from http://files.kff.org/attachment/issue-brief-medicaid-moving-forward

Paradise, J., Lyons, B., & Rowland, D. (2015, May). *Medicaid at 50*. Washington, DC: Kaiser Commission on Medicaid and the Uninsured. Retrieved from http://files.kff.org/attachment/report-medicaid-at-50

Pear, R. (2014, October 26). Is the Affordable Care Act working?: 6. How has the expansion of Medicaid fared? *New York Times*. Retrieved from http://www.nytimes.com/interactive/2014/10/27/us/is-the-affordable-care-act-working.html#medicaid

Philipps, D. (2015, April 22). Few people lost jobs with VA in scandal. *New York Times*. Retrieved from http://www.nytimes.com/2015/04/23/us/few-people-lost-jobs-with-va-in-scandal.html?_r=0

Pozgar, G. (2007). *Legal aspects of health care administration*. Sudbury, MA: Jones and Bartlett.

Purcell, P., & Staman, J. (2008, April 10). *Summary of the Employee Retirement Income Security Act (ERISA)*. Washington, DC: Congressional Research Service. Retrieved from http://www.nccmp.org/resources/pdfs/other/Summary%20of%20ERISA.pdf

Quealy, K. & Sanger-Katz, M. (2014, October 29). Obama's health law: Who was helped most. *New York Times*. Retrieved from http://www.nytimes.com/interactive/2014/10/29/upshot/obamacare-who-was-helped-most.html

Rowland, D., Lyons, B., Salganicoff, A., & Long, P. (1994, Spring). A profile of the uninsured in America. *Health Affairs*, *13*(2), 283–289.

Ryu, A. J., Gibson, T. B., McKellar, M. R., & Chernew, M. E. (2013). The slowdown in health care spending in 2009-11 reflected factors other than the weak economy and thus may persist. *Health Affairs*, *32*(5), 835–840.

Sack, K. (2010, July 27). Texas battles health law even as it follows it. *New York Times*. Retrieved from http://www.nytimes.com/2010/07/28/health/policy/28texas.html

Sanger-Katz, M. (2014, October 26). Is the Affordable Care Act working?: 1. Has the percentage of uninsured people been reduced? *New York Times*. Retrieved from http://www.nytimes.com/interactive/2014/10/27/us/is-the-affordable-care-act-working.html#uninsured

Schwartz, J. (2010, August 2). Virginia suit against health care law moves forward. *New York Times*. Retrieved from http://www.nytimes.com/2010/08/03/us/03virginia.html?scp=1&sq=virginia%20suit&st=cse

Shear, M. D. & Philipps, D. (2015, March 13). Progress is slow at V.A. hospitals in wake of crisis. *New York Times*. Retrieved from http://www.nytimes.com/2015/03/14/us/obama-va-hospital-phoenix.html

Sisko, A. M., Keehan, S. P., Cuckler, G. A., Madison, A. J., Smith, S. D., Wolfe, C. J., ... & Poisal, J. A. (2014). National Health Expenditure projections, 2013–23: Faster growth expected with expanded coverage and improving economy. *Health Affairs*, *33*(10), 1841–1850.

Snyder, L., & Rudowitz, R. (2015, May). *Medicaid financing: How does it work and what are the implications?* Washington, DC: Kaiser Commission on Medicaid and the Uninsured. Retrieved from http://files.kff.org/attachment/issue-brief-medicaid-financing-how-does-it-work-and-what-are-the-implications

Social Security and Medicare Boards of Trustees. (2014). *A Summary of the 2014 Annual Reports*. Retrieved from http://www.ssa.gov/oact/trsum/

Starr, P. (1982). *The social transformation of American medicine*. New York, NY: Basic Books.

TRICARE. (2007). *Anytime, anywhere, keeping warfighters ready, for life: 2007 TRICARE stakeholders report*. Falls Church, VA: TRICARE Management Activity. Retrieved from http://www.tricare.mil/stakeholders/downloads/stakeholders_2007.pdf

TRICARE. (2008). *Caring for America's heroes: 2008 MHS stakeholders' report*. Falls Church, VA: TRICARE Management Activity. Retrieved from http://www.tricare.mil/stakeholders/2007/downloads/stakeholders_2008.pdf

TRICARE. (2010a). *Sharing knowledge: Achieving breakthrough performance: 2010 MHS stakeholders' report*. Falls Church, VA: TRICARE Management Activity. Retrieved from http://www.tricare.mil/stakeholders/downloads/2010stakeholders-final.pdf

TRICARE. (2010b). *TRICARE for life*. Retrieved from http://www.military.com/benefits/tricare/retiree/tricare-for-life.html

Troy, T. (2015, October 12). The 'Cadillac Tax' makes everyone sick. *Wall Street Journal*. Retrieved from http://www.wsj.com/articles/the-cadillac-tax-makes-everyone-sick-1444691323

Truffer, C. J., Keehan, S., Smith, S., Cylus, J., Sisko, A., Poisal, J. A., Lizonitz, J. & Clemens, M. K. (2010, March). Health spending projections through 2010: The recession's impact continues. *Health Affairs, 29*(3), 522–529.

Truffer, C. J., Klemm, J. D., Wolfe, C. J., Rennie, K. E., & Shuff, J. F. (2013). *2013 actuarial report on the financial outlook for Medicaid*. Washington, DC: U.S. Department of Health & Human Services.

U.S. Census Bureau. (2013). *Health Insurance historical tables—HIB series*. Retrieved from http://www.census.gov/hhes/www/hlthins/data/historical/HIB_tables.html

U.S. Department of Health & Human Services (DHHS). (2015, March 10). *Health insurance marketplaces 2015 open enrollment period: March enrollment report*. Retrieved from http://aspe.hhs.gov/health/reports/2015/MarketPlaceEnrollment/Mar2015/ib_2015mar_enrollment.pdf

U.S. Department of Veterans Affairs. (2009, September 15). *All enrollment priority groups*. Retrieved from http://www.va.gov/healthbenefits/resources/priority_groups.asp

U.S. Department of Veterans Affairs. (2015). *2015 Congressional budget submission. Summary—volume I*. Retrieved from http://www.va.gov/budget/docs/summary/fy2015-volumei-summary.pdf

U.S. Department of Veterans Affairs, Health Administration Center. (2009, June). *Fact sheet 01-06: The spina bifida health care program*. Retrieved from http://www.va.gov/PURCHASEDCARE/docs/pubfiles/factsheets/FactSheet_01-06.pdf

U.S. Department of Veterans Affairs, Veterans Health Administration (VHA). (n.d.) About VHA. Retrieved from http://www.va.gov/health/aboutVHA.asp

U.S. Department of Veteran Affairs, Veterans Health Administration (VHA). (2014, September 21). *Blueprint for excellence*. Retrieved from http://www.va.gov/HEALTH/docs/VHA_Blueprint_for_Excellence.pdf

Wachino, V. (2007, June). *The new Medicaid integrity program: Issues and challenges in ensuring program integrity in Medicaid—Executive summary*. Menlo Park, CA: Kaiser Family Foundation. Retrieved from https://kaiserfamilyfoundation.files.wordpress.com/2013/01/7650es.pdf

Wilensky, G. R. (2006, January/February). Consumer-driven health plans: Early evidence and potential impact on hospitals. *Health Affairs, 25*(1), 174–185.

CHAPTER 10

Managing Costs and Revenues

Kevin D. Zeiler

LEARNING OBJECTIVES

By the end of this chapter, the student will be able to:

- Evaluate the importance, purpose, and major objectives of financial management in health care organizations;
- Compare and contrast tax status implications of for-profit versus not-for-profit health care entities;
- Assess the primary methods of reimbursement to providers;
- Apply methods for classifying and controlling costs;
- Evaluate determinants and initial processes considered by health care managers in setting charges/prices for products and services;
- Appraise the purposes, primary sources, and major problems associated with managing working capital;
- Analyze some of the important issues and major processes involved in managing accounts receivable in health care organizations;
- Examine the importance, basic tenets, and commonly accepted methods for managing materials and inventory;
- Analyze the major characteristics and types of budgets utilized by health care managers;
- Critique the basic tenets of health care billing and coding principles; and
- Discuss special research issues related to managing costs and revenues.

INTRODUCTION

The purpose of this chapter is to give a general overview of the various components of financial management within health care organizations, providing examples and applications. Students in health care management and administration frequently become apprehensive about dealing with the financial management aspects of the field. However, it cannot be emphasized enough that an understanding of finance is critical to any student who desires to better understand the business function. The entry-level management position will, at the very least, require an understanding and grasp of the basic concepts of accounting and finance principles, budgets, billing and coding, and forecasting goals and techniques. Each section of this chapter will provide an overview that will help with future studies and lay the groundwork for continued research and application.

WHAT IS FINANCIAL MANAGEMENT AND WHY IS IT IMPORTANT?

Health care financial management is the process of providing oversight for the health care organization's day-to-day financial operations as well as planning the organization's long-range financial direction. Put simply, it involves working to increase the revenues and decrease the costs of the organization. This involves making organizational forecasts, while taking into consideration numerous external environmental variables such as the economy, insurance company policy changes, legislative rules and regulations, and so on. These can have profound impacts on the financial forecast. Ultimately, it is the goal of the finance department to put the organization in the best position possible.

Finally, in the dawn of health care reform, all students, health providers, and financial personnel must understand that financial management will be an ever-changing field that will continually be affected by outside influences. According to a recent poll concerning health care reform, "[n]early three-quarters of health care executives say health care reform will have a negative financial impact on their facilities" (Ledue, 2010, p. 1). This statement does not mean reform is going to ruin the industry; instead, it means that the savvy financial manager will need to stay on top of industry changes in order to maintain the financial health of the organization.

Most health care organizations attempt to meet their economic goals by charging their finance departments with both accounting and finance tasks. These functions help to establish the groundwork for reaching the aforementioned goals.

Accounting consists of two types:

1. **Managerial accounting**, in which financial data are provided concurrently or prospectively to internal users (managers, executives, and the organization's governing board); and

2. **Financial accounting**, in which data are provided retrospectively to external users (stockholders, lenders, insurers, government, and suppliers).

Finance generally includes:

1. Borrowing and investing funds; and
2. Analyzing accounting information to evaluate past decisions and make sound decisions that will affect the future of the organization.

While Nowicki (2004) emphasizes financial management's primary purpose as being "to provide both accounting and finance information that assists healthcare managers in accomplishing the organization's purposes" (p. 4), Berger (2002) takes this description of purpose one step further by noting that "a primary role of financial management [is] helping to analyze the financial implications of the data across the healthcare organization's setting" (p. 7). The latter implies the importance of involving managers at *all* levels of the organization in financial analysis and decision-making. For example, the manager in the radiology unit of a hospital should be directly involved in looking at both the **revenues**, i.e., the amount of money generated by procedures (X-rays, ultrasound procedures, CT scans, etc.) performed in the department and the **expenses** incurred (i.e., money that is spent) in running the department, in addition to being involved in hiring personnel, managing appropriate staffing ratios, making decisions involving the replacement or purchase of equipment, and so on.

TAX STATUS OF HEALTH CARE ORGANIZATIONS

In order to fully comprehend the financial needs and constraints of any given health care organization, it is important to first determine the tax status of that organization. Although health care organizations are primarily categorized as either for-profit or not-for-profit, Berger (2002) discusses three major types: one for-profit and two not-for-profit. For the student's clearer understanding, they have been arranged somewhat differently below, and additional comments have been included:

- **For-profit, investor-owned health care organizations**: These organizations are owned by investors or others who have an interest in making a profit from the services that are provided. These are normally viewed as the for-profit organizations that are required to pay taxes as a cost of doing business. Traditionally, this has included most physician practices and skilled nursing facilities.
- **Not-for-profit health care organizations**: Historically, these organizations have taken care of the poor, needy, and indigent residents of communities and thus have been granted tax-exempt status. They include the following two groups:

1. *Business-oriented (private) organizations*, which are characterized as private enterprises with no ownership interests, that are self-sustaining from fees charged for goods and services, are exempt from income taxes and may receive tax-deductible contributions from those who support their mission, and must provide a certain amount of charity care or community service. Based on their relationships with religiously affiliated organizations, it is not surprising that this group has included an overwhelming majority of hospitals.

2. *Government-owned organizations and public corporations*, which are influenced by political interests but are exempt from taxation and have the ability to issue directly (rather than through a state or municipal authority) debt that pays interest exempt from federal taxation. Included in this group are government-owned hospitals (especially research and training institutions or those serving the medically indigent) and public health clinics.

In addition, there are significant differences in financial management goals based on tax status, which can be summarized as follows:

- Financial goals in for-profit organizations: According to Berman, Weeks, and Kukla (1986), "management must administer the assets of the enterprise in order to obtain the greatest wealth for the owner" (p. 4). That is, the goal is to maximize earnings and profits while minimizing risk to the organization.

- Financial goals in not-for-profit organizations: According to Berger (2002), while these entities must still "produce the best possible bottom line . . . they simply need to do so in the context of providing optimal patient care in the most efficient manner" (p. 6). However, both Berger and Nowicki (2004) emphasize that nonprofit health care providers still place somewhat greater emphasis on community services and other social goals.

Table 10-1 delineates the primary differences between for-profit and not-for-profit health care organizations.

FINANCIAL GOVERNANCE AND RESPONSIBILITY STRUCTURE

The organizational structures of these health care organizations may also be affected by their tax status, although the largest differences are probably seen in the structures of their governing bodies, or boards of directors or trustees. While similar types of professionals (or "volunteers," in the case of not-for-profit boards) are specifically charged with financial accountability and stewardship, in smaller organizations one individual may perform several of the separate functions. Knowing the organizational structure of the financial components of the organization

TABLE 10-1 Comparison of For-Profit and Not-for-Profit Organizations

For-Profit	Not-for-Profit
Serve private interests	Serve public or community interests
Pay federal and state income taxes on profits, state and local sales taxes, and property taxes	Are exempt from taxes; health care organizations receive 501(c)(3) designation if they meet federal IRS criteria
Must file an annual for-profit tax return	Must file the IRS 990 annual corporate tax return, including a community services benefits report
Are motivated by profit, with income benefitting individuals	Revenues cannot benefit individuals, beyond payment of reasonable salaries
Must pay business fees	Are exempt from paying most business fees and licenses
Must adhere to taxable bond yields	Can access tax-exempt bond markets to raise capital
May participate in political campaigns and influence legislation	May not participate in political campaigns or influence legislation
Able to issue stock to raise capital and offer stock options to recruit and retain staff	May not issue stock or offer stock options to staff
Have limited obligation to provide indigent care	Must provide designated amounts of community benefit, including indigent care

will allow all managers to access the appropriate individual(s) in order to make judicious financial decisions for their departments or divisions. In order of responsibility:

- **The Governing Body, or Board of Directors**: As described by the American Hospital Association (1990) and reiterated by Nowicki (2004), in its "fiduciary" role (persons in a position of trust), the board is ultimately "responsible for the proper development, utilization, and maintenance of all resources in the healthcare organization" (p. 30). In for-profit organizations, board members may be paid, but board members serve strictly as volunteers in not-for-profit organizations.
- **The chief executive officer (CEO)** is hired and delegated authority by the board and serves as chief administrator of the operations of the entire organization. The CEO's fiscal performance is monitored through the board's Finance Committee.
- **The chief operating officer (COO)**, often the senior vice president, is responsible for the day-to-day operations of the organization.
- **The chief financial officer (CFO)**, who may also serve as a vice president, is responsible for the entire financial management function of the organization. The CFO is in charge of two primary financial branches, involving (1) the accounting function and (2) management of financial assets. The CFO directly supervises two officers (and occasionally one other) directly in charge of these functions. In some organizations, the COO and the CFO may be the same person.

- **The controller (also called the comptroller)** is the chief accounting officer responsible for the accounting and reporting functions, including financial record keeping. He or she oversees such departments and activities as patient accounts, accounts payable, accounts receivable, cost analysis, budgets, tax status, the generation of financial reports, and sometimes internal auditing.
- **The treasurer** is charged with the stewardship of the organization's financial assets, including cash management, commercial bank relations, investment portfolios, management of pensions or endowment funds, capital expenditures, management of working capital, and long-term debt obligations.
- **The internal auditor** is often a separate staff position from the CFO in large health care organizations and is responsible for ensuring that the accounting, bookkeeping, and reporting processes are performed in accordance with **generally accepted accounting principles (GAAP)**, the nationally accepted rules that determine how financial information is recorded and reported. GAAP includes, among other things, the overarching ideas of conservatism, consistency, and matching of revenues and costs. The internal auditor protects the organization's assets from fraud, error, and loss.
- **The chief information officer (CIO)**, present in many large health care organizations, is the corporate officer responsible for all information and data processing systems, including medical records, data processing, medical information systems, and admitting. The CIO reports either to the CFO or directly to the CEO.
- **The independent auditor**, generally a large accounting firm, is retained by the health care organization to ensure that all financial reports sent to external entities are accurate as to format, content, and scope in presenting the organization's true financial position.

All managers in a health care organization are financial managers to the extent that they consider asset selection, charges, financing, reimbursement, and/or department budgets. This shared responsibility at all levels of the organization serves to maximize efficiency and accountability.

MANAGING REIMBURSEMENTS FROM THIRD-PARTY PAYERS

One of the major objectives of financial management involves facilitating and managing third-party reimbursements, which is vital to generating revenues for the daily operations, growth, and competitiveness of the health care organization. This section will discuss both the methods of payment to providers by managed care organizations (MCOs) and other private insurers and reimbursements to providers from public entities such as Medicare and Medicaid.

What Are the Primary Methods of Payment Used by Private Health Plans for Reimbursing Providers?

Private health care plans use a variety of methods for reimbursing the providers servicing the plan's enrollees. Some are utilized more frequently than others for payments to different provider groups. They are classified according to the amount of financial risk assumed by health care organizations and whether reimbursements are determined after or before health care services are delivered.

Retrospective Reimbursement

Under **retrospective reimbursement**, the amount of reimbursement is determined after the delivery of services, providing little financial risk to providers in most cases. It can involve the following methods:

- **Charges**, most commonly called **fee-for-service**: Health care providers are paid close to or at 100% of their submitted prices or rates for care provided. Because there is virtually no financial risk to providers, these are no longer common. Where full charges persist are with private-pay patients and uninsured individuals, who do not have insurance companies to negotiate discounted rates on their behalf.
- **Charges minus a discount or percentage of charges**: Health care organizations offer discounted charges to third parties in return for large numbers of patients. This is the second most common form of reimbursement to hospitals.
- **Cost plus a percentage for growth**: Health care institutions receive the cost for care provided, plus a small percentage to develop new services and products.
- **Cost**: The organization is reimbursed for the projected cost, expressed as a percentage of charges. While this method provides the smallest amount of reimbursement to providers, there is little risk unless full costs (**direct costs** of providing care plus **indirect costs** or overhead for running the organization) are not recognized.
- **Reimbursement modified on the basis of performance**: The provider is reimbursed based on quality measures, patient satisfaction measures, and so on. Obviously, this method poses more risk for providers.

Prospective Reimbursement

This method of reimbursement to providers is established before the services are provided to patients. These are the primary methods utilized by managed care organizations (MCOs):

- **Per diem**, in which a defined dollar amount per day for care is provided. This is the most common method of reimbursement to hospitals. It presents risks and incentives.

It tends to be bad for acute-only patients, for whom greater costs are incurred earlier in care without the opportunity to make up differences later, when less intense services may be needed.

- **Per diagnosis**, in which a defined dollar amount is paid per diagnosis. It provides risks and incentives. Most common are those similar to the rates utilized by the Centers for Medicare & Medicaid Services (CMS) for Medicare reimbursements, including **Diagnosis-Related Groups (DRGs)** for hospitals, **Resource Utilization Groups (RUGs)** for nursing homes, and **Home Health Resource Groups (HHRGs)** for home health care. Additional rates have more recently been determined for outpatient and inpatient rehabilitation hospital services. In virtually all cases, fewer patient treatments or visits, and/or shorter hospital stays, are now being provided for any given diagnosis.

- **Accountable Care Organizations (ACOs)**: The model of the ACO is based on the idea that groups of providers come together and take responsibility for delivering care to a defined patient population (Colla, Lewis, Shortell, & Fisher, 2014). This approach uses a primary care physician (PCP) to orchestrate the care delivered. The ACO is encouraged to deliver efficient and appropriate care and to keep patients healthy. The approach relies heavily on information technology, so that providers have access to medical records, particularly test results, which is intended to prevent duplication. If those goals are achieved and costs are reduced, the ACO is eligible to share in the savings with Medicare. ACOs differ from HMOs in that the PCP doesn't act as a gatekeeper and patients have the choice of going out of network to receive care (Gold, 2014).

- **Bundled Payments**: This model is based on the idea of providing a single payment for a specific episode of care or a specific procedure. Instead of paying multiple providers to perform their specific tasks in, for example, a surgery such as a knee replacement, a single payment is made. Under this model, "a group of providers receives a fixed payment that covers the average cost of a bundle of services" (Ridgely, de Vries, Bozic, & Hussey, 2014, p. 1345). CMS has developed four models of payment under its Bundled Payments for Care Improvement Initiative, which is being used to test different methods of reimbursement (retrospective and prospective), as well as different types of bundling (CMS, 2013). The models are being phased in at different times "to assess whether the models being tested result in improved patient care and lower costs to Medicare" (CMS, 2014, para. 4). The Advisory Board Company (2014) reported that many provider groups have signed up to participate in this program as of summer 2014, but a report on an early demonstration in California indicated that problems existed with the program and that few contracts were signed to continue after the initial phase of the demonstration; specific concerns were with "a number of barriers, such as administrative burden, state regulatory uncertainty, and disagreements about bundle definition and assumption of risk" (Ridgely et al., 2014, p. 1345).

- **Fee schedule by Current Procedural Terminology (CPT) code, or procedure code**, which is the most common method for reimbursement of specialty physicians. In general, the more complex and time-consuming the procedure, the higher the rate of reimbursement.
- **Capitation** is an agreement under which a health care provider is paid a fixed amount per enrollee per month by a health plan in exchange for a contractually specified set of medical services in the future. Negotiated capitated payments are based on perceptions of expenses for a population. Thus, capitation shifts the risk of coverage from the insurer to the provider of care, providing the most financial risk but also the most opportunity. It is the most common reimbursement method for primary care physicians in MCOs, providing penalties and withholdings for too much care and bonuses as an incentive for ordering lower levels of care.
- **Medical Home:** This model also focuses on connecting patients to primary care, linking them to all types of services, and developing a system that encourages and assures quality of care. The concept of the medical home, which is also referred to as the patient-centered medical home (PCMH), is not new, as it was initially devised in 1967 to provide care to children with special needs (Health Resources and Services Administration [HRSA], n.d.). What is new is that it has been adapted for coordinating the care of adults and other children. The Affordable Care Act "contains various provisions that support implementation of the medical home model including new payment policies, Medicaid demonstrations, and the creation of Accountable Care Organizations—which are similar to medical homes, on a larger scale" (National Conference of State Legislatures, 2012, para. 7).

The medical home model is based on the following seven principles as adopted by the American Academy of Family Physicians, the American College of Physicians, and the American Osteopathic Association:

1. Personal physician: patients are linked to a primary care physician (PCP).
2. Physician directed medical practice: a team of care givers works with the PCP to provide and be responsible for care; this includes nurses, social workers, nutritionists, etc.
3. Whole person orientation: the PCP and the team take a holistic approach to the patient and assume responsibility for all types of care across the person's entire life, including primary care, behavioral health, chronic care, etc.
4. Care is coordinated and/or integrated: all types of providers within the health care system and community can become involved in the provision of care in order to assure that appropriate care is provided.

5. Quality and safety are hallmarks of the medical home: providers and patients work collaboratively to assure quality and good outcomes.

6. Enhanced access to care: practices make access more accessible through offering expanded hours and improved communication with patients.

7. Payment: payment includes coverage of the management of care, specific provider visits, inpatient procedures and stays, as well as the sharing of any savings derived from the management of care (HRSA, n.d.; National Conference of State Legislatures, 2012).

A recent survey of 172 patient-centered medical home initiatives found extensive expansion in the number between 2009 and 2013. The study also found that private insurers, Medicaid, and Medicare participated; used different types of payment reform incentives, such as FFS, pay for performance bonuses, per member per month (PMPM) payments, and various combinations of these; covered almost 21 million people; and concluded that the "model is likely to continue to both become more common and to play an important role in delivery system reform" (Edwards, Bitton, Hong, & Landon, 2014, p. 1823).

The third-party reimbursement system in the health care arena has become so complex, many health care providers (including hospitals and large physician practices) have been forced to hire employees specializing in different contract types within their insurance/finance departments to negotiate the labyrinth of rules and regulations. Accuracy is critical in today's health care industry, where improper coding or billing or untimely filing can lead to missed opportunity—or charges of fraud. Thus, reimbursement is a form of risk for the organization. Simply put, think about the risk as the way in which reimbursement affects profits and how it is uncertain (Gapenski, 2009). Remember, finance is forecasting, so you can see how a complex reimbursement system can and will affect an organization financially if billing is not done correctly.

What Are the Primary Methods of Payment Used for Reimbursing Providers by Medicare and Medicaid?

The largest government-sponsored health care programs in the U.S. are Medicare and Medicaid, as discussed in Chapter 9. Different methods are used to provide reimbursement to various providers of care by these programs, as discussed further below. The current regulations regarding reimbursement to providers in these programs are, however, reflective of various cost-containment efforts. It is also worth mentioning that health reform has also affected Medicare and Medicaid by creating the **Center for Medicare and Medicaid Innovation (CMI)**, which was established to test innovative payment and service delivery models (Shafrin, 2010). As you enter the field or continue to study health care finance, keep in mind that reimbursement will continue to change and adapt to the numerous factors listed earlier in this chapter. Cost-containment issues will continue to arise and will continue to force financial managers to adapt and change to this volatile environment.

Reimbursement to Hospitals and Contractual Allowances

Due to rapidly rising health care expenditures based on an initial retrospective, charge-based reimbursement system to providers, Congress passed the Tax Equity and Fiscal Responsibility Act (TEFRA) in 1982, with particular emphasis on Medicare cost controls. Included among its provisions was a mandate to hospitals for a prospective payment system (PPS) with reimbursement rates established up-front for certain conditions, the option of providing managed care plans to Medicare beneficiaries, and the requirement that Medicare become the secondary payer when a beneficiary has other insurance.

Like most third-party payers for hospital services, CMS substantially reduces reimbursement to hospitals (from original hospital charges to beneficiaries) based on a system of contractual allowances. As defined by McLean (2003), a **contractual allowance** is the "difference between the charge for a bed-day in the adult medicine unit and the amount that the hospital has agreed to accept from the patient's insurance carrier" (p. 53).

In the case of Medicare-eligible patients, CMS reimburses a fixed amount per admission and per diagnosis, based on the patient's **Diagnosis-Related Group, or DRG**. For example, a patient being admitted for heart bypass surgery would receive a higher reimbursement rate than a patient admitted for observation after a fall in which he or she suffered a fractured humerus (arm bone). Berger (2002) asserts that the International Classification of Diseases, ninth edition (ICD-9 codes) was "the most important element" in creating the DRG for reimbursement of an inpatient stay (p. 127). Furthermore, the Omnibus Budget Reconciliation Act of 1990 later folded capital costs into DRG rates as well, with hospitals risking significant reimbursement losses if their buildings and equipment are not properly utilized (Nowicki, 2004).

On the other hand, the Medicaid reimbursement rate to hospitals for any given service varies from state to state, but in all cases includes a substantial contractual allowance. Individual states implement cost controls for Medicaid payments, using either DRGs (like Medicare) or case mix to set reimbursement rates. **Case mix**, also referred to as **patient mix**, is usually related to the mix of patients served by an organization based on the severity of illnesses. An example of differences in this type of reimbursement would be a nursing unit primarily serving patients on ventilators that would be reimbursed at a substantially higher rate than a nursing unit serving patients with orthopedic problems, due to the greater expenses incurred by the former. In all cases, providers must accept reimbursement as payment in full and follow designated efficiency and quality standards.

Reimbursement to Physicians

A **Resource-Based Relative Value System (RBRVS)** was implemented in 1992 for reimbursement for physician office services rendered to Medicare beneficiaries. This system pays a prospective flat fee for physician visits and is based on the **Healthcare Common Procedure Coding System (HCPCS)** codes used by outpatient health care providers and medical suppliers to code their professional services and supplies. Current Procedural Terminology (CPT) (American Medical Association, 2010) is the generally accepted coding methodology utilized. An example of this system is the higher reimbursement rate afforded to a physician for an extended initial patient visit to fully assess a patient's medical condition, versus the lower reimbursement provided for a brief follow-up visit to assess how well a prescribed medication was working.

However, recent legislation (April 2015) passed through both houses and will set up a new way to pay physicians. The current plan will allow physicians to see pay increases over the next five years until a new, merit based program is approved (Carey, 2015). Therefore, the reimbursement formula from that 1990's mentioned above, will become a thing of the past.

Because Medicare serves over 54 million Americans, it was important to pass such legislation so the program can continue into the future (Cornwell & Humer, 2015). Furthermore, the new system will be focused on, "quality, value and accountability" (Carey, 2015). Similarly, state Medicaid programs have implemented cost controls for reimbursement to physicians, initially through fee schedules, but with many states more recently requiring beneficiaries to enroll in capitated managed care plans. As defined by Gapenski (2003), **capitation** is "a flat periodic payment per enrollee to a healthcare provider; it is the sole reimbursement for providing defined services to a defined population. . . . Generally, capitation payments are expressed as some dollar amount per member per month (PMPM)" (p. 576).

Medicare Reimbursements to Other Providers

Despite reductions in reimbursements for hospital admissions and physician visits, Medicare expenditures continued to soar throughout the 1990s. Congress passed the Balanced Budget Act of 1997 in an attempt to control costs for other health care services. Prospective payment systems were implemented in other settings beginning in 1998, as follows:

- *Skilled nursing facilities (SNFs)*, in 1998, with RUGs (Resource Utilization Groups);
- *Home health agencies (HHAs)*, in 2000, with HHRGs (Home Health Resource Groups); and
- *Outpatient hospitals and clinics*, in 2002, with OPPS (Outpatient Prospective Payment System).

How Are Providers Reimbursed by Private Pay Patients and Individuals with No Health Insurance?

As discussed above, those individuals who are not covered by any type of health plan, whether private or public, are often billed for full charges (generally well above costs) by the health care organization delivering the care. This is largely due to the inability of the individual to negotiate a discounted rate for his or her care that is usually afforded patients covered by group health plans. This phenomenon has had the consequence of substantially increasing the number of personal bankruptcies related to medical bills. As revealed in a frequently-cited article in the journal *Health Affairs*, approximately half of the 1.458 million personal bankruptcies filed in 2001 were related to medical bills caused by injury and illness (Himmelstein, Warren, Thorne, & Woolhandler, 2005). A more recent study found little change in these findings, stating that in 2013, "1.7M Americans live in households that will declare bankruptcy due to their inability to pay their medical bills" (LaMontagne, 2015, para. 3). As a direct result, there have been increases in the amount of uncompensated, or unreimbursed, care.

Not-covered or **uncompensated care** is a measure of total hospital care provided without payment from the patient or an insurer. This accounted for between 5.8% and 6.1% of hospital total expenses between 2007 and 2013 (American Hospital Association, 2015). The two major types include:

- **Bad debt**, in which the health care organization bills for services but receives no payment. These operating expenses are based on charges, not costs, and are written off by the organization. This term is usually used with for-profit organizations.
- **Charity care**, in which the not-for-profit organization provides care to a patient who it knows will be unable to pay. Level of charity care (based on either costs or charges) must be documented in footnotes to the financial statements; otherwise, the organization's tax status can be questioned.

Although uncompensated care may be written off as bad debt or charity care by the health care organization, and although it is even required to a certain extent with a not-for-profit organization to maintain its 501(c)(3) status, it is important for managers to recognize that providing too much of this type of care could serve to financially cripple the organization, both in terms of difficulty in maintaining current operations and inability to maximize investment opportunities. Some for-profit organizations question the tax status of not-for-profit organizations and their ability to write off debt as "charity care." They also decry the use of the term "bad debt," because it implies that the manager who extended the credit used poor judgment. This is a controversial topic and one that bears watching.

CODING IN HEALTH CARE

After a patient receives any type of health care service, a bill is generated. Typically, after an encounter with a physician, ambulatory surgery center, or other provider, diagnosis and procedure codes are assigned to the bill. Codes also represent symptoms and medications in order to process a claim properly. The bill is then submitted to the payer, often a health insurance company, in order to receive payment for services rendered. This interaction is known as the **billing cycle** or **revenue cycle** and can take several days to several months to complete.

The **diagnosis codes** and **procedure codes** assist the insurance company in determining the medical necessity of the services and whether the services are covered and should be paid. Usually, a **medical coder** abstracts information from documentation in the patient's medical record, assigns the appropriate codes, and creates the claim to be paid by the commercial insurance company or government agency such as the CMS (American Association of Professional Coders [AAPC], 2015).

Since the late 1800s, an international system of classification for diseases and other health problems has been used to record vital records such as death certificates (World Health Organization [WHO], 2015). Since 1948, WHO has assumed responsibility for managing and publishing this **International Classification of Diseases (ICD)** (WHO, 2015). This is the standard tool for categorizing diseases and health problems for clinical and epidemiological purposes such as mortality statistics as well as for reimbursement decisions around the world. It is updated every ten years. **ICD-10** is the 10th revision of the classification system and increases the number of codes from more than 17,000 to 69,000 different codes (Centers for Disease Control and Prevention[CDC], 2015). The latest compliance date for ICD-10 has been set as October 1, 2015, according to a regulation published by the DHHS on August 4, 2014 (AMA, 2015b). The CMS announced in July 2015 that it will make several changes during the first year of ICD-10 implementation to prevent Medicare claims denials and other penalties, thus making in the changeover less disruptive for physician practices (Stack, 2015).

In 1966, the AMA created the **Common Procedural Terminology (CPT)** set, which it updates every year (AMA, 2015a). CPTs describe medical procedures and other services. In the 1970s, the federal government released the **Healthcare Common Procedure Coding System (HCPCS)**, pronounced as "hick picks," which is based on the AMA's CPT codes for Medicare payment. This coding is necessary for Medicare, Medicaid, and other health insurance programs (AMA, 2015a). Currently, HCPCS has two levels of coding: Level 1 is the CPT code and Level 2 is alphanumeric and includes non-physician services like ambulances, devices, and supplies.

Until the 1980s, claims were submitted using paper forms when electronic submission of bills began. Now, Medicare bills must be sent electronically, and payment is transmitted to providers electronically, as well. Over the years, coding has become more sophisticated and covers more services and specialties such as dental care and skilled nursing facilities. Because of the complexity of this, medical billing and coding specialists must pass examinations to become certified and may even specialize in areas such as outpatient coding or interventional radiology coding (AAPC, 2015). Auditing and compliance are essential aspects of the billing and coding process to ensure quick and accurate claims submission, faster reimbursement, fewer denials, and better-managed practices. Here are some examples.

Question: What is the ICD-10 code for acute appendicitis?
Answer: K35.2 is a billable ICD-10-CM code that can be used.
Question: What is the ICD-10 code for leprosy?
Answer: A30.9 is the billable ICD-10 code.
Question: What is the HCPCS code for 15 minutes of medical nutrition therapy initial assessment and intervention?
Answer: The CPT code is 97802. This code can only be used once a year.
Question: What is the CPT code for hepatitis A vaccination?
Answer: The CPT code is 90632 for monovalent Hepatitis A vaccine for adults (ICD 10 Data, 2015).

Any manager in health care needs to understand the importance of billing and coding classification systems in receiving payment based on accurate and prompt claim submission. Meticulous processing of records related to office visits, planned surgery, or outpatient procedures will ensure compliance with insurance requirements and federal regulations.

In summary, almost every medical condition, procedure, service, and supply can be identified by a numeric code, primarily because Medicare and other third-party payers require numeric coding on claim forms. Accurate coding is the key to prompt reimbursement for services. Knowing the difference between a diagnosis code of 280 (iron deficiency anemia) and 820 (a fracture of the neck of the femur) will help protect a practice from fraud and abuse investigations, as well as help ensure getting paid appropriately and in a timely manner.

CONTROLLING COSTS AND COST ACCOUNTING

Historically, health care organizations, especially hospitals, have been provided strong financial incentives to maximize reimbursements rather than control costs. However, as can be seen in the preceding discussion, there has been a major movement during much of the past two decades to decrease the levels of reimbursement to providers in almost all sectors of the industry. It has thus become increasingly important for health care organizations to understand how to estimate and manage their costs. This changing environment has also resulted in separation of "cost accounting systems from financial accounting systems" and movement "from traditional allocation-based cost systems to activity-based cost systems" (Zelman, McCue, Millikan, & Glick, 2003, p. 15).

While Nowicki (2004) describes its purpose as providing managers with cost information for such reasons as "setting charges and profitability analysis" (p. 145), it is important to note that cost accounting ultimately leads to decision making. This might include enhancing departments that are making money, eliminating services that are losing money, and carefully managing loss leaders (i.e., procedures provided cheaply or below cost to attract customers to the organization). Cost accounting also provides methods for classifying and allocating costs, as well as more precisely determining product costs, all of which will be described briefly in this section.

Classifying Costs

Although there are a number of ways in which costs may be classified, the purpose of Table 10-2 is to illustrate a sampling of the most frequently utilized methods. The importance of such systems is merely to provide a point of departure for controlling costs.

While many authors provide a concise summary of the major methods of classifying costs, such as those shown in Table 10-2 (Nowicki, 2004; Zelman et al., 2003), they do not show how these classifications are often combined by managerial accountants to demonstrate the complexity of cost analysis within health care organizations. For example, concerning salaries and wages in hospitals, the salaries of radiology department managers are both direct and fixed, the wages of on-call nurses are direct but variable, and the salaries of the CEO and CFO are fixed but indirect.

Allocating Costs

Cost allocation involves the determination of the total cost of producing a specified health care service through assigning costs into revenue-producing departments and then further allocating the costs down to the unit-of-service or procedure level based either on departmental revenue or volume. The purpose of this methodology is:

- To ensure that patients are paying [theoretically] "for only the costs of the services and products they received" (Nowicki, 2004, p. 147); and
- "To separate costs at the unit-of-service level to allow managers to:
  - Measure the effects of change in intensity and case mix;
  - Identify those costs that can be converted from fixed to variable; and
  - Identify inefficient functions and demonstrate the nature of the problem, such as price, volume, or practice" (Berger, 2002, p. 216).

TABLE 10-2 Frequently Utilized Methods of Classifying Costs

METHOD	CLASSIFICATION	EXAMPLE
By behavior	**Fixed costs**—stay the same in relation to changes in volume of services	Electricity for lighting
	Variable costs—change directly in relation to changes in volume	Number of sutures used to close incisions
	Semivariable costs—partially fixed and partially variable	Labor costs are the same for patients 1–8; then with The Joint Commission standards, need another RN to take care of the ninth person
By traceability	**Direct costs**—can be traced to a particular patient, product, or service	Gauze pads used in dressing a wound
	Indirect costs (overhead)—cannot be traced to a particular patient or service	Amount of water used during a typical hospital stay
	Full costs—both direct costs and indirect costs	Treatments provided plus utilities used
By decision-making capability	**Controllable costs**—under the manager's influence	Wages of certified nursing assistants (CNAs) per shift
	Uncontrollable costs—cannot be controlled by the manager	Upper administrative hours allocated to department
	Sunk costs—already incurred and cannot be influenced further	Cost of insurance paid in advance
	Opportunity costs—proceeds lost by rejecting alternatives	No purchase of X-ray machine if money spent on new ultrasound machine

Although a number of methods have been identified for cost-allocation purposes, in each case the process ends when all of the organization's costs (including those generated in non-revenue-producing departments, such as housekeeping and medical records) are allocated to the cost centers of revenue-producing departments (radiology, pediatrics, and so forth). These methods have been widely used for pricing and reimbursement purposes in the past but are beginning to be replaced by more accurate methods of determining product costs.

Determining Product Costs

A number of methods for determining **product costs** (e.g., home health visits or patient days) have been posed, each of which crosses department lines of responsibility. However, one method, **activity-based costing (the ABC method)**, has enjoyed increasing popularity in health care organizations because of its greater accuracy. This change in methodology is also due to the fact that cost allocations are no longer made on the basis of cost center characteristics (e.g., number of office visits or percentage of square feet) but rather on the basis of **cost drivers**, or "the activities that go on in preparation for and during a unit of service" (McLean, 1997, p. 142). As explained by Zelman et al. (2003), "ABC is based on the paradigm that activities consume resources and products consume activities. Therefore, if activities or processes are controlled, then costs will be controlled" (p. 426).

Break-Even Analysis

The ultimate goal of managing costs is minimally to break even and not run a deficit. **Break-even analysis** is the method of determining at what level of volume the production of a good or service will equal the revenues created. It is used by health care managers for the purpose of determining profit or loss. The **break-even point** is the volume of production in units and sale of goods or services where total costs equal total revenue. As noted by Nowicki (2004), "After the break-even point has been reached and fixed costs have been covered, each subsequent unit produced contributes to profit" (p. 159). McLean (2003), however, emphasizes that the break-even quantity (e.g., total number of visits) does not necessarily need to be reached for a health care organization to decide to keep a specified service. He states, "If [a] unit covers its direct costs (fixed and variable) and makes any contribution to overhead, it is worth keeping, even in the long run," since the organization would incur overhead expenses even without the unit (McLean, 2003, p. 142). In the long run, "if the unit cannot meet its own (direct) total costs, it should be eliminated unless some outside entity or another revenue center is to subsidize it" (McLean, 2003, p. 142).

SETTING CHARGES

Only after costs have been determined can health care organizations go about the business of setting rates or charges for their services and products. While the earlier section on "Managing Reimbursements from Third-Party Payers" describes a number of methods used by third-party payers and health care organizations to negotiate payments for services, a more complete picture of what is involved when setting charges should be taken into consideration by any provider.

A first step in this discussion might be to differentiate the meanings of charges versus actual prices set by the organization. The Robert Wood Johnson Foundation defines **charges** as the "amount of money a provider would charge absent discounts" (Painter, Chernew, & Dunn, 2012, p. 9). In other words, charges do not reflect costs and are often published simply for reporting purposes. They do not reflect what the consumer will pay or the true value of the services.

Prices in health care, on the other hand, involve opportunity costs, what consumers or third-party payers give up in order to acquire medical goods or services, including:

- Money actually spent.
- The perceived value of:
  - These goods or services;
  - Time sacrificed in acquiring these services; and
  - Other opportunities forgone (purchases, activities).

In other words, charges posted by the organization do not necessarily translate into actual prices paid for services.

Other Determinants of Setting Charges and Prices

Although not claiming to be all-inclusive, the following factors are provided to make sure that the health care manager gives due consideration to each when involved in setting prices for services or products.

- State and federal laws and regulations;
- The Joint Commission and other accrediting body regulations;
- Antitrust and other fair-pricing laws; and
- Profit-oriented pricing, including profit maximization, satisfactory profits, or break-even strategies.

Setting charges or rates remains a highly complex activity within any health care organization due to the need to consider a huge number of variables, both internal and external to the organization. While individual health care managers may be involved in providing substantial input into this process, larger organizations employ experts dedicated to this task in order to sustain revenue maximization and competitiveness in the health care market.

MANAGING WORKING CAPITAL

"**Working capital** refers both to **current assets**," that is, inventory, cash on hand, accounts receivable, and other such items that can be converted to cash in less than one year, "and to **current liabilities**," meaning "those liabilities that will be paid within the current accounting period" (McLean, 2003, p. 288). Virtually all experts, however, define net working capital as "current assets minus current liabilities," a concept that seems to remind us that health care organizations are never without accumulation of debt.

What Are the Purposes of Working Capital Management?

There are two sets of purposes in managing working capital. The end result of the first set of purposes is to increase revenues and reduce expenses in order to:

- Serve as the "catalyst" to make capital assets (buildings and equipment) productive by wisely managing such current assets as labor and inventory.
- Control the volume of resources committed to current assets. McLean (2003) states that "financing working capital by the least costly means available can allow one's organization to deliver the same amount of care at lower cost, or can allow an organization with a limited budget to deliver a greater amount of care" (p. 288).
- Conserve cash by cutting the organization's financing costs in order to take advantage of short-term investments.
- Manage cash flow, that is, the amount of inflows and outflows, and the cash conversion cycle, which is the process (measured in days) through which initial cash is converted into the inventory, labor, and supplies needed in health care operations that in turn generate accounts receivable and that finally are collected in the form of cash revenues.
- Manage the liquidity of an organization, that is, "how quickly assets can be converted into cash" (Zelman et al., 2003, p. 488).

The second set of purposes involves enhancing "goodwill" toward the organization by:

- Paying vendors and employees on time; and
- Demonstrating to lenders that the organization is "creditworthy" by showing it has sufficient resources to repay loans or at least pay interest on short-term funds.

Why Is Working Capital Management in Health Care Environments Problematic?

Managing working capital tends to be more problematic with health care organizations because, with the exception of patient copays, which are miniscule in the big picture of the organization's finances, health care organizations generate very little immediate cash. This is largely due to the huge preponderance of third-party payers and the substantial delays in payment. Also, even if paid by private parties, the large costs incurred for most medical services result in payment after the billing cycle, by credit card, or in negotiated installments.

Another area of concern for many health care financial managers is how best to make decisions in managing working capital when faced with such a wide array of options. Even new and inexperienced managers might take heart by heeding the advice of Sachdeva and Gitman (1981), who offer a simple decision rule when faced with alternative choices between possible means of managing current assets and liabilities: "Undertake changes in working capital management practices that *add value* to the organization" (p. 45).

MANAGING ACCOUNTS RECEIVABLE

Accounts receivable (AR) have been defined as a "current asset, created in the course of doing business, consisting of revenues recognized, but not yet collected as cash" (McLean, 2003, p. 352). Zelman et al. (2003) estimate that AR comprise "approximately 75 percent of a healthcare provider's current assets" (p. 175). Also called **patient accounts** in many health care organizations, accounts receivable provide no interest for the provider unless they have been converted into interest-bearing loans to allow patients to pay out their debts for services over time. Therefore, management of AR becomes exceedingly important in order to collect revenues generated to ensure cash flow for management of the operations of the organization. It is essential to note that the ultimate collection of AR becomes less likely as the amount of time since services were rendered increases. More and more providers are becoming aggressive about collecting these revenues, sometimes resorting to telephone scripts more typical of collection agencies to obtain payments.

Major Steps in Accounts Receivable Management

Managing accounts receivable involves collaboration and cooperation among almost all departments of a health care organization, although some departments are more directly involved than others. Table 10-3 provides examples of involvement in a typical hospital setting.

TABLE 10-3 Hospital Departmental Involvement in Managing Accounts Receivable

Department	AR Involvement
Contracts	Relationships and contract negotiation with third-party payers
Admissions/registration	Precertification, preadmission, insurance verification
Patient care unit (nursing, lab, radiology, rehab, etc.)	Documentation capture, charge capture for services rendered
Medical records	Coding, utilization review, QA (quality assurance audits)
Billing	Bill preparation, billing audits
Compliance	Fraud and abuse internal audits
Collections	Collection policy and procedures, financial counseling, third-party, and self-pay follow-up
Legal	Contracts, litigation policy, federal regulations, patient rights

Some additional thoughts and clarification are warranted concerning the "overriding importance" of managing accounts receivable in all departments:

- **Documentation capture** emphasizes the importance of the quality of the written or electronic record of patient care by all health care professionals.
- Ultimately, interdependence among departments affects the reduction in the AR collection period. For example, accurate documentation supports the coding, and the timeliness of the coding greatly affects the ability of the billing department to send out a timely bill. Cooperation among managers is essential.
- AR outcomes are often measured by first determining a baseline of the progress to be measured and then monitoring the outcomes periodically by looking at the organization's balance sheet and income statements. This process is often referred to as "benchmarking," in which the current year's results can be measured against prior results to see whether things are getting better or worse.

MANAGING MATERIALS AND INVENTORY

Formerly referred to as **inventory management** and more recently designated as **supply chain management**, materials management refers to the process of managing the clinical and non-clinical goods and inventory purchased and used by the personnel of a health care organization in order to perform their duties.

Why Is Materials Management Important?

There are at least three reasons why materials management is so important to the health care organization. The first involves delivery of appropriate patient care, for which the organization must have the right kind and right amount of supplies, delivered in the right time frame. **Stock-outs** (not having enough of a product) are considered totally unacceptable in health care organizations, as they may result in unnecessary deaths or poor outcomes. A second reason involves cost control. Inventory, a nonproductive asset, loses value over time, increasing the costs to the health care facility. If items spend too much time in inventory, they may become contaminated, lost, stolen (referred to as "shrinkage"), or expired. Furthermore, cash tied up in excessive inventory cannot be used for assets that produce income. The third reason involves improvement of the organization's profitability. Skillful materials management can improve the organization's bottom line through such techniques as reducing utilization of overused supplies, obtaining best pricing for supplies and equipment through negotiation, and standardizing the organization's supplies to provide purchasing discounts (Berger, 2002).

What Are the Basic Tenets of Materials Management?

It is also important to adopt the most appropriate method for stocking inventory. This includes keeping a safety stock level of inventory, below which the health care facility will not allow units on hand to fall. It further involves understanding and adopting one of the commonly accepted methods for valuing inventory:

- **FIFO, or "first-in, first-out,"** in which the first item put in inventory is the first taken out; it produces an inventory of newer items and thus values the cost of inventory at the price paid for the newest items;
- **LIFO, or "last-in, first-out,"** in which the last item put in inventory is the first taken out; it produces an inventory of older items and thus values the cost of inventory at the price paid for the oldest items;
- **Weighted average**, in which the average cost of inventory items is multiplied by the number of units in inventory; and
- **Specific identification**, in which the actual cost of each item is included. This tends to be used with high-cost (and relatively few) items.

Finally, adopting the most appropriate method for stocking inventory includes application of either the JIT or ABC inventory methods in terms of when to order or deliver products to the health care facility:

- **Just-in-time (JIT)**: With this technique, products are literally delivered to the organization "just in time" for use. This method is preferred by Berger (2002) in order to decrease the "chance for obsolescence and shrinkage (theft)" (p. 306) and to reduce holding costs associated with warehousing items in the health care facility.
- **ABC inventory method**: With activity-based costing (ABC), each supply item is categorized as belonging to one of three groups. Group A includes very expensive items that must be monitored closely, such as certain expensive drugs. Group B consists of intermediate-cost items, where order and inventory quantities change "as interest rates and unit prices vary." Group C, the largest group, consists of items that represent little cost but are important to the day-to-day operations of the health care organization (e.g., bandages, tissues, pain relievers). Zelman et al. (2003) and Nowicki (2004) describe the ABC method in detail, providing examples of how it is applied.

While it may be the ultimate responsibility of the materials manager to ensure that all goods needed by both the clinical and non-clinical users in a health care facility are available when required and in the most cost-efficient manner, every manager in the organization must be held accountable for timely ordering and judicious use of materials.

Physicians and other users of high-cost equipment and supplies should also be educated about the procedures involved in the ordering and stocking process. Table 10-4 provides examples of the most commonly used inventory management techniques.

TABLE 10-4 Inventory Management Techniques

FIFO Example

Date	Purchased	Sold	Balance
August 3			200 @ $10 = $2,000
August 9		100 @ $10 = $1,000	100 @ 10 = 1,000
August 11	300 @ $11 = $3,300		100 @ 10 = 1,000
			300 @ 11 = 3,300
August 12		100 @ 10 = 1,000	200 @ 11 = 2,200
		100 @ 11 = 1,100	
August 20	50 @ 14 = 700		200 @ 11 = 2,200
			50 @ 14 = 700
August 26		200 @ 11 = 2,200	50 @ 14 = 700
August 29	200 @ 12 = 2,400		50 @ 14 = 700
			200 @ 12 = 2,400
Total August 30	550 $ 6,400	500 $ 5,300	250 $ 3,100

2,000 + 6,400 − 5,300 − 3,100 = 0

IIFO Example

Date	Purchased	Sold	Balance
August 3			200 @ $10 = $2,000
August 9		100 @ $10 = $1,000	100 @ 10 = 1,000
August 11	300 @ $11 = $3,300		100 @ 10 = 1,000
			300 @ 11 = 3,300
August 12		200 @ 11 = 2,200	100 @ 10 = 1,000
			100 @ 11 = 1,100
August 20	50 @ 14 = 700		100 @ 10 = 1,000
			100 @ 11 = 1,100
			50 @ 14 = 700
August 26		50 @ 14 = 700	
		100 @ 11 = 1,100	
		50 @ 10 = 500	50 @ 10 = 500
August 29	200 @ 12 = 2,400		50 @ 10 = 500
			200 @ 12 = 2,400
Total August 30	550 $ 6,400	500 $ 5,500	250 $ 2,900

2,000 + 6,400 − 5,500 − 2,900 = 0

TABLE 10-4 Inventory Management Techniques (Continued)

Weighted-Average Example

Date	Purchased	Sold	Balance
August 3			200 @ $10 = $2,000
August 9		100 @ $ 10 = $1,000	100 @ 10 = 1,000
August 11	300 @ $11 = $3,300		400 @ 10.75 = 4,300
August 12		200 @ 10.75 = 2,150	200 @ 10.75 = 2,150
August 20	50 @ 14 = 700		250 @ 11.40 = 2,850
August 26		200 @ 11.40 = 2,280	50 @ 11.40 = 570
August 29	200 @ 12 = 2,400		250 @ 11.88 = 2.970
Total August 30	550 $ 6,400	500 $ 5,430	250 $ 2,970

2,000 + 6,400 – 5,430 – 2,970 = 0

MANAGING BUDGETS

One of the most critical functions for managers in health care organizations is management of the departmental or division budget. While the facility's Finance Department is generally involved in working with the manager in developing both operational and capital budgets for the department, it is the responsibility of each manager to ensure that expenditures (for items such as labor, equipment, and supplies) and revenues (if the department supplies services or products for patients/consumers) are monitored carefully on an ongoing basis.

Sorting Out the Definitions and Distinguishing Characteristics of Budgeting

Budgeting means different things to different people, even in health care organizations, and it does not help that not all authors or organizations utilize the same terms in discussing their budgeting processes. The purpose of the current section is to try to sort out some common budgeting terms that are used in the financial management departments of health care entities.

Budgeting is, quite simply, the process of converting the goals and objectives of the organization's operating plan into financial terms: expenses, revenues, and cash flow projections. The budget, then, is a financial plan for turning these objectives into programs for earning revenues and expending funds. Listed below are characteristics of budgeting important to health care managers.

- The budget should be a dynamic working document, to be utilized on an ongoing basis by every manager in the organization.

- Managers must have access to a budget manual and last year's data regarding volumes, revenues, expenses, and cash flows on a monthly basis to provide guidance for their departments' budgeting process.
- Budgets provide a tool for *ex post facto* evaluation of managers concerning their performance in efficiently running their departments and for assessing how well the organization as a whole has met its financial performance goals.
- The budget period is the time frame for which a budget is prepared, often one fiscal year (McLean, 2003).
- The budget calendar is a planning tool used to design and maintain all of the organization's projects falling under the budget, with separate calendars being prepared for the operating and capital budgets (Berger, 2002). Included in this calendar are the budget activities, time-frame expectations, the parties responsible, and follow-up meeting times.

What Are the Specific Types of Budgets?

The **operating budget** generally refers to the annual budget that follows the strategic financial and operating plan. Berger (2002) describes 24 steps in preparing the operating budget, including five distinct "segments": strategic planning, administrative, communications, operational planning, and budgeting segments. He further asserts that these steps "involve managers in every facet of operations. In addition, a critical set of stakeholders who must be accessed, solicited, and appeased are the physicians linked to the organization, either in an employment capacity or in an affiliate relationship" (pp. 145–148).

Cash budget is a term sometimes used interchangeably with "operating budget," but it is specifically distinguished from the latter by some authors and organizations. Prepared by the finance department staff, this budget is described by Berger (2002) as "the necessary step that allows the organization to determine how to optimize the value of the cash being generated by its operations" (p. 235). McLean (1997) more specifically defines a cash budget as "a forecast of cash inflows, cash outflows, and net lending or borrowing needs for the months ahead" (p. 355). This 52-week budget attempts to forecast the receipts (most often from third-party payers) and disbursements (expenses) of the organization. These budgets comprise the following:

- An **expense budget**, which is a prediction of the total expenses that the organization will incur, typically includes such items as labor, supplies, and acuity levels (case mix) and is included on the left-hand side (the debit side) of accounting entries. Remember, an expense is an outflow or an asset that has been used up, and a cost is the resources necessary to provide the service or product you are producing.

- A **revenue budget**, shown on the right-hand (credit) side of accounting entries, includes data on forecasted utilization of specific services within the organization and third-party payer mix.

Three other terms generally associated with cash budgets are:

- **Cash outflows**, which include such expenses as mortgage payments or rents, salaries and wages, benefits, utilities, supplies, and interest paid out;
- **Cash inflows**, which include cash payments up front, 30-day and 60-day collections, government appropriations, donations, and any interest earned each month; and
- **Ending cash**, which comprises both the cash balance at the end of the month and the following month's beginning cash level. The following formula is used to determine this amount: Ending cash = Beginning cash + Cash inflows – Cash outflows.

There are two other types of budgets with which health care managers should become familiar. The term **statistics budget** is given to the initial statistics delineated in the operating plan that forecasts service utilization (by service type, acuity level or case mix, and payer mix), resource use, and policy data (employment data, occupancy rates, staffing ratios, etc.). The **capital budget** refers to the plan for expenditures for new facilities and equipment (often referred to as fixed assets). The following discussion will focus on the latter.

The Importance of Capital Budgeting

Capital budgeting may be defined as the process of selecting long-term assets, whose useful life is greater than one year, according to financial decision rules. The capital budget determines funding amounts, what capital equipment will be acquired, what buildings will be built or renovated, depreciation expenses, and the estimated useful life to be assigned to each asset. Berger (2002) states that its main purpose "is to identify the specific capital items to be acquired. The problem in almost all healthcare organizations is which capital projects should be funded" in light of scarce resources (p. 157). McLean (2003) further asserts that "[t]he basic question that any capital budgeting system must ask is, 'Does this asset or project, in a time value sense, at least pay for itself? If not (if it requires a subsidy), is there a subsidy forthcoming?' If the answer is yes, then the project is worth doing" (p. 189).

The following are types of items typically included in such budgets:

- Land acquisition, including land to be used for expansion of service offerings;
- Physical plant or facility construction, expansion, acquisition, renovation, or leasing, possibly including medical office space for physician practices;
- Routine capital equipment, including items used in clinical areas (radiology, lab, surgery, rehab, and nursing departments);

- Information technology infrastructure or upgrades for financial systems, medical records, and clinical use; and
- Recruitment and acquisition of staff physicians (more recently included), either through purchasing existing physician practices or establishing new practices by employing physicians.

While the capital budgeting process often involves substantial outlays of time by managers at different levels of the organization, it is important to consider some essential steps that are frequently followed. Determination of the capital budget often begins with a wish list of various items requested by staff, physicians, or any other individuals who must obtain or use equipment within the department. It is important to note that engaging physician leaders in this process cannot be overemphasized, because they ultimately make the majority of diagnostic and clinical decisions regarding patient care in health care organizations.

Department managers must then complete and submit designated capital budget requests to the Finance Department. Once all requests have been submitted, the finance staff reviews them for consistency and completeness. Reviewers of the technical aspects of the capital requests make sure each contains all of the data required. This group often includes accounting staff, information systems management, materials management, and facilities management. Designated evaluators assess the merits of the requests, how each compares to all other project requests on a criteria basis, and whether each adheres to strategic plan criteria. Administrative approval and approval by the governing body completes the process.

While there are a number of methods utilized to make capital budgeting decisions, most health care organizations establish criteria-based decision rules. These range from a simple accept/reject decision, which merely addresses "whether or not to acquire an asset or initiate a project," to capital rationing, in which a fixed dollar amount is placed on annual capital spending by governing bodies and those with the highest profitability index are selected (McLean, 2003, pp. 193–195). However, as a "safety valve" in the decision process, some organizations have found that it is necessary to include a mechanism that allows some needed capital acquisitions "to be purchased no matter what," that is, despite not being able to meet formal evaluation criteria. Berger (2002) calls this non-criteria-based capital budgeting.

OPPORTUNITIES FOR RESEARCH ON MANAGING COSTS AND REVENUES

Opportunities for in-depth research on managing costs and revenues exist in a variety of venues, including your own health care organization. Many of the resources used in writing this chapter also include extensive research holdings and data sets which are available to students and academic researchers to utilize. Herewith is a partial listing of some resources.

- Agency for Healthcare Research and Quality;
- American College of Healthcare Executives;
- Centers for Medicare and Medicaid Services, particularly the reimbursement and fee schedules;
- Healthcare Financial Management Association;
- Health Services Research Information Central (HSRIC);
- Internal Revenue Service, particularly areas on charity, non-profits, and tax exemptions; and
- Social Security Administration.

CONCLUSION

Managing costs and revenues in the health care arena is a complex and often technical process that involves understanding of the interrelatedness of the processes involved, the interplay of many departments and managers within the organization, and the importance of influences external to the organization. This chapter has addressed the importance and objectives of financial management and the impacts of tax status and organizational structure and has taken a cursory look at how effective management of a variety of organizational support functions contribute to maximizing revenues and controlling costs. More specifically, the chapter has provided the health care administration student with a non-financial career path a basic understanding of managing costs, reimbursements from third-party payers and other sources, budgeting, capital acquisition, working capital, accounts receivable, setting charges and prices, and managing materials and inventory. Managers at all levels of the organization are often involved in addressing these functions.

What this chapter did not address more specifically were investment decisions, short-term versus long-term financing, managing endowments, financial ratios, or financial statement preparation and analysis. This is largely due to the fact that these functions are most often handled by professionals within the Finance Department of the health care organization, who in turn provide managers with pertinent related information on an as-needed basis. However, for health care managers more directly involved in financial management as a major part of their jobs, it is imperative that they avail themselves of this and other detailed financial management information to help ensure the financial viability of their organizations.

All managers employed within the health care arena must continue to monitor the changes taking place in health care and, more precisely, with health care reform. The key to understanding health care finance is to take the concepts one step at a time until you are able to build them into one cohesive unit of understanding. Furthermore, getting involved and applying what you have learned in the classroom and through the textbook is an excellent way to hone your financial skills. Never pass up the opportunity to put your financial skills to work in a real-world setting, as this is how you will learn to apply the principles discussed in this chapter.

DISCUSSION QUESTIONS

1. Define health care finance and provide several examples of how it affects managers at all levels within the organization.

2. Compare and contrast the different inventory management techniques and discuss how each technique might play a role within different health care organizations.

3. How are health services paid for? Provide a definition for the term "third-party payer," discuss the different payers currently operating in the market, and assess the importance of each.

4. Define and give examples (other than from the table in the text) of fixed, variable, and semivariable costs, along with examples of ways to control the costs in your examples.

5. Explain why budgets are important to all organizations. Expand this discussion by illustrating how different types of budgets are used.

6. How is working capital important to the health care organization of today? Why is it different in health care as opposed to other industries?

7. Discuss the various ways in which health care reform has affected and may affect the financial delivery of health care today and into the future.

8. How do medical billing and coding specialists keep up-to-date with changes in ICD and CPT?

9. Why is it so important to have accurate medical billing and coding?

Cases in Chapter 18 related to this chapter include:

- Piecework
- Problems with the Pre-Admission Call Center
- Medical Center: Let's All Just Get Along
- I Want to Be a Medical Coder
- Managing Costs and Revenues at Feel Better Pharmacy

Case study guides are available in the online Instructor's Materials.

REFERENCES

Advisory Board Company. (2014, August 1). Thousands of providers join Medicare's bundled pay program. Retrieved from https://www.advisory.com/daily-briefing/2014/08/01/providers-join-medicare-bundled-pay-program-what-it-means

American Association of Professional Coders (AAPC). (2015). *Certified Professional Coder.* Retrieved from https://www.aapc.com/certification/cpc/

American Hospital Association (AHA). (1990). *Role and functions of the hospital governing board.* Chicago, IL: Author.

American Hospital Association (AHA). (2015, January). *Uncompensated hospital care cost fact sheet.* Retrieved from http://www.aha.org/content/15/uncompensatedcarefactsheet.pdf

American Medical Association (AMA). (2010). *Current procedural terminology (CPT).* Retrieved from http://www.ama-assn.org/ama/pub/physician-resources/solutions-managing-your-practice/coding-billing-insurance/cpt.shtml

American Medical Association (AMA) (2015a). *History timeline.* Retrieved from http://www.ama-assn.org/ama/pub/about-ama/our-history/ama-history-timeline.page

American Medical Association (AMA). (2015b). *ICD-10 code set to replace ICD-9.* Retrieved from http://www.ama-assn.org/ama/pub/physician-resources/solutions-managing-your-practice/coding-billing-insurance/hipaahealth-insurance-portability-accountability-act/transaction-code-set-standards/icd10-code-set.page

Berger, S. (2002). *Fundamentals of health care financial management: A practical guide to fiscal issues and activities* (2nd ed.). San Francisco, CA: Jossey-Bass.

Berman, H. J., Weeks, L. E., & Kukla, S. F. (1986). *The financial management of hospitals* (6th ed.). Chicago, IL: Health Administration Press.

Carey, M. A. (2015). Congress just passed a Medicare doc fix. *Kaiser Health News.* Retrieved from http://time.com/money/3823180/medicare-doc-fix-congress/

Centers for Disease Control and Prevention (CDC). (2015, October 1). International Classification of Diseases, (ICD-10-CM/PCS) transition—background. Retrieved from http://www.cdc.gov/nchs/icd/icd10cm_pcs_background.htm

Centers for Medicare & Medicaid Services (CMS). (2013). Bundled Payments for Care Improvement (BPCI) Initiative: General information. Retrieved from http://innovation.cms.gov/initiatives/bundled-payments/

Centers for Medicare and Medicaid Services (CMS). (2014, January 1). Fact sheets: Bundled Payments for Care Improvement Initiative fact sheet. Retrieved from http://www.cms.gov/Newsroom/MediaReleaseDatabase/Fact-sheets/2014-Fact-sheets-items/2014-01-30-2.html

Colla, C. H., Lewis, V. A., Shortell, S. M., & Fisher, E. S. (2014). First national survey of ACOs finds that physicians are playing strong leadership and ownership roles. *Health Affairs, 33*(6), 964–971.

Cornwell, S., & Humer, C. (2015). U.S. House okays bipartisan bill to fix Medicare doctor payments. *Reuters.* Retrieved from http://www.reuters.com/article/2015/03/26/us-usa-congress-medicare-idUSKBN0MM27B20150326

Edwards, S. T., Bitton, A., Hong, J., & Landon, B. E. (2014). Patient-centered medical home initiatives expanded in 2009-13: Providers, patients and payment incentives increased. *Health Affairs, 33*(10), 1823–1831.

Gapenski, L. C. (2003). *Understanding healthcare financial management* (4th ed.). Chicago, IL: Health Administration Press.

Gapenski, L. C. (2009). *Fundamentals of health care finance*. Chicago, IL: Health Administration Press.

Gold, J. (2014, April 16). FAQ on ACOs: Accountable care organizations, explained. *Kaiser Health News*. Retrieved from http://www.kaiserhealthnews.org/stories/2011/january/13/aco-accountable-care-organization-faq.aspx

Health Resources and Services Administration (HRSA). (n.d.). *What is a medical home? Why is it important?* Retrieved from http://www.hrsa.gov/healthit/toolbox/Childrenstoolbox/BuildingMedicalHome/whyimportant.html

Himmelstein, D. U., Warren, E., Thorne, D., & Woolhandler, S. (2005, February). Market watch: Illness and injury as contributors to bankruptcy. *Health Affairs*, *10*(W5), 63–73, Web exclusive.

ICD10DATA.COM (2015). ICD-10 CM Codes. Retrieved from http://www.icd10data.com/ICD10CM/Codes

LaMontagne, C. (2015, April 28). NerdWallet Health finds medical bankruptcy accounts for majority of personal bankruptcies. *NerdWallet Health*. Retrieved from http://www.nerdwallet.com/blog/health/2014/03/26/medical-bankruptcy/

Ledue, C. (2010, April 23). Healthcare executives believe reform will negatively affect facilities. *Healthcare Finance News*. Retrieved from http://www.healthcarefinancenews.com/news/healthcare-executives-believe-reform-will-negatively-affect-facilities

McLean, R. A. (1997). *Financial management in health care organizations*. Clifton Park, NY: Thomson Delmar Learning.

McLean, R. A. (2003). *Financial management in health care organizations* (2nd ed.). Clifton Park, NY: Thomson Delmar Learning.

National Conference of State Legislatures. (2012, September). The medical home model of care. Retrived from http://www.ncsl.org/research/health/the-medical-home-model-of-care.aspx

Nowicki, M. (2004). *The financial management of hospitals and healthcare organizations* (3rd ed.). Chicago, IL: Health Administration Press.

Painter, M. W., Chernew, M. E., & Dunn, D. (2012). Counting change: Measuring health care prices, costs and spending. *Robert Wood Johnson Foundation*. Retrieved from http://www.rwjf.org/content/dam/web-assets/2012/03/counting-change

Ridgely, S. M., de Vries, D., Bozic, K. J., & Hussey, P. S. (2014). Bundled payment fails to gain a foothold in California: The experience of the IHA bundled payment demonstration. *Health Affairs*, *33*(8), 1345–1352.

Sachdeva, K. S., & Gitman, L. J. (1981). Accounts receivable decisions in a capital budgeting framework. *Financial Management*, *10*(4), 45–49.

Shafrin, J. (2010, June 30). Center for Medicare and Medicaid Innovation. *Healthcare Economist*. Retrieved from http://healthcare-economist.com/2010/06/30/center-for-medicare-and-medicaid-innovation/

Stack, S. J. (2015, July 6). CMS to make ICD-10 transition less disruptive for physicians. *AMA Wire*. Retrieved from http://www.ama-assn.org/ama/ama-wire/post/cms-icd-10-transition-less-disruptive-physicians

World Health Organization (WHO). (2015). International Classification of Diseases (ICD) information sheet. Retrieved from http://www.who.int/classifications/icd/factsheet/en/

Zelman, W. N., McCue, M. J., Millikan, A. R., & Glick, N. D. (2003). *Financial management of health care organizations: An introduction to fundamental tools, concepts and applications* (2nd ed.). Malden, MA: Blackwell.

CHAPTER 11

Managing Health Care Professionals

Sharon B. Buchbinder and Dale Buchbinder

LEARNING OBJECTIVES

By the end of this chapter, the student will be able to:

- Distinguish among the education, training, and credentialing of physicians, nurses, nurse aides, midlevel practitioners, and allied health professionals;
- Deconstruct factors affecting the supply of and demand for health care professionals;
- Analyze reasons for health care professional turnover and costs of turnover;
- Propose strategies for increasing retention and preventing turnover of health care professionals;
- Create a plan to prevent conflict of interest in a health care setting;
- Examine issues associated with the management of the work life of physicians, nurses, nurses' aides, midlevel practitioners, and allied health professionals; and
- Investigate sources of data for health workforce issues.

INTRODUCTION

Health care organizations employ a wide array of clinical, administrative, and support professionals to deliver services to their patients. The Bureau of Labor Statistics (BLS) indicated that there were close to 16 million jobs in hospitals, offices of health practitioners, nursing and residential care facilities, home health care services, and outpatient settings (Torpey, 2014).

The largest employment setting in health care is hospitals and the largest category of health care workers is registered nurses, with 2.7 million jobs, 61% of which are in hospitals (BLS, 2014h). According to the BLS, there were 691,400 physicians and surgeons who held jobs in 2012 (BLS, 2014e). Increasingly, physicians are choosing to practice in large groups or to be employed by hospitals, rather than in solo or small practices. In 2013, Jackson Healthcare re-conducted a survey of physicians and found 26% were employed by hospitals, an increase of 6% over the previous year. Ownership stakes in practices, solo practices, and independent contractor statuses all declined in the same period (Vaidya, 2013). Employment offers physicians a safe haven in a volatile health care environment. Under the umbrella of a hospital or other large health care organization, they have better work hours, benefits, and time off, which they could not always afford in small or solo practice. It is expected the proportion of employed physicians will continue to grow in the coming decade. In 2012, physician assistants held 86,700 jobs, over 55% of which were in ambulatory health care services, including physician practices, about 20% were in hospitals, and the rest in nursing care facilities and government settings (BLS, 2014f). Allied health professionals constitute a broad array of 28 health science professions, including, but not limited to, anesthesiologist assistants, medical assistants, respiratory therapists, and surgical technologists (Commission on Accreditation of Allied Health Education Programs, 2015).

These statistics mean that, as a health care manager, in many instances you will be working with a mix of people with either more or less education than you have. It also means you will not have the clinical competencies that these health care providers have—an intimidating scenario, to say the least. Instead of clinical expertise, however, you will bring a background that enables you to enhance the environment in which these highly specialized personnel deliver health care services. You will be the person responsible for making sure nurses, doctors, and other health care professionals have the resources to provide safe and effective patient care. Your role will be to provide and monitor the infrastructure and processes to make the health care organization responsive to the needs of the patients and the employees. The more you understand clinical health care professionals, the better prepared you will be to do your job as a health care manager. The purpose of this chapter is to provide you with an overview of who your future colleagues are, how they were trained, and ways to manage the quality of their work environment.

PHYSICIANS

Physicians begin their preparation for medical school as undergraduates in premedical programs. Premedical students can obtain a degree in any subject; however, the Association of American Medical Colleges (AAMC) (2015) indicates that the expectation is that they will graduate with a strong foundation in mathematics, biology, chemistry, and physics. Entry into medical school is competitive; applicants must have high grade point averages and high scores on the Medical College Admission Test (MCAT).

There are some shorter, combined Bachelor of Science/Medical Doctor (BS/MD) programs; however, the majority of medical school graduates will have 8 years of post–high school education before they go through the National Residency Matching Program (NRMP), a matching process whereby medical students interview and rank their choices for graduate medical education (GME), also known as residencies, and the residency training programs do the same (NRMP, 2015). Once matched with a residency training program, physicians are prepared in specialty areas of medicine. Depending on the specialty, the length of the residency training program can be as short as 3 years (for family practice) or as long as 10 years (for cardio-thoracic surgery or neurosurgery). According to the Accreditation Council for Graduate Medical Education (ACGME), "When physicians graduate from a residency program, they are eligible to take their board certification examinations and begin practicing independently. Residency training programs are sponsored by teaching hospitals, academic medical centers, health care systems and other institutions" (ACGME, 2015, para. 4–5). Due to recent GME legislation working on the physician shortage, there will be a gradual increase of residency training positions over the coming years with a priority on primary care physician residency spots (AMA Wire, 2015a). Some authors have begun to question the need for lengthy training programs, given the presence of shorter pre-medical programs, competency based education, the looming shortage of physicians, and levels of debt incurred by medical students (Duvivier, Stull, & Brockman, 2012; Emanuel & Fuchs, 2012). Regardless of the specialty, length of physician training programs, or number of trainees, depending on the type of health care organization where you are employed, you may be working with residents-in-training and medical students, as well as physicians who have been in independent practice for decades.

In addition to having a long time before they can practice independently, residents work extensive hours as part of their training programs. At one time, it was not uncommon for residents to be on call continuously for 48 hours, because ceilings on hours of work for residents varied by residency training program. However, that all changed due to the death of Libby Zion, an 18-year-old college student, who was seen at the Cornell Medical Center in 1984 and allegedly died due to resident overwork (AMA, Medical Student Section, n.d.). Although the hospital and resident were exonerated in court, the battle over resident work hours had begun. New York was the first state to institute limits on resident work hours in 1987. Over the past two decades, various specialty societies, medical associations, and legislators fought over the definition of "reasonable" work hours for physicians in training. The battle has continued, and new rules have been updated from those published in 2003. Per these new rules, hospitals and residency training program directors will be required to limit resident work hours to no more than "80 hours per week, averaged over a four-week period, inclusive of in-house call activities and all moonlighting" (i.e., side jobs in addition to the 80 hours per week) (ACGME, 2014, p. 4). First-year residents (PGY-1) are not permitted to moonlight (ACGME, 2011).

"Sponsoring institutions and programs must ensure and monitor effective, structured hand-over processes to facilitate both continuity of care and patient safety" (ACGME, 2014, p. 13). This mandate means when the resident goes home, the next person taking care of the patient must be briefed to ensure that the patient care team has all relevant information. Despite the restrictions on work hours, residents are not permitted to walk out the door without communicating this important patient care information. At times, this means a delicate balancing act to ensure compliance with all standards, which also emphasize the need for interpersonal and communication skills, professionalism, systems-based practice as components in a culture of safety and patient-centric care.

When the work-hour rules first went into effect, physicians who trained under the "work until you drop" mentality protested that professionalism would decline and residents would miss out on learning opportunities associated with continuity of the care from patient admission to discharge. Surgeons, in particular, protested, fearing walk-outs in the middle of long cases, a reflection of a time-clock-punching and a shift-work mentality. Ethnographic research conducted among medical and surgical residents in two hospitals did not find evidence for those fears. Over the course of three months, Szymczak, Brooks, Volpp, and Bosk (2010) followed residents, observed behaviors, and conducted in-depth face to face interviews. These researchers found that rather than leave at a critical juncture, the residents were, on occasion, more inclined to stay—off the clock. Interviews elucidated thoughtful, analytical rationales for the non-compliant behaviors, as well as a respect for the work-hour rules. Residents were mindful of the implications of their behaviors and the implications of non-compliance and were conflicted about under-reporting their hours, i.e., lying about their time on duty. These work-hour rules and patient handoff protocols underscore the fact that residents are in the hospital for education, not to provide service to the hospital, a major departure from the way graduate medical education was conducted a few decades ago. More time is needed to see if the pendulum will swing back to longer duty-hours in light of actual behaviors.

The implications of limits on resident work hours are multifold. While residency training program directors are responsible for monitoring resident work hours, they must be in compliance with the health care institution's policies as well. You may be responsible for ensuring compliance by collecting work-hour data for your managers. Health care managers are obligated to ensure adequate coverage of the hospital with physicians. Resident work-hour restrictions may mean that you need to employ more physicians or midlevel practitioners—physician assistants and nurse practitioners. And your organization may need to hire ancillary staff and allied health professionals, such as intravenous therapists and surgical assistants, to do tasks previously covered by resident physicians.

Most physicians are eligible to obtain a license to practice medicine after one year of postgraduate training. **Licensure**, granted by the state, is required for physicians, nurses, and others to practice and demonstrates competency to perform a scope of practice (National Council of State Boards of Nursing [NCSBN], 2015a). Limited licensure is granted for PGY-1s in hospital practice under supervision. State Boards of Physician Quality Assurance (BPQA) establish the requirements for medical licenses. These requirements are lengthy and strenuous. For example, the state of Maryland requires the following (Annotated Code of Maryland, 2015):

- Good moral character;
- Minimum age of 18 years;
- A fee;
- Documentation of education and training; and
- Passing scores on one of the following examinations:

  - All parts of the National Board of Medical Examiners' examinations, and/or a score of 75 or better on a FLEX exam, or a passing score on the National Board of Osteopathic Examiners, or a combination of scores and exams; or
  - State Board examination;
  - All steps of the U.S. Medical Licensing Examination (USMLE).

Candidates must demonstrate oral and written English-language competency and supply the following:

- A chronological list of activities beginning with the date of completion of medical school, accounting for all periods of time;
- Any disciplinary actions taken by licensing boards, denying application or renewal;
- Any investigations, charges, arrests, pleas of guilty or *nolo contendere*, convictions, or receipts of probation before judgment;
- Information pertaining to any physical, mental, or emotional condition that impairs the physician's ability to practice medicine;
- Copies of any malpractice suits or settlements, or records of any arrests, disciplinary actions, judgments, final orders, or cases of driving while intoxicated or under the influence of a chemical substance or medication; and
- Results of all medical licensure, certification, and recertification examinations and the dates when taken.

In addition to the above requirements, many states also mandate Continuing Medical Education (CME) in such topics as domestic violence, child abuse, drug abuse, and quality assurance, to name but a few. A new commission is working to help streamline the process for those physicians seeking licensure in multiple states. The eligible physician designates her "principle state of licensure and selects other states in which she desires licensing" (AMA Wire, 2015b, para 3). At the time of this writing, seven states were participating in this compact. It is anticipated that with the rise of telemedicine, more states will join the Federation of State Medical Boards, Inc. (FSMB)–initiated agreement.

Physicians must also undergo criminal background checks (CBCs) in all but a few states. As of 2014:

- "45 state medical boards conduct criminal background checks as a condition of initial licensure;
- 39 state medical boards require fingerprints as a condition of initial licensure;
- 43 state medical boards have access to the Federal Bureau of Investigation database; and
- The Minnesota Board of Medical Practice will conduct criminal background checks and require fingerprinting (including access to the FBI National Crime Information Center [NCIC]) by January 1, 2018" (FSMB, 2014, p. 1).

The reasons for increasing numbers of medical boards requiring CBCs are numerous and include, but are not limited to, increasing societal concerns about alcohol and drug abusers, sexual predators, and child and elder abusers. If a CBC contains information about convictions, the state licensure board will examine the application on a case-by-case basis. The reviewers will be looking for level and frequency of the criminal behavior, basing their decision on that, along with other materials submitted by the applicant, such as proof of alcohol and drug rehabilitation.

In addition to obtaining a license, physicians may voluntarily submit documentation of their education, training, and practice to an American Board of Medical Specialists (ABMS) member board for review (ABMS, 2015). Upon approval of the medical specialty board (i.e., successful completion of an approved residency training program), the physician is then allowed to sit for examination. Successful completion of the examination(s) allows the physician to be granted certification, and she is designated as **board certified** in that specialty (e.g., a board-certified pediatrician or a board-certified general internist). Certificates are time-limited; physicians must demonstrate continued competency and retake the exam every 6 to 10 years, depending on the specialty. The purpose of American Board of Medical Specialties **Maintenance of Certification** (ABMS MOC) is to ensure that physicians remain up-to-date in their specialties (ABMS, 2015). Board certification is a form of **credentialing** a physician's competency in a specific area. For staff privileges and hiring purposes, most hospitals, HMOs, and other health care organizations require a physician to be board certified or **board eligible** (i.e., preparing to sit for the exams) because board certification is used as a proxy for determining the quality of health professionals' services. This assumption of quality is based on research that more education and training leads to a higher quality of service (Donabedian, 2005; Tamblyn et al., 1998). Lipner, Hess, and Phillips (2013) conducted a meta-analysis of the perceptions of the value of ABMS MOC on stakeholders. The authors found patients and health care organizations valued MOC and participation across the boards was high, perhaps due in large part to hospitals requiring it for privileging. However, not all physicians were not convinced re-certification was useful. The same literature review found the association between physician board certification and quality of care to be positive, but "modest in effect sizes and are not unequivocal" (Lipner et al., 2013, p. S20). Since the ABMS MOC is still a relatively new requirement, it remains to be seen if the impact on quality of care will grow over time.

Most states require that physicians complete a certain number of **continuing medical education (CME)** credits to maintain state licensure and to demonstrate continued competency. Additionally, hospitals may require CME credits for their physicians to remain credentialed to see patients (National Institutes of Health [NIH], 2015). Seven organizations, the ABMS, the American Hospital Association (AHA), the AMA, the Association of American Medical Colleges (AAMC), the Association for Hospital Medical Education (AHME), the Council of Medical Specialty Societies (CMSS), and the FSMB, are members of the **Accreditation Council for Continuing Medical Education (ACCME)** (ACCME, 2015b). The ACCME establishes criteria for determining which educational providers are quality CME providers and gives its seal of approval only to those organizations meeting their standards. The ACCME also works to ensure "uniformity in accreditation" of educational offerings to maintain the quality of continuing physician education and now requires educational providers to reapply for maintenance of recognition (ACCME, 2015a).

Physician credentialing is the process of verifying information a physician supplies on an application for staff privileges at a hospital, HMO, or other health care organization. Most health care organizations have established protocols, and as a health care manager, you will be required to follow that protocol. Physicians are tracked by the AMA from the day they graduate from medical school until the day they die. Information about every physician in the U.S. is in the AMA Physician Masterfile, which has been in existence for more than 100 years. Originally created on paper index cards to establish biographic records on physicians, "the Masterfile…serves as a primary resource for professional medical organizations, universities and medical schools, research institutions, governmental agencies, and other health-related groups" (AMA, 2015b, para. 5). Physician credentialing is a time-consuming, labor-intensive, costly process that must be repeated every two years.

When physicians apply for privileges at a hospital, they must specify what they want by specialty and, within the surgical specialties, by procedure. For example, a general surgeon who wants to do laparoscopic cholecystectomies (i.e., removal of the gall bladder through a very small incision, using an instrument like a tiny telescope) would apply for both general surgery privileges and for that specific procedure. Using extensive documentation, the surgeon must demonstrate competency for those privileges.

Normally, physician credentialing criteria are established by the department where the physician would be affiliated. **Core privileges** cover a multitude of activities that a physician is allowed to do in a health care services organization. Using family practice (FP) as an example, the Department of Family Practice in a hospital would establish the criteria for privileges. Core privileges for a FP might include: admission, evaluation, diagnosis, treatment and management of infants and children, adolescents, and adults for most illnesses, disorders, and injuries (American Academy of Family Practice [AAFP], 2015b). **Specific privileges** would be those activities outside the core privileges and would require documentation of required additional training and expertise in a procedure. In this example, if the FP also wanted to be allowed to deliver babies at a hospital, that FP would be required to provide documentation of that training and might be subject to observation or proctorship to ensure he or she had the requisite competencies (AAFP, 2015a). If there are two departments with physicians who do the same thing (e.g., Obstetrics and Gynecology and Family Practice), each department is responsible for its own criteria. The Medical Staff Office would enforce, but not establish, the criteria. A hospital must conduct diligent research on physicians before granting privileges, or it can be held liable in a court of law for allowing an incompetent physician on its staff, should there be a bad outcome. The same is true for HMOs, ambulatory care centers, and other health care delivery organizations. In *Taylor v. Intuitive*, lawyers for the estate of Fred Taylor alleged Intuitive, the company that created the daVinci robotic surgery system, failed to provide adequate training for the surgeon, which led to major complications and the death of the patient. Intuitive argued it had no responsibility for assessing the surgeon's competency in using the technology. The jury agreed with the defense, underscoring the importance the hospital's legal liabilities associated with negligent credentialing and privileging (Pradarelli, Campbell, & Dimick, 2015).

It is preferable to obtain primary, meaning firsthand, verification and documentation by contacting each place of education, training, and employment individually by phone and obtain original documents, such as transcripts with raised seals. Verification can include, but is not limited to, the following elements (Government Accountability Office [GAO], 2010):

- Name, address(es), and telephone numbers;
- Birthdate and place of birth;

- Medical school;
- Residency training program and other graduate education, including fellowships;
- State licensure details, including date of issue and expiration;
- Specialty and subspecialty, including board certification and eligibility;
- Continuing medical education;
- Educational and employment references;
- Drug Enforcement Agency (DEA) registration status; and
- Licensure, Medicare/Medicaid, and other state or federal sanctions.

The importance of primary verification of these elements has been underscored by an audit of the credentials of physicians employed by six Veterans' Affairs Medical Centers (VAMCs) (GAO, 2010). The auditors "looked for evidence of omissions by physician applicants related to medical licenses, malpractice, and at five of six VAMCs visited, gaps in background greater than 30 days" (GAO, 2010, p. 42). They found that of 180 physician files they reviewed, 29 lacked proper verification of state licensure and 21 physicians failed to disclose malpractice information (GAO, 2010).

An entire industry of companies who conduct physician credentialing for a wide array of requirements now exists for physicians and health care organizations. Regardless of who completes the work, it still must be reviewed and approved by the organization where the physician will be practicing. As a health care manager, you may find yourself working in the physician relations and credentialing department of a hospital, HMO, or other health care delivery organization, and you may be responsible for determining whether the credentials offered by a physician are legitimate. Physician credentialing requires excellent interpersonal skills, organizational skills, persistence, an eye for details, and the ability to identify inconsistencies in data.

Since physicians are tracked from the moment they graduate from medical school, the first thing to verify is that there are no gaps in their resumes. Physicians rarely take time off "to find themselves." If there is a significant gap between educational or employment placements (e.g., nothing on the resume for four years between a residency training program and an evening-shift job working at a clinic with a poor reputation), you need to question what has transpired in this individual's life. Physicians are human, and they can have events in their lives such as mental illness, addiction, or imprisonment. Since you will be responsible for safe, effective patient care, you must be mindful about who is providing that care. The first clue will be in the credentials, especially in the chronology of life events.

Occasionally, you will come across an individual who claims to be a physician but is not. In this Internet and computer age, physician imposters can obtain fraudulent credentials from medical schools in other countries, or even in the U.S. Physician imposters are rare, but potentially dangerous, individuals. There is no substitute for personal interaction with the institution where someone claims to have been educated or employed. This is where an eye for details and inconsistencies and interpersonal skills come into play. You will be required to handle telephone inquiries with the utmost tact to ensure that you obtain verification. If no one at an institution knows the individual, or if the medical school has "burned down, leaving no records," alarm bells should be ringing in your head, and you should notify your manager immediately there may be a problem with the application.

A comprehensive review of a physician's credentials involves making electronic queries to the **National Practitioner Data Bank (NPDB), aka "the Data Bank."** At one time, physicians who were disciplined or lost their license in one state could simply move to another state and get a license there. Other than person-to-person contacts, there were few ways to track "bad docs" who moved across state borders. The NPDB was created to have a system whereby state licensing boards, hospitals, professional societies, and other health care entities could identify, discipline, and report those who engage in unprofessional behavior. "The National Practitioner Data Bank (NPDB) is an electronic information repository created by Congress. It contains information on medical malpractice payments and certain adverse actions related to health care practitioners, entities, providers, and suppliers. Federal law specifies the types of actions reported to the NPDB, who submits the reports, and who queries to obtain copies of the reports" (National Practitioner Data Bank, 2015, para. 1). One of the main criticisms of the NPDB is that a physician can be reported for having been sued, but the outcome of the lawsuit, even when dismissed, is not reported, and the lawsuit remains on the physician's record. In an era of increasingly litigious consumers of health care, this is not a minor complaint. Physicians may dispute the report, but it can take much time and effort, much like trying to get a correction on a credit report. Hence, the information in the Data Bank should be used along with other data to look for patterns of deviation from professional behaviors.

When credentialing physicians, it is critical to have other physicians review the application to ensure that experts who understand the nuances of the data contained in an application render the final judgment as to whether to approve or disapprove privileges. Using the example of a surgeon applying for general surgical privileges at a hospital, after the physician credentialing department receives a physician's application for privileges and conducts due diligence in verifying each and every claim on the application, the materials are submitted to a surgical credentialing committee. Unless the hospital is very small, each department will have its own credentialing committee. In this case, if the department of surgery's credentialing committee approves the application, it then recommends that the documents be forwarded to a medical executive committee, which is a subcommittee of the hospital board of directors. The subcommittee then makes a recommendation to the board, which then approves or disapproves the application. Under certain circumstances, temporary credentials can be granted. Usually, however, the time from submission of the application to final approval can take three to six months. If there are problems with the application or missing documents, the process can take even longer.

Some hospital systems are now instituting system-wide credentialing processes to ensure standardization across multiple settings. Regardless of protocol or process, physician credentialing is one of the most important jobs in any health care delivery setting. By approving a physician's privileges, the health care organization indicates that it believes that this physician will provide safe, effective patient care. It is not a responsibility to be taken lightly. The lives of patients and the financial survival of the health care organization depend on how well this process has been done.

International Medical Graduates

International Medical Graduates (IMGs), formerly referred to as Foreign Medical Graduates (FMGs), can be U.S. citizens who attend school abroad or foreign-born nationals who come to the U.S. seeking educational and professional opportunities and filling voids in health care services delivery for the U.S. population. IMGs represent 25% of the total physician population in the U.S. physician workforce, or approximately 245,005 physicians (Traverso & McMahon, 2012). In 2009, the top country sending foreign-born physicians to the U.S. was India (AMA, 2015a).

Researchers have repeatedly demonstrated that IMGs are more likely to go where U.S. medical graduates (USMGs) prefer *not* to go (i.e., inner-city and rural areas) and to serve populations increasingly at risk of medical abandonment (Hagopian, Thompson, Kaltenbach, & Hart, 2003; Hallock, Seeling, & Norcini, 2003; Mick & Lee, 1999a, 1999b; Mick, Lee, & Wodchis, 2000; Polsky, Kletke, Wozniak, & Escarce, 2002; Thompson, Hagopian, Fordyce, & Hart, 2009). In 2008, nearly 60% of the IMGs in the U.S. were in primary care (internal medicine, pediatrics, family medicine) or specialized in psychiatry, anesthesiology, obstetrics/gynecology, general surgery, or cardiovascular disease (Smart, 2010). More than three-quarters of the IMGs in practice were in direct patient care. At one time, the quality of care provided by non-USMGs was a major concern. Over the past decades, however, a formidable system of checks and balances has been implemented, and foreign-trained and foreign-born medical graduates (FBMGs) are now required to pass rigorous English-language and written and clinical skills assessment examinations prior to being allowed to apply for GME, that is, residency training positions (Whelan, Gary, Kostis, Boutlet, & Hallock, 2000). This arrangement has improved the quality of the IMG applicant pool that continues to fill graduate medical education positions still left unfilled by USMGs (Cooper & Aiken, 2001; McMahon, 2004). Additionally, a study examining quality of care provided by IMGs in Pennsylvania found the quality of care provided to be as good as or better than that given by graduates from U.S. medical schools (Norcini et al., 2010).

We are now facing a shortage of physicians across all specialties. This shortage of physicians is a result, in part, from the aging of the Baby Boomer population, physician retirements, changing ethnic and racial demographics, increased access to care with the implementation of the Affordable Care Act (ACA), increased utilization of services, advances in health care technology, a hostile malpractice environment, and medical school graduates (both female and male) who desire reasonable work hours (Bureau of Health Professions, 2003; Cooper, 2002, 2003). While some experts argue over the exact numbers of physicians in the workforce and whether to use the American Medical Association Masterfile or the U.S. Census Bureau Current Population Survey for workforce projections, they agree that the physician workforce will be younger and work fewer hours per week regardless of gender (Steiger, Auerbach, & Buerhaus, 2009, 2010).

In response to the predicted workforce shortage, U.S. medical schools have increased enrollments and new medical schools have opened their doors. This upsurge in production of U.S. trained physicians is predicted to bump international medical graduates, both foreign and U.S. born, out of graduate medical education programs. An increase in supply in U.S. medical graduates creates new questions about of the diversity of residents in training and their ability to provide culturally responsive care as well as the education and training of international medical graduates whose home countries have relied on them to return home to provide high quality care (Traverso & McMahon, 2012). As residency training programs begin to reduce acceptances of IMGs, the question still remains: who will provide medical care to an aging U.S. population?

Even with attempts to ramp up the physician workforce, there is a pipeline effect. Students admitted to medical school in 2010 will not be prepared to provide primary care until 2017, at the earliest. Despite increases in residency training positions, longer specialty training means longer wait times for the population needing to be served and greater mortality rates. The American College of Physicians (2008) estimated "the addition of one primary care physician per 10,000 population in the U.S. resulted in 3.5 fewer people dying each year" (p. 7). In the meantime, with the increase of chronic disease, longer lifespans, and re-merging epidemics, health care managers will struggle with recruitment, retention, and optimal utilization of physicians, whether USMG or IMG. According to the BLS (2014e), employment of physicians will increase by 18% over the next decade due to expansion of the health care industry. Some of the issues you will be most likely to encounter with IMGs will surround the physician credentialing process and the J-Visa, which provides legal entry to the U.S. for training purposes. Physicians who graduate from foreign medical schools will have to provide, in some instances, additional documentation and verification that the information they have provided is true and correct. The Educational Commission for Foreign Medical

Graduates (ECFMG) offers online credential verification services that can ease some of the burden but not all of the responsibility or liability in the granting of privileges (ECFMG, 2011).

In summary, physicians are critical to the provision of safe, effective patient care. Ensuring the quality of the physicians practicing in an organization is one of the roles of the health care manager. To fulfill this responsibility, you will need to know all the steps in the education, training, and credentialing of physicians. It will take attention to detail, organizational skills, and excellent interpersonal skills to do it well.

Employed Physicians and Turnover

At one time, the majority of physicians in the U.S. were self-employed, solo practitioners, or in partnership with one or two other physicians. Recent data suggest that the old images of the independent physician practitioner need to be updated to reflect the growing numbers of physicians who are now employed by organizations such as hospitals and large single- or multispecialty group practices (Isaacs, Jellinek, & Ray, 2009). One recruiter reported that in some communities, as many as 90% of the physicians may be employees (Butcher, 2008). In 2008, about one-third of all physicians, male and female, between the ages of 45 and 54 were full-time hospital employees (Smart, 2010). A 2013 survey of 3,456 physicians found the number of employed physicians was up by 6% from the previous year and the number of solo practitioners was down by the same proportion (Vaidya, 2013). Continued robust growth in physician hospital employment reflects the desire of these organizations to improve their bottom lines by becoming **accountable care organizations (ACOs)**, i.e., health care providers that focus on continuity and quality of care of a given population. Medicare rewards ACOs with shares of savings from reduced health care utilization. This increased demand for hospitalists and other employed physicians arrives at the same time newer generations of medical school graduates are expecting a balanced work–family life.

Combined with the consolidation of physicians' practices and enrollment growth in managed care organizations, these trends will continue to accelerate. However, employment goes hand in hand with **turnover** (i.e., the proportion of job exits or quits from a facility in a year). Buchbinder, Wilson, Melick, and Powe (2001), using data from a nationally representative sample, studied a cohort of 533 post-resident, non-federal, employed PCPs who were younger than 45 years of age, had been in practice between two and nine years, and had participated in national surveys in 1987 and 1991. They combined data from this sample with a national study of physician compensation and productivity and physician recruiters to estimate recruitment and replacement costs associated with turnover. The authors found that by the 1991 survey, slightly more than half ($n = 279$, or 55%) of all PCPs in this cohort had left the practice in which they had been employed in 1987;

20% (*n* = 100) had left two employers in that same five-year period. Estimates of recruitment and replacement costs for individual PCPs for the three specialties were $236,383 for family practice (FP), $245,128 for internal medicine (IM), and $264,645 for pediatrics (Peds). Turnover costs for all PCPs in the cohort by specialty were $24.5 million for FP, $22.3 million for IM, and $22.2 million for Peds. They concluded turnover was an important phenomenon among the PCPs in this cohort and that PCP turnover has major fiscal implications for PCP employers. Loss of PCPs causes health care organizations to lose resources that could otherwise be devoted to patient care, as well as potentially sidelining their goal to becoming an ACO.

A physician retention study conducted by Cejka Search and American Medical Group Association (AMGA) reported physician turnover remained at about the same level from the previous year, however, primary care physician turnover increased by 9% and specialist physician turnover increased by 6% in 2013 (Cejka Search & AMGA, 2013). Retirements escalated, with 18% of physicians in the survey indicating that reason for leaving employment. Women and new physicians appeared to be more vulnerable to turnover, in general. Women were more likely to leave practices with 3 to 50 physicians. Both genders were equally likely to turnover in practices with over 500 physicians. The vast majority of the groups surveyed indicated they "offered flexible schedules, less than a full-time schedule, and extended time off" (Cejka Search & AMGA, 2013, p. 18). Most medical groups indicated they plan to hire more physicians, as well as **advanced practice clinicians, or APCs,** such as physician assistants and nurse practitioners. The majority of the groups plan to focus on ensuring their physicians "are working at their maximum efficiency with our APCs" (Cejka Search & AMGA, 2013, p. 11). These are clearly management issues related to physician recruitment, retention, turnover, and utilization.

Employee turnover has been clearly linked to job dissatisfaction and job burnout. **Job satisfaction** is the "pleasurable or positive emotional state resulting from the appraisal of one's job or job experiences" (Locke, 1983, p. 1300). **Job burnout** is "a prolonged response to chronic emotional and interpersonal stressors on the job" (Maslach, 2003, p. 189). In the past, most solutions to job burnout involved removing the affected individual from the job. However, it is the *organization* that is the primary cause of job burnout (due to heavy workload, poor relations with coworkers, etc.) and job dissatisfaction. Therefore, it is the health care manager's role to address these issues. Health care managers employed in these kinds of settings must be alert to signs of physician job dissatisfaction and burnout, the harbingers of turnover (Dunn, Arnetz, Christensen, & Homer, 2007). "Achieving a patient-centered and professionally satisfying culture and closing the quality chasm in cost-effective ways depend on accountable organizational arrangements, strong primary care, and effective team performance" (Mechanic, 2010, p. 556). As a health care manager in a hospital or physician owned medical group practice, you will be expected to work with the physicians to help create a positive practice environment and to provide recommendations for interventions to improve retention.

Employed Physicians and Conflict of Interest

There has long been a requirement for researchers to disclose funding sources for biomedical research because of concerns that the outcomes of the research could be biased in favor of the company that has, in essence, paid for the research. The NIH and the majority of biomedical journals require investigators to disclose any financial relationships that might exist between the researcher and the funding entity (Drazen et al., 2010; NIH, 2014). Related to these concerns have been growing fears about the influence of gifts and other financial incentives on physicians' prescribing practices and purchasing behaviors. Some states, such as Massachusetts, Minnesota, and Vermont, enacted laws earlier than others to prohibit pharmaceutical or medical device companies from giving more than $100 in gifts to a physician (Ross et al., 2007). These laws and **Open Payments, aka, the Sunshine Act**, have led to a more transparency in health care as well as greater urgency for organizations to create their own conflict of interest policies for physicians employed by health care organizations.

Open Payments, aka, the Sunshine Act, which was created as part of the Affordable Care Act, requires medical device manufacturers and **group purchasing organizations (GPOs)** (entities that work with multiple health care organization to buy in large volumes to decrease costs) to report any payments and "transfers of value" to physicians' or teaching hospitals, as well as any ownership of investment interest physicians or immediate family members have in a company. This information must be reported annually. These "transfers of value" can be as small as $7.77 for coffee and donuts. Records of these gifts are maintained on the Centers for Medicare and Medicaid Services (CMS) website and are open to anyone with access to the Internet, hence, the name "Open Payments" (CMS, 2015; Dreger, 2013). It is imperative that physicians periodically check this website to ensure the accuracy of these reports. If there is a discrepancy, physicians and hospitals have the right to appeal. Physicians who do not want to give even the appearance of impropriety are now telling sales representatives to desist in bringing food. Office staff who looked forward to free lunches from sales representatives are sometimes resentful of this loss in "benefits." As managers in physician offices and teaching hospitals, it will be up to you to be vigilant about ensuring your employer's integrity by deterring these gifting behaviors.

Conflict of interest is a term used to describe when an individual can be influenced by money or other considerations to act in a way that is contrary to the good of the organization for whom he or she works or the patient for whom he or she should be advocating in their best interests. In most health care organizations, conflict of interest disclosures are required for all employees who make purchasing decisions—including physicians and administrators—and include a series of questions to which the individual must respond no or, if yes, must explain. These questions include but are not limited to the topics of:

- Personal gifts;
- Meals, invitations, and entertainment;
- Attendance at industry-sponsored (and third-party industry sponsored) conferences, education sales, or promotional events;
- Industry-sponsored scholarships and other education support for trainees;
- Speaking, consulting arrangements, and advisory services with industry;
- Fiduciary, management, or other financial interests with industry;
- Detailing, tying, switching, or ordering;
- Conflicts of commitment;
- Site or facility access by industry representatives;
- Publications/ghost-writing/ghost-authoring; and
- Free drug/product samples.

There must be full disclosure if a conflict exists, and the individual must remove himself or herself from the decision-making role. The individual must certify his or her responses to all of the above questions are complete and accurate to the best of their knowledge and, if anything changes, they must update their disclosure document. Conflict of interest documents must be updated annually (Medstar Health, 2015).

Your job as a health care manager will be to ensure that first and foremost you complete the same type of document you expect physicians to complete. Even the appearance of any potential conflict of interest should be avoided. Your reputation and the reputation of the health care organization where you are employed depend on ethical behaviors of all employees.

REGISTERED NURSES

At one time, all nurses were trained in hospital-based programs and received diplomas upon graduation. Before 1917, nursing was essentially an apprenticeship, without a set curriculum, which then morphed into hospital-based diploma schools that produced their own nursing workforce. The hospital-based diploma nursing school is part of a passing era; in 2011, they represented only 10% of the nursing programs in the U.S. (American Association of Colleges of Nursing [AACN], 2011). Currently, the majority of nursing education is provided in degree-based settings. Over half the nursing workforce holds baccalaureate, four-year degrees; many of these RNs began with associate degrees and returned to school to earn a bachelor's of science in nursing (BSN) to improve their opportunities for career advancement (Health Resources and Services Administration [HRSA],

2013). "Between 2007 and 2011, nursing master's and doctoral graduates increased by 67 percent" (HRSA, 2013, p. ix). This increase in advanced degree nurses means increased production capabilities of undergraduate nurses. Indeed, the overall numbers of RNs has increased; however, due to aging, nurses continue to retire faster than they can be replaced in the workforce.

Nurses with BSNs can continue their education and enter a wide array of graduate educational programs including, but not limited to, post-baccalaureate certificates; masters of science in nursing (MSN) degrees for community health nursing and nurse education; advanced practice degrees (nurse practitioner, clinical nurse specialist, nurse midwife, nurse anesthetist); and doctoral degrees, such as the nursing doctorate (ND), doctorate in nursing science (DNS), or a doctor of philosophy (PhD).

The undergraduate nursing school curriculum (BSN) is rigorous and demands a good understanding of the biological sciences. At Stevenson University, for example, students are eligible to continue to the third year of the program only after completing a specific sequence of courses and maintaining a 3.0 or B average overall GPA and in all science courses (Stevenson University, 2015).

The current shortage of nursing faculty means fewer slots for nursing students—there are fewer faculty to teach (AACN, 2014b). "In the 2014–2015 academic year, 265,954 completed applications were received for entry-level baccalaureate nursing programs (a 1.9% decrease from 2013) with 170,109 meeting admission criteria and 119,428 applications accepted. This translates into an acceptance rate of 44.9%" (AACN, 2014a, para. 12). Due to a crisis-level national nursing shortage and demands for workers, state legislators are pressuring universities and colleges to increase the number of graduates from nursing programs. However, unlike other undergraduate degrees, nursing students must learn clinical skills and be carefully supervised in health care organizations by master's or doctorally prepared nursing faculty. The nursing faculty clinical supervisor is only allowed to have a specific number of student nurses. Exceeding that number could endanger the lives of patients and the faculty member's nursing license.

As nursing students progress through their program of study, meeting state requirements for licensure and passing the National Council Licensure Examination (NCLEX) is uppermost in everyone's mind. A student must pass the NCLEX to become a licensed registered nurse (RN) in the U.S., and nursing programs' pass rates on the NCLEX are used as a proxy for the quality of their educational curriculum. With the current nursing shortage, many graduating nurses have a job offer in hand before graduating—contingent upon obtaining state licensure and passing the NCLEX (NCSBN, 2015b).

As of 2012, 40 boards of nursing out of 55 required CBCs for nurse applicants for licensure (Council of State Governments [CSG], 2012). The CSG has called for fingerprinting to be added to the CBC requirements for nurses based on evidence that RNs with criminal backgrounds do not always self-disclose and go undetected without fingerprinting (CSG, 2013). Again, the reasons are multifold and include but are not limited to increasing societal concerns about alcohol and drug abusers, sexual predators, and child and elder abusers. If a criminal background check contains information about convictions, the licensure board will examine the application on a case-by-case basis. As noted previously, the reviewers will be looking for level and frequency of the criminal behavior, basing their decision on that, along with other materials submitted by the applicant, such as proof of alcohol and drug rehabilitation and a monitoring program utilizing random drug testing reported to the state board of nursing.

After graduation, RNs, unlike physicians, do not have postgraduate programs that last from 3 to 10 years. In the past, new RNs have been hired to work in hospitals or other health care organizations, given a brief orientation, then placed on a nursing unit and left to sink or swim. This Darwinian approach to nurse staffing led, in part, to massive turnover. Although the vast majority of nurses are female (only 9% are male), women now have career choices other than nursing, teaching, or homemaking; older nurses continue to retire faster than new ones come into the field (HRSA, 2013; Steiger, Auerbach, & Buerhaus, 2000). Nursing turnover costs have been estimated to be 1.3 times the salary of a departing nurse, or an average of $65,000 per lost nurse (Department for Professional Employees AFL-CIO, 2010; Jones & Gates, 2007). Multiply that by the number of nurses who quit their jobs, and the costs can be in the millions of dollars for health care organizations. Health care managers cannot afford to ignore the loss of nurses from the workforce.

Any strategy that improves the retention of nursing staff saves the organization the costs of using agency or traveler nurses, replacing lost nurses and training new ones, as well as the loss of productivity from burdening the remaining staff. A survey conducted among 67 new nurses from 13 hospital departments indicated that new graduates were concerned about communicating with physicians and were afraid of "causing accidental harm to patients." Additionally, this group identified a desire for "comprehensive orientation, continuing education and mentoring" (Boswell, Lowry, & Wilhoit, 2004, p. 76). Nurse residency programs (NRPs) were created in response to low satisfaction levels and high turnover rates among new graduates. The University HealthSystem Consortium (UHC)/AACN Residency Program has 92 practice sites in 30 states that offer the year-long post-baccalaureate residency. As of this writing, more than 26,000 nurses have completed the program. Satisfaction, as reflected by a 95.6% retention rate versus previous turnover rates of 30%, serves as a strong indicator of the success of this program (AACN, 2015). While much work has been done to develop a model with a strong curriculum and excellent outcomes, thus far the participants are only in academic health centers and large health systems. NRPs need to be replicated beyond these elite and well-endowed settings to community hospitals where much of the health care is provided in the U.S.

A difficult transition into practice isn't the only reason that nurses leave health care organizations. Nurses quit jobs where they feel overworked, underpaid, and disrespected by their coworkers and managers. Using national focus groups, on behalf of the Robert Wood Johnson Foundation, Kimball and O'Neil (2002) found RNs are concerned about being unable to physically continue to do the work, increases in their daily workloads, and the lack of ancillary staff to support them. These groups also indicated they were confused about health care financial issues, felt powerless to change things in their work environments, and thought their nurse managers were overextended and unable to help them. The respondents gave a list of suggestions to improve the retention of nurses, including:

- Decreasing workloads;
- Providing support staff;
- Empowering nurse managers;
- Increasing salaries;
- Encouraging physicians to treat nurses as colleagues;
- Improving the orientation process; and
- Providing paid continuing education (Kimball & O'Neil, 2002, p. 46).

Overwork of nurses and high patient-to-nurse ratios lead to patient mortality, nurse burnout, and job dissatisfaction (Aiken, Clarke, Sloane, Sochalski, & Silber, 2002). Aiken et al.'s (2002) benchmark article reported "that the difference from 4 to 6 and from 4 to 8 patients per nurse would be accompanied by 14% and 31% increases in mortality, respectively" (p. 1991). The Joint Commission (2002) report called a high patient-to-nurse ratio "a prescription for danger" and indicated that "staffing levels have been a factor in 24% of 1,608 sentinel events (unanticipated events that result in death, injury, or permanent loss or function)" (p. 6). In addition, Aiken and her colleagues reported that more nurse education and training led to higher quality of service and lower patient mortality (Aiken, Clarke, Cheung, Sloane, & Silber, 2003). A recent longitudinal survey of predictors of turnover among newly licensed RNs found Magnet Hospital Status was not related to turnover, but on the job injuries *were* directly predictive. This means implementing policies to prevent strains and sprains can reduce nursing turnover (Brewer, Kovner, Greene, Tukov-Shuser, & Djukic, 2012). In light of these data, it makes financial sense to employ more RNs per patient, to protect them from on the job injury and to hire RNs with a baccalaureate level or higher. Given the nursing shortage, the health care manager's next best choice would be to hire RNs with an associate degree, provide tuition assistance, and create incentives for them to return to school for their BSN.

Conflict and Communication: Creating a Culture of Safety

Encouraging physicians to treat nurses as colleagues has always been a challenge. Recommendations for collaborative practice between physicians and nurses have been in place for decades, going back to nursing shortages in the 1980s and the National Commission on Nursing's 1983 *Summary Report and Recommendations*, calling for nurse-physician joint practice (National Commission on Nursing, 1983). One of the problems in this dyad has been the gap between physician and nursing education. In previous years, when diploma schools dominated nursing education, physicians had at least 20 more years of formal education than the RNs they worked with. In that era, when a physician walked into a room, a nurse would stand as a sign of respect—and give him her chair. Nurses now have formal educational programs in degree-granting settings, and the educational gap between the two health care professional groups is diminishing. Women have also "come of age" since the women's rights movement in the 1970s, and nurses are no longer the doctor's handmaidens. They, too, are health care professionals.

Teamwork is essential to a culture of safety. Physician resistance to acknowledging nurses as professionals and colleagues leads to poor teamwork and interpersonal conflict and can result in poor patient outcomes. One study found that physicians and nurses differed widely in their opinions about teamwork in an ICU setting. Almost three-quarters of the physicians reported high levels of teamwork with nurses, but less than half of the nurses felt the same way (Sexton, Thomas, & Helmreich, 2000). Despite demonstrated need and effectiveness of interdisciplinary teamwork, formal educational training in this important skill for physicians and nurses is rare (Baker, Salas, King, Battles, & Barach, 2005; Buchbinder et al., 2005). A poll conducted in 2004 by the American College of Physician Executives (ACPE) revealed that about one-quarter of the physician executive respondents were seeing problem physician behaviors almost weekly (Weber, 2004). Approximately 36% of the respondents reported conflicts between physicians and staff members (including nurses), and 25% reported that physicians refused to embrace teamwork.

It is no longer an option for physicians or nurses to refuse to play well with other health care professionals. The operating room and the ICU are two units that must rely on teamwork to accomplish life-saving procedures. An orthopedic surgery symposium emphasized the need to address problem physicians' behavior immediately and warned that avoidance of confrontations enables toxic personalities to continue to create hostile workplaces (Porucznik, 2012). Teamwork in the ICU is critical, yet despite studies that document associations between positive caregiver interactions and positive patient outcomes, an extensive review of the literature failed to determine a one best approach to improving teamwork (Dietz et al., 2014). No doubt this inability to have a one-size-fits-all approach is due, in part, to the wide variety of tasks and teams, not to mention organizational settings. Other authors have reported that combining the Agency for Healthcare Research and Quality (AHRQ) training program, TeamSTEPPS, with specialty team protocols improves role delineation and communication among team members, leading to better patient outcomes (Gupta, Sexton, Milne, & Frush, 2015; Tibbs & Moss 2014). Regardless of how the team arrives at improved performance, it must include respectful communication and behaviors from all team members.

Intimidating and disruptive behaviors include "overt actions such as verbal outbursts and physical threats as well as passive activities such as refusing to perform assigned tasks or quietly exhibiting uncooperative attitudes during routine activities" (The Joint Commission, 2008, p. 1). Disruptive behaviors, whether from physicians or nurses, are unacceptable and counterproductive to a patient-centric culture of safety. Disruptive behavior is considered a **sentinel event**, i.e., "a Patient Safety Event that reaches a patient and results in any of the following: death; permanent harm; severe temporary harm and intervention required to sustain life" (The Joint Commission, 2014, para. 2).

People who behave like schoolyard bullies in health care organizations must be dealt with through counseling sessions, disciplinary actions, or terminations. Trust and good communication are central to excellence in health care delivery.

Communication between physicians, nurses, and other health care professionals is critical to a culture of safety. The Joint Commission established new standards to address communication and published a book for clinicians and health care managers with strategies to improve communication between staff members, patients, and teams (The Joint Commission, 2009). In this book, as well as in peer-reviewed articles, physicians and nurses are tasked to focus on patient-centered care and patient safety (Levinson, Lesser, & Epstein, 2010; Nadzman, 2009). However, nurses and physicians rarely receive education on effective communication in their professional programs. While it is hoped that medical and nursing school curricula will respond to the need for this important skill, those courses are not in place at this time. For this reason, it may become *your* duty as a health care manager to ensure that resources such as educational seminars and teamwork training are in place to support a culture of safety at your health care organization.

Organizational climate is critical to promoting job satisfaction and retention of nursing staff. Laschinger and Finegan (2005) found that nurses who perceived that they had access to opportunity, experienced honest relationships and open communication with peers and managers, and trusted their managers were more likely to be retained and to have higher job satisfaction. The American Association of Colleges of Nursing (AACN, 2002) published a white paper titled *Hallmarks of the Professional Nursing Practice Environment*. The attributes of hospitals with work environments that support professional nursing practice were reviewed and the questions a new graduate should ask were listed. They are: Does your potential employer:

- Manifest a philosophy of clinical care, emphasizing quality, safety, interdisciplinary collaboration, continuity of care, and professional accountability?
- Recognize the contributions of nurses' knowledge and expertise to clinical care quality and patient outcomes?
- Promote executive-level nursing leadership?
- Empower nurses' participation in clinical decision making and organization of clinical care systems?
- Maintain clinical advancement programs based on education, certification, and advanced preparation?
- Demonstrate professional development support for nurses?
- Create collaborative relationships among members of the health care provider team?
- Utilize technological advances in clinical care and information systems?

The AACN also recommends that applicants inquire about RN staff education, vacancy, tenure, and turnover rates; patient and employee satisfaction scores; and the percentage of registry/traveler nurses used. The questions posed by the AACN challenge health care organizations to rise to higher standards and to reach for American Nurses Credentialing Center Magnet Recognition Program status (ANCC, 2014a). Unless these questions are answered in the affirmative, nursing turnover will continue to be one of the largest human and financial costs that the health care manager will be forced to control.

Like physicians who sit for board certification examinations, RNs can take ANCC's or other nursing specialty organizations' (e.g., the Wound, Ostomy, and Continence Nurses' Society; the American Association of Critical Care Nurses, etc.) examinations to demonstrate additional competence in a specialty, after they have earned a baccalaureate or higher degree and practiced for a specific number of hours in a specialty area. Thus, nurses can be certified in a large number and variety of specialty areas. Nurses who are credentialed in specialty areas must demonstrate continuing competency by fulfilling requirements for certification renewal via one or several of the following mechanisms: continuing education hours, academic courses, presentations and lectures, publications and research, or preceptorships.

In many states, nurses are required to obtain nursing continuing education units (CEUs) to renew and maintain their nursing licenses. The ANCC Commission on Accreditation, the credentialing unit of the American Nurses Association (ANA), reviews and approves providers of nursing CEUs (ANCC, 2015).

There are literally hundreds of providers of nursing CEUs and multiple ways to obtain nursing CEUs, including but not limited to online courses; magazine or journal articles; workshops and conferences; audiotapes, CDs, and DVDs; and the previously noted academic courses, presentations and lectures, publications and research, or preceptorships. Nurses can even attend other health care providers' workshops that have been approved for awarding nursing CEUs. There is no dearth of opportunities for nurses to obtain continuing education. It is the responsibility of the RN to maintain his or her license. Your role as health care manager will be to ensure that resources (i.e., money and time) are available for nurses to participate in these educational opportunities.

Foreign Educated Nurses

The nursing shortage, caused by a confluence of the aging of the U.S. nursing workforce, declining enrollments in nursing schools, higher average age of new graduates from nursing school, and organizational retention and turnover difficulties, would have been difficult enough for health care managers on its own. However, we have what some people call "the perfect storm" in health care because the nursing shortage is now combined with demographic forces and market forces, such as aging Baby Boomers, increasing racial and ethnic diversity, increased demand for health care services, increasing longevity of U.S. citizens, new treatments for chronic diseases that used to kill people (like asthma, diabetes, hypertension), and educated and demanding health care consumers (AACN, 2014b; HRSA, 2013).

Since U.S. health care organizations are experiencing a crisis in the nursing workforce and cannot survive without nurses to deliver care, it is not surprising that foreign-educated nurses are coming to the U.S. to fill gaps in nursing services. However, the annual number of internationally educated NCLEX passers has declined from nearly 23,000 in 2007 to only 6,100 in 2011 (HRSA, 2013). In 2010, the majority of internationally trained nurses who took the NCLEX came from the Philippines, trailed by South Korea, India, Canada, and Nigeria (NCSBN, 2010). According to the Commission on Graduates of Foreign Nursing Schools (CGFNS) (2015) for nurses educated outside the U.S., all U.S. State Boards of Nursing require credentials evaluation, certification, or verification as a first-step in the application process. The CGFNS International Certification Program provides a credentials review, a qualifying exam of nursing knowledge, and an English-language proficiency examination. The CGFNS International Certification Program is required for licensure by a number of State Boards of nursing licensure and can be utilized for federal Visa screening requirements for immigration. The CGFNS Certification Program removes a major burden from an employer. However, as a health care manager, your job may require you to ensure that foreign-educated nurses are who they say they are, have fulfilled all the requirements of the State Board of Nursing, and are legally allowed to work in the U.S. (McFarlane, 2013).

Due to the stringent requirements the U.S. has for RN licensure, concerns about the U.S. depleting other nations of their nursing workforce are not based on hard data (Aiken, Buchan, Sochalski, Nichols, & Powell, 2004). However, these types of misperceptions can influence coworker relationships and may contribute to conflicts between U.S.-educated and foreign-educated nurses and between physicians and foreign-educated nurses. Different cultures bring varying expectations to the work setting. These expectations may well be at odds with those of their coworkers. Excellent interpersonal skills, conflict management, cultural proficiency, and sensitivity to diversity issues are critical for you to be able to be an effective health care manager for these employees.

LICENSED PRACTICAL NURSES/LICENSED VOCATIONAL NURSES

In 2012, there were about 738,400 **Licensed Practical Nurses (LPNs) or Licensed Vocational Nurses (LVNs)** working under the supervision of physicians and nurses in the U.S. According to the BLS (2014c), they were employed in nursing homes and extended care facilities, hospitals, physicians' offices, and private homes. Most work full time. After graduation from high school, LPNs are trained in one-year, state-approved programs. Most are trained in technical or vocational schools, although some high schools offer it as part of their curriculum. In order to be employed as an LPN, students must graduate from a state-approved program, then pass the LPN licensing exam, the NCLEX-PN (BLS, 2014c). LPNs are trained to do basic nursing functions such as checking vital signs, observing patients, and assisting patients with **activities of daily living (ADLs)**, such as bathing, dressing, feeding, and toileting. With additional training, where state laws allow, they can also administer medications. LPNs are the backbone of the long-term care (LTC) sector of the health care industry, providing around-the-clock care and supervision of **certified nurse's assistants (CNAs)** in nursing homes and convalescent centers. Many LPNs go on to earn their RN, and in some states, LPNs can take challenge examinations to earn their RN licensure. LPNs are an important part of the health care team and should be included in the health care manager's tuition assistance plan to encourage key personnel to return to school for additional education.

NURSING ASSISTANTS AND ORDERLIES

In 2012, there were over 1.5 million nursing assistants and orderlies employed in nursing and residential care facilities and in hospitals (BLS, 2014d). Nursing aides, nursing assistants, certified nursing assistants (CNAs), orderlies, and other unlicensed patient attendants work under the supervision of physicians and nurses. They answer call bells, assist patients with toileting, change beds, serve meals, and assist patients with ADLs. Regardless of employment setting, aides are frontline personnel. Since nursing aides held the most jobs, at 1.5 million, and were employed most often by nursing care facilities, that will be the focus of the remainder of this section.

Nurse's aides have made the news in negative ways in recent years. In the past, CNAs were not required to have CBCs, and elder abusers, sexual predators, and thieves saw the elderly population as easy prey. Now the majority of states and employers require CBCs. However, a clean CBC doesn't guarantee that the person hasn't abused or won't abuse a patient. Therefore, it is incumbent upon the health care organization to have policies about neglect and abuse prevention in place, and the health care manager must enforce them. Some nursing homes have installed "granny-cams," video surveillance systems to keep an eye on caregiver behavior and to document misbehavior. When working with vulnerable populations, the health care manager must be in a state of constant vigilance for neglect and abuse.

CNAs are often trained on the job in 75 hours of mandatory training and are required to pass a competency examination. CNAs provide direct care to patients over long periods of time and are often the most overlooked group of workers in terms of pay, benefits, and opportunities for advancement. Seavey (2004) conducted a literature review and found that estimates of turnover from LTC facilities ranged from 40% to 166%, with indirect and direct costs per lost worker ranging from $951 to $6,368. She estimated a minimum direct cost of $2,500 per lost worker. Ribas, Dill, and Cohen (2012) utilized longitudinal data collected between 1996 and 2003 and found 73% of the sample working in occupations other than nurse's aide over time. Over half those who left nurse aide work moved into higher paying occupations; however, when they excluded those who became RNs from the sample the number dropped to 35% (p. 2189). The researchers pointed to lack of clear career paths and lack of career ladders for these workers, resulting in lower wages.

It's a vicious cycle: poor quality of work life begets turnover, which begets poor quality of work life, which begets more turnover. And it's not just the CNAs and other aides who are affected. Once the CNAs are gone, the LPNs will go, then the RNs will be stressed, become emotionally burned out, and leave (Kennedy, 2005). Then who will provide the care? The job of the health care manager is to improve retention to slow down or stop turnover by addressing the quality of work life. The place to start is with a comparable market wage analysis. Are the workers being paid the same as or better than workers with comparable jobs at other comparable facilities? Nursing home administrators have confided that CNAs will leave one facility to go to another one for a pay raise of 25 cents per hour. Is the pay fair? Does the facility pay tuition assistance for CNAs? What kind of benefits package is being offered? Are there career paths and ladders presented to the CNAs to encourage them to move up?

After looking at these basic items, the health care manager then needs to assess the work environment, including employee job burnout and satisfaction, preferably using an outside organization so workers can respond freely without fear of retribution. While not an exhaustive list, some of the items to be included in a work life analysis include worker perceptions of:

- Job autonomy, variety, and significance;
- Fairness of pay and benefits;
- Opportunities for promotion and advancement;
- Relationships with supervisors;
- Relationships with coworkers;
- Level of job burnout; and
- Overall job satisfaction.

All health care workers, not just nurses, want to be treated as colleagues and with respect. If you conduct a survey of the organizational climate—as seen by the workers—you must be prepared to respond and intervene. If you do nothing, you will lose employees' trust, and the revolving door of turnover will continue.

HOME HEALTH AIDES

In 2012, there were 875,100 home health aides employed in the U.S. (BLS, 2014b). Hospitals continue to discharge patients quicker and sicker, which means more and more health care that used to be provided strictly in hospital settings is now given at home (Landers, 2010). In addition, due to the demographic tsunami of aging Baby Boomers who wish to age in place (i.e., at home) and due to the increasing longevity of individuals with chronic diseases and disability, this area of employment is expected to grow dramatically over the next decade. Many of the same issues associated with nursing aides will come along with this dramatic employment surge in home health aides. Since these individuals go to people's homes to provide their services, all of the concerns noted above related to the need for CBCs, prevention of abuse of vulnerable populations, and turnover apply here as well. In addition,

> home health aides who work for agencies that receive reimbursement from Medicare or Medicaid must get a minimum level of training and pass a competency evaluation or receive state certification. Training includes learning about personal hygiene, reading and recording vital signs, infection control, and basic nutrition. Aides may take a competency exam to become certified without taking any training. These are the minimum requirements by law; additional requirements for certification vary by state. (BLS, 2014b, para 3)

Many hospitals and health care organizations have branched out into home health care services. While you may think you will be employed by a hospital and work only on inpatient services, the reality is you may very well become a manager for these outpatient, in-home services. It will be your responsibility to ensure that the people who are hired for these jobs are trustworthy and competent.

MIDLEVEL PRACTITIONERS

Midlevel practitioners include advanced practice nurses (APNs), such as nurse practitioners (NPs), clinical nurse specialists (CNS), nurse anesthetists, and nurse midwives, as well as physician assistants (PAs). "Between 2001–2011, the number of NP graduates grew from 7,261 to 12,273, a growth of approximately 69 percent" (HRSA, 2013, p. 50). According to Bureau of Labor Statistics, PAs held about 86,700 jobs in 2012 (BLS, 2014f). These health care professionals are called **midlevel practitioners** because they work midway between the level of an RN and that of an MD. Midlevel practitioners serve in a variety of settings, including hospital emergency rooms or departments, community health clinics, physician offices, and health maintenance organizations. They may also cover hospital floors for physicians. Midlevel practitioners are usually less expensive than physicians, often replacing MDs at a 2:1 ratio. Although APNs were resisted by many state medical societies early in the 1970s, over time physicians realized that APNs could increase their productivity and ease their workload. Midlevel practitioners are much sought after by health care organizations because they can provide many of the same services as physicians at a lower cost.

Advanced Practice Nurses

There are many organizations and accrediting bodies that certify advanced practice nurses (APNs). The following discussion is not intended to be an exhaustive listing of the specialty certifications that are available. Rather, it is meant to be illustrative of the variety of roles that APNs can assume. In addition to the educational preparation noted below, all APNs must demonstrate continuing competency by obtaining CEUs. APN certification must be renewed every five years, either by documenting evidence of practice or by retaking the examination. Below are some examples of APNs.

Nurse practitioners (NPs) are prepared, according to the American Association of Nurse Practitioners (AANP), in either an NP MSN, a post-master's certificate, or a doctoral program (AANP, 2010). To become certified in Adult, Family, and Adult-Gerontology Primary Care by the AANP's Certification Program (AANPCP), candidates must provide documentation that they are graduates of an accredited college or university's master's or post-master's level adult, gerontologic, and family nurse practitioner program (AANPCP, 2015, p. 9) They must also take a competency-based exam. "The certification program is recognized by all State Boards of Nursing, the Centers for Medicare and Medicaid Services (CMS), the Veterans Administration, private managed care organizations, institutions, and health care agencies for credentialing purposes" (AANPCP, 2015, p. 6). This means they can bill for services rendered, as can the organization that employs them. NPs can also become certified in areas of care that include but are not limited to acute, adult psychiatric/mental health, advanced diabetes management, family psychiatric/mental health, medical-surgical, school, and pediatric. They must pass a certification exam and maintain their competency through continuing nursing education and recertification exams (AANPCP, 2015). To respond to changes in the field, some examinations are retired (the Gerontologic NP) or being retired (the Adult NP). Qualified NPs can elect to apply for conversion to the Adult-Gerontology Primary Care Nurse Practitioner (AANPCP, 2015, p. 9). On May 12, 2015, Maryland became the 21st state to enact the full practice law, which enables nurse practitioners to evaluate patients, diagnose, order and interpret diagnostic tests, initiate and manage treatments, including prescribing medications, under the exclusive licensure authority of the state board of nursing (AANP, 2015). In light of the physician shortage, it is anticipated more states will follow suit and enact full practice laws for NPs.

Clinical nurse specialists (CNSs) have in-depth education in the clinical specialty area at a master's or doctoral degree level. To be certified as a CNS, the RN must have all of the same educational qualifications as an NP, but in their area of focus, plus a minimum number of hours of supervised clinical practice as specified by each specialty area. Areas of certification include:

- ACNS-BC (Adult CNS - Board Certified);
- GCNS-BC (Gerontological CNS - Board Certified);
- HHCNS-BC (Home Health CNS - Board Certified);
- PCNS-BC (Pediatric CNS - Board Certified); and
- PMHCNS-BC (Psychiatric Mental Health CNS - Board Certified)—used for both Child/Adolescent and Adult (ANCC, 2015, para 3).

They, too, must pass a certification exam and maintain their competency through continuing nursing education and recertification exams (ANCC, 2015).

Certified registered nurse anesthetists (CRNAs) are APNs who specialize in providing anesthesia. Between 2001 and 2011, their numbers grew from 1,159 graduates to 2,447 graduates (HRSA, 2013). According to the American Association of Nurse Anesthetists (AANA), nurses have been providing anesthesia care since the U.S. Civil War (AANA, 2015). They work in cooperation with anesthesiologists, surgeons, dentists, and other health care professionals. Education and experience required to become a Certified Registered Nurse Anesthetist (CRNA) include:

- A Bachelor's of Science in Nursing (BSN) or other appropriate baccalaureate degree.
- A current license as a registered nurse.
- At least one year's experience in an acute care nursing setting.
- Graduation from an accredited graduate school of nurse anesthesia. These educational programs range from 24–36 months, depending upon university requirements, and offer a master's degree.
- All programs include clinical training in university-based or large community hospitals.
- Pass a national certification examination following graduation.

It takes a minimum of seven calendar years of education and experience to prepare a CRNA. The average student nurse anesthetist completes almost 2,500 clinical hours and administers about 850 anesthetics (AANA, 2015, para 1–3). "As of Nov. 1, 2014, there were 114 accredited nurse anesthesia programs in the U.S. utilizing more than 2,500 active clinical sites; 32 nurse anesthesia programs are approved to award doctoral degrees for entry into practice" (AANA, 2015, para 6).

A review of six years of data from the Centers for Medicare & Medicaid Services (CMS) found no adverse outcomes in states where nurse anesthetists were allowed to practice solo, that is, without the supervision of a physician (Dulisse & Cromwell, 2010). Other researchers made a strong case for the cost-effectiveness of nurse anesthetists as well as the quality of care provided (Hogan, Seifert, Moore, & Simonson, 2010; Mackey, Hogan, Seifert, Moore, & Simonson, 2010). Nurse anesthetists and anesthesiologists have similar postgraduate training; these data provide evidence that the positive health outcomes for patients of solo nurse anesthetists are similar to those of physicians and cost-effective.

Certified nurse midwives (CNMs) are licensed as independent practitioners in all 50 states, the District of Columbia, American Samoa, Guam, and Puerto Rico. CNMs provide prenatal care and deliver babies. They are defined as primary care providers under federal law (American College of Nurse-Midwives [ACNM], 2014). More than 80% of all nurse midwives have master's degrees; another 4.8% have doctoral degrees. Nurse midwives were introduced to the U.S. in 1925 with the Frontier Nursing Service (FNS), founded by Mary Breckenridge (FNS, 2015). As of 2010, all CNM applicants were required to have graduate degrees and to graduate from a nurse-midwifery education program accredited by the ACNM and pass a national certification examination (ACNM, 2014).

Physician Assistants

According to the BLS (2014f), in 2012 there were 86,700 employed PAs in the U.S. PAs were created in the 1960s in response to a primary care physician shortage in the U.S. Vietnam veteran medical corpsmen were selected for a "fast-track" training program and trained to assist physicians wherever they practiced (American Academy of Physician Assistants [AAPA], 2015b). Once a male-dominated profession, now over two-thirds (67%) are female. In 2015, there were 196 accredited PA educational programs that must confer graduate degrees (Accreditation Review Commission on Education for the Physician Assistant, Inc., 2015). Only graduates of accredited PA programs are eligible to take the Physician Assistant National Certifying Examination (PANCE). PAs must demonstrate competency and be recertified every 10 years and must earn 100 CME hours every two years (National Commission on Certification of Physician Assistants, 2015). PAs are certified to practice with a team of physicians and can prescribe medication in every state in the U.S., the District of Columbia, and most U.S. territories. A physician assistant's responsibilities depend on state laws, practice setting, their experience, and the physician's scope of practice (AAPA, 2015a, 2015c). PAs practice in every conceivable setting, although the major employers of PAs are hospitals, followed by single- and multi-specialty physician group practices (AAPA, 2013). PAs are versatile and valuable members of the health care team and are highly sought after by hospitals, physician practices, and other employers.

ALLIED HEALTH PROFESSIONALS

The term **allied health professionals** refers to more than 2,000 programs in 28 health science occupations (Commission on Accreditation of Allied Health Education Programs [CAAHEP], 2015). A full list of allied health occupations is provided at the CAAHEP website, www.caahep.org. Each has its own body of knowledge, program requirements, and competency expectations. Allied health professionals assist physicians and nurses in providing comprehensive care to patients in a variety of settings. Many of the occupations, such as anesthesiologist assistant and surgical assistant, have grown from the unmet demand for help in the highly specialized operating room environment. Other occupations, such as perfusionist and electroneurodiagnostic technician, have grown out of the technological boom and the need for people to operate highly specific equipment. Radiologic technologists and technicians (often shortened to "rad techs") assist radiographers in imaging technologies, which are changing with dizzying speed. The rate of accreditation of licensed rad techs is not keeping up with the speed of change in technology, and shortages are predicted for this high-demand field (BLS, 2014g).

Laboratories that analyze clinical specimens with increasingly sophisticated technologies need to be staffed with qualified personnel. The National Accrediting Agency for Clinical Laboratory Sciences (NAACLS) is responsible for maintaining the quality of programs in the clinical laboratory sciences. "Accredited programs include Clinical Laboratory Scientist/Medical Technologist, Clinical Laboratory Technician/Medical Laboratory Technician, Cytogenetic Technologist, Diagnostic Molecular Scientist, Histologic Technician, Histotechnologist, and Pathologists' Assistant" (NAACLS, 2015). The BLS (2014a) indicates that job growth will be brisk in the coming years for clinical laboratory technologists and technicians and that the majority of this growth will occur in hospitals; however, other settings will need these workers as well.

Respiratory Therapists (RTs)

This section will address one allied health occupation in greater detail: respiratory therapists (RTs). In 2012, RTs held about 119,300 jobs, with most employed by hospitals (BLS, 2014i). RTs evaluate, treat, and care for patients with respiratory disorders, such as asthma, emphysema, pneumonia, and heart disease. An associate's degree is required for entry into the field to become a certified respiratory therapist (CRT). Additional education is required for advanced practice and eligibility for the registered respiratory therapist (RRT) designation. RTs are certified by the National Board for Respiratory Care (NBRC), and registration is available only to graduates of accredited programs in respiratory care of the Commission on Accreditation for Respiratory Care (CoARC; NBRC, 2015). All states except Alaska, as well as the District of Columbia and Puerto Rico, require RTs to obtain a license (AARC, 2010; BLS, 2014i). In addition, most employers require cardiopulmonary resuscitation (CPR) certification because RTs are usually members of hospital rapid response teams.

Shortages exist in almost all the allied health occupations, but respiratory therapy continues to be particularly affected. With a vacancy rate of 9% that translates to a national shortage of 12,000 respiratory therapists, recruitment and retention are critical matters (Brady & Keene, 2008). The authors, who are respiratory therapists, paint a disturbing picture of work life for these health care professionals. Understaffed and overwhelmed, the demands of a high patient load can be tipped into disaster when a code is called and all the other less critical patients have to wait—with anxious and angry family members who don't understand why their loved one's treatment is delayed. Brady and Keene (2008) recommend strategies to retain RTs, beginning with appreciating the important work they are doing. They also recommended approaches to assess and assign workload more evenly and expressed concerns that overwork and short staffing compromises patient care. Since recruitment and retention are under the domain of the health care manager, you will be expected to come up with creative approaches to address this ongoing dilemma.

OPPORTUNITIES FOR RESEARCH ON HEALTH CARE PROFESSIONALS

Staffing shortages across all health care professions will continue to be an issue, along with recruitment, retention, job satisfaction, burnout, and turnover. Maintenance of currency and the relevance of an up-to-date health care workforce will always be an evergreen topic for researchers and health care managers alike. Many of the resources used in writing this chapter also include extensive research holdings and data sets that are available to students and academic researchers. Herewith is a partial listing of these resources.

- Agency for Healthcare Research and Quality TeamSTEPPS®: Strategies and Tools to Enhance Performance and Patient Safety;
- Bureau of Labor Statistics (BLS) Occupational Outlook Handbook Healthcare;
- Centers for Disease Control and Prevention (CDC) Collaboration Primer;
- Foundation for the Advancement of International Medical Education and Research;
- Hospital Consumer Assessment of Healthcare Providers and Systems;
- Hospital Research and Educational Trust (HRET);
- Inter-university Consortium for Political and Social Research (ICPSR);
- Open Payments;
- The Robert Wood Johnson Foundation; and
- U.S. Department of Health and Human Services Health Resources and Services Administration (HRSA) Coordinating Center for Interprofessional Education and Collaborative Practice (CC-IPECP).

You will have an abundance of information at your fingertips at any one of these websites.

CONCLUSION

This chapter has described the education, training, and credentialing of physicians, nurses, nurses' aides, midlevel practitioners, and allied health professionals and has given an overview of the supply of and demand for health care professionals. In addition, some of the reasons for health care professional turnover and costs of turnover have been discussed, along with some strategies for increasing retention and preventing turnover. Conflict of interest as it relates to employed physicians has been addressed, and issues related to the management of the work life of physicians, nurses, nurses' aides, midlevel practitioners, and allied health professionals have been interwoven through all of these topics. These are issues that can and should be addressed by you, the health care manager, with respect for each and every health care professional. The challenges await you; there will be no shortage of problems for you to solve.

DISCUSSION QUESTIONS

1. Delineate the steps in attaining state licensure for physicians.

2. Describe the steps in attaining state licensure for nurses.

3. Compare and contrast licensure and credentialing.

4. Distinguish between core privileges and specific privileges in physician credentialing.

5. Why is physician credentialing one of the most important jobs in a hospital?

6. What is the National Practitioner Data Bank, and why was it created?

7. What is an international medical graduate, and what populations have they traditionally been most likely to serve?

8. Why might we begin to see fewer foreign-educated nurses in the U.S.?

9. Why might we begin to see fewer foreign-educated physicians in the U.S.?

10. Define the following terms: "job burnout," "job satisfaction," "retention," and "turnover." Why are they of importance in managing health care professionals? What can health care managers do to minimize physician burnout?

11. What is the "Sunshine Law," how does it relate to conflict of interest, and why is it important among employed physicians?

12. What is the relationship among nursing education, nursing burnout, job dissatisfaction, and patient mortality? What can health care managers do to minimize nursing burnout?

13. What are the attributes of hospitals that support professional nursing practice?

14. Distinguish among the following: advanced practice registered nurse, certified registered nurse, and physician assistant.

15. Distinguish among licensed practical nurses, certified nurses' assistants, and home health aides. What are some of the health care manager's challenges with these groups?

16. Who are allied health professionals? What are some health care management issues in working with them?

Cases in Chapter 18 that are related to this chapter include:

- United Physician Group
- Death by Measles
- Full Moon or Bad Planning
- The Brawler
- I Love you...Forever
- Managing Health Care Professionals—Mini-Case Studies
- Such a Nice Young Man
- The New Toy at City Medical Center

Case study guides are available in the online Instructor's Materials.

REFERENCES

Accreditation Council for Continuing Medical Education (ACCME). (2015a). *Maintenance of recognition.* Retrieved from http://www.accme.org/accreditors/maintenance-of-recognition

Accreditation Council for Continuing Medical Education (ACCME). (2015b). *Member organizations.* Retrieved from http://www.accme.org/about-us/collaboration/members-organizations

Accreditation Council for Graduate Medical Education (ACGME). (2011, July 1). *Common program requirements.* Retrieved from http://www.acgme.org/acgmeweb/Portals/0/PDFs/Common_Program_Requirements_07012011%5B2%5D.pdf

Accreditation Council for Graduate Medical Education (ACGME). (2014). *Frequently asked questions: ACGME Common duty hour requirements: July 1, 2011, updated June 18, 2014.* Retrieved from http://www.acgme.org/acgmeweb/Portals/0/PDFs/dh-faqs2011.pdf

Accreditation Council for Graduate Medical Education (ACGME). (2015). *ACGME fact sheet.* Retrieved from http://www.acgme.org/acgmeweb/tabid/276/About/Newsroom/FactSheet.aspx, para 4–5.

Accreditation Review Commission on Education for the Physician Assistant, Inc. (ARC-PA). (2015). *Accredited PA programs.* Retrieved from http://www.arc-pa.org/acc_programs/

Aiken, L. H., Buchan, J., Sochalski, J., Nichols, B., & Powell, M. (2004, May/June). Trends in international nurse migration. *Health Affairs, 23*(3), 69–77.

Aiken, L. H., Clarke, S. P., Cheung, R. B., Sloane, D. M., & Silber, J. H. (2003). Educational levels of hospital nurses and surgical patient mortality. *Journal of the American Medical Association, 290*(12), 1617–1623.

Aiken, L. H., Clarke, S. P., Sloane, D. M., Sochalski, J., & Silber, J. H. (2002). Hospital nurse staffing and patient mortality, nurse burnout, and job dissatisfaction. *Journal of the American Medical Association, 288*(16), 1987–1993.

AMA Wire. (2015a, May 20). *4 things students should know about the new GME bill.* Retrieved from http://www.ama-assn.org/ama/ama-wire/post/4-things-students-should-new-gme-bill

AMA Wire. (2015b, May 19). *New commission to help streamline medical licensure.* Retrieved from http://www.ama-assn.org/ama/ama-wire/post/new-commission-streamline-medical-licensure

American Academy of Family Practice (AAFP). (2015a). *AAFP-ACOG joint statement on cooperative practice and hospital privileges.* Retrieved from http://www.aafp.org/about/policies/all/aafp-acog.html

American Academy of Family Practice (AAFP). (2015b). *Family medicine specialty.* Retrieved from http://www.aafp.org/about/the-aafp/family-medicine-specialty.html

American Academy of Physician Assistants (AAPA). (2013). *AAPA national survey report.* Retrieved from https://www.aapa.org/WorkArea/DownloadAsset.aspx?id=2902

American Academy of Physician Assistants (AAPA). (2015a). *Become a PA.* Retrieved from https://www.aapa.org/Become-a-PA/

American Academy of Physician Assistants (AAPA). (2015b). *History.* Retrieved from https://www.aapa.org/threeColumnLanding.aspx?id=429

American Academy of Physician Assistants (AAPA). (2015c). *I'm a PA.* AAPA Brochure. Retrieved from https://www.aapa.org/workarea/downloadasset.aspx?id=889

American Association for Respiratory Care (AARC). (2010). *State licensure.* Retrieved from http://www.aarc.org/advocacy/state/licensure_matrix.html#matrix

American Association of Colleges of Nursing (AACN). (2002, January). *Hallmarks of the professional nursing practice environment.* AACN white paper. Retrieved from http://www.aacn.nche.edu/Publications/positions/hallmarks.htm

American Association of Colleges of Nursing (AACN). (2011). *Fact sheet.* Retrieved from http://www.aacn.nche.edu/media-relations/fact-sheets/nursing-fact-sheet

American Association of Colleges of Nursing (AACN). (2014a). *New AACN data confirm enrollment surge in schools of nursing.* Retrieved from http://www.aacn.nche.edu/news/articles/2015/enrollment#Findings

American Association of Colleges of Nursing (AACN). (2014b, August 18). *Nursing faculty shortage.* Retrieved from http://www.aacn.nche.edu/media-relations/fact-sheets/nursing-faculty-shortage

American Association of Colleges of Nursing (AACN). (2015). *Nurse residency program.* Retrieved from http://www.aacn.nche.edu/education-resources/nurse-residency-program

American Association of Nurse Anesthetists (AANA). (2015). *Certified registered nurse anesthetists fact sheet.* Retrieved from http://www.aana.com/ceandeducation/becomeacrna/Pages/Nurse-Anesthetists-at-a-Glance.aspx

American Association of Nurse Practitioners (AANP). (2010). *What is a nurse practitioner?* Retrieved from http://www.aanp.org/all-about-nps/what-is-an-np

American Association of Nurse Practitioners (AANP). (2015). *State regulatory map.* Retrieved from http://www.aanp.org/images/documents/state-leg-reg/stateregulatorymap.pdf

American Association of Nurse Practitioners Certification Program (AANPCP). (2015, February). *Candidate handbook and renewal of certification handbook.* Retrieved from https://www.aanpcert.org/ptistore/resource/documents/2013%20CandidateRenewalHandbook%20-Rev%2011%2025%202013%20forNCCA%28FINAL%29.pdf

American Board of Medical Specialists (ABMS). (2015). *Board certification and maintenance of certification.* Retrieved from http://www.abms.org/board-certification/

American College of Nurse-Midwives (ACNM). (2014). *Essential facts about midwives.* Retrieved from http://www.midwife.org/Essential-Facts-about-Midwives

American College of Physicians. (2008). *White paper: How is a shortage of primary care physicians affecting the quality and cost of medical care? A comprehensive evidence review.* Retrieved from https://www.acponline.org/advocacy/current_policy_papers/assets/primary_shortage.pdf

American Medical Association (AMA) International Medical Graduates' Section. (2015a). *IMGs in the United States.* Retrieved from http://www.ama-assn.org/ama/pub/about-ama/our-people/member-groups-sections/international-medical-graduates/imgs-in-united-states.page?

American Medical Association (AMA). (2015b) *AMA physician masterfile.* Retrieved from http://www.ama-assn.org/ama/pub/about-ama/physician-data-resources/physician-masterfile.page

American Medical Association (AMA) Medical Student Section, Committee on Legislation and Advocacy (COLA), Subcommittee on Medical Education. (n.d.). *Resident work hours.*

American Nursing Credentialing Center (ANCC). (2014a). *ANCC certification center.* Retrieved from http://www.nursecredentialing.org/certification.aspx#

American Nurses Credentialing Center (ANCC). (2014b). *Magnet recognition program overview.* Retrieved from http://www.nursecredentialing.org/Magnet/ProgramOverview

American Nursing Credentialing Center (ANCC). (2015). *ANCC announces new credentials for clinical nurse specialists.* Retrieved from http://www.nursecredentialing.org/FunctionalCategory /AboutANCC/Headlines/NewCredentialsforClinicalNurseSpecialists.html

Annotated Code of Maryland (COMAR). (2015). *Licensure: Qualifications for initial licensure.* Retrieved from http://www.dsd.state.md.us/comar/getfile.aspx?file=10.32.01.03.htm

Association of American Medical Colleges (AAMC). (2015). *Aspiring docs: The basics.* Retrieved from https://www.aamc.org/students/aspiring/basics/

Baker, D. P., Salas, E., King, H., Battles, J., & Barach, P. (2005, April). The role of teamwork in the professional education of physicians: Current status and assessment recommendations. *Journal on Quality and Patient Safety, 31*(4), 185–202.

Boswell, S., Lowry, L. W., & Wilhoit, K. (2004). New nurses' perceptions of nursing practice and quality patient care. *Journal of Nursing Care Quality, 19*(1), 76–81.

Brady, S., & Keene, S. (2008). Respiratory therapists can facilitate positive change with institutional support. *The Internet Journal of Healthcare Administration 6*(1), 1–5.

Brewer, C. S., Kovner, C. T., Greene, W., Tukov-Shuser, M., & Djukic, M. (2012). Predictors of actual turnover in a national sample of newly licensed registered nurses employed in hospitals. *Journal of Advanced Nursing, 68*(3), 521–538.

Buchbinder, S. B., Alt, P. M., Eskow, K., Forbes, W., Hester, E., Struck, M., & Taylor, D. (2005). Creating learning prisms with an interdisciplinary case study workshop. *Innovative Higher Education, 29*(4), 257–274.

Buchbinder, S. B., Wilson, M. H., Melick, C. F., & Powe, N. R. (2001). Primary care physician job satisfaction and turnover. *American Journal of Managed Care, 7*(7), 701–713.

Bureau of Health Professions (BHPr). (2003, Spring). *Changing demographics: Implications for physicians, nurses and other health workers.* Washington, DC: U.S. Department of Health and Human Services, Health Resources and Services Administration, Bureau of Health Professions, National Center for Health Workforce Analysis. Retrieved from http://www.nachc.org/client/documents/clinical /Clinical_Workforce_Changing_Demographics.pdf

Bureau of Labor Statistics (BLS). (2014a). Clinical laboratory technologists and technicians. *Occupational outlook handbook, 2014–15 edition.* Retrieved from http://www.bls.gov/ooh/healthcare /medical-and-clinical-laboratory-technologists-and-technicians.htm

Bureau of Labor Statistics (BLS). (2014b). Home health aides. *Occupational outlook handbook, 2014–15 edition.* Retrieved from http://www.bls.gov/ooh/healthcare/home-health-aides.htm#tab-4

Bureau of Labor Statistics (BLS). (2014c). Licensed practical and licensed vocational nurses. *Occupational outlook handbook, 2014–15 edition.* Retrieved from http://www.bls.gov/ooh/healthcare /licensed-practical-and-licensed-vocational-nurses.htm

Bureau of Labor Statistics (BLS). (2014d). Nursing assistants and orderlies. *Occupational outlook handbook, 2014–15 edition.* Retrieved from http://www.bls.gov/ooh/healthcare/nursing-assistants.htm #tab-1

Bureau of Labor Statistics (BLS). (2014e). Physicians and surgeons. *Occupational outlook handbook, 2014–15 edition.* Retrieved from http://www.bls.gov/ooh/healthcare/physicians-and-surgeons.htm

Bureau of Labor Statistics (BLS). (2014f). Physician assistants. *Occupational outlook handbook, 2014–15 edition.* Retrieved from http://www.bls.gov/ooh/healthcare/physician-assistants.htm

Bureau of Labor Statistics (BLS). (2014g). Radiologic and MRI technologists. *Occupational outlook handbook, 2014–15 edition.* Retrieved from http://www.bls.gov/ooh/healthcare/radiologic-technologists.htm

Bureau of Labor Statistics (BLS). (2014h). Registered Nurses. *Occupational outlook handbook, 2014-15 edition.* Retrieved from http://www.bls.gov/ooh/healthcare/registered-nurses.htm.

Bureau of Labor Statistics (BLS). (2014i). Respiratory therapists. *Occupational outlook handbook, 2014–15 edition.* Retrieved from http://www.bls.gov/ooh/healthcare/respiratory-therapists.htm

Butcher, L. (2008, July). Many changes in store as physicians become employees. *Managed Care.* Retrieved from http://www.managedcaremag.com/archives/0807/0807.physicians.html

Cejka Search & American Medical Group Association (AMGA). (2013). *2013 Benchmarks for retention, recruitment and growth.*

Centers for Medicare & Medicare Services (CMS). (2015). *Open payments.* Retrieved from http://www.cms.gov/openpayments/

Commission on Accreditation of Allied Health Education Programs (CAAHEP). (2015). *About CAAHEP.* Retrieved from http://www.caahep.org/Content.aspx?ID=63

Commission on Graduates of Foreign Nursing Schools (CGFNS). (2015). *The certification program.* Retrieved from http://www.cgfns.org/services/certification-program/

Cooper, R. A. (2002). There's a shortage of specialists. Is anyone listening? *Academic Medicine, 77,* 761–766.

Cooper, R. A. (2003). Medical schools and their applicants: An analysis. *Health Affairs, 22*(4), 71–84.

Cooper, R. A., & Aiken, L. H. (2001). Human inputs: The health care workforce and medical markets. *Journal of Health Politics, Policy and Law, 26,* 925–938.

Council of State Governments (CSG). (2012). *Proposed policy resolutions.* Retrieved from http://www.csg.org/2012NationalConference/documents/Resolution%20Supporting%20Criminal%20Background%20Checks%20for%20Nurses%20Applying%20for%20State%20Licensure.pdf

Council of State Governments (CSG). (2013, July). *Capitol facts & figures: Nurse licensure criminal background checks.* Retrieved from http://knowledgecenter.csg.org/kc/system/files/nurse_licensure.pdf

Department for Professional Employees AFL-CIO (DPEAFLCIO). (2010). *Fact Sheet: The costs and benefits of safe staffing ratios.* Retrieved from http://dpeaflcio.org/pdf/DPE-fs_2010_staffratio.pdf

Dietz, A. S., Pronovost, P. J., Mendez-Tellez, P. A., Wyskiel, R., Marsteller, J. A., Thompson, D. A., & Rosen, M. A. (2014). Administration/Teamwork: A systematic review of teamwork in the intensive care unit: What do we know about teamwork, team tasks, and improvement strategies? *Journal of Critical Care, 299,* 908–914. doi:10.1016/j.jcrc.2014.05.025

Donabedian, A. (2005). Evaluating the quality of medical care. *The Milbank Quarterly, 83*(4), 691–729.

Drazen, J. M., de Leeuw, P. W., Laine, C., Mulrow, C., DeAngelis, C., Frizelle, F. A., …Zhaori, G. (2010). Toward more uniform conflict disclosures—the updated ICMJE conflict of interest reporting form. *New England Journal of Medicine, 363,* 188–189.

Dreger, A. (2013, February 6). What the Sunshine Act means for health care transparency. *The Atlantic.* Retrieved from http://www.theatlantic.com/health/archive/2013/02/what-the-sunshine-act-means-for-health-care-transparency/272926/

Dulisse, B., & Cromwell, J. (2010, August). No harm found when nurse anesthetists work without supervision by physicians. *Health Affairs, 29*(8), 1469–1475.

Dunn, P. M., Arnetz, B. B., Christensen, J. F., & Homer, L. (2007). Meeting the imperative to improve physician well-being: assessment of an innovative program. *Journal of General Internal Medicine, 22*(11), 1544–1552.

Duvivier, R. J., Stull M. J., & Brockman, J. A. (2012). Shortening medical education. *Journal of the American Medical Association, 308*(2), 133–136. doi:10.1001/jama.2012.7022

Educational Commission for Foreign Medical Graduates (ECFMG). (2011). *International credentials services.* Retrieved from http://www.ecfmg.org/eics/index.html

Emanuel, E. J., & Fuchs, V. R. (2012). Shortening medical training by 30%. *Journal of the American Medical Association, 307*(11), 1143–1144. doi:10.1001/jama.2012.292

Federation of State Medical Boards (FSMB). (2014). *Criminal background checks: Board by board overview.* Retrieved from http://library.fsmb.org/pdf/grpol_criminal_background_checks.pdf

Frontier Nursing Service (FNS). (2015). *Frontier nursing service.* Retrieved from https://frontiernursing .org/History/History.shtm

Government Accountability Office (GAO). (2010, January). *VA health care: Improved oversight and compliance needed for physician credentialing and privileging processes.* Report number GAO-10-26. Washington, DC: Author. Retrieved from http://www.gao.gov/new.items/d1026.pdf

Gupta, R. T., Sexton, J. B., Milne, J., & Frush, D. P. (2015, January). Practice and quality improvement: Successful implementation of TeamSTEPPS tools into an academic interventional ultrasound practice. *American Journal of Roentgenology, 204*(1), 105–110.

Hagopian, A., Thompson, M. J., Kaltenbach, E., & Hart, L. G. (2003). Health departments' use of international medical graduates in physician shortage areas. *Health Affairs, 22*(5), 241–249.

Hallock, J. A., Seeling, S. S., & Norcini, J. J. (2003). The international medical graduate pipeline. *Health Affairs, 22*(4), 64–96.

Health Resources and Services Administration (HRSA). Bureau of Health Professions National Center for Health Workforce Analysis (2013, April). *The U.S. nursing workforce: Trends in supply and education.* Retrieved from http://bhpr.hrsa.gov/healthworkforce/reports/nursingworkforce /nursingworkforcefullreport.pdf

Hogan, P. F., Seifert, R. F., Moore, C. S., & Simonson, B. E. (2010). Cost effectiveness analysis of anesthesia providers. *Nursing Economic$, 28*(3), 159–169.

Isaacs, S. L., Jellinek, P. S., & Ray, W. L. (2009). The independent physician—going, going… *New England Journal of Medicine, 360,* 655–657.

Jones, C., & Gates, M. (September 30, 2007). The costs and benefits of nurse turnover: A business case for nurse retention. *The Online Journal of Issues in Nursing, 12*(3), Manuscript 4. Retrieved from http://www.nursingworld.org/MainMenuCategories/ANAMarketplace/ANAPeriodicals/OJIN /TableofContents/Volume122007/No3Sept07/NurseRetention.aspx

Kennedy, B. R. (2005, December). Stress and burnout of nursing staff working with geriatric clients in long-term care. *Journal of Nursing Scholarship, 37*(4), 381–382.

Kimball, B., & O'Neil, E. (2002, April). Health care's human crisis: The American nursing shortage. *Robert Wood Johnson Foundation.* Retrieved from http://www.rwjf.org/content/dam/web-assets /2002/04/health-care-s-human-crisis

Landers, S. H. (2010). Why health care is going home. *New England Journal of Medicine, 363*(18), 1690–1691.

Laschinger, H. K. S., & Finegan, J. (2005). Using empowerment to build trust and respect in the workplace: A strategy for addressing the nursing shortage. *Nursing Economic$, 23*(1), 6–13.

Levinson, W., Lesser, C. S., & Epstein, R. M. (2010). Developing physician communication skills for patient-centered care. *Health Affairs, 29*(7), 1310–1316.

Lipner, R. S., Hess, B. J., & Phillips, R. L. (2013). Specialty board certification in the United States: Issues and evidence. *Journal of Continuing Education In The Health Professions, 33*, S20–S35. doi:10.1002/chp.21203

Locke, E. A. (1983). The nature and causes of job satisfaction. In M. Dunnette (Ed.), *Handbook of industrial and organizational psychology* (pp. 1297–1349). New York, NY: John Wiley & Sons.

Mackey, B., Hogan, P. F., Seifert, R. F., Moore, C. S., & Simonson, B. E. (2010). Cost effectiveness analysis of anesthesia providers. *Nursing Economic$, 28*(4), 287.

Maslach, C. (2003, October). Job burnout: New directions in research and intervention. *Current Directions in Psychological Science, 12*(5), 189–190.

McFarlane, J. (2013). Freeze on foreign nurses as NHS chiefs admit they have no idea how many lied about qualifications and experience using fake IDs. *Daily Mail*. Retrieved from http://www.dailymail.co.uk/news/article-2290920/Freeze-foreign-nurses-NHS-chiefs-admit-idea-lied-qualifications-experience-using-fake-IDs.html

McMahon, G. T. (2004). Coming to America: International medical graduates in the United States. *New England Journal of Medicine, 350*, 2435–2437.

Mechanic, D. (2010). Replicating high-quality medical care organizations. *Journal of the American Medical Association, 303*(6), 555–556.

Medstar Health. (2015). *Guidance on interaction with industry*. Retrieved from http://www.medstarhealth.org/mhs/about-medstar/disclosure-of-outside-interests/guidance-on-interactions-with-industry/#q={}1.Medstar-COI-and-Interactions-with-Industry.pdf

Mick, S. S., & Lee, S. D. (1999a, Winter). Are there need-based geographical differences between International Medical Graduates and US Medical Graduates in rural US counties? *The Journal of Rural Health, 15*(1), 26–43.

Mick, S. S., & Lee, S. D. (1999b). International and US medical graduates in US cities. *Journal of Urban Health: Bulletin of the New York Academy of Medicine, 76*(4), 481–496.

Mick, S. S., Lee, S. D., & Wodchis, W. P. (2000). Variations in geographical distribution of foreign and domestically trained physicians in the United States: "Safety nets" or "surplus exacerbation." *Social Science & Medicine, 50*, 185–202.

Nadzman, D. M. (2009). Nurses' role in communication and patient safety. *Journal of Nursing Care Quality, 24*(3), 184–188.

National Accrediting Agency for Clinical Laboratory Sciences (NAACLS). (2015). *Programs*. Retrieved from http://www.naacls.org/program-center/

National Board for Respiratory Care (NBRC). (2015). *Examinations*. Retrieved from https://www.nbrc.org/Pages/examinations.aspx

National Commission on Certification of Physician Assistants. (2015). *Maintaining certification*. Retrieved from http://www.nccpa.net/CertificationProcess

National Commission on Nursing (NCN). (1983). *Summary report and recommendations*. Chicago, IL: Hospital Research and Educational Trust.

National Council of State Boards of Nursing (NCSBN). (2010). *Quarterly examination statistics. Volume, pass rates & first-time internationally educated candidates' countries*. Retrieved from https://www.ncsbn.org/NCLEX_Stats_2010.pdf

National Council of State Boards of Nursing (NCSBN). (2015a). *History*. Retrieved from https://www.ncsbn.org/history.htm

National Council of State Boards of Nursing (NCSBN). (2015b). *Number of candidates taking NCLEX examination and percent passing, by type of candidate*. Retrieved from https://www.ncsbn.org/Table_of_Pass_Rates_2015_%283%29.pdf

National Institutes of Health (NIH). (2014). *Financial conflict of interest*. Retrieved from http://grants.nih.gov/grants/policy/coi/

National Institutes of Health (NIH). (2015). *Frequently asked questions*. Retrieved from http://www.nih.gov/news/calendar/calendarfaq.htm#cmecredit

National Practitioner Data Bank (NPDB). (2015). *National practitioner data bank: About us*. Retrieved from http://www.npdb.hrsa.gov/topNavigation/aboutUs.jsp

National Residency Matching Program (NRMP). (2015). *Match process*. Retrieved from http://www.nrmp.org/match-process/

Norcini, J. J., Boulet, J. R., Dauphinee, W. D., Opalek, A., Krantz, I. D., & Anderson, S. T. (2010). Evaluating the quality of care provided by graduates of international medical schools. *Health Affairs*, *28*(8), 1461–1468.

Polsky, D., Kletke, P. R., Wozniak, G. D., & Escarce, J. (2002). Initial practice locations of international medical graduates. *HSR: Health Services Research*, *37*, 907–928.

Porucznik, M. A. (2012). How to deal with the "problem physician": Fall meeting symposium focuses on crucial conversation tips. *AAOS Now*. Retrieved from http://www.aaos.org/news/aaosnow/jan13/managing3.asp

Pradarelli, J. C., Campbell, D. A., Jr., & Dimick, J. B. (2015). Hospital credentialing and privileging of surgeons: A potential safety blind spot. *Journal of the American Medical Association*, *313*(13), 1313–1314. doi:10.1001/jama.2015.1943

Ribas, V., Dill, J. S., & Cohen, P. N. (2012, Dec.) Mobility for care workers: job changes and wages for nurse aides. *Social Science & Medicine*, *75*(12), 2183–2190. doi: 10.1016/j.socscimed.2012.08.015

Ross, J. S., Lackner, J. E., Lurie, P., Gross, C. P., Wolfe, S., & Krumholz, H. M. (2007). Pharmaceutical company payments to physicians: early experiences with disclosure laws in Vermont and Minnesota. *Journal of the American Medical Association*, *297*(11), 1216–1223.

Seavey, D. (2004, October). *The cost of frontline turnover in long-term care*. Retrieved from http://www.directcareclearinghouse.org/download/TOCostReport.pdf

Sexton, J. B., Thomas, E. J., & Helmreich, R. L. (2000). Error, stress, and teamwork in medicine and aviation: Cross sectional surveys. *British Medical Journal*, *320*, 745–749.

Smart, D. R. (2010). *Physician characteristics and distribution in the US*. Chicago, IL: AMA Press.

Steiger, D. O., Auerbach, D. I., & Buerhaus, P. I. (2000). Expanding career opportunities for women and the declining interest in nursing as a career. *Nursing Economic$*, *18*(5), 230–236.

Steiger, D. O., Auerbach, D. I., & Buerhaus, P. I. (2009). Comparison of physician workforce estimates and supply projections. *Journal of the American Medical Association*, *302*(15), 1674–1680.

Steiger, D. O., Auerbach, D. I., & Buerhaus, P. I. (2010). Trends in the work hours of physicians in the United States. *Journal of the American Medical Association, 303*(8), 747–753.

Stevenson University. (2015). *Nursing program.* Retrieved from http://www.stevenson.edu/academics /undergraduate-programs/nursing/

Szymczak, J. E., Brooks, J. V., Volpp, K. G., & Bosk, C. L. (2010). To leave or to lie? Are concerns about a shift-work mentality and eroding professionalism as a result of duty-hour rules justified? *Milbank Quarterly, 88*(3), 350–381. doi:10.1111/j.1468-0009.2010.00603.x

Tamblyn, R., Abrahamowicz, M., Brailovsky, C., Grand'Maison, P., Lescop, J., Norcini, J.,... & Haggerty, J. (1998). Association between licensing examination scores and resource use and quality of care in primary care practice. *Journal of the American Medical Association, 280*(11), 989–996.

The Joint Commission (TJC). (2002). *Health care at the crossroads: Strategies for addressing the evolving nursing crisis.* Retrieved from http://www.jointcommission.org/assets/1/18/health_care_at_the _crossroads.pdf

The Joint Commission (TJC). (2008, July 9). Behaviors that undermine a culture of safety. *Sentinel Event Alert*, Issue 40. Retrieved from http://www.jointcommission.org/sentinel_event_alert_issue _40_behaviors_that_undermine_a_culture_of_safety/

The Joint Commission (TJC). (2009). *The Joint Commission guide to improving staff communication* (2nd ed.). Oak Brook, IL: Joint Commission Resources.

The Joint Commission (TJC). (2014, November). *Sentinel event policy and procedure.* Retrieved from http://www.jointcommission.org/sentinel_event_policy_and_procedures/

Thompson, M. J., Hagopian, A., Fordyce, M., & Hart, L. G. (2009). Do international medical graduates (IMGs) "fill the gap" in rural primary care in the United States? A national study. *The Journal of Rural Health, 25*(2), 124–134. doi:10.1111/j.1748-0361.2009.00208.x

Tibbs, S., & Moss, J. (2014, Nov.). Promoting teamwork and surgical optimization: Combining TeamSTEPPS with a specialty team protocol. *AORN Journal, 100*(5), 477–488. doi: 10.1016/j .aorn.2014.01.028. Epub 2014 Oct 25.

Torpey, E. (2014, Spring). Healthcare: Millions of jobs now and in the future. *Occupational Outlook Quarterly.* Retrieved from http://www.bls.gov/careeroutlook/2014/spring/art03.pdf

Traverso, G., & McMahon, G. T. (2012). Residency training and international medical graduates: Coming to America no more. *Journal of the American Medical Association, 308*(21), 2193–2194. doi:10.1001/jama.2012.14681

Vaidya, A. (2013, June 18). Survey: Number of hospital-employed physicians up 6%. *Becker's Hospital Review.* Retrieved from http://www.beckershospitalreview.com/hospital-physician-relationships /survey-number-of-hospital-employed-physicians-up-6.html

Weber, D. O. (2004, September–October). Poll results: Doctors' disruptive behavior disturbs physician leaders. *The Physician Executive, 30*(5), 6–14.

Whelan, G. P., Gary, N. E., Kostis, J., Boutlet, J. R., & Hallock, J. A. (2000). The changing pool of international medical graduates seeking certification training in US graduate medical education programs. *Journal of the American Medical Association, 288*, 1079–1084.

The Strategic Management of Human Resources

Jon M. Thompson

LEARNING OBJECTIVES

By the end of this chapter, the student will be able to:

- Delineate why human resources management includes strategic and administrative actions;
- Assess current environmental forces influencing human resources management;
- Analyze the key role of employees as drivers of organizational performance;
- Summarize major federal legislation affecting human resources management;
- Contrast human resources functions that address employee workforce planning/ recruitment and employee retention;
- Differentiate between the key responsibilities of human resources management staff and line management staff in recruitment and retention;
- Classify methods of compensating employees;
- Compare methods of evaluating employees;
- Discuss examples of human resource management issues in health care settings; and
- Identify current research areas in human resources management.

INTRODUCTION

The management of human resources is one of the most important and challenging responsibilities within health services organizations. Health services organizations need to be high-performing organizations, and human resources are considered the most important factor in creating such organizations (Pfeffer, 1998). A high-performing health services organization provides high-quality services and excellent customer service, is efficient, has high productivity and reliability, and is financially sound.

Human resources management involves both administrative and strategic elements. From a strategic perspective, health services organizations compete for labor. They desire an adequate labor supply and the proper mix of quality and committed health care professionals to provide needed services. The strategic perspective acknowledges that organizational performance is contingent on individual human performance. Health services organizations need to view their human resources as a strategic asset that helps create competitive advantage (Becker, Huselid, & Ulrich, 2001). Additionally, organizations must have the capability to understand their current and future manpower needs and develop and implement a clear-cut strategy to meet those needs to achieve the organizational business strategy. Administratively, there are a number of specific functions and action steps that need to be carried out in support of managing the human resources of the health services organization to ensure high levels of performance.

Fundamentally, **human resources management** addresses the need to ensure that qualified and motivated personnel are available to staff the business units operated by the health services organization (Hernandez, Fottler, & Joiner, 1998). Human resources management encompasses a variety of functions and tasks related to recruiting, retaining, and developing staff in the health services organization. These staff include administrative staff who carry out nonclinical administrative functions such as patient accounting, quality management, and community relations; clinical staff who provide diagnostic, treatment, and rehabilitation services to patients; and support staff who assist in the delivery of clinical, administrative, and other facility services. The human resources activities that support administrative and clinical staff are carried out by dedicated human resources personnel who work in human resources or personnel departments, and are also carried out by line managers who have primary responsibility for directing staff and teams and who are charged with hiring, supervising, evaluating, developing, and, when necessary, terminating staff.

Management of human resources is complex, and human resources actions address a variety of issues and situations. Consider the following examples of human resources management in various health services organizations:

- A large physician practice is in need of hiring someone to head up its information management area. The practice has grown from seven to 23 physicians in the past five years, and the practice administrator has realized the clinical and financial records' needs of the practice have outpaced current administrative expertise. The administrator wants to define the job by analyzing job duties and then recruiting personnel to fill the position.

- A large system-affiliated hospital desires to train patient care technicians to assist in direct clinical care of patients. The hospital has experienced a shortage of RNs in the past three years and has found that a multidisciplinary team approach using patient care technicians will help the organization meet patient and manpower needs. The Vice President of Patient Care desires to know the best way to train these teams.
- An assisted living facility is developing a new position for a marketing specialist, who will be tasked with marketing the facility in an effort to increase its census. The facility administrator desires to conduct a job analysis to determine the specific responsibilities of the marketing specialist's job.
- An ambulatory care clinic plans to add new diagnostic imaging equipment in order to compete for more patients in its service area. The purchase of this equipment raises several questions for the organization, including: What are the specific human resources needed to staff the new technology, and are they available? How will the addition of new technology and services affect the operating budget and the achievement of the business strategy of the clinic?

Each of these scenarios provides a good illustration of the diverse nature of human resources activities from both strategic and administrative perspectives and suggests how these activities contribute to the effective performance of the organization.

This chapter provides an overview of the specific activities that take place strategically and administratively to manage the human resources of the health services organization. First, environmental forces affecting the management of human resources in health services organizations will be reviewed. Second, the importance of employees as drivers of organizational performance will be addressed. Key functions within human resources management will then be identified and discussed. Finally, conclusions regarding management of human resources in health services organizations will be presented.

ENVIRONMENTAL FORCES AFFECTING HUMAN RESOURCES MANAGEMENT

There are several key environmental forces that affect the availability and performance of human resources within health services organizations (HSOs) (see Table 12-1). The **environment** for HSOs is the external space beyond the organization that includes other organizations and influences that affect the organization.

First, *declining reimbursements* from government payers and other third parties have reduced the revenues coming to HSOs. In efforts to contain their expenses, the Medicare and Medicaid programs, private insurance, and managed care organizations have reduced their payments on behalf of covered beneficiaries. Declining reimbursements for health

TABLE 12-1 Environmental Forces and Impacts on Human Resources Management

Force	Impact
Declining reimbursement	Less resources to recruit, compensate, and develop workforce
Declining supply of workers	Shortage of skilled workers, changes in recruiting and staffing specialized services, lower satisfaction of workers
Increasing population need	Increased volumes of patients and workload for HSOs
Increasing competition among HSOs	Competition for health care workers and pressure for higher wages
External pressure on HSOs	HR must ensure high performance in HSO for accountability and performance

services organizations have left HSOs with fewer resources to recruit, compensate, and develop their workforces. Because other organizations in local and regional markets are also competing for the same labor, this has made recruitment and retention of staff more difficult for many HSOs.

Second, the *low supply of health care workers*—particularly highly specialized clinical personnel—has made recruitment of needed health care personnel very challenging (Fottler, Ford, & Heaton, 2002). Many areas of the country have experienced shortages of nursing, diagnostic, and treatment personnel, a phenomenon that has left many HSOs understaffed, requiring remaining staff to work longer hours per week (Shanahan, 1993). This has also contributed to lower levels of staff satisfaction and higher rates of turnover in certain staff positions, which has in turn increased human resources costs to the HSOs (Izzo & Withers, 2002; Shanahan, 1993). In addition, recruiting staff members who are highly specialized and who are in short supply tends to raise human resources costs as HSOs have to pay these staff members' higher wages and provide other incentives to appeal to these potential workers (Shanahan, 1993).

Third, *competition among health services organizations* has increased dramatically in the past 20 years due to an increase in supply of traditional HSOs, such as hospitals and nursing homes, as well as the influence of newly emerging HSOs, such as retirement communities, assisted living facilities, and ambulatory care programs. HSOs have engaged in service competition and, to a lesser degree, price competition in trying to outperform their rivals. Competition in services and competition for labor has contributed to increased demands on human resources management.

Fourth, *the population's needs for health and medical care* have increased in the past two decades and will continue to grow during the next 25 years as the population ages and Baby Boomers approach retirement and qualify for Medicare. Older adults require more health services, and therefore, HSOs will require more health care workers to care for the increasing volumes of patients served at their facilities. This is further complicated by the fact that much of the current health care workforce is nearing retirement age themselves (Burt, 2005). Thus, in the future, health services organizations will be faced with declining workforces due to retirements, on the one hand, and expanded demands from the population on the other hand. Projections of the future number of health care workers show significant opportunities for employment (see Table 12-2). However, this puts HSOs in a difficult situation: additional workers are needed to care for the increased patient workload, while the supply of workers in many categories continues to be low. This creates additional challenges for recruiting as well as retaining HSO staff.

Finally, *increasing regulation and scrutiny of health services organizations* by external organizations have increased pressures for high-quality and high-performing organizations. While licensing and accrediting organizations monitor HSO conformance to standards, they also make these performance indicators available to the public, legislators, and other stakeholders. In addition, reimbursement organizations and government payers, like Medicare and Medicaid, are increasing requirements on HSOs for accountability and performance by mandating reports on quality, morbidity, and mortality, as well as efficiency and costs. For HSOs, this means that human resources management must help the HSO become a high-performing, high-quality organization that can demonstrate quality processes and outcomes to these external stakeholders. Human resources can help accomplish this by hiring staff that are high quality, retaining those that are high quality, and reinforcing the culture of a high-performing organization.

TABLE 12-2 Projected Growth in Health Care Occupations Employment, 2012–2022

Occupation	Total Employment, 2012	Projected Total Employment, 2022	Difference (percentage)	Median Annual Earnings in 2012
Physician Assistants	86,700	120,000	33,300 (38%)	$90,930
Physical Therapists	204,200	277,700	73,500 (36%)	$79,860
Physicians and Surgeons	691,400	814,700	123,300 (18%)	$187,200
Registered Nurses	2,711,500	3,238,300	526,800 (19%)	$65,470
Medical and Health Services Managers	315,500	388,800	73,300 (23%)	$88,580

Bureau of Labor Statistics, 2014.

In addition to the noted external factors, internal factors also affect human resources management. Increasingly, senior management of HSOs view human resources in terms of its contribution to the success of the HSO and look to human resources indicators in their assessment of overall organizational performance (Becker et al., 2001; Galford, 1998; Griffith, 2000; Pieper, 2005). As they do with other departments and services, HSO senior management wants to see a return on their investment in human resources functions and a contribution to the bottom line (Becker et al., 2001). Although a support function to the core focus of delivery of patient care services, human resources activities are evaluated in terms of the contribution to recruitment, training, and development for staff, as well as employee satisfaction and retention. Therefore, human resources strategies and programs to address recruitment and retention needs are being developed and assessed, not in terms of whether they look good or because other organizations are doing them, but rather because they contribute to the organization's mission and goals for the creation of a high-performing, high-quality organization.

UNDERSTANDING EMPLOYEES AS DRIVERS OF ORGANIZATIONAL PERFORMANCE

The core services provided by HSOs—patient care services—are highly dependent on the capabilities and expertise of the organization's employees. It has been said that successful business strategy is directly connected to having committed, high-performance employees (Ginter, Swayne, & Duncan, 2002). HSOs are only as good as their employees. Why is this so for health services organizations?

There are three primary reasons why this is the case. First, HSOs are service organizations, unlike traditional businesses or manufacturing firms that make and distribute a specific product. Being a service organization means providing a service that is needed and/or desired by a consumer who decides to take advantage of what the HSO has to offer. Providing services involves doing things to help others, and HSOs require employees who have a desire to help others—a "service orientation" (Fottler et al., 2002). Second, HSOs are highly specialized service organizations that provide a range of specific services that include inpatient, outpatient, surgical, rehabilitation, diagnostic, therapeutic, and wellness services. To provide these specialized services, health care workers need to carry out many highly specialized tasks, and they need to have the proper knowledge, training, and experience to do those tasks well. Finally, because of the variety of services provided in HSOs and the fact that specialized staff provide only specific "pieces" of the overall service experience, health care workers from different departments and units must work together to provide a comprehensive service that meets all the needs of each patient (Liberman & Rotarius, 2000). Staff must work together as teams to ensure that all required services are provided and that the total needs of the patient or health care client are met. Therefore, teamwork is necessary for the HSO to provide the high-quality, coordinated, and comprehensive services that are required for it to be a high-performing organization.

In essence, all HSO employees need to work together to ensure the best service possible, centered on the patient's needs. Managers, therefore, must be able to hire good people with the proper knowledge, skills, and attitudes and provide them the resources and support necessary to do their jobs effectively and efficiently.

KEY FUNCTIONS OF HUMAN RESOURCES MANAGEMENT

In this section, the major functions within human resources management will be reviewed. The primary areas of human resources management activity include job analysis; workforce planning; establishing position descriptions; recruitment, selection, and hiring of employees; orienting new employees; managing employee relations and engagement; providing training and development; managing compensation and benefits; assessing performance; offering leadership development programs; providing employee assistance services; and offering employee suggestion programs. Typically, these key functions can be collapsed into two major domains called **workforce planning/recruitment** and **employee retention** (see Table 12-3). In the discussion that follows, the reader should note that activities in these

TABLE 12-3 Human Resources Functions

Function	Related Tasks
Workforce Planning/Recruitment	Job analysis
	Manpower planning
	Job descriptions
	Recruitment, selection, negotiation, and hiring
	Orientation
Employee Retention	Employee relations and engagement
	Training and development
	Compensation and benefits
	Employee assistance programs
	Assessing performance
	Labor relations
	Leadership development
	Employee suggestion programs

two domains are typically carried out by human resources staff professionals who are under the supervision of a vice president, director, or manager of human resources. In some HSOs, this office may be called "personnel," but most health services organizations—particularly large HSOs—now have a department or office of human resources that reflects both a strategic and administrative focus.

The human resources department or office develops and maintains all employee policies and procedures that reflect hiring, evaluating, promoting, disciplining, and terminating employees. In addition, policies and procedures related to assessing employee satisfaction, giving employee awards, compensating employees, and providing benefits are also developed and managed by the human resources staff. Furthermore, all employee records are maintained in the human resources office and in the human resources information system.

It should be noted that many federal and state laws affect human resources management in HSOs. There is a lengthy history of federal legislation that has been enacted to protect the rights of individual employees and to ensure nondiscrimination in the hiring, disciplining, promoting, compensating, and terminating of employees on the basis of age, sex, religion, color, national origin, or disability. Many states have also enacted specific laws that protect employees. Other employment issues such as sexual harassment, whistleblowing (identifying wrongdoing), and workplace harassment are also addressed under federal and state law and offer employees protection. The legal environment for HSOs related to human resources management is constantly changing, and employers must carry out their activities with full knowledge of applicable laws and emerging rulings from court cases. Table 12-4 provides a summary of key federal legislation affecting human resources management in HSOs.

WORKFORCE PLANNING/RECRUITMENT

Human resources functions carried out within the workforce planning/recruitment domain are directed to analyzing jobs needed within the HSO; identifying current and future staffing needs; establishing position descriptions; recruiting, selecting, negotiating, and hiring employees; and orienting new employees.

Job Analysis

One of the fundamental tasks of human resources is to conduct an analysis of all jobs or positions that are a part of the HSO. Every position in the HSO—whether administrative, support, or clinical—needs to be justified in terms of its specific responsibilities and day-to-day activities. **Job analysis** involves identifying those unique responsibilities, duties,

TABLE 12-4 Key Federal Legislation Affecting Human Resources Management

1935	**National Labor Relations Act** (as amended in 1974). Provides for bargaining units and collective bargaining in hospitals and health services organizations.
1938	**Fair Labor Standards Act** (as amended many times). Employees who are nonexempt from minimum wage and overtime provisions must be paid minimum wage and time and a half for hours beyond 40 hours per week. Special provisions for health services organizations.
1963	**Equal Pay Act.** Prohibits discrepancies in pay between men and women who perform the same job.
1964	**Civil Rights Act** (as amended many times). Prohibits discrimination in screening, hiring, and promotion of individuals based on gender, color, religion, or national origin (Title VII).
1967	**Age Discrimination in Employment Act.** Prohibits employment discrimination against employees age 40 and older.
1970	**Occupational Safety and Health Act.** Requires employers to maintain a safe workplace and adhere to standards specific to health care employers.
1973	**Rehabilitation Act.** Protects the rights of handicapped people (physically or mentally impaired) and protects them from discrimination.
1974	**Employee Retirement Income Security Act (ERISA).** Grants protection to employees for retirement benefits to which they are entitled.
1978	**Pregnancy Discrimination Act.** Requires employers to consider pregnancy a "medical condition" and prohibits exclusion of pregnancy in benefits and leave policies.
1986	**Consolidated Omnibus Budget Reconciliation Act (COBRA).** Gives employees and their families the right to continue health insurance coverage for a limited time due to various circumstances such as termination, layoff, death, reduction in hours worked per week, and divorce.
1986	**Immigration Reform and Control Act.** Establishes penalties for employers who knowingly hire illegal aliens.
1987	**Worker Adjustment and Retraining Notification Act.** Requires employers who will make a mass layoff or plant closing to give 60 days' advance notice to affected employees.
1989	**Whistleblower Protection Act.** Protects employees who report employer misconduct or wrongdoing with respect to compliance with federal and state law.
1990	**Americans with Disabilities Act (ADA).** Gives people with physical and mental disabilities access to public services and requires employers to provide reasonable accommodation for applicants and employees.
1993	**Family and Medical Leave Act (FMLA).** Permits employees in organizations to take up to 12 weeks of unpaid leave each year for family or medical reasons.
2003	**Health Insurance Portability and Accountability Act (HIPAA).** Affords employee protection from outside access to personal health information and limits employers' ability to use employee health information under health insurance plans.
2010	**Patient Protection and Affordable Care Act (PPACA or ACA).** Enacts various health insurance reforms, including requiring employers to offer coverage, prohibiting denial of coverage/claims based on preexisting conditions, and extending insurance coverage for dependent children to age 26.

Data from: Busse, 2005; Kaiser Family Foundation, 2010; Lehr, McLean, & Smith, 1998; U.S. Department of Labor, 2006.

and activities specific to every position in the HSO. This is necessary to clarify individual responsibilities but is also critical to avoid duplication of tasks and responsibilities across positions. The outcome of job analysis is to clearly state the responsibilities, duties, and tasks of every position within the HSO.

Human resources experts have suggested that HSOs should focus on those positions that contribute most directly to the completion of the organization's business objectives (Huselid, Beatty, & Becker, 2005). This is important because filling these critical positions with the best personnel—"A" players—will then increase the organization's ability to perform.

Workforce Planning

For every position established for the HSO, there needs to be an estimate of the number of staff members needed to carry out those responsibilities at the present time, as well as projections of the number of staff members needed at some future target date. For example, how many RNs does our hospital currently need for all the various services that we currently offer, and how many will we need in five years? This is a very complex decision process, and it must be based on consideration of many factors. For example, consider a hospital. Will the hospital be downsizing or eliminating any services in the next five years? Will the facility be adding any new services that are not presently offered? How will changes in regulations, the addition of new technology, or the addition of nursing assistants affect the need for RNs in the future, across all services of the hospital?

Identifying current numbers of staff is based on volume statistics that reflect the current performance of the HSO. The need for clinical staff is based typically on patient care statistics, such as the number of patients admitted, number of outpatient visits, or the number of patients receiving a specific service. In some cases, need will be determined by licensure standards that govern the minimum number of staff for certain services. For non–patient care areas, including such support functions as medical records, information technology, and financial services, the number of staff needed is contingent on the current volume of records and patient accounts that must be processed. Each support person in these areas can handle a minimum number of accounts or records per day, which becomes the basis for estimating current need. This is called a **ratio method of determining needs**. The managers in various units calculate these estimates and forward them to human resources for the development of aggregate estimates of staffing needs for the total facility.

Projections of staffing needs for a future target date are based on a similar method. Projections of future service volumes are made and associated staffing requirements are projected as well to serve that anticipated volume. Again, line managers usually develop these projections. Future volumes are typically determined through a consensus-based strategic planning process where there is agreement on future service volumes. In this process, consideration is also made for retiring staff, transfers, and service changes (such as eliminations or expansions of beds and services) to arrive at the needed number of staff to recruit or to acquire on a temporary basis from outside staffing firms. Once the projected staffing needs are identified for the total facility, strategies and timeframes are established for recruiting. Projections of staffing needs are revisited every year as annual performance is assessed to see if projections remain accurate.

Accuracy of projections has important implications for preparing budgets and evaluating financial performance of the HSO. For example, future staffing levels may be unrealistic if forecast revenues don't match projected expenses. Therefore, planned positions may remain unfilled and flexible staffing arrangements used as necessary. In addition, if demand shifts occur, some services may not realize projected patient volumes, and cutbacks in staffing arrangements may be necessary. Conversely, if there is an influenza or other contagious disease epidemic, the facility may find itself seriously short staffed. In conclusion, projections of future staffing requirements are just that— projections that may or may not hold up given the uncertain and dynamic nature of the health services environment. Many factors affect these projections, and a thorough and periodic assessment is needed to ensure that projections are realistic and revised as appropriate.

Establishing Job Descriptions

Position descriptions or job descriptions are required for every position within the HSO. **Job descriptions** are necessary to define the required knowledge, skills, responsibilities, training, experience, certification or licensure, and line of reporting for a specific job within the HSO. Such descriptions are important to both the organization and employee. The position description elaborates on the findings from the job analysis and provides a means by which the organization clarifies each position in terms of expectations, locus within the organizational structure, and how it contributes to the organization's overall performance. For the employee, the position description clarifies expectations and duties and allows prospective employees a means to evaluate the "fit" between a position and their own individual knowledge, skills, and experience.

Position descriptions are developed through joint efforts of line managers and human resources staff. Line managers specify job requirements; human resources staff keep job descriptions in a consistent format and ensure accuracy of the positions as they are included in the HSO's Human Resources Information System. An example of a position description for a hospital is shown in Figure 12-1.

BON SECOURS HEALTH CORPORATION
St. Francis Medical Center
POSITION DESCRIPTION

TITLE:	Environmental Services Aide	JOB CODE: 950
DEPARTMENT:	Environmental Services	
REPORTS TO:		FLSA: Non-exempt

I. GENERAL PURPOSE OF POSITION:
The primary responsibility of this position is to perform cleaning tasks to maintain designated areas in a clean, safe, orderly and attractive manner. The employee is expected to follow detailed instructions and/or written task schedules to accomplish assigned duties. This position serves all populations of visitors, employees, physicians and patients.

II. EMPLOYMENT QUALIFICATIONS:
1. Ability to communicate and interpret assignments issued through a computerized paging system.
2. Dependability and flexibility demonstrated through previous work or school history.
3. Previous housekeeping work experience preferred.

III. ESSENTIAL JOB FUNCTIONS:
1. Communicates all hospital-related issues to Supervisor.
2. Performs the duties necessary to maintain the sanitary conditions of the hospital, including routine cleaning and maintenance of all floor types.
3. Prepares patient rooms for new admissions through the proper utilization of the Bedtracking® system. (Login|Logout)
4. Cleans and sanitizes isolation rooms and other contaminated areas following written techniques appropriate for that type of isolation (i.e., tuberculosis, HIV, hepatitis).
5. Performs general cleaning tasks using the 7 Steps process.
6. Follows hospital policy regarding storage and security of housekeeping chemicals.
7. Accurately uses Bedtracking® system to meet departmental response and cleaning time standards.
8. Responsible for the use and care of equipment and other hospital property. Maintains equipment by proper cleaning and storage; reports dangerous or broken equipment to team leader. Makes sure EVS cart is clean, box locks, and wringer free of lint.
9. Understands basic safety procedures. (RACE, PASS, MSDS, etc.)

IV. OTHER JOB EXPECTATIONS:
1. Actively participates in the hospital's Continuing Educational Improvement programs (i.e., Essential Skills, Safety Fairs, etc.)
2. Assists in the orientation of new employees in departmental methods and procedures.
3. Responds to unusual occurrences such as flood, spillage, etc.

V. WORKING CONDITIONS:
Works in all areas of the hospital and off-site properties. May be exposed to hazardous chemicals, but potential for harm is limited, if safety precautions are followed.
The individual performing this job may reasonably come into contact with human blood and other potentially infectious materials. The individual in this position is required to exercise universal precautions, use personal protective equipment and devices, when necessary, and learn the policies concerning infection control.

VI. BON SECOURS MISSION, VALUES, CUSTOMER ORIENTATION AND CONTINUOUS QUALITY IMPROVEMENT FOCUS:
It is the responsibility of all employees to learn and utilize continuous quality improvement principles in their daily work.
All employees are responsible for extending the mission and values of the Sisters of Bon Secours by understanding each customer, treating each patient, staff member, and community member in a dignified manner with respect, kindness, and understanding, and subscribing to the organization's commitment to quality and service.

VII. APPROVALS   DATE

Department Manager

Administration ———————————————————

Human Resources

The above statements are intended to describe the nature and level of work being done by individuals assigned to this classification and are not to be construed as an exhaustive list of all job duties. This document does not create an employment contract, and employment with Bon Secours Richmond Health System is "at will".

FIGURE 12-1 Position Description

Reprinted with permission from Bon Secours St. Francis Medical Center, Midlothian, Virginia.

Recruitment, Selection, Negotiation, and Hiring of New Employees

A key principle of human resources recruitment is making ensuring HSO positions are filled with competent and highly skilled personnel. Once recruitment needs are made known by line managers, it is the responsibility of human resources to follow the appropriate procedures to fill those positions. In some cases, existing employees will have an interest in a new position for which they are qualified, and internal candidates will be considered. Human resources recruitment personnel use a standard process for external recruiting. These steps include advertising, screening applicants, determining those to be interviewed, conducting interviews, selecting the candidate, negotiating, and hiring. Activities for both human resources staff and line managers related to recruitment are identified in Table 12-5.

Advertising

Different modes of **advertising** are used to target candidates and generate interest. These sources include local newspapers and electronic media including radio and television, organizational websites, and Internet job search engines, for example, monster.com and CareerBuilder.com. The human resources department uses standards for communication that address the position, required degrees, training and/or certification, experience, functional line of reporting, and general expectations of the position. Applicants submit information in response to the advertising and submit their credentials electronically to

---

TABLE 12-5 Responsibilities of HR Staff and Line Managers in Recruitment

HR Staff Person

Prepares position description

Prices jobs

Prepares advertisements/recruitment materials

Keeps track of applicants/maintains HR Information System

Checks applicant references

Maintains personnel files

Narrows candidate pool

Line Manager

Clarifies job function/provides input into position description

Interviews candidates

Ranks candidates

Selects candidate

Negotiates with candidate

Hires candidate

---

be reviewed and evaluated by human resources staff. Sometimes candidates are referred personally to the hiring manager or to the human resources staff. These candidates are informed that they need to make formal application through the organization's online job application system.

The use of social media and website employment sites such as Indeed.com and CareerBuilder.com offer health services organizations innovative, non-traditional ways to advertise job openings and to identify candidates based on candidate posting and submission of resumes (Sarringhaus, 2011). While health care organizations have been slow to adopt the use of innovative communications found in social media, more organizations are adding social media sites and reaching out to their employees, patients, and potential employees (Hawn, 2009).

Candidates are recruited also through **private recruitment** or **headhunter** firms, and these may include firms that engage in general staff recruiting or firms that specialize in health services organization staff by recruiting nurses, technicians, financial analysts, or office personnel. Arrangements with recruiters usually involve paying a percentage of the first-year salary to the recruiter if the candidate referred by the recruitment firm is selected for the position. This method of recruiting will result in costs that exceed the normal expected costs of filling position vacancies. However, this technique may be a necessary option when recruiting for highly specialized positions where the candidate pool is limited.

Another frequently used option in recruiting is to work with educational programs that prepare specialized health personnel, such as nurses, physical therapists, and diagnostic technicians (Shanahan, 1993). Sending announcements of positions to these educational programs, attending recruitment open houses, and developing important referral relationships with faculty and staff of these programs is helpful in building interest and identifying candidates. Other sources include placing ads in targeted professional journals that are read by health care professionals, disseminating recruitment materials to health care workers identified through association membership listings, and attending regional or annual meetings of professionals where human resources representatives can meet with interested candidates. A final option to identify interested candidates is for human resources staff to attend **health care recruitment or job fairs** held locally or regionally, or for the HSO to hold its own.

Some observers have suggested that HSOs use a pre-employment assessment by the candidate of the fit between their credentials and the job (Liberman & Rotarius, 2000). This is recommended to ensure that only appropriate, well-qualified applicants apply.

Interviewing, Selection, Negotiation, and Hiring

Most applications for positions in HSOs are handled online through the organization's employment website, and tracking is also handled online. Human resources staff complete the preliminary review and analysis of candidates based on their applications, check candidate references, and identify past employers' satisfaction with the candidates. As a result, human resources staff narrow down the pool to those candidates that provide the best fit for the position based on training, experience, and other factors such as motivation and attitude. These applicants are then discussed with the line manager to select those to be interviewed. The candidates are invited to come to the organization and interview and spend some time with management, staff, and others. From the HSO's perspective, this is important for two reasons. It enables the HSO to assess firsthand the candidates and verify their knowledge and skills; also, it enables the assessment of the candidates' fit and compatibility with the organization and staff with whom they would be working. From the candidate's perspective, an interview is important to get a close look at the organization and staff and to assess their fit and interest in the position and the organization.

Depending on the position, human resources staff may participate in candidate interviews, and line managers will definitely participate in interviews with candidates. **Structured interviews** with clearly defined questions are thought to be best for assessing candidates (Foster & Godkin, 1998). Increasingly, peer interviews and behavioral-based interview questioning are used to assess candidates (Studer, 2003). **Behavioral-based questioning** focuses on the candidate's response to questions that yield insight into actions taken in particular situations (e.g., "Tell me a time when a project could not be completed and how you resolved the problem," or "Describe a situation in the past where you have experienced conflict with co-workers or a supervisor, and how you resolved the conflict"). Responses to behavioral-based questions yield important clues about the candidates' attitudes and behaviors in past situations, their experiences in dealing with complex and difficult situations, and how they respond to questions under pressure.

Subsequent to the interviews, the staff who have interviewed candidates meet to review the candidates, determine how the candidates match with position requirements, and rank order candidates. Once the staff agree on the applicant they would like to hire, an offer is extended.

An **offer of employment** is made in writing, and the offer letter must specify the position for which the offer is made, start date, associated salary/compensation and benefits, and any other key information regarding the offer. Offers of employment are typically contingent on a successful background check. Although an offer has been extended, the recruitment process is not complete. Depending on the position, there may be a period of negotiation over salary, benefits, start time, flexible scheduling, and other issues. Once agreement is reached, the position is assumed filled, and the candidate responds with a formal letter of acceptance agreeing to the position and conditions of acceptance. Background checks, physical examinations, drug tests, and proof of immunizations are frequently required. In addition, human resources reviews social media (e.g., Facebook,

LinkedIn, and Twitter) as part of a background check to look for evidence of behaviors, published statements, and or pictures that may yield more information about a candidate and their "fit" for the open position.

Completion of hiring paperwork is necessary at the time that the person starts the job. This typically includes issuance of an identification badge and keys. It should be noted that if agreement is not reached with the first-choice candidate, then the offer would be extended to the next best candidate, and then the next, until agreement with a suitable candidate is reached.

Orientation

One of the key requirements of a new staff member is to attend an **orientation program** coordinated by human resources. This program is important for several reasons. An orientation program informs the new employee of policies, procedures, and requirements, and it offers an opportunity for the new employee to ask questions and clarify understanding about the organization. The Employee Staff Manual is provided to each new employee. During orientation, various policies and procedures are highlighted, including expectations for the work day, proper attire and behavior, employee assessment, disciplinary actions and grievances, probationary period, and opportunities for training and development. The organization's values, mission, vision, and goals are reviewed, as are strategic and long-range plans. Standards of behavior and codes of conduct are reviewed. Standards of behavior and codes of conduct specify attitudes and behaviors that each employee will exhibit in carrying out their position. These behaviors include such actions as providing excellent customer service and using resources in a cost-effective manner. Specific employee benefits are identified and reviewed, and employees are informed about options concerning benefits and associated costs. Safety and security policies and practices are reviewed, and in large HSOs, such as hospitals and nursing homes, special codes are revealed so that employees know when and how to respond to emergency situations such as fires, patient medical emergencies, patient problems, intruders, and chemical and environmental emergencies. With the passage of the Health Insurance Portability and Accountability Act (HIPAA) in 1996, training in the requirements of this law regarding confidentiality of health information has been incorporated into many HSO's employee orientation sessions. Training in compliance with Medicare rules and regulations, along with the dissemination of Whistleblower Protection Act of 1989 information, is also becoming a part of new employee orientation in many HSOs.

Orientation is usually held once a month to coincide with the start date for new employees. Part-time, full-time, and short-term temporary employees are typically required to attend orientation. New employees have an opportunity to meet the senior management team, who typically provide an overview of their respective management domains during orientation. This helps new staff gain an understanding of their respective roles in the HSO. Subsequent to the formal orientation session, most HSOs now require new employees to complete a required number of online and in-person courses related to the organization and other pertinent topics, such as sexual harassment, communications, customer service, and teamwork. Employees are tested on their knowledge after completing the training and must show competency as a part of their employment.

EMPLOYEE RETENTION

Employee retention functions include all of those key activities that address care, support, and development of employees to facilitate their long-term commitment to the organization. The key functions under **employee retention** include employee relations and engagement, training and development, managing compensation and benefits, providing employee assistance programs, assessing performance, managing labor relations, providing leadership development programs, and offering employee suggestion programs.

Employee Relations and Engagement

The purpose of employee relations and engagement efforts coordinated by the human resources staff is to identify and address the needs of employees so that they will be satisfied, perform at a high level, and remain with the organization. Increasingly, human resources staff use **predictive analytics** to identify employee needs, factors driving employee satisfaction, and factors that lead to employee retention (Davenport, Harris, & Shapiro, 2010). It has been shown through empirical study that satisfied workers provide better service and care (Angermeier, Dunford, Boss, & Boss, 2009). As a result, HSOs have increased their efforts recently to address staff concerns, improve the work environment, and redesign jobs and administrative structures to provide for personal learning and professional growth (Becker et al., 2001; Osterman, 1995). Initiatives to increase participative management, through greater employee decision making about aspects of their work and sharing of organizational metrics about performance with employees, have been shown to increase **employee satisfaction and engagement** and lessen the likelihood of leaving the organization (Angermeier et al., 2009). Also, there have been major efforts at implementing recognition and reward programs, such as employee of the month, staff appreciation events, and greatest improvement by department or unit in balanced scorecard measures. In addition, organization-wide events are used to celebrate renewed accreditation or noteworthy achievements such as Magnet status by the American Nurses Credentialing Center, and top performance as recognized by such groups as Truven Health Analytics and HealthGrades.

The human resources department works with managers to determine appropriate employee relations activities, and typically, cross-functional committees are established to spearhead these efforts. Employee engagement and satisfaction surveys are commonly used to assess satisfaction and to help human resources staff and individual managers identify operational areas in need of improvement. Sometimes HSOs contract with consulting firms to survey employees in an anonymous fashion, usually once a year; to collect employee perceptions and suggestions; and to assess progress on addressing prior issues. Improvements in communications and teamwork, in addition to common areas of concern, such as compensation and benefits, are issues that are frequently identified through engagement surveys.

Another common tactic for HSOs to gauge employee perceptions and satisfaction is through manager walk-arounds, town hall meetings, employee neighborhood meetings, daily huddles, and employee focus groups. These efforts can be used in addition to engagement surveys, and those organizations that practice high-involvement employee relations will use these additional techniques with regularity. These methods allow for greater clarity of employee issues and concerns through dialogue with a manager. Follow-up responses to employees by managers are critical to closing the loop on concerns and suggestions. Moreover, observation of work units and meeting with employees through rounding creates a connection between management and employees that signals managerial interest in employees and a greater sense on the part of management as to employee daily job tasks and challenges (Studer, 2003). Observations are recorded on logs or diaries and are used to identify needed improvements. Sometimes, employees may feel constrained in their input and discussion with managers—particularly their own manager—as they may view their input as complaining. However, in most HSOs where there is a positive relationship between management and staff, and where input and exchange is a key part of the organizational culture, employees will feel open to expressing their concerns. In addition, some senior administrators now use blogs and intranet postings to inform staff about decisions and solicit input on key issues.

Training and Development

Training and development of the workforce are extremely important human resources functions for several reasons. First, the organization's need for specific knowledge and skills is always changing because of the rapid changes being experienced by HSOs. For example, HSOs frequently add new medical technologies that require different technical skills of employees. Another example of additional skills needed is in the information technology area, where new computer information systems, electronic medical records, databases, and integrated patient and financial data systems are being acquired to generate, store, and retrieve patient-level and organizational information. Second, training is necessary to provide for continuing education of some staff. For clinical staff who require continuing education as part of their licensure and/or certification, HSOs may coordinate the provision of hands-on training that is provided either on-site or at remote locations. Some clinical training and training for nonclinical staff can be provided online through the organization's intranet or a third party's website. While it is clear not all training and development needs of staff can be met due to resource limitations, the human resources staff determines priorities for annual training and education efforts and implements and manages those programs. Human resources staff typically accomplish this through organization-wide needs assessments or through identification of specific training needs that are made known to human resources staff by managers. Typically, the cost of training and development programs is provided for in the human resources budget; in some cases, other departments or services within the HSOs may cover the cost of training that is coordinated by human resources. In most cases, the costs of training can be reduced if the training is provided online.

The goal of any training or development effort is to provide value for the organization by returning benefits, such as increased productivity, greater effectiveness, higher quality, greater coordination of care, and enhanced patient or customer service. Therefore, training and development programs are evaluated by human resources for cost-effectiveness to ensure training is effective in terms of return on investment and methods of training are appropriate (Phillips, 1996). Training programs cover a range of topics, including technical training on equipment and software programs, customer service training, and training to improve interpersonal communications and leadership skills, among others. Training and development of teams within HSOs are also increasingly common, as HSO staff work frequently in teams to coordinate the delivery of care. The effectiveness of team leaders has been shown to influence team learning, development, and performance (Edmonson, Bohmer, & Pisano, 2004).

Managing Compensation and Benefits

The following sections describe the management of employee compensation and benefits in health care organizations and how it can contribute to a high-performing organization.

Compensation

The human resources department has the specific responsibility of managing the pay or **base compensation** and **benefits** associated with all positions held within the HSO. This is no easy task, as specific pay ranges and benefits must be established for each position, which in the hospital industry includes more than 300 distinct jobs or major job classifications (Metzger, 2004). The management of compensation begins with a clear definition of the HSO's compensation philosophy, which reflects the organization's mission, values, and strategy regarding human resources, as well as consideration of internal (e.g., equity) and external (e.g., competitive) factors (Gering & Conner, 2002; Joiner, Jones, & Dye, 1998).

Determining compensation refers to the establishing of a specific financial value for a job. Compensation for each position is set based on the consideration of a number of factors, including the specialized knowledge and skills associated with the position, the experience required for the position, the relative availability of skilled individuals to fill the position, and average wages that are specific to the local labor market. This is called **job pricing** (Joiner et al., 1998). Some positions are hourly rated (i.e., nonexempt and eligible for overtime pay), where a compensation rate per hour of work is established (e.g., for maintenance staff and floor nurses). Some positions are salaried (i.e., exempt and not paid overtime), where an annual salary is paid the employee (e.g., nurse managers and other managerial staff). In short, compensation is set to account for the special skills and experiences required of employees and to enable the organization to be competitive in the market in securing and retaining needed employees. Pay ranges will vary by type of position, but within a position class there must be equity. However, HSOs typically account for differences in training, experience, and special considerations of the job (working weekends or evenings) by allowing for pay/shift differentials. Also, some jobs are subject to significant external market pricing, because the skill set is unique and the market is national or international.

The typical large HSO, such as a hospital or hospital system, has a separate, designated staff to handle the administration of compensation on the one hand and benefits on the other. Human resources staff responsible for compensation keep records of wages and salaries, compensation adjustments, and the basis for compensation adjustments in individual employee personnel files and in the Human Resources Information System. Every few years, human resources administers a compensation or salary survey for positions within the HSO for **benchmarking** their current compensation to local and regional markets. This comparative market analysis of wages is then used to adjust salary ranges for positions as appropriate to remain competitive.

Job pricing is used to establish equitable pay scales by position within HSOs, but reward systems beyond base pay are frequently considered of greater importance to employees (Joiner et al., 1998). In addition to base compensation tied to expectations for a specific job, many HSOs have embraced **incentive compensation**. While compensation plans focus on individual performance and allocating rewards such as raises to high performers based on individual performance, incentive plans are designed to improve organizational performance (Gibson, 1995). In an incentive or pay-for-performance plan, the purpose of the plan is to stimulate employees to higher levels of achievement and performance that benefit the organization. Meaningful measures such as profits (return on investments), productivity, attendance, safety, quality, and customer satisfaction are a few examples of financial and nonfinancial organization-wide performance indicators that can be used in developing incentive plans. The incentive plan would work in the following way. The organization would set target goals for performance in a specific time period. At the end of that time period, the organization would collect and review relevant information to measure the status of performance. If the measurement of performance on specific indicators met the target goals, the organization would then reward employees for the "organization-wide" performance. These programs are also known as **bonus, gainsharing, or goal-sharing** programs, and payouts (revenues derived from savings, increased productivity or volumes, increased customer retention, and quality) would be shared with employees as a bonus for their contributions to high performance within the HSO (Gomez-Mejia, Welbourne, & Wiseman, 2000).

Incentive compensation plans have long been thought to be associated with higher levels of organizational performance (Bonner & Sprinkle, 2002). The theory behind this approach is that use of incentives such as compensation bonuses positively affects motivation, which leads to higher performance (Gibson, 1995). Many health services organizations have begun to follow the lead of businesses and industries that pioneered these programs, but published literature addressing the impact of incentive compensation on organizational performance in health care is limited (Griffith & White, 2002). There is evidence to show that more HSOs are using incentive programs for executives that are tied to organizational performance (Healthcare Financial Management Association, 2001). However, other research in the business literature has shown the relationship between incentive pay and performance may not hold up.

Beer and Katz (2003) found in their survey of senior executives from many firms that bonuses have little to no positive effect on performance and their real function may be to attract and retain executives. They looked at firms that had implemented executive bonus compensation systems and assessed relationships to performance and found the only key explanatory factor was that the incentive system promoted teamwork. Similarly, Luthans and Stajkovic (1999) found in their analysis of research on pay-for-performance that social recognition and administrative feedback to employees on performance were just as influential as pay-for-performance in achieving higher levels of performance in a manufacturing setting. Moreover, Beer and Cannon (2004) found many senior managers view incentive compensation programs with concern and question whether the benefits outweigh the costs. However, none of the studies cited above were specific to health services organizations.

Benefits

The human resources staff is responsible for managing benefits provided to employees working in an HSO. A **benefit** is defined as any type of compensation provided in a form other than salary or direct wages, that is paid for totally or in part by an employer

(Jenks & Zevnik, 1993). As benefits extended to workers, in general, have increased over the past two decades, the number and type of benefits made available to HSO employees have increased as well (Griffith & White, 2002; Runy, 2003). However, the HSO is faced with a dilemma. On the one hand, HSOs are under pressure to manage costs, and employee benefits have been a high-cost item for HSOs, which directly affects the HSO's cost management strategy, financial status, and competitive position. On the other hand, benefits as a portion of total compensation have increased in importance, as more and more employees indicate that benefits are important in their choice of an employer (Runy, 2003).

Benefits may differ by level within the organization, as management may receive one set of benefits to offset the higher level of skill needed to complete the job, versus lower-level employees who may receive fewer benefits due to a lower level of skills required for the job. The availability of benefits, as well as the percentage of employee cost sharing, varies widely by HSO. Typical benefits offered by HSOs include the following:

- *Sick leave.* A certain number of days per year are allocated for the employee being unable to be on the job due to illness or injury.
- *Vacation.* A certain number of vacation days are allocated to employees for them to use as free time. In many HSOs, this is combined under a paid-time-off (PTO) plan with sick leave days and holidays.
- *Holidays.* Designated national holidays are given to employees with pay as part of their benefits.
- *Bereavement leave.* Paid leave of a specified duration is provided to employees due to a death of a family member or significant other.
- *Health insurance.* Medical, behavioral health, and prescription drug coverage for the employee and optional coverage for dependents are typically made available. Depending on the type of health insurance plan offered to employees (and there may be one or more plans offered by the HSO), the total plan cost for the employee may be shared by the employer and employee. HSOs, like other organizations, have turned to managed care plans as a way to reduce health benefits expense for the HSO. Typical health insurance plans offered include a Preferred Provider Organization (PPO), a Health Maintenance Organization (HMO), and/or a High Deductible Health Plan (HDHP). Typical plan features include greater cost-sharing and out-of-pocket expenses for employees, along with the trend of increased access to out-of-network and specialty care. In addition, much of the coverage by health insurers today focuses on the management of certain chronic clinical conditions, such as cardiovascular problems and diabetes. These disease management programs are offered in an attempt to help the employee or dependent manage their conditions to promote better quality of life and reduce cost.

- *Life insurance.* Coverage is provided that will help offset the loss of earnings for a limited time and to cover burial and other expenses related to the death of an employee. The employee is typically provided a base amount of life insurance with an option to increase coverage for an additional cost.
- *Flexible health benefits.* Flexible or "cafeteria" benefits are increasing in popularity as they are offered to employees as options. Flexible benefits most often include health insurance, dental insurance, vision coverage, and other health benefits (such as disability insurance and long-term care insurance) and provide the employee with a choice of benefits for specific costs. Flexible benefits offer advantages to the employee in that the employee can tailor benefits to meet individual needs at varying costs (Joiner et al., 1998). For the HSO, overall benefit costs can be reduced under flexible benefit plans due to the fact that the employer is no longer paying for a specific base package of benefits for all employees (Joiner et al., 1998).
- *Retirement benefits.* Many HSOs have retirement plans in place where employees are granted a certain percentage of their compensation over and above their compensation that is put into a retirement fund. This fund can be a pension fund that is set up specific to the HSO or, more likely, a 401(k) or 403(b) plan where employees can manage their retirement dollars in mutual fund investments (Jenks & Zevnik, 1993). Many HSOs also have included the option in the retirement plan of offering to "match" employees' contributions to the plan with employer-paid funds up to a maximum amount. Retirement funds can only be accessed at the age of retirement, or fund withdrawals are subject to penalties.
- *Flexible spending accounts.* These are also called reimbursement accounts and are offered by the HSO to help the employee and their dependents by allowing pre-tax dollars to be placed in a health care or dependent care account. These accounts are then used to reimburse for out-of-pocket costs incurred by the employee and dependents that are not covered under other benefits or for the care of a child or dependent, disabled parent (Jenks & Zevnik, 1993).
- *Other benefits.* Several other categories of benefits are also made available to HSO employees, although the degree to which they are offered and the scope of coverage will vary considerably. These benefits may include discounted personal health benefits (complementary and alternative health care, yoga, Pilates, weight control and health classes, wellness/fitness center memberships, health education programs, personal health risk appraisals, and fitness coaches and food coaches); transportation (use of a van pool); educational reimbursement (tuition assistance for employee's or dependent's college, parenting classes); employee incentives (profit sharing, stock options, sign-on bonuses, relocation/moving assistance); service and event discounts, such as free or discounted financial planning services and corporate

discounts on movie tickets, events, and merchandise; flexible work scheduling, part-time work, job-sharing, and telecommuting; child care assistance and on-site child care; back-up child care assistance; elder care assistance; concierge services for information and referral on a variety of personal services; and savings programs (matched savings plans), among many others (Jenks & Zevnik, 1993; Halzack, 2014). Flexible scheduling, part-time work, telecommuting, job sharing, childcare assistance, and elder care assistance are examples of what many employee-focused organizations offer employees in terms of work–life balance benefits. These benefits are viewed as a means to strengthen the commitment to the organization, reduce turnover, increase satisfaction, and provide flexibility in order to meet personal needs of employees (Osterman, 1995). Part-time work and telecommuting through a "virtual office" have increased in HSOs for some staff, and offer several benefits for the individual and the HSO, which include lower absenteeism, increased morale, greater schedule flexibility, creation of a wider talent pool, perception of fewer distractions, and perceived higher productivity (Corwin, Lawrence, & Frost, 2001; Hill, Miller, Weiner, & Colihan, 1998; Kurland & Bailey, 1999). However, challenges resulting from this workplace practice include social and professional isolation, where employees believe that interactions with others and promotional opportunities are limited (Cooper & Kurland, 2002). Managerial resistance to part-time workers and telecommuters, as well as unsupportive cultures, have also been identified as key barriers mitigating use of flexible work arrangements (Corwin et al., 2001; Kossek, Barber, & Winters, 1999). Perceived inequity among employees in terms of job structure and oversight may be another dilemma for management that results from adoption of this policy. Certainly, not all direct-care HSO employees could even consider telecommuting, due to their skills needed where the patient or client is located. For some HSO employees—such as information technology, business development and marketing, and finance—such flexible scheduling options may work well. In general, offering of these benefits is linked to several advantages, including lower turnover, higher satisfaction, and greater financial performance (Huselid, 1995; Konrad & Mangel, 2000; Perry-Smith & Blum, 2000),

- *Occupational safety and health.* The human resources department contributes to the organization's efforts to maintain a safe and healthy work environment. Responsibilities are carried out in several ways to address this concern. First, workers' compensation coverage is required for organizations under state law, in order to protect workers who may get sick due to the job or become injured or incapacitated due to working conditions. This coverage is separate from any health insurance provided. Second, the HSO monitors federal and state regulations for occupational safety, monitors risk in the organization, and works to eliminate safety risks. Sometimes these human resources staff activities are conducted in conjunction with the risk management activities within the HSO.

Employee Assistance Programs

Employee assistance programs (EAPs) are HSO-sponsored programs that are made available to employees, and in many cases their dependents, to assist with personal or family problems that also affect the employee's job performance (Howard & Szczerbacki, 1998). Such problems include stress and mental health problems; parenting issues; family dysfunction and divorce; alcohol and substance abuse problems; financial problems; legal issues; physical and emotional abuse; poor work relationships; and adjustment issues stemming from a death in the family, loss of a job, or severe illness. In addition, the patient care services provided in an HSO are often challenging and stressful, and providing care to individuals who are sick, injured, and in some cases dying or near death is very trying and stress inducing for employees (Blair, 1985). This may lead to feelings of helplessness, guilt, or grief that negatively affect attendance and threaten the employee's focus, effectiveness, and productivity. **Second victim programs** to address clinicians' guilt and trauma associated with medical errors have also grown out of the quality management and patient safety movement (Wu, 2000). Workplace stress may also be exacerbated by personal and family stress outside the HSO. As a result, HSOs have recognized the value of EAPs to help employees in their times of need by making available counseling, stress reduction programs, health education programs, and other interventions based on need to lessen the impact of these problems. A problem-free, happy employee is an employee who is more likely to be focused and productive on the job. This results in positive performance for the individual employee as well as the HSO. The cost of services to the employee will vary depending on how the EAP is structured; some of the needed EAP services may be covered under other current employee benefits. EAP services can be offered on-site at the HSO or offered at remote locations under contract with other providers, which facilitates greater confidentiality for users. Employees are also afforded protection from harassment and job loss due to use of the EAP.

In summary, the benefit package has become more important to employees in recent years as employees balance tradeoffs between compensation and an appropriate array of benefits that are important to the employee and his/her dependents. For example, many employees with young families may be more interested in a broad range of benefits, such as those discussed above, rather than the highest salary possible. Such benefits help employees meet their own unique needs and become a significant factor in employee recruitment and retention. In the end, benefits may be one of the most critical factors in making the HSO competitive in attracting and retaining staff.

Assessing Employee Performance

The human resources department is charged with developing and maintaining a system for measuring employee performance for all employees of the HSO. The central theme of this chapter is that organizational performance is paramount and that individual employee performance in an HSO is highly contributory to organization-wide performance. Therefore, assessing individual employee performance is critical to understanding and achieving high levels of organizational performance.

Under human resources department leadership, a performance appraisal system is established for the HSO. **Performance appraisal** means assessing the job performance of an individual employee. In order for the HSO to know how individuals are performing and to develop a plan and program for employees to improve performance, an annual performance assessment is required. The assessment form includes several criteria that are determined to be important for the HSO in evaluating performance. These criteria may include measures of work productivity, quality, and quantity as specified in the position description and include technical skill assessment as well as other criteria that address the employee's motivation, attitude, and interpersonal skills in carrying out their respective work. Human resources, in conjunction with senior management of the HSO, will determine what specific criteria are included in the performance appraisal. Increasingly, managers use the results of computer monitoring systems to conclude how much work time is lost due to employee engagement in non-work activity (Buchbinder, 2015). Performance appraisals also include an assessment of the degree to which an individual's annual goals and objectives have been achieved as spelled out in the yearly management plan. See Figure 12-2 for an example of a performance appraisal used by Bon Secours St. Francis Hospital.

Kirkpatrick (2006) argues that a performance appraisal system must be part of the organization's efforts for continuously improving performance. Performance assessment is conducted by line managers for their subordinates on an annual basis, at the time of the employee's anniversary date or, more commonly, at a standard time to coincide with the budget development process for the upcoming year. Using the agreed-upon form, the manager will complete an assessment of each subordinate's performance for the assessment period. The manager then will sit down with the employee and review the appraisal and discuss areas of favorable performance, as well as areas of improvement opportunity. This will also give the subordinate an opportunity to express any concerns and/or seek clarification as to the basis for the evaluation ratings. Many managers also ask subordinates to complete a self-evaluation for the performance period under review, using the same criteria, for discussion at the meeting. It should be noted that good managers communicate with their subordinates about employee performance regularly throughout the year, with an interest in monitoring, correcting, and improving performance on an ongoing basis.

At the designated annual performance appraisal meeting between a manager and a subordinate, a meaningful exchange can be carried out in order to frankly discuss performance, identify opportunities for improving performance, and develop a specific plan for achieving higher levels of performance. A two-way discussion of these matters is the most fruitful for both parties, as the employee will understand the manager's concern and interest in the employee and the sincere desire for improving performance. In addition, the employee can express likes and dislikes about the job, which the manager needs to know (Butler & Waldroop, 2005). However, it is essential that clarity be provided in communicating performance, as perceived by the supervisor, so that there is no confusion as to the intent of the evaluation (Timmreck, 1998). A key outcome of the performance evaluation is the setting of performance improvement goals, actions to achieve the improvements, and priorities for action (Kirkpatrick, 2006). In addition to an annual performance appraisal, the HSO may require some or all employees to be reviewed for satisfactory performance at the end of their first 90 days of employment (often referred to as the **probationary period**) and at other times as specifically requested by a manager or if conditions warrant.

Performance appraisals are helpful to management and employees in the following ways (Longest, Rakich, & Darr, 2000):

- The manager can compare absolute as well as relative performance of staff;
- Together, the manager and employee can determine a plan for improving performance if such improvement is needed;
- Together, the manager and employee can determine what additional training and development activities are needed to boost employee performance;
- The manager can use the findings to clarify employee desires to move up to higher-level positions and/or expand responsibilities;
- The manager can document performance in those cases where termination or reassignment is necessary;
- The manager can determine adjustments to compensation based on performance; and
- The manager can determine promotional or other advancement opportunities for the employee.

In addition to the traditional method of assessing performance described above, many HSOs are now employing **360-degree performance appraisal systems**. While this method also includes a manager–subordinate evaluation, it provides for multisource feedback on employee performance from a number of other stakeholders—including peers, the employee's subordinates, and internal and external customers, if applicable. Feedback is aggregated and communicated to the employee through a neutral third party such as a human resources staff member. The advantages to using the 360-degree evaluation are reduction of fear of repercussion from evaluative comments and a greater range of feedback

Management Summary Form

Confidential

Development Level:
1 = Performs below standard
2 = Inconsistently meets the standard
3 = Consistently meets the standard
4 = Frequently exceeds the standard
5 = Consistently exceeds the standard

_____ Annual Review

_____ Other

(For the initial review, please use the "Introductory Performance Review" Form)

Instructions: The Performance Improvement Plan is a tool designed to assist in managing, developing and reviewing an employee's effectiveness and efficiency. It also provides a common understanding of job expectations for present and future performance review periods. ***Please note all supporting comments on the Development Plan.***

I. Values (includes integration of Quest for Excellence Behaviors) *(see page 6-7 of the Process Guide)*

		Developmental Level				
A.	Respect - commitment to treat people well (e.g., responsive - returns calls/emails). Justice - supporting and protecting the rights of all people. Integrity - honest in dealings (e.g., honors commitments, keeps promises). Compassion - experiencing empathy with another's life situation.	1	2	3	4	5
B.	Stewardship - responsible use of Bon Secours resources (e.g., consistently on time). Innovation - creating or managing new ideas, methods, processes and/or technologies. Quality - continuous improvement of service; involved in Gallup/Quest planning. Growth - developing and improving services and promoting self-renewal; completion of previous year's Development Plan. (e.g., thinks "Big Picture").	1	2	3	4	5

Average Developmental Level for Section I (A + B/2):

II. Leadership Competencies (see page 10-14 of the Process Guide)

	Developmental Level				
Change Management & Organization Development - planning & designing change strategies as needed; integrating individual dev. & organizational dev. into strategies.	1	2	3	4	5
Communication & Interpersonal Skills - listening & responding in constructive manner; promoting understanding while building productive working relationships.	1	2	3	4	5
Critical Thinking - examining underlying causes & determining best course of action.	1	2	3	4	5
Human Resource Development - facilitating others to achieve professional dev. goals.	1	2	3	4	5
Planning & Strategic Direction Setting - determining shape of present & future job environment; efficiently maintaining & improving practices; setting direction for dept./org.; **developing Gallup Impact, PRC, Quest for Excellence Plans.**	1	2	3	4	5
Promotion of Mission & Values - setting an example by integrating org. standards into day-to-day functions; guiding others to a common Mission & Vision.	1	2	3	4	5
Self-Knowledge & Insight - using personal understanding to promote positive self-change.	1	2	3	4	5
Team Building - promoting teamwork to accomplish dept./org. objectives.	1	2	3	4	5
Proficiency in Field - subject matter expert in field; resource to others.	1	2	3	4	5

Average Developmental Level for Section II (Sum of 9 Leadership Competency Dev. Levels/9):

III. Essential Job Functions
(This section is determined by the Job Description and will vary with the Position being evaluated)

Average Developmental Level for Section III:

Overall Average: *(Average Level for Section I x .5) + (Average Level for Section II x .25) + (Average Level for Section III x .25)*

FIGURE 12-2 Performance Evaluation

Reprinted with permission from Bon Secours St. Francis Medical Center, Midlothian, Virginia.

Development Plan

Name: _____

Facility & Dept.: _____

The Purpose of the Development Plan is to aid in the process of developing specific skills and behaviors. The Plan is reviewed and finalized during the performance review meeting. At a minimum, progress toward reaching agreed-upon goals should be discussed once during the year. ***This form must be completed by each employee and returned prior to the performance review.***

1 **Previous Objectives, Goals, and Accomplishments.** Review learning and development objectives, goals, and accomplishments achieved since last performance review; include knowledge and skill strengths used to accomplish objectives and goals.

_____

_____

_____

_____

_____

_____

2 **New Objectives and Goals.** Identify new learning and development objectives and goals for the coming year, which include addressing opportunities for growth. Include issues, which may need to be addressed and opportunities needed to successfully implement, including implementation of Quest/Team Player improvements.

_____

_____

_____

_____

_____

_____

3 **Employee and/or Manager's Comments.** Additional comments may be made on a separate sheet of paper and attached to this form.

_____

_____

_____

_____

_____

_____

_____

_____

FIGURE 12-2 Performance Evaluation (*Continued*)

from a larger number of observers of the employee/manager (Garman, Tyler, & Darnall, 2004). However, there are some disadvantages as well. These include the higher cost of administration of a 360-degree evaluation, compared to a traditional evaluation, and the lack of an instrument suitable for health services managers (Garman et al., 2004). In addition, peer feedback included in 360-degreee evaluation may also be biased or inaccurately given, due to difficulties in determining an individual's contribution to the unit or service or fear of providing negative feedback to a colleague (Peiperl, 2005).

One of the most challenging outcomes of the performance appraisal process is the need to terminate an employee. Although the goal of human resources management is to retain high-performing staff, not all employees will be retained. There are many reasons why an employee can be discharged, but in every case, the primary reason must relate to performance deficiency. Terminating an employee is not easy and is uncomfortable at times for managers who have the authority to discharge an employee. However, failure to act decisively will jeopardize the HSO's performance and will certainly reflect negatively on the manager's ability as a leader (Hoffman, 2005). In situations where an employee is not likely to be retained, it is essential that the manager not wait until the appraisal to assess the employee's performance. In fact, ongoing monitoring of performance, efforts to correct performance problems, and documentation of the steps taken in any corrective processes are all typically required prior to discharge. This process should be done by the line manager in close consultation with the human resources manager. The HSO policies and procedures must be adhered to carefully to prevent subsequent allegations of wrongful discharge and potentially avert a lawsuit against the HSO and/or the line manager.

Managing Labor Relations

Labor relations is a general term that addresses the relationships between staff (labor) and management within HSOs. Labor relations is associated with collective bargaining where a union, if certified (i.e., voted in by the workers), represents the interests of employees who become members of that union. Nationally, about 20% of HSOs have at least one union represented in their organizations (Longest et al., 2000). In the period 1980–1994, there were 4,224 certification elections held in health services organizations: 31% of these were in hospitals, 40% in nursing homes, and 29% were in other health care facilities (Scott & Lowery, 1994). Union elections in health services organizations vary by type of health care setting, but overall about 60% of elections result in a union being approved (Deshpande, 2002). Unions have a higher-than-average win rate in hospitals, and hospitals have been the focus of increased union organizing efforts in recent years (Deshpande, 2003). In 2009, union membership in health care was about 14% of the health care workforce (Malvey, 2010). However, this represents an increase of 270,000 unionized health care workers since 2000, with much of the growth occurring in registered nurse and other non-physician occupations (Malvey, 2010).

Why do unions get involved in HSOs? As seen in manufacturing, the fundamental reason for unionization in health care is that employees are dissatisfied with some aspects of the work and/or the work environment and feel that management is insensitive to their needs. Unions often step in where management has failed to do its job and become the "voice" of the employees. If staff are strongly dissatisfied with various aspects of the HSO, view senior management as poor communicators, and/or perceive that management is insensitive to staff issues, they may believe that a union is the only way to have their voices heard and needs met. If elected to represent employees in an HSO, a union is then authorized to engage in collective bargaining with management of the HSO regarding wages, working conditions, promotion policies, and many other aspects of work (Longest et al., 2000).

The National Labor Relations Act of 1935, as amended, enables union organizing and collective bargaining in health services organizations. The Act also created the **National Labor Relations Board (NLRB)**, which recognizes several bargaining units for health care employees, including nurses, physicians, other professional employees, and nonprofessional employees, among others. The NLRB has the authority to oversee and certify the results of union elections. There are many rules and regulations that must be followed in unionization activity, and there are certain restrictions placed on management as well as staff that govern what can and cannot happen regarding union discussions, organizing, and elections.

The presence of a union creates significant challenges for management of an HSO. From management's perspective, unions create an unnecessary third party in decisions that affect the employment relationship and work of the HSO's staff, which raises potential for conflict. Union requirements may restrict the administrator's ability to use the number and type of staff in desired ways, and compensation negotiated by the union may reduce management's ability to directly control staffing expenses. Labor unions can also limit an HSO's discretionary authority to make changes in the workplace and in workplace practices (Holley, Jennings, & Wolters, 2001). Also, some research has shown that productivity may be negatively affected after unionization (Holley et al., 2001).

Beyond general impact on administration, unionization has been shown to significantly affect the human resources function in HSOs. Deshpande (2002) found in a study of hospital unionization activity that the presence of unions resulted in higher numbers of employees who were screened, a higher number of employee training programs, a greater number of job classifications, greater use of employee performance appraisal methods, and lower productivity, as reported by CEOs of hospitals.

Various strategies have been discussed with respect to the administrative stance vis-à-vis unions (Deshpande, 2003). To reduce the possibility of union discussions and union organizing, administrators are encouraged to keep communication open and fluid, provide competitive salaries and benefits, establish grievance policies and procedures, and ensure staff participation and involvement in decision making as much as possible. In all respects, administrators and human resources staff should continuously assess staff satisfaction and needs, as well as opportunities for staff and management to work together for the betterment of the organization and larger community. There are many challenging issues that affect HSOs, including lowered reimbursements from managed care and government payers, cost reduction practices, and lower staffing ratios. These can lead to employee dissatisfaction, and management needs to be cognizant of the negative impact of some of their decisions on staff motivation, satisfaction, and commitment.

If one or more unions are certified to represent employees in an HSO, then much of the time and effort of the human resources staff will be spent in addressing unionization issues. These include negotiating (bargaining) aspects of the union contract, ensuring that specific aspects of the contract are met, communicating with union representatives, and being the focal party in carrying out all union discussion and negotiation under the auspices of federal labor law (Longest et al., 2000).

Leadership Development

It is widely accepted that health services managers must practice effective leadership in order for their staffs, and thus their organizations, to perform at the highest possible level. Leadership and leadership practices are increasingly addressed in the current health care literature, and leadership is seen as one of the key competencies of health services managers. Because of the complexity and rapid change within the environment of HSOs and within HSOs themselves, managers need to engage in learning consistently to upgrade their knowledge and skills so that they can be effective leaders (Squazzo, 2009; Sukin, 2009).

Many HSOs have followed the lead of business and industry and are now embracing the concept of **leadership development** for their managers. Recent data show that about one-half of hospitals and health systems have a leadership development program for mid-level managers and senior executives (Kim & Thompson, 2012; McAlearney, 2010). Leadership development includes both formal and informal efforts. The formal efforts include completion of courses with satisfactory scores on assessment, usually on an annual basis, which are required to advance to higher levels of management within the HSO or to keep knowledge and skills current. Formal efforts may also include structured mentoring, 360-degree feedback, and coaching (Thompson & Kim, 2013). Some HSOs separate leadership development for existing managers, executive managers, and aspiring managers. Courses and self-study may be completed online through organizational staff Web portals or through seminars with trainers who are either HSO staff or contracted consultants. Required training may include topics that are priorities of the HSO, such as customer service or process improvement, or it may reflect special topics of executing leadership, such as organizational change, effective communications, and building effective teams. Many times, leadership development training is tied to a personal development plan for a manager, or conversely, for an aspiring manager. Informal methods are where the HSO has its executive and mid-level managers work unofficially with selected staff through mentoring, advising, and coaching. This also may include job enlargement based on successful job performance, where the staff member may be assigned additional work tasks or tasks that reflect cross-discipline work where that staff member can gain different perspectives and gain visibility throughout the organization.

Leadership development efforts in HSOs, as noted in Chapter 1, are also employed to provide for **succession planning** for senior/executive and mid-level managers. Because many senior executives are nearing retirement, and given the high demand for health care managers across all sectors of the industry due to keen competition for leadership talent, organizations have decided to groom from within. Providing for succession to positions by filling from within offers several advantages. These include seamless continuation of organizational leadership, proven fit with the organizational culture, commitment to the organization, and prior demonstration of effective working relationships across disciplines.

Leadership development initiatives also serve as a recruitment tool for bringing highly qualified candidates to the organization in both clinical and nonclinical roles. For example, clinical staff who have an interest in management may find that the organization that provides extensive leadership development and career track options is better than those that do not. Accordingly, leadership development can serve as a differentiator for HSOs. This has been a strategy of businesses for many years, where individuals with bachelor's and master's degrees can begin their careers with an organization that will provide opportunities for leadership development and advancement.

Employee Suggestion Programs

Employee suggestion programs (ESPs) are increasingly being considered by HSOs in an effort to encourage creativity on the part of employees and to identify needed improvements in processes and outcomes. Employee suggestion programs have been in existence for quite some time (Carrier, 1998), but the primary locus has been in manufacturing and other business enterprises as opposed to HSOs.

An ESP works simplistically by soliciting employee suggestions for change and acknowledging and rewarding those suggestions that offer the most potential to meet organizational goals and implementing those suggestions. These programs usually are formally structured, widely communicated throughout the organization, and managed by human resources staff. Current ESPs have gone far beyond the old suggestion box model and include elements of electronic submission and Web-based applications, as well as formal recognition and reward (Fairbank, Spangler, & Williams, 2003).

ESPs are part of an overall effort by HSOs to stimulate innovation and creativity by generating ideas that will help the HSO. The underlying rationale for the program is that employees of HSOs, as key providers of its services and activities, are in the best position to know what can be improved and may have good ideas as to how such improvements can be made. ESPs are built on the premise that innovation in organizations can be understood from a problem-solving approach (Fairbank et al., 2003). Goals of ESPs can include organizational improvements, such as reducing costs, improving methods and procedures, improving productivity, improving equipment, and cutting waste, as well as increasing job satisfaction and organizational commitment on the part of employees (Carrier, 1998). This second goal of ESPs is very important and should not be overlooked by the human resources staff. Part of the overall satisfaction in working in an HSO is the belief that management understands and appreciates its employees and is interested in their input. ESPs are not, however, without their limitations. Drawbacks to the program include difficulties in designing a program, effectively administering it, and sustaining the program over several years (Kim, 2005).

RESEARCH IN HUMAN RESOURCES MANAGEMENT

Many administrators and researchers consider effective human resource management to be the single most important factor affecting organizational performance. Because of the importance of human resource management to the success of the health services organization, there are many areas of research in human resources. Three lines of important research have emerged recently and the results are informing human resources management policies and practices. The first is understanding the nature of high-performance work systems in health care organizations. McAlearney et al. (2013) and Garman et al. (2011) have investigated the work practices of successful health care organization and identified best practices that can lead to high levels of organizational performance. These practices have been identified at both the organization-wide (macro-level) and the sub-organizational level (micro-level). These researchers found that best practices reflect four areas: staff engagement, staff acquisition and development, staff frontline empowerment, and leadership alignment and development. Practices specific to each are as follows:

- Staff engagement: information sharing, employee involvement in decision-making, and performance-driven regard and recognition;
- Staff acquisition and development: rigorous recruiting, selective hiring using assessments of cultural fit and behavioral standards, staff training, and career development using mentoring and leadership development;
- Frontline employee empowerment: employment security through redeployment, use of teams, and decentralized decision-making; and

- Leadership alignment and development: leadership training, succession planning, and performance-contingent rewards.

Similar to this research, Griffith (2015) and Griffith and White (2005) have examined characteristics associated with high-performing organizations that have met the Baldrige criteria for health care quality excellence. Griffith and White (2005) found human resources practices such as recognition of employee contributions, strategies to promote retention of employees, and continuous training of staff are emphasized in these high-performing organizations. Griffith (2015) found Baldrige winners as high-reliability organizations with a workforce that is more effective than the norm, and that training of staff in quality performance improvement and offering of rewards in conjunction with accomplishment of quality goals is critical to high performance.

The second line of research has examined the role of strategic human resources management in organizational strategic planning and its role in ensuring organizational success. This area of research ties closely to the view of human resources management as a strategic initiative that seeks to enhance organizational performance. Recent research examined the extent to which human resources management strategies were included in organizational strategic planning, the association between the involvement of senior human resources professionals in strategic planning, and the use of innovative human resources practices in hospitals (Platonova and Hernandez, 2013). They found significant associations between human resources management strategy inclusion in the strategic planning process and senior human resources professionals' involvement in organizational strategic planning as reflected in three innovative human resources activities: finding talent in advance for key job openings, stressing organizational culture and values in the selection process, and basing individual or team compensation on goal-oriented results (Platonova & Hernandez, 2013). In addition, the researchers found innovative human resources practices were underused in some hospitals, but those hospitals that emphasized effective human resources management were more likely to use some of the innovative human resources approaches.

A third area of emerging human resources management research is the area of **predictive analytics or human resources analytics**. Using large internal datasets that include information on employee skills, capabilities, and business performance, firms can identify needs and better manage their human resources. Davenport, Harris, and Shapiro (2010) state that human resources analytics can help the organization in various ways, including predicting performance based on employee engagement, understanding why employees choose to stay or leave, and developing models based on key statistics to boost retention rates. The analysis of employee data can also aid in planning for staff vacancies and succession planning, developing effective staffing models based on anticipated business volume, and assessing current employees and identifying issues that may impact turnover and promotion. In addition, the field of human resources analytics can provide meaningful information on measures of actual employee engagement, such as the amount of work occurring outside of normal working hours, the percentage of time participating in ad hoc meetings and initiatives, and the percent of a manager's time spent with work teams (Fuller, 2014). This allows HSOs to measure actual engagement rather than employee perceptions of engagement, and can be used to modify manager practices to increase employee engagement. However, human resource analytics must be based on quality data and must be actionable for effective use by managers and leaders (Collins, 2013). Also, large HSOs can use third-party databases, typically made available by consultants, and compare employment patterns and organizational characteristics to regional or national benchmarks. They can also use this information to help in recruitment of staff that have greater opportunity to "fit" and remain with the organization.

Finally, given the importance of value-based purchasing programs being implemented by government and insurers that pay hospitals and physicians on the basis of quality and patient satisfaction, it is critical for additional research to be conducted on employee engagement and how employee satisfaction and engagement are related to patient satisfaction. Prior research has found that satisfied employees are associated with higher levels of patient satisfaction, but specific understanding of the actions that organizations are taking to increase employee satisfaction and engagement is needed. See Chapter 11 for specific organizations that conduct research on health care professionals and their human resource issues.

CONCLUSION

The management of human resources is an important function within HSOs because the performance of HSOs is tied directly to the motivation, commitment, knowledge, and skills of clinical, administrative, and support staff. Human resources actions of HSOs are undertaken for both strategic and administrative purposes. A variety of activities are included within the human resources area, and these activities typically fall within the domains of workforce planning/recruitment and employee retention. While human resources serves as a support function for line managers within HSOs, line managers and staff managers carry out human resources management roles as well, because they are involved in hiring, supervising, evaluating, promoting, and terminating staff. Therefore, human resources staff and other managers work closely to ensure that HSOs perform well. The contribution of the human resources management function is increasingly being evaluated by senior management, similar to other organizational functions, to determine the net contribution of human resources staff to organizational success. It is likely that management of human resources will increase in importance in the future, as HSOs face heightened external and internal pressures to recruit and retain committed and high-performing staff.

DISCUSSION QUESTIONS

1. Contrast strategic and administrative actions within human resources management.

2. For each human resources scenario described in the introduction to the chapter, identify the steps you would take to address the specific human resources issue being faced. From your perspective, which is the most challenging issue, and why?

3. Two key domains of human resources management are workforce planning/recruitment and employee retention. Describe several human resources functions that fall under each and describe their importance to human resources management.

4. Identify and describe some environmental forces that affect human resources functions in health services organizations.

5. Contrast "employee assistance programs" and "employee suggestion programs."

6. Why do HSOs offer incentive compensation programs? How do these programs differ from base compensation programs?

7. Describe the importance of employee relations and engagement efforts by HSOs, and give some examples of these activities.

Cases in Chapter 18 that are related to this chapter include:

- Metro Renal
- The Condescending Dental Hygienist
- The Brawler
- I Love You...Forever
- Such a Nice Young Man
- The Magic Is Gone
- Sustaining an Academic Food Science and Nutrition Center Through Management Improvement
- Emotional Intelligence in Labor and Delivery
- Communication of Patient Information During Transitions in Care
- Multidrug-Resistant Organism (MDRO) in a Transitional Care Unit
- Recruitment Challenge for the Middle Manager

Case study guides are available in the online Instructor's Materials.

REFERENCES

Angermeier, I., Dunford, B. B., Boss, A. D., & Boss, R. W. (2009). The impact of participative management perceptions on customer service, medical errors, burnout, and turnover intentions. *Journal of Healthcare Management, 54*(2), 127–142.

Becker, B. E., Huselid, M. A., & Ulrich, D. (2001). *The HR scorecard.* Boston, MA: Harvard Business School Press.

Beer, M., & Cannon, M. D. (2004, Spring). Promise and peril in implementing pay-for-performance. *Human Resources Management, 43*(1), 3–48.

Beer, M., & Katz, N. (2003). Do incentives work? The perceptions of a worldwide sample of senior executives. *Human Resource Planning, 26*(3), 30–44.

Blair, B. (1985). *Hospital employee assistance programs.* Chicago, IL: American Hospital Publishing, Inc.

Bonner, S. E., & Sprinkle, G. B. (2002). The effects of monetary incentives on effort and task performance: Theories, evidence and a framework for research. *Accounting, Organizations and Society, 27,* 303–345.

Buchbinder, S. B. (2015). Big Brother is watching. [Blog post]. Retrieved from http://blogs.jblearning .com/health/2015/04/06/big-brother-is-watching/

Bureau of Labor Statistics. (2010). *Employment and wage estimates and projections between 2008 and 2018.* Retrieved from http://www.bls.gov/emp/ep_projections_methods.htm

Burt, T. (2005, November/December). Leadership development as corporate strategy: Using talent reviews to improve senior management. *Healthcare Executive, 20*(6), 14–18.

Busse, R. C. (2005). *Your rights at work.* Naperville, IL: Sphinx Publishing.

Butler, T., & Waldroop, J. (2005). Job sculpting: The art of retaining your best people. In *Harvard Business Review on appraising employee performance* (pp. 111–136). Boston, MA: Harvard Business School Press.

Carrier, C. (1998, June). Employee creativity and suggestion programs: An empirical study. *Creativity and Innovation Management, 7*(2), 162–172.

Collins, M. (2013). Change your company with better HR analytics. *Harvard Business Review.* Retrieved from https://hbr.org/2013/12/change-your-company-with-better-hr-analytics/

Cooper, C. D., & Kurland, N. B. (2002). Telecommuting, professional isolation, and employee development in public and private organizations. *Journal of Organizational Behavior, 23,* 511–532.

Corwin, V., Lawrence, T. R. B., & Frost, P. J. (2001, July/August). Five strategies of successful part-time work. *Harvard Business Review, 79*(7), 121–127.

Deshpande, S. P. (2002). The impact of union elections on human resources management practices in hospitals. *Health Care Manager, 20*(4), 27–35.

Deshpande, S. P. (2003). Labor relations strategies and tactics in hospital elections. *Health Care Manager, 22*(1), 52–55.

Davenport, T. H., Harris, J., & Shapiro, J. (2010). Competing on talent analytics. *Harvard Business Review, 88*(10), 52–58. Retrieved from https://hbr.org/2010/10/competing-on-talent-analytics

Edmondson, A., Bohmer, R., & Pisano, G. (2004). Speeding up team learning. In *Harvard Business Review on teams that succeed* (pp. 77–97). Boston, MA: Harvard Business School Press.

Fairbank, J. F., Spangler, W. E., & Williams, S. D. (2003, September/October). Motivating creativity through a computer-mediated employee suggestion management system. *Behavior and Information Technology, 22*(5), 305–314.

Foster, C., & Godkin, L. (1998, Winter). Employment selection in health care: The case for structured interviewing. *Health Care Management Review, 23*(1), 46–51.

Fottler, M. D., Ford, R. C., & Heaton, C. (2002). *Achieving service excellence: Strategies for healthcare.* Chicago, IL: Health Administration Press.

Fuller, R. (2014). A primer on measuring employee engagement. *Harvard Business Review.* Retrieved from https://hbr.org/2014/11/a-primer-on-measuring-employee-engagement

Galford, R. (1998, March/April). Why doesn't this HR department get any respect? *Harvard Business Review, 76*(2), 24–32.

Garman, A. N., Tyler, J. L., & Darnall, J. S. (2004, September/October). Development and validation of a 360-degree-feedback instrument for healthcare administrators. *Journal of Healthcare Management, 49*(5), 307–322.

Garman, A. N, McAlearney, A. S., Harrison, M.I., Song, P. H., & McHugh, M. (2011) High-performance work systems in health care management, Part 1: Development of an evidence-informed model. *Health Care Management Review, 36*(3), 201–213.

Gering, J., & Conner, J. (2002, November). A strategic approach to employee retention. *Healthcare Financial Management, 56*(11), 40–44.

Gibson, V. M. (1995, February). The new employee reward system. *Management Review, 84*(2), 13–18.

Ginter, P. M., Swayne, L. E., & Duncan, W. J. (2002). *Strategic management of health care organizations* (4th ed.). Malden, MA: Blackwell.

Gomez-Mejia, L. R., Welbourne, T. M., & Wiseman, R. M. (2000). The role of risk sharing and risk taking under gainsharing. *Academy of Management Review, 25*(3), 492–507.

Griffith, J. R. (2000, January/February). Championship management for healthcare organizations. *Journal of Healthcare Management, 45*(1), 17–31.

Griffith, J. R. (2015). Understanding high-reliability organizations: Are Baldrige recipients models? *Journal of Healthcare Management, 60*(1), 44–62.

Griffith, J. R., & White, K. R. (2002). *The well-managed healthcare organization* (5th ed.). Chicago, IL: Health Administration Press/AUPHA Press.

Griffith, J. R., & White, K. R. (2005). The revolution in hospital management. *Journal of Healthcare Management, 50*(3), 170–190.

Halzack, S. (2014, June 22). Something extra—top workplaces 2014. *Washington Post*, pp. 27–31.

Hawn, C. (2009). Take two aspirin and tweet me in the morning: How Twitter, Facebook, and other social media are reshaping health care. *Health Affairs, 28*(2), 361–368.

Healthcare Financial Management Association (HFMA). (2001, August). More healthcare organizations using quality measures to reward executives. *Healthcare Financial Management, 55*(8), 22–25.

Hernandez, S. R., Fottler, M. D., & Joiner, C. L. (1998). Integrating management and human resources. In M. D. Fottler, S. R. Hernandez, & C. L. Joiner (Eds.), *Essentials of human resources management in health services organizations.* Albany, NY: Delmar Publishers.

Hill, E. J., Miller, B. C., Weiner, S. P., & Colihan, J. (1998). Influences of the virtual office on aspects of work and work/life balance. *Personnel Psychology, 51*, 667–683.

Hoffman, P. B. (2005, November/December). Confronting management incompetence. *Healthcare Executive, 20*(6), 28–30.

Holley, W. H. Jr., Jennings, K. M., & Wolters, R. S. (2001). *The labor relations process* (7th ed.). Orlando, FL: Harcourt College Publishers.

Howard, J. C., & Szczerbacki, D. (1998). Employee assistance programs in the hospital industry. *Health Care Management Review, 13*(2), 73–79.

Huselid, M. A. (1995). The impact of human resource management practices on turnover, productivity, and corporate financial performance. *Academy of Management Journal, 38*(3), 635–672.

Huselid, M. A., Beatty, R. W., & Becker, B. E. (2005, December). "A players" or "A positions"? The logic of workforce management. *Harvard Business Review, 83*(12), 110–117.

Izzo, J. B., & Withers, P. (2002). Winning employee-retention strategies for today's healthcare organizations. *Healthcare Financial Management, 56*(6), 52–57.

Jenks, J. M., & Zevnik, B. L. P. (1993). *Employee benefits*. New York, NY: Collier Books/Macmillan Publishing Company.

Joiner, C. L., Jones, K. N., & Dye, C. F. (1998). Compensation management. In M. D. Fottler, S. R. Hernandez, & C. L. Joiner (Eds.), *Essentials of human resources management in health services organizations*. Albany, NY: Delmar Publishers.

Kaiser Family Foundation. (2010). *Summary of new health reform law*. Retrieved from www.kff.org/healthreform/upload/8061.pdf

Kim, D-O. (2005, July). The benefits and costs of employee suggestions under gainsharing. *Industrial and Labor Relations Review, 58*(4), 631–652.

Kim, T. H., & Thompson, J. M. (2012). Organizational and market factors associated with leadership development programs in hospitals: A national study. *Journal of Healthcare Management, 57*(2), 113–132.

Kirkpatrick, D. L. (2006). *Improving employee performance through appraisal and coaching* (2nd ed.). New York, NY: American Management Association/AMACOM.

Konrad, A. M., & Mangel, R. (2000). The impact of work-life programs on firm productivity. *Strategic Management Journal, 21*, 1225–1237.

Kossek, E. E., Barber, A. E., & Winters, D. (1999, Spring). Using flexible schedules in the managerial world: The power of peers. *Human Resource Management, 38*(1), 33–46.

Kurland, N. B., & Bailey, D. E. (1999, Autumn). Telework: The advantages and challenges of working here, there, anywhere and anytime. *Organizational Dynamics, 28*(2), 53–67.

Lehr, R. I., McLean, R. A., & Smith, G. L. (1998). The legal and economic environment. In M. D. Fottler, S. R. Hernandez, & C. L. Joiner (Eds.), *Essentials of human resources management in health services organizations*. Albany, NY: Delmar Publishers.

Liberman, A., & Rotarius, T. (2000, June). Pre-employment decision-trees: Jobs applicant self-election. *The Health Care Manager, 18*(4), 48–54.

Longest, B. B., Rakich, J. S., & Darr, K. (2000). *Managing health services organizations and systems*. Baltimore, MD: Health Professions Press.

Luthans, F., & Stajkovic, A. D. (1999, May). Reinforce for performance: The need to go beyond pay and even rewards. *The Academy of Management Executive, 13*(2), 49–57.

Malvey, D. (2010). Unionization in healthcare—background and trends. *Journal of Healthcare Management, 55*(3), 154–157.

McAlearney, A. S. (2010). Executive leadership development in U.S. health systems. *Journal of Healthcare Management, 55*(3), 206–224.

McAlearney, A. S., Robbins, J., Garman, A. N., & Song, P. H. (2013). Implementing high performance work practices in healthcare organizations: Qualitative and conceptual evidence. *Journal of Healthcare Management, 58*(6), 446–462.

Metzger, N. (2004). Human resources management in organized delivery systems. In L. F. Wolper (Ed.), *Health care administration* (4th ed.). Sudbury, MA: Jones and Bartlett.

Osterman, P. (1995). Work/family programs and the employment relationship. *Administrative Science Quarterly, 40*, 681–700.

Peiperl, M. A. (2005). Getting 360-degree feedback right. In *Appraising employee performance* (pp. 69–109). Boston, MA: Harvard Business School Press.

Perry-Smith, J. E., & Blum, T. C. (2000). Work-family human resource bundles and perceived organizational performance. *Academy of Management Journal, 43*(6), 1007–1117.

Pfeffer, J. (1998). *The human equation.* Boston, MA: Harvard Business School Press.

Phillips, J. (1996, April). How much is the training worth? *Training and Development, 50*(4), 20–24.

Pieper, S. K. (2005, May/June). Reading the right signals: How to strategically manage with scorecards. *Healthcare Executive, 20*(3), 9–14.

Platonova, E. A., & Hernandez, S. R. (2013). Innovative human resource practices in U.S. hospitals: An empirical study. *Journal of Healthcare Management, 58*(4), 290–303.

Runy, L. A. (2003, August). Retirement benefits as a recruitment tool. *Hospitals and Health Networks, 77*(8), 43–49.

Sarringhaus, M. M. (2011). The great divide: Social media's role in bridging healthcare's generational shift. *Journal of Healthcare Management, 56*(4), 235–244.

Scott, C., & Lowery, C. M. (1994, Winter). Union election activity in the health care industry. *Health Care Management Review, 19*(1), 18–27.

Shanahan, M. (1993). A comparative analysis of recruitment and retention of health care professionals. *Health Care Management Review, 18*(3), 41–51.

Squazzo, J. D. (2009, November/December). Cultivating tomorrow's leaders: Comprehensive development strategies ensure continued success. *Healthcare Executive, 24*(6), 8–20.

Studer, Q. (2003). *Hardwiring excellence.* Gulf Breeze, FL: Fire Starter Publishing.

Sukin, D. (2009, Winter). Leadership in challenging times: It starts with passion. *Frontiers of Health Services Management, 26*(2), 3–8.

Thompson, J. M., & Kim, T. H. (2013). A profile of hospitals with leadership development programs. *The Health Care Manager, 32*(2), 179–188.

Timmreck, T. C. (1998, Summer). Developing successful performance appraisals through choosing appropriate words to effectively describe work. *Health Care Management Review, 23*(3), 48–57.

Wu, A. W. (2000). Medical error: The second victim: The doctor who makes the mistake needs help too. *British Medical Journal, 320*(7237), 726–727.

CHAPTER 13

Teamwork

Sharon B. Buchbinder
Jon M. Thompson

LEARNING OBJECTIVES

By the end of this chapter, the student will be able to:

- Distinguish between a face to face team, a virtual team, a task force, and a committee;
- Compare and contrast disciplinary, interdisciplinary, and cross-functional teams;
- Discuss the challenges associated with teamwork in health care organizations;
- Compare and contrast the benefits and costs of face to face and virtual teamwork;
- Summarize research findings on the importance of effective teamwork in health care;
- Analyze differences between tame and wicked problems;
- Assess ways to fit into a team and to select team members;
- Apply current thinking on emotions to teamwork scenarios;
- Critique strategies for managing communication and conflict on a team;
- Create a personal development plan for becoming an effective team member; and
- Investigate sources of research on teamwork.

INTRODUCTION

Unless you've lived alone your entire life, by the time you obtain your first job in the health care arena, you will have been on a team. Family teams organize chores, vacations, and household projects. In school, students are assigned tasks—almost from the sandbox—that require small group work and cooperation. Extra-curricular activities—Girl Scouts, Boy Scouts, Junior Achievement, Habitat for Humanity—all require young people to work in cooperative groups. And let us not forget the soccer moms and dads, who chauffeur their offspring from preschool through high school to participate in sports teams. So why does the thought of teamwork assignments make entire classes of health care management students cringe? Despite years of teamwork experiences, few students in any discipline are actually educated and trained in the "how-to" of working in teams. Yet in health care management, from the day you enter the door of your first job, your role will include being part of a team. Teamwork requires leadership, strategic thinking, diverse groups of people with different perspectives and disciplines, excellent organizational and interpersonal skills, and a good sense of humor. The purpose of this chapter is to help you understand the formation and operation of teams, the benefits and costs of teams, and tools to navigate the sometimes tricky waters of teamwork.

WHAT IS A TEAM?

Most simply, a **team** is a group of people working together to achieve a common goal (Grumbach & Bodenheimer, 2004). Teams typically include individuals with complementary skills who are committed to a common approach for which they hold themselves mutually accountable (Katzenbach & Smith, 2005). The formation and operation of teams are central to the effective functioning of health care organizations. In health care organizations, teams can be composed of one or more disciplines, for example, the nursing team, the physician leader team, the management team, or the quality improvement team. In Chapter 1, you learned about the internal structure of health care organizations. For example, a senior Vice President has several directors who report to him, which constitutes a management team. Likewise, the administrator or CEO and all Vice Presidents that report to her comprise an executive team.

One of the distinguishing characteristics of health care organizations is that the professional staff needs to work closely and collaboratively to meet patient needs. In other words, the tasks of individual employees affect, and are dependent upon, the work of others. This is known as task interdependency. Because the health care needs of patients cut across an organization's different disciplines or functions, it is important that interdisciplinary clinical teams be set up to ensure the delivery of safe, effective, and timely care. Clinical teams can be classified according to a number of factors, including client or patient population, disease type, or care delivery setting (e.g., inpatient or outpatient) (Blackmore & Persaud, 2012). In addition, teams can be organized to address a short-term, quality assurance problem, such as "Why did Mrs. Jones fall out of bed?" or long-term problems, such as preventing harm to all patients in all aspects of care (Ball, 2005) (see Textbox 13-1). Moreover, **cross-functional teams (CFTs)** are common in health care organizations to address specific organizational needs, such as service excellence, environmental sustainability and green initiatives, and clinical services marketing (Thompson, 2010). Cross-functional teams also help health care organizations carry out performance improvement activities and focus the organization on service enhancements (Studer, 2003). These CFTs include representatives from clinical and nonclinical areas of the organization. Health care organizations are considered high-reliability organizations, with hazardous environments where the consequences of errors are high (Baker, Day, & Salas, 2012). It is widely believed that the use of clinical and cross-functional teams will become more critical in the future as health care organizations become more complex and the demands for effective patient management increase (Jain, Thompson, Chaudry, McKenzie, & Schwartz, 2008) (see Textbox 13-2).

TEXTBOX 13-1. TEAM FUNCTIONING ACROSS ORGANIZATIONS: IMPROVING TRANSITIONS FROM THE HOSPITAL TO SKILLED NURSING FACILITIES TO REDUCE AVOIDABLE REHOSPITALIZATIONS

Pierce County, Washington, located just south of Seattle, is the second most populous county in Washington State. The county is made up of urban areas in and around the city of Tacoma as well as less-populated towns. Pierce County also has the highest county-wide readmission rate within the state for hospital patients discharged to skilled nursing facilities (SNFs). In 2011, the average Washington State readmission rate for Medicare fee-for-service patients discharged to SNFs was 19.0 percent. In Pierce County, this rate was 20.6 percent.

In early 2011, MultiCare Health System created an interdisciplinary team focused on improving care transitions and reducing readmissions from SNFs. The team, originally involving three area SNFs, evolved to over ten participating SNFs by the end of the year. Health care systems in Pierce County have a long history of working together to improve the health of county residents. As such, in January 2012, MultiCare Health System, one of the four hospital systems in the county, invited key stakeholders from Pierce County and several neighboring counties to propose a partnership for improving care transitions and reducing readmissions for their shared patients. What developed out of these early discussions was a series of active work teams focusing on populations at risk for readmissions.

The Pierce County STAAR & Beyond Team quickly gained traction with its efforts focused on SNF patients. The team comprises two groups—a Case Management/SNF Working Group and a Provider Working Group. The Case Management/SNF Working Group includes administrators and directors of nursing from SNFs across the county (12 organizations and 32 individual facilities), as well as care managers from the four area health systems. This group is convened monthly and facilitated by the Medical Director of Care Management at MultiCare Health System. The Provider Working Group, also facilitated by the Medical Director of Care Management, includes physicians from the four health systems, primary care physicians, area SNFs, and hospital emergency departments.

(Continued)

During the STAAR & Beyond Team meetings, participants share data, identify opportunities for improvement, identify and agree upon best practice standards, and report out on PDSA cycles (tests of change) underway. These meetings serve as a forum for collaboration and shared learning focused on accelerating the progress of all. Operational practice changes made included:

1. Ensure SNF Staff Are Ready and Capable to Care for the Resident
2. Reconcile the Treatment Plan and Proactively Plan for Condition Changes
3. Engage the Resident and Their Family Caregivers in a Partnership to Create an Overall Plan of Care

The results were significant. Pierce County's STAAR and Beyond Team decreased their aggregate 30-day readmission rate for Medicare patients discharged to SNFs by about 13 percent—from a baseline of 21.1 (Q4 2009 to Q3 2012) to a median rate of 18.3 in the most recent four quarters (Q4 2009 to Q3 2012).

Pierce County SNFs are also working to improve the care conferences that occur with residents and their family caregivers upon admission to the facility. SNFs are conducting tests to improve the timing and reliability of care conferences and ensure important topics, such as advance care directives and palliative care needs, are discussed and implemented.

Herndon L, Bones C, Bradke P, Rutherford P. How-to Guide: Improving Transitions from the Hospital to Skilled Nursing Facilities to Reduce Avoidable Rehospitalizations. Cambridge, MA: Institute for Healthcare Improvement; June 2013. Available at www.IHI.org.

Task forces require teamwork, but don't have the life of a **committee**. A blue-ribbon task force may be commissioned for several years by a professional association or institute to examine issues in health care services delivery, such as medical errors and patient safety (Institute of Medicine [IOM], 2001). These groups focus on a specific agenda, have a limited term of tenure, and disband when a report or book is issued. At the intra-organizational level, a quality assurance committee comprised of individuals from many departments may have people appointed to three-year terms. At the end of that time, a person whose term has expired steps down, but the committee and the work of the committee lives on. Committees such as these usually have a person for whom this area is their full-time job, but representatives of multiple disciplines and areas of the organization are required to examine problems and to implement organizational policy decisions.

TEXTBOX 13-2. MULTIDISCIPLINARY CARE TEAMS IN INTENSIVE CARE UNITS

It is known that critically ill patients are medically complex and may benefit from a multidisciplinary approach to care. More than 4 million intensive care unit (ICU) admissions occur annually in the U.S. These patients are often at high risk of death: mortality for critical illness syndromes such as acute lung injury and sepsis ranges from 25% to 50%, and 20% of Americans die while receiving intensive care services. One approach to lowering ICU mortality is to optimize the organization of ICU services. For example, a large body of literature indicates that the presence of trained intensivist physicians is associated with improved survival, leading many policy makers to call for expansion of the intensivist-led model of critical care. A potential complement to intensivist staffing is a multidisciplinary care model in which physicians, nurses, respiratory therapists, clinical pharmacists, and other staff members provide critical care as a team. A multidisciplinary approach acknowledges the complexities of modern critical care and the important role of communication between health care providers in delivering comprehensive care.

Researchers conducted a study to determine the effect of multidisciplinary care teams completing daily rounds and 30-day mortality. The researchers conducted a population-based retrospective cohort study of medical patients admitted to Pennsylvania acute care hospitals (N = 169) from July 1, 2004, to June 30, 2006, linking a statewide hospital organizational survey to hospital discharge data. Multivariate logistic regression was used to determine the independent relationship between daily multidisciplinary rounds and 30-day mortality.

A total of 112 hospitals and 107,324 patients were included in the final analysis. Results indicate that overall 30-day mortality was 18.3%. After adjusting for patient and hospital characteristics, multidisciplinary care was associated with significant reductions in the odds of death (odds ratio [OR], 0.84; 95% confidence interval [CI], 0.76–0.93 [P = .001]). When stratifying by intensivist physician staffing, the lowest odds of death were in intensive care units (ICUs) with high-intensity physician staffing and multidisciplinary care teams (OR, 0.78; 95% CI, 0.68–0.89 [P < .001]), followed by ICUs with low-intensity physician staffing and multidisciplinary care teams (OR, 0.88; 95% CI, 0.79–0.97 [P = .01]), compared with hospitals with low-intensity physician staffing but without multidisciplinary care teams. The effects of multidisciplinary care were consistent across key subgroups including patients with sepsis, patients requiring invasive mechanical ventilation, and patients in the highest quartile of severity of illness.

Source: The Effect of Multidisciplinary Care Teams on Intensive Care Unit Mortality. Michelle M. Kim, Amber E. Barnato, Derek C. Angus, Lee F. Fleisher, and Jeremy M. Kahn, (2010). *Archives of Internal Medicine, 170*(4), 369–376.

THE CHALLENGE OF TEAMWORK IN HEALTH CARE ORGANIZATIONS

Originally, hospitals grew out of religious orders, and nuns and monks provided health care to the poor. If you were wealthy, uneducated nurses tended to you at home, and physicians made house calls. Prior to the late 1700s and early 1800s, medical training was an apprenticeship, and there were no university-trained nurses. The U.S. Civil War and the Crimean War fueled the development of the nursing profession. The first nurse training school in the U.S. was created in 1798 at New York Hospital, by a physician. Florence Nightingale, a nurse, founded the first training school for nurses at St. Thomas Hospital in England in 1860 after the Crimean War and published her landmark book, *Notes on Nursing*, in 1890 (Donahue, 1985). Over time and as the field of nursing evolved, nursing education moved out of strictly hospital-training programs into university-based settings (Donahue, 1985).

The American Medical Association (AMA) was formed in 1842, and its first meeting was to discuss the appalling lack of quality in U.S. medical schools and their products—physicians. The AMA Council on Medical Education was formed in 1847. Abraham Flexner, working at the Carnegie Foundation, traveled around the U.S. and Canada to examine the structure, processes, and outcomes of the more than 300 medical schools that existed at that time. His 1910 report, *Medical Education in the United States and Canada*, often referred to as "The Flexner Report," called for dramatic reorganization in the medical education system. Those schools that were at the "A" level (such as the Johns Hopkins School of Medicine) were the standards by which all other schools were evaluated. The report recommended that "B"-level schools either get the resources to become "A"-level schools or go out of business. Flexner urged all "C"-level schools, which were considered substandard (some had no books!), to cease production of physicians (Flexner, 1910).

Compared to medicine and nursing, health care management is a young discipline. The University of Chicago founded the first program in health administration in 1934 under the leadership of Michael M. Davis, who had a PhD in sociology. Davis recognized that there was no formal training for hospital managers and that an interdisciplinary program of education was needed. Envisioning the role of the health care manager as both a business and social role, he utilized the expertise of medical, social service administration, and business faculty to create an interdisciplinary model that has been replicated repeatedly across the U.S. and throughout the world (University of Chicago School of Social Service Administration, n.d.). Schools with a degree in health care management or administration were originally all master's degree programs, geared to preparing hospital administrators. Now, in addition to master's degrees, there are baccalaureate and doctoral programs in health care management. More jobs in health care management are being created outside of hospital settings than within (Bureau of Labor Statistics, 2010). Increasing specialization of health care, burgeoning allied health care disciplines, a diversity of health care organizations, greater variety in jobs, higher expectations for health care outcomes, and demanding consumers mean that health care organizations must be able to respond appropriately, effectively, and efficiently. Interdisciplinary teams and teamwork provide the mechanism for improved responses to these demands.

Despite demonstrated need and effectiveness of interdisciplinary teams, formal educational training in this skill for physicians and nurses is rare (Baker, Salas, King, Battles, & Barach, 2005; Buchbinder et al., 2005). A poll conducted in 2004 by the American College of Physician Executives (ACPE) revealed that about one-quarter of the physician executive respondents were seeing problem physician behaviors almost weekly (Weber, 2004). Thirty-six percent of the respondents reported conflicts between physicians and staff members (including nurses), and 25% reported that physicians refused to embrace teamwork. The IOM (2001) has recommended that health care organizations develop effective teams. Physicians and nurses work from a clinical framework of advocating at the individual level for patients and families. Health care managers, on the other hand, are trained to look at population-level and organization-wide issues. Sometimes, clinicians and managers have head-on collisions due to these contrasting worldviews (Edwards, Marshall, McLellan, & Abbasi, 2003). Developing teams and facilitating team activities are recognized competencies for health care managers (Stefl, 2008). However, there is little formal preparation in teamwork in undergraduate and graduate health care management education programs (Leggat, 2007), and therefore, much of the manager's understanding of team dynamics and operations is learned on the job. Developing and managing teams is a skill that you will want to build as you progress in your health care management career.

Health care executives recommend that to engage medical staff managers need to promote alignment between hospitals and physicians. This alignment can be accomplished through the use of shared goals, especially those relating to patient safety (Sherman, 2006). Understanding physicians is key to getting them on board with teamwork and reducing medical errors. Physicians are pulled in multiple directions by multiple demands, and their time is at a premium. Valuing a physician's time means organizations must have competent team members in place to whom physicians can delegate tasks that they might otherwise have to do themselves. Promoting interdependence on trustworthy teammates is critical in achieving safe, effective patient care. As a health care manager, you will be responsible for working with and encouraging all health care professionals to become good team members. It will not always be an easy task, but in the long run, it will be rewarding.

THE BENEFITS OF EFFECTIVE HEALTH CARE TEAMS

One of the best ways to convince a clinician that interdisciplinary teamwork is important is to show them the relationship to patient care. According to Mickan (2005), some of the benefits of effective teams include improved coordination of care, efficient use of health care services, increased job satisfaction among team members, and higher patient satisfaction. Ruddy and Rhee (2005) echoed these findings in their literature review of primary care for the underserved. When a group of researchers convened experts to identify key factors in successful and unsuccessful teams, they noted that successful teams had the following attributes:

- "Champions to drive the change management process;
- Clarity regarding roles on the parts of all team members;
- Trust, respect, value, and being valued within the teamwork setting; and
- Cultural readiness within the setting" (Clement, Dault, & Priest, 2007, p. 31).

In contrast, the teams that failed demonstrated:

- "A lack of time to bring people together to reflect and to change;
- Insufficient inter-professional education, including continuing education, and the persistence of silos;
- Systems of payment that do not reward collaboration;
- Few links between collaborative practice and individual goals; and
- The absence of efforts to capture evidence for success and to communicate this to key stakeholders, including the public" (Clement, Dault, & Priest, 2007, p. 32).

Roblin, Vogt, and Fireman (2003) demonstrated that primary health care teams in ambulatory care settings could improve quality of care and corporate productivity when employees were empowered to be innovative and rewarded for performance. Additional benefits of teams include sharing different areas of knowledge and expertise, learning from different perspectives, and realizing innovative ideas that come from other team members (Quinlan & Robertson, 2010; Thompson, 2010). For example, Alexander and colleagues (2005) found in their study of teams providing treatment to mental health patients that patients experienced greater improvements in activities of daily living when teams had higher levels of sharing and staff participation. Clinical and non-clinical (e.g., business development) hospital services also can benefit from cross-functional team approaches that show increased trust among staff, shared goals, and greater patient satisfaction (see Textboxes 13-3 and 13-4).

Clinical research has underscored the importance of excellence in teamwork in the operating room (OR). A multisite retrospective study of 74 Veterans Health Administration

TEXTBOX 13-3. CROSS-FUNCTIONAL TEAM FOR PATIENT-CENTERED ROUNDING AT CINCINNATI'S CHILDREN'S HOSPITAL, CINCINNATI, OHIO

The Cincinnati Children's Hospital has developed a cross-functional care team model that extends beyond caregivers. The team is formed of the patient and their family, and the hospital physicians, nurses, administrative staff, and others. The care process includes conducting family and patient-centered rounds for all patients. Team members provide integrated, comprehensive care for patients and their families in the hospital in-patient setting.

The hospital uses an integrated, cross-functional multi-disciplinary clinical team process. The patient and family are integrated as full members of the team, active in conversations and decisions. Hospital staff members meet with the patient and family during morning rounds to discuss the patient's condition, care plan, and progress. Team members clearly explain their role on the team, refrain from using medical jargon, ask for the feedback, and elicit questions and clarifications from the patient and family.

Effective team functioning of caregivers is based on effective communication. Effective communicators are deep listeners—actively listening to the contributions of others on the team, including the patient and family. Individuals on the team need to be able to listen actively and model this for others on the team by clarifying or elaborating key ideas, reflecting thoughtfully on value-laden or controversial "hot-button" issues. Team members may need to help each other improve this skill either through team exercises or individual conversations. Patients and families often participate more as listeners on the team; their contributions may need to be facilitated through the active listening of other team members. Teams that perform patient- and family-centered rounds at Cincinnati Children's Hospital engage listening at many levels. First and foremost, central to rounds is the elicitation, on the first day, of the patient and family's preference for participation (or nonparticipation) in team rounds. Whatever option patients and families choose, the plan of care and daily work are defined by the goals and concerns expressed by the patient and family. Active listening—with confirmation of information transfer—is fundamental to the rounds.

Source: Mitchell, P., Wynia, M., Golden, R., McNellis, B., Okun, S., Webb, C.E., Rohrbach, V., & Von Kohorn, I. (2012). Core Principles & Values of Effective Team-Based Health Care. Discussion Paper. Institute of Medicine: Washington, DC. Reprinted with permission from the National Academy of Sciences, Courtesy of the National Academies Press, Washington, D.C.

(VHA) facilities found that "participation in the VHA Medical Team Training program was associated with a lower surgical mortality rate" (Neily et al., 2010, p. 1693). By *lower*, the authors mean an 18% reduction in annual mortality rates. The findings from this study are significant not only in a research sense, but also in a true clinical sense; that figure represents lives saved through improved teamwork. Dissemination of this

TEXTBOX 13-4. COLLABORATION AMONG BUSINESS DEVELOPMENT, ADMINISTRATIVE, AND CLINICAL STAFF AT THE UPPER CHESAPEAKE HEALTH SYSTEM

Business development efforts at the Upper Chesapeake Health System in Bel Air, Maryland, illustrate the need for and value of collaboration between business development staff, administrative functions and clinical leadership.

In 2009, Michael Boblitz, MBA, Director of Planning, was requested by his CEO to develop business plans for seven outpatient clinical services to be located in a medical office building connected to the Upper Chesapeake Medical Center. The total space available for the seven programs was 24,837 square feet. The medical office building was under construction on the campus of the system's largest hospital at the start of the business planning process. The space occupied one of two floors and was adjacent to the main hospital with direct access via pedestrian walkways via a bridge and ground level. Boblitz was appointed as Project Manager for the new service development efforts and provided leadership as an internal consultant.

Boblitz' first action was to form several Operations Planning Teams, one for each service. Each team was comprised of several relevant clinical and administrative support managers who, under Boblitz' leadership and facilitation, would be tasked to design, strategically and operationally, the services that would be offered. This is an example of marketing/business development staff coordinating a new service development function within a single facility through a series of cross-functional, integrated teams.

Such a collaborative structure is necessary, according to Boblitz, because "clinical services have special needs and requirements that only clinical managers know." For example, the outpatient cancer center was to provide clinical support services that required the expertise of nurse managers. Furthermore, the rehabilitation department manager was instrumental in defining the spatial needs of the new outpatient rehabilitation center that reflected dedicated space needed for various therapies, such as fitness equipment, hydrotherapy and speech therapy services.

Based on set timelines, the Operations Planning Teams met in several working sessions over a seven month period to finalize revenue projections, operating expenses, capital requirements, space and adjacency needs. Boblitz served as the facilitator of this planning and implementation process for new business development, but relied on the contributions of clinical and administrative staff members to ensure that the services were effectively designed for optimal patient care. Each Operations Planning Team included the following representatives:

- Operations Director
- Planning Director
- IT Director
- Reimbursement Director
- Facilities Director

- Patient Access Director
- Materials Management Director
- Human Resources Director
- Marketing Director

Source: Personal Communication, Michael Boblitz, MBA, Director of Planning, Upper Chesapeake Health System, Bel Air, MD. From *Collaboration Across the Disciplines in Health Care*, Freshman, B., Rubino, L., & Reid Chassiakos, Y. (Eds), Sudbury, MA: Jones and Bartlett Publishers.

information throughout all surgical training programs in the U.S. will require enormous effort because surgeons often believe "they alone are responsible for patient outcomes" (Pronovost & Freischlag, 2010, p. 1721). It will take a major culture shift to move many physicians and surgeons from this solo savior mentality to the "there is no I in teamwork" approach.

Clinicians are not always the reluctant team builders. Sometimes higher-level management is uncertain that teamwork is worth the effort and short-term costs. For this audience, the answer lies in the bottom line: improved communication, increased productivity, increased job satisfaction, and decreased nursing turnover (Amos, Hu, & Herrick, 2005; Institute for Healthcare Improvement, 2004). In an era when nurses are retiring faster than new ones are coming into the field, health care managers cannot afford to ignore the loss of nurses from the workforce (Health Resources and Services Administration 2003, 2004, 2010). Nursing turnover costs have been estimated to be 1.3 times the salary of a departing nurse or an average of $65,000 per lost nurse, as noted in Chapter 11 (Department for Professional Employees AFL-CIO, 2010; Jones & Gates, 2007). Multiply that by the number of nurses who quit their jobs and the costs can be in the millions of dollars for health care organizations.

Any strategy that improves the retention of nursing staff saves the organization the costs of using agency or traveler nurses, replacing lost nurses and training new ones, and the loss of productivity from burdening the remaining. In a large system, like the Veterans Health Administration, High Involvement Work Systems that include teamwork can mean lower service costs in the millions of dollars (Harmon et al., 2003). Show higher-level management improvements in patient satisfaction scores, as well as the money to be saved in the long run with effective teamwork, and their approvals will follow.

THE COSTS OF TEAMWORK

Despite all the benefits of teamwork noted previously, there can be a downside with its associated costs. The costs of teamwork include the costs of having meetings, along with a place to meet and food and coffee; the costs of trying to arrange a time that's convenient for most of the participants; time spent in meeting and the accompanying opportunity costs, that is, how that time might have been better spent; the hard-to-measure interpersonal costs associated with having to work with other people (such as a perceived loss of autonomy and the need for compromise, which can be difficult for some people); the development of mutually respectful behaviors and trust; the costs of risk taking associated with letting go of one's turf; and the potential embarrassment of looking bad in a group. Clinical teams have the added burden of ensuring good customer service and patient safety. Some clinicians report that coordinated, team care can be difficult and that it may increase medical errors (Mitchell et al., 2012). Additional factors that may adversely affect clinical and or cross-functional teams include lack of experience or expertise, staff preferences to work in specific areas or "silos," hierarchical decision-making in teams, poor infrastructure to support teams, and reimbursements that are not aligned with clinical team work (Mitchell et al., 2012; Weinberg, Cooney-Miner, Perloff, Babington, & Avgar, 2011).

Tuckman (1965) conducted a comprehensive literature review of small group behavior in therapy group, t-group, natural, and laboratory group studies. After examining the literature, he devised a classification scheme for small group dynamics. In this classic article, Tuckman provided the following five stages that teams go through: **forming, storming, norming, performing, and adjourning**. When teams are **forming**, they are getting oriented to the team goals and each other, finding out what the tasks are and who they will be working with. Then the **storming** begins. With storming, there is intragroup conflict; there can be attempts at dominance, passive-aggressive behavior along with information withholding, and other forms of resistance to team tasks and goals. Peace breaks out when the storming stage passes, and team members actually begin working together and agreeing on things in the **norming** stage, where expectations and roles become codified, either formally or informally. They then move on to **performing** the work at hand, have open dialogue with one another, and share information to accomplish the team's goals. Winding down and **adjourning** brings its own emotional turbulence. Team members who may have disliked each other at the start have worked together over a long period of time and have developed respect for one another. There is often a reluctance to let go and move on to the next task because they have become comfortable working with each other. They've grown to like each other as individuals and the team as a whole and become sad that they are disbanding (Tuckman, 1965).

When teams don't work well together, there are significant costs to the organization in terms of human resources and opportunity costs. These costs mean that teamwork may not always be as efficient as other forms of problem solving and decision making. According to Drinka and Clark (2000), "To become efficient. . . the team members must learn to define the scope of the problem. . . and select the least disciplines needed to address the problem well" (p. 36). The more is not always the merrier. Efficient team function can only occur when each carefully selected team member knows the goal(s) of the team. It takes less time (usually) for one person to decide on a potential strategy than a group of people. However, without having team advocates in each of the areas affected by the decision, implementing a unilateral decision can become a health care manager's worst nightmare.

One of the emerging trends in health care organizations is the use of virtual teams. With the availability of the Internet and other innovative communication technologies, virtual teams are gaining popularity for some activities in health care organizations (Tompkins & Orwat, 2010). Most patient care cannot be addressed effectively through virtual or remote teams, however. Some positive results from virtual teams are related to the use of telemedicine, which promotes health care interventions over geographic distances (Tompkins & Orwat, 2010). For some staff in nonclinical areas of health care organizations who have flexible work schedules and can telecommute, such communication technologies allow for less face-to-face team activities and more remote team activities (as noted in Chapter 12). This can work both for and against team unity, and the manager must guard against problems in employee relationships and team effectiveness that may result from the use of remote and virtual teams.

ELECTRONIC TOOLS AND REMOTE AND VIRTUAL TEAMS

The exponential growth of Internet devices and applications in business and health care settings has created new opportunities for team work and workers. Many Internet-based companies have employees who work remotely from home on teams, whether responding to order fulfillment, customer service, or working on strategic plans. All levels of organizations have taken advantage of the flexibility associated with having a cyber-office in the home. However, there have been some abuses of this innovative approach to work, from both the worker and management sides of the computer screen. While on the employer's clock, workers check and respond to personal emails, update their status in social media websites, participate in personal virtual messages and chats, check sports scores, and go shopping, to name but a few of the abuses that contribute to decreased worker productivity (Ciocchetti, 2011; Sanders, Ross, & Pattison, 2013).

In response to this loss in productivity, some organizations have instituted **electronic performance monitoring and control systems (EMPCS)**, observation tools that enable an employer to keep an eye on its employees to ensure they remain productive. These systems include audio and video recordings of customer service calls, keystroke logging, Internet filters, Internet search term monitoring, screen warnings that pop up and remind the employee about policies related to personal usage, email monitoring, and monitoring of employee social media posts and interactions, to name some of the more common tracking methods.

When the employee is physically based at the organization, it is easier to understand why these strategies would be enacted. However, when the employee works out of her home, the issues become murkier and productivity becomes an even bigger issue to the employer. In February 2013, Yahoo, Inc. announced: "To become the absolute best place to work, communication and collaboration will be important, so we need to be working side-by-side," the memo said. "That is why it is critical that we are all present in our offices" (Pepitone, 2013, para. 3). Employer surveillance techniques have evoked worker concerns about justice and privacy. In McNall and Roch's study (2007), Internet surveillance was perceived as the most procedurally just and direct physical monitoring of employees by supervisors and as the most invasive of privacy. When the employee is physically present, it is easier to see if someone is doing their job, even in the absence of having a supervisor looking over the worker's shoulder. It is also easier to assess whether someone is an effective member of a team. The next section of this chapter will address the pros and cons of face to face versus virtual teams.

FACE TO FACE VERSUS VIRTUAL TEAMS

In rural areas, space stations, and Antarctic research operations, to name but a few possibilities, it may be physically impossible to "go to the home office" to work with your team. Additionally, the health care industry has a large non–direct care sector that has worked from remote work opportunities for such areas as revenue recovery, billing, and customer service. For those with disabilities, elderly parents, or small children, work from home opportunities can provide opportunities for employment and work–life balance. Some of the other benefits of virtual teamwork identified by Plump & Ketchen (2013) include: less interpersonal conflict, reduced travel, and access to diverse employees and talents regardless of geography. Kulesza (2015) echoes these benefits, and emphasizes the need for careful selection of team members; frequent communication with the team and one-on-one with individual team members; and emails between meetings to summarize, clarify, and move a project along. He also urged team leaders to be sensitive to diversity. Assertion is valued in the American culture, but that is not true across cultures. Cultural competency is key to respecting and engaging all team members.

Virtual teams have emerged recently in the provision of direct care to patients by health care professionals. Virtual teams communicate via email, phone, and other technology to maximize communication among members of a treatment team. These virtual teams can exist in acute care settings, such as a hospital radiologist reading images from remote locations, and in long-term care settings addressing patients with chronic illness. The virtual format enables team members to focus on the core information to be discussed while limiting extraneous information that might otherwise distract from the focus on care, facilitating highly efficient team communication (BRIGHTEN, 2015). It has been shown that virtual teams can save resources, including staff time, as well as provide the patient with helpful perspectives often not available from an individual staff member (Rothschild & Lapidos, 2003). See an example of a clinical virtual team in Textbox 13-5.

TEXTBOX 13-5. THE BRIGHTEN PROGRAM—EXAMPLE OF A VIRTUAL TEAM

The BRIGHTEN Program (**B**ridging **R**esources of an **I**nter-disciplinary **G**eriatric **H**ealth **T**eam via **E**lectronic **N**etworking) was developed to address depression and anxiety among older adults by integrating existing health care resources and technologies to overcome the barriers characteristic of health care delivery. BRIGHTEN is a patient-centered assessment and treatment program that relies on a "virtual" team communication and treatment planning. The virtual process was based on the Virtual Integrated Practice (VIP) model, which addresses the pervasive lack of collaborative, coordinated care for patients with chronic, complex medical and other needs in small, community based medical clinics.

Because older adults often have a variety of health issues that interact with symptoms of depression, the BRIGHTEN team goes beyond those who typically treat mental health problems. The BRIGHTEN virtual team includes staff from psychology, social work, psychiatry, physical therapy, occupational therapy, dietetics, and pharmacy, as well as a Chaplain and the patient's primary physician. Physicians whose patients are screened into BRIGHTEN are integral team members and receive updates on their patients' progress during treatment. Each of these disciplines contributes a unique perspective on healing for older adults with depression and anxiety. The goal of the team is to support and treat older adults with depression and anxiety by integrating health care resources and delivery.

Older adults who screen positive for depression or anxiety complete a comprehensive evaluation with a BRIGHTEN mental health clinician, including standardized measures. The clinician and team members correspond virtually to develop care recommendations, collaboratively develop a treatment plan, and aid the older adult in implementing the plan.

Sources: BRIGHTEN, 2015; Mitchell et al., 2012.

Hoch and Kozlowski (2014) conducted research among 101 virtual teams. They examined the leadership role in these new frameworks and found "shared leadership enhanced team performance." Along with recommendations for increased training and support for these virtual team leaders, they suggested implementation of a "fair and reliable reward structure," among other things. The positive findings associated with shared leadership were a surprise, one which drove the researchers to recommend this for all teams, not just virtual ones (p. 399).

Plump and Ketchen (2013), however, urged caution and provided suggestions for avoiding legal problems with employees in these roles. While Hoch and Kozlowski (2014) extoll the virtues of shared team leadership, Plump and Ketchen point to the fact that virtual teams make it difficult to tell who the supervisor is—which can have legal ramifications.

Traditionally, supervisors are considered agents of the organization and there is a higher standard of behavior expected of a manager. In a "leaderless" or co-led virtual team, if there are charges of harassment, discrimination, or any other violation of Title VII of the Civil Rights Act of 1986, the question is who is the boss? Who is more liable? Likewise, work hours and wages are usually set by a supervisor, who acts as the agent of the organization. The Fair Labor Standards Act of 1938 established minimum wages and overtime standards. If your team mate tells you that the project is on a deadline and he doesn't care how late you work, will you get paid overtime? And will the wages be fair?

The Family and Medical Leave Act of 1983 (FMLA) provides for classes of employees to take unpaid leave and still have a job upon their return. Again, does this apply in a virtual team? Who determines whether the employee is eligible to take the time off? Will a job still be there when she comes back from maternity leave? Who monitors the employee's leave time and checks the physician documentation for validity? The Americans with Disabilities Act of 1990 (ADA) prohibits discrimination against people with disabilities, actual, perceived, or associated. Employers must provide reasonable accommodations to perform their jobs. What does that mean when the employee works from home? Who handles these requests? How are they managed? These labor laws and several others are addressed in greater detail in Chapter 12.

Finally, **intellectual property (IP) laws** constrain the use of other people's copyrighted materials, patents, trademarks, and proprietary secrets, such as the secret ingredients in a recipe. How does the company ensure the employee complies with these laws? What if a team member lives in a country where the laws do not apply? Are they allowed to sell company secrets because they don't live in the U.S.?

Plump and Ketchen (2013) recommend a clear delineation of authority and roles and responsibilities to prevent confusion. Policies and procedures must be set by the organization and communicated to all employees. In virtual teams, as in face to face teams, someone has to be the identified leader—or co-leader—and have the ultimate authority and responsibility. As the sign on Harry Truman's desk said, "The buck stops here."

REAL-WORLD PROBLEMS AND TEAMWORK

Tame Versus Wicked Problems

Real-world health care problems are vexing—complex, complicated, and messy (Buchbinder, 2009a). Rittel and Webber (1973) wrote on planning, and first dubbed these "wicked problems" (p. 160). Drinka and Clark (2000) wrote about "tame versus wicked problems" (p. 37). **Tame problems** can be defined and, while not easy, they can be solved. **Wicked problems** are difficult to define and not easily resolved—and sometimes can never be truly solved due to multiple layers of issues, such as we see in health care. Rittel and Webber (1973) described 10 key features of wicked problems:

1. "There is no definitive formulation of a wicked problem.
2. Wicked problems have no stopping rule.
3. Solutions to wicked problems are not true-or-false, but good-or-bad.
4. There is no immediate and no ultimate test of a solution to a wicked problem.
5. Every solution to a wicked problem is a 'one-shot operation;' because there is no opportunity to learn by trial-and-error, every attempt counts significantly.
6. Wicked problems do not have an enumerable (or an exhaustively describable) set of potential solutions, nor is there a well-described set of permissible operations that may be incorporated into the plan.
7. Every wicked problem is essentially unique.
8. Every wicked problem can be considered to be a symptom of another problem.
9. The existence of a discrepancy representing a wicked problem can be explained in numerous ways. The choice of explanation determines the nature of the problem's resolution.
10. The planner has no right to be wrong" (pp. 161–166).

Most health care problems fall along the continuum of tame to wicked, with many levels of messiness along the way. Conklin (2008) speaks of fragmentation as a result of vexing, wicked problems interacting with social complexity. By having only one discipline examining an issue, problems can actually be *exacerbated*, rather than ameliorated. When different factions stare at their pieces of the puzzle and don't attempt to see the perspectives of others, problems are addressed in a piecemeal, not holistic, manner.

Here are some examples of wicked problems:

- An 80-year-old woman has had hip replacement surgery and used up her post-op Medicare paid days at the skilled nursing facility (SNF). Her walking has improved but is not back to pre-injury status. In her home, her bedroom is on the second floor and she has a flight of stairs to climb to get to her front door. Her only daughter lives in another state and has two teenagers (one of whom is struggling with depression), and her husband just lost his job.

- A Hispanic man has sustained burns over much of his upper torso, including his arms. He is uninsured and needs extensive therapy to prevent contracture (immobilization) of his arms. Neither he nor his family members are fluent in English. They don't understand what he needs or how to access health care resources to help him return to his activities of daily living (ADLs).
- A young woman who is addicted to heroin gives birth. The baby is born with low Apgar scores (a numerical score on a scale from 1 to 10, given at 1 and 5 minutes after birth; a lower score indicates a sicker newborn) and is in withdrawal. Eventually, the baby is ready for discharge. The social services department is not keen on handing the baby over to the mother, who is still using heroin. However, the mother's mother (the baby's grandmother) says *she* can take care of the baby—except grandmother arrives to pick up the infant drunk (she failed to mention that she was an alcoholic) and her husband (the grandfather) is also high when he arrives because he is addicted to prescription painkillers.

As you can see from the above examples, wicked problems cannot be solved by one person or one discipline. You need to have every involved area's input to analyze a wicked problem, because it won't be solved by one person—or one discipline. Because of these complexities, members of a team must be selected with care.

All accountable care organizations (ACOs) are moving toward improved teamwork to address these kinds of issues. In addition to ACOs, Medical Homes, Comprehensive Primary Care Initiatives, Gerontology Primary Care Programs, and many other new models of care are based on teams to provide comprehensive and coordinated care to patients. Not only is it about the bottom-line, but also about clinical effectiveness and patient-centric care. We cannot continue to function in silos, in fact, that will be the death knell of any health care organization. More of information on ACOs can be found in Chapter 10.

WHO'S ON THE TEAM?

When you first start out in health care management, it is unlikely that you will be able to choose your teammates. It will be *your* job to learn the culture of the organization and to determine how best to fit into a team. Some of the questions that you can ask when you are assigned to a team are:

- What are the goals of the team?
- How will they be measured?
- What are the short-term and long-term deadlines?

- When and where does the team meet?
- To whom do I report? (Sometimes staff members are loaned to teams, so this is an important issue to resolve.)
- What is my role on the team?
- What are my responsibilities in that role?

Good managers don't mind if a new staff member makes a list of questions and asks for clarification and direction. Coaching, mentoring, and guiding are all part of the manager's role, and health care management is a continuous learning experience. Managers *do* mind, however, if you don't ask questions and go off and do the wrong thing. Additionally, good managers want thoughtful observations from a new perspective: yours.

Over time, as you assume more responsibilities and learn the organization, you may be asked to recommend team members or to convene a team to address a specific organizational issue. Getting the right people on a team is one of the most critical tasks a health care manager can have. Kulesza (2015) likens selecting team mates to making a soup: "Choosing the right members is synonymous with choosing the right ingredients" (p. 19). When this opportunity comes, ask for counsel and advice from your manager and your coworkers. The last thing you want to do is exclude the chairman of surgery on a team that's addressing operating room productivity. As noted previously, real-world health care management problems are complex, complicated, and messy. As a health care manager, you will need to assess the strengths and weaknesses of each potential team member before inviting him or her onto your team. You will need to ask the following questions.

Does this person:

- Belong to an area that's affected by the problem at hand?
- Have the knowledge, skills, and disposition to do the tasks at hand?
- Have a clearly defined role on the team?
- Have the authority to make decisions and implement recommendations?
- Follow through on assignments and tasks and meet deadlines?
- Think beyond the confines of a department or discipline?
- Work collaboratively and respectfully with other disciplines?
- Have the ability to defuse tensions and de-escalate conflict?
- Have a sense of humor?
- Have a good reputation within the organization as a team player?
- Value perceptions and ideas of others?
- See organizational goals as superseding individual goals?

One tool that is sometimes used for understanding differences in team members' personalities is the **Myers-Briggs Type Indicator (MBTI)**, a personality inventory based on

Jung's theory of psychological types (Rideout & Richardson, 1989). The MBTI assesses four domains and four subsets within those domains on a four-by-four grid (Wideman, 2003). On the vertical axis of this grid is the Introvert-Extrovert scale; on the horizontal axis is the Sensing-Intuitive scale. Within each of the four quadrants of this grid are two more axes—the Perceiving-Judging axis and the Thinking-Feeling axis. After taking this paper-and-pencil, self-administered inventory, the individual finds her "Myers-Briggs Type" on a large square. The types are designated by letters, so when a search firm is looking for a strong executive, they would want an "ESTJ," someone who is "responsible, dependable, highly organized, likes to see things done correctly, tends to judge in terms of standard operating procedures, realistic, matter-of-fact, and loyal to institutions" (Wideman, 2003, p. 11).

Other instruments have been used to determine goodness of fit for team members, as well. Emergenetics® is similar to the Myers-Briggs Type Indicator in that it assesses how people think (Browning, 2006). The difference is it also assesses how people behave. Using the "four ways of thinking" and "three ways of behaving," people are assigned to color coded categories. The results of these assessments have been demonstrated to be stable over time. Once a person is identified in a certain manner, it is likely that individual will continue to behave that same way in future events and interactions. With respect to team building, this is helpful in identifying what traits are needed for a specific project.

When building a team, you may not want everyone to be a leader. If there is an urgent matter that requires quick and decisive action, you probably don't want to have the over-analytical, slow to act, unassertive person in charge of that team. You probably want that person on a research project that requires integration of a lot of data and comprehensive reporting, leaving no stone unturned. You also need good followers, that is, people who are willing to bring their strengths to the group process, who may be more on the sensing, introverted, intuitive end of the axis on the MBTI, rather than the extroverted end (noted in Chapter 2). Wideman (2003) suggests that, while project management and teamwork are becoming mandatory in most employment settings, not everyone in the workforce population is suited, by their personality type, to function well on a team. He suggests judicious use of the MBTI to see where people fit in the leadership versus followership mode and to be cautious about who is placed on a team.

Many health care recruiters utilize the MBTI to help them select candidates for health care placements. In addition, many health care management professional organizations offer seminars and workshops for individuals to learn about their personality styles using the MBTI, Emergenetics, and other instruments. The key thing to know about these popular tools is that they are not the only way to understand health care team members. Oftentimes, experience and the oral history of the health care organization where you work is the best predictor of selecting good team members.

EMOTIONS AND TEAMWORK

Psychological researchers have known for decades that infants learn emotions through observation and mimicry of caregivers' facial expressions (Buchbinder, 2009b). In addition, Laird and Bresler (1992) demonstrated in laboratory research that when subjects' faces were arranged into frowns, the subjects reported feeling angry—even in the absence of any cues that would induce such emotions. Muscle memory appeared to create the mood associated with the facial expressions. Recently, neuroscientists have discovered that a cluster of premotor and parietal cells called "mirror neurons" or the "mirror neuron system" (MNS) is responsible for enabling humans to learn motor skills, language, communication, and social behaviors (Chi, 2008; Iacoboni & Depretto, 2006; Rizzolatti & Craighero, 2004).

According to Hatfield, Cacioppo, and Rapson (1993), people who are emotionally in tune with others can read emotions within *nanoseconds* of observing facial expressions. The ability to read other people's emotions has been measured through the **Emotion Contagion (EC) scale**. Doherty, Orimoto, Singelis, Hatfield, and Hebb (1995) found women and physicians scored higher on the EC scale and that there were significant correlations between self-report of "catching emotion" and "judges' ratings of participants' actual emotional reactions" (p. 369).

When Totterdell, Kellett, Teuchmann, and Briner (1998) looked at the relationship between mood and work groups of community nurses, they discovered "significant associations between people's moods and the moods of their teammates at work over time" (p. 1513). The term used by these researchers and others for why this happened was "emotional contagion." In other words, the teammates caught each other's moods.

To summarize:

- We are hardwired to learn emotions through mimicry and mirroring.
- Emotions are communicated in a flash—literally within microseconds.
- Women and people in the helping professions are more sensitive to reading emotions.
- Emotions are contagious and can spread within moments.

Kanter (2004) found that optimistic leaders focus on specific tasks ahead, rather than dwelling on past failures and negativity. Although we are experiencing challenging times in health care, leaders *can* moderate the impact of this volatile environment. With all the women and helping professionals in health care settings, the majority of employees are highly sensitive to other people's moods. Enthusiasm, confidence, and optimism are critical to leading others. Emotionally aware team members can change an organization's emotional environment and improve the quality of employees' and patients' lives by helping others to become "infected" with positive emotions (Buchbinder, 2009c).

Emotional intelligence (EI), the concept made famous by Daniel Goleman in the late 1990s (and as noted in Chapter 2), encompasses self-awareness, self-regulation, self-motivation, social awareness, and social skills, and within each of these areas, specific skill sets (Consortium on Research for Emotional Intelligence in Organizations, 2009; Goleman, 1998). In 2006, Goleman moved to the terminology *social intelligence* (SI) to separate out the last two components of EI, social awareness and social skills, and began using the term "social facility" instead of "social skills" (Goleman, 2006). These two are defined as:

"**Social Awareness**
Primal empathy: Feeling with others; sensing nonverbal emotional signals.
Attunement: Listening with full receptivity; attuning to a person.
Empathic accuracy: Understanding another person's thoughts, feelings, and intentions.

Social Facility
Synchrony: Interacting smoothly at the nonverbal level.
Self-presentation: Presenting ourselves effectively.
Influence: Shaping the outcome of social interactions.
Concern: Caring about others' needs and acting accordingly" (Goleman, 2006, p. 84).

Currently there is a controversy in the industrial-organizational psychology literature regarding the definitions, models, and measurement of EI, SI, and now, **emotional social competencies (ESC)**. Cherniss (2010) defined ESC as "those emotional abilities, social skills, personality traits, motivations, interests, goals, values, attachment styles, and life narratives that can contribute to (or detract from) effective performance across a variety of positions" (p. 184). The bottom line is that being aware of one's emotional and social skills and being able to effectively use them is an important ability for leaders and followers. In health care, these competencies and the ability to assess when and how to utilize these competencies are essential to good leadership and effective teamwork. Protocols such as the EI360, a 360-degree assessment of an individual's EI, help to identify an individual's emotional and social strengths and weaknesses (Buchbinder, 2009b). With coaching and specific behavioral goals that are applied in the workplace, health care managers can learn how to move to the next level of their EI, SI, and ESC abilities—and how to best apply them in the workplace.

TEAM COMMUNICATION

Frequent, positive communications improve team interactions and increase trust. Organizations that empower their employees promote employee job satisfaction. Laschinger and Finegan (2005) found that nurses who felt they had access to opportunity, honest relationships, open communication with peers and managers, and trusted their managers were more likely to be attached to their organizations and have higher job satisfaction. Similarly, it has been shown that health care employees who view their work unit climate as participative as opposed to authoritarian provide higher levels of customer service, commit fewer clinical errors, and express less likelihood of leaving the organization (Angermeier, Dunford, Boss, & Boss, 2009).

Dreachslin, Hunt, and Sprainer (1999) conducted research to assess how diversity affected patient-centered team communication and to improve communication and patient care. Focus groups were convened to elicit key issues and to develop recommendations. The authors concluded that health care managers should facilitate open and honest dialogue between management and care production teams and within the teams themselves. The process should involve care production team members in process improvement. To improve relationships between team members and nurse managers, more training is needed, both in the clinical and relationship management arenas. Diversity training has to be part of team and leadership training. The **patient-centered care model** must emphasize caring for patients, as well as 360-degree feedback, where nurses and technicians evaluate each other, which should be implemented for assessment, communicated to team members, and used as a management tool for continuous quality improvement.

In a classic article on management teams, Eisenhardt, Kahwajy, and Bourgeois (1997) observed teams in 12 technology companies. Much like health care today, these companies operated in a high-stakes, fast-paced environment, where today's technology is tomorrow's dinosaur. Teams had to be lightning fast in their responses and almost precognitive to stay ahead of the competition. The authors found that teams with minimal interpersonal conflict had the same six strategies. "Team members: worked with more, rather than less information, and debated facts; developed multiple alternatives to enrich the level of debate; shared commonly agreed upon goals; injected humor into the decision process; maintained a balanced power structure; and resolved issues without forcing consensus" (Eisenhardt et al., 1997, p. 78). By keeping the focus on the facts and not on personalities, and communicating in an open, honest, and safe forum, the teams were able to have fun and be productive.

The airline industry has become a model of how to build teams in hospitals and other health care organizations (Nance, 2008). Pilots are trained to be team players because a plane full of people may die if they don't pay attention to their teammates' observations. **Crew resource management (CRM)** has been developed to address attitudes, change behavior, and improve performance. Anyone can and should speak up if they have safety concerns, from co-pilot to flight attendant. Sexton, Thomas, and Helmreich (2000) have applied crew resource management research to hospitals, where stakes are also high and lives depend on the smooth functioning of the health care team. Senior surgeons were least likely to be in favor of teamwork and flat hierarchies. Medical staff responded that teamwork was imperative, but that they were not encouraged to report safety concerns. Doctors and nurses differed widely in their opinions regarding teamwork. Almost three-quarters of surveyed intensive care physicians reported high levels of teamwork with nurses, but less than half of the nurses felt the same way. These results point to the need for a more realistic appraisal of safety concerns, improved communication between team members, and enhanced team training for health care professionals, in all disciplines and specialties.

In 2003, Morey and colleagues published their findings on the implementation of CRM in a quasi-experimental, multi-site prospective study over the period of a year. The researchers, funded by a U.S. Army Research Laboratory contract, utilized nine emergency departments (EDs), six in the intervention arm and three in the control group. Four of the EDs were military, three in the experimental arm and one in the control arm. Clinical staff (physicians, nurses, and technicians) in the EDs in the intervention arm participated in extensive teamwork training based on the principles of CRM. Post-tests revealed improved teamwork in all experimental EDs as demonstrated by decreased clinical errors, increased positive attitudes toward teamwork, and staff perceptions of support. The authors recommended an initial training, followed by "dosing," i.e., interjecting shorter coaching and mentoring sessions on teamwork in the clinical setting after the first classroom based educational sessions. They also recommended refresher courses on a regular basis for all staff.

The military and aviation concepts of CRM and interprofessional teamwork training were picked up and expanded into **TeamSTEPPS** by the Agency for Healthcare Research and Quality (AHRQ). Per the AHRQ TeamSTEPPS (2015) website:

"TeamSTEPPS is a teamwork system designed for health care professionals that is:

- A powerful solution to improving patient safety within your organization.
- An evidence-based teamwork system to improve communication and teamwork skills among health care professionals.
- A source for ready-to-use materials and a training curriculum to successfully integrate teamwork principles into all areas of your health care system.
- Scientifically rooted in more than 20 years of research and lessons from the application of teamwork principles.
- Developed by Department of Defense's Patient Safety Program in collaboration with the Agency for Healthcare Research and Quality.

TeamSTEPPS provides higher quality, safer patient care by:

- Producing highly effective medical teams that optimize the use of information, people, and resources to achieve the best clinical outcomes for patients.

- Increasing team awareness and clarifying team roles and responsibilities.
- Resolving conflicts and improving information sharing.
- Eliminating barriers to quality and safety" (para. 1–2).

The Hospital Research & Educational Trust (HRET) now manages the national implementation of TeamSTEPPS, which is funded by the AHRQ. "The core components include: master training courses; annual national conference; community support and engagement through the online portal; and updates to the TeamSTEPPS curriculum" (HRET, 2015, para. 2).

METHODS OF MANAGING TEAMS OF HEALTH CARE PROFESSIONALS

Effective leadership, addressed in the second chapter of this book, is needed at every level of the health care organization, but especially in teamwork. Because, by definition, interdisciplinary health teams are made up of people from different fields, it's the health care manager's job to take the lead and to establish team guidelines and foster good communication. It's the responsibility of the team leader to establish communication networks. At the first meeting, the leader should obtain names, all phone numbers, email addresses, and any other ways the team members can be contacted. One of the things a team leader can do to facilitate good communication early in the life of the team is to establish guidelines for expected behaviors, processes, and outcomes in a written document. A manager can facilitate effective team functioning within her unit by providing support for struggling teams and by allowing teams to share their successes in improving teamwork and team results (Scott, 2009).

As can be seen in Figure 13-1, Guidelines for Teamwork, the document does not have to be complicated. This tool can be used to evaluate the performance of individual members of the team, thus avoiding the **social loafer** or **free-rider syndrome**, where a member of the team does nothing but gets credit for the work done by others. Managing social loafers and other problem teammates can be the biggest part of managing a team. As an effective team leader, your job is to get the best out of each team member. Attaining top performance requires understanding who your teammates are, what they need, and the ability to build consensus, being aware that you may not have 100% agreement on every decision.

After introductions and establishing the purpose of the team in a written document, Maginn (1995) recommends that the team leader go around the table and ask each person his or her ideas about the problem. The leader should acknowledge each idea, recording it as the team member speaks. Be sure to wait for people to respond to the question—and

---

The purpose of Team XYZ is to _____ <**goals**> _____.

Our deadline for solving this problem is _____ <**date**> _____.

The team will meet _____ <**number of times or frequency of meetings**> _____.

Representatives from each affected area have been asked to serve on Team XYZ.

Those representatives are: _____ <**List names of team members**> _____

Team members will:
- Attend all team sessions, unless there is an emergency;
- Prepare for each session;
- Listen to each other with respect;
- Work collaboratively to identify and meet session goals;
- Be an active participant in group discussions;
- Keep an open mind, be willing to modify opinions or conclusions to keep the project moving forward;
- Present ideas concisely;
- Be considerate and tactful when participating in group discussions;
- Submit/delegate work on time and fulfill responsibilities as agreed; and
- Work actively to achieve group consensus on issues and problems.

By _____ <**deadline**> _____, Team XYZ will have the following outcomes:*
- Reports of proceedings, data analyses, recommendations, and an evaluation plan for implementation of the recommendations.

Note: The Leader of Team XYZ is responsible for presentation of this report, with all team members present, if possible, to the administration for review and approval.

Interim deadlines may be needed, so consider those as you discuss these guidelines.

FIGURE 13-1 Guidelines for Teamwork

to each other. Don't interrupt, and don't let others interrupt a person when he/she has the floor. Ask critics for ideas and suggestions, getting those negative comments out on the table so they can be addressed. Remain calm, open-minded, and nondefensive. At the end of each meeting, thank everyone for their thoughtful comments, summarizing what you thought you heard and asking for clarification.

Before the meeting ends, it's time to ask people to do some homework. Who is willing to do what task? Will there be research needed? What process should be used for reporting to each other? Send a summary of the meeting to everyone on the team, and include a list of steps that need to be taken before the next meeting. Communication that includes everyone is key. Establish an email list and be sure all correspondence regarding the project goes through it. The more information team members have, the more buy-in and cooperation will occur.

To build trust, meet commitments and do what you say you are going to do. Bring reliable information to the team. Accurate data and demonstrated skill at your work inform the team members that you are competent—and trustworthy (Maginn, 1995). Even when team members trust each other, conflict happens. At some point in time, there will be disagreement about which choices and decisions the team should make. Maginn (1995) recommends five potential strategies for conflict resolution in teams: **bargaining, problem solving, voting, research, and third-party mediation**.

Bargaining is when someone says, "If you go along with me this time, I'll back you up next time." If the choices are equally good, then bargaining can be a good tool; if the choices aren't equal, then it may not be a good tool. **Voting** is democratic, but also bears the weight of potentially taking a team to the incorrect choice. **Problem solving** may be the better way to go. This means taking time to answer the "what if" scenarios of each alternative. "If we do this, then what might happen?" How will you assess if it's the right option? You may not know until you try it. Doing more **research**, i.e., additional study to find out if others have created a solution to the problem or if there are factors that have been overlooked by the team, is safe. However, time pressures may preclude the team from doing an in-depth study. When all else fails, **third-party mediation** is probably a win-win, especially if the third party is the boss. Oftentimes, the team presentation to the boss will include choices that have been laid out, like a menu, for an upper-level manager to select. The alternatives are listed, the pros and cons of each alternative are provided, and the assessment plan for each alternative is in place. You win, your team wins, and your organization wins.

OPPORTUNITIES FOR RESEARCH ON EMERGING ISSUES

This chapter has discussed some of the research on teamwork and health care management being conducted. Our nation continues to move toward ACOs and other organizational models that demand the use of teams to provide safe, effective patient-centric care. Simultaneously, consumers, providers, payers, and other stakeholders are demanding to know what the data say about the outcomes of these new models of care. Opportunities for in-depth research on these emerging issues exist in a variety of venues, including your health care organization. Many of the resources we used in writing this chapter also include extensive research holdings and courses available to students and academic researchers. Herewith is a partial listing of these resources.

- Agency for Healthcare Research and Quality (AHRQ) TeamSTEPPS;
- Centers for Disease Control and Prevention (CDC) Collaboration Primer;
- Hospital Research and Educational Trust (HRET) TeamSTEPPS national implementation;
- Inter-university Consortium for Political and Social Research (ICPSR);
- Institute for Healthcare Improvement (IHI) Open School: Free Courses for University Students; and
- World Health Organization: Team Tools.

CONCLUSION

This chapter has described what a team is and some of the challenges associated with teamwork in health care organizations. Some current trends in using teams and the benefits of teamwork, as well as costs, have been described. Tame and wicked problems were defined and related to the need for interdisciplinary teams to solve them. Fitting into teams and selecting team members were discussed, along with the Myers-Briggs Type Indicator personality inventory. The importance of emotional contagion, emotional and social intelligence, and emotional and social competencies was discussed in relation to effective teamwork. In addition, communication on teams and some methods of managing teams of health care professionals have been reviewed. And, finally, some examples of teams in health care settings have been presented. You have the background and tools; now you can begin to build your team. Throughout this chapter, we have noted places where you can obtain research data and publications related to teamwork.

DISCUSSION QUESTIONS

1. What are the differences among an onsite team, a virtual team, a task force, and a committee? What are some of the potential differences in dynamics between people in these different groups?

2. What are the pros and cons of virtual teams? What are some of the potential legal issues an organization can encounter with virtual teams?

3. Compare and contrast disciplinary, interdisciplinary, and cross-functional teams.

4. The hospital where you are completing your internship is located in an inner city neighborhood with a multi-lingual, diverse population. Recently, the local newspaper has been running a series about the lack of input the community has into the hospital. A number of anonymous interviewees complained they felt like dollar signs, not people. Your internship mentor is the Director of Public Relations. She tasks you with finding the top three evidence-based, cost-effective tools to facilitate communication with the community and increase patients' and families' input into hospital management and processes.

5. What are some of the unique challenges associated with teamwork in health care? How do you see teamwork fitting in with the accountable care organization (ACO)

mandates? Describe three benefits and three costs of teamwork in health care organizations.

6. After working in a hospital for 6 months, you have been selected to head up the team to conduct hand-washing audits on all the nursing units. Whom do you want on your team and why? A month later, a member of the hand-washing audit team comes to you and complains that another team member is not pulling her weight. This individual is not your employee, but she is on your team. What should you do?

7. List and describe five potential strategies for conflict resolution in teams. Which method is likely to be most successful if your manager likes to be involved in every decision?

8. What are the five stages of team development? Describe each stage and how those stages may appear as behaviors in a health care setting.

9. Based on the past year's patient grievances which identified significant staff attitude issues in the ED, the VP for Service Excellence at Brownsville Community Hospital has decided the ED needs improved teamwork. He tasks you with finding an evidence-based intervention. Which cost-effective, evidence-based educational programs will you recommend to address these issues? Provide a rationale for your recommendations.

10. Over the past month, every member of the Intravenous (IV) Therapy Team has complained to you about the IV Team supervisor. Her direct reports, all RNs, agree that she is technically superb. However, their comments include statements that she is "hyper-critical," "demeaning," and that they "feel bad" about coming to work. It would be extremely difficult to find a replacement for this supervisor; however, if you don't do *something*, it looks as if the entire IV Team will resign. What should you do?

Cases in Chapter 18 that are related to this chapter include:

- The "Easy" Software Upgrade at Delmar Ortho
- Problems with the Pre-Admission Call Center
- The Magic Is Gone
- Madison Community Hospital Addresses Infection Prevention
- Emotional Intelligence in Labor and Delivery
- The New Toy at City Medical Center

Case study guides are available in the online Instructor's Materials.

REFERENCES

Alexander, J. A., Lichtenstein, R., Jinnett, K., Wells, R., Zazzali, J., & Liu, D. (2005). Cross-functional team processes and patient functional improvement. *Health Services Research, 40*(5), 1335–1355.

Amos, M. A., Hu, J., & Herrick, C. A. (2005, January/February). The impact of team building on communication and job satisfaction of nursing staff. *Journal for Nurses in Staff Development, 21*(1), 10–16.

Angermeier, I., Dunford, B. B., Boss, A. D., & Boss, R. W. (2009). The impact of participative management perceptions on customer service, medical errors, burnout, and turnover intentions. *Journal of Healthcare Management, 54*(2), 127–141.

Baker, D. P., Day, R., & Salas, E. (2006). Teamwork as an essential component of high-reliability organizations. *Health Services Research, 41(4 Part 2)*, 1576–1598.

Baker, D. P., Salas, E., King, H., Battles, J., & Barach, P. (2005, April). The role of teamwork in the professional education of physicians: Current status and assessment recommendations. *Journal on Quality and Patient Safety, 31*(4), 185–202.

Ball, M. J. (2005, October 25). Culture of safety. *Advance for Nurses, 7*(23), 31–32.

Blackmore, G., & Persaud, D. D. (2012). Diagnosing and improving functioning in interdisciplinary health care teams. *The Health Care Manager, 31*(3), 195–207.

BRIGHTEN. (2015). *Bridging Resources of an Inter-disciplinary Geriatric Health Team via Electronic Networking.* Retrieved from http://brighten.rush.edu

Browning, G. (2006). *Emergenetics (R): Tap into the new science of success.* New York, NY: HarperBusiness.

Buchbinder, S. B. (2009a, September 17). Can we tame the wicked problems in health care? [Blog post]. Retrieved from http://blogs.jblearning.com/health/2009/09/09/can-we-tame-wicked-problems-in-health-care/

Buchbinder, S. B. (2009b, July 29). Emotional intelligence and leadership. [Blog post]. Retrieved from http://blogs.jblearning.com/health/2009/07/29/emotional-intelligence-and-leadership/

Buchbinder, S. B. (2009c, November 23). Infectious leadership. [Blog post]. Retrieved from http://blogs.jblearning.com/health/2009/11/23/infectious-leadership/

Buchbinder, S. B., Alt, P. M., Eskow, K., Forbes, W., Hester, E., Struck, M., & Taylor, D. (2005). Creating learning prisms with an interdisciplinary case study workshop. *Innovative Higher Education, 29*(4), 257–274.

Bureau of Labor Statistics, U.S. Department of Labor. (2014). Medical and health services managers. *Occupational outlook handbook, 2014-15* edition. Retrieved from http://www.bls.gov/ooh/management/medical-and-health-services-managers.htm

Chi, K. (2008, November 20). Beyond mirror neurons. *SFARI: Simons Foundation Autism Research Initiative.* Retrieved from http://sfari.org/news-and-opinion/conference-news/2008/society-for-neuroscience-2008/beyond-mirror-neurons

Ciocchetti, C. A. (2011). The eavesdropping employer: A twenty-first century framework for employee monitoring. *American Business Law Journal, 48*(2), 285–369.

Cherniss, C. (2010). Emotional intelligence: New insights and further clarifications. *Industrial and Organizational Psychology, 3*, 183–191.

Clement, D., Dault, M., & Priest, A. (2007, January). Effective teamwork in healthcare: Research and reality. *HealthcarePapers, 7(SP)*, 26–34. doi:10.12927/hcpap.2013.186

Conklin, J. (2008). Wicked problems and social complexity. Retrieved from http://www.cognexus.org/wpf/wickedproblems.pdf

Consortium on Research for Emotional Intelligence in Organizations. (2009). *The emotional competence framework.* Retrieved from http://www.eiconsortium.org/reports/emotional_competence _framework.html

Department for Professional Employees AFL-CIO (DPEAFLCIO). (2010). *Fact sheet: The costs and benefits of safe staffing ratios.* Retrieved from http://dpeaflcio.org/pdf/DPE-fs_2010_staffratio.pdf

Doherty, R. W., Orimoto, L., Singelis, T. M., Hatfield, E., & Hebb, J. (1995). Emotional contagion: Gender and occupational differences. *Psychology of Women Quarterly, 19*, 355–371.

Donahue, M. P. (1985). *Nursing: The finest art: An illustrated history.* St. Louis, MO: CV Mosby.

Dreachslin, J. L., Hunt, P. L., & Sprainer, E. (1999). Communication patterns and group composition: Implications for patient-centered care team effectiveness. *Journal of Healthcare Management, 44*(4), 252–268.

Drinka, T. J. K., & Clark, P. G. (2000). *Health care teamwork: Interdisciplinary practice and teaching.* Westport, CT: Auburn House.

Edwards, N., Marshall, M., McLellan, A., & Abbasi, K. (2003, March 22). Doctors and managers: A problem without a solution? *British Medical Journal, 326*(7390), 609–610.

Eisenhardt, K. M., Kahwajy, J. L., & Bourgeois, L. F. (1997). How management teams can have a good fight. *Harvard Business Review, 75*(5), 77–85.

Flexner, A. (1910). *Medical education in the United States and Canada.* New York, NY: Carnegie Foundation for the Advancement of Teaching.

Goleman, D. (1998, December). What makes a leader? *Harvard Business Review, 76*(6), 93–102.

Goleman, D. (2006). *Social intelligence.* New York, NY: Bantam Books.

Grumbach, K., & Bodenheimer, T. (2004). Can primary health care teams improve primary care practice? *Journal of the American Medical Association, 291*(10), 1246–1251.

Harmon, J., Scotti, D. J., Behson, S., Petzel, R., Neuman, J. H., & Keashly, L. (2003, November/ December). Effects of high-involvement work systems on employee satisfaction and service costs in veterans healthcare. *Journal of Healthcare Management, 48*(6), 393–406.

Hatfield, E., Cacioppo, J. L., & Rapson, R. L. (1993). Emotional contagion. *Current Directions in Psychological Sciences, 2*, 96–99.

Health Resources and Services Administration (HRSA). (2003, Spring). *Changing demographics: Implications for physicians, nurses and other health workers.* Washington, DC: U.S. Department of Health and Human Services, Health Resources and Services Administration, Bureau of Health Professions, National Center for Health Workforce Analysis.

Health Resources and Services Administration (HRSA). (2004). *The registered nurse population: Findings from the March 2004 national sample survey of registered nurses.* Retrieved from http://bhpr.hrsa.gov /healthworkforce/rnsurveys/rnsurvey2004.pdf

Health Resources and Services Administration (HRSA). (2010, March). *The registered nurse population: Initial findings from the 2008 national sample survey of registered nurses.* Retrieved from http://bhpr .hrsa.gov/healthworkforce/rnsurveys/rnsurveyfinal.pdf

Herndon, L., Bones, C., Bradke, P., & Rutherford, P. (2013). *How-to guide: Improving transitions from the hospital to skilled nursing facilities to reduce avoidable rehospitalizations.* Cambridge, MA: Institute for Healthcare Improvement.

Hoch, J. E., & Kozlowski, S. J. (2014). Leading virtual teams: Hierarchical leadership, structural supports, and shared team leadership. *Journal of Applied Psychology, 99*(3), 390-403. doi:10.1037/a0030264

Hospital Research and Educational Trust (HRET). TeamSTEPPS national implementation. Retrieved from http://www.teamsteppsportal.org/

Iacoboni, M., & Dapretto, M. (2006). The mirror neuron system and the consequences of its dysfunction. *Nature Reviews: Neuroscience, 7*, 942–951.

Institute for Healthcare Improvement. (2004). *Transforming care at the bedside.* Retrieved from http ://www.ihi.org/IHI/Results/WhitePapers/TransformingCareattheBedsideWhitePaper.htm

Institute for Healthcare Improvement. (2015). Open school. Retrieved from http://app.ihi.org/lms /home.aspx?CatalogGuid=4cc435f0-d43b-4381-84b8-899b35082938

Institute of Medicine (IOM). (2001). *Crossing the quality chasm: A new health system for the 21st century.* Washington, DC: National Academies Press.

Jain, A. K., Thompson, J. M., Chaudry, J., McKenzie, S., & Schwartz, R. W. (2008). High-performance teams for current and future physician leaders: An introduction. *Journal of Surgical Education, 65*(2), 145–150.

Jones, C., & Gates, M. (September 30, 2007). The costs and benefits of nurse turnover: A business case for nurse retention. *OJIN: The Online Journal of Issues in Nursing, 12*(3). doi:10.3912/OJIN .Vol12No03Man04

Kanter, R. M. (2004). *Confidence: How winning streaks and losing streaks begin and end.* New York, NY: Crown Books.

Katzenbach, J. R., & Smith, D. K. (2005). The discipline of teams. *Harvard Business Review, 83*(7), 162–171.

Kim, M. M., Barnato, A. E., Angus, D. C., Fleisher, L. F., & Kahn, J. M. (2010). The effect of multidisciplinary care teams on intensive care unit mortality. *Archives of Internal Medicine, 170*(4), 369–376.

Kulesza, B. (2015). Leading global teams virtually. *Strategic Finance, 97*(4), 19–21.

Laird, J. D., & Bresler, C. (1992). The process of emotional feeling: A self-perception theory. In M. Clark (Ed.), *Review of personality and social psychology* (Vol. 13). Newbury Park, CA: Sage. As cited by Hatfield, E., Cacioppo, J. L., & Rapson, R. L. (1993). Emotional contagion. *Current Directions in Psychological Sciences, 2*, 96–99.

Laschinger, H. K. S., & Finegan, J. (2005). Using empowerment to build trust and respect in the workplace: A strategy for addressing the nursing shortage. *Nursing Economic$, 23*(1), 6–13.

Leggat, S. G. (2007). Teaching and learning teamwork: Competency requirements for healthcare managers. *The Journal of Health Administration Education, 24*(2), 135–149.

Maginn, M. (1995). *Effective teamwork.* West Des Moines, IA: American Media Publishing.

McLaughlin, C. P. (2004). West Florida Regional Medical Center. In J. S. Rakich, B. B. Longest, & K. Darr (Eds.), *Case in health services management* (4th ed.). Baltimore, MD: Health Professions Press, Inc., pp 317-338.

McNall, L. A., & Roch, S. G. (2007). Effects of electronic monitoring types on perceptions of procedural justice, interpersonal justice, and privacy. *Journal of Applied Social Psychology, 37*(3), 658–682.

Mickan, S. M. (2005). Evaluating the effectiveness of health care teams. *Australian Health Review, 29*(2), 211–217.

Mitchell, P., Wynia, M., Golden, R., McNellis, B., Okun, S., Webb, C. E., … Von Kohorn, I. (2012). *Core principles & values of effective team-based health care.* Washington, DC: Institute of Medicine. Retrieved from https://www.nationalahec.org/pdfs/VSRT-Team-Based-Care-Principles-values.pdf

Morey, J. C., Simon, R., Jay, G. D., Wears, R. L., Salisbury, M., Dukes, K. A., & Berns, S. D. (2002). Error reduction and performance improvement in the emergency department through formal teamwork training: Evaluation results of the MedTeams project. *Health Services Research, 37*(6), 1553–1581.

Nance, J. (2008). *Why hospitals should fly*. Bozeman, MT: Second River Healthcare Press.

Neily, J., Mills, P. D., Young-Xu, Y., Careney, B. T., West, P., Berger, D. H.,…Bagian, J. P. (2010). Association between implementation of a medical team training program and surgical mortality. *Journal of the American Medical Association, 304*(15), 1693–1700.

Pepitone, J. (2013, February 25). Marissa Mayer: Yahoos can no longer work from home. *CNN Money*. Retrieved from http://money.cnn.com/2013/02/25/technology/yahoo-work-from-home/

Plump, C. M., & Ketchen, D. J. Jr. (2013). Navigating the possible legal pitfalls of virtual teams. *Journal of Organization Design, 2*(3), 51–55. doi:10.7146/jod.2.3.13463

Pronovost, P. J., & Freischlag, J. A. (2010). Improving teamwork to reduce surgical mortality. *Journal of the American Medical Association, 304*(15), 1721–1722.

Quinlan, E., & Robertson, S. (2010). Mutual understanding in multi-disciplinary primary health care teams. *Journal of Interprofessional Care, 24*(5), 565–578.

Rideout, C. A., & Richardson, S. A. (1989, May). A teambuilding model: Appreciating differences using the Myers-Briggs Type Indicator with developmental theory. *Journal of Counseling and Development, 67*(9), 529–533.

Rittel, H., & Webber, M. (1973). Dilemmas in a general theory of planning. *Policy Sciences, 4*, 155–169. In N. Cross (Ed.). (1984), *Developments in design methodology* (pp. 135–144). Chichester, UK: Wiley & Sons.

Rizzolatti, G., & Craighero, L. (2004). The mirror-neuron system. *Annual Review of Neuroscience, 27*, 169–192.

Roblin, D. W., Vogt, T. M., & Fireman, B. (2003, January–March). Primary health care teams: Opportunities and challenges in evaluation of service delivery innovations. *Journal of Ambulatory Care Management, 26*(1), 22–35.

Rothschild, S., & Lapidos, M. (2003). Virtual integrated practice: Integrating teams and technology to manage chronic disease in primary care. *Journal of Medical Systems, 27*(1), 85–93.

Ruddy, G., & Rhee, K. (2005). Transdisciplinary teams in primary care for the underserved: A literature review. *Journal of Health Care for the Poor and Underserved, 16*, 248–256.

Sanders, D. E., Ross, J. K., & Pattison, P. (2013). Electronic snoops, spies, and supervisory surveillance in the workplaces. *Southern Law Journal, 23*(1), 1–27.

Scott, G. (2009). Teamwork. *Healthcare Executive, 24*(2), 46–47.

Sexton, J. B., Thomas, E. J., & Helmreich, R. L. (2000). Error, stress, and teamwork in medicine and aviation: Cross sectional surveys. *British Medical Journal, 320*, 745–749.

Sherman, J. (2006, March/April). Patient safety: Engaging medical staff. *Healthcare Executive, 21*(2), 20–23.

Stefl, M. (2008). Common competencies for all healthcare managers: The healthcare leadership alliance model. *Journal of Healthcare Management, 53*(6), 360–374.

Studer, Q. (2003). *Hardwiring excellence*. Gulf Breeze, FL: Fire Starter.

TeamSTEPPS. (2015). TeamSTEPPS: Strategies and tools to enhance performance and patient safety. Retrieved from http://teamstepps.ahrq.gov/about-2cl_3.htm

Thompson, J. M. (2010). Collaboration in health care marketing and business development. In B. Freshman, L. Rubino, & Y. R. Chassiakos (Eds.), *Collaboration across the disciplines in health care*. Sudbury, MA: Jones and Bartlett.

Tompkins, C., & Orwat, J. (2010). A randomized trial of telemonitoring heart failure patients, *Journal of Healthcare Management, 55*(5), 312–323.

Totterdell, P., Kellett, S., Teuchmann, K., & Briner, R. B. (1998). Evidence of mood linkage in work groups. *Journal of Personality and Social Psychology, 74*, 1504–1515.

Tuckman, B. W. (1965, June). Developmental sequence in small groups. *Psychological Bulletin, 63*(6), 384–399.

University of Chicago School of Social Service Administration. (n.d.). About GPHAP. Retrieved from http://gphap.uchicago.edu/aboutgphap.shtml

Weber, D. O. (2004, September–October). Poll results: Doctors' disruptive behavior disturbs physician leaders. *The Physician Executive, 30*(5), 6–14.

Weinberg, D. B., Cooney-Miner, D., Perloff, J. N., Babington, L., & Avgar, A. C. (2011). Building collaborative capacity: Promoting interdisciplinary teamwork in the absence of formal teams. *Medical Care, 49*(8), 716–723.

Wideman, M. (2003). *Project teamwork, personality profiles and the population at large: Do we have enough of the right kind of people?* Retrieved from http://maxwideman.com/papers/profiles/profiles.pdf

CHAPTER 14

Addressing Health Disparities: Cultural Proficiency

Nancy K. Sayre

LEARNING OBJECTIVES

By the end of this chapter, the student will be able to:

- Assess the concepts of health disparities, social determinants, cultural competency, and cultural proficiency;
- Propose a cogent argument for addressing health disparities;
- Analyze trends in demographics in the U.S. and the expected impact on the patient population and the health care workforce;
- Examine initiatives to foster cultural proficiency within health care organizations and explain the benefits; and
- Evaluate new paradigms relating to health disparities in research and practice.

INTRODUCTION

Unprecedented scientific and medical discoveries, continuous innovation, and new evidence-based interventions have improved the health and life expectancy of many American residents. Simultaneously, participants in the public and private sectors of the health care economy have made enormous investments, and Americans' health care utilization and spending have increased. Not all individuals, groups, or organizations have benefited, however, from these scientific breakthroughs or these financial investments in diagnosis and treatment. For decades, there has been, and even now there continues to be, a disproportionate burden of illness and injury among **vulnerable populations** who are not well integrated into the health care system. Also viewed as **underserved populations**, the

U.S. Department of Health and Human Services' Health Resources and Services Administration (HRSA, 1995) defines an underserved population as a group with economic barriers or cultural and/or linguistic barriers to primary medical care services. Researchers have compared segments of the population in the U.S. and have found very different measures of life expectancy, wellness, health care utilization, and outcomes of illnesses and injuries. These differences called **health disparities** are complicated, and the causes are multifactorial.

A term widely used in public health, health disparity has different definitions; in general, health disparities represent significant differences between one population and another. Developed in September 1999 by the National Institutes of Health (NIH, 2010c), the definition of health disparities is "differences in the incidence, prevalence, mortality and burden of diseases and other adverse health conditions that exist among specific population groups in the United States" (para. 1). The Agency for Healthcare Research and Quality (AHRQ, n.d.) considers these **priority populations** in terms of research, policy, support, and funding to include women; children; racial and ethnic minorities; the elderly; low-income; inner-city; rural; and those with special health care needs, such as those who have disabilities, need chronic care, or need end-of-life health care. Also recognized on the federal level, health disparities occur among lesbian, gay, bisexual, and transgender (LGBT) individuals, but limited data collection diminishes recognition of the full extent of the issue.

Outside the U.S., in countries such as the United Kingdom and Australia, the terms **health inequality** or **health inequity** are more commonly used. An inequality refers to conditions being unequal, whereas an inequity signifies a subjective value judgment of or unjustness. The ethical judgment of the fairness of a health disparity and whether one is avoidable leads to the sometimes subjective nature of the term. Most experts would agree that a **health disparity** signifies a difference in access, utilization, quality of care, health status, health environment, or health outcome between groups.

Some of the most striking disparities include shorter life expectancy and higher rates of substance abuse, infant mortality, and birth defects, as well as a higher incidence of diseases such as asthma, cancer, diabetes, stroke, cardiovascular disease, sexually transmitted diseases, and mental illness, when comparing a reference group to other populations in the U.S. The U.S. Department of Health and Human Services, Office of Minority Health; the Centers for Disease Control and Prevention, National Center for Health Statistics; and the National Institutes of Health have published numerous reports and important data on health disparities; the following are but a few examples.

- *Diabetes*—Diabetes affects nearly 26 million Americans (8.3% of the population) and about 79 million adults (35%) are at risk of developing diabetes. Racial and ethnic minorities have a higher burden of the disease, worse control of diabetes, and are more likely to experience complications (for example, the death rate from diabetes among Hispanics is 50% higher than for non-Hispanic whites). Among American Indians/Native Americans, 17.5% of the population has diabetes, and research continues as to why this group has such a high risk, with contributing factors such as genetics and the environment (U.S. Food and Drug Administration, 2014).

- *Infant mortality*—Among African Americans, the infant mortality rate is 2.3 times higher than non-Hispanic whites. African American infants are almost four times as likely to die due to complications related to low birth weight as compared to white infants (Office of Minority Health, 2014c).

- *Heart disease and stroke*—Heart disease is the leading cause of death in the U.S., and racial and ethnic minorities and individuals with low socioeconomic status are greatly affected. African American adults are 40% more likely to have high blood pressure, but half as likely as whites to have it under control (NIH, 2010a; Office of Minority Health, 2014b). African American adults are twice as likely to have a stroke when compared to white adults and death rates are higher as well (Office of Minority Health, 2014d).

- *Cancer*—Cancer deaths vary by gender, race, and ethnicity. In general, whites have higher survival rates than many racial and ethnic groups for cancers. Asian Americans suffer disproportionately higher rates of stomach and liver cancers (Office of Minority Health, 2013b).

- *Mental health*—American Indians and Alaska Natives suffer disproportionately from mental health disorders (nervousness, restlessness), and suicide is the second leading cause of death in those between the ages of 10 and 34 in this population (Office of Minority Health, 2013a).

- *Suicide*—LGBT youth are at increased risk for suicidal thoughts, behaviors, attempts, and suicide. A nationally representative study of adolescents in grades seven through 12 found these individuals to be more than twice as likely to have attempted suicide as their heterosexual peers (Russell, 2001).

- *Eye disease*—Researchers have found Latinos develop visual impairment and blindness at the highest rate of any ethnic group in the country, when compared with estimates from other U.S. population-based studies (National Eye Institute, 2010, NIH, 2010d). Retinopathy, cataracts, and glaucoma found in this population are often related to the presence of diabetes.

- *HIV and AIDS*—Racial and ethnic minorities are disproportionately affected by the AIDS epidemic. "African Americans comprised 13% of the U.S. population in 2007, but accounted for nearly half of persons living with HIV/AIDS. HIV/AIDS rates (cases per 100,000) were 77 among Black/African Americans, 35 among Native Hawaiians/Other Pacific Islanders, 28 among Hispanics, 13 among American Indians/Alaska Natives, 9.2 among whites and 7.7 among Asian Americans" (NIH, 2010a, para 7).

As illustrated by the preceding examples, health disparities can be measured by comparing the health of one group to a reference group, although who should be included in the comparison group is often debatable. Another complicating factor in health disparities is the fact that knowledge of *why* they exist is complicated. The causes are multifactorial, but the largest contributors are related to **social determinants** outside the health care delivery system. These include living or working conditions, geographic isolation, income and socioeconomic status, education, and access to insurance. Access to health insurance is often identified as one of the most serious contributing factors in better health outcomes. Of the 45.7 million non-elderly Americans without health insurance in 2008 (prior to the implementation of the Affordable Care Act), more than half of the citizens affected were racial and ethnic minorities (Thomas & James, 2009). Researchers have found a statistically and economically significant relationship between insurance coverage stability and access to care (Buchmueller, Orzol, & Shore-Sheppard, 2014). Age, race, ethnicity, sexual orientation, biology, genetics, individual behaviors, health beliefs, and attitudes all may play a complex interrelated role in health disparities. Separating the underlying social determinants from the individual and medical issues is difficult with health disparities. The complicated interrelationships among these variables and their causal contributions continue to be investigated.

Addressing health disparities is important from a social justice standpoint, but also to improve the overall health of the U.S. population. Vulnerable populations have higher rates of health conditions and experience worse health outcomes. According to one report by the Kaiser Family Foundation (2012), one benefit of addressing health disparities is a decrease in overall costs because 30% of direct medical costs for Blacks, Hispanics, and Asian Americans are excess costs due to health inequities.

Cultural competence is one strategy to begin to counter health disparities and to drive toward equity in health and health care. It is just one competency among many needed by health care managers to be proficient in the workplace. Health care managers must evaluate whether the delivery of care is aligned with the program or institutional priorities related to the health outcomes of the populations they serve. Similar to health disparities, the term "cultural competence" has many definitions, interpretations, and limitations. In 1989, the seminal work of Cross and colleagues established a foundation for the discipline and provided a definition of cultural competence. Since then, the definition has been adapted and modified; however, the core concepts remain applicable today. Cross defined **cultural competence** as a set of congruent behaviors, attitudes, and policies that come together in a system or agency or among professionals and enable the system, agency, or professions to work effectively in cross-cultural situations (Cross, Bazron, Dennis, & Isaacs, 1989). According to the National Center for Cultural Competence (n.d.), cultural competence requires that organizations have a defined set of values and principles and demonstrate behaviors, attitudes, policies, and structures that enable them to work effectively cross-culturally. "Cultural competency helps organizations work effectively in cross-cultural situations and provide the best possible service to clients from various racial and ethnic backgrounds and who speak different languages," according to the Office of Minority Health (2014a, para 2). According to The Joint Commission, cultural competence requires organizations and their personnel to do the following: (1) value diversity, (2) assess themselves, (3) manage the dynamics of difference, (4) acquire and institutionalize cultural knowledge, and (5) adapt to diversity and the cultural contexts of individuals and communities served (The Joint Commission, 2014). A **culturally competent organization** is vigilant and addresses disparities in triage, screening, prescriptions, procedures, recommendations, and health outcomes. Generally, cultural competency refers to the ability and willingness to respond respectfully and effectively to people of all cultures, classes, races, ages, sexual orientations, geographic regions, ethnic backgrounds, and religions in a manner that recognizes and values the dignity and worth of all. Cultural competence includes both interpersonal and organizational interventions for overcoming differences.

Concerns with the term cultural competence are prevalent among practitioners, public health experts, and sociologists. One concern is whether anyone or any organization can truly be culturally competent because culture changes over time and the attitudes and skills needed change as well. Another limitation of the term is the implication that prior to training or at some point in time, people may have been culturally incompetent, obviously a negatively charged sentiment. Cultural competence is really a growth process or a journey, not a destination. It is a continuum starting with cultural destructiveness and blindness leading to competence and then proficiency (Rose, 2011). It is challenging to demonstrate that individuals have achieved cultural competence because it is extremely difficult to measure. While many have published surveys or scales to measure this important ability, a 20-year study of cultural competency measures published between 1980 and 2003 found that *none* of the instruments had been validated (Gozu et al., 2007). Among nurses, 11 instruments were found to examine cultural competence in one study. The reviewed instruments measured nurses' self-perceptions or self-reported level of cultural competence, but offered no objective measure of culturally competent care from a patient's perspective, which was viewed as problematic (Loftin, Hartin, Branson, & Reyes, 2013). Other terms that are sometimes used include "culturally effective care," "cultural conditioning," "cultural sensitivity," "cultural humility," or "cultural excellence training." The term preferred by this author is **cultural proficiency**, because just like other skills, cultural proficiency needs continual updating. The terms cultural competence and cultural proficiency will be used interchangeably here. No matter what terminology is used and whether it can be ultimately attained, the underlying principles of cultural competence for health care managers remain salient and timely. Health care organizations and health care professionals must journey toward delivering culturally effective care and work toward reduction in disparities.

CHANGING U.S. DEMOGRAPHICS AND PATIENT POPULATIONS

In 2012, there were more than 300 million people living in the U.S. and projections indicate that the country will reach 400 million in 2051. According to the U.S. Census Bureau, by midcentury, the population will be much older. Between 2012 and 2060, the population aged 65 and older is expected to more than double (U.S. Census Bureau, 2012). Also, the nation will be more racially and ethnically diverse. In 1900, the U.S. had a population of 76 million and the percentage of whites was 90% or more in all but two states (Hobbs & Stoop, 2002). "The U.S. will become a plurality nation, where the non-Hispanic white population remains the largest single group, but no group is in the majority" (U.S. Census Bureau, 2012). The U.S. is projected to become a **majority-minority nation** for the first time in 2043. Now 37% of the U.S. population, minorities are projected to comprise the majority, representing 57% of the population in 2060, as shown in Figure 14-1. The Hispanic

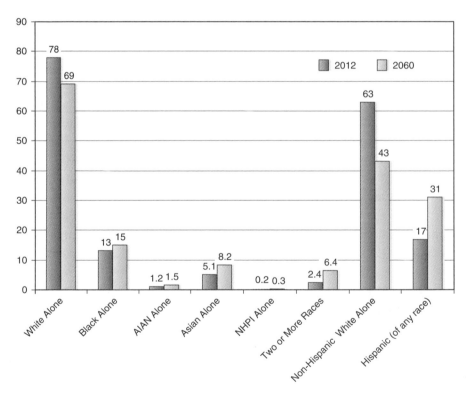

AIAN = American Indian and Alaska Native; NHPI = Native Hawaiian and Other Pacific Islander

FIGURE 14-1 Changing Demographics—Population by Race and Hispanic Origin: 2012 and 2060

Reproduced from: U.S. Census, 2012.

American (fastest growing group), Asian American, American Indian and Alaska Native, and African American populations are all expected to increase (U.S. Census Bureau, 2012).

As the U.S. becomes older and more diverse, health care systems will increasingly see patients of every race, ethnicity, age, culture, language, sexual orientation, and language proficiency. Patients may present symptoms differently from textbooks, may not speak or read English as their primary language, or may have varying beliefs and attitudes about health and illness. Health care organizations and health care managers must be ready to understand and address these issues.

ADDRESSING HEALTH DISPARITIES BY FOSTERING CULTURAL COMPETENCE IN HEALTH CARE ORGANIZATIONS

Until the 1980s and 1990s, the field of health disparities and cultural competency was ill-defined. In 1986, the Office of Minority Health was established by the U.S. Department of Health and Human Services and was reauthorized by the Affordable Care Act. Its focus is on public health programs affecting American Indians and Alaska Natives, Asian Americans, Blacks/African Americans, Hispanics/Latinos, Native Hawaiians, and other Pacific Islanders. In 1992, the results of a study conducted by the American College of Healthcare Executives (ACHE) on diversity in health care management spurred the creation of the Institute for Diversity in Health Management, an affiliate of the American Hospital Association (AHA). In 1998, the First National Conference on Quality Health Care for Culturally Diverse Populations was held in New York City. These served as watershed events because they placed the issues of health and health care delivery for vulnerable and underserved populations front and center on the national agenda.

In 2000, the U.S. Congress passed Public Law 106-525, also known as the "Minority Health and Health Disparities Research and Education Act." This established the National Center on Minority Health and Health Disparities to lead, coordinate, support, and assess NIH efforts to eliminate health disparities, and in this early work, a definition of health disparity was determined, as previously mentioned (NIH 2010b, 2010c). In 2010, the National Center on Minority Health and Health Disparities (NCMHD) transitioned to the National Institute on Minority Health and Health Disparities (NIMHD). This organization established the National Standards on Culturally and Linguistically Appropriate Services (CLAS) in 2000 and these were updated in the fall of 2010, in order to reflect the past decade's advancements, expand their scope, and improve their clarity to ensure understanding and implementation, as shown in Table 14-1. These guidelines are intended to inform, guide, and facilitate culturally and linguistically appropriate practices across the continuum of health care services.

TABLE 14-1 National Standards on Culturally and Linguistically Appropriate Services (CLAS)

Principal Standard:

1. Provide effective, equitable, understandable, and respectful quality care and services that are responsive to diverse cultural health beliefs and practices, preferred languages, health literacy, and other communication needs.

Governance, Leadership, and Workforce:

2. Advance and sustain organizational governance and leadership that promotes CLAS and health equity through policy, practices, and allocated resources.

3. Recruit, promote, and support a culturally and linguistically diverse governance, leadership, and workforce that are responsive to the population in the service area.

4. Educate and train governance, leadership, and workforce in culturally and linguistically appropriate policies and practices on an ongoing basis.

Communication and Language Assistance:

5. Offer language assistance to individuals who have limited English proficiency and/or other communication needs, at no cost to them, to facilitate timely access to all health care and services.

6. Inform all individuals of the availability of language assistance services clearly and in their preferred language, verbally and in writing.

7. Ensure the competence of individuals providing language assistance, recognizing that the use of untrained individuals and/or minors as interpreters should be avoided.

8. Provide easy-to-understand print and multimedia materials and signage in the languages commonly used by the populations in the service area.

Engagement, Continuous Improvement, and Accountability:

9. Establish culturally and linguistically appropriate goals, policies, and management accountability, and infuse them throughout the organization's planning and operations.

10. Conduct ongoing assessments of the organization's CLAS-related activities and integrate CLAS-related measures into measurement and continuous quality improvement activities.

11. Collect and maintain accurate and reliable demographic data to monitor and evaluate the impact of CLAS on health equity and outcomes and to inform service delivery.

12. Conduct regular assessments of community health assets and needs and use the results to plan and implement services that respond to the cultural and linguistic diversity of populations in the service area.

13. Partner with the community to design, implement, and evaluate policies, practices, and services to ensure cultural and linguistic appropriateness.

14. Create conflict and grievance resolution processes that are culturally and linguistically appropriate to identify, prevent, and resolve conflicts or complaints.

15. Communicate the organization's progress in implementing and sustaining CLAS to all stakeholders, constituents, and the general public.

Office of Minority Health, n.d. Retrieved from http://minorityhealth.hhs.gov/omh/browse.aspx?lvl=2&lvlid=53

During the past three decades (1990, 2000, 2010), *Healthy People* has served as an agenda for public health in the U.S. Created by the U.S. Department of Health and Human Services, *Healthy People* is an initiative to provide science-based, measurable objectives for achieving health equity for all Americans. *Healthy People 2020* delineates a set of health objectives (600 objectives with 1,200 measures) for the nation to achieve. These objectives include eliminating health disparities, addressing social determinants of health, improving access to health services, improving the dissemination of health information, strengthening public health services, reducing or eliminating diseases, and other new objectives such as addressing the health of lesbian, gay, bisexual, and transgender individuals (Centers for Disease Control and Prevention, 2011; U.S. Department of Health and Human Services, 2015).

With the establishment of these standards and a public health agenda, the field of health disparities and cultural competency has evolved significantly—new data emerges and new solutions are proposed. Grants have been provided to support innovation and research, standards and policies have been adopted at state and national levels, and accrediting bodies and professional associations have established common practices. All medical schools in the U.S. are now required by the Association of American Medical Colleges to integrate cultural competence into their curricula. Similarly, residency programs are also adhering to cultural competence standards of the American Council on Graduate Medical Education, and the American Nurses Association supports the agenda as well (Betancourt, Green, Carillo, & Park, 2005). The AHA has also joined forces to improve care and eliminate disparities for minority populations. One AHA study reported that most hospitals are actively collecting patient demographic data—97% collect data on race, 94% on ethnicity, and 95% on primary language. In addition, 86% of hospitals provide cultural competency training to clinical staff, while nearly 65% require all employees to attend diversity training. Nearly one-third of hospital patients were from a minority group. The AHA suggests that hospitals and health systems should:

1. Increase the collection and use of race, ethnicity, and language preference data to identify where disparities exist;
2. Increase cultural competency training to ensure caregivers and other staff have a deeper understanding of diverse patients and their individual needs; and
3. Increase leadership and governance diversity (AHA, 2014).

The recommendations on data collection were reinforced by the Institute of Medicine (2014) report, *Capturing Social and Behavioral Domains in Electronic Health Records, Phase 2*, which had been undertaken as part of the Affordable Care Act's mandate to reduce health disparities. This calls for adding these and other data to the EHR (see Chapter 8 for details).

The National Committee for Quality Assurance (NCQA), which accredits and certifies health care organizations, specifically health insurance plans, released its Multicultural Health Care Standards in 2010 (NCQA, 2010). These standards pertain to data collection of race/ethnicity and language; language services; cultural responsiveness and accountability; and quality improvement, including using data to improve culturally and linguistically appropriate services. In a similar manner, The Joint Commission developed patient-centered communication standards to advance the issues of effective communication, cultural competence, and patient- and family-centered care. The standards for hospitals were fully implemented in July 2012 and are published in the *Comprehensive Accreditation Manual for Hospitals (CAMH)*. The standards address topics such as qualifications for language interpreters and translators, identifying and addressing patient communication needs, collecting patient race and ethnicity data, patient access to a support individual, and non-discrimination in care (The Joint Commission, 2014). Health care managers should monitor both The Joint Commission's and NCQA's requirements to develop or modify organization-specific initiatives to ensure compliance. In addition to complying with standards, mandates, and recommendations, driving toward cultural competence in a health care organization is simply a good business practice.

Cultural proficiency is becoming a standard of care in delivering quality service. The Provider's Guide to Quality and Culture, a joint project of the Management Sciences for Health and the U.S. Department of Health and Human Services' Health Resources and Services Administration and Bureau of Primary Health Care, assists health care organizations in providing high-quality, culturally competent services to multiethnic populations (Manager's Electronic Resource Center, 2008). A toolkit is also available from the AHA and provides a framework and resources to help hospital leaders accelerate the elimination of health care disparities and ensure their leadership teams and board members reflect the communities they serve (AHA, 2015). Initiatives addressing cultural competence have the potential to make care more effective, as well as improve staff productivity, customer satisfaction, and market share for hospitals or medical practices.

BEST PRACTICES

Health care managers must recognize the issues of health disparities and build a framework to link interventions to eliminating disparities despite the fact that much remains to be learned about the most effective interventions. Cultural proficiency requires that organizations and interdisciplinary staff value diversity and manage the dynamics of difference. Health care organizations should pursue initiatives to acquire the awareness, knowledge, and skills in continual pursuit of greater cultural competence and operational excellence. Essential components of a culturally proficient health care organization include:

1. A diverse health care workforce;
2. Management practices including supportive leadership, organizational values and culture, and appropriate human resource policies;
3. Assessment;
4. Education and training for all staff;
5. Effective multilingual services and support materials;
6. System capacities such as evaluation and research data collection for tracking health outcomes; and
7. The ability to adapt to the context of and respond to and engage the community served.

The Health Care Workforce

Approximately 13.5% of physicians identify as Black or African-American, American Indian or Alaska Native, and Hispanic or Latino; only 14% of physician assistants identify as nonwhite; and minority nurses make up only 16.8% of the total nurse population (Association of American Medical Colleges, 2015; Loftin et al., 2013). It is generally recognized that a more diverse clinical health care workforce is an important component in the delivery of quality, competent care throughout the nation. However, moving towards greater diversity is not keeping pace with the nation's demographic shift, and this includes health care managers and executives. In 1992, the ACHE joined with the National Association of Health Services Executives (NAHSE), an association of African American health care executives, to investigate the career advancement of their members. The study found that minorities held less than 1% of top management positions, although they represented more than 20% of hospital employees. It also documented that African American health care executives made less money, held lower positions, and had less job satisfaction than their white counterparts. A 1997 follow-up study, expanded to include Latinos and Asians, found that, although the gap had narrowed in some areas, not much had changed (Institute for Diversity in Health Management, 2012). A study by Weil (2009) confirmed these findings; however, newer data is certainly needed. A more recent survey by the AHA found minorities comprise 14% of hospital trustees, 12% of executive leadership, and 17% of first- and mid-management positions (AHA, 2014). While positive results are occurring, continued progress is required towards matching clinical and management employees with a diverse community. Given U.S. demographic trends, achieving greater diversity in the health care workforce will continue to be a challenge for leaders. For individuals, organizations, and society, the reported benefits are to better reflect the makeup of increasingly diverse communities; to enhance the patient experience; to become a more culturally competent workforce; to allow greater access to care for the underserved; to foster research in neglected areas; to enrich the pool of talent to meet future needs of society; and to generate cost savings by decreasing turnover, absenteeism, and the number of lawsuits (Cordova, Beaudin, & Iwanabe, 2010). The Institute for Diversity in Health Management (http://www.diversityconnection.org) is a good resource for strategies, programs, and leadership initiatives in the area of workforce diversity. The ultimate goal is to have the entire health care workforce in the U.S. reflect the makeup of the communities served.

Management Practices

Cultural competence needs to be incorporated into many aspects of the health care organization, particularly to be embraced by the leadership, human resource management, administration, and service delivery. It requires cross-disciplinary health care professionals who are sensitive and respectful of others to collaborate and advance the cause of cultural proficiency within an organization. Cultural proficiency means being able to understand the organizational forces that either support or negate achieving cultural sensitivity. Management must ensure that there is not differential access to resources, opportunities, and influence. In order for managers to be change agents, they must understand the implications of power and privilege within the institution.

First and foremost, the leaders of an organization need to be role models in cultural sensitivity and establish a supportive culture for diversity and cultural competence initiatives. Health care executives should incorporate underlying principles into the mission and vision of the organization and place initiatives in the organization's strategic plan to underscore their importance. Assessing the return-on-investment of cultural proficiency training can be a worthwhile exercise. Researchers have examined the positive business benefits of diversity management in health care (Dreachslin, 2007). Although some benefits can be intangible and others can be long term and difficult to quantify, specific measures, such as better customer satisfaction, enhanced employee productivity, greater market share, or fewer malpractice claims, can be evidence supporting the business rationale. Managers need to be wary of falling into the trap of cultural proficiency training becoming the "fad" project of the month. This important competency development must be a long-term commitment of the management team in order to make progress on the issue.

Human resource policies play a key role in addressing diversity in the workforce. Health care managers must ensure that salary, benefit, recruitment, and promotion practices are fair to all regardless of age, race, gender, sexual orientation, religion, or ethnic background. Racially and ethnically diverse employees represented a small percentage of the health care management workforce in one study, but the author suggested that organizations offer residencies and fellowships, embrace mentoring, encourage transparency in organizational decisions, develop programs that diversify managerial ranks, and promote professional societies' policy statements on equal employment (Weil, 2009).

Structural barriers to care sometimes arise when patients are facing a complex, bureaucratic organization. Even relatively simple changes like expanding hours of operation to match work schedules or adding questions about gender identification and sexual orientation to intake forms can bring greater access and acceptance. The clinical patient–provider encounter must be appropriately cross-cultural. Studies have shown communication between providers and patients is directly related to patient satisfaction, adherence to treatment regimens, and ultimately outcomes (Betancourt et al., 2005). Organizations should design and implement patient services that offer equal access and are nondiscriminatory, tailored to match the needs of the community they serve, and determined by client-preferred choices. Managers must monitor the impact of these programs; developing reports to examine inequalities in care may be a good management practice. The National Center for Cultural Competence translates policy into specific practices and provides helpful advice for programs and personnel in health care delivery.

Assessment

To address disparities and work toward cultural sensitivity in a health care organization, assessment must occur on several personal and organizational levels. The first step is self-reflection. Health care leaders should examine their own personal biases in order to become role models. Informal self-assessment of one's own attitudes and behaviors should include questions such as: What is my worldview and what are my biases? Am I aware of my prejudices toward other cultural groups? Do I seek out encounters with individuals who are different from me? How do I react when someone does not speak English? An online assessment tool has been designed by the National Center for Cultural Competence (n.d.) for health care practitioners. Although not designed for health care managers, the tool can be used as part of the learning experience for all individuals working in the health care system, as well as another tool designed for clinical investigators (O'Brien et al., 2006). An easy-to-use assessment tool for executives, staff, and providers has been prepared by a health educator in her textbook (Rose, 2011). Other assessment tools are often used in conjunction with consultants in this field. These instruments and their results should be interpreted with care, as they provide a snapshot of an individual at that particular moment in time on a test and may not reflect the individual's real-world application of the needed information. After examining these issues on a personal level, the organization must also reflect on and assess whether it appropriately reflects and serves its community.

On an organizational level, assessment in terms of tracking patient data on race, ethnicity, and language is currently being performed by 78% of hospitals in the U.S. Although some cite limitations due to self-reporting or observational reporting, the data are a start-ing point. Sadly, less than 20% of surveyed hospitals report tying patient race and ethnicity information to patient outcomes and quality improvements (Armada & Hubbard, 2010). If health care organizations want to be top-notch, then they need to keep racial, ethnic, and language assessment data at the forefront of management's attention. After all, how can an organization deliver best practices in clinical care if they don't know who their patients are? Toolkits and guides are available for collecting racial and ethnic data in a culturally competent manner (Martin, 2007).

The ACHE partnered with three other national organizations to develop a *Diversity and Cultural Proficiency Assessment Tool for Leaders* (AHA, 2004). This tool helps orga-nizations address the issue of cultural competence and presents case studies of successful diversity and cultural proficiency programs from America's hospitals. Action steps are pre-sented as well. Other assessment tools are available for health care organizations (Andrulis, Delbanco, Avakan, & Shaw-Taylor, n.d.).

An assessment can provide a tool to understand what an organization does well in delivering care to diverse populations, where there are gaps, and how it can determine an agenda for improving services. Most importantly, assessment can lead to a dialogue on diversity and cultural proficiency within the organization. The very act of conducting an assessment indicates to the workforce that the organization values diversity and wishes to increase its cultural competence.

Education and Training

Workplace education centers on building knowledge, skills, and attitudes surrounding cul-tural competence. Currently, there is no consensus on how cultural competence should be taught even among medical school faculty; considerable variability exists in the design and implementation of cross-cultural education. Building awareness and changing behaviors are recognized as crucial, regardless of the approach. (Curtis, Dreachslin, & Sinioris, 2007). Interactive and stimulating courses can be employed to train all health care person-nel about health disparities and cultural competence. Learning about cultural competence is not easy. Culture happens within a context; memorizing simple facts about disparities can lead to stereotyping. Health care professionals who have typically been trained in the absolute of scientific methodology sometimes have a difficult time learning how to tolerate gray areas, particularly in human interactions. Cultural proficiency implies being open and accepting ambiguity. Training can include watching videos or having speakers present on health disparities or cultural competence. Former patients who have encountered situa-tions of intolerance or professionals who have participated in health care for underserved groups make for interesting presentations. In addition to the didactics, opportunities should be provided for self-reflection, practicing cross-cultural communications through role playing, and developing conflict resolution skills with observation and feedback. Some institutions embrace mentoring as a way to encourage cultural sensitivity or use consultants to introduce new training programs. The training should be documented and evaluated for effectiveness using outcome measurement tools. Cultural proficiency training in health care should be for everyone regardless of an individual's background.

Multilingual Services

According to the AHA, 80% of members frequently encountered an individual with limited English proficiency, 43% reported daily encounters, and 20% weekly encounters (Armada & Hubbard, 2010). To understand an organization's starting place in terms of competency in this area, the American Medical Association (AMA, n.d.) has developed a self-assessment tool for patient-centered communications called the *C-CAT*, the *Communication Climate Assessment Toolkit*. The goal is to help physicians and hospitals assess their organizations to determine how well they communicate with diverse patient populations. It focuses on those groups at risk of poor health outcomes because of vulnerability to ineffective communication during patient encounters.

Health care professionals need to be able to effectively communicate and convey information in an easily understood manner to a diverse audience, including people of limited or no English proficiency; those who are illiterate or disabled; and those who are deaf or hard of hearing. **Linguistic competency** requires staff to be able to interact with and respond to the community they serve. AHRQ (2014) released explicit standardized instructions for taking medications in six languages that improve patients' understanding and medication adherence and possibly reduce errors. Two publications that may be helpful to health care managers are the AMA's (n.d.) *Office Guide to Communicating with Limited English Proficient Patients* and *Bridging the Language Divide: A Pocket Guide to Working Effectively with Interpreters in Health Care Settings* (Grey, Yehieli, & Rodriguez-Kurtovic, 2006). Health care organizations must have the policies, practices, and resources to support this capacity. Services need to be delivered in the preferred language of the population served. Those qualified to be medical interpreters should be bilingual with superior language proficiency, have studied medical vocabulary, have training in interpreting techniques, and be culturally sensitive. Written materials need to be modified to meet the needs, reading abilities, and preferences of the community. When necessary, they should be translated from English into other languages. Interpretation and translation services need to comply with federal, state, and local mandates as well as the requirements of accrediting agencies. In addition to meeting compliance standards, language services may improve the outcome of the patient/provider encounter, decrease medical errors, equalize health care utilization, and increase patient and provider satisfaction. Consumers of health care services should be engaged in evaluating language and communication services of the health care organization to ensure quality and satisfaction. An organization should monitor its performance regularly using structure, process, and outcome measures, and make appropriate adjustments as needed.

Evaluation

Interventions addressing health disparities and fostering cultural proficiency should be evaluated for their impact. Questions to be addressed include: Did the intervention achieve its goal? Did it affect the process of care? Was utilization improved? Did it affect patient behavior or satisfaction? Was practitioner, manager, or patient satisfaction improved? How were the patient health outcomes impacted? Was the cost-effectiveness of delivery altered? What were the tangible and intangible benefits to the organization? The evaluation of interventions can provide managers with insights about how to address health disparities and improve cultural proficiency within their organizations.

Research

Research findings are used to justify evidence-based practice in health care. In the area of culturally competent interventions, the research has not kept pace in terms of documenting disparities and the outcomes of implementing new measures. Greater collection and reporting on patient data related to race, ethnicity, sexual orientation, and culture are needed, particularly identifying sources of disparities. The Office of Minority Health and AHRQ both support investigations on how cultural competency initiatives affect health care delivery and health outcomes. Other organizations, such as the National Center for Healthcare Leadership, are investigating the impact of improved culturally competent health care leadership on patient safety and other measures of organizational performance. This additional research is required to document the impact of culturally competent health care interventions and their outcomes. In 2006, the federal government established the Federal Collaboration on Health Disparities Research in the Office of Minority Health, with the purpose of supporting and disseminating research aimed at reducing or eliminating disparities (Rashid et al., 2009). Organizations on national and local levels must continue to pursue research to support an evidence-based approach for cultural competency interventions in health care and eliminate inequities in health.

Community Outreach and Engagement

The environment in which people live and work, as well as their lifestyles and behaviors, can influence the incidence of illness within a population. A community can achieve health improvements when people work together to effect change. Involving members of the community is a cornerstone of public health improvement, particularly on important issues such as obesity and smoking cessation. Consequently, a health care organization should demonstrate inclusivity with the community it supports. **Community engagement** is the process of working collaboratively towards well-being with and through groups of people affiliated by geography, special interest, or a common cause. It includes exchanging information, ideas, and resources between individuals, community members, nonprofit organizations, and corporations. Participation is essential for community engagement including education, input, advisory, and partnership. To pursue community engagement, health care managers may put into action a network of concerned individuals, a public health promotion campaign, the use of a focus group or an advisory panel, a community health fair, or employment of community health workers (NIH, 2011).

ADDRESSING HEALTH DISPARITIES BY ENHANCING PUBLIC POLICY

Public health experts would contend that a public discussion among policy makers is needed to address whether health inequalities can be reduced or eliminated. Many would argue that improvements in social determinants may significantly affect health outcomes in the nation. By working to establish policies that positively influence social and economic conditions such as eliminating toxic exposure, creating safe spaces for recreation, or enabling access to nutritious foods, we can improve health for many people in ways that can be sustained over time. Improving the conditions in which we live, learn, work, and play through sound public policy will create a healthier workforce, population, and society. One organization that works to influence the public discourse on health disparities and social determinants is the American Public Health Association (APHA). This member-driven organization develops statements on key public health topics to shape policy for legislation and regulation. For example, in 2014, a policy statement was developed on the reduction of bullying to address health disparities among lesbian, gay, bisexual and transgender (LGBT) youth (APHA, 2014). Freudenberg and Olden (2010) have proposed specific public policies to decrease disparities, including:

- *Improve access to primary care*—Lack of access to primary care has been reported to contribute to health disparities. A change in the U.S. health care system toward greater investment in primary care, including screening and counseling, could address the burden of chronic disease in underserved populations.
- *Enforce consumer and environmental protection laws*—Consumer and environmental policies leave vulnerable populations more exposed to risks. For example, manufacturers of unhealthy products like tobacco or high-fat fried foods have directed their marketing efforts at vulnerable populations, contributing to chronic disease and exacerbating health disparities.

Policy is an important component of resolving health disparities and so is the obligation of health care providers, nonprofit associations, and government agencies to be responsive to the communities they serve. Even relatively simple steps can be taken, such as ensuring hospitals have respectful visitation policies and that visitation rights are not denied based on race, color, national origin, religion, sex, sexual orientation, gender identity, or disability. Health for all is a complex and complicated undertaking, and it can only be achieved by creating a culturally proficient workforce within these organizations. The interrelationships are illustrated in Figure 14-2. Health care managers can help the nation move toward the long-term goal of health equity for all Americans.

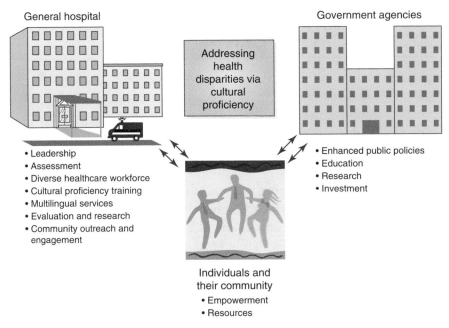

FIGURE 14-2 Interrelationships Needed for Cultural Proficiency

OPPORTUNITIES FOR RESEARCH ON HEALTH DISPARITIES AND CULTURAL PROFICIENCY

As the U.S. grows older and more diverse, health disparities and cultural proficiency will continue to be twin issues, joined by the need for recruitment and retention of more diverse health care professionals who are culturally sensitive and willing to become proficient. There is an urgent need for development and maintenance of databases of current applied research on addressing health disparities and improving cultural proficiency. Many of the resources used in writing this chapter also include extensive research holdings and data sets, which are available to students and academic researchers. Herewith is a partial listing of these resources.

- Agency for Healthcare Research and Quality (AHRQ);
- American Public Health Association (APHA);
- Centers for Disease Control and Prevention (CDC);
- *Healthy People 2020*;
- Hospital Research and Educational Trust (HRET);
- Institute for Diversity in Health Management (IDHM);
- Inter-university Consortium for Political and Social Research (ICPSR);
- Kaiser Family Foundation;
- Manager's Electronic Resource Center;
- National Center for Cultural Competence (NCCC);
- National Center for Health Statistics;
- National Committee for Quality Assurance;
- National Institute on Minority Health & Health Disparities;
- Office of Minority Health;
- The Joint Commission;
- The Robert Wood Johnson Foundation; and
- U.S. Census Bureau.

You will have an abundance of data and research resources at your fingertips at any one of these websites. However, more research is needed and you will be called upon to contribute.

CONCLUSION

Major gaps exist in understanding the causal relationships in complicated health disparities, and more research is needed to support the cost and quality improvements from cultural competency initiatives. Health care managers who are committed to the issues of diversity, equity, and equality need to be aware of and implement best practices in cultural competency. Health care managers must take leadership roles within their institutions to facilitate developing cultural proficiency within their staffs. Although cultural proficiency alone may not solve the problems of health disparities, managers who understand the diversity of their communities will be better able to serve diverse patient populations and ensure that their organizations both reflect and support the communities they serve.

DISCUSSION QUESTIONS

1. Explain why cultural competence alone cannot address health disparities.

2. What are the benefits of implementing programs to address cultural competence within a health care organization? What are the costs of *not* implementing such programs?

3. What are some of the limitations of the term "cultural competence"? Which term do you prefer and why?

4. Describe a time when you witnessed or experienced cultural incompetence in the delivery of health care. Knowing what you now know, what do you think could have been done to avoid that incident?

5. Describe how you would put in place initiatives for cultural proficiency at an inner city pediatric clinic.

6. How do you convince a reluctant health care professional to participate in cultural proficiency training?

7. What public policies might help to address health inequities or the social determinants of health?

Cases in Chapter 18 that are related to this chapter include:

- Are We Culturally Aware or Not?
- Where Do You Live? Health Disparities Across the United States

Case study guides are available in the online Instructor's Materials.

REFERENCES

Agency for Healthcare Research and Quality (AHRQ). (n.d.). *Priority populations*. Retrieved from http://www.ahrq.gov/health-care-information/priority-populations/index.html

Agency for Healthcare Research and Quality (AHRQ). (2014, December*). Explicit and standardized prescription medicine instructions*. Retrieved from http://www.ahrq.gov/professionals/quality-patient-safety/pharmhealthlit/prescriptionmed-instr.html

American Hospital Association (AHA). (2004). *Strategies for leadership: Does your hospital reflect the community it serves? A diversity and cultural proficiency assessment tool for leaders*. Retrieved from http://www.aha.org/aha/content/2004/pdf/diversitytool.pdf

American Hospital Association (AHA). (2014). *Diversity and disparities: A benchmark study of U.S. hospitals 2013*. Retrieved from https://aharesourcecenter.wordpress.com/category/health-care/health-disparities/

American Hospital Association (AHA). (2015, February 10). *HPOE toolkit targets health care disparities.* Retrieved from http://news.aha.org/article/hpoe-toolkit-targets-health-care-disparities

American Medical Association (AMA). (n.d.a). *C-Cat.* Retrieved from http://www.ama-assn.org/ama /pub/physician-resources/medical-ethics/the-ethical-force-program/patient-centered-communication /organizational-assessment-resources.page?

American Medical Association (AMA). (n.d.b). *Office guide to communicating with limited English proficient patients* (2nd ed.). Retrieved from http://www.nyhq.org/doc/Page.asp?PageID=DOC000306

American Public Health Association (APHA). (2014). *Public health policy statements.* Retrieved from http://www.apha.org/policies-and-advocacy/public-health-policy-statements

Andrulis, D., Delbanco, T., Avakan, L., & Shaw-Taylor, Y. (n.d.). *Conducting a cultural competence self-assessment.* Retrieved from http://www.consumerstar.org/pubs/Culturalcompselfassess.pdf

Armada, A. A., & Hubbard, M. F. (2010). Diversity in health care: Time to get real! *Frontiers of Health Services Management, 26*(3), 3–17.

Association of American Medical Colleges. (2015). *Diversity in the physician workforce: Facts and figures 2014.* Retrieved from http://aamcdiversityfactsandfigures.org/

Betancourt, J. R., Green, A. R., Carillo, J. E., & Park, E. R. (2005, March). Cultural competence and health care disparities: Key perspectives and trends. *Health Affairs, 24*(2), 499–505.

Buchmueller, T., Orzol, S. M., & Shore-Sheppard, L. (2014, February). Stability of childrens' insurance and implications for access to care: Evidence from the survey of income and program participation. *International Journal of Health Care Finance and Economics, 14*(2). Retrieved from http://www .hcfo.org/publications/stability-children%E2%80%99s-insurance-coverage-and-implications -access-care-evidence-survey-in

Centers for Disease Control and Prevention (CDC). (2011). *Healthy People 2020.* Retrieved from http ://www.cdc.gov/nchs/healthy_people/hp2020.htm

Cordova, R. D., Beaudin, C. L., & Iwanabe, K. E. (2010). Addressing diversity and moving toward equity in hospital care. *Frontiers of Health Services Management, 26*(3), 19–34.

Cross, T. L., Bazron, B. J., Dennis, K. W., & Isaacs, M. R. (1989). *Towards a culturally competent system of care* (Vol. 1). Washington, DC: CASSP Technical Assistance Center, Georgetown University Child Development Center.

Curtis, E. F., Dreachslin, J. L., & Sinioris, M. (2007). Diversity and cultural competence training in health care organizations: Hallmarks of success. *Health Care Manager, 26*(3), 255–262.

Dreachslin, J. L. (2007). Diversity management and cultural competence: Research, practice, and the business case. *Journal of Healthcare Management, 52*(2), 79–86.

Freudenberg, N., & Olden, K. (2010). Finding synergy: Reducing disparities in health by modifying multiple determinants. *American Journal of Public Health, 100*(Supp 1), S25–S29.

Gozu, A., Beach, M. C., Price,. E G., Gary, T. L., Robinson, K., Palacio, A., …Cooper, L. A. (2007). Self-administered instruments to measure cultural competence of health professionals: A systematic review. *Teaching and Learning in Medicine, 19*(2), 180–190.

Grey, M. A., Yehieli, M., & Rodriguez-Kurtovic, N. (2006). *Bridging the language divide: A pocket guide to working effectively with interpreters in health care settings.* Cedar Rapids, IA: University of Northern Iowa.

Health Resources and Services Administration (HRSA). (1995). *Medically underserved areas/populations: Guidelines for MUA and MUP designation.* Retrieved from http://www.hrsa.gov/shortage/mua /index.html

Hobbs, F., & Stoop, N. (2002). *Demographic trends in the 20th century.* U.S. Census Bureau, Census 2000. Special Reports, Series CENSR-4. Washington, DC: U.S. Government Printing Office.

Institute for Diversity in Health Management. (2012). About the institute. Retrieved from http://www .diversityconnection.org/diversityconnection/about-us/About-the-Institute.jsp

Institute of Medicine. (2014). *Capturing social and behavioral domains in electronic health records. Phase 2.* Washington, DC: National Academies Press.

Kaiser Family Foundation. (2012, December). *Focus on health care disparities: Key facts.* Retrieved from https://kaiserfamilyfoundation.files.wordpress.com/2013/01/8396.pdf

Loftin, C., Hartin, V., Branson, M., & Reyes, H. (2013). Measures of cultural competence in nurses: An integrative review. *The Scientific World Journal, 2013*, 1–11. doi:10.1155/2013/289101

Manager's Electronic Resource Center. (2008). The provider's guide to quality and culture. Retrieved from http://erc.msh.org/mainpage.cfm?file=1.0.htm&module=provider&language=English

Martin, C. (2007). *Reducing racial and ethnic disparities: Quality improvement in Medicaid managed care toolkit.* Hamilton, NJ: Center for Health Care Strategies, Inc. Retrieved from http://www .chcs.org/resource/reducing-racial-and-ethnic-disparities-quality-improvement-in-medicaid-managed -care-toolkit/

National Center for Cultural Competence. (n.d.). Cultural competence: Definition and conceptual framework. Retrieved from http://nccc.georgetown.edu/foundations/frameworks.html

National Committee for Quality Assurance (NCQA). (2010). About NCQA. Retrieved from http ://www.ncqa.org/tabid/675/Default.aspx

National Institutes of Health (NIH). (n.d.). *NIH health disparities strategic plan, fiscal years 2004–2008, Volume 1.* Retrieved from http://www.ncbi.nlm.nih.gov/books/NBK57031/

National Institutes of Health (NIH). (2010a). *Fact sheet: Health disparities.* Bethesda, MD: Author. Retrieved from http://report.nih.gov/nihfactsheets/Pdfs/HealthDisparities(NIMHD).pdf

National Institutes of Health (NIH). (2010b). National Institutes of Health statement of organization, functions, and delegations of authority. *Federal Register.* Retrieved from http://www.federalregister .gov/articles/2010/09/13/2010-22666/national-institutes-of-health-statement-of-organization -functions-and-delegations-of-authority

National Institutes of Health (NIH). (2010c). NIH announces Institute on Minority Health and Health Disparities. Retrieved from http://www.nih.gov/news/health/sep2010/nimhd-27.htm

National Institutes of Health (NIH). (2011). *Principles of community engagement* (2nd ed.). Retrieved from http://www.atsdr.cdc.gov/communityengagement/pdf/PCE_Report_508_FINAL.pdf

National Institutes of Health (NIH), National Eye Institute. (2010). *U.S. Latinos have high rates of developing vision loss and certain eye conditions.* Retrieved from https://www.nei.nih.gov/news /pressreleases/050110

O'Brien, R. L., Kosoko-Lasaki, O., Cook, C. T., Kissell, J., Peak, F., & Williams, E. H. (2006). Self-assessment of cultural attitudes and competence of clinical investigators to enhance recruitment and participation of minority populations in research. *Journal of the National Medical Association, 98*(5), 674–682.

Office of Disease Prevention and Health Promotion. (2005). *Healthy People 2010: The cornerstone for prevention*. Retrieved from: http://www.healthypeople.gov/2010/

Office of Minority Health. (n.d.). The national CLAS standards. Retrieved from http://minorityhealth.hhs.gov/omh/browse.aspx?lvl=2&lvlid=53

Office of Minority Health. (2013a). Mental health and American Indians/Alaska Natives. Retrieved from http://minorityhealth.hhs.gov/omh/browse.aspx?lvl=4&lvlID=39

Office of Minority Health. (2013b). Cancer and Asians/Pacific Islanders. Retrieved from http://minorityhealth.hhs.gov/omh/browse.aspx?lvl=4&lvlID=46

Office of Minority Health. (2014a). Cultural competency assistance. Retrieved from http://minorityhealth.hhs.gov/omh/browse.aspx?lvl=3&lvlid=31

Office of Minority Health. (2014b). Heart disease and African Americans. Retrieved from http://minorityhealth.hhs.gov/omh/browse.aspx?lvl=4&lvlid=19

Office of Minority Health. (2014c). Infant mortality and African Americans. Retrieved from http://minorityhealth.hhs.gov/omh/browse.aspx?lvl=4&lvlID=23

Office of Minority Health. (2014d). Stroke and African Americans. Retrieved from http://minorityhealth.hhs.gov/omh/browse.aspx?lvl=4&lvlid=28

Rashid, J. R., Spengler, R. F., Wagner, R. M., Skillen, E. L., Mays, R. A., Heurtin-Roberts, S., & Long, J. A. (2009). Eliminating health disparities through transdisciplinary research, cross-agency collaboration, and public participation. *American Journal of Public Health, 99*(11), 1956–1961.

Rose, P. R. (2011). *Cultural competency: For health administration and public health*. Sudbury, MA: Jones and Bartlett.

Russell, S., & Joyner, K. (2001). Adolescent sexual orientation and suicide risk: Evidence from a national study. *American Journal of Public Health, 91*, 1276–1281.

The Joint Commission. (2014). *Advancing effective communication, cultural competence, and patient-and-family-centered care: A roadmap for hospitals*. Retrieved from http://www.jointcommission.org/assets/1/6/ARoadmapforHospitalsfinalversion727.pdf

Thomas, M., & James, C. (2009). The role of health coverage for communities of color. *Kaiser Family Foundation Issue Brief*. Retrieved from https://kaiserfamilyfoundation.files.wordpress.com/2013/01/8017.pdf

U.S. Census Bureau. (2012, December 12). U.S. Census Bureau projections show a slower growing, older, more diverse nation a half century from now. *U.S. Census Bureau News*. Retrieved from http://www.census.gov/newsroom/releases/archives/population/cb12-243.html

U.S. Food and Drug Administration. (2014, March 25). Fighting diabetes' deadly impact on minorities. *FDA Consumer Health Information*. Retrieved from http://www.fda.gov/ForConsumers/ConsumerUpdates/ucm389919.htm

U.S. Department of Health and Human Services. (2015). How to use healthypeople.gov. Retrieved from https://www.healthypeople.gov/2020/about/How-To-Use-HealthyPeople.gov

Weil, P. (2009). A racial/ethnic comparison of career attainments in healthcare management: By taking action, healthcare executives can help narrow the gaps. *Healthcare Executive, 24*(6), 22–31.

Ethics and Law
Kevin D. Zeiler

LEARNING OBJECTIVES

By the end of this chapter, the student will be able to:

- Critique the distinctions and overlaps between ethics and law;
- Characterize the concepts of respect for persons, beneficence, nonmaleficence, and justice;
- Differentiate among common law, statutes, rules, regulations, and executive orders;
- Distinguish between civil and criminal law;
- Analyze the elements of a contract and describe the relationship to torts;
- Assess the types of torts;
- Appraise malpractice;
- Provide an overview of patient and provider rights and responsibilities;
- Examine some of the legal issues in managed care, biomedical care, and beginning- and end-of-life care; and
- Investigate key research data repositories for health care law and bioethics.

INTRODUCTION

Ethics and the law are often mentioned in the same breath, but for all of the instances in which they are similar, there are many ways in which they are different. In this chapter, we will discuss the meaning of each as well as how they work together and apart to form and shape the legal system in the U.S. The topics surrounding law and ethics are extremely important to the aspiring health care manager as they touch and affect the daily activities of every organization. Our discussion will begin with a definition of both ethics and law so a foundation can be laid in order to proceed more easily through the chapter.

The two categories, law and ethics, overlap, with ethical principles underlying the development of laws, but they approach the world of health care from somewhat differing perspectives. In America, laws are publicly enforced standards and rules created by courts, legislatures, executive orders, and administrative agencies. Each of those bodies has a unique process, creating laws in varying ways. There are also differences between the authority of federal and state lawmaking entities. Ethical viewpoints, on the other hand, stem primarily from family, community, and religious traditions. It is worth noting that this is how we get many of our laws; the rights and wrongs that we hold dear to our hearts often become the laws of our country. Therefore, it must be noted that those who write and enforce our laws bring their ethical beliefs to the table when making decisions affecting the law. Even though the premise behind legal decision making is to be an unbiased adjudicator, it is extremely difficult to leave your personal, ethical beliefs behind. As we have seen in such cases as that of Terri Schiavo, clashes between and among individuals' deeply held ethical principles and legal interpretations can cause major disruptions in the health care system (Dresser, 2004). Before continuing, take a look at Table 15-1 to see the ways in which law and ethics differ.

TEXTBOX 15-1. TERRI SCHIAVO CASE

Terri Schiavo suffered a heart attack in 1990 that led to a massive brain injury from a lack of oxygen. A court battle ensued and lasted nearly 16 years, dealing with issues surrounding the right to life and who had the legal right to make such decisions on behalf of Terri. Furthermore, the case addressed issues surrounding life-sustaining treatment, as well as the withdrawal of such treatment. Ultimately, Terri Schiavo died in 2005 after her feeding tube was removed.

Source: Conigliaro, 2005.

TABLE 15-1 Legal and Ethical Comparison

LEGAL	ETHICAL
Action is required by law.	No legal requirements to act, but professional organizations may require it.
Legal consequences may occur if no action is taken.	Censure by the governing body may occur if unethical behavior occurs.
Many professionals have a duty to report based on law, that is, physicians, nurses, social workers, and so on.	Ethics oftentimes helps to define the duty of care owed to a patient by a professional caregiver.
Results from numerous areas of law such as rules of professional responsibility, legislative action, court rulings, and so on.	Standards are defined by governing bodies that license professionals.
Individuals may face criminal sanctions if they deviate from the law.	Violation of standards may result in loss of license or professional privileges.

There are numerous examples like the Schiavo case, but most recently, health care reform followed this same pattern. Many believe every individual is entitled to health care, while others feel it must be earned, and in the middle, numerous constitutional and other legal precedents tug at the issue as well. In this sense, law and ethics are inseparable, but this is exactly what makes the law in the U.S. work. However, on many occasions law and ethics are at polar opposites and lead to much controversy. Without a doubt, many of you have heard the statement that it is legal, so it must be ethical. This is where the line between the two disciplines becomes distorted, and in health care organizations, questions between law and ethics force managers to make difficult decisions.

This chapter will begin by defining **ethics** and **law** as they apply to health care, and then will discuss patient, provider, and organizational rights and responsibilities. Ethical management will be examined in the broad sense so the reader can see how it affects the overall health delivery system. Also, in the wake of health care reform, the chapter will focus on how changes in ethical and legal thought have brought us to this current point in health care. Finally, ethical management will be examined, with a particular focus on managed care settings, and we will discuss some biomedical areas of ethical and legal concern and provide an overview of a few key beginning- and end-of-life issues affecting the administration of health care services. Table 15-2 illustrates the overlap of perspectives on what is legal and ethical in health care settings. There is very little absolute agreement about what actions belong in each cell, but in health care, these types of choices must be made on a daily basis.

LEGAL CONCEPTS

In order to provide a solid background for understanding the law, legal concepts will be discussed first, then we will move to a discussion of ethical considerations. Many of us may feel we have a good handle on the law in the U.S., but to fully understand the way

TABLE 15-2 Overlap of Legal and Ethical Activities

	Is it legal?		
Is it ethical?	Yes	Uncertain	No

in which law is carried out, we must learn how law is developed, what entity enforces it, and when it applies. First and foremost, we must understand what the law does. Pozgar (2007) provides a usable definition that is easy to understand. "**Laws** govern the relationships between private individuals and organizations and between both of these parties and government" (p. 1).

Thus, the law is used to help determine our actions and the actions of others when it comes to dealing with individuals, organizations, and other such entities. Look at the law as a body of official rules of conduct, subject to interpretation and change over time. In most cases, federal laws take precedence over state laws; this is called **preemption**. In other words, federal law trumps state or local law if the federal government has passed legislation in the field of law being disputed. Also, states can always be more stringent than the federal government, meaning that they may enforce laws that are "tougher" than what the federal government has mandated. In addition to the U.S. Constitution (National Archives, n.d.), each state also has a state constitution, setting the basic principles for its legal system. It is these constitutions that form the basis for legal decisions in our country.

The constitutions provide a basic understanding of what our laws are, but how can a constitution possibly cover every single issue that arises in society? The answer is that we use **interpretive justice** or **judicial authority** to set precedents in order to have a sound understanding of what the law says. As the judiciary interprets previous precedents for each particular case, they create what is known as **common law**. The common law was developed through court decisions and is used to ensure that fairness and consistency exist when similar issues are faced by the court (Pozgar, 2007). Remember, **judge-made law**, or

---

TEXTBOX 15-2. KEY TERMS

Common law: A form of law that depends on judicial decisions as opposed to legislative acts. It is often referred to as **judge-made law**.

Interpretive justice: An academic approach to defining the justice system so that legal standards can be better understood—for example, defining what the U.S. Constitution means and how it applies to specific cases.

Precedent: The term "precedent" refers to legal cases (at common law) that were decided by judges. When issues arise that are similar to those in a previous case, those same principles will be used to decide the current case.

common law, sets what is known as a **precedent**, and it is this precedent that is followed by courts in similar cases. Before we leave the common law, think about how a judge's decision not only follows the law when setting precedent, but how his or her own ethical viewpoints may help to create the law. It is easy to see how the line between law and ethics can be extremely thin.

Another way in which laws are created is by the **legislature**. Legislatures create law by passing **statutes**, which will be able to overrule common law findings for a given jurisdiction unless the judiciary finds the statutes to be unconstitutional. Think about ways in which politicians attempt to stop, for example, Supreme Court decisions that they are not happy with. Oftentimes, statutes are used to gain an advantage over precedent by creating such statutes and forcing society to abide by the new law. However, constitutional challenges exist, and the statutes must be able to pass this review. Also, laws are created by **administrative agencies**, which establish the necessary rules and regulations to carry out statutes. Administrative agencies exist to govern numerous industries in society, and health care is no exception. Administrative agencies dictate many of the ways in which health care organizations do business. Finally, **executive orders** are also used on occasion to establish a **binding policy**, rather than waiting for the legislature or courts to act.

In health care, there are numerous regulatory agencies that promulgate rules for health care organizations to follow. There are also many accrediting agencies as well as professional organizations and state and local regulations that health care must adhere to. Table 15-3 tracks a few of the larger agencies that regulate health care at the macro level. A total list of state, local, and professional organizations is too large to include here.

As if the previous variants on the law weren't confusing enough, we must also keep in mind the distinction between civil and criminal laws. **Criminal law** is concerned with wrongs against society as a whole, even if only a particular individual is harmed. There appears to be a growing willingness to use criminal law charges in the health care field, including in cases of malpractice, Medicare fraud, abortion, and the unlicensed practice of medicine. **Civil law**, on the other hand, is concerned with wrongs against a particular person or organization. It encompasses contractual violations involving voluntary agreements between two or more parties. **Torts** also fall under civil law, as a category of "wrongful acts" committed against another person without a preexisting contract, for which courts seek to determine and apply remedies. The following sections will address tort and contract law in more detail, as they are important in the delivery of health services.

TABLE 15-3 Health Care Regulatory and Accrediting Agencies

Regulatory/Accrediting Agency	Type	Charge/Web Link
The Joint Commission (TJC)	Independent, Not-for-profit	Accredits and certifies health care organizations. http://www.jointcommission.org/default.aspx
The National Committee on Quality Assurance (NCQA)	Independent, Not-for-profit	Accredits and sets standards for health plans. http://www.ncqa.org/
Agency for Healthcare Research and Quality (AHRQ)	U.S. Government Agency (DHHS)	Performs research to improve health care quality. http://www.ahrq.gov
Centers for Disease Control and Prevention (CDC)	U.S. Government Public Health Agency	Focuses on safety and health threats both foreign and domestic. http://www.cdc.gov
Department of Health and Human Services (DHHS)	U.S. Government Agency	Provides essential health and human services, and oversees many of the federal agencies listed here. http://www.hhs.gov
Food and Drug Administration (FDA)	U.S. Government Agency	Protects public health by ensuring the safety of human and veterinary pharmaceuticals. http://www.fda.gov
Centers for Medicare and Medicaid Services (CMS)	U.S. Government Agency (HHS)	Administers the Medicare program and assists states with the Medicaid program. http://www.cms.gov
Occupational Safety and Health Administration (OSHA)	U.S. Government Agency	Assures safe and healthy work conditions. https://www.osha.gov
Accreditation Commission for Health Care (ACHC)	Independent, private organization	Accreditation to improve business operations and the quality of health care. http://www.achc.org
United States Agency for Toxic Substance and Disease Registry (ATSDR)	U.S. Government Agency	Performs public health assessments on environmental hazards. http://www.atsdr.cdc.gov

TEXTBOX 15-3. KEY TERMS

Legislature: The legislature is the government body that makes rules and laws that society abides by. Normally, legislators are elected officials such as congressional or state representatives and senators.

Statutes: A statute, in this context, refers to an act by a legislative body such as a law. The statute is the form in which the law is expressed.

Executive orders: An executive order is a requirement that the President makes of individuals or organizations under the jurisdiction of the executive branch of government. It is respected much like a law.

Binding policy: A policy is a requirement that an organization, group, or government agency adopts to make its organization run more smoothly. Therefore, a binding policy means that the policy is final and must be followed when it applies.

TORT LAW

Tort law is viewed by some as an area of the law that is in need of reform, but this type of law is common and touches many everyday events. Tort law plays an important role in the delivery of health services.

Tort law encompasses several key areas within the health care industry, including:

1. **Negligence**, which involves the unintentional commission or omission of an act that a reasonably prudent person would or would not do under the same circumstances;
2. **Intentional torts**, such as assault and battery, false imprisonment, defamation of character, and invasion of privacy; and
3. The **infliction of mental distress**.

Managers must understand tort law and its implications to the organization. It is an active area of the law that affects many aspects of health care.

In order for **negligence** to be proven, there must be four key factors involved: (1) the negligent party must have a **duty** toward the harmed party. In health care, this includes the practitioner exercising the level of skill expected in routine practice while treating a person with whom he/she has a patient–provider relationship; (2) there must have been a **breach of duty**, by failing to meet the appropriate **standard of care**; (3) the plaintiff must prove that he or she suffered injury or damages from the interaction; and (4) **causation** must be proven. In other words, the breach of duty has to have been directly connected to the harm that occurred. Negligence charges are usually brought against the practitioner involved, but they can also be brought against an organization under the doctrine of ***respondeat superior*** (meaning that organizations can be liable for harm caused by their employees or agents). There are various types of negligent acts:

- **Misfeasance**, or performing the correct action incorrectly and causing injury;
- **Malfeasance**, or performing an unlawful act (such as a procedure that is illegal in a particular state); and
- **Nonfeasance**, or failing to act where there is a duty that a reasonably prudent person would have fulfilled (perhaps failing to test for an obvious cause of a person's symptoms).

Intentional tort cases depend on proving that the harm was committed deliberately. In assault and battery cases, for example, there must be a deliberate threat on one person by another for **assault** to apply, and actual physical contact for the situation to be considered **battery**. One example in the health care field would be surgery mistakenly performed on an unconscious patient without his/her consent. **False imprisonment** is another form of intentional tort. This could include inappropriately restraining a patient or keeping someone in a more restrictive level of care than necessary. **Defamation of character** can be slander or libel—oral or written false representations of a person's character that will hold that person up to shame or ridicule. Another important aspect of intentional torts in health care settings is **invasion of privacy**, which violates the right to privacy implicit in the Constitution. **Confidentiality** of patient records (more on this later in this chapter) constitutes a major concern under this heading, as does the need to evaluate when a "need to know" overrides privacy, as in the legal requirement to report child or elder abuse, sexually transmitted diseases, or other public health concerns.

MALPRACTICE

A major emphasis of tort law in health care involves medical **malpractice**. Malpractice is the negligence or carelessness of a professional person; it can be either a civil (tort) concern or a criminal one, depending on whether it involved "reckless disregard" for the safety of another (criminal) or simple carelessness (civil). The legal dictionary definition states that "malpractice is a professional's improper or immoral conduct in the performance of duties, done either intentionally or through carelessness or ignorance. Furthermore, the term is commonly applied to a physician, surgeon, dentist, lawyer, or public officer to denote the negligence or unskillful performance of duties resulting from such person's professional relationship with patients or clients" (Gifis, 1996, p. 303). For a health care administrator, this is a central concern in hiring, training, and monitoring the performance of employees and those with admitting privileges, both in order to protect the patients from harm and out of concern for the reputation and financial stability of the organization itself.

Again, as has been discussed earlier in this chapter, tort reform, health care reform, and other legislative and legal actions are all focused on eliminating many of the medical malpractice claims in the U.S. today. However, many people believe medical malpractice claims in and of themselves help to deter malpractice by forcing the organization or individual to focus on poor outcomes and be more cognizant of best practices and patient outcomes (Shi & Singh, 2008). It may be true the threat of being sued is a deterrent to many, but this is not always the case. The downside of malpractice is that fear of litigation has actually led to many organizations hiding the truth and ignoring patient harms, as they don't want to face fines, sanctions, or in some cases prison time (Shi & Singh, 2008). In addition, fear of malpractice can also drive up costs of care when practitioners order unnecessary tests so they won't miss something—or out of fear of malpractice suits (Bishop, Federman, & Keyhani, 2010).

Medical malpractice will continue to be a problem in the U.S. as long as individuals perceive they have been harmed. According to the Kaiser Family Foundation (2005), "in some states the problems associated with medical malpractice are called a crisis," (p. 1) and the costs were "estimated to be $55.6 billion in 2008 dollars" (Mello, Chandra, Gawande, & Studdert, 2010, p. 1569). This area of law carries with it both legal and ethical implications and is very difficult to control. The fact that many look at this issue as a crisis should make you aware that as a manager it is critical to understand the law surrounding this topic and work within your organization to ensure that training and education are being provided to mitigate the risk.

CONTRACT LAW

No legal discussion would be complete without discussing the law of contracts. Much like most areas of the law, contracts can be very specialized and difficult to understand, but most of us have been a party to one kind of contract or another. The easiest example is that of a patron who walks into a restaurant and orders a meal. He or she has what is considered an **implied contract**, which means that by ordering a meal and consuming it, they have agreed to pay for their purchase. This example also helps to illustrate that a contract does not have to be in writing, and this is very important when it comes to issues in health care. Let's begin by looking at the necessary elements of a contract.

In order for a **contract** to exist, there must be four key elements:

1. The agreement must be between two or more parties;
2. The parties must both be competent to consent to such an agreement;
3. The agreement must be for something of value; and
4. The agreement must be lawful.

If any of these elements are missing, the parties are not bound by their agreement. These elements are used to inform each party that they are bound by either a written or verbal agreement. In complex organizations, such as the health care industry, contracts are usually written documents and are signed by both parties. The purpose of this practice is to force the parties to ensure that they are getting what they bargained for and to help eliminate undue litigation, cost, and time to both parties (Pozgar, 2007).

Contract law is another area that requires the attention of health care managers, and Table 15-4 delineates several of the differences between contract and tort law and ways in which the two interrelate.

TABLE 15-4 Contract and Tort Law

CONTRACT	TORT
Duties are determined by the parties who are privy to the contract	Duties are determined by law
Parties are known as those that have been contracted with	Parties are generally unknown
Consented to	Individuals do not consent
No legal action for the contract itself	Legal action is available
The damages awarded are not for the contract itself, only for the particular breach that occurred	Damages are awarded and are the only remedy
Damages are normally determined by the writing contained in the contract; in other words, the intent of the contracting parties will determine the legal remedy	Damages are normally decided by a judge or jury that makes a decision based on the evidence

---

TEXTBOX 15-4. KEY TERM

Competence: Competence speaks to an individual's ability to make decisions or perform tasks. For example, an individual must be competent to agree to a medical procedure, meaning that they are of sound mind, of legal age, and so on. Competent also means that a professional has the skills to perform a task, that is, a surgeon is educated, trained, and licensed to practice surgery.

ETHICAL CONCEPTS

"Ethics" is a term that has been used in many different (sometimes contradictory) ways. We talk of **ethical behavior**, meaning the ability to tell the difference between right and wrong. But where does one's "sense of right and wrong" come from? At an individual level, ethical perspectives generally come from family upbringing and/or religion. We are also members of communities (ethnic, residential, national) and of professions that have codes, traditions, and practices setting out standards of ethical behavior. At the organizational level, we speak of similar standards, which may vary depending on the type of organization under examination (public/private; for-profit/nonprofit; religiously based/nonsectarian). In all these settings, we must also distinguish between "normative" ethics, which set a standard of what ought to be done, and "descriptive" ethics, illustrating what is actually done.

On the theoretical level, ethics discussions in health care hark back to moral philosophies such as, among others, utilitarianism, deontology, natural law, and the hybrid philosophy of John Rawls (which uses portions of several of these philosophical approaches to address a particular issue or problem, i.e., ethics). As crises in human subject research came to the public's attention in the 20th century, a whole new field of "bioethics" emerged, examining not just the physician–patient relationship, but also areas such as the allocation of scarce resources, genetics, transplantation, and end-of-life care.

In documents, including the World Medical Association's 1964 Declaration of Helsinki and the 1978 report of the National Commission for the Protection of Human Subjects of Biomedical and Behavioral Research, a simplified listing of key ethical principles for health care research was created and widely circulated. Callahan and Jennings (2002) and many others make a persuasive argument for the application of those same ethical principles to a much wider array of health care settings. These central principles are: respect for persons, beneficence, nonmaleficence, and justice.

Respect for Persons

Several key aspects of medical ethics fall under this heading, including **autonomy**, **truth-telling**, **confidentiality**, and **fidelity**. Individuals have the right to make informed decisions about and consent to their care when they are competent to do so and to have respectful guardianship when they cannot be self-determining. The principle of truth-telling implies that those involved in health care are to be honest with patients/clients as much as possible. Confidentiality, which requires keeping information about others involved in the health care interaction private, is a critical part of any health care manager's job and is being closely scrutinized in the electronic world. Fidelity, the fourth element of the respect-for-persons concept, requires keeping one's word. This includes practitioners' and administrators' responsibility to provide care as promised, whether a formal contract exists or not.

Beneficence and Nonmaleficence

Beneficence and nonmaleficence are common ethical principles and will be discussed briefly as they are key to understanding medicine and ethics. **Beneficence** requires doing the best one can for the recipient of one's services. Stemming from the Hippocratic tradition, it requires a positive duty to care. In other words, it is a balancing of treatment versus the risks and cost involved. For a health administrator, this would mean approaching cost–benefit analysis carefully, and always with the requirement of putting the patient's welfare first. Under this standard, practitioners are to use the full array of their skills for all patients, regardless of demographic or cultural factors that might separate them and (as much as possible) regardless of the ability to pay.

The parallel concept, **nonmaleficence**, is the "do no harm" or at least "don't make it worse" principle, as opposed **maleficence** or doing harm. Health care workers and administrators are admonished to not increase patients' difficulties by their actions (or inactions). Of course, this principle can't always be followed to the letter, as some risks and harms may be inevitable in the attempt to make the situation better. Such tradeoffs are acceptable only with patient understanding and consent. Where possible, practitioners and organizations are to minimize risk and need to always protect against active, intentional harm to patients.

Justice

As a health care principle, justice is a bit harder to pin down than the preceding three. **Justice**, however, is tied to ethical philosophy and implies fairness. Authors and policy makers have defined "fairness" according to an array of definitions, ranging from exactly equal treatment for all to having individuals receive the treatment they "deserve." For example, if someone pays for an item, they would receive the item as opposed to the person not paying for it. Thus, not all are equal. In health care, justice and ethics, as a theory, are often very complicated.

It may seem that ethics and the law are further apart than ever after reading the previous sections, but one only needs to look through a newspaper or view the nightly news in order to see that the values system in this country is on the decline. Pozgar (2010) hit the nail on the head when he described instances that include "questionable political decisions, numbers-cooking executives with exorbitant salaries, health care executives working for both profit and non-profit organizations," among others (p. 238). What can we do to remedy this? Will more laws help us get on track ethically, or will better ethics lead to more enforcement of our existing laws? It is a dilemma that every health care executive must face, and it is critical to the success of any organization. Law and ethics are very much intertwined, and the savvy manager must find a way to walk the thin line between the two in order to bring order and discipline to the organization.

PATIENT AND PROVIDER RIGHTS AND RESPONSIBILITIES

Providers

Both the health care provider and the patient have rights and responsibilities in a host of different areas relating to the provision of care, compliance, respect, and numerous other areas. Of course, as noted above, one key provider responsibility is to avoid harming patients and to use one's skills to (ideally) better their situation. This has both legal and ethical underpinnings and is directly connected to concerns about malpractice. The legal notion of "duty" is critical, as it flows both from the provider's training and professional oath and from the existence of a relationship (contractual or implied) with the patient.

In the case of people seeking emergency care, for instance, the federal **Emergency Medical Treatment and Active Labor Act** (**EMTALA**) of 1985 requires that hospitals participating in Medicare must provide screening examinations and treatment in their emergency departments unless they can prove that a patient requested a transfer (having been fully informed about EMTALA) and/or that the hospital cannot provide the necessary care for the patient's condition.

It needs to be understood that EMTALA is not exclusive to hospitals. There has been much legal debate over the years as to what type of organization EMTALA rules apply. Many have questioned whether the work carried out at urgent care centers falls under EMTALA rules and regulations, so the topic is worth exploring.

As with many areas of law, answers aren't always black and white. There is no definitive answer as to an urgent care center falling under EMTALA or not. According to McguireWoods (2012), "Determining whether EMTALA applies to your urgent care center is a fact-based analysis" (para. 5). However, the DHHS (2003) does believe that most provider-based urgent care centers will fall under the revised definition of an emergency center.

Ultimately, competent legal counsel should handle these types of decisions, so that the organization is operating legally. The ability to determine the plain meaning of language is critical when determining these types of legal questions and counsel is the best way to protect the organization.

Another critical responsibility of the health care organization itself is its fiduciary duty to the patient. **Fiduciary duty** means that people or organizations have an obligation to those who have placed their trust in them. The health care organization, its board of trustees, and its staff are in a position of relative power with the patients. This entails fiduciary duties to protect the organization's assets, abide by its articles of incorporation, and refrain from personal gain at the organization's or patient's expense.

Marketing presents numerous concerns as well and can be a particularly sticky ethical area for any organization or practitioner. Some issues to consider in this regard are:

- How far is it acceptable to go in convincing potential patients that they "need" your services?
- When does providing public information cross over into creating demand in order to increase your own income?
- Is it ethical to attract or keep patients in your institution or professional practice when they might be served better elsewhere?

In addition to their responsibilities to patients, health care organizations have the responsibility to ensure all employees and attending staff are treated fairly and with dignity. Providers are to be protected from sexual or other harassment and have been generally allowed to excuse themselves from patient care with which they disagree, although this is an area under litigation and pressure for legislative change (Stein, 2006).

Individual medical providers are obliged to abide by the requirements of their licenses, living up to the standards of their professions. This includes protecting patient information, providing the best quality of care, serving as advocates for their patients within the health care organization, keeping their own training up-to-date, and reporting any unethical behavior by their coworkers.

Patients

For their part, patients have the responsibility to understand and consent to care, to ask questions of their care providers, to provide accurate information to them (including insurance information, medications, etc.), and to attempt to follow the directions and take prescriptions given for their care.

In America, legal and ethical standards support the notion of **patient self-determination** as a central aspect of health care. Closely linked to this concept is the requirement for confidentiality of patient information. The federal Health Insurance Portability and Accountability Act (HIPAA) of 1996 is one effort to protect patient information in the modern hospital. According to the DHHS (2003), a portion of HIPAA was designed to protect patient privacy and confidentiality in secure environments, particularly through electronic transactions. The regulations protect medical records and other individually identifiable health information, whether on paper or in electronic or oral communications. Key provisions of these new standards include rules and regulations regarding access to medical records, notice of privacy practices, limits on the use of personal and medical information, prohibitions on marketing, stronger state laws, confidential communications, and provisions for patient complaints in case they feel their rights have been violated.

Long before HIPAA, however, there was an acknowledged legal right of patients to make informed decisions about their own care. **Consent** cannot be considered valid if the person giving it did not fully understand the situation, including the potential benefits and risks involved. Adult patients (or their surrogates) also have an absolute right to decline care, even if medical practitioners disagree.

TEXTBOX 15-5. KEY TERM

Patient self-determination: Patient self-determination is a law that requires health care organizations to inform patients of their rights as they pertain to their ability to determine their own health care. For instance, a patient would be informed about their right to consent, their ability to accept and refuse care, and advanced directives.

LEGAL/ETHICAL CONCERNS IN MANAGED CARE

By definition, "managed" care imposes limits on patient and provider choices. When it was originally developed, the goal was to avoid "unnecessary" care and to encourage the use of preventive care as much as possible. However, the more recent concerns are that care is being "rationed," that doctors' hands are tied, and/or that managed care disproportionately harms those dependent on public funding for their care (hence unable to pay higher premiums to ensure a wider range of choices). As most employers have moved to requiring some version of managed care for their employees, the last concern (of unfair treatment of recipients of medical assistance) has waned somewhat. But the issues of rationing and physicians' divided loyalties remain.

In order to be able to treat patients in a managed care plan, the physician must be found acceptable to the plan because of his/her treatment record and charges. Once in the plan, a physician is expected to use only approved medications (also called a formulary), treatments, and referrals in order to save money and to stay within the plan's budgetary restrictions—and good graces. Such cases as *Wickline v. California* (1986) established that physicians are obliged to act as advocates for their patients and resist inappropriate care determinations made by managed care organizations. Other cases have reiterated the point that both the physician and the managed care organization are legally liable for harm caused to the patient by inadequate care due to cost containment. Managed care organizations are also obliged to hire and retain competent physicians and to ensure that they remain qualified to practice (Perry, 2002).

Health care organizations are in the somewhat unique situation of choosing which managed care plans to belong to as providers, as well as choosing which to offer to employees in their own health benefits packages. This can bring home rather bluntly the cost–benefit decisions involved. However, the new health care reform law may be changing the landscape for these organizations, as it is felt that they may be in a better position to offer more competitive benefits to recipients. Because managed care organizations have successfully fought off a national health plan, the opportunity to service more individuals under the umbrella of the new health care reform may bring new prosperity and expansion to the industry (Kaiser Health News, 2010).

BIOMEDICAL CONCERNS

While health care managers do not have to personally make life-and-death medical decisions, the organization's policies can strongly influence what happens under its supervision. One area of ongoing concern is the question of resource allocation implicit in most health care decisions and explicit in managed care settings. As long as equal access to particular levels of care and/or treatments is not available, this will continue to occur. It is possible health care reform will answer some of these questions, but nonetheless, these will still be the types of questions that managers will need to address.

Another overarching issue is that of consent. As mentioned above, informed **consent** is a keystone of medical practice, requiring the practitioner to provide the patient with sufficient information to participate in decisions about his/her care. With laws such as the Americans with Disabilities Act, this responsibility has been expanded to require providing information that is understandable to the patient or, if the patient is not able to decide, to a surrogate decision maker. Particularly in highly emotional situations, such as beginning- and end-of-life care decisions, this process needs to occur. Most hospitals have **patient advocate** offices for the specific purpose of having staff dedicated to walking through difficult decisions with patients and their families.

BEGINNING- AND END-OF-LIFE CARE

As medical science has advanced, the variety and complexity of decisions to be made has also expanded. Two places where this is particularly apparent are in beginning- and end-of-life care. When *Roe v. Wade* was decided in 1966, morning-after pills and various forms of nonsurgical abortions weren't available. In vitro fertilization didn't exist, and medical science wasn't able to keep infants alive when they were born many months early. Provision and funding of contraception; provision and funding of abortion; and balancing parental, societal, and practitioner rights and responsibilities are all issues to be discussed in the context of an organization's mission, vision, and values.

Likewise, end-of-life care has become more complicated than in previous eras. Health care organizations now must pay close attention to obtaining advance directives and identifying surrogate decision makers; providing ethical care in the absence of clear directives; making crucial decisions about life-sustaining treatment; and balancing familial, societal, and practitioner rights and responsibilities.

Similarly, the previous end-of-life cases would have been much more complicated with today's increased array of end-of-life technologies. Also, we now face divergence between state and federal law about physician-assisted suicide. Of course, not every health care organization has the desire or the facilities to provide complicated care. In addition, the particular organization's mission and values will shape what it is willing to provide. Aside from the requirements of EMTALA for those hospitals with emergency facilities and/or obstetrics departments, facilities are free to decide and publicize the types of care that their (often religious) standards will or will not allow them to provide.

In 2014 and 2015, a new movement called **Right to Try Laws** has captured steam and is moving forward with as many as 14 states signing on as of April 2015. Additionally, it is believed that as many as 20 additional states are looking at passing similar laws (Tenth Amendment Center, 2015). These laws are nullifying many of the FDA laws already on the books, so patients have an opportunity to try experimental drugs that would otherwise not be available to them. There are several safeguards built in, particularly for physicians doing the prescribing, to help alleviate lawsuits (Richardson, 2015). A prescribing physician will advise the patient about the medication and will then fill out appropriate FDA paperwork, so a chain of information is present. Patients must have a terminal illness to use the experimental drugs and they must be administered under the care of a physician (Richardson, 2015).

Even though these laws seem to represent progress for patient rights, many still believe it is too dangerous. Numerous federal bills are being drafted, so that additional safeguards are in place. There is still much concern about experimental drugs and many don't believe that those with terminal conditions are able to properly consent (Richardson, 2015).

It is clear that beginning- and end-of-life care and patient rights will continue to be a hot button topic. This will be an area to continue following as legislation will play a major role in the development of these laws, so changes are inevitable.

OPPORTUNITIES FOR RESEARCH IN HEALTH CARE ETHICS AND LAW

In-depth references to law and bioethical consideration in health care, as well as data are available to the public and include, but are not limited to:

- Ascension Health;
- The Center for Ethics and Advocacy in Health Care, Georgetown University Institute of Ethics;
- The Hastings Center;
- The Healthcare Ethics Consortium;
- Islamic Medical and Scientific Ethics Project (ISME);
- NIH Office of Clinical Research and Bioethics; and
- World Health Organization.

As technology advances, we will confront new and potentially divisive questions about what it means to be human. Science fiction is now science fact. We could soon be dealing with questions about whether a human clone is the same or different from the copy, or at what percentage of body replacement after a trauma does a person become a cyborg or a robot and what does that mean with respect to his or her legal rights? You may think these are frivolous concerns, but you need only turn on your TV set to see fiction writers are already posing these questions.

CONCLUSION

Health care is one of the most regulated industries in the nation. Laws have been put in place to protect patients based on ethical concerns and precedents. Every time an organization provides health care services, the potential for legal violations of patients' rights should loom large in the health care manager's consciousness. This chapter has provided you with the vocabulary and some context for addressing legal issues in health care organizations. Since these laws can change and the cases vary, it is incumbent upon the health care manager to stay abreast of developments in health care ethics and law. Furthermore, the new health care reform act of 2010 will provide numerous changes that will affect all health care providers and organizations. Innovations in science, technology, and health care bring new legal and ethical considerations. It is critical for managers to be able to understand the complex issues presented in these new laws and apply them in a both just and ethical manner.

DISCUSSION QUESTIONS

1. Provide several examples of legal behavior and ethical behavior. In what instances are the two similar, and in what instances are they different?

2. How do the legal concepts discussed in this chapter, that is, criminal, tort, civil, and so on, work to dictate the ways in which organizations must operate?

3. As you think about the new health care reform bill, what type of lawmaking action instituted it? In other words, was it developed from the common law, executive order, or legislative process? Was this the best way to institute the new reform? Explain your answer.

4. Think of several examples of both ethical and legal circumstances where you can apply the concepts of beneficence and nonmaleficence. How do these concepts work within your examples to provide protection to both the organization and the patient?

5. There are numerous end-of-life issues that we have all heard about in the news, but how are these laws established? Is it okay for a patient and provider to make these decisions on their own, outside of the law? Aren't these privileged physician–patient decisions?

6. What do you see for the future of health care reform as the law applies? Will health care reform spawn new laws, or will new laws be enacted to guide reform?

7. Return to the tort section in your text and answer the following question based on the information provided by the chapter. Is reporting child abuse a legal obligation or an ethical one? Does it matter what your position is within the organization, i.e., nurse, manager, clerk, and so on? What if you find out about child abuse from a patient encounter, but the law does not allow you to report from the official record? Do you have an ethical obligation to do so?

8. Look back at Table 15-2 and try to determine where tort and contract law come together and in what areas there may be conflict between law and ethics. Explain your thinking and final decisions.

9. In thinking about biomedical issues, address the following questions: How do we decide which patient will receive an organ transplant? Can we be positive that a particular combination of genetics, age, demographics, and lifestyle factors will enable one person to have a longer and more productive life than another? Should we be influenced by the available level of family support, or by the family's need to be involved in a relative's care? How can a health care organization best reflect the ethical preferences of its community while abiding by the law? Should the ability to have care reimbursed affect the decision to provide it?

10. Why have "Right to Try" laws been more successful than right to die laws?

11. Is an expansion of EMTALA policies better or worse for patients?

12. Stephen Hawking, the world-renowned physicist, and occasional guest star on a popular comedy TV show was diagnosed with motor neuron disease in 1963 at the age of 21 and was given two years to live (http://www.hawking.org.uk/). A scientific genius with a literary flair and a wicked sense of humor, he has survived and thrived despite what physicians told him. Which ethical principles do you hypothesize his specialists were following when they advised him and his young wife to get his affairs in order?

Cases in Chapter 18 that are related this chapter include:

- United Physician Group
- Death by Measles
- Full Moon or Bad Planning?
- The Condescending Dental Hygienist
- Sundowner or Victim?
- You Will Do What You Are Told

Case study guides are available in the online Instructor's Materials.

REFERENCES

Bishop, T. F., Federman, A. D., & Keyhani, S. (2010). Physicians' views on defensive medicine: A national survey. *Archives of Internal Medicine, 170*(12), 1081–1083.

Callahan, D., & Jennings, B. (2002). Ethics and public health: Forging a strong relationship. *American Journal of Public Health, 92*(2), 169–176.

Conigliaro, M. (2005). The Terri Schiavo information page. *Abstract Appeal.* Retrieved from http ://abstractappeal.com/schiavo/infopage.html

Dresser, R. (2004). Schiavo: A hard case makes questionable law. *Hastings Center Report, 34*(2), 8–9.

Gifis, S. H. (1996). *Barron's law dictionary.* Hauppauge, NY: Barron's Educational Series.

Kaiser Family Foundation. (2005). *Medical malpractice law in the United States.* The Henry J. Kaiser Family Foundation Online. Retrieved from https://kaiserfamilyfoundation.files.wordpress .com/2013/01/medical-malpractice-law-in-the-united-states-report.pdf

Kaiser Health News. (2010). Health law having affects on managed-care firms, medical suppliers. *KHN Morning Briefing.* Retrieved from http://www.kaiserhealthnews.org/Daily-Reports/2010/May/28 /Health-Overhaul-and-Business.aspx

McGuireWoods. (2012). EMTALA and urgent care: Three things you need to know. Retrieved from http://www.mcguirewoods.com/Client-Resources/Alerts/2012/11/EMTALA-Urgent-Care -3-Things-Know.aspx

Mello, M. M., Chandra, A., Gawande, A. A., & Studdert, D. M. (2010). National costs of the medical liability system. *Health Affairs, 29*(9), 1569–1577.

National Archives. (n.d.). *United States Constitution.* Retrieved from http://www.archives.gov/exhibits /charters/constitution.html

Perry, F. (2002). *The tracks we leave: Ethics in healthcare management.* Chicago, IL: Health Administration Press.

Pozgar, G. D. (2007). *Legal aspects of health care administration* (10th ed.). Sudbury, MA: Jones and Bartlett.

Pozgar, G. D. (2010). *Legal and ethical issues for health professionals* (2nd ed.). Sudbury, MA: Jones and Bartlett.

Richardson, E. (2015, March 5). Right to try laws. *Health Affairs.* Retrieved from http://www.healthaffairs .org/healthpolicybriefs/brief.php?brief_id=135

Shi, L., & Singh, D. A. (2008). *Delivering health care in America* (4th ed.). Sudbury, MA: Jones and Bartlett.

Stein, R. (2006, January 30). Health workers' choice debated: Proposals back right not to treat. *Washington Post,* p. A01.

Tenth Amendment Center. (2015). 14 states and counting. [Blog post]. Retrieved from http ://blog.tenthamendmentcenter.com/2015/04/14-states-and-counting-north-dakota-right -to-try-act-signed-into-law-effectively-nullifies-some-fda-restrictions-on-terminal-patients/

U.S. Department of Health and Human Services (DHHS). (2003a). *Fact sheet: Protecting the privacy of patient's health information.* Retrieved from http://dlthede.net/informatics/chap20ehrissues /privacyfactsapril03.pdf

U.S. Department of Health and Human Services (DHHS). (2003b). *Medicare program; Clarifying policies related to the responsibilities of Medicare-participating hospitals in treating individuals with emergency medical conditions.* Retrieved from http://www.cms.gov/Regulations-and-Guidance /Legislation/EMTALA/downloads/cms-1063-f.pdf

Wickline v. California. 192 Cal. App. 3d 1630, 1636, 239 Cal Rptr 810 (2d Dist. 1986).

CHAPTER 16

Fraud and Abuse

Kevin D. Zeiler

LEARNING OBJECTIVES

By the end of this chapter, the student will be able to:

- Characterize the difference between fraud and abuse;
- Produce examples of fraud and abuse and compare the extent of occurrences;
- Distinguish between the types of civil and criminal penalties incurred for violating rules and regulations;
- Analyze the history of the False Claims Act and its application to health care;
- Assess the managerial and organizational implications of the Emergency Medical Treatment and Active Labor Act (EMTALA);
- Critique the major objectives of the U.S. antitrust laws related to the health care industry;
- Examine the major provisions of the Stark I and Stark II laws and safe harbor regulations;
- Appraise the major components of compliance, risk management, and internal control programs;
- Assess *qui tam* and the whistle-blower role;
- Examine the desirable roles of a health care manager in fraud and abuse cases; and
- Utilize key research data bases for fraud and abuse.

INTRODUCTION

Fraud and abuse have always been a concern to the federal government with regard to Medicare, Medicaid, and other federally funded health care programs. Many remedies have been implemented through the years. In 1995, **Operation Restore Trust**

(ORT) was put in motion by the U.S. Congress to give the Department of Health and Human Services (DHHS) the investigative and enforcement authority necessary to deal with fraud and abuse violations. With ORT in place, the delivery of health care in the U.S. has dramatically and definitively changed for the provider, the beneficiary, and the payer of federally funded health care benefits. Whether these measures were taken for political, fiscal, or quality-of-care reasons, the landscape has changed. The DHHS **Office of Inspector General (OIG)** reported to government officials in 2010 that "the sums lost each year to fraud and abuse reached into the tens of billions of dollars, though there's little agreement on a specific estimate" (Blesch, 2010, para. 10). These numbers are staggering and still seem to be rising. As you try to understand the fact that tens of billions of dollars are lost to fraud, is it the number that is troublesome or the fact that nobody can agree on an estimate? What is being and can be done to reduce the fraud and prevent it? Clearly, this is a major issue facing health care managers.

This chapter will focus on the beginnings of the fraud and abuse prevention programs that started with the decentralized **home health agencies (HHA)** and have broadened to include various types of compliance programs. The chapter will also look at the investigative processes used to uncover fraud and abuse, the enforcement role of governmental programs, and the responsibilities of employees of health care organizations.

For the federal government, ORT was successful, but it still wasn't enough. New programs such as the Tax Relief and Healthcare Act of 2006, which instituted **Recovery Audit Contractors (RAC)** and the **Health Care Fraud Prevention and Enforcement Action Team (HEAT)** in 2009, have continued to turn up the heat and keep the pressure on fraud and abuse in the health care industry. Furthermore, the new health care reform bill, passed in March 2010, provided an additional $350 million in new funding to fight fraud and abuse over the next 10 years (Lexology, 2010).

WHAT IS FRAUD AND ABUSE?

Fraud is an intentional act of deception, while **abuse** consists of improper acts that are unintentional but inconsistent with standard practices. Oftentimes, abuse is so labeled because the investigator cannot determine if fraud occurred, or in other words, if the party acted willfully. The more common forms of fraud and abuse are providers billing for services that were not provided or did not meet medical necessity criteria (false claims), submitting duplicate bills, upcoding services to receive higher reimbursement, and receiving kickbacks for referrals.

HISTORY

The history of compliance as it relates to health care fraud and abuse dates back to the Civil War. **The False Claims Act (FCA)**, also called the **Lincoln Law**, was enacted in 1863 by the federal government as the primary civil remedy for fraudulent or improper health care claims. In 1986, the first major amendments were added to the FCA. These changes removed the clause requiring that there be specific intent to defraud the federal government and that the government need only show that the claim submitted is false and submitted knowingly. Violations of this act include fines of $5,500 to $11,000 per claim, plus up to three times the amount of the damages caused to the federal program (31 USC, 1986a). The Act's *qui tam* **provision** permits private individuals to file false claims actions on behalf of the federal government and receive 15% to 30% of any recovery (31 USC, 1986b). A *qui tam* (Latin for "who as well") is used to indicate that the plaintiff is bringing the action on behalf of the government as well as himself. This individual is also known as a "whistle-blower" or a "relator." The *qui tam* provision has been key to getting individuals to come forward, as it offers monetary incentives and shelter from backlash and/or prosecution.

While the number of civil health care fraud cases rose dramatically in the 1990s, the rate of increase in the number of cases has stabilized since then, but the dollars recovered in suits and investigations has increased. "The 2.3 billion in health care fraud recoveries in fiscal year 2014 marks five straight years the department has recovered more than $2 billion in cases involving false claims against federal health care programs such as Medicare, Medicaid and TRICARE" (Department of Justice, 2014, para. 11).

Operation Restore Trust

Operation Restore Trust (ORT) started in 1995 to counter charges about health care fraud and abuse. Initially, the program involved the five states with the heaviest volume of Medicare beneficiaries. The first services investigated were those provided outside of normal treatment facilities (e.g., hospices, home health agencies, etc.). These investigations led to recovery of $190 million from fraudulent health care activities. In 1997, the program was expanded to include 12 more states.

Operation Restore Trust now includes all 50 states, and more health care delivery systems are covered. The program not only investigates and applies penalties for fraud, but also provides advisories to prevent violations. It uses statistical data to select claims for audits and investigations. DHHS has organized state and federal agencies to monitor activities under ORT.

The Tax Relief and Health Care Act of 2006

In 2009, the Centers for Medicare & Medicaid Services (CMS) introduced **Recovery Audit Contractors (RACs)** in response to the continuing fraud and abuse problem faced by both programs. The beauty of the RAC program is that examiners work on a contingency basis, meaning they only get paid when they find a mistake (CMS, 2009). The RAC program is the biggest effort since ORT in the mid-1990s. The goal is to use computer systems to find data that will lead to discrepancies so information can be obtained, leading to a monetary recovery. Since contractors are not being paid unless the program is recovering money, the incentive to uncover fraud and abuse is very large. Time will tell if this program is able to generate as much return as ORT, as it was not used in all 50 states until sometime during 2010 (CMS, 2009).

As of May 2015, RAC is going through significant changes. First, the Medicare RAC program is struggling to return funds to the program, but the state Medicaid Fraud Control Units (MFCUs) have been very successful in returning funds (Spencer, 2015). Second, the Medicare Audit Improvement Act of 2015 was introduced to Congress with a goal of fixing the ailing RAC system (Dundon, 2015). Specifically, the biggest concern has been the way that RAC contractors are reimbursed. The bill will end contingency payments to contractors and also provide ample time for health care organizations to file paperwork with Medicare (Dundon, 2015).

However, all is not doom and gloom for the program. In the 2015 fraud case filed in 2012, Davita, a Denver-based renal care company, settled its third Medicare lawsuit and will be paying out nearly $1 billion dollars (Chuang, 2015). Perhaps this is a drop in the bucket when it comes to the overall cost of Medicare fraud, but it sends a strong message to other organizations. In addition, whistleblower statutes are beginning to make a difference when it comes to fraud and abuse cases.

Battling fraud and abuse in the Medicaid and Medicare system will not go away overnight. It is clear that stronger legislation will continually need to be applied and a constant monitoring of the problem will be necessary.

Health Care Fraud Prevention and Enforcement Action Team

The newest member to the fraud and abuse team is President Obama's **Health Care Fraud Prevention and Enforcement Action Team**, or **HEAT**, as it is known. This program, much like the others, is geared toward stopping fraud and abuse of Medicare and Medicaid claims. However, HEAT is different in the sense that the President is also using it as an enforcement tool against the agencies directed to stop such fraud and abuse (Blesch, 2010). In the past, CMS acted to investigate fraud and abuse, but this action gives muscle to agencies and assists CMS with enforcement against those individuals or organizations that are violating the law and attempting to defraud the system. Since so many agencies are working to reduce this problem, it is only reasonable that some type of accountability must take place. Time will tell if a more concerted government effort will prove to be the difference in this ongoing battle.

THE SOCIAL SECURITY ACT AND THE CRIMINAL-DISCLOSURE PROVISION

The **Criminal-Disclosure Provision of the Social Security Act** makes it a felony for a health care provider or beneficiary to possess "knowledge of the occurrence of any event affecting his initial or continued right to any such benefit or payment, or the initial or continued right to any such benefit or payment of any other individual in whose behalf he has applied for or is receiving such benefit or payment conceals or fails to disclose such event with an intent fraudulently to secure such benefit or payment either in a greater amount or quantity than is due or when no such benefit or payment is authorized" (42 USC, 1987a). Violation of this provision is a felony and may include punishment of up to 5 years in prison and/or fines of up to $25,000 (42 USC, 1987a).

This provision of the Social Security Act (SSA) also imposes a requirement to disclose overpayments to the government regardless of intent at the time the claim was submitted (42 USC, 1987a). By obligating this disclosure, the government may start collection efforts. If the provider acts in good faith to reimburse the program, it may limit its liability under the False Claims Act (FCA). It does not, however, loosen any criminal liability under this provision.

There are at least two cases that follow the Criminal-Disclosure Provision of the Act. These include several defendants who were charged with conspiracy to knowingly misstate certain interest expenses on providers' cost reports filed with the government. Documents show the conspiracy involved the defendants knowingly failing to notify the government of the fiscal intermediary's audit error concerning interest expense. The defendants were convicted on the conspiracy count, but no separate finding was made on the failure-to-disclose allegation (42 USC, 1987b).

Another case involves three individuals in California charged with conspiracy to defraud the U.S. government in connection with a scheme to submit fraudulent medical necessity certification for certain medical equipment. It is critical for all health care managers, whether it be the highest ranking executive, the line, or the unit manager, to understand that the federal government intends to prosecute these types of cases to the fullest extent of the law. *All* members of an organization are now going to be held liable for the actions or inactions of those within the organization and will be held to standards established by criminal statutes. In other words, it is getting more and more difficult for CEOs or high-ranking executives to hide behind the corporate shield.

THE EMERGENCY MEDICAL TREATMENT AND ACTIVE LABOR ACT

The **Emergency Medical Treatment and Active Labor Act (EMTALA)** was enacted in 1986 to prevent patient dumping. It is also known as the Anti-Dumping Act. It was used to prevent emergency rooms from refusing treatment or transferring a patient to another facility because of the patient's inability to pay for treatment. The Act mandates that an appropriate **medical screening exam (MSE)** be given to any patient who presents to any department that is established as a provider of emergent or urgent care. If an MSE is performed and shows an emergency condition exists, the patient must be either treated and discharged or admitted as an inpatient and transferred from the dedicated emergency department. The EMTALA obligations cease at this point. However, EMTALA also restricts the emergency room staff from discussing financial or insurance information until *after* the MSE has been performed and the emergent condition has been stabilized. As long as the treatment is not delayed, hospitals may continue the registration process.

The CMS has the authority to enforce EMTALA and can impose financial penalties on providers who do not comply. In addition, the OIG has separate authority to impose sanctions for EMTALA violations. Violators may incur monetary penalties of up to $50,000 per violation and have their Medicare program participation terminated. The final EMTALA rule became effective on November 10, 2003.

Hospital Compliance with EMTALA

To avoid EMTALA violations, providers should:

- Require all clinical, administrative, and contract staff to review and understand the EMTALA requirements and to document this training;
- Ensure all patients who have an emergent admission and either "refuse," decline, or withdraw treatment are offered a medical screening exam and treatment before they leave the hospital and that declining or refusal to accept treatment is documented (informed consent);
- Ensure ER staff understands all statutory rules regarding transfer of patients to another facility; and
- Enforce the requirement that prevents staff from asking for financial and accounting information before the medical screening exam has been completed and the patient is stabilized.

Review the chart shown in Table 16-1 so you have a good understanding of the Acts that have been covered thus far in the chapter.

TABLE 16-1 Criminal Disclosure Provisions

ACT	FUNCTION
Criminal-Disclosure Provisions of the Social Security Act	a) Provider must disclose overpayments so that the government can initiate collection efforts.
	b) Imposes penalties for failure to disclose such payment information.
	c) Disclosure may provide a defense if the government attempts to collect.
	d) Provider liability includes: Felony offense Up to $25,000 fine Up to five years in jail
False Claims Act	a) Federal government's primary civil remedy for fraudulent claims.
	b) Providers who make improper claims are fined $5,500–$11,000 per claim.
	c) The Act is also applied to improper billing, claims for services not rendered, unnecessary services, misrepresenting credentials, and substandard quality of care.
Emergency Medical Treatment and Active Labor Act (EMTALA)	a) Requires all Medicare and Medicaid hospitals with an emergency department to provide appropriate medical screening to all seeking emergency care.
	b) Often referred to as the anti-dumping law because it prohibits hospitals from transferring an emergency patient to another hospital because of an inability to pay.

Data from: Cleverley & Cameron, 2007, pp. 75–77.

ANTITRUST ISSUES

Antitrust laws were implemented to protect the citizenry from the negative effects of monopolies. Three Acts form the basis of antitrust law.

- **The Sherman Antitrust Act**—Section 1 prohibits all conspiracies or agreements that restrain trade.
- **The Clayton Act**—Section 7 of the Act prohibits mergers and acquisitions that may substantially lessen competition "in any line of commerce . . . in any section of the country." This was enacted in 1914.
- **The Federal Trade Commission Act**—Section 5 of the Act prohibits various types of unfair competition, such as collusion, price fixing, and the like.

The Department of Justice (DOJ) and the **Federal Trade Commission (FTC)** revised the Statements of Antitrust Enforcement Policy in Health Care in 1996. The revision was intended to ensure that policies did not interfere with activities that reduce health care costs.

In order to prevent violations of the Antitrust Act, Congress passed the Hart-Scott-Rodino **Antitrust Improvements Act of 1976.** This required hospitals and all other parties who enter into certain mergers, acquisitions, joint ventures, or tender offers to notify the DOJ and FTC before finalizing all agreements. This is a requirement for hospitals with assets greater than $100 million acquiring a hospital with more than $10 million in assets. The DOJ and FTC then decide if the transaction should be approved.

Table 16-2 provides an overview of the main antitrust Acts and their functions.

PHYSICIAN SELF-REFERRAL/ANTI-KICKBACK/SAFE HARBOR LAWS

Two laws have been enacted to prevent conflicts of interest in Medicare patient referrals. The Physician Self-Referral Laws are also known as **Stark I and Stark II.** The **Stark II Law** "prohibits physicians from referring patients to providers with which the physician has a financial relationship" (Furrow et al., 2004, p. 1034). This law is an extension of the **Stark I Law,** which only applies to physicians referring to laboratories in which they have a financial interest. Examples of violations of the Stark Laws include paying a physician for a referral and a hospital offering rental space to a physician below fair market value. Physicians who receive benefits not given to other doctors or staff may be considered in violations of the rule, too.

The second law is the **Anti-Kickback Act** (42 USC, 1987a), which is designed to prevent the offer or payment of bribes or other remuneration as an inducement to refer

TABLE 16-2 Antitrust Acts

ACT	FUNCTION
Sherman Antitrust Act	a) Applies to agreements that unreasonably restrain trade. These include, but are not limited to: price fixing, boycotting other organizations, dividing market territories, and using coercive tactics with the intent to harm or injure another party.
	b) Applies to virtually all businesses in the country, including health care.
Clayton Act	a) Prohibits mergers and acquisitions that may lessen competition.
	b) Unlike the Sherman Act, the Clayton Act only imposes civil penalties.
Federal Trade Commission Act	a) Prohibits unfair methods of competition. This may include techniques such as larger businesses using their size to gain lower prices from suppliers and suppliers giving discounts to larger companies without providing the same for smaller ones.

Data from: Cleverley & Camerson, 2007, pp. 78 and 82.

Medicare patients for treatment or services (Manning, 1996). These rules, especially the Anti-Kickback statute, were so stringent that many providers were being wrongly accused of conduct that was not inherently illegal, leading Congress to ask CMS to develop and enforce **safe harbor** provisions, under which physicians can receive remuneration in specific instances. Each of these is discussed further in this section.

Under Stark II, if a physician or immediate family member has a specified financial relationship with an entity, the physician may not refer Medicare or Medicaid patients to that entity to receive health services (Furrow et al., 2004, p. 1034). Thus, the provision may be implicated when a referring physician has an ownership or investment interest, or when a physician or immediate family member receives compensation or other remuneration from the entity providing health care services. Additionally, the recipient of the referral may not present a claim for any designated health services provided due to this referral.

Before continuing in with this section, take a moment to expand your knowledge as it applies to Stark I and II, as shown in Table 16-3.

The Anti-Kickback Act, formerly known as the **Medicare and Medicaid Anti-Kickback Act**, is the law of choice for federal enforcement authorities. This Act imposes criminal liability for the knowing and willful payment, solicitation, or receipt of remuneration (i.e., any kickback, bribe, or rebate, direct or indirect, overt or covert, in cash or in kind, and any ownership interest or compensation interest) in exchange for referring an individual to another entity for the purpose of obtaining reimbursement from the federal health care program. These referrals can be for purchasing, leasing, ordering, arranging for, or recommending, the purchase, lease, or ordering of items or services reimbursable by Medicare or Medicaid. This Act affects a vast array of health care industry business relationships.

The Anti-Kickback Act has broadened the original Act's reach to encompass all federal health care programs, excluding the Federal Employees Health Benefits Program, which is the health plan for federal employees. This was done in 1996 with the passage of the

TABLE 16-3 Stark Laws

STARK I	STARK II
Enacted to deal with physician self-referrals.	Expanded Stark I laws.
Often referred to as the Ethics in Patient Referrals Act.	Any amounts billed illegally must be refunded.
Makes it illegal for a physician to make a Medicare-financed referral to an organization in which he or she or a family member has a financial interest.	Applies to Medicaid services as well as Medicare.
Also prohibits billings by a laboratory for services provided pursuant to illegal referrals.	Knowingly billing or failing to make a refund is subject to a civil fine of $15,000 per item billed.

Furrow et al., 2004, p. 1033.

Health Insurance Portability and Accountability Act (HIPAA). In addition, the Balanced Budget Act of 1997 imposes civil monetary penalties of $50,000 for each violation of the Anti-Kickback Act and damages of up to three times the total amount of remuneration offered, paid, solicited, or received in violation of the Act.

Federal enforcement authorities continuously review application of the Act. They are currently reviewing doctors and drug samples, incentives for therapeutic switches, and provision of free goods or value-added services to nursing homes. OIG staffers have stressed that the most important aspect of the Anti-Kickback Act violation is the intent to induce referrals and that no safe harbor exists for conduct that may also benefit patients because enforcement authorities do not believe that such services are provided with only patients' interests in mind. In contrast to the Anti-Kickback Act, Stark I and II describe prohibited conduct explicitly. Unlike the Anti-Kickback Act, Stark I and II are strict liability statutes, meaning that individuals or organizations are liable "for damages that their actions or products cause regardless of fault on their part"; they do not require proof of intent, nor do they have regulatory safe harbors that give rise to gray areas (Pozgar, 2007, p. 46).

Safe harbor regulations were put in place in 1987 by DHHS after a congressional mandate. Initially, 11 safe harbor provisions were implemented in 1991. These gave guidelines that, when complied with in full, would ensure compliance with this very vague statute. The goal of the safe harbors laws is to "immunize certain payment and business practices that are implicated by the anti-kickback statute from criminal and civil prosecution under the statute" (OIG, 1999, para. 4). "In 1993, the OIG proposed to include within the list of safe harbor provisions, payments made to surgeon-investors in **Ambulatory Surgery Centers (ASCs)**, provided that the facility was wholly owned by the referring surgeons and that these surgeons performed the surgery themselves on patients they had referred to the ASC, so this safe harbor could be justified because the ASC facility was an extension of the referring surgeon's practice and of little risk for fraud and abuse" (Kinkade, 2000, para. 3).

On November 19, 1999, the OIG published a final rule, which established 8 new safe harbors and clarified 6 of the original 11 that went into effect in 1991 (Kinkade, 2000). The following key points, as delineated by Kinkade (2000), help to outline the standards established by the safe harbor rules:

1. Both surgeon-owned and single-specialty ASC safe harbors, which differ only by types of physicians who may hold ownership interest in the ASC, impose an additional requirement that examines each investor's income from the ASC. Under this rule, one-third of each physician-investor's medical practice income for the previous year must be derived from the physician's performance of surgical

procedures at an ASC or hospital surgical setting. According to the OIG, this will ensure that a physician's investment in an ASC actually represents an extension of the physician's office.

2. The multispecialty ASC safe harbor is identical to surgeon-owned and single-specialty ASC safe harbors, but requires that at least one-third of the physician's surgical procedures are performed at the ASC in which they are investing. Like the practice income test applicable to surgeon-owned and single-specialty ASCs, this requirement is intended to prohibit passive investment among physicians in different specialties. This situation, according to the OIG, creates the greatest risk of prohibited payments or other remuneration for referrals.

3. The hospital/physician ASC is somewhat different from the above-described safe harbors. This safe harbor requires the same five criteria, but does not require the examination of practice income arising from the facility. Instead, the safe harbor imposes three stringent requirements on the hospital investor that may well keep all hospital/physician ASCs outside the scope of the safe harbor.

4. Perhaps the most important feature of the new ASC safe harbor is the OIG's decision to do away with a requirement of 100% physician ownership. Under the final safe harbor, individuals who are neither an existing nor potential source of referrals are permitted to invest in the facility.

5. Also significant in the new safe harbors is the OIG's decision not to expand the scope of the safe harbor to include facilities that are not traditionally considered "surgical" facilities, such as lithotripsy centers, end-stage renal disease facilities, comprehensive outpatient rehabilitation facilities, radiation oncology facilities, cardiac catheterization centers, and optical dispensing facilities, despite support for inclusion (para. 6–10).

Recent studies have shown safe harbor rules may not actually be reforming medical malpractice, but they may improve patient safety. A study that looked at 266 claims that occurred between 2002 and 2009 concluded that only 1% of liability outcomes would have changed because of legislation (Kachalia, Little, Isavoran, Crider, & Smith, 2014). Nevertheless, the threat of such legislation may actually push more physicians to act in accordance with the law, which provides better patient outcomes. Ultimately, the question that must be answered is how much policy is too much? If the policy is costing more than its impact is achieving, is it worth the investment?

The government has successfully prosecuted cases under the FCA by contending that either the Stark laws or Anti-Kickback Statute violation constitute making a false statement. These cases have primarily been ones in which a provider submits claims to the government certifying that, either implicitly or explicitly, all services or items were provided according to applicable laws (Kinkade, 2000).

MANAGEMENT RESPONSIBILITY FOR COMPLIANCE AND INTERNAL CONTROLS

According to the **Committee of Sponsoring Organizations (COSO)** of the Treadway Commission (2010), internal control is "a process, effected by an entity's board of directors, management, and other personnel, designed to provide reasonable assurance regarding the achievement of objectives in the following categories: 1. Effectiveness and efficiency of operations. 2. Reliability of financial reporting. 3. Compliance with applicable laws and regulations" (para. 5).

Under the new structure of corporate compliance, it is important to note the internal control of compliance programs is now the responsibility of the board, management, and other internal personnel. The responsibility clearly rests in the hands of management. The CEO is no longer able to merely place the blame on the executive staff. The COSO (2010) lists five interrelated components of internal control:

- Control environment sets the tone of an organization, influencing the control consciousness of its people. It is the foundation for all other components of internal control, providing discipline and structure.
- Risk assessment is the entity's identification and analysis of relevant risks to achievement of its objectives, forming a basis for determining how the risks should be managed.
- Control activities are the policies and procedures to help ensure that management directives are carried out.
- Information and communication—pertinent information must be identified, captured, and communicated in a form and time frame that enable people to carry out their responsibilities.
- Monitoring [is] a process that assesses the quality of the system's performance over time (p. 2).

CORPORATE COMPLIANCE PROGRAMS

The OIG strongly recommends the adoption of a corporate compliance plan as it helps limit the risk of compliance errors and limits the liability of management and directors. An effective program can also limit liability under the Federal Sentencing Guidelines, which are rules that demand consistency in sentencing as it applies to felonies only, not misdemeanors. Most importantly, an effective corporate compliance plan gives employees the guidelines necessary to follow the laws and allows management to know that the laws are being followed. In addition, more and more organizations are appointing a designated corporate compliance officer as opposed to the past when it was often tasked to numerous individuals. In 2006, the OIG released an integrated approach to corporate compliance that helps organizations understand the roles and responsibilities of all involved in the discipline.

The OIG has published a list of eight essential elements of an effective compliance program. They are part of the Federal Sentencing Guidelines and are shown in Table 16-4.

For the compliance plan to be effective, all employees must be aware of the plan. The OIG will survey employees when auditing an institution to measure compliance knowledge and awareness. To develop an effective plan, the first step is to conduct a risk assessment facing the organization.

TABLE 16-4 Effective Compliance Program Essentials

ELEMENT	REQUIREMENT
1) Written policies, procedures, and standards of conduct.	These must speak to the organization's commitment to comply with all applicable federal and state standards.
2) Designation of a compliance officer.	Sponsor must have: a) compliance officer in place b) compliance committee in place c) established protocol for overview d) compliance officer if responsible for fraud and abuse program
3) Training and education.	Must have a training and education program in place.
4) Effective lines of communication throughout the organization.	Sponsor must have: a) organized lines of communication to effectively provide information as it pertains to compliance issues b) mechanisms are in place for capturing concerns and risks
5) Enforcement procedures.	Must enforce standards through disciplinary guidelines.
6) Procedures for effective internal monitoring and auditing.	These requirements are as follows: a) must have a monitoring and auditing program b) must monitor and audit contractors c) must allow CMS to audit financial records d) must allow the federal government to perform an onsite audit e) contractors must allow CMS access to their records
7) Procedures for corrective action.	The organization must ensure: a) prompt response to violations b) appropriate corrective action is taken
8) Fraud and abuse plan must be in place.	Must have a plan in place to detect and prevent fraud and abuse.

The greatest threat to health care compliance is erroneous or fraudulent billing. A snapshot of the corporation's billing practices should be created for a risk analysis under the supervision of the organization's attorneys, and once the risk areas are identified, a written compliance plan should be developed. This plan should be distributed to all personnel, with all employees being trained to follow it. Once the plan is in force and operational, it will only be effective if it has management support, as well as effective communication, continuous monitoring, and accountability. Also, a key to making a compliance program work is to provide the appropriate organizational response to a violation (OIG, 2004). Without proper reporting, the program is merely an expensive tool to the organization.

OPPORTUNITIES FOR RESEARCH IN FRAUD AND ABUSE

Thanks to the greater transparency requirements of new laws relating to fraud and abuse, the federal government and other entities have created resources and databases that offer students of health care opportunities for research in fraud and abuse. In-depth references to fraud and abuse regulations, as well as data on efforts to combat these crimes, are available to the public and include, but are not limited to:

- Centers for Medicare and Medicaid Services (CMS) regulations and guidance pages;
- Federal Trade Commission (FTC);
- Office of Inspector General (OIG) Centers for Medicare and Medicaid Services, where photos of OIG's Most Wanted Fugitives for health care fraud can be seen; and
- U.S. Department of Justice.

In addition, non-governmental partnerships with industry, such as the National Health Care Anti-Fraud Association (n.d.), provide education and training to health care organization compliance officers and law enforcement personnel. With larger databases and the enthusiastic cooperation of health care insurance companies, big data analytics and health information technology offer researchers, compliance officers, and law enforcement officers opportunities for discerning trends in fraud and determining where to invest their efforts most wisely. Foster (2012) stated:

> Big-data tools can be used to review large healthcare claims and billing information to target the following:
>
> 1. Assess payment risk associated with each provider
> 2. Over-utilization of services in very short-time windows
> 3. Patients simultaneously enrolled in multiple states
> 4. Geographic dispersion of patients and providers

5. Patients traveling large distances for controlled substances
6. Likelihood of certain types of billing errors
7. Billing for "unlikely" services
8. Pre-established code pair violation
9. Up-coding claims to bill at higher rates (para. 13).

For anyone interested in a blend of forensic sciences and health care management, fraud and abuse identification, investigation, and prosecution is a rapidly growing area that needs ethical people.

CONCLUSION

Fraud and abuse are constantly changing in response to the environment. For instance, as new statutes or laws are passed, clever violators find new ways to get around them. It is for this reason that all health care managers must be cognizant of even the most subtle changes within their organization. The key to handling fraud and abuse issues is to keep the staff informed, prepared, and ready and willing to work together in order to protect not only the organization but the industry as well. New initiatives utilizing big data are assisting with the identification, investigation, and prosecution of health care fraud.

This chapter has merely provided an overview of the many complicated laws and issues surrounding fraud and abuse. Recent laws, statutes, and health care reform all are proposing new ways to address this difficult issue, but there are no easy answers. As Furrow et al. (2004) state, "the particular statutes, regulations, cases and interpretive rulings and guidelines that fraud has spawned, are also bewilderingly complicated and have generated confusion and cynicism in the health care industry" (p. 976). Therefore, a diligent compliance program is the best way to combat this growing problem.

DISCUSSION QUESTIONS

1. Discuss the differences between fraud and abuse. During your discussion, provide examples of each and how health care managers might deal with them.

2. How has the history of health care compliance changed since its inception? (Hint: Look at the ways in which penalties have increased in various ways.) What do you think will be the key to getting control of the issue of fraud and abuse in the future?

3. Choose one of the recent laws that have been enacted that are included in the chapter and discuss why it is or isn't an effective stop-gap to health care fraud and abuse.

4. EMTALA is a far-reaching act; explain several of its benefits and describe how it is effective at preventing fraud and abuse as opposed to detecting it.

5. Describe your responsibilities as a health care manager as they apply to fraud and abuse. What if you were a unit manager? A department manager? A member of the executive division?

6. As you try to understand the fact that tens of billions of dollars are lost to fraud, is it the number that is troublesome or the fact that nobody can agree on an estimate? What is being done and can be done to reduce fraud and prevent it?

7. You are the new compliance manager for a health care organization. Describe the steps you will take to ensure that your compliance plan is legal and effective.

8. A physician and his colleague decide to set up a laboratory owned by a dummy corporation in their wives' names and begin to refer patients to this laboratory. What (if any) laws have they violated?

9. A psychiatrist bills for 10 hours of psychotherapy and medication checks for a deceased woman. Has he committed fraud or abuse? Can the deceased woman's estate press charges if the bills were sent to Medicare, and not to the family?

10. An attorney sees a plastic surgeon and is so happy with her face-lift that she begins to refer all her friends and family. At her 6-month follow-up, she says, "So, Doc, I've sent you all these patients, where's my 30% cut of your fees?" What should the plastic surgeon do?

11. While working on your homework for this course and surfing the Internet to check out all the fascinating links, you realize the person who manages the branch of the new durable medical equipment company (DMExcellence) where you work looks just like someone on the OIG Most Wanted list. He even has the same first name! And he has a wife who looks like the woman on the list with him! While you really need this new job to help pay your way through school, you have a sinking feeling all is not good at DMExcellence. What do you do?

Cases in Chapter 18 that are related this chapter include:

- Who You Gonna Call?

Case study guides are available in the online Instructor's Materials.

REFERENCES

Balanced Budget Act of 1997 (Public Law 105-33). Title IV, Subtitle D, Chapter 1, Section 4304 (b) (2).

Blesch, G. (2010). Targeting fraud. *Modern Healthcare*. Retrieved from http://www.modernhealthcare.com/article/20100621/MAGAZINE/100619919

Centers for Medicare & Medicaid Services (CMS). (2009). *Recovery audit contractor overview*. Retrieved from http://www.cms.gov/Research-Statistics-Data-and-Systems/Monitoring-Programs/Medicare-FFS-Compliance-Programs/Recovery-Audit-Program/Downloads/RACSlides.pdf

Chuang, T. (2015, May 4). DaVita will pay $495 million to settle Atlanta whistle-blower case. *The Denver Post*, p. 1A. Retrieved from http://www.denverpost.com/business/ci_28046592/davita-will-pay-495-million-settle-atlanta-whistleblower?source=pkg

Cleverley, W. O., & Cameron, A. E. (2007). *Essentials of health care finance* (6th ed.). Sudbury, MA: Jones and Bartlett.

Committee of Sponsoring Organizations (COSO) of the Treadway Commission. (2010). *Internal control-integrated framework*. Retrieved from http://www.coso.org/documents/Internal%20Control-Integrated%20Framework.pdf

Dundon, E. (2015). From Washington: Graves introduces bill to reform the Medicare audit system. [Blog post]. *Hannibal Courier-Post*. Retrieved from http://www.hannibal.net/article/20150505/BLOGS/150509495

Foster, R. (2012, May 14). Top 9 fraud and abuse areas big data tools can target. *Government HealthIT*. Retrieved from http://www.govhealthit.com/news/part-3-9-fraud-and-abuse-areas-big-data-can-target

Furrow, B. R., Greaney, T. L., Johnson, S. H., Jost, T. S., & Schwartz, R. L. (2004). *Health law: Cases, materials and problems* (5th ed.). St. Paul, MN: Thomson-West.

Kachalia, A., Little, A., Isavoran, M., Crider, L. M., & Smith, J. (2014). Greatest impact of safe harbor rule may be to improve patient safety, not reduce liability claims paid by physicians. *Health Affairs*, *33*(1), 159–166.

Kinkade, W. A. (2000). Anti-kickback Act safe harbor provisions finalized. Retrieved from http://library.findlaw.com/2000/Dec/8/126843.html

Lexology. (2010). The fraud-and-abuse provisions of the health care reform act. Retrieved from http://www.lexology.com/library/detail.aspx?g=1a1ece1c-87bf-41c4-b4c7-65adc56b3d67

Manning, W. L. (1996). *Summary of the Medicare and Medicaid Patient Protection Act of 1987 (42 U.S.C. 1320a-7b)*. Retrieved from http://www.hackensackumc.org/assets/1/7/Anti_kickback_statute.pdf

National Health Care Anti-Fraud Association. (n.d.). Who we are. Retrieved from http://www.nhcaa.org/about-us/who-we-are.aspx

Office of Inspector General (OIG). (1999). *Federal anti-kickback law and regulatory safe harbor*. Retrieved from http://oig.hhs.gov/fraud/docs/safeharborregulations/safefs.htm

Office of Inspector General (OIG). (2004). *An integrated approach to corporate compliance: A resource for health care organization Boards of Directors*. Retrieved from http://oig.hhs.gov/fraud/docs/complianceguidance/Tab%204E%20Appendx-Final.pdf

Office of Inspector General (OIG). (2006). *Prescription drug plan sponsors' compliance plans*. Retrieved from http://oig.hhs.gov/oei/reports/oei-03-06-00100.pdf

Office of Inspector General (OIG). (2015). OIG most wanted fugitives. Retrieved from http://oig.hhs .gov/fraud/fugitives/index.asp

Pozgar, G. D. (2007). *Legal aspects of health care administration* (10th ed.). Sudbury, MA: Jones and Bartlett.

Spencer, J. P. (2015). Medicaid fraud control units yielding results. *RAC Monitor.* Retrieved from http ://www.racmonitor.com/rac-enews/1825-medicaid-fraud-control-units-yielding-results.html

Title 31 United States Code (31 USC). 31 U.S.C. §§ 3729 (7) et seq. (1986a).

Title 31 United States Code (31 USC). 31 U.S.C. §3730 (d1). (1986b).

Title 42 United States Code (42 USC). 42 U.S.C. 1320a-7b, 1903m; Title 42 Consolidated Federal Registry (CFR) § 1001.952. (1987a).

Title 42 United States Code (42 USC). 42 U.S.C. CFR 489.24 and 42 CFR 413.65. (1987b).

U.S. Department of Justice (DOJ). (2014, November 20). *Justice Department recovers nearly $6 billion from False Claims Act cases in fiscal year 2014.* Retrieved from http://www.justice.gov/opa/pr /justice-department-recovers-nearly-6-billion-false-claims-act-cases-fiscal-year-2014

CHAPTER 17

Special Topics and Emerging Issues in Health Care Management

Sharon B. Buchbinder and Nancy H. Shanks

LEARNING OBJECTIVES

By the end of this chapter, the student will be able to:

- Discuss the potential impact of re-emerging outbreaks on a health care organization;
- Analyze potential risks for bioterrorism in a health care organization;
- Propose strategies for addressing violence in health care settings;
- Examine the role of the health care manager in combatting human trafficking;
- Create a plan to incorporate medical tourism and consumer directed health care into the mission, vision, and values of a health care organization; and
- Investigate key research data repositories for topics covered in this chapter.

INTRODUCTION

Health care managers stand at the intersection of social, public health, and medical issues, and must be able to deal with everyone who arrives at the Emergency Department with compassion and clarity. The purpose of this chapter is to bring some special topics and emerging issues, many of which are torn from today's headlines, to your attention. You will be challenged to examine and analyze these sometimes volatile issues with thoughtful sensitivity and reflection. **TRIGGER WARNING: This book chapter, or pages it links to, contains information about sexual assault and/or violence which may be triggering to survivors**. Due to space constraints, this chapter will not delve into each one with the depth of preceding chapters. Instead, we will provide you with an overview to entice you to dig deeper into one or more of these areas which you find intriguing, unsettling, or provocative. In this chapter, we will address: re-emerging outbreaks, human trafficking, violence in health care settings, medical tourism, and consumer directed health care. In addition we will direct you to where you can find more research data bases and repositories on these topics.

RE-EMERGING OUTBREAKS, VACCINE PREVENTABLE DISEASES, AND DEATHS

With the return of Ebola to center stage in world health and the promising early outcomes of vaccine trials for this disease in West Africa, it is easy to forget old diseases and debates (Clottey, 2015; Kuehn, 2015). **Vaccines** work by imitating an infection and stimulating the body's immune system to respond as if it were a real infection (Centers for Disease Control and Prevention [CDC], 2012). Vaccinations created by man, not by natural disease processes, have historically engendered controversy. According to Link (2005), "vaccines are counterintuitive. What sense does it make to inject a well-baby with a potent, biologically active vaccine that contains elements of the very disease it is supposed to prevent?" (p. 38).

Over the past decades, since the publication of the now retracted 1998 Wakefield and colleagues *Lancet* article asserting a link between measles, mumps, and rubella vaccines and childhood autism, fears of making well babies sick, rather than protecting them, have swelled. Some of the fears are founded in well-grounded research and concerns about special populations and faulty vaccine preparation. Other fears are based on theories that big Pharma is conspiring to make money by killing our children. Unfortunately, what has remained in some health care consumers' and parents' minds is *not* the fact that the physician falsified data and was discredited, but the notion that all vaccinations are bad, including those that have withstood the test of time.

Due to lack of immunization in other countries, porous borders, global travel, and parental refusals to vaccinate their children in this country, diseases we once thought we vanquished with vaccines are making a comeback, often in tragic ways. We are now seeing a resurgence of measles, polio, pertussis, and our old friend, influenza. While our eyes and fears have been focused on Ebola, the rise of vaccine-preventable outbreaks has grown. In response to these outbreaks, California passed vaccination legislation requiring all children to be vaccinated against diseases, including measles and pertussis (McGreevy & Lin, 2015). Here are a few scientific facts about these diseases:

- **Measles** is highly contagious virus and can be transmitted via aerosolization, i.e., breathing the droplets of the virus in the same air as someone who has measles. The virus can live in a room for up to two hours in the airspace after an infected person has coughed or sneezed in the space.
- **Pertussis** is a highly contagious respiratory disease caused by the bacterium *Bordetella pertussis*. It can also be transmitted via aerosolization, i.e., breathing the droplets of the virus in the same air as someone who has pertussis.
- "**Polio virus** is very contagious. It spreads through contact with the stool of an infected person and droplets from a sneeze or cough. If you get stool or droplets from an infected person on your hands and you touch your mouth, you can get infected. Also, if you put objects, like toys, that have stool or droplets on them into your mouth, you can get infected." (CDC, 2014, para. 11).
- **Ebola virus** can only be transmitted through direct contact with body fluids that contain the virus. Health care workers who take care of the sickest, dying, and dead Ebola victims are at greater risk than the general population.
- **Immunization**, i.e., stimulating the body with vaccines to create antibodies against a disease, currently prevents an estimated two to three million deaths every year (World Health Organization [WHO], 2015).
- Measles, polio, pertussis, and influenza by themselves kill more people annually than Ebola has at the height of the latest outbreak.

An interactive map of Vaccine Preventable Outbreaks from 2008 to the present can be found at the Council on Foreign Relation website at http://www.cfr.org/interactives/GH_Vaccine_Map/#map. As you can see from this dynamic model, the rise of outbreaks directly corresponds with declines in vaccinations, thanks in large part to the spread of "Wakefieldism," and in some parts of the world, attacks on vaccinators and public health workers by terrorists (Garrett & Builder, 2014; Harlow & Summers, 2014). The following table provides an overview of selected vaccine preventable diseases, the number of cases in the U.S., and the number of global cases and deaths.

What About Ebola?

The video of the Ebola cases time series, https://youtu.be/XdYyvR3DJ-A, makes a visual statement that in the fall of 2014, a wild fire of disease was spreading across Guinea, Liberia, and Sierra Leone. Those of us in the U.S. felt safe until the day Thomas Eric Duncan arrived in the Texas Presbyterian Emergency Department on September 24, 2014. The hospital had

TABLE 17-1 Diseases by Cases and Deaths in the U.S. and Globally

Disease	Cases in U.S.	Global Cases and Deaths
Measles	173 cases, 21 states and District of Columbia 5 outbreaks in 2015[a]	In 2013, 145,700 deaths; About 400 deaths every day, or 16 deaths every hour.[b]
Pertussis	10,000–40,000 cases each year; 10–20 children's deaths[c]	16 million cases in 2008; 195,000 children's deaths[d]
Polio	None; free of disease for 30 years due to vaccine.[e]	416 reported cases in 2013; One in 200 infections leads to irreversible paralysis. Of those, 5% to 10% die when their breathing muscles become immobilized[f]
Influenza	98,680 cases 2014/15[g] 125 pediatric deaths in U.S., 90% unvaccinated[h]	250,000 to 500,000 deaths (all ages)[h]
Ebola virus	4 cases, 1 death[i]	10 countries; 20,272 cases; 7,953 deaths[i]

[a]CDC,2015d	[d]WHO, 2011	[g]CDC, 2015
[b]WHO, 2015	[e]CDC, 2014	[h]CDC, 2015b
[c]CDC, 2013b	[f]WHO, 2014	[i]WaveWeb, 2015

just received Ebola training the week before, yet the man's signs, symptoms, and history were discounted, and he was sent home. Four days later, he returned to the ED and was admitted to the hospital. From the time he was admitted until his death, nurses changed his dirty linens, assisted him when he vomited, and inserted IV lines and endotracheal tubes. Two of the nurses who cared for Mr. Duncan contracted the disease. The head of the CDC implied the nurses had used sloppy procedures and contaminated themselves, a blame-the-victim response that outraged nurses across the country (Steenhuysen, 2014a).

A survey conducted in early October 2014 among 400 nurses by National Nurses United found over half (60%) indicated their hospitals were "not prepared to handle patients with Ebola and over three-quarters (80%) indicated their administration had not communicated with them any policy regarding the disease" (para. 16). In addition, almost one-third (30%) of the nurses indicated they had insufficient protective personal equipment (PPE) gear (e.g., eye goggles and fluid resistant gowns) on hand to protect themselves from bodily fluids, the main method of transmission of the disease (Steenhuysen, 2014b).

After the backlash against the federal agency, the CDC revised the PPE donning and doffing procedure. This new process delineates the roles and responsibilities of the caregivers and their supervisors, and establishes a procedure for a buddy to assist with donning and doffing, as well as an observer who stands by with a checklist to ensure no steps are missed (CDC, 2015c). Although there is tremendous *awareness* of the Ebola virus, and the CDC has launched a multi-media website called "The Road to Zero: the CDC's Response to the 2014 Ebola Epidemic" (see online resources), it is improbable that every hospital, ambulatory care clinic, and physician practice in the U.S. has the correct PPE resources; been trained to a level of automatic PPE competency; and inculcated the proper protocols into nursing staff, ancillary staff, custodial staff, supervisors, and health care managers. According to one source (Gary Hicks, personal communication, April 18, 2014) the costs of setting up rooms and an area in the ED to isolate an Ebola patient prior to transfer to a CDC-approved Ebola treatment facility are quite high. The new construction costs for the space required to hold an Ebola patient and family members who accompany him to the ED, plus his contaminated linens, can be a minimum of $35,000. This does not include the labor costs associated with the estimated 21 people per shift required to care for the patient. Although the list of CDC-approved sites for caring for Ebola patients has grown to 55 hospitals as of February 18, 2015, this is only a small proportion of hospitals in the U.S. (CDC, 2015a).

As a health care manager, you will be responsible for ensuring your organization is prepared for contagious outbreaks, from measles to Ebola. You will be required to work with clinicians to establish appropriate training and protocols in the event of an outbreak or epidemic. Part of this training must include an emphasis on teamwork and on "**just culture**," which puts the focus on "what went wrong, not who caused the problem" (Barnsteiner, 2011, para. 6). When CDC Director Frieden blamed nurses in Texas for contaminating themselves, he demonstrated a punitive approach. The nurses were not consciously reckless; the *system* set them up for failure. Just culture distinguishes between:

- "**Human error**, an inadvertent action ... a slip, lapse, or mistake;
- **At-risk behavior**, a behavioral choice that increases risk where risk is not recognized or is mistakenly believed to be justified; and,
- **Reckless behavior**, a behavioral choice to consciously disregard a substantial and unjustifiable risk" (Pennsylvania Patient Safety Authority, 2012, slide 4).

Hospitals must have sufficient resources on hand to take care of infectious patients if they present to the ED. Lacking these resources and appropriate quarantine facilities, nurses and health care managers have an obligation to collaborate and speak up (Buchbinder, 2014).

It is critical to ensure our communities and the populations we serve are informed about the importance of vaccinations. To protect the health of our nation, we must move our patients and communities to become protected against vaccine preventable diseases. As health care managers we must remember:

- **Herd immunity**, also known as **community immunity** or **indirect immunity**, which is conferred when most of the population has been vaccinated, is not the same as a closed colony. In the latter situation, no one new comes in and no one leaves the protective bubble. This is not a realistic approach to thinking about immunizations. We are an open society, with global connections. Disease does not respect national borders or state boundaries (CDC, 2013a).

- Vaccines are not new. Nor are parent advocates. Lady Mary Wortley Montagu visited Turkey in 1717 and wrote letters home about the women healers who vaccinated children against smallpox using nutshells full of the infectious material. She asserted she would not leave the country without having her son "engrafted" and vowed to take the treatment to England. She also swore to fight physicians if needed to bring the innovation to her beloved country (Halsall, 1998).

- Using disease for warfare is not new, either. An eyewitness account of pustule-covered bodies being tossed over the walls of the city of Caffa gave rise to a theory that the Black Plague spread through Europe as a result of biological warfare. The author concluded that it really only gave bubonic plague to the city, not all of Europe. Still, it was an effective weapon (Wheelis, 2002).

- We should be very concerned about ensuring the next generation is protected. Something as easy to prevent as measles, mumps, polio, pertussis, and influenza can be used as biological warfare against unvaccinated populations (Southern Illinois School of Medicine, 2012).

Vaccinations and Health Care Managers

At this point, a few of you may be saying, "Aside from ensuring my employees have their flu shot, this is not my job." That would be a misperception. Anywhere a health care manager is responsible for the health of a population, such as in **Accountable Care Organizations (ACOs)** which are "organized groups of physicians, hospitals or other providers jointly accountable for caring for a defined patient population" (Lake, Stewart, & Ginsburg, 2011, para. 1), she is responsible for the health care provided by those physicians. Likewise, as the proportion of physicians employed by hospitals continues to rise, the buck for the quality of the health care delivered stops with the CEO and the Board of Trustees (Vaidya, 2013). We haven't even mentioned the **Healthcare Effectiveness Data and Information Set (HEDIS)**, one of the most widely used sets of health care performance measures in the U.S. used in organizations like health care insurance companies, ambulatory care centers, public health clinics, or urgent care centers, where health care managers are employed (National Committee for Quality Assurance, 2015). Health care organizations with large data bases have the ability to conduct big data analyses and to implement the recommendations from the 2013 Institute of Medicine report, *Best Care at Lower Cost: The Path to Continuously Learning Health Care in America.* They also have the ability to use better health literacy approaches to improve communication between health care providers and families. Where there is good team work, there is no disconnect between health care managers and health care providers. This, too, is the responsibility of health care managers. The bottom line is health care managers *are* responsible for the health of populations and for ensuring vaccinations are provided for a healthier population today and for future generations (Buchbinder, 2015).

BIOTERRORISM IN HEALTH CARE SETTINGS

Several years ago, one of the chapter authors asked the question, "Are health care professionals prepared for disasters?" and closed with the following:

> *In light of intelligence findings that smaller targets will be next, we can no longer pretend that it won't happen to us. We cannot undo the horrific events of 9–11, Hurricane Katrina or the earthquakes in Haiti. We can, however, learn from them and take action as citizens and as healthcare professionals. It's time for us all to get involved and get prepared before disaster hits* (Buchbinder, 2010, para. 9).

At the time, the focus of Homeland Security's anti-terrorist efforts in the U.S. was on large symbolic targets. Now, however, we know "softer" targets, such as sports stadiums, amusement parks, schools, and hospitals, are potential sites for attacks (Blair, 2005). A **bioterrorism** attack could be as subtle as a patient walking into the emergency department with a highly contagious disease, one not easily amenable to vaccinations or treatment. Posing as patients, terrorists could be planted as human time bombs carrying deadly contagion (CDC, 2007).

If you think such a scenario couldn't happen in your local hospital or ambulatory care center, perhaps you should read the work of Elin A. Gursky, ScD (2004, 2012). Her 2004 report on bioterrorism readiness in rural hospitals commissioned by the National Defense University reads like a litany of what health care managers should *not* do. This in-depth case study approach examined five rural hospitals' preparedness for biologically induced mass casualties. Hospitals were selected for their "proximity to military installations, nuclear or chemical plants, large-scale agricultural production, an international border, or major waterways" (Gursky, 2004, p. 15). In interviews with key informants, Dr. Gursky found unprepared staff and out-of-date facilities which could be overwhelmed with small numbers of casualties, much less large ones. Here is a partial listing of her findings on what these facilities lacked:

- Training on how to identify early signs of potential biological hazards;
- Reliable communication equipment, especially in areas where cell phones are not usable;
- Vaccinations, such as smallpox, due to travel distances to vaccination programs;
- Quarantine facilities or up to date facilities;
- Personal protective equipment (PPE) and knowledge of how to use it;
- Emergency inventory in case the facility is unable to bring in materials;
- Security, e.g., some hospitals left doors open 24/7, some had *no* security guards; and
- Suspicion, e.g., the feeling that everyone in town was "like family."

Many of these shortcomings are under the control of hospital administrators. As noted previously in the section on vaccinations, the survey conducted among 400 nurses by National Nurses United found over half (60%) indicated their hospitals were "not prepared to handle patients with Ebola" (Steenhuysen, 2014b). Health care managers are responsible for planning, organizing, controlling, and monitoring resources. Staffing, training, equipment, inventory, communication trees, inventory control, and security measures—all of these are under the purview of health care managers. As the national "See Something, Say Something" campaign has demonstrated, people can be trained to become more cautious and alert, with positive results (Gendar, Parascandola, Deutsch, & Goldsmith, 2010; Nationwide Suspicious Activity Reporting Initiative, 2015).

Per the American College of Healthcare Executives (2013), health care managers are expected to be prepared to take action in times of disaster. The Federal Bureau of Investigation (FBI) and CDC work closely together in all cases of suspected bioterrorism (FBI, CDC, & Department of Justice [DOJ], 2011). The United Nations Environmental Programme (UNEP) (2014) reported natural and man-made disasters are increasing in frequency and size of impact. UNEP is responding with disaster prevention and preparedness educational training programs. As health care managers, it is incumbent upon you to join in this global work and to educate your staff on better ways to respond to and prepare for all hazards emergencies, including bioterrorism.

HUMAN TRAFFICKING

While **human trafficking** takes a wide variety of forms and occurs in a multitude of industries, the most widely accepted definition of the phenomenon is that of the United Nations 2000 Protocol to Prevent, Suppress and Punish Trafficking in Persons, Especially Women and Children, Supplementing the United Nations Convention Against

Transnational Organized Crime. First proposed in 2000, the Trafficking in Persons, or TIP, Protocol, was "open to all States for signature from 12 to 15 December 2000 in Palermo, Italy, and thereafter at United Nations Headquarters in New York until 12 December 2002" (UN, 2000).

The heart of the TIP Protocol are articles 2 and 3, the Statement of Purpose and the Definitions of Terms (p. 2), which state:

Article 2

Statement of purpose

The purposes of this Protocol are:

(a) To prevent and combat trafficking in persons, paying particular attention to women and children;
(b) To protect and assist the victims of such trafficking, with full respect for their human rights; and
(c) To promote cooperation among States Parties in order to meet those objectives.

Article 3

Use of terms

For the purposes of this Protocol:

(a) "Trafficking in persons" shall mean the recruitment, transportation, transfer, harbouring or receipt of persons, by means of the threat or use of force or other forms of coercion, of abduction, of fraud, of deception, of the abuse of power or of a position of vulnerability or of the giving or receiving of payments or benefits to achieve the consent of a person having control over another person, for the purpose of exploitation. Exploitation shall include, at a minimum, the exploitation of the prostitution of others or other forms of sexual exploitation, forced labour or services, slavery or practices similar to slavery, servitude or the removal of organs;
(b) The consent of a victim of trafficking in persons to the intended exploitation set forth in subparagraph (a) of this article shall be irrelevant where any of the means set forth in subparagraph (a) have been used;
(c) The recruitment, transportation, transfer, harbouring or receipt of a child for the purpose of exploitation shall be considered "trafficking in persons" even if this does not involve any of the means set forth in subparagraph (a) of this article;
(d) "Child" shall mean any person under eighteen years of age.

The TIP Protocol is not new. It has been in existence and promoted in all anti-trafficking efforts for over a decade (United Nations Office of Drugs and Crime [UNODC], 2000a). As of 2015, the list of countries that have signed the protocol still has over a dozen unsigned lines (UNODC, 2000b). Why wouldn't a country agree to the TIP Protocol? Likewise, why would a country sign the TIP Protocol, then not enforce it? Scholars and activists alike are working on this issue, with mixed results. In this section we will explore the reasons why modern slavery persists and what you can do as a health care manager.

Culture Predicts the Business Model

Worldwide, human trafficking follows cultural approaches to business. In Asia, there is a trade and development model, and humans are used to build national economy. In Eurasia and Eastern Europe, it is a natural resource model. Furs, oil, lumber, and humans are sold as commodities. In Europe, the violent entrepreneur model takes center stage with Balkan Crime Groups. Humans are disposable goods; in fact, victims are often tattooed to show which gang owns them. In the U.S., the American pimp model follows a high consumption, low savings route. Runaways and street children are lured by male and female traffickers. Victims, often minority women in poverty-stricken homes, are told they'll live the high life, and find out later it is the low life. In Latin America, there is a supermarket approach. Lots of women and children provide opportunities for low cost and high volume. If one dies, no worries, there are more where they came from. Illegal immigration and people smuggling can lead to trafficking if the "customer" can't pay the smuggler. Africa combines traditional slavery with high technology. The state of Edo, Nigeria is at the center of trafficking and follows the old slave routes (Buchbinder, 2014; Carling, 2005; Shelly, 2010). The International Labour Organization (2012) estimates there are 20.9 million victims of human trafficking globally, including 5.5 million children; 55% are women and girls.

The enormous profit that can be made from this transnational crime facilitates the push and pull factors. This is a $150 billion a year business. The money is good, the risks are low, and in many countries the consequences, even if a trafficker is caught, are minor. In many nations, politicians and police are corrupt and profit from trafficking and border patrols are often complicit in crime. Higher levels of poverty predict great levels of human trafficking. In places like India, if you are born into a brothel, you will remain in a brothel (Buchbinder, 2013; Red Light Films, HBO Cinemax, Sundance Institute Documentary Film, Briski, & Kauffman, 2004).

You may wonder why it persists. The bottom line is as long as women and children are considered chattel, i.e., "a movable article of personal property, or slave," it will continue. Patriarchy, lower education for women, and lower status of women predict greater levels of trafficking with one exception. Some clients want educated women so they can feel they have a "high class call girl." The value of the trafficked person depends on the part of the world, but more often than not, the trafficked person is treated poorly. There is a higher mortality rate among trafficked women and children. In Southeast Asia, if a slave contracts the HIV virus and AIDS, she will not be treated. She will be tossed out onto the street to die.

TABLE 17-2 The Push and Pull of Human Trafficking

Push Factors of Human Trafficking	Pull Factors of Human Trafficking
Poverty, low educational levels, patriarchy; High birth rate →low value of human life; Street children unsupervised by parents; Runaways and abused children susceptible; Destabilization of governments (e.g., Syria, Iraq, Soviet Union, Latin America, Africa); Rise of organized crime from former soldiers and enforcers (Russian mob, MS-13); and Natural disasters leave women and children unprotected.	Demand for sex in areas with large numbers of unmarried men (mining, agricultural); Sex tourism, demand for children both male and female; Demand for compliant soldiers (<12 years); Demand for cheap labor (global competition), domestic servants, agricultural workers; Criminal demand for children for begging; and Demand for babies and body parts.

Data from: International Labour Organization, 2012; Polaris.org, 2015; Shelley, 2010.

The average life expectancy of a woman or child post-trafficking is seven years (Hauser & Castillo, 2013). If they survive and are freed and not jailed, they continue to have mental health issues. Some return to their traffickers because they have no other life skills. If you can't read, write, or have skills to support yourself in an alternative way, your options are extremely limited.

Perhaps at this point, you're thinking, "This is *not* happening where I live." You would be wrong. Activists estimate at least 100,000 people are trafficked in the U.S. (Polaris, 2015). The majority are women and children trafficked for sex. Many organized U.S. crime rings and gangs have diversified from drug and gun trafficking to human trafficking. They can only sell a drug or gun once, but they can resell a human many times over. Among other major roads, the I-95 corridor from Florida to Boston is a main artery for trafficking. An activist recently told one of the authors that due to crack-downs at rest-stops and truck stops, the traffickers are moving to less beaten paths and routes that parallel the corridor.

With the Trafficking Victims Protection Act (TVPA) of 2000, which echoes the definitions of trafficking in the TIP protocol now in effect in all 50 states, you would think we'd have a better handle at stopping this crime, as well as good data (Government Printing Office, 2000). The answer is we're not great, but we're getting better. One of the problems with examining human trafficking is that it is inherently a covert activity. The National Institute of Justice (NIJ, 2010) states, "Due to the underground nature of trafficking, the number of victims is unknown (para. 1)." While attempting to improve data comparability, we still have a wide variety of agencies collecting data in different ways, making it difficult to compare the data, i.e., the apples to oranges and pineapples problem

(Farrell et al., 2012). What we do know is that in 2014, per the U.S. State Department Trafficking in Persons report:

- "In 2013, U.S. Immigration and Customs Enforcement (ICE) Homeland Security Investigations (HSI) reported opening 1,025 investigations possibly involving human trafficking, an increase from 894 in Fiscal Year (FY) 2012.
- The Federal Bureau of Investigation (FBI) formally opened 220 human trafficking investigations concerning suspected adult and foreign child victims, a decrease from 306 in FY 2012, and additionally initiated 514 investigations involving the sex trafficking of children, an increase from 440 in FY 2012.
- The Department of Social Services (DSS) reported investigating 159 human trafficking-related cases worldwide during FY 2013, an increase from 95 in FY 2012.
- The Department of Defense (DoD) reported investigating nine human trafficking-related cases involving military personnel, an increase from five in FY 2012.
- The Department of Justice (DOJ) reported a total of 161 federal human trafficking prosecutions in FY 2013, charging 253 defendants. Of these, 222 defendants engaged predominately in sex trafficking and 31 engaged predominately in labor trafficking, although multiple defendants engaged in both.
- In FY 2013, DOJ's Civil Rights Division, in coordination with U.S. Attorney's Offices (USAOs), initiated 71 prosecutions involving forced labor and sex trafficking of adults by force, fraud, or coercion. Of these, 53 were predominantly sex trafficking and 18 predominantly labor trafficking; several cases involved both.
- During FY 2013, DOJ convicted a total of 174 traffickers in cases involving forced labor, sex trafficking of adults, and sex trafficking of children, compared to 138 such convictions obtained in FY 2012. Of these, 113 were predominantly sex trafficking and 25 were predominantly labor trafficking, although several involved both. These totals do not include child sex trafficking cases brought under non-trafficking statutes. In these cases, penalties imposed ranged from probation to life imprisonment plus five years. During the reporting period, federal prosecutors secured life sentences and other significant terms of imprisonment against traffickers in multiple cases" (p. 398).

The U.S. now has an interagency strategic plan to combat trafficking in persons, a first in this country, which strives to align efforts, improve understanding, expand access to services, and improve outcomes. One of these improved outcomes is to treat the trafficked person as a victim, not as a criminal (President's Interagency Task Force to Monitor and Combat Trafficking in Persons, 2014). One of the agencies on this task force is the Department of Health and Human Services (DHHS). The DHHS has pledged to:

- "leverage the work of DOJ's National Institute of Justice to identify targeted screening tools for human trafficking for specific use within medical and health systems (including community clinics and emergency rooms), child welfare systems, mental health and substance abuse treatment providers, providers of services to homeless populations, human services programs, and other systems likely to encounter potential victims.
- explore the development of standardized health care protocols for intake (including increased focus on medical history and past intimate partner violence), evaluation/ examination, referrals, evidence collection, and long-term care (physical, oral, and mental) in human trafficking situations" (President's Interagency Task Force to Monitor and Combat Trafficking in Persons, 2014, p. 23).

All health care organizations in the U.S. ultimately report to the DHHS. Efforts are underway now through the Administration for Children & Families (ACF), a branch of the DHHS, and professional organizations to educate nurses and physicians about the signs of a trafficking victim (ACF, 2015; Munoz, 2012; Patel, Ahn, & Burke, 2010). These victims, much like domestic violence and child abuse victims of the past, have been invisible in our EDs. With increased training, they will become visible and need medical and social services. As a health care manager, your job will be to ensure your clinicians are trained for the signs and to have referrals in place to assist the victim to become free and stay free. Collaborating with state and local law enforcement agencies, as well as social services, mental health, and other agencies, will be critical to helping these individuals. Many non-governmental organizations are short-handed and poorly funded. Your health care organization may be called upon to partner with community voluntary groups to ensure their long-term survival, as well as that of the survivors of human trafficking. Human trafficking *is* in your back yard.

VIOLENCE IN HEALTH CARE SETTINGS

Almost daily, it seems the media outlets are filled with reports of violence, so much so that we almost become numb to them. An active shooter in a popular mall. A disgruntled employee returns to his former place of employment armed to kill. A student with mental health problems murders a favorite teacher, a classroom full of students, or goes on a campus rampage. However, when violence hits in health care settings, we are shocked and ask, "*How did this happen?*" These institutions, these sacred places, are supposed to serve and care for our loved ones. Yet in many instances they cannot protect our loved ones because of the nature of the settings themselves. The purpose of this section is to provide a brief overview of violence in health care settings, raise your awareness of this phenomenon, and encourage you to be aware of and find ways to address and prevent violence when you are health care managers.

What Is Violence in Health Care Settings?

One of the challenges in writing about statistics on violence in health care settings is the data are not always collected in the same manner, using the same definitions across various reporting agencies and authors. For this discussion, we chose to use data from the Bureau of Labor Statistics (BLS); the Bureau of Justice Statistics (BJS); the Centers for Disease Control and Prevention (CDC), the National Institute for Occupational Safety and Health (NIOSH); the National Violence Against Women Survey; and peer-reviewed literature published by epidemiologists, physicians, nurses, attorneys, law enforcement officers, criminologists, and forensic psychologists, as well as important papers from professional organizations.

NIOSH (2002) defines **workplace violence** as "violent acts (including physical assaults and threats of assaults) directed toward persons at work or duty" (p. 1). In reality, violence in health care settings can occur against workers, clients/residents, visitors, relatives, i.e., *anyone* physically present in a health care setting. In 2015, the Occupational Safety and Health Administration (OSHA) reported that while "under 20% of all workplace injuries happen to health care workers, health care workers suffer over 50% of all assaults" (p. 3). In 2007, the BLS Census of Fatal Occupational Injuries data showed health care settings had the following fatality rates: ambulatory health care services, 48 per 6,013,000 workers, or a fatality rate of 0.8; hospitals, 29 per 5,169,000 workers, or a fatality rate of 0.6; and nursing and residential care facilities, 18 per 2,256,000 or a 0.8 fatality rate.

These rates are low when compared to workplace violence statistics overall. Consistent with the BLS data, the BJS found homicides represented less than 1% of workplace violent crimes, or about 900 work-related homicides annually. "Between 1993 and 1999 in the United States, an average of 1.7 million violent victimizations per year were committed against persons age 12 or older who were at work or on duty, according to the National Crime Victimization Survey (NCVS)" (Duhart, 2001, p. 1). Workplace violence accounted for almost a fifth (18%) of all violent crime during the time period under review. In other words, victims of violent crimes have a one in five chance of being at work when the attack occurs. In 2010, The Joint Commission (TJC) reported "significant increases in reports of assault, rape and homicide, with the greatest number of reports in the last three years: 36 incidents in 2007, 41 in 2008 and 33 in 2009" (para. 2). Preventing this workplace violence is the responsibility of the health care manager.

Types of Workers

For the same time period (1993 to 1999), physicians experienced a rate of 16.2 per 1,000 workers of violent victimizations in the workplace and nurses experienced a rate of 21.9 per 1,000. While the rate was not statistically different from that of physicians, it was "72% higher than medical technicians and more than twice the rate of other medical field workers" (Duhart, 2001, p. 4). Mental health workers experienced higher rates of violence than their peers, and have "higher assault rates than all other occupations—except law enforcement" (Duhart, 2001, p. 5). Rates for these workers were: mental health professional workers, 68.3 per 1,000; mental health custodial workers, 69.0 per 1,000; and other mental health workers, 40.7 per 1,000 (Duhart, 2001).

Mental health and emergency room workers have similar risks in part due to the fact that violence from the street often follows patients into the ER; however, the data on ER workers are dearth. According to the Emergency Nurses Association (2010), threats and violence are underreported because some employees assume that it's part of the job, or are fearful of reporting the incident to their supervisor because they are afraid of poor performance appraisals. In 2005, the Michigan College of Emergency Physicians Workplace Violence Taskforce surveyed ER physicians and asked how often members experienced work-related violence in the past year. Of the 171 physicians who completed the survey, three-quarters indicated they were victims of verbal abuse, slightly over a quarter indicated they were physically assaulted, and 3.5% indicated they were stalked (Kowalenko, Walters, Khare, & Compton, 2005). Clearly, more and better data are needed to have a better understanding of the patterns and perpetrators of violence in these volatile areas of health care.

Types of Crimes

Between 1993 and 1999, the "majority (94%) of workplace crimes were simple and aggravated assaults" (Duhart, 2001, p. 5). There were four simple assaults for every aggravated assault. Assault rates, as noted before, were highest among mental health care workers. ER physicians also reported high rates of assault, with one in four responding physicians having been physically assaulted (Kowalenko, Walters, Khare, & Compton, 2005). The BJS found assailants were most likely to be male, most likely to be of a similar racial group to the victim, most likely to be young, and had about a one in three chance of being under the influence of alcohol or drugs at the time of attack (Duhart, 2001).

Stalking

Stalking is defined as:

> a course of conduct directed at a specific person that would cause a reasonable person to feel fear. … This can include: unwanted phone calls, texts, letters, emails, social media posts, following or spying on the victim, showing up at places without a legitimate reason, waiting at places for the victim, leaving unwanted items, presents, or flowers; posting information or spreading rumors about the victim. (Baum, Catalano, & Rose, 2009, p. 1)

In the National Violence Against Women Survey noted earlier, using a strict definition of stalking, i.e., the victim felt a high level of fear, the authors found that "8 percent of the women surveyed were stalked versus 2 percent of men have been stalked at some point in their life" (Tjaden & Thoennes, 1998, p. 3). About half of the victims of stalking, both male and female, reported their concerns to police. Police were more likely to intervene when the victim was a woman. Of those who did not report their complaints, the top three reasons for non-reporting were: "did not think it was a police matter, thought police couldn't do anything, or feared reprisal from stalker" (Tjaden & Thoennes, 1998, p. 10). When compared to individuals who had never been stalked, stalking victims reported "more fears for their personal safety and being stalked, carried something on them for personal safety, and felt things had gotten worse in general for men and women with regard to personal safety" (Tjaden & Thoennes, 1998, p. 11).

Stalking is an underreported phenomenon (Davis & Chipman, 1997; Logan, 2010). Victims are embarrassed, unwilling to disclose their concerns for fears of being ridiculed or worse, and fear losing their job. In addition, victims are often in the throes of domestic troubles that may have already spilled over into violence, and fear reprisal from their stalkers. Stalking can last an average of two years and can escalate into aggravated assault and homicide, especially if the stalker is an intimate partner (Logan, 2010; Tjaden & Thoennes, 1998). Concannon (2005) found "individuals who engaged in stalking behaviors with greater frequency over the course of one year were significantly more likely to be violent than were those who did not engage in such behaviors or who engaged in such behaviors on a less frequent basis" (p. vi). Fear of the stalker, feelings of helplessness, and being overwhelmed contribute to the victim's fear of job loss—if they dare to share their terror. The National Center for Victims of Crime has a Stalking Resource Center (see online resources), which includes definitions, data, and resources for stalking victims.

In the case of health care professionals, stalkers are more common among mental health professionals. One of the few available studies on the actual prevalence of stalking of mental health professionals found that "5% of counseling center staff had been stalked by current or former clients, 8% had a family member stalked, and over half (65%) had experienced harassment" (Romans, Hays, & White, 1996, p. 595). Stalking can last over a period of a few months to several years (McIvor & Petch, 2006; Mullen, Mackenzie, Ogloff, Pathé, McEwan & Purcell, 2006). The obsessive stalker can be male or female, personality disordered and/or substance abusing, and may be in search of "intimacy or are ex-partners unwilling to abandon the lost relationship" (Mullen et al., 2006, p. 440).

Homicide

With respect to females, while their overall numbers were lower than males for violent crime, when they were targets of violence in the workplace, women are more likely to be *killed at work* and were more likely to be *killed by someone they know and/or an intimate partner.* These homicides do not appear in a vacuum. Oftentimes, victims have reported domestic violence incidents to the police and have obtained restraining orders against their partners. Employers may take the easy route and fire an employee who has issues with domestic violence (DOJ, FBI, 2002). In health care settings, this type of callous response is unconscionable. The next time a supervisor sees that employee, she could be dead on arrival in the ED.

According to NIOSH (2014), "homicide accounts for 40% of all workplace deaths among female workers; over 25% of the homicide victims are assaulted by people they know, and 16% are victims of domestic violence that spills over into the workplace" (para. 1). At some point in a tumultuous relationship, intimate partners became murderers. Oftentimes before the murder occurs, there have been warning signs, such as harassment; emotional, psychological, and physical abuse; and stalking. Many women are reluctant to tell co-workers they are going through an ugly separation or divorce. This shame can cost them their lives and the lives of others.

Consequences, Costs, and Planning

In addition to the physical consequences of assault, emotional and mental sequelae take a significant toll on victims and witnesses of violence (Gillespie, 2008). From a financial perspective, workplace violence has a large impact on the bottom line of an organization, causing increasing absences from work, greater use of workers' compensation claims, sick time, and personal injury lawsuits. From a business perspective, it makes good sense to have a violence prevention plan in the workplace, which means when you become health care managers, you will need to be prepared to develop or update these plans.

The Joint Commission (2010) has a list of recommended actions that encompass improved risk assessment, training of staff, improved communication, crime reporting, and root cause analysis of the incident. Many excellent resources for developing workplace violence prevention plans are available online. The Emergency Nurses Association (ENA) (2010) has an *ENA Workplace Violence Toolkit*, which provides health care professionals with a step-by-step plan for addressing violence in the ED. In addition, OSHA (2015) has *Guidelines for Preventing Workplace Violence for Health Care & Social Service Workers*, and the New York Department of Labor (2009) has *Workplace Violence Prevention Program Guidelines*, to name but a few. The video from the Department of Homeland Security (2013) on active shooter scenarios is also an excellent resource. Whether we want to think about it or not, workplace violence in health care settings is a real phenomenon that won't go away by ignoring it. As health care managers, it is incumbent upon us to protect our workers, employees, patients, and families from those intent on bringing violence to health care settings.

MEDICAL TOURISM

Medical Tourism Defined

Medical tourism relates to patients traveling to seek and receive medical care. Some consider it to be out-of-country travel, but the Deloitte Center for Health Solutions' classification of medical tourists provides a more comprehensive definition. Their three groups include:

- "Outbound: U.S. patients traveling to other countries for medical care
- Inbound: Foreign patients traveling to the U.S. for medical care
- Intrabound: U.S. patients traveling domestically for medical care" (Keckley & Underwood, 2009, p. 3)

The Inbound group has been very common for some hospitals in the U.S. that are known internationally for certain centers of excellence and market their expertise to people around the world. This type of medical tourism has been in existence for many years with people from other countries bringing sick children to a specialty children's hospital for treatment of a rare heart condition or cancer or with people accessing institutions like the Mayo Clinic or MD Anderson Cancer Center for diagnosis and treatment. The Intrabound tourists are also very common, with U.S. citizens going to these same places, as well as to the National Institutes of Health, seeking care. So, what's new about medical tourism?

First, we have not referred to these types of access to care as medical tourism, but that is technically what it is. Second, medical tourism of the Outbound patient has become a new growth industry not just in the U.S., but around the world as well. Third, while in the past most of the care provided was highly specialized care, now the care being sought and provided also includes regular types of care, such as dental care, and relatively common types of procedures, such as dental implants, plastic surgeries, or knee replacements. There are also different types of health-related tourism, including dental tourism, wellness tourism (for preventative care), Lasik tourism, and tourism for all different types of medical procedures. Thus, what was once a one-way street with people coming to the U.S. for care has now become a global network of people traveling all over the world for medical care.

Drivers of Medical Tourism

There are clearly many economic, social, and political factors that impact the continuing development of the medical tourism industry. Dollars and cents are major contributors to this trend. The high cost of health care in the U.S. is a major factor that drives citizens to seek care elsewhere, whether across the border in Mexico or traveling to Asia for a procedure. As discussed throughout this textbook, U.S. health care costs have risen significantly over the last 50 years, making it difficult for some people to purchase health insurance and/or to be able to afford care. The economics of providing care make it much easier for health care providers in other countries to offer medical care at a much lower price than in the U.S. Some examples of the price differentials are provided in Textbox 17-1. As those data suggest, "serious savings" are to be found in seeking care outside the U.S. (Smith, 2012). These lower costs may serve as an incentive for individuals (both insured and uninsured) to travel to receive care, and it also may provide incentives for health insurers and self-insured companies to encourage insureds and employees to use these lower-priced locations.

Many entrepreneurs have seen opportunities to invest in and develop service expertise in different areas, thereby attracting patients of all different types to their facilities. Some health care professionals have trained in the U.S., become highly skilled, and either returned home or moved their practices to other countries where it is far less expensive to run a practice, and they stand to make a good return on their investment. In addition, "many foreign facilities involved in medical tourism have affiliations, agreements or sponsorships with trusted U.S. entities such as the Cleveland Clinic and the Memorial Sloan-Kettering Cancer Center, as well as prestigious universities, including Harvard, Duke, Johns Hopkins, Cornell and Columbia. In addition, Christus Health System in Texas operates numerous hospitals and clinics in Mexico through a joint venture, Christus Muguerza" (Ryan, 2011, p. 20).

There are several social factors that impact medical tourism. In some countries, medical care is just not available, resulting in unmet needs and forcing those with resources to seek

---

TEXTBOX 17-1. COMPARISON OF COSTS BY PROCEDURE

Gastric Sleeve Surgery
  Costa Rica, $17,386–U.S., $30,000 (Edelheit, 2014)
Heart Bypass
  Thailand, $11,000–U.S., $130,000 (Ryan, 2011)
Heart Valve Replacement
  Singapore, $12,500–U.S., $160,000 (Ryan, 2011)
Hip Replacement
  Belgium, $13,660–U.S., $125,000 (Rosenthal, 2013)
Hysterectomy
  India, $3,000–U.S., $20,000 (Ryan, 2011)
Knee Replacement
  Costa Rica, $23,531–U.S., $59,000 (Edelheit, 2014)
Spinal Fusion
  Malaysia, $6,000–U.S., $62,000 (Ryan, 2011)

Data from: Edelheit, 2014; Rosenthal, 2013; Ryan, 2011.

care elsewhere. Others may consider the quality of care in the U.S. higher and travel to receive it. Health insurance also impacts medical tourism in several ways. Those in other countries with national health care systems, such as Canada or England, may face long wait lists for certain procedures like hip or knee replacements. Rather than waiting years, those with resources may opt to pay out-of-pocket and go elsewhere for care. Similarly, uninsured U.S. citizens may be able to afford less expensive care and find it more cost-effective to travel to another country for care.

Privacy provides yet another incentive for traveling for care. Celebrities from the U.S. may travel to another country for plastic or other types of surgery to avoid media attention. The reverse is also true for celebrities and dignitaries from other countries coming to the U.S.

Political issues play a role in medical tourism. The U.S. health care system is heavily regulated, while providing care in other countries is not regulated to the same degree. This provides incentives to set up practices and facilities elsewhere. It also means that some procedures or medications are more available in other countries, when they have not yet been approved and made available in the U.S. Additionally, the restrictions on certain types of procedures, such as transplants, may be significantly less in other countries, where organs for transplantation are more readily available (Underwood & Makadon, 2010). This leads to other concerns about both political and ethical issues relating to obtaining human organs. As pointed out by Leggat (2015), "a number of unethical practices have been described … in 2006, for example, 4000 prisoners in China were executed to provide 8000 kidneys and 3000 livers, mainly for foreign patients purchasing these organs" (p. 18).

On the other side of the political coin, some medical tourists may deem stricter regulation to be an indicator of higher quality and thus opt to travel to the U.S. for care. Laws such as EMTALA also provide impetus for people to come to the U.S. to seek care. Since U.S. hospitals cannot turn away patients from their emergency rooms, this is a huge incentive for patients. Some countries, such as Canada, are concerned that inbound medical tourists utilize resources that should be devoted to Canadian citizens and have recommended banning medical tourism (Glauser, 2014). A final political issue relates to political unrest in some countries, which may serve as a disincentive for attracting medical tourists to those areas and as an incentive to travel elsewhere for care.

Industry Size

Patients Beyond Borders is an organization that collects and reports data and information on medical tourism around the world. They estimate that 11 million patients travel each year, with the number of U.S. travelers being estimated at 1.2 million; this is expected to result in expenditures of $38.5–$55 billion (Patients Beyond Borders, 2014). Others have suggested these expenditures are even higher; "it has been estimated that medical tourism is a global industry of around $100 billion and growing at the rate of 20–30% per annum" (Bartold, 2014, p. 279). The CDC (2015e) reported a lower estimated number of 750,000 U.S. residents who partake in medical tourism on an annual basis. The Medical Tourism Association (2014) also collects data on medical tourism and reports statistics from many countries around the world. A few examples are:

- "The number of medical tourists traveling to Asia is expected to surpass 10 million by 2015 with Thailand, India and Singapore expected to control more than 80% market share" (para. 9).
- "The medical tourism industry in Malaysia generated approximately 20 million USD in revenue in 2013" (para. 13).
- "In 2014 Taiwan's medical tourism industry is expected to pump over 400 million USD into the economy" (para. 17).
- "According to 'Why International Medical Tourism is Growing', a 2013 article from *D Magazine*, the Mexican Government expects the number of U.S. medical tourists to reach 650,000 by 2020" (para. 29).
- "In 2012 400,000 Americans crossed international borders for dental care. For 2013, they project a growth rate of approximately 20 percent" (para. 29).

The increased number of facilities around the world that attract medical tourists is a huge part of the industry's growth. For example, many facilities in other countries that have become known as "world-class facilities," including Bumrungrad International Hospital in Bangkok, "one of the biggest, boasting more than 400,000 international patient visits per year" (Smith, 2012, p. 66). Other facilities include Hospital Clinica Biblica in Costa Rica, the Barbados Fertility Centre, and Hospital Punta Pacific in Panama City, Panama, "which is affiliated with Johns Hopkins Medicine International" (Smith, 2012, p. 68). These hospitals are all accredited by The Joint Commission International (JCI, 2015), whose "mission to improve global health" is achieved by providing "expertise to countries striving to establish national and regional quality and safety standards and country-specific accreditation" (p. 16). As of February 2015, JCI has awarded its *Gold Seal of Approval to* more than 700 accredited organizations in 62 countries (JCI, 2015) and has established a website to connect patients to these facilities (see http://www.worldhospitalsearch.org/).

Precise data are not available on the numbers of providers of care, costs, and utilization of medical tourism facilities. There are clearly sites all over the world that serve large numbers of medical tourists, which in turn infuses millions of dollars into the economies of these countries. While growth has occurred, it has not reached levels that were anticipated in 2010. This is attributed to Americans not wanting to travel to obtain care, employers not being willing to push for this lower priced option, concerns about non-clinical medical tourism facilitators, and problems with HIPAA (Mitchell, 2015). Many, particularly those affiliated with the industry, continue to be quite optimistic that the growth in medical and wellness tourism will continue (Stephano, 2014).

To Be or Not to Be a Medical Tourist?

Several researchers point out that the decision to become a medical tourist is a complex one for patients, as well as for companies seeking to control their health care expenditures by outsourcing care. Most frequently, the rationale for becoming a medical tourist is based on an unmet need for care; the level of pain; cost of care; and issues about the delivery of that care, such as accreditation and quality of facilities and health care professionals (Runnels & Carrerra, 2012; Stanley, 2010). To assist in the decision-making process the American Medical Association (AMA) developed a set of guiding principles in 2008 to help promote safety, as shown below (see Textbox 17-2).

An important set of considerations regarding medical tourism for both patients and companies relates to quality and the concomitant risks to patients, such as those delineated by the CDC (2015e) that include: communication concerns and language barriers, unsafe injection practices that could lead to communicable diseases, counterfeit or poor quality medications, exposure to antibiotic resistant bacteria, safety and quality of the blood supplies, and complications related to vacationing and/or flying following surgery. The CDC (2015e) recommends trying to address these issues prior to travel and specifically

---

TEXTBOX 17-2. AMA GUIDELINES FOR PATIENTS GOING OVERSEAS FOR CARE

- Medical care outside the U.S. should be voluntary.
- Financial incentives should not inappropriately limit diagnostic and therapeutic alternatives, or restrict treatment or referral options.
- Financial incentives should be used only for care at institutions accredited by recognized international accrediting bodies.
- Local follow-up care should be coordinated and financing arranged to ensure continuity of care.
- Coverage must include the costs of follow-up care upon return.
- Patients should be informed of rights and legal recourse before traveling.
- Patients should have access to physician licensing and outcomes data.
- Transfer of patient medical records should be consistent with HIPAA guidelines.
- Patients should be informed about potential risks of combining surgical procedures with long flights and vacation activities.

Source: "Medical Care Outside the United States," AMA Council on Medical Service Report 1 (A-08), as adopted.

seeking assistance from a "travel medicine practitioner" to address the process, risks, and procedures; checking credentials for facilities and other providers; having a written agreement detailing what will be done, what is covered, what the costs are, etc.; specifying who will be liable if there are problems; securing copies of medical records, prescriptions, follow-up care instructions, etc. to bring home; and arranging for follow-up care at home. As pointed out by both the AMA and CDC, it is also important for care to be coordinated by clinically-trained medical professionals, not just by a medical tourism facilitator with no clinical background (Mitchell, 2015).

Implications of Medical Tourism

While many people have questioned the need to travel for health care when the U.S. is thought to have the highest quality health care in the world, there are clearly some overriding issues that impel individuals to become medical tourists. Companies that are "dissatisfied with the value they receive in return for the investment they make in the health of their employees" are opting to change their health coverage to self-funded plans, to thereby assume the risk for the health care coverage of their employees, and to encourage the use of medical tourism as a vehicle for saving on expenditures (Edelheit, 2014). Others have suggested that medical tourism is the ultimate form of outsourcing for U.S. companies to save money. Marlowe and Sullivan (2007) caution companies to carefully consider the following:

- Quality of care,
- Public perceptions,
- ERISA fiduciary obligations,
- Plan sponsor liability,
- HIPAA privacy issues,
- Travel-related exposure,
- Protected groups, and
- Tax implications.

Just the idea of further outsourcing of the production of services from America also carries negative connotations for some (Perfetto & Dholakia, 2010). Health insurers and companies that self-fund coverage would do well to have worked out these details prior to adopting an outsourcing policy.

Medical tourism results in an outflow of dollars from the U.S. for outbound tourists, but this may be offset by inbound patients. Given the data, it is not clear what the net results of this will be. For health care managers there are several issues to be aware of. The bottom line is that the old adage that "all health care is local" is no longer true; and while other countries have much to learn from the U.S., we also can learn from other countries (Thomas, 2014).

Employees may consider using medical tourism for elective procedures that are not covered by health insurance policies. Organizations may move to become self-insured. As mentioned earlier, organizations may opt to develop expertise in specific specialty areas in order to attract inbound and intrabound tourists in order to develop new business.

CONSUMER-DIRECTED HEALTH CARE

Think about health care and how you go about obtaining it. Do you purchase it in the same way as you do other goods and services? Is the same process used as when you go to buy groceries or a car? If it is not the same, what are the factors that make health care different from other goods?

Most consumers typically shop for goods and services and purchase on the basis of the quality, value, and the price point they can afford. For example, when buying food some people only buy organic items that are thought to be healthier and higher quality and only then do prices, which are usually higher, become a consideration. On the other hand, other people (perhaps most people) shop on the basis of price and then try to get what they think is giving them the best bang for their buck, such as a name brand rather than a generic brand. The same is true of purchasing a new automobile, where price is for most people the most important starting point. If you cannot afford a Cadillac or Range Rover, you're not going to go to those dealerships and instead will opt for the best value and quality Chevy, Toyota, Kia, or whatever brand you opt for that is within your price range.

Health care has not typically been consumed in the same way in the past. That results from the facts that most people have no idea what the cost of health care is, how to judge the quality of that care, and/or whether it is a good value. This is not the consumer's fault, however, because information on cost has typically not been provided, comparison shopping hasn't been possible, and information on quality has been superficial at best. Furthermore, most people do not purchase health care directly. That is, most consumers have health insurance coverage through employment and have not needed to pay much attention to either price or quality in their decision making. In fact, if a patient needed to see a physician, an appointment was made and the patient showed up, paid a deductible or copay, saw the doctor, and went on their way. If a patient needed surgery, their physician would recommend a surgeon who was affiliated with a particular hospital or health system and whose office would arrange for that procedure, leaving it to the patient to take care of pre-op testing and other details and then show up for the surgery, again making a copay or deductible to the hospital. The consumer would most likely assume the quality would be good based on the physician's recommendation and would have no idea about the cost until bills (often difficult to understand) started coming in from the hospital and a host of other health care professionals who participated in the procedure. For many people, this is the way they have consumed health care in the past and may continue to do so in the future.

How did we get to this point? Several authors have suggested it is inherent to our health care system. Callahan (2012) stated the "fee-for-service model … encourages patients to be ignorant of and indifferent to costs" (para. 4), and Cowles (2011) suggested "the health care community, insurance industry and, of course, government … have worked together, perhaps unwittingly, toward a common goal: the disempowerment of the American consumer" (para. 6). Callahan (2012) went on to state, "a patient's relationship with his doctor is not the same as with an auto salesman" (para. 9) and both authors have further indicated this situation was not likely to change. While that was the case a few years ago, health care has begun to change radically.

Disruptive Innovation in Health Care

Several authors, including Butcher (2015b), Kaufman and Grube (2015), Main and Slywotzky (2014), Price Waterhouse Coopers (PwC) (2014), and Townsend (2013), to name just a few, have begun suggesting that health care is being impacted by what Clayton Christensen has termed **disruptive innovation**, i.e., "the phenomenon by which an innovation transforms an existing market or sector by introducing simplicity, convenience, accessibility, and affordability where complication and high cost are the status quo" (Christensen Institute, n.d., para. 2). The characteristics of disruptive innovation have not been common in health care in the past, with its high level of complexity, ever increasing costs, lack of transparency, and access concerns for many. In the last couple of years, however, things have begun to change with several areas of disruption leading the way.

The Affordable Care Act, while experiencing many problems with its rollout, is one such disrupter. Its goals are to increase access and affordability by over time decreasing costs. Wanamaker (2013) points out that both the individual and employer mandates, as well as the minimum benefit package and the insurance exchanges, are changing the way consumers access coverage. The rollout of the Act has led to innovations; for example, "Amazon-style public and private exchanges, along with shopping tools like Castlight and ZocDoc, are already sparking consumer choice for healthcare providers" (Main & Slywotzky, 2014, p. 11).

Other evidence of disruptions comes from many new suppliers of services intended to make health care easier, more accessible, more convenient, and more affordable. Many of them are retailers who are new to the health care market place. Examples of a few of the many both large and small organizations who are disrupters include:

- Walgreens, who has become the "nation's second-largest provider of flu shots after the federal government" (Butcher, 2015b);

- Target, who has begun partnering with Kaiser Permanente to provide clinic sites in several of its stores in southern California (Packer-Tursman, 2015);

- Walmart, who has become a major player with its Care Clinics, where visits cost only $40 (Butcher, 2015b);

- Sarrell Dental, a non-profit health care organization, who is providing dental services in numerous locations across Alabama to a low-income Medicaid population, while accepting Medicaid reimbursement and being able to run a "sustainable business" in the process (Townsend, 2013);

- Golden Bison, "the third largest bison company in the U.S.," who opened a weight management clinic in July 2015 (Smith, 2015); and

- Time Warner Cable Business Class, who "announced a 'virtual visit' experiment with Cleveland Clinic caregivers [to] interact with patients using secure video technology" (PwC, 2014).

These examples indicate how several existing health care providers, like Kaiser and Cleveland Clinic, are partnering with retail entities to delivery care in new ways, or are expanding their scope beyond being just a drug store, like Walgreens. A leading example of a disrupter is CVS, which at one time was only a retail pharmacy and has now morphed into one of the largest players in the industry. Through numerous acquisitions in the last several years, CVS Health now operates "about 9,600 retail stores, or about one out of seven retail pharmacies" across the country, has 900 clinics already operating in its stores, intends to add another 600 clinics by 2017, and has become "the country's biggest operator of health clinics" (Tabuchi, 2015). This is part of a broad strategic initiative that also includes the corporate decision to discontinue the sale of and forego the revenue generated from tobacco products in an effort to focus entirely on health and wellness. The other big player in the consumerism movement is the health IT industry, which has seen a boom in new products, such as apps, fitness trackers, and all sorts of wearable devices and clothing, that are becoming very common in the health and wellness sector. "There are the apps for smartphones and tablets, tens of thousands of them, to count your steps, track your blood sugar, connect you to a community of patients with similar concerns, provide health information, or let you compete with your friends on who burns the most calories" (Main & Slywotzky, 2014, pp. 3–4)

These are just a few of many new entrants who are leading the way as disruptors on the supply-side of health care. As Johnson (2014) points out, "retail health is here" (para. 16); he goes on to say that "the market has gone from B2B to B2B2C" (para. 18). In support of this contention there is evidence from Merchant Medicine LLC, as reported by Packer-Tursman (2015), that the number of retail clinics increased from 258 to 1,866 between January 2007 and January 2015. PwC's (2014) recent report has characterized what is going on, stating "the race is on to become the Amazon.com of healthcare" (p. 3). Main and Slywotzky (2014) also suggest that one indicator that this growth will continue is that "the surest sign that an industry is about to undergo wrenching change is a sudden influx of tech entrepreneurs backed by venture capital investment" (p. 3), and go on to say that "all in all, the past two or three years have seen an outpouring of innovation and investment in health and healthcare that is simply remarkable, and all the more so for its pace – easily ten times faster than anything healthcare has seen before" (pp. 4–5). Health care providers and organizations are clearly taking notice as physicians, such as Nash (2015), and insurance associations, like the American Health Insurance Plans (Kutscher, 2015), have echoed the existence of significant disruption and growth of consumerism in health care.

Who Are the New Consumers and What Are Their Expectations?

The changes indicate a shift from control by the supply side of health care to the demand side. These new consumers are younger individuals, "basically the 18–54 age group" (Butcher, 2015b). They are health care shoppers who are very comfortable going online to shop and research illness, wellness, and care issues. They are people who approach care differently and are unwilling to wait for weeks to get a doctor's appointment or other access to care. Main and Slywotzky (2014) and others point out that many are newly covered consumers, who gained access to insurance through the health care exchanges and don't have primary care physicians, but are part of the what they have termed the **quantified-self movement**, i.e., those who are using various electronic health IT gadgets and devices to monitor their own health status and link them to other consumer information. And, they want "their online healthcare and insurance shopping experience to be as easy as other online shopping experiences" (Conn, 2014, para. 1).

Estupiñan, Fengler, and Kaura (2014) reported the findings of a Strategy& and PwC survey in their report, *The Birth of the Healthcare Consumer: Growing Demands for Choice, Engagement and Experience*. The results from surveying 2,339 U.S. residents indicated changes in expectations from the past, a willingness to trust non-traditional sources of care, and a desire for the industry to work like the other digital companies with which they do business. A list of consumer expectations has been compiled from their findings and the following sources: Butcher (2015a, 2015b), Conn (2014), Huckman and Kelley (2013), Johnson (2014), Lewis (2014), and Sarasohn-Kahn (2015a, 2015c). These expectations include:

- Convenience
- Simplicity/hassle-free and seamless transactions
- Clear, concise, transparent information and data
- Personalized, customer-oriented service
- A range of choices

- Low cost
- Providers (particularly retailers) they trust
- A voice in clinical discovery and decision making

It's important to think of them as consumers, not patients. Butcher (2015a) points out that "a health system's patients are people who have been treated there in the past; consumers are those who may – or may not – choose to seek care there in the future" (para. 9). While the goal may be to turn them into patients, providers will need to change how they go about doing this.

Unlike other patients, these new consumers will be quite knowledgeable consumers when shopping for a health care provider. Butcher (2015c) suggests that they will already know the following six things:

- What does the doctor really think?
- How do your costs compare?
- How does your quality of care stack up?
- What do your patients say about you?
- What does personalized medicine mean to them?
- Is your hospital safe for patients?

In addition to this knowledge, consumers may seek out care from providers other than physicians, such as nurse practitioners, physician assistants, and others (Parikh, 2013). Those with High Deductible Health Plans (HDHPs) may self-ration by making decisions to not even seek care that is not deemed valuable. (Coughlin, Wordham, & Jonash, 2015; Sarasohn-Kahn, 2015b). They are also pushing for more "mobile-centric," as opposed to "inpatient-centric" care (Kaufman & Grube, 2015). Finally, these consumers want to be heard and to discuss their care and treatment with their providers. They no longer want to be treated like "know-nothings" by paternalistic providers.

Implications for Providers and Management

Change is upon us and it is predicted to be happening very fast. Main and Slywotzky (2014) see this as a shift from Health Market 1.0, the existing health care delivery model, to Health Market 2.0. This new model is characterized by transparency, smart care teams delivering care to the quantified-self consumer, and engaged consumers who bring different expectations and knowledge and information to their health care and wellness experience. The result will be an environment where a value-based health care system is the focus and "healthcare professionals actually accomplish their most important goal: keeping people well and giving them more years of productive, good life" (Main & Slywotzky, p. 37). They state, "the speed of change in Health Market 2.0 is something the healthcare industry has never had to imagine or manage through before. If hospitals and insurers want to survive, they need to step on the gas" (p. 25).

Some suggestions for what health care managers and providers can do include:

- Hospitals, Kaufman and Grube (2015) suggest, should not adopt a "business as usual" strategy, but instead should focus on revamping their "outpatient and telehealth-based delivery system[s]" (p. 53) and develop new ways of providing care to consumers. In doing so, organizations will need to develop new "blueprints to guide change," as well as metrics for measuring progress.
- Competition from new entrants to the market needs to be assessed and understood as being very different from the past (Coughlin et al., 2015).
- Given expectations and the long-term calls for transparency, organizations need to be moving to increase transparency and provide understandable information on both pricing and quality (Mulvany, 2014; Schultz, 2014).
- Beyond this Coughlin et al. (2015) propose creating "strategies that build upon five factors:

  - Embedded enhanced transparency and clearly articulated value into corporate culture, services and processes.
  - Focus change and innovation efforts on educating, informing and supporting consumers as they learn how to engage with the health care system.
  - Ensure that organizations have the right insights into consumers' distinctive behaviors and preferences.
  - Think through the broader ecosystem and connect with new players using new relationships.
  - Achievement of the above requires different talent – creative designers, data scientists, and behavioral economists – and a different way of thinking about the future" (pp. 177–178).

- Zeckhauser and Sommers (2013) suggest that clinicians themselves need to become informed about consumerism, understand what their patients know and are thinking, compare their own thoughts and diagnosis with the patients', and make sure they are not ignoring what they are being told.
- Providers need to start collecting data on their patients beyond what is typically in their medical records, such as preferences about communication, diet, religion, care givers, etc., which in turn will allow them to communicate better and provide more personalized care (Institute for HealthCare Consumerism, n.d.).
- An approach to fully understanding consumer behavior is to become one by acting like and doing the things that consumers do (Schultz, 2014).

- "Hospitals and health systems should be prepared to compete on value by lowering the cost to produce these services [i.e., lab tests, imaging, and outpatient procedures] while simultaneously maintaining or improving quality" (Mulvany, 2014, p. 38).

Change is clearly happening very quickly in health care. The message is that this does not appear to be some kind of blip; everyone needs to start understanding the changes, thinking strategically about their impacts and how this may impact their organizations, and taking steps to not be left behind in the reshuffle. While some consider this a generational issue, many older people are also becoming savvier, using the Internet to assess their conditions, and becoming digitally-competent consumers. These changes are likely to have major positive impacts for traditional patients and new consumers alike.

OPPORTUNITIES FOR RESEARCH ON EMERGING ISSUES

This chapter has brought some of the most current topics impacting health care management to your attention. Opportunities for in-depth research on these emerging issues exist in a variety of venues, particularly in those areas where data are sparse due to the early identification of the issue, such as medical tourism or consumer-driven health care, or in those areas that are illicit, illegal, or embarrassing, such as bioterrorism, human trafficking, stalking, and violence in health care. With respect to vaccinations and re-emerging diseases, an abundance of data are available from a variety of sources. Many of the resources we used in writing this chapter also include extensive research holdings and data sets that are available to students and academic researchers. Herewith is a partial listing of these resources.

- Consumer driven health care: Institute for HealthCare Consumerism;
- Human trafficking: Polaris.org; HumanTrafficking.org; UNICEF; U.S. Immigration and Customs Enforcement (ICE); the World Health Organization; U.S. Department of Health and Human Services (DHHS); U.S. Department of Justice (DOJ); the Federal Bureau of Investigation (FBI);
- Medical tourism: Joint Commission International; the Medical Tourism Association; Patients Beyond Borders;
- Violence in health care settings: U.S. Department of Justice; Bureau of Justice Statistics; U.S. Office of Violence Against Women; Occupational Safety and Health Administration (OSHA); the Federal Bureau of Investigation (FBI); and
- Bioterrorism: ANSER; Centers for Disease Control and Prevention (CDC); the Federal Bureau of Investigation (FBI); the UMPC Center for Health Security.

The only thing that constrains you in investigating these topics is your imagination.

DISCUSSION QUESTIONS

1. Looking at the chart of vaccine-preventable contagious diseases, provide a prioritized list of required vaccinations for health care employees. Be sure to provide a rationale for your rankings, as well as examples of why exceptions might be granted, along with appropriate references.

2. A patient presents in the ED complaining of vague discomforts: nausea, vomiting, stomach pain, watery diarrhea, fever, and chills. The patient reports he has not travelled outside of the U.S. Since it occurs at the height of the norovirus season, the ED physician assumes it is another run of the mill case. When the lab reports return a quick test of cholera, the public health department is called in. Could this be a potential bioterrorism attempt? Why or why not? Provide a solid rationale for your response along with appropriate references.

3. Request an interview with a health care executive and explore his perceptions of risk and disaster preparedness for his organization. Ask to see the health care organization's all hazards plan. Based on your interview and review of the plan, create a report to your professor on the organization's preparedness. Provide rationales for your assessment, along with appropriate references.

4. The nurses in the ED of your hospital have recently suffered an increase of injuries from assaultive patients and family members. One nurse had to be hospitalized with head injuries after the most recent assault. Upon interview in the ICU, her co-workers inform you that the security guard in the ED has been less visible of late. They have complained to their nurse manager, to no avail. Using the resources and references provided in this chapter, create a plan for a root cause analysis of this latest incident and an injury prevention plan.

5. A young woman presents to the ED with an older woman accompanying her. The older woman acts as the younger woman's interpreter and states her charge fell down a flight of stairs. The triage nurse becomes suspicious when she observes the girl's downcast demeanor and evidence of unhealed cigarette burns on her torso. She calls the administrator on call (you!) to inform you that she believes the girl is a victim of human trafficking. Using the resources and references provided in this chapter to guide you, what are your next steps?

6. Would you opt to become a medical tourist yourself or have a family member become one? Provide the rationale for your decision.

7. Should organizations become involved in outbound medical tourism? Why or why not?

8. Thinking about the location where you live, provide an example of inbound and/or intrabound medical tourism and explain what expertise that organization provides and who utilizes their services.

9. What type of consumer are you? How do you approach the health care system? Are there ways you can become a better consumer?

10. What changes do you see that are indicators of retailers entering the health care delivery market in your community? Provide specific examples and justification for them.

Cases in Chapter 18 that are related this chapter include:

- Death by Measles
- Full Moon or Bad Planning?
- How Do We Handle a Girl Like Maria?
- The Brawler
- I Love You … Forever
- Such a Nice Young Man
- Sundowner or Victim?
- To Partner or Not to Partner with a Retail Company
- Wellness Tourism: An Option for your Organization?

Case study guides are available in the online Instructor's Materials.

REFERENCES

Adler, F., Mueller, G. O. W., & Laufer, W. S. (2004). Types of crimes. In F. Adler, G. O. W. Mueller, & W. S. Laufer (Eds.), *Criminology and the criminal justice system* (pp. 237–258). New York, NY: McGraw-Hill.

Administration for Children & Families (ACF). (2015). SOAR to health and wellness training. Retrieved from http://www.acf.hhs.gov/programs/endtrafficking/initiatives/soar

American College of Healthcare Executives (ACHE). (2013, November 16). Healthcare executives' role in emergency preparedness: Policy statement. Retrieved from http://www.ache.org/policy/emergency_preparedness.cfm

American Medical Association (AMA) Council on Medical Services. (2007, June). Report B. Medical travel outside the U.S. Retrieved from http://www.medretreat.com/templates/UserFiles/Documents/AMA%20Report%20June%202007.pdf

Bartold, P. M. (2014). Medical tourism – an established problem. *Australian Dental Journal 59*, 279.

Basile, K. C., Smith, S. G., Breiding, M. J., Black, M. C., & Mahendra, R. R. (2014). Sexual violence surveillance: Uniform definitions and recommended data elements version 2.0. Atlanta, GA: Centers for Disease Control and Prevention, National Center for Injury Prevention and Control. Retrieved from http://www.cdc.gov/violenceprevention/pdf/sv_surveillance_definitionsl-2009-a.pdf

Barnsteiner, J. (2011, September 30). Teaching the culture of safety. *OJIN: The Online Journal of Issues in Nursing, 16*(3). Retrieved from http://www.nursingworld.org/MainMenuCategories /ANAMarketplace/ANAPeriodicals/OJIN/TableofContents/Vol-16-2011/No3-Sept-2011 /Teaching-and-Safety.html

Baum, K., Catalano, S., & Rose, K. (2009). Stalking victimization in the United States. U.S. Department of Justice (DOJ), Office of Justice Programs, Bureau of Justice Statistics, Special Reports. Retrieved from https://www.victimsofcrime.org/docs/src/baum-k-catalano-s-rand-m-rose -k-2009.pdf?sfvrsn=0

Blair, J. D. (2005, September). Is the healthcare industry prepared for terrorism? All-hazards "HVA" for non-federal healthcare CBRNE readiness: A level playing field? *Inside Homeland Security, 3*(5), 4–9.

Buchbinder, S. (2010a, October 6). Bioterrorism and health care managers. [Blog post]. Retrieved from http://blogs.jblearning.com/health/2014/10/06/bioterrorism-and-health-care-managers/

Buchbinder, S. (2010b, May 1). Are healthcare professionals prepared for disasters? [Blog post]. Retrieved from http://blogs.jblearning.com/health/2010/05/01/are-health-care-professionals-prepared-for -disasters/

Buchbinder, S. (2013a, Summer/Fall). Truth in advertising: Human trafficking in Southeast Asia. *The Islamic Monthly*, 78–81.

Buchbinder, S. (2013b, August 7). When women traffic other women. *The Daily Beast*. Retrieved from http://www.thedailybeast.com/witw/articles/2013/08/07/when-women-are-found-trafficking -other-women.html

Buchbinder, S. (2014a, November 2). *Just culture and speaking up.* [Blog post]. http://blogs.jblearning .com/health/2014/11/02/just-culture-and-speaking-up/

Buchbinder, S. (2014b, Fall/Winter). Sex, lies, and crime: Human trafficking in the Middle East. *The Islamic Monthly*, 92–96.

Buchbinder, S. (2015a, April 18). *Re-emerging outbreaks: Ebola, measles—what's next?* Presentation. Nursing and Healthcare Management Symposium, Stevenson University, Owings Mills, MD.

Buchbinder, S. (2015b, February 2). Vaccinations and health care managers. [Blog post]. Retrieved from http://blogs.jblearning.com/health/2015/02/02/vaccinations-and-health-care-managers/

Butcher, L. (2015a, February 10). Is your hospital ready to answer consumer demands? *H&HN (Hospitals & Health Networks)*. Retrieved from http://www.hhnmag.com/Magazine/2015/Feb/cob -health-care-consumer

Butcher, L. (2015b, April 14). The modern day health care disruptors. *H&HN (Hospitals & Health Networks), 89*. Retrieved from http://www.hhnmag.com/Magazine/2015/Apr/feature-new -healthcare-consumers-disruption

Butcher, L. (2015c, June 9). Six things consumers will know about you. *H&HN (Hospitals & Health Networks), 89*. Retrieved from http://www.hhnmag.com/Magazine/2015/June/feature-new-health -care-consumer-need-to-know

Caffarini, K. (2008, July 7). AMA meeting: Guidelines target safety of medical tourists. *American Medical News*. Retrieved from http://www.amednews.com/article/20080707/profession/307079957/7/

Callahan, D. (2012). *The roots of bioethics: Health, progress, technology, death.* Oxford, England: Oxford University Press.

Carling, J. (2005, July 1). Trafficking in women from Nigeria to Europe. *The Online Journal of the Migration Policy Institute.* Retrieved from http://www.migrationpolicy.org/article/trafficking-women-nigeria-europe

Centers for Disease Control and Prevention (CDC). (2007). Bioterrorism overview. Retrieved from http://emergency.cdc.gov/bioterrorism/overview.asp

Centers for Disease Control and Prevention (CDC). (2012). How vaccines prevent diseases. Retrieved from http://www.cdc.gov/vaccines/parents/vaccine-decision/prevent-diseases.html

Centers for Disease Control and Prevention (CDC). (2013a). Glossary: Community immunity. Retrieved from http://www.cdc.gov/vaccines/about/terms/glossary.htm#commimmunity

Centers for Disease Control and Prevention (CDC). (2013b, December 9). Pertussis (Whooping Cough). Frequently asked questions. Retrieved from http://www.cdc.gov/pertussis/about/faqs.html

Centers for Disease Control and Prevention (CDC). (2014, August 11). Polio disease: Questions and answers. Retrieved from http://www.cdc.gov/vaccines/vpd-vac/polio/dis-faqs.htm

Centers for Disease Control and Prevention (CDC). (2015a, February, 18). Current Ebola treatment centers. Retrieved from http://www.cdc.gov/vhf/ebola/healthcare-us/preparing/current-treatment-centers.html

Centers for Disease Control and Prevention (CDC). (2015b). *FluView: Weekly U.S. Influenza surveillance report: 2014–2015 Influenza season week 32 ending August 15, 2015.* Retrieved from http://www.cdc.gov/flu/weekly/index.htm#S3

Centers for Disease Control and Prevention (CDC). (2015c, April 25). Guidance on personal protective equipment to be used by healthcare centers for workers during management of patients with Ebola virus disease in U.S. hospitals, including procedures for putting on (donning) and removing (doffing). Retrieved from http://www.cdc.gov/vhf/ebola/healthcare-us/ppe/guidance.html

Centers for Disease Control and Prevention (CDC). (2015d, June 2). Measles cases and outbreaks. Retrieved from http://www.cdc.gov/measles/cases-outbreaks.html

Centers for Disease Control and Prevention (CDC). (2015e, February 23). Medical tourism. Retrieved from http://www.cdc.gov/features/medicaltourism/

Centers for Disease Control and Prevention (CDC). (2015f, March 6). Update: Influenza activity: United States, September 28, 2014–February 21, 2015. *Mortality Morbidity Weekly Report, 64*(08), 206–212. Retrieved from http://www.cdc.gov/mmwr/preview/mmwrhtml/mm6408a2.htm

Centers for Disease Control and Prevention (CDC), National Institute for Occupational Safety and Health (NIOSH). (2001). *Women's safety and health issues at work.* Retrieved from http://www.cdc.gov/niosh/docs/2001-123/pdfs/2001-123.pdf

Centers for Disease Control and Prevention (CDC), National Institute for Occupational Safety and Health (NIOSH). (2002). *Violence: Occupational hazards in hospitals.* Retrieved from http://www.cdc.gov/niosh/docs/2002-101/pdfs/2002-101.pdf

Centers for Disease Control and Prevention (CDC), National Institute for Occupational Safety and Health (NIOSH). (2014). Occupational violence. Retrieved from http://www.cdc.gov/niosh/topics/violence/pubsrelated.html

Christensen Institute. (n.d.). Disruptive innovation. Retrieved from http://www.christenseninstitute.org/key-concepts/disruptive-innovation-2/

Clottey, P. (2015, July 15). Sierra Leone welcomes ebola vaccine trial outcome. *Voice of America.* Retrieved from http://www.voanews.com/content/sierra-leone-welcomes-ebola-vacine-trial-outcome/2890451.html

Concannon, D. (2005). *The association between stalking and violence in interpersonal relationships.* (Doctoral dissertation, Alliant International University, Fresno, CA, 2005). *Dissertation Abstracts International: Section B: The Sciences and Engineering, 67* (2-B), 2006, 1203.

Conn, J. (2014, October 21). Consumers want an improved online healthcare experience. *Modern Healthcare.* Retrieved from http://www.modernhealthcare.com/article/20141021/blog/310219995

Coughlin, S., Workham, J., & Jonash, B. (2015). Rising consumerism. *Deloitte Review, 16,* 164–179.

Cowles, D. (2011, September 1). Who killed consumer-directed health care? *Employee Benefit News, 25*(22), 27–28.

Davis, J. A., & Chipman, M. A. (1997, Dec.). Stalkers and other obsessional types: a review and forensic psychological typology of those who stalk. *Journal of Clinical Forensic Medicine, 4*(4), 166–72.

Duhart, D. T. (2001). *Violence in the workplace, 1993–1999.* U.S. Department of Justice, Office of Justice Programs, Bureau of Justice Statistics, Special Report. Retrieved from http://www.bjs.gov/content/pub/pdf/vw99.pdf

Edelheit, J. (2014). *Self-funding: Passport to medical tourism for U.S. employers.* Palm Beach Gardens, FL: Medical Tourism Association. Retrieved from http://www.medicaltourismassociation.com/upload/upload_SELF%20FUNDED%20WHITEPAPER.pdf

Emergency Nurses Association. (2010). *ENA workplace violence toolkit.* Retrieved from http://www.ena.org/practice-research/Practice/ViolenceToolKit/Documents/toolkitpg1.htm

Estupiñan, J., Fengler, K., & Kaura, A. (2014). *The birth of the healthcare consumer: Growing demands for choice, engagement, and experience.* New York, NY: Strategy& and PwC.

Farrell, A., McDevitt, J., Pfeffer, R., Fahy, S., Owens, C., Dank, M., & Adams, W. (2012, April). Identifying challenges to improve the investigation and prosecution of state and local human trafficking cases. *National Criminal Justice Reference Service.* Retrieved from https://www.ncjrs.gov/pdffiles1/nij/grants/238795.pdf

Federal Bureau of Investigation (FBI), Centers for Disease Control and Prevention (CDC), & U.S. Department of Justice (DOJ). (2011). *Criminal and epidemiological investigation handbook.* Retrieved from https://www.fbi.gov/about-us/investigate/terrorism/wmd/criminal-and-epidemiological-investigation-handbook

Garrett, L., & Builder, M. (2014, February 12). The Taliban are winning the war on polio. *Foreign Policy.* Retrieved from http://foreignpolicy.com/2014/02/12/the-taliban-are-winning-the-war-on-polio/

Gendar, A., Parascandola, R., Deutsch, K., & Goldsmith, S. (2010, May 1). Time Square car bomb: Cops evacuate heart of NYC after 'potential terrorist attack.' *New York Daily News.* Retrieved from http://www.nydailynews.com/news/crime/time-square-car-bomb-cops-evacuate-heart-nyc-potential-terrorist-attack-article-1.444423

Gillespie, G. L. (2008). Consequences of violence exposures by emergency nurses. *Journal of Aggression, Maltreatment & Trauma, 16*(4), 409–418.

Glauser, W. (2014, September 16). Medicare advocates decry medical tourism. *Canadian Medical Association Journal, 186*(13), 977.

Government Printing Office (GPO). (2000, October 28). Victims of Trafficking and Violence Protection Act of 2000. Public Law 106-386. Retrieved from http://www.gpo.gov/fdsys/pkg/GPO-CDOC-106sdoc30/pdf/GPO-CDOC-106sdoc30-2-9-8.pdf

Gursky, E. A. (2004). *Hometown hospitals: The weakest link? Bioterrorism readiness in America's rural hospitals.* Washington, DC: Center for Technology and National Security Policy of the National Defense University.

Gursky, E. A., & Fierro, M. F. (2012). *Death in large numbers: The science, policy, and management of mass fatality events.* Chicago, IL, American Medical Association.

Halsall, P. (1998, July). *Modern history sourcebook: Lady Mary Wortley Montagu (1689–1762): Smallpox vaccination in Turkey.* Retrieved from http://legacy.fordham.edu/halsall/mod/montagu-smallpox.asp

Harlow, J., & Summers, H. (2014, February 16). Measles legacy of disgraced doctor. *The Sunday Times U.K.* Retrieved from http://www.thesundaytimes.co.uk/sto/news/uk_news/Health/article1376354 .ece?CMP=OTH-gnws-standard-2014_02_15

Hauser, A., & Castillo, M. (2013, August 26). A heavy toll for the victims of human trafficking. *CNN.* Retrieved from http://www.cnn.com/2013/08/25/us/miami-sex-trafficking/

Huckman, R. S., & Kelley, M. A. (2013). Public reporting, consumerism, and patient empowerment. *New England Journal of Medicine, 369*(20), 1875–1877.

International Labour Organization. (2012). *New ILO global estimate of forced labour: 20.9 million victims.* Retrieved from http://www.ilo.org/global/about-the-ilo/newsroom/news/WCMS_182109 /lang–en/index.htm

Institute for HealthCare Consumerism. (n.d.). *The Consumerization of healthcare: What patient experience means to our future.* Retrieved from http://www.theihcc.com/en/communities/health _care_consumerism/the-consumerization-of-healthcare-what-patient-exp_h333dkhj.html

Institute of Medicine (IOM). (2013). *Best care at lower cost: The path to continuously learning health care in America.* Washington, DC: National Academies Press.

Johnson, A. M. (2014, November 6). Where health care consumerism is headed (and what that means for brokers). *Benefits Pro.* Retrieved from http://www.benefitspro.com/2014/11/06/where-health -care-consumerism-is-headed?page_all=1

Joint Commission International (JCI). (2015). *Improve care. Empower change.* Oakbrook, IL: Author.

Kaufman, K., & Grube, M. E. (2015, January). Succeeding in a disruptive healthcare environment. *Healthcare Financial Management, 69*(1), 49–55.

Keckley, P. H., & Underwood, H. R. (2009). *Medical tourism: Consumers in search of value.* Washington, DC: Deloitte Center for Health Solutions.

Kienast, J., Lakner, M., & Neulet, A. (2014, December 20). The role of female offenders in sex trafficking organizations. *Regional Academy of the United Nations (RAUN).* Retrieved from http://www.ra-un .org/uploads/1/6/7/1/16716340/the_role_of_female_offenders_in_sex_trafficking_organizations.pdf

Kowalenko, T., Walters, B. L., Khare, R. K., & Compton, S. (2005). Workplace violence: A survey of emergency physicians in the state of Michigan. *Annals of Emergency Medicine, 46,* 142–147.

Kuehn, B. M. (2015). As Ebola epidemic begins to slow, trials of drugs and vaccines speed up. *JAMA, 313*(10), 1000–1002. doi:10.1001/jama.2015.0942.

Kutscher, B. (2015, June 4). AHIP Institute highlights growing focus on consumerism. *Modern Healthcare.* Retrieved from http://www.modernhealthcare.com/article/20150604/blog/150609954

Lake, T. K., Stewart, K. A., & Ginsburg, P. B. (2011, January). *Lessons from the field: Making accountable care organizations real.* NIHCR Research Brief No. 2. Retrieved from http://hschange.com /CONTENT/1179/?words=accountable%20care%20organanizations

Leggat, P. (2015). Medical tourism. *Australian Family Physician, 44* (1–2), 16–21.

Lewis, D. (2014, November 16). The new health care consumer expects transparency, simplicity and convenience. *The Morning Consult.* Retrieved from http://morningconsult.com/opinions/new -health-care-consumer-expects-transparency-simplicity-convenience/

Link, K. (2005). *Vaccine controversy: The history, use, and safety of vaccinations.* Westport, CT: Praeger.

Logan, T. (2010). *Research on partner stalking: Putting the pieces together.* Lexington, KY: University of Kentucky, Department of Behavioral Science & Center on Drug and Alcohol Research. Retrieved from http://www.victimsofcrime.org/docs/Common%20Documents/Research%20 on%20Partner%20Stalking%20Report.pdf

Main, T., & Slywotzky, A. (2014). The patient-to-consumer revolution. *Oliver Wyman.* Retrieved from http://www.oliverwyman.com/content/dam/oliver-wyman/global/en/images/insights/health-life -sciences/2014/October/The-Patient-To-Consumer-Revolution.pdf

Marlowe, J., & Sullivan, P. (2007). Medical tourism: The ultimate outsourcing. *Human Resource Planning, 30*(2), 8–10.

McGreevy, P., & Lin, R. G. II. (2015, June 25). California assembly approves one of the toughest mandatory vaccination laws in the nation. *LA Times.* Retrieved from http://www.latimes.com/local/political /la-me-pc-vaccine-mandate-bill-up-for-vote-thursday-in-california-assembly-20150624-story.html

McIvor, R. J., & Petch, E. (2006). Stalking of mental health professionals: An underrecognized problem. *British Journal of Psychiatry, 188*, 403–404.

Medical Tourism Association. (2014). *Research/Surveys/Statistics.* Retrieved from http://www .medicaltourismassociation.com/en/research-and-surveys.html

Mitchell, J. W. (2015, January 21). Medical tourism – health care disrupter or fringe service? *Dotmed Daily News.* Retrieved from http://www.dotmed.com/news/story/24812

Mullen, P. E., Mackenzie, R., Ogloff, J. R. P., Pathé, M., McEwan, T., & Purcell, R. (2006). Assessing and managing the risks in the stalking situation. *Journal of the American Academy of Psychiatry Law, 34*(4), 439–450.

Mulvany, C. (2014). The march to consumerism: The evolution from patient to active shopper continues. *Healthcare Financial Management, 68*(2), 36–38.

Munoz, J. (2012, November 18). Red flags: Identifying sex trafficking victims in the ED. *Emergency Physicians Monthly.* Retrieved from http://www.epmonthly.com/features/current-features/red-flags -identifying-sex-trafficking-victims-in-the-ed-/

Nash, D. B. (2015, February). N=1. *American Health & Drug Benefits, 8*(1), 12–13.

National Committee for Quality Assurance. (2015). *HEDIS quality measurement: HEDIS measures.* Retrieved from http://www.ncqa.org/HEDISQualityMeasurement/HEDISMeasures/HEDIS2015.aspx

National Institute of Justice (NIJ). (2010, May 29). Human trafficking: How big is the problem? Retrieved from http://www.nij.gov/topics/crime/human-trafficking/pages/problem.aspx

Nationwide Suspicious Activity Reporting Initiative (NSI). (2015). Retrieved from http://nsi.ncirc.gov/

National Center for Victims of Crime Stalking Resource Center. (n.d.) Stalking resource center. Retrieved from http://www.victimsofcrime.org/our-programs/stalking-resource-center

New York State Department of Labor. (2009). *Workplace violence prevention program guidelines.* Retrieved from http://www.labor.ny.gov/workerprotection/safetyhealth/PDFs/PESH/WPV%20 Violence%20Prevention%20Guidelines.pdf

Occupational Safety and Health Administration (OSHA). (2015). *Guidelines for preventing workplace violence for health care & social service workers.* Retrieved from https://www.osha.gov/Publications /osha3148.pdf

Packer-Tursman, J. (2015, February 17). Consumerism increases retail opportunities and access to coverage and care. *Managed Healthcare Executive.* Retrieved from http://managedhealthcareexecutive .modernmedicine.com/managed-healthcare-executive/news/consumerism-increases-retail -opportunities-and-access-coverage-and-care-0?page=full

Parikh, R. B. (2013, November). The empowered patient: Consumerism in American medicine. *AMA Journal of Ethics, 15*(11), 923–925.

Patel, R. B., Ahn, R., & Burke, T. F. (2010). Human trafficking in the emergency department. *Western Journal of Emergency Medicine, 11*(5), 402–404.

Patients Beyond Borders. (2014). *Medical tourism statistics & facts.* Retrieved from http://www.patientsbeyondborders.com/medical-tourism-statistics-facts

Pennsylvania Patient Safety Authority. (2012). Just Culture™: Are hospitals doing what they say? Retrieved from http://www.acmq.org/presentations/Impact%20of%20Teamwork%20Clarke.pdf

Perfetto, R., & Dholakia, N. (2010). Exploring the cultural contradictions of medical tourism. *Consumption Markets & Culture, 13*(4), 399–417.

Polaris. (2015). Human trafficking: Overview. Retrieved from http://www.polarisproject.org/human-trafficking/overview

President's Interagency Task Force to Monitor and Combat Trafficking in Persons. (2014). *Federal strategic action plan on services for victims of human trafficking in the United States, 2013–2017.* Retrieved from http://www.ovc.gov/pubs/FederalHumanTraffickingStrategicPlan.pdf

Price Waterhouse Coopers (PwC). (2014). *Healthcare's new entrants: Who will be the industry's Amazon.com?* Retrieved from http://www.pwc.com/us/en/health-industries/healthcare-new-entrants/assets/pwc-hri-new-entrants.pdf

Red Light Films, HBO Cinemax, Sundance Institute Documentary Film (Producers), & Zana Briski and Ross Kauffman (Directors). (2004). *Born into Brothels.* USA: HBO Cinemax.

Romans, J. S. C., Hays, J. R., & White, T. (1996). Stalking and related behaviors experienced by counseling center staff members from current or former clients. *Professional Psychology: Research and Practice, 27*(6), 595–599.

Rosenthal, E. (2013, August 3). In need of a new hip, but priced out of the U.S. *New York Times.* Retrieved from http://www.nytimes.com/2013/08/04/health/for-medical-tourists-simple-math.html

Rugala, E. (2002, September 26). *Emerging trends in employment and labor law.* [Congressional Testimony]. Retrieved from http://www.fbi.gov/news/testimony/emerging-trends-in-employment-and-labor-law

Runnels, V., & Carrerra, P. M. (2012). Why do patients engage in medical tourism? *Maturitas, 73,* 300–304.

Ryan, K. J. (2011). Medical tourism: Is now the time to offer this benefit? *Benefits Magazine, 48*(7), 20–25.

Sarasohn-Kahn, J. (2015a, April 6). Consumers trust retailers and techs to manage their health – as much as health provider. *HEALTHPopuli.* Retrieved from http://healthpopuli.com/2015/04/06/consumers-trust-retailers-and-techs-to-manage-their-health-as-much-as-health-provider/

Sarasohn-Kahn, J. (2015b, June 30). It's still the prices stupid – health care costs drive consumerism. *HEALTHPopuli.* Retrieved from http://healthpopuli.com/2015/06/09/its-still-the-prices-stupid-health-care-costs-drive-consumerism/

Sarasohn-Kahn, J. (2015c, June 30). People-powered health/care – celebrating patient independence & empowerment. *HEALTHPopuli.* Retrieved from http://healthpopuli.com/2015/06/30/people-powered-healthcare-celebrating-patient-independence-empowerment/

Schultz, D. (2014, January). *Meet the new health care consumer: Reluctant. Anxious. Looking for help.* Albany, NY: Media Logic.

Shelly, L. (2010). *Human trafficking: A global perspective.* New York, NY: Cambridge University Press.

Smith, A. K. (2012). Health care bargains abroad. *Kiplinger's Personal Finance, 66*(1), 65–68.

Smith, T. (2015, July 11). Denver-based bison company opens weight-management clinic. *Denver Post.* Retrieved from http://www.denverpost.com/business/ci_28467391/denverbased-bison-company -opens-weightmanagement-clinic

Southern Illinois School of Medicine. (2012, October 30). Overview of potential agents of biological terrorism. Retrieved from http://www.siumed.edu/medicine/id/bioterrorism.htm

Spector, P. E., Coulter, M. L., Stockwell, H. G., & Matz, M. W. (2007, Apr–Jun). Perceived violence climate: A new construct and its relationship to workplace physical violence and verbal aggression, and their potential consequences. *Work & Stress, 21*(2), 117–130.

Stalking Resource Center. (2012). Stalking resource center. Retrieved from http://www.victimsofcrime .org/our-programs/stalking-resource-center

Stanley, M. (2010). Anywhere but here. *National Underwriter, 114*(18), 22–25.

Steenhuysen, J. (2014a, October 13). U.S. CDC head criticized for blaming "protocol breach" as nurse gets Ebola. *Reuters.* Retrieved from http://www.reuters.com/article/2014/10/13/us-health-ebola -usa-nurse-idUSKCN0I206820141013

Steenhuysen, J. (2014b, October 3). U.S. nurses say they are unprepared to handle Ebola patients. *National Nurses United.* Retrieved from http://www.nationalnursesunited.org/news/entry/us-nurses -say-they-are-unprepared-to-handle-ebola-patients/

Stephano, R-M. (2014). *Wellness tourism: Trillion dollar future?* Palm Beach Gardens, FL: Medical Tourism Association. Retrieved from http://www.medicaltourismcongress.com/wp-content /uploads/2014/04/WELLNESS_WHITEPAPER.pdf

Tabuchi, H. (2015, July 11). How CVS quit smoking and grew into a health care giant. *New York Times.* Retrieved from http://www.nytimes.com/2015/07/12/business/how-cvs-quit-smoking-and-grew -into-a-health-care-giant.html?_r=0

The Joint Commission. (2010, June 3). *Preventing violence in the health care setting.* Sentinel event alert. Issue 45. Retrieved from http://www.jointcommission.org/assets/1/18/sea_45.pdf

Thomas, S. (2014, June 10). All health care is local – or is it? [Blog post]. Retrieved from http://blogs. deloitte.com/centerforhealthsolutions/2014/06/my-take-all-health-care-is-local-or-is-it.html# .VZNZX_Pnbug

Tjaden, P., & Thoennes, N. (1998). *Stalking in America: findings from the National Violence against Women Survey,* Research in Brief, Washington, D.C.: U.S. Department of Justice, National Institute of Justice, Publication No.: NCJ 169592. Retrieved from http://www.ncjrs.gov /pdffiles/169592.pdf

Townsend, J. C. (2013, April 23). Disruptive innovation: A prescription for better health care. *Forbes.* Retrieved from http://www.forbes.com/sites/ashoka/2013/04/23/disruptive-innovation-a -prescription-for-better-health-care/

Underwood, H. R., & Makadon, H. J. (2010). Medical tourism: Game-changing innovation or passing fad? *Healthcare Financial Management, 64*(9), 112–118.

United Nations Environmental Programme. (2014). Disaster risk reduction. Retrieved from http://www .unep.org/disastersandconflicts/Introduction/DisasterRiskReduction/tabid/104159/Default.aspx

United Nations Office on Drugs and Crime (UNODC). (2000a). *Protocol to prevent, suppress and punish trafficking in persons, especially women and children, supplementing the United Nations convention against transnational organized crime.* New York, NY: United Nations. Retrieved from https://www.unodc.org/documents/treaties/UNTOC/Publications/TOC%20Convention /TOCbook-e.pdf

United Nations Office on Drugs and Crime (UNODC). (2000b). *Signatories to the Protocol to prevent, suppress and punish trafficking in persons, especially women and children, supplementing the United Nations convention against transnational organized crime*. Retrieved from http://www.unodc.org/unodc/en/treaties/CTOC/countrylist-traffickingprotocol.html

U.S. Department of Homeland Security. (2013, January 25). *Options for consideration: Active shooter training video*. Retrieved from http://youtu.be/oI5EoWBRYmo

U.S. Department of Justice (DOJ), Federal Bureau of Investigation (FBI). (2002). Workplace violence: Issues in response. Retrieved from https://www.fbi.gov/stats-services/publications/workplace-violence

U.S. Department of Justice (DOJ), Federal Bureau of Investigation (FBI). (2004). *Uniform crime reporting Handbook*. Retrieved from https://www2.fbi.gov/ucr/handbook/ucrhandbook04.pdf

U.S. Department of Labor, Bureau of Labor Statistics (BLS), Census of Fatal Occupational Injuries (2007). *Fatal occupational injuries, employment, and rates of fatal occupational injuries by selected worker characteristics, occupations, and industries, 2007*. Retrieved from http://www.bls.gov/iif/oshwc/cfoi/CFOI_Rates_2007.pdf

U.S. State Department. (2014, June). *Trafficking in persons report*. Retrieved from http://www.state.gov/j/tip/rls/tiprpt/2014/index.htm

Vaidya, A. (2013, June 18). Survey: Number of hospital-employed physicians up 6%. *Becker's Hospital Review*. Retrieved from http://www.beckershospitalreview.com/hospital-physician-relationships/survey-number-of-hospital-employed-physicians-up-6.html

RETRACTED: Wakefield, A. J., Murch, S. H., Anthony, A., Linnell, J., Casson, D. M., Malik, M., Berelowitz, M., Dhillon, A.P., Thomson, M.A., Harvey, P., Valentine, A., Davies, S.E., & Walker-Smith, J. A. (1998, February). Ileal-lymphoid-nodular hyperplasia, non-specific colitis, and pervasive developmental disorder in children. *The Lancet*, 28, 351(9103), 637–641. doi: 10.1016/S0140-6736(97)11096–0)

Wanamaker, S. (2013, September 26). Disruptive innovation and the Affordable Care Act. [Blog post]. *The Health Care Blog*. Retrieved from http://thehealthcareblog.com/blog/2013/09/26/disruptive-innovation-and-the-affordable-care-act/

Wattendorf, G. E. (2000, March). Stalking-investigation strategies. *FBI Law Enforcement Bulletin*, 69(3), 10–14. Retrieved from https://leb.fbi.gov/2004-pdfs/leb-november-2004

WaveWeb. (2015, June 19). Ebola app. Retrieved from http://appshopper.com/travel/ebola-app

Wheelis, M. (2002, September). Biological warfare at the 1346 siege of Caffa. *Emerging Infectious Diseases*, 8(9), 971–975.

World Health Organization (WHO). (2011, June 21). Immunizations, vaccines, and biologicals: Pertussis. Retrieved from http://www.who.int/immunization/topics/pertussis/en/

World Health Organization (WHO). (2014, October). Poliomyelitis fact sheet. Retrieved from http://www.who.int/mediacentre/factsheets/fs114/en/

World Health Organization (WHO). (2015, February). Measles fact sheet. Retrieved from http://www.who.int/mediacentre/factsheets/fs286/en/

Zeckhauser, R., & Sommers, B. (2013, November). Consumerism in health care: Challenges and opportunities. *AMA Journal of Ethics*, 15(1), 988–992.

CHAPTER 18

Health Care Management Case Studies and Guidelines[1]

Sharon B. Buchbinder, Donna M. Cox, and Susan Casciani

INTRODUCTION

A case study is the presentation of an organizational scenario. The case will usually present a description of the organization as well as the major players in the organization and their interactions regarding a specific situation. The objective in analyzing a case study is to develop and test a proposed "solution" to address the described situation. As praised in the *Case Study Handbook from the Harvard Business School*, "The case method is not only the most relevant and practical way to learn managerial skills, it's exciting and fun" (Hammond, 2002, p. 1). Hammond states further:

> Simply stated, the case method calls for discussion of real-life situations that business executives have faced. Casewriters, as good reporters, have written up these situations to present you with the information available to the executives involved. As you review their cases, you will put yourself in the shoes of the managers, analyze the situation, decide what you would do, and... [be] prepared to present and support your conclusions. (Hammond, 2002, p. 1)

[1]Each case study is followed by a list of related chapters. These chapters are listed in order of relevance, the first listed is most closely related to the case study. In addition, each case study has an online instructor's guide.

Case studies are thus widely used as learning methods in the education of health care managers and administrators. Cases require the student to think, reason, develop critical thinking and analytic skills, identify underlying causes of problems, use creative abilities, make decisions, and, in the case of group work, deal with personality conflicts and change. Generally, health care management utilizes two types of case studies: diagnostic and descriptive. In a diagnostic case study, a major issue or problem will need to be identified and addressed. A descriptive case study usually presents a theme or describes a situation or series of events. There is not necessarily a major problem presented, and thus the objective is more of discussing the theme in terms of management challenges. Regardless of the type, case studies can be daunting at first, and a good strategy for how to tackle the case study is needed.

CASE STUDY ANALYSIS

Based on more than two decades of experience using the case study method in the classroom and in faculty workshops, we recommend that students work in teams and use the following guidelines for case studies.

- Read (or watch) the case carefully several times. The first time you read it, read it quickly, trying to pick up the high-level issues and players. In successive readings, become absorbed in the situation in such a way that you see yourself intimately involved with the personalities, problems, and conflicts.

  TIP: Highlight sentences that may be important in identifying the main issue or theme of the case, and strike out those sentences that are "nice to know" but not critical to the issues in the case. This will help you to filter out the "noise" in the case.

- As the case starts to become more familiar to you, begin to ask yourself the following types of questions and jot down your thoughts:

  1. What is *really* going on this case? Generally speaking, what types of managerial issues are there (e.g., human resources, leadership, legal, confidentiality, quality control, conflict management, etc.)?
  2. Can you describe *in one sentence* the major issue/problem? Make a list of all of the problems you can identify. Analyze this list to see if you can determine how these problems relate to each other. Are some problems the *cause* of other problems? If so, highlight the causal problems to see if a pattern develops. For example, a problem that is usually rather easy to identify is a loss of revenue, but you must dig deeper—*why* is there a loss of revenue? What is causing it?

- This will lead you to begin to understand the secondary, or underlying, issues. It is important to note here that you may end up with more than one "major" problem; your challenge is to identify the one that has the greatest potential to alter the situation for the better if addressed successfully.

  TIP: Sketch out the relationships between your major and secondary problems in a flowchart-like manner. Apply reasoning to how and why the problems developed; always answer the question, "WHY?" While we only know what the case tells us, we need to think about underlying motivators while we read. Play "devil's advocate" to test these causal relationships to help ensure you are on the right track.

- Conduct some initial research on your identified major problem/issue. The research will likely help frame the major problem and reinforce its relationships to your potential secondary problems. For example, if the problem you have identified deals with employee supervision, research what types of things need to be considered when supervising employees (e.g., performance reviews, hiring/firing processes, related potential legal issues, discrimination and/or diversity issues, mentoring, confidentiality, etc.). Be sure to consider any potential diversity issues and the impact they may have. Only by gaining an understanding of the relevant management issues surrounding the major problem can you begin to develop potential solutions.

  TIP: Utilize academic and trade journals as the major focus of your research. Websites can only get you so far, and academic/trade journals will provide you with more in-depth and directly relevant information

- *Important note:* If you are working in teams on the case study, we highly recommend you complete all of the above steps *individually*, and then come together as a group to compare notes. This will help to ensure you have done the best job of analyzing the case.

- Now that you have identified the major problem, decide from which management level you want to "solve" the problem. Is the problem best addressed from a departmental perspective (e.g., supervisor, director, manager), a senior executive perspective (e.g., vice presidents), an organizational perspective (e.g., CEO, board of directors), or perhaps from an outside perspective (e.g., consultant)? Note that in order to make this decision, you *must* understand the roles and responsibilities of each of these levels as they relate to the problem and identify the strengths and weaknesses of each approach.

- Identify at least two, but no more than three, potential alternative "solutions" to address the major problem *from the management level you have selected*. This is where you are being asked to "think outside of the box." Were there possibilities not suggested by the text? How would each of these solutions improve the situation, and to what degree? Identify the strengths and weaknesses of each approach. The best choice may not be affordable; as managers we have to "satisfice," that is, make the best choice available at that time. Is one more cost-effective than the other(s)? Would one of them take too long to implement before experiencing the needed results? Do you have the expertise and resources to implement the solution? In developing your alternative solutions, keep in mind the strengths and weaknesses of the organization *as they relate to the major problem*. Having a great community reputation, for example, will likely have little bearing on whether you should fire the head of surgery. However, significant financial reserves may be relevant in trying to increase access for patients in outlying areas. Remember, there is no one right or wrong solution, only better or worse solutions. The difference will be in how you analyze and present them.

- Select the best alternative solution to implement. In the step above, you analyzed each potential alternative in terms of the strengths and weaknesses of each. Through this process it should have become evident which alternative has the best chance of successfully addressing the major problem. Your final challenge is to identify *how* and *when* you will know whether your proposed alternative solution worked. To do this, you must identify ways to evaluate your solution. For example, if the desired outcome of your solution is increased revenue, when will this occur, and to what degree? Increased revenue will be one of your evaluation metrics, but you will need to outline specifically what you expect to happen. A sufficient response in this example could be "increase revenue by 5% by end of third quarter." Note that regardless of which metrics you choose, you need to be able to *measure* them. At this point in the case it may be necessary to "assume" some things. For example, if a desired outcome is increased patient satisfaction, you can assume the organization already measures this and simply state your expected quantitative improvement and time frame (e.g., "improve patient satisfaction by 10 percentage points within six months"). However, be sure to *state any assumptions* you are making (e.g., "We assume the organization already tracks patient satisfaction and it is currently at 30%").

CASE STUDY WRITE-UP

Prepare a written report of the case using the following format.

Background Statement

What is going on in this case *as it relates to the identified major problem*? What are (only) the key points the reader needs to know in order to understand how you will "solve" the case? Summarize the scenario in your own words—do not simply regurgitate the case. Briefly describe the organization, setting, situation, who is involved, who decides what, and so on.

Major Problems and Secondary Issues

Specifically identify the major and secondary problems. What are the real issues? What are the differences? Can secondary issues become major problems? Present analysis of the causes and effects. Fully explain your reasoning.

Your Role

In a sentence or short paragraph, declare from which role you will address the major problem, whether you are a senior manager, departmental manager, or an outside consultant called in to advise. Regardless of your choice, you *must* justify in writing *why* you chose that role. What are the advantages and disadvantages of your selected role? Be specific.

Organizational Strengths and Weaknesses

Identify the strengths and weaknesses that exist *in relation to the major problem*. Again, your focus here should be in describing what the organization is capable of doing (and not capable of doing) with respect to addressing the major problem. Thus, the identified strengths and weaknesses should include those at the managerial level of the problem. For example, if you have chosen to address the problem from the departmental perspective and the department is understaffed, that is a weakness worthy of mentioning. Be sure to remember to include any strengths/weaknesses that may be related to diversity issues.

Alternatives and Recommended Solutions

Describe the two to three alternative solutions you came up with. What feasible strategies would you recommend? What are the pros and cons? State what should be done—why, how, and by whom. Be specific.

Evaluation

How will you know when you've gotten there? There must be measurable goals put in place with the recommendations. Money is easiest to measure; what else can be measured? What evaluation plan would you put in place to assess whether you are reaching your goals?

TIP: Write this section as if you were trying to "sell" your proposed solution to the organization. Convince the reader that your proposed solution is the best available and that it will work as planned. Make sure the goals you identify are worth the effort required to achieve them!

TEAM STRUCTURE AND PROCESS FOR COMPLETION

We recommend that teams select a team leader and a team recorder, although *all* should take notes. The team should decide how to divide the tasks to be accomplished. In our classes, we expect to see written responses to the aforementioned questions, and the written, typed case studies to be a minimum of five pages long. Teams should indicate who had responsibility for different tasks/sections on the written materials that are handed in.

Team findings should be presented in no more than 10 minutes to the rest of the class. Individual grades are given for each of the student's designated sections and a group grade for the case study as a whole from peers on the presentation, plus teammates are required to grade each other's efforts and teamwork within the group. The average of the three grades becomes each individual's case study grade. Copies of forms utilized for each evaluation (individual sections, group presentation, and teamwork) are provided in this chapter (Figure 18-1, Figure 18-2, and Figure 18-3).

Guidelines for Effective Participation

1. Attend all team sessions. Eighty percent of life is showing up. It's important here too.
2. Prepare before coming to team sessions, and take careful notes. Think about the project and be prepared for each session.
3. Help establish the purpose of the session and the direction to be followed by the group.
4. Have an open mind and be willing to modify your conclusions. Welcome the stimulation of having your ideas challenged.
5. Strike a balance between your speaking time and that of others.
6. Be respectful, considerate, and tactful of the feelings of others—especially when you disagree.
7. Present the substance of your thinking concisely and to the point.
8. Help the team reach some conclusions within the allotted time.
9. Really pull your weight on the team. Assist in accomplishing the work of the team by putting the needs of the group ahead of your own needs.
10. *Have fun!*

	A Level	B Level	C Level	D Level
Introduction (10 pts)	The section introduction: • Was well organized • Smoothly pulled the reader into the topic • Presented the main focus of the case study section • Included adequate content • Was written for the correct audience	The section introduction had one limitation: • Disorganized • Not smooth • Did not present the main focus of the case study section • Too detailed or too sketchy • Rocky first sentences	The section introduction had two of these limitations: • Disorganized • Not smooth • Did not present the main focus of the case study section • Too detailed or too sketchy • Rocky first sentences	The section introduction had three or more limitations listed at left or required major changes.
Content (20 pts)	The content of the case study section: • Was clear • Had a unified focus • Focused on important information • Adequately explained concepts • Was correct	The content of the case study section had one of these limitations: • Hard to understand • Included irrelevant or too much detailed information • Failed to explain concepts • Had a disjointed focus • Incorrect information	The content of the case study section had two of these limitations: • Hard to understand • Included irrelevant or too much detailed information • Failed to explain concepts • Had a disjointed focus • Incorrect information	The content of the case study section was not clearly written and difficult to understand OR had three or more limitations listed at left.
Paragraph organization (20 pts)	Paragraphs in the case study section: • Had clear topic sentences • Were about a single topic • Were organized at the paragraph level • Had transitions from one paragraph to another	Paragraphs in the case study section had one of these limitations: • Poor topic sentences • Run-on paragraphs or paragraphs were too brief • Lacked organization within the paragraph • Lacked transitions from one paragraph to another	Paragraphs in the case study section had two of these limitations: • Poor topic sentences • Run-on paragraphs or paragraphs were too brief • Lacked organization within the paragraph • Lacked transitions from one paragraph to another	Paragraphs in the case study section had three or more of the limitations at left.
Case study section organization (20 pts)	The case study section's organization: • Was easy to follow • Was presented in a logical manner • Integrated information • Summarized information when needed • Used headers	The case study section had one of the following limitations: • Organization was not logical • Information was not consistently integrated together • Information was not summarized when needed • Headers were missing	The case study section had two of the following limitations: • Organization was not logical • Information was not consistently integrated together • Information was not summarized when needed • Headers were missing	The case study section was disorganized and illogical OR had three or more of the limitations listed at left.
Writing style (10 pts)	The style of writing is professional • Easy to understand • Uses appropriate vocabulary • Shows mature syntax style	Writing is affected by one of the following limitations: • Jargon • Wordiness • Redundant phrasing • Awkward syntax structures • Choppy sentences • Run-on sentences • Incorrect use of vocabulary	Writing is affected by two of the following limitations: • Vocabulary jargon • Wordiness • Redundant phrasing • Awkward syntax structures • Choppy sentences • Run-on sentences • Incorrect use of vocabulary	Writing is affected by three or more limitations occurring three or more times.
Writing mechanics (10 pts)	The case study section is free of spelling, grammar, and punctuation errors.	The case study section has fewer than 5 errors in spelling, grammar, or punctuation.	The case study section has 6–10 errors in spelling, grammar, or punctuation.	The case study section has more than 10 errors in spelling, grammar, or punctuation.
APA (10 pts)	All APA rules are followed for citations, numbers, quotes, references, headers, etc.	The case study section has fewer than 5 APA rule errors.	The case study section has 6–10 APA rule errors.	The case study section has more than 10 APA rule errors.

FIGURE 18-1 Detailed Rubric for Grading Written Case Studies

Courtesy of Sharon Glennen

PEER EVALUATION CRITERIA FOR CASE STUDY PRESENTATIONS SCORING SHEET	
Presentation Title and Author's Name	**Your Name**
Use a scale of 1 to 10, where 1 is poor and 10 is excellent. (You must explain any scores below 3 and above 8.)	
How well did the presenter:	**Points**
Indicate the purpose of the presentation and its relevance to the course?	0
Ensure the presentation was relevant to the current state of health care?	0
Demonstrate knowledge about the *case study*?	0
Contribute to peer knowledge?	0
Use proper grammar, punctuation, and vocabulary?	0
Adhere to length constraints (*10 slides maximum*, excluding references)?	0
Use current references and cite properly in presentation?	0
Provide appropriate main points?	0
Use legible fonts with appropriate colors/background and clip art?	0
Accomplish the stated objectives?	0
TOTAL	0
Comments	

FIGURE 18-2 Peer Evaluation Criteria for Group Presentations

CONFIDENTIAL TEAMMATE EVALUATION CRITERIA			
Use a scale of 1 to 10, where 1 is poor and 10 is excellent. (Do NOT evaluate yourself.)			
How well did your teammates:	**Name**	**Name**	**Name**
Attend all team sessions?	0	0	0
Prepare for each session?	0	0	0
Work collaboratively to identify and meet session goals?	0	0	0
Actively participate in group discussions?	0	0	0
Keep an open mind or modify opinions or conclusions to keep the project moving?	0	0	0
Present ideas concisely?	0	0	0
Submit assigned work on time?	0	0	0
Interact with teammates in a respectful, considerate, and tactful manner?	0	0	0
Fulfill responsibilities as agreed?	0	0	0
Work actively to achieve group consensus on issues/problems?	0	0	0
TOTAL	0	0	0
Would you be willing to work with this teammate again on another team? (YES or NO)			
(You must evaluate ALL teammates and explain any scores below 3 and above 8.)			

FIGURE 18-3 Confidential Teammate Evaluation Form

REFERENCES

Hammond, J. S. (2002, April 16). Learning by the case method. *Harvard Business Review*, Industry and Background Note 9-376-241. Retrieved from http://hbr.org/product/learning-by-the-case-method /an/376241-PDF-ENG?N=0&Ntt=Case±method&referral=00269&cm_sp=endeca-_-spotlight-_-link

Metro Renal—Case for Chapters 12 and 2

Mohamad A. Ali

"Dr. Griffith, Dr. Williams called and asked if you would join him on the golf course this afternoon," Sandra the office manager said to Dr. Griffith.

"Of course I'll be there, I may have to cancel my afternoon patients."

Metro Renal is a reputable nephrology clinic in Urbana, IL headed by the Chief Medical officer of the group, Dr. Rosenberg. The group has two internists, Dr. James and Dr. Campbell, and it has also two nephrologists, Dr. Griffith and Dr. Rosenberg. Metro Renal Clinic was acquired last year by a well-known physician management company MRA, Metro Renal Associates. As a part of the acquisition, Dr. Rosenberg was chosen as the chief medical officer. Even though Dr. Rosenberg sees patients two days a week, he was offered a generous incentive from the management company to ensure that the practice is efficient and maintaining high returns.

Dr. Rosenberg has established a strict policy when it comes to scheduling and seeing patients which requires all physicians to be double booked. No cancellations are allowed except for family emergencies, in which case Dr. Rosenberg is to be notified directly. In order for Dr. Rosenberg to make sure the practice is running accordingly, he asked his scheduler, Tanya, to tell him everything that happened with other physicians in the group and their patients without anybody knowing.

Dr. Griffith and Sandra have been working together for four years and have a good personal relationship. Dr. Griffith is a renowned physician and his patients admire and respect him. No complaints were ever filed against him, and he gets the highest satisfaction scores. Dr. Griffith didn't think it was a big deal to cancel his afternoon patients and enjoy the nice weather with his friend on the golf course. Sandra agreed with him, since they can be rescheduled early next week instead. Sandra went ahead and cancelled the afternoon schedule and didn't mention anything to Dr. Rosenberg.

Tanya overheard the conversation between Dr. Griffith and Sandra and called Dr. Rosenberg to notify him.

The next day, Dr. Rosenberg showed up unexpectedly and asked Sandra to come to his office. He had prepared a written warning for violating his policy. He handed it to her and asked her to sign it. Sandra felt betrayed, but she didn't know who could have done this to her. She told Dr. Rosenberg that he should communicate that with Dr. Griffith.

Dr. Rosenberg ignored her request and never discussed the subject with Dr. Griffith. Sandra notified Dr. Griffith of what happened, however, he wouldn't comment on the subject either.

Dr. Griffith knew he violated the practice policy and didn't want to have a heated conversation with Dr. Rosenberg.

Sandra called the regional manager and complained. The regional manager told Sandra not to worry about it, she would discuss it with Drs. Rosenberg and Griffith. However, the issue was never brought up in any meeting or ever addressed. Sandra has decided to leave the practice since she felt she was treated unfairly.

You are the regional manager. You were notified by Sandra that she is submitting her two weeks' notice. She is a good manager and you don't want to lose her. However, you don't want to get involved in a heated conversation with the practicing physicians at the same time.

DISCUSSION QUESTIONS

1. What are the facts of this case?

2. What are the management implications of this case?

3. What are the legal obligations the practice has to its employees and how do they apply to this case?

4. How would you address her letter of resignation? You want to keep Sandra and avoid confrontation with the physicians. Is that feasible?

5. Create a script for discussing this situation with Sandra.

United Physician Group—Case for Chapters 5, 9, 11, and 15

Mohamad A. Ali

Allen Smith is a recent graduate of one of the most reputable schools in the North East Region. He completed his Master's in Health Administration and his undergraduate studies in Economics. Allen has no work experience in health administration except for the internship he completed with a small physician office as a part of his capstone training.

Upon graduation, Allen was offered a job as a practice administrator in Buffalo, New York with United Physician Group, UPG. The long-term practice administrator, John Delaphena, has decided to retire by the end of the month after being with the practice for 20 years. He believes health care has become more challenging than ever before. He believes hiring a new graduate as a practice administrator would be a good option to assist the practice in overcoming these new challenges. Mr. Delaphena interviewed Allen and found him to possess a high level of analytical and problem-solving skills. He discussed the interview results with Dr. Wilson, the Chief Medical Officer, and they decided to give Allen a chance to demonstrate his managerial skills.

UPG is a small physician group practice which consists of five physicians. The group was founded by Dr. Larry Wilson 20 years ago along with John Delaphena who started out as an administrative assistant. Dr. Wilson dedicated 20 years of his professional life to his practice with the hope of getting a rewarding return on his investment once he decides to sell his practice. Dr. Wilson is being offered a non-compete offer from Heathway Medical System to buy his practice. All the staff will continue to work in the practice for another five years before management restructuring takes place. Dr. Wilson is worried the Affordable Care Act (ACA) will have a negative impact on small medical groups like his. Such an impact could eventually force them to close the practice and be hired by larger medical groups or an affiliated hospital, such as Heathway Medical System. Dr. Wilson has requested Allen to study the law and to explore the different options United Physician Group has in terms of preparing for the impact of the ACA.

UPG represents five different specialties: primary care, physical medicine, orthopedics, neurology, and orthopedic surgery. In addition to the physicians, the group has five other employees: a front desk person, an RN, an LPN, a billing coordinator, and a medical assistant.

Dr. Wilson talked to Dr. Smith, the practice neurologist, who is seven years younger than Dr. Wilson, about the possibility of buying Dr. Wilson's share of the practice. Dr. Wilson was going to transfer the leadership role to Dr. Smith once Dr. Wilson retired. Dr. Wilson proposed to stay as a non-executive chairman to help Dr. Smith through the transition phase. Initially, Dr. Smith showed interest in taking over the group, but once the ACA was passed, Dr. Smith also had concerns about the future of their practice. He has requested Dr. Wilson wait until they can find out more about the impact of the ACA on medical groups.

Dr. Adams, an orthopedic surgeon, has a strong relationship with Heathway Medical System and its chair of Orthopedic Surgery at its hospital. He made a recommendation during their last quarter meeting to consider an offer from Heathway Medical System which enables them to sell the practice to Heathway Medical System and become employees of the hospital for five years. However, the buyout proposed by Heathway Medical System was 28% below the expectations of Dr. Wilson, so he rejected the offer. Dr. Adams thinks that it is the only option available to them since the practice is doomed to fail with the cuts in reimbursement and the growing regulations of the Centers for Medicare and Medicaid Services (CMS). Over the past year, the practice was highly affected with a 15% cut in Medicare reimbursement; 70% of the practice patients are from Medicare.

Dr. Wilson was greatly concerned about the future of the practice and the future of his investment. That concern made him seek advice and recommendations from Allen regarding the best option to pursue in handling this dilemma. Allen has promised Dr. Wilson that he will do his best conducting market research, reviewing the ACA, and conducting financial analysis to identify the best option for the group. Allen, however, is leaning towards selling the practice since those who are in a similar role like his and who are working for Heathway Medical System make $15,000 more in annual compensation than he currently makes with the practice.

DISCUSSION QUESTIONS

1. How should Allen go about conducting his market research?

2. What kind of financial information is essential to identify, gather, and study?

3. What are some of the issues that the Affordable Care Act presents? Are they serious threats to the practice?

4. Do you think there could be a conflict of interest in Allen's case?

5. Is Dr. Wilson doing the right thing by hiring a new graduate to provide analysis and recommendations? Why or why not?

6. If you were Dr. Wilson, how would you handle this situation?

7. Which of the options available to UPG seems to be the best? Provide the rationale for your response.

Piecework—Case for Chapters 9 and 10

Dale Buchbinder

Dr. Jones develops an outpatient vascular surgical procedures center attached to his office. He equips the center with a fluoroscopy unit, and all the requirements for a single specialty operating room have been maintained. He hires a nurse anesthetist to give anesthesia and monitor the patients. In addition, he has a small recovery area with a nurse to follow the patients postprocedure. He learns he can be reimbursed an up to $20,000 facility fee for every procedure performed. He has decided that since his overhead is anywhere from 40%–60%, the more procedures he performs, the higher his profit ratios will be.

Therefore, when Mr. Smith is in need of a lower extremity revascularization, he is brought in for diagnostic angiogram. The angiogram reveals he has an external iliac and a superficial femoral artery stenosis on the left side. These two lesions probably account for the patient's symptoms. The patient returns the following week, and Dr. Jones performs an iliac artery angioplasty with a balloon. In approximately 10 days, the patient returns for one of three procedures in which he has his superficial femoral artery also treated with a balloon angioplasty.

The patient has now had three procedures totaling $60,000 in revenue. The overhead for these procedures was approximately 40%, providing a $36,000 profit. Had these procedures been done in a regulated space (i.e., a hospital), the physician would have probably performed the diagnostic angiogram as well as the definitive angioplasties of both external iliac and superficial femoral arteries at the same time. The physician's fees for these procedures would have been approximately $2,000. Also, it is possible that in a regulated facility the doctor would have chosen to at least place a stent or would have performed an atherectomy or even used a drug-coated balloon in one or both of these lesions. However, in the free-standing outpatient vascular surgery center, the use of these devices would have greatly driven up the cost of the procedure and decreased the profits.

It is not uncommon for these types of procedures to be performed in an unregulated space with no hospital quality control or supervision. While they drive up the cost of treating the patient, they are extremely profitable for the doctor. In order to gain this profit, the physician has subjected the patient to three procedures with three different anesthesia procedures, tripling the risk of any anesthetic complications for the patient. Furthermore, if an adverse event occurs in these settings, there is no rapid response team available to resuscitate the patient.

DISCUSSION QUESTIONS

1. What are the facts of this case?

2. Compare and contrast the impact on Dr. Jones revenue stream for patients covered by the following insurance plans: HMO (closed or open panel), IPA model HMO, Network Model HMO, PPO, POS, Medicare, and Medicaid.

3. Based on your analysis of the above, which plan(s) do you think he is targeting for his revenues?

4. What are the legal and ethical obligations Dr. Jones has to his patients and how do they apply to this case?

5. What are the advantages and disadvantages for the consumer in this scenario?

6. What are the advantages and disadvantages for Dr. Jones in this scenario?

7. If an adverse event occurs, what do you think will happen to Dr. Jones and his facility?

8. Is Dr. Jones gambling with patients' lives? Provide a rationale for your responses.

Building a Better
MIS-Trap—Case for Chapter 8

Sharon B. Buchbinder

You are the CEO of a large health services organization (HSO) in Florida. Your HSO has inpatient and outpatient facilities, home health care services, and every other service your patient population needs. You also have a world-renowned AIDS treatment center that has been considered by many to be a model for the rest of the U.S. Your HSO has always enjoyed an excellent reputation, and your quality of care is known to be excellent. You have been very happy in your work, knowing that your HSO provides good care to people who truly need it in a caring and cost-effective manner.

Your HSO has recently been featured in every media vehicle known to every man, woman, and child in the U.S. and beyond. The reason: someone downloaded the names of 4,000 HIV+ patients who had been seen in your world-renowned HIV clinic and sent the list to newspapers, magazines, and the Internet.

You and your board of trustees are completely blown away. The board is furious and wants to fire you. You have been able to convince them that they need to keep you on to fix the HSO's management information system (MIS). Their last words to you were "You had *better* come back with plans for building a better MIS, or you're fired!"

You hire a computer security consultant, and she comes into your organization under disguise as a nurse manager to help you determine where the security leak might be. She returns to you in three days with the following report.

"While I was undercover in your organization for a mere three days, I observed the following breaches in computer security. These are the highlights (or lowlights):

- Nurses log in with their passwords, walk away, and leave the system open and up and running;
- Dr. Jones leaves his password taped to the PC on a piece of paper;
- Fax machines and printers are often in areas of high traffic and in rooms without locks;

- With my one password, I had remote access to every database in the hospital, including Human Resources' personnel files, from my home;
- There are no programs reminding people to change their passwords on a regular basis;
- When I pretended to forget my password, other nurses gave me theirs; and
- When I requested sensitive patient files on flash drive, even after this incident, people rarely questioned me.

In short, you have a major problem with your MIS—and your staff!"
What should you do?

DISCUSSION QUESTIONS

1. What law is being violated by the employees at this health services organization?

2. Why was this law enacted?

3. What are the penalties for violating this law?

4. If an employee shares confidential medical information about a celebrity and is caught, what should the penalty be?

5. Do you think you should be updating your résumé and looking for a new job?

Death by Measles—Case for Chapters 17, 11, and 15

Sharon B. Buchbinder

In July 2015, an elderly woman being treated for several health issues attended a local health clinic. The medications for her chronic diseases placed her in an immuno-compromised status. While waiting to be seen by her primary care physician, a child came in with his mother, sneezing and coughing. Nothing more was thought of it until the woman died from pneumonia—caused by measles. This was the first death in the U.S. from measles in 12 years.

DISCUSSION QUESTIONS

1. What are the facts of this case?

2. What would have been the potential impact on the woman if the child had the following diseases: pertussis, polio, influenza, or Ebola?

3. What are the management implications of this case? Should there be separate waiting rooms for people with an immuno-compromised status?

4. What are the legal and ethical obligations of the parent of the unvaccinated child?

5. What are the legal and ethical obligations the clinic has to its patients and how do they apply to this case? Should the woman's family seek legal remedies?

6. An RN who works at the clinic refuses to have an influenza vaccination. She does not have allergies, nor does she have religious objections. She "doesn't believe in them." Create a script for a conversation with this employee, urging her to reconsider, and detailing the consequences of her continued refusal.

Full Moon or Bad Planning?—Case for Chapters 17, 11, and 15

Sharon B. Buchbinder

Greenville Community Hospital (GCH) was located in an affluent suburb of a metropolitan area. A large psychiatric hospital was geographically adjacent. In fact, the two hospitals shared facilities, such as a conference center and some office buildings. Thanks to good teamwork between the two, a consistent pattern of admitting patients via the Emergency Department (ED), then to the psychiatric hospital had emerged.

Lately, however, an uptick of substance abuse-related ED admissions had created a large backlog in GCH. The patients could not be admitted to the psychiatric hospital because they were short on beds for long-term rehab. Drug rehabilitation facilities in the area were either too expensive ($24,000–$40,000 for 28 days), if private pay, or overbooked, if Medicaid supported. In the meantime, the patients had multiple health issues secondary to drug use. The patients were now being placed on a non-secure unit, along with routine medical–surgical patients.

On a night lit by a full moon, Rosemary, a floor nurse, went in to take vital signs on a young female patient who had been admitted for a heroin overdose. She found the girl in bed with her boyfriend, having sex. When she told the boy visiting hours were over and he had to leave, he leaped up, screamed obscenities, and chased her out of the room. Rosemary ran for the nursing station and help. Fortunately for her, he was ataxic and uncoordinated due to his own illegal drug ingestion. She made it to the desk and called security just as he collapsed to the floor. Then she called for a rapid response team to revive the boyfriend.

She wondered how much longer she could do this job. There was no way to call for help, no safe place or room for staff to hide from aggressive patients. It was only a matter of time before she was injured—or killed.

DISCUSSION QUESTIONS

1. What are the facts of this case?

2. What are the management implications of this case? What should management be doing to protect their employees?

3. If Rosemary had been injured, who would have been responsible? What if the visitor attacked another patient? What are the legal and ethical obligations GCH has to its employees and to its patients and how do they apply to this case?

4. What would be the optimum physical space for these patients? How much do you think it would cost to install a panic alarm in the patients' rooms? At the nurse's station? A safe room? What are the costs of doing nothing?

5. Create an emergency plan for the staff in this unit while they await administration's decision on renovations.

How Do We Handle a Girl Like Maria?—Case for Chapters 17 and 4

Sharon B. Buchbinder

It was Saturday evening and Joe Johnson, VP of Patient Services, was relaxing with his family after dinner and watching a situation comedy. As the administrator on call (AOC), he was grateful things had been quiet—so far. The last time he was AOC, a psychiatric patient attacked a nurse in the middle of the night and tried to choke her to death. He really didn't want another one of *those* nights. His phone vibrated and he was chagrined to see the Emergency Department (ED) number.

Please, not another attack on a nurse.

"Hey Joe, this is Liz. We've had a bit of a situation here." It was the head of the ED, Elizabeth Watkins, a woman he liked and respected. Joe breathed a sigh of relief. Liz was a competent emergency physician and could handle just about anything.

She's probably just calling to give me a heads up. No biggie.

Joe kept his eyes on the TV and smiled at the last joke. "What's up?"

"I've called the police. I think we have things handled for the moment. I just have one question—"

He jumped up from the sofa and went into the kitchen. "Things? What things?"

"An older man brought in a young woman, a girl really. We think she's about twelve or thirteen, she doesn't speak English, so it's hard to tell. She's been beat up pretty badly. He said she fell. But, her injuries were inconsistent with his description of what occurred. She was dressed in a short skirt, spike heels, and wore a ton of make-up. When I told him he had to leave the room so I could examine her in private, he refused to leave." She blew out a long breath. "I told him to hold on, I needed to get some paperwork. I lied."

"You what?" Joe's head was about to explode.

"I got the off duty police officer who serves as our security guard in the ED to come back with me and escort the man to another room. The guy wasn't happy, started yelling at me in Spanish. I knew enough to understand he wasn't calling me nice names."

Joe ran his hand over his head. "What made you do that? Do you really think it's necessary to get a cop when a patient's family member won't leave the room? She's a minor, her father has a right to be present. He could sue us."

"He's not her father. He's her pimp."

Words escaped him. After several long breaths, at last he was able to get something out. They were in an affluent county, not in an urban area. Things like that didn't happen in his community, not in his back yard.

"This sounds like a stretch, Liz. We're not in the city. What made you decide that?"

"You know that human trafficking course I insisted everyone take? The one you missed? She had all the hallmarks of an enslaved minor child."

"Okay, okay. So the police are on the way to arrest the guy. What about the girl?"

"That's what I was calling you about, Joe. Did you make a plan for these types of victims? That was your job. Who am I supposed to call? How do we handle a girl like Maria?"

DISCUSSION QUESTIONS

1. What are the facts of this case?

2. What were the clues to Liz that the girl was being trafficked?

3. What were Joe's attribution errors in this scenario?

4. What are the management implications of this case? What should Joe have done to prepare for this situation?

5. What should the ED staff do with Maria?

The Condescending Dental Hygienist—Case for Chapters 7, 12, 15, and 4

Sharon B. Buchbinder

Dr. Rose, a 65-year-old woman, goes to her six month appointment for a dental cleaning. Upon arrival, the receptionist requests her insurance card, driver's license, and an updated health form. On the form, Dr. Rose indicates a lengthy list of allergies, including a scrub used for surgeries. The previous summer, after a minor in-office procedure, she discovered this new allergy to chlorhexidine, so she is careful to include it on all her allergy lists.

The dental hygienist, Chrissy, a new 21-year-old employee, inquires about Dr. Rose's profession. When she tells the hygienist she is a registered nurse and a university professor, Chrissy pats her shoulder and says, "Oh, that's nice, dear."

The hygienist instructs Dr. Rose to rinse her mouth out with an antibacterial mouthwash for 30 seconds. While she is having her teeth cleaned, Dr. Rose notices a letter "C" on the bottle of mouthwash and turns it around. It is chlorhexidine, the very ingredient she was allergic to in the surgical scrub. She informs the hygienist immediately and begins to rinse her mouth with water repeatedly.

Chrissy protests and tells Dr. Rose she is mistaken, it is not the same thing, "dear," that scrub is "what you wash your hands with." She pats Dr. Rose's arm again, telling her to be a "good patient" and to open her mouth for cleaning.

Dr. Rose gets out of the chair, grabs her smartphone, points to the surgical scrub and the active ingredient. She uses her albuterol nebulizer and takes a dose of prednisone. Chrissy continues to insist it is not the same substance when the dentist enters the room and asks what is going on.

Between puffs on her nebulizer, Dr. Rose relays the incident to the dentist.

Chrissy continues to protest until the dentist tells her she is wrong, it is the same active ingredient. The dentist offers Dr. Rose a shot of epinephrine, which she declines. Dr. Rose leaves the office as quickly as she can and returns home, grateful she didn't swallow the mouthwash and annoyed by the dental hygienist's condescending behaviors.

Upon arrival at home, Dr. Rose receives a phone call from Chrissy, asking, "How are you feeling, dear?"

DISCUSSION QUESTIONS

1. What are the facts of this case?

2. Review the quality improvement tools in Chapter 7 and select the appropriate one to analyze this problem.

3. What are the top three management issues in this case?

4. What are the legal and ethical obligations a health care professional has to his or her patients and how do they apply to this case?

5. What attribution error did Chrissy make about Dr. Rose? How did that influence her communication with her patient?

6. Who should be held responsible for addressing these problems?

7. What obligations does the dentist have to Dr. Rose?

The "Easy" Software Upgrade at Delmar Ortho—Case for Chapters 8 and 13

Sharon B. Buchbinder

Delmar Orthopedics is a 42-physician orthopedic group; its physicians command the local market in terms of the orthopedic specialty—operating in several of the nearby hospitals and seeing patients in their five sites around the city. Delmar works like a machine. The physicians, the structure around their practice, and the employees who support them are extremely efficient and predictable. Recently, their margins have declined due to reductions in reimbursement, but they have been doing a good job of squeezing every penny out of each clinical day. And, they finally smoothed things out after the somewhat rocky implementation of their electronic medical records (EMR) system the prior year. Everything seemed to be under control.

Patrick McCain joined Delmar Orthopedics a month ago as the practice manager. Prior to joining the practice, he'd been managing a bank for two years after working his way up through the teller ranks in his college years. A hard worker, Patrick felt relatively comfortable in his ability to manage people and a budget. He was excited about his new job with the challenge of managing a large team—more than 40 people—and having responsibility for all practice administrative functions excluding finance, legal, and information technology (IT).

Years ago, the practice instituted a bimonthly meeting of the leadership (management team members and a number of the key physicians) to discuss volumes and patient care issues and announce upcoming activities/events. Yesterday's meeting was Patrick's second since joining. During the meeting, it appeared that a number of the physicians were not paying attention. One played a game on his smart phone during the entire meeting, and another one kept leaving the meeting to take phone calls. Two of the team members had a running sidebar conversation about their weekend plans, and a third one actually fell asleep. Although the meeting was relatively noneventful—and, in fact, this seemed to be the team's usual meeting behavior—there *was* one item that concerned him.

Terry, the practice's IT director, announced to the group that it was time for the annual upgrade of the system. The schedule wasn't yet finalized, but he recommended completion within the next 90 days. This would be their first upgrade to the system and would require five hours of downtime for the vendor to complete. Plus, it had to occur on a weekday, when physicians would be seeing patients. Terry did say that this would be their first time the system had been down since it was installed the prior year; however, he did not provide any additional details or offer contact information for follow-up.

Patrick knew this upgrade would be an important chance to prove himself, but he was the "new kid" on the block. He worried that there might be alliances of which he was unaware and "sacred cows" that no one wanted to disturb. He lived through many systems upgrades in the banking world and was painfully aware that these supposedly "easy" upgrades never were. He wanted to alert the practice to the problems that could occur and how to avoid them. As he sat at his desk thinking about all the issues, Terry strolled by, grinned at him and said, "Don't worry, I've got it all under control." At those words, Patrick's heart sank.

As he learned more about the project, it was clear that all of the staff and physicians needed to be retrained. And there had been no accommodations made for testing the changes. He increasingly felt as though Terry had not appropriately informed the leadership team about the scope and risk of the upgrade. Terry appeared to be held in high regard by the practice.

DISCUSSION QUESTIONS

1. How can Patrick address these risks without embarrassing Terry?

2. Why do you think that a number of the team members don't pay attention to this important event? As a future manager, what do you think should have occurred in this meeting?

3. How would you handle the discussion that needs to take place with Terry? What measures might you take to plan for the worst?

4. What research should Patrick do on the prior year's project that might assist him in assessing the risk in the upgrade?

5. How might Patrick ensure that he understands the impact of the project before putting too much time and effort into it himself?

6. What are some of the questions Patrick should pose to understand how this upgrade would affect his staff? The physicians? Delmar's patients?

7. Are the physicians "team players"? Explain your response.

8. Reread this case. Using Figure 18-3, the Confidential Teammate Evaluation Form at the start of this chapter, compare the behavior of these physicians and managers with the expected behaviors of teammates. Score each one as if he or she were your teammate. What scores did they earn?

The Brawler—Case for Chapters 11, 12, and 17

Sharon B. Buchbinder and Dale Buchbinder

Dr. O'Connor was known for his hot temper and drinking. Although he claimed never to come to work under the influence, nurses, physicians, and other coworkers had their doubts, and several expressed their alarm to their supervisors. The emergency room needed coverage, and it was hard to find physicians who would work the graveyard shift, so little was done to address these concerns. One night, Dr. O'Connor walked across a clearly marked wet floor that the custodian had just mopped. When the angry janitor protested loudly and pointed to the bright yellow sign and the offending footprints, Dr. O'Connor took a swing at the other man and a fistfight ensued.

DISCUSSION QUESTIONS

1. What should the hospital do to deal with the good doctor? Who should handle this?

2. What role, if any, did the janitor play in this incident? What could he have done differently?

3. Where should Dr. O'Connor be referred—anger management, Alcoholics Anonymous, psychiatric evaluation? Provide a rationale for your response.

4. How can this incident be turned into a "teachable moment" for the staff, physicians, and others?

5. How could this have been prevented?

I Love You ... Forever—Case for Chapters 17, 12, and 11

Sharon B. Buchbinder and Dale Buchbinder

Nurse Practitioner Nancy Masters broke up with her control freak boyfriend, Joe Jerque, after a three-year relationship that was going nowhere but down. Despite her repeated pleas for counseling, he refused help, and his short temper and terrifying tantrums were only getting worse. Fearful of retaliation, she moved out while he was at work, didn't leave a forwarding address, and changed her phone number and e-mail address. One evening as she walked to her car in the poorly lit parking lot next to the clinic where she worked, Joe showed up and confronted her, begging to be taken back. She told him it was over and to please leave her alone. The following night, Joe appeared again, and again she told him to go away. On the third evening, she asked the security guard to walk her to her car. When she arrived at her vehicle, she found a note under her windshield wiper alongside an envelope: "I will never let you go. You are mine forever, even in death." Inside the envelope was a .38 caliber bullet. Terrified, she immediately called the police to report the incidents, and the security guard took the matter to his supervisor. The clinic administrator told Nancy and the security guard that it was a personal matter to pursue with the police and the legal system, and that the clinic was not responsible for her safety once she left the premises. Nancy is terrified; she is familiar with the stalking literature. There is a direct association between the number of stalking incidents and the likelihood of violence—including homicide. She petitions the court and obtains a restraining order against Joe, but worries that he will violate it. She is considering getting a permit to carry a concealed weapon for self-protection.

DISCUSSION QUESTIONS

1. What is the clinic's responsibility in these types of situations?

2. What could the clinic do to help remedy the situation?

3. What do you recommend that Nancy do above and beyond what has already been done?

4. Do you think Nancy is wise in considering carrying a gun to the clinic?

5. What laws in your state are applicable with regard to concealed carry in general and in health care facilities specifically?

Managing Health Care Professionals— Mini-Case Studies for Chapter 11

Sharon B. Buchbinder and Dale Buchbinder

1. You are a new administrator at Jonestown Medical Center. You receive a telephone call from the nurse manager of the emergency room. Dr. Smith, an emergency room physician who is an employee of your hospital, has just reported for duty. The nurse manager suspects that Dr. Smith is intoxicated. What do you do?

2. You are the CEO of Sleepy Hollow Retirement Community and Nursing Center. A resident's family has come to you to complain that their loved one, who is on pain medication, is in intolerable pain. Her medications appear not to be working anymore. One of the family members states, "My 90-year-old mother saw the nurse put the pain medicine in her pocket." What do you do?

3. You are the practice manager of Docs R Us, Ltd., a large multispecialty medical practice employing more than 100 physicians. You are conducting a random review of billing for doctors in the practice and you discover that one of the internists in your group who treats mostly Medicare recipients has been checking off the wrong code for her procedures on the billing form. The procedures on the patient record do not match the billing form codes. You pull up her files for the past 3 months and find a pattern of upcoding. When you meet with her to review this miscoding, she becomes very defensive and angry. What do you do? How could you have prepared better for the meeting with the physician?

4. You are the assistant director of the hospital medical staff office at the Rural Outreach Community Hospital in a tiny town in Arkansas. It is your job to verify physician credentials for staff privileges. Your hospital receives an application from a physician for staff privileges. On his application, it states that he graduated from medical school in El Salvador. When you call to verify this, you are told that the medical school burned down two years ago and all the records were destroyed. What do you do?

5. You are a new administrator at a hospital, well known for pulmonary medicine. The physicians in the ICU, the ER, and the department of pulmonary medicine have demanded to meet with you about the shortage of respiratory therapists. You stall them for 48 hours so you can gather data. What types of information will you need to collect to have an intelligent conversation with this powerful group of physicians?

6. Dr. White ordered an unusual dose of a medication. May Patterson, RN, sees the order and believes it to be the wrong dose. She calls Dr. White, who insists that she give the medication—as written. Nurse Patterson calls you, the administrator on call for the weekend, to resolve this crisis. What do you do?

Problems with the Pre-Admission Call Center—Case for Chapters 13 and 10

Sharon B. Buchbinder and Dale Buchbinder

South Street Hospital (SSH) is one of 12 hospitals in the Great West Hospital System, a not-for-profit health care system. SSH serves a largely blue-collar and elderly population. This patient-centric hospital prides itself on high patient satisfaction scores and good financial management.

Dr. Canton is a busy colorectal surgeon who has brought hundreds of cases to SSH in the past year. The day before one of his patients, Mr. Gutsy, was scheduled for an extensive bowel resection, Dr. Canton's office received an irate phone call from the patient stating that he was not having the surgery "because a woman from SSH called and demanded he bring money to the admitting center." Shocked, Dr. Canton personally called the patient to find out what happened.

Mr. Gutsy stated that a woman "insisted that I bring cash or credit cards with me to pay my copayment. I have Medicare and other insurance. There are *no* copays. The more I tried to explain that to the woman, the nastier she became."

Dr. Canton apologized and asked if Mr. Gutsy was able to recall the woman's name.

"No, she didn't give me a name, but she sure gave me attitude." Despite Dr. Canton's best efforts, the patient said he wasn't going *anywhere* that made these types of demands.

Dr. Canton complained to the chairman of surgery, Dr. Kutup, who in turn called the head of SSH pre-admissions, Mrs. Mintz. She was appalled and said, "No one makes those calls from *this* hospital. Great West has a corporate call center for all 12 hospitals in the system. They're *supposed* to be following a script." Mrs. Mintz told Dr. Kutup she'd look into it and get back to him ASAP.

A short time later, Dr. Kutup was scrubbing for his next case and related the story to an anesthesiologist, Dr. Gasser.

Dr. Gasser laughed and said, "Tell your patient they did the same thing to me—but they told me to bring $2,000 in cash to admissions. I almost asked them if they wanted it in unmarked bills."

"Did you bring the money?"

"No, I did *not*. I knew I had coverage, so I just agreed with the woman and ignored her."

"Well, you work here, you're one of their physicians, and they told you that—which makes me think they're doing this to everyone." Dr. Canton shook his head. "Will you tell Mrs. Mintz about this with me?"

"Sure, just don't ask me for my credit card or gold bullion."

The next day, Drs. Kutup, Canton, and Gasser sat down with Mrs. Mintz.

"When I talked to Mr. Count de Money at headquarters, he said the call center used a script and they were 'just following it.'" Mrs. Mintz shook her head. "I tried to tell him that it wasn't true, that they were *harassing* people and patients were complaining—but more will just vote with their feet and go elsewhere. He asked me if I thought the system should lose money on these deadbeats? I tried to reason with him, but he hung up on me! Great West talks a good game about how we're a '*team with 12 hospitals*.' He didn't treat me like a member of the team. He was nasty—and he's in charge of the call center!"

Dr. Canton said, "I have privileges at another hospital. If they don't stop this, I'll be taking my cases there."

Dr. Kutup pointed at his colleague. "This guy is one of our busiest surgeons. SSH is going to lose a *lot* of business if something isn't done about this."

DISCUSSION QUESTIONS

1. Who should Dr. Kutup and Mrs. Mintz approach next with this problem? Provide a rationale for your choice(s).

2. Is Mr. Count de Money responding in an emotionally intelligent way to Mrs. Mintz and her concerns? What aspects of emotional contagion do you think apply to this case?

3. What type of team should SSH form to address this problem? Who should be selected to be on this team? Provide a rationale for your choices.

4. Identify and delineate the top three issues that the team should address in its deliberations.

5. Since SSH is part of the larger hospital system, who should be the person designated to take the matter to corporate headquarters?

6. How should the team evaluate whether a change in corporate policy is needed? Who should take the lead on this evaluation?

Such a Nice Young Man—Case for Chapters 17, 11, and 12

Sharon B. Buchbinder and Dale Buchbinder

Mrs. Davenport is a vivacious septuagenarian living in Whispering Willows Continuing Care Retirement Community. An attractive lady, she spends her days with a large group of friends, playing cards and going on day trips to museums and shows. She enjoys kidding around with the staff, especially Joe, who works in the dining room. A handsome young man, she tells him that he reminds her of her dearly departed husband and calls him "eye-candy." One day, when she doesn't appear for her bridge game, her best friend, Mrs. Atkins, goes to her apartment and knocks on her door—which swings open. Mrs. Davenport is in bed, sobbing. When Mrs. Atkins asks her what's wrong, all Mrs. Davenport can say is, "I thought he was such a nice young man." Mrs. Atkins summons help, and the Nursing Home Administrator (NHA) arrives with an RN from the Nursing Center. Mrs. Davenport will not get out of bed and refuses to get out from under the covers. The NHA is very concerned and suspicious. To Mrs. Davenport's horror, the NHA calls the police. Mrs. Davenport refuses to speak to the RN or the female police officer and sits in her bed, weeping. The NHA tries to convince the shaken resident to go to the ER. Mrs. Davenport shakes her head and says, "No, no, no! It's too shameful. I brought it on myself. Just go away. Please. Just leave me alone." Leaving the RN at the bedside to secure the scene, the NHA and the police officer step out into the hall to discuss the next steps. The police officer asks to speak with Joe. The NHA sends the Administrator in Training (AIT) to find Joe and bring him to the NHA's office—but the AIT returns and reports he is not in the dining room, and a coworker reported seeing Joe jump into his car and take off like a "bat out of hell." Upon review of Joe's criminal background check at hire, all that appear are minor misdemeanors. Can Whispering Willows be sure they are not responsible for hiring a sexual predator? Or is Joe just a victim of circumstances?

DISCUSSION QUESTIONS

1. What are the facts in this situation? What is known and not known so far?

2. What steps should be taken to investigate this further?

3. Do you think the NHA did the correct thing by bringing in the police?

4. Do we know if elder sexual abuse has taken place?

5. Circumstantial evidence seems to point to Joe as the perpetrator of this offense. What does the police officer have to do to ensure collection of physical evidence to support her case?

6. What should the facility do to train the staff and try to prevent these types of incidents from happening again?

7. What liability does Whispering Willows have in this case?

Sundowner or Victim?—Case for Chapters 15 and 17

Sharon B. Buchbinder and Dale Buchbinder

Mr. Nathan, an elderly male patient hospitalized for prostatic surgery, woke up in the middle of the night, dressed himself, and attempted to leave the nursing unit. An RN approached him to ask him where he was going and tried to detain him. He shoved the woman into a wall and she struck her head, sustaining a concussion. The unit clerk called for help. The patient ran toward the exit and was stopped by two male orderlies and a security guard. As they took him by the arms, he screamed, "I'm being held prisoner! I have the right to leave!" A physician wrote restraining orders to be checked in an hour, and the patient was given an intramuscular sedative. Mr. Nathan sustained some bruises and abrasions in the struggle. The nurse was taken to the ER and was out of work for two weeks. The patient is now suing the hospital for false imprisonment and aggravated assault.

DISCUSSION QUESTIONS

1. What are the known facts in this situation? What else may be going on?

2. What are the responsibilities of the hospital with regard to caring for Mr. Nathan?

3. What should the hospital do about the nurse's injuries?

4. Was the physician justified in giving the patient a sedative and ordering physical restraints? Provide a rationale for your position.

5. Do you think his suit will hold up in court? Why or why not?

Last Chance Hospital—Case for Chapters 5 and 6

Susan Casciani

Last Chance Hospital (LCH) is a 254-bed, community hospital located in a small, affluent suburb just outside of San Diego, California. The hospital has historically been well-received by the local community, which demographically has a higher concentration of older age groups than most other local areas. The greater San Diego area is densely populated, and over 25 hospitals operate in the larger geographic area. Historically, LCH had always been financially sound, and had managed to remain independent as their local competitors joined larger systems. But that was then, and this is now. About a year ago, Last Chance Hospital undertook a strategic planning process to encompass the next five years. At the time, the hospital was doing okay financially, but was starting to dip into their cash reserves more often than the Board of Trustees liked; LCH was in need of an ideal strategy to bring them ahead of the market before things got out of hand.

As the strategic planner for LCH, Russ Newmarket reported indirectly to the CEO, Marvelous Marvin, but his immediate boss was Courtney Graveyard—and she had a lot on her plate. LCH did not have a chief nursing officer, and as COO, Graveyard was responsible for all of the nursing departments as well as surgical services, facilities, and information technology. A nurse by background, Graveyard spent the majority of her time trying to find different ways to recruit much-needed nursing staff.

During the development of the strategic plan, Russ called together the usual group of senior executives, Board members, and key physician leaders. He diligently developed the SWOT using their input and applying their assumptions. During his market research, Russ became aware of some patient-centric trends emerging across the country, but he was also aware that LCH had always strategically catered more to physicians due to the notion that physicians were the ones who ultimately referred patients to the hospital. Through the strategy development process, it became clear that senior management was stuck on this physician-centric mindset. Russ, ambitious and eager to make a name for himself, found and presented valid information that concurred with management's mindset. At the end of the planning process, Marvelous Marvin felt confident that their physician-focused strategy would give them a market lead—the plan was to attract more surgeons—and increase OR volumes. Graveyard was under intense pressure from Marvelous Marvin to make sure the operating rooms were as efficient as possible to handle the planned increase in volume, as OR efficiency would be a key recruitment issue for surgeons. The LCH physician recruiter was under the gun as well. The remainder of the executive staff breathed a collective sigh of relief that their areas were not part of the strategic initiative. Russ suspected LCH needed more of a strategy than attracting new surgeons, but he convinced himself that senior management knew best.

After the Board approved the strategic plan, Graveyard immediately met with her OR Director and charged him with increasing the efficiency of the ORs. She then turned her focus back to her first love, nursing. The physician recruiter hit the ground running, developing an elaborate plan to increase surgeon recruitment. From all appearances, LCH was on a roll.

Over the next several months, the OR Director was able to reduce the OR's operating budget by 13%, a result that made Marvelous Marvin very happy. At the same time, Graveyard made great strides in increasing LCH's exposure to and status in the nursing community, and was able to decrease the nursing vacancies by over 6%. In a time of nursing shortages, the Board was impressed with Graveyard's results. The physician recruiter was having only moderate success at recruiting surgeons, however, and her targeted volume projections were noticeably under budget. Marvelous Marvin approved her request to increase her staff, adding approximately $250,000 to her budget line. Overall, patient volumes were steadily decreasing at what was becoming an alarming rate, and thus the financial picture for LCH was in critical condition. Marvelous Marvin couldn't help but wonder aloud, "Why isn't the LCH strategic plan working?"

DISCUSSION QUESTIONS

1. In Russ's role as strategic planner for LCH, what should he have done differently that would have positively affected the outcome of the strategic plan execution?

2. What should Marvelous Marvin have done differently as CEO in order to avoid the current situation?

3. What political factors created bias and clouded judgments in this situation?

4. Who's to blame for the bad outcomes of this strategic plan?

5. If you were one of the OR Director's direct reports/managers, what should your involvement in the organization's strategy have been?

The Magic Is Gone—Case for Chapters 3, 12, and 13

Amy Dore

Windmill Long Term Care is a regional corporation serving the Midwest, "the Great Plains" region of the U.S. They are known for their top-notch consulting in which they provide industry-specific expert advice for the following service lines:

- Product development
- Succession planning
- Merger and acquisitions services
- Provider support
- Financial services

Windmill LTC has held a market presence for over 35 years with corporate headquarters located in Dallas, Texas and regional offices located in Wichita, Kansas and Pierre, South Dakota. It has a total workforce of 240 employees along with a board of directors.

The long-established Financial Services department, which has always been one of the largest and most successful areas, has been experiencing significant discontent among its employees. The department proudly held the well-earned reputation within the organization of being the "Magic Team" by getting projects done on time, within the required scope and expectations, and at a remarkably high quality. The employees feel that the cohesiveness, camaraderie, and synergy of the existing department disappeared when the organization hired new graduates and restructured the departmental hierarchy and team structures. The department is also adjusting to a shift in reporting structure as a handful of executive team members retired and three additional team members are midway through their phased-retirement agreement with Windmill LTC. Additionally, for the first time in the organization's history, an internship program was established, bringing the opportunity for high school students and college students to volunteer at Windmill LTC to gain experience in a growing industry. Each department is expected to accept a minimum of two student volunteers each year.

Taking into consideration the differing areas of expertise and the typical hiccups experienced when working in a group (or team), the Financial Services department must figure out how to work well together and bring back the magic. Create a proposal to be submitted to organizational executives with your recommendations for creating the optimal team, utilizing the information provided in Chapters 3, 12, and 13. Use the following guidelines in preparing your proposal:

1. The team must include a minimum of five and a maximum of eight people. The team must include a cross-section of age groups and at least one student volunteer.
2. Provide your recommendations regarding the composition of the team including:

   i. Number of team members
   ii. Gender of each team member
   iii. Age of each team member
   iv. Experience level and/or job title of each team member

3. To which generation does each team member belong?
4. Describe the workplace characteristics for each team member, utilizing the information in Chapter 3, particularly Table 3–1.
5. Provide details of the motivational preferences for each team member.
6. Employers do not have the power to force a person to act. However, employers can work to provide various types of incentives and rewards in an effort to influence employees and encourage improved employee performance and increased employee morale. The ultimate goal is to provide support to each team in working together to help the organization achieve its goals. To accomplish this, include a *Team Motivation and Engagement Plan*. The plan will describe your recommendations for helping the team to reach organizational goals by keeping the team motivated and engaged. Justify your recommendations.
7. The proposal must be submitted in a business proposal format. Examples of business proposals can be found online:

   a. https://owl.english.purdue.edu/owl/resource/656/02/
   b. http://www.wikihow.com/Write-a-Business-Proposal

Set Up for Failure?—Case for Chapter 3

Amy Dore

Allison began her health care career with an established general dentistry practice consisting of one dentist, Dr. Gable. Shortly after she started her job, Dr. Gable decided to add a second dentist, even though his past ventures with adding a partner had not been successful. Dr. Gable hired an expensive consulting firm to handle all the specifics, such as developing the contract with this new dentist, helping with hiring additional staff, purchasing additional equipment, and helping the current staff adapt during the transition. Even though Allison was new to the dental field, Dr. Gable kept her up-to-date with the process, but only to a certain point. Furthermore, Allison's input was not wanted, so she politely stepped back and observed the process. Both dentists had big ideas for a successful partnership and expected instant success. They even looked for land to build and move the current practice because they expected the practice to double or triple in size since there would be two dentists to serve their expanding patient base.

Watching the beginning of the partnership develop was exciting for Allison, and she was anxious for the partnership to succeed. The thought of managing such a large, successful practice would certainly be good experience for her. However, Allison noted a couple of negative factors that made her question the wisdom of adding a second dentist. Those factors included:

1. The new partner had just graduated from dental school and did not have a patient base to bring to the practice.
2. The discussions between the two dentists and the consulting firm did not indicate how the new dentist would market himself.
3. The new dentist would be paid a set salary, increasing each year, without consideration of how much revenue he actually generated.

Furthermore, several issues quickly came to the surface:

1. Expenses quickly exceeded profits.

   a. The new dentist wanted all the best and newest equipment, which was very expensive.

b. Increased staff for the new dentist meant a larger salary expense (not to mention the salary of the new dentist).

2. The new dentist was neither motivated to nor interested in marketing himself. He was drawing a salary, which would increase each year, so he was not motivated to seek new patients.

a. This meant he was treating the existing patients and, therefore, taking away business from Dr. Gable.
b. In turn, little additional revenue was being generated, and expenses were going through the roof.

3. The morale of the office quickly deteriorated.

a. The tension between the dentists and staff was obvious. Due to the increased expenses, the year-end bonuses for staff were eliminated and employee hours were cut.
b. Allison was also feeling demoralized.

Now, after keeping Allison out of this process, both dentists expect her to fix the situation. Allison feels like her job is on the line, along with the morale of the staff and the outcomes of the practice. Plus, Allison is positive neither dentist will be open to accepting responsibility for the situation. She is trying to decide what to do and how to address these problems.

DISCUSSION QUESTIONS

1. How might she draw upon and apply the theories of management and motivation to address these issues?

2. How might she approach the dentists?

3. What are the most urgent issues?

4. What actions might she suggest to improve the situation?

5. What strategies might be used to motivate the dentists and the employees in working to begin to address the issues?

6. Should Allison be updating her résumé and looking for another job? Explain your response.

Sustaining an Academic Food Science and Nutrition Center Through Management Improvement—Case for Chapters 2 and 12

Ritamarie Little and Louis Rubino

Introduction

It was my first time sitting on the other side of the desk. I have been asked by my Dean to serve as the Interim Director of the Marilyn Magaram Center (MMC), a Food Science, Nutrition, and Dietetics collaborative on our large state University campus. For a dozen years I have served as an "outside-the-area" advisory board member consulting in my area of expertise (health administration). I met several times with the very competent Director concerning the Center's initiatives but my focus and involvement had only been confined to broad oversight. Now she has accepted a national position within a food service industry professional association. It is up to me to "maintain the ship" for the nine months before I begin my sabbatical. How deep will I dive into what is happening within the Center itself while I maintain my regular teaching and program director responsibilities? The extra pay being given to me while I lead the Center will be nice, and I would like to make a difference, but to do that I will need to be more actively involved in operations. Am I able to use my administrative expertise to help this Center improve or will I just be a caretaker until a new Director is recruited since food is not my thing?

History

Marilyn Magaram was a graduate student in Food Science and Nutrition at California State University, Northridge (CSUN). She earned her Master's Degree in 1984 and after graduation she began teaching at CSUN. Later she opened a private practice as a Registered Dietitian, where she specialized in low-calorie, gourmet cooking. In 1989, during a trip to Australia, Marilyn died in a rafting accident. The Marilyn Magaram Center for Food

Science, Nutrition, and Dietetics (MMC) was established in 1991 through the support of Marilyn's husband, Phil, in honor of his late wife. The purpose of the Center was to provide research support and community service in the areas of food science and nutrition, while educating future professionals.

Operated under the auspices of the Department of Family & Consumer Sciences in the College of Health and Human Development, the Magaram Center has engaged in a variety of nutrition and food science-related research, education, and community service projects. These activities utilize the knowledge and expertise of faculty, the energy and talents of students, and the extensive and diverse resources of the San Fernando Valley community. The Center provides a framework for collaboration among students, faculty, professionals, businesses, and community organizations in the food and nutrition field.

Mission, Vision, and Goals

The mission of the MMC is to enhance and promote health and wellbeing through research and education in the fields of nutrition and food science. Its vision is to be a recognized Center of Excellence in research and education in the fields of food science and nutrition in the global community. In adhering to its mission and working towards its vision, MMC has had an impact in many places in the community. It provides nutrition education and outreach through community events, health fairs and research projects in area schools, health departments, farmers' markets, children's centers, senior centers, and health care centers, just to name a few. It has engaged hundreds of graduate and undergraduate students in real-world, professional projects, providing them practical skills and knowledge which they cannot gain in a classroom. In this way, it ensures that the academic work can have meaningful, practical impact on all sides.

To more specifically guide the Center, the MMC Advisory Board has set the following goals:

1. Promote the professional growth and development of faculty, students, and professionals in the fields of nutrition and food science.
2. Provide education related to food science, nutrition, health, and wellbeing to diverse communities.
3. Pursue scholarly projects in the fields of nutrition and food science.
4. Form (and maintain) alliances with professional organizations and community agencies to raise awareness of the critical role nutrition plays in health and wellbeing.
5. Ensure long-term viability of the Center.

Ongoing Programs

MMC provides specific services to help it meet these stated goals. These include:

- **PEP:** The MMC Professional Experiences Program (PEP) is the mechanism by which students are placed to work in MMC's various projects. These opportunities provide "real-world" experiences for future nutrition professionals so that they may gain knowledge and professional skills in practical settings, things that are not often taught in a classroom. Students volunteer in dietetics departments of local hospitals, promote good nutrition and fresh produce at local farmers' markets, and plan and host educational events related to nutrition and food science on campus.

- **NCB:** The Nutrition College Bowl (NCB) is an annual event hosted by the Center for over 15 years. Students from all over the state compete in this game show–style competition focusing on nutrition and dietetics subject areas. The goals of the NCB are to promote teamwork and leadership, enhance critical thinking skills, foster enthusiasm for learning, and create a community for nutrition scholars and future professionals.

- **Health Assess:** MMC offers valuable health evaluation services to community members using industry standard BodPod equipment to measure body composition (% fat vs. % lean mass) and The Food Processor Nutritional Analysis software to analyze dietary intake as well as provide recipe nutrient analysis.

- **CSA:** The Community Supported Agriculture (CSA) program allows community members to purchase boxes of fresh locally grown produce each week. The boxes are delivered to campus from a local farm one day each week and are picked up the same day by CSA members. Members have the option to sign up for monthly, quarterly, or annual memberships and can choose from either a large or small box depending on their needs.

- **Consulting:** MMC outreaches to the professional community with recipe analysis projects, which provide nutrition facts label information to food industry partners. Additionally, it offers food product analysis services that help to evaluate shelf stability (such as pH and/or flavor profiling) to companies developing new food products.

- **Training:** The food safety management training program provides vital food safety education to students and food industry professionals. Individuals can become certified through this fee-supported program, and many CSUN students who have become certified become instructors and administer the course on MMC's behalf. The course is offered in English, Spanish, and Korean.

Stakeholders

The Center is staffed with four people. The core team of Executive Director, Associate Director, Project Manager, and Administrative Assistant are responsible for the organizational and administrative support required to develop and ensure the success of MMC's programs and activities.

The Executive Director directs the center on a path of continued evolution and growth. Traditionally, this position takes on the "network leader" role with more of an external focus connecting people across disciplines and organizational departments, securing grants and contracts, and developing new community partners. She interfaces with the MMC Advisory Board, comprised of industry leaders and academics, who keep MMC on track with fulfilling its mission and accomplishing its goals. In this way, she is also taking on, along with the Advisory Board, a "strategic leader" role. She also meets with top level University administration and is held accountable for MMC's operation. She leads the MMC staff in pursuit of Center goals.

The Associate Director has more of an internal focus identified as the "operational leader." She collaborates, once appropriate projects and opportunities for the Center are identified, on project planning, navigation of contracts, risk management, budget development, and oversight, as well as project and expense reporting. She also plays a key role in the operational management of the Center including staff and student oversight and project implementation. She plans for and coordinates new projects, ensuring they are implemented in accordance with University policy, helping to develop the specifics of contracts and budgets as well as risk management. She also provides direction and oversight for the Project Manager and Administrative Assistant to ensure that projects are properly carried out with regards to volunteer recruitment and coordination as well as tracking of activities, contacts and use of funds.

The Project Manager is also a current student in the Nutrition, Dietetics and Food Science Department at the University. As such, she is the direct link from the Center to the students that it serves. She keeps the Center abreast of the needs and concerns of the students, helping to link students to projects by identifying the types of activities and experiences that they are interested in. She directly recruits and oversees student volunteers on projects. She is responsible for developing work schedules for services as well as for the Center's participation in outside health fairs and other events. She works with clients and PEP students to ensure that all Center services are provided in a timely and professional manner. An interesting challenge of this position is that it is continually vacated and re-staffed as students graduate from the University.

The Administrative Assistant provides administrative support to all staff in the Center. He is responsible for completing all financial paperwork as well as tracking/documenting spending for each project. He also helps to coordinate schedules for services offered, such as the food safety manager training course and Health Assess services. He manages the office facility and maintains inventory of resources.

In order to carry out their many services and activities, the Center relies heavily on student volunteers. Some of these positions are formalized, such as the Professional Experiences Program (PEP) students who are assigned to specific positions (i.e., overseeing the CSA program or providing Health Assess services) each semester. However, it also has student volunteers who work as needed, at health fairs or one-time community events. Other students may actually become part-time employees of the Center in which they engage in work that is grant funded. As with all academic disciplines, students in the Nutrition, Dietetics and Food Science options are encouraged to partake in professional experiences during their education. In fact, for those focusing on dietetics and planning to continue on into a dietetic internship after graduation to obtain the Registered Dietitian (RD) credential, professional experience in the field (above and beyond that required as part of academic coursework) is required. Thus, MMC provides students with a myriad of opportunities in community, clinical, and food service settings. This helps students to apply their knowledge and skills gained in the classroom, as well as develop a sense of the specific areas in the field in which they are most interested.

Unique Nature of Academic Units

Academic units can vary greatly from the very sophisticated, large grant-funded research institutes to small, specialized, distinct-focus endowed centers. All campuses seem to have them so the faculty can receive extra compensation for their research or buy out from their teaching load. Most faculty would like to concentrate on their scholarly interests not only for financial gain but also to build their personal reputation in their field of study and therefore advance their careers. Sometimes these institutes and centers are given space (laboratories, conference room, technology, etc.) to facilitate these pursuits. This partnership, created for higher education, has many benefits not only to the faculty but also to the institution. The University's status in the specific field researched could be enhanced. Also, securing indirect funds from certain grant awards can be used to supplement operations at the University.

The MMC is a relatively large Center for what is considered a "teaching" school. Research is becoming much more important as the state-dependency mindset is giving way to more accountability and much needed accessibility to funds to fulfill the mission. The Center was started with two generous donations that were placed into an endowment. It was never intended that these funds would actually cover direct services but that the interest they would gain would be available to use to cover operating expenses. Most of the MMC projects have needed to be self-supporting, either through fees for service or through grants written for the specific project. This has often left a gap for core operating expenses.

Interim Director's Assessment

A large initial donation has provided our Center with the ability to continue, yet the question remains as to what happens when the funds are expended? Who will pay for the ongoing costs of engaged faculty and employed staff when the "soft" money runs out? It is becoming much more competitive to be selected for grant awards and without consistent inflowing funds, the University would have to guarantee the Center's continued existence through budget allocations. This will just not happen in these austere times. How does our Center continue to survive when there is no money going back into operations? What can be done to make the Center sustainable into the future? How can I lead this effort? While it is clear that the work in which our Center engages is of value to students and the surrounding community alike, the funding that supports these projects is just not properly in place. One could say of our five strategic goals listed, the one that is most in need of attention at this time is the last one: ensuring the long-term viability of the center.

Sustainability

MMC is held in high regard yet there is one fundamental flaw which hits most of these research-based centers. Most of the monies obtained through grants and donations are earmarked for specific things (building, equipment, projects). People and agencies like to donate or grant awards for something tangible, all the better if the donor's name(s) can be somehow associated with the entity/project. This is wonderful and welcomed, of course, but what is also needed for a Center like MMC is to have money to pay for operations. The Center's mission and goals may be fulfilled through funds being provided by very generous benefactors, but the costs associated with the faculty time to coordinate both the assisting students' pay and the supplies needed are typically how the donations and awards are allocated.

This is where management intervention can help. A complete analysis of the operations must be conducted to see what opportunities exist for improvements, which will secure the future. An evidence-based management approach is necessary so that the right things are done right (McAlearney & Kovner, 2013). Costs are to be examined and reduced. New funds that are not targeted for projects need to be obtained. A partnership needs to be created which will support the Center and allow it to accomplish its mission and goals without jeopardizing its very existence.

Management Improvement Plan

The Center receives no funding through the University and therefore needs to be self-sustaining. There are essentially three revenue streams: private donations, grants, and fees collected for the services provided. While there have been two large private donations made in the past, the donations that are received today are very small and do not serve as major support for the Center. The Center has pursued both project specific grants to support certain activities and programs as well as some grants for core operating support. Other measures must be taken to secure the Center's position.

Improvements Identified

1. **Initiation of employee evaluations:** Employees of the Center have not ever had formal evaluations completed and so have received no feedback on their performance and little to no direction as far as expectations of management and goals. Initial evaluations were completed collaboratively with input from both the employee and management. The process started with a review of each job description and within that context, areas of strengths and weaknesses were identified. This process helped to clearly identify goals for each employee that met both their professional aspirations and the needs of the Center. The process has been formalized so that each employee is evaluated every 6 months.

2. **Staff changes:** All staff at the Center were part-time employees and the Associate Director was the only benefitted position. This left the Center with fewer staff than needed to cover basic office needs on a regular basis. An increase of the Associate Director position to 80% time (4 days per week) allowed for a redesigned role to include more responsibility for grant writing and financial management and oversight, which was required by a recent audit. The Administrative Assistant was also given a full-time, benefitted position. This provided more office coverage during the week to support revenue-generating services. Due to these changes, the Center staff was able to take on a collaborative effort to conduct program evaluation for a multi-agency community intervention grant, which collected new revenue for the Center. Further, these changes also allowed more time for important Center management-related activities such as service contact tracking, formalizing and implementing policy and procedure, and developing training materials. Key to the success, though, was providing the Associate Director a sense of empowerment to take on the new challenges and become more independent, implementing her management changes. This embraces the philosophy of the Institute for Healthcare Improvement (www.ihi.org) for building improvement capacity and stresses the importance of equipping health care professionals, at all levels, with the right (and appropriate) knowledge and skills to effect change.

3. **Staff meetings:** Weekly staff meetings were implemented to ensure effective communication about ongoing projects, milestones, and planning activities among the small but active Center staff. Previously, the staff, often operating in silos,

looked only at the specific project that they may be assigned. Regular meetings have facilitated communication about the many moving parts of the Center so that all projects are clear to all staff. The weekly staff meeting agenda is used as a master task list that keeps the Center on track with ongoing projects and activities. This includes standing agenda items for particular items such as activity/contact tracking and financial reports. (See Figure 18-4.)

4. **Formalization of policies and procedures:** As the staff has been quite small, there has been an informal system of policies and procedures dictating how the day-to-day operations are carried out. Recent changes have necessitated more formalized policies and procedures for Center operations. A recent financial audit highlighted the need for documented procedures for cash handling and reporting. The involvement of the Center in many diverse projects has necessitated standard operating procedures for fund reimbursement, event and activity tracking, volunteer management, complaint handling, and educational materials check out. Changes in Center staff positions necessitate procedures for time-off requests and employee evaluations. Standard policies and procedures have also provided excellent training materials for new volunteers as well as potential staff.

May 26, 2014

1. Event forms for submission: (to Project Manager)
2. **First meeting of each month**: Financial reports (Admin Asst)
   a. CATCH budget
   b. Whole Kids budget
3. **Second meeting of each month**: Contacts and hours reports (Project Mgr and Admin Asst)
4. Website Review
5. PEPS Update:
   a. New placements for Fall 2014—applications due 5/27
6. DeFeo's Tomato Sauce samples:
   a. pH testing needs to be done by 6/12
   b. recipe nutrient analysis done by 6/20
7. Health Assess:
   a. Appoint scheduling needed for softball team
8. Tracking Magaram Center Projects/Activities
   a. Can we develop a written policy and instructions for how this is done so we have training materials?
9. CPHIZ:
   a. Contract for Dr. Barrack Gardner
   b. Program Evaluation: Lindsey Marx
10. Lactation Affinity Group—Graduate student to oversee project on behalf of MMC

FIGURE 18-4 MMC Staff Meeting Agenda

5. **Comprehensive system for tracking activities and contacts:** The diverse nature of the Center's activities (research projects, health fairs, professional development workshops, CSA, NCB) has made consistent tracking and reporting of activities a challenge. However, it is imperative for us to be able to report the types of activities that we engage in as well as the number of people that we reach in a concise and efficient manner. To address this, the task of collecting this data was specifically assigned to the Project Manager, who created a formalized policy. An Event Form was developed which allows for all pertinent information about a particular event to be recorded in a more readily usable manner. At the start of each weekly staff meeting, all current activities are reviewed and each staff member is asked to provide any and all Event Forms to the Project Manager who then enters the information into a database where it is more easily managed and reported as needed. (See Figure 18-5.)

6. **Dashboard reporting:** In an effort to better communicate with the Advisory Board, the Center has adopted a dashboard, which clearly presents the activities of the Center and connects each back to the Center goals (listed above). For each goal set for the Center, the dashboard clearly delineates the tactics used to meet that goal and measures progress towards it. (See Figure 18-6.)

7. **New partnerships:** Opportunities across campus were evaluated. Being a large urban University, collaborations could be formed to continue improvement activities. One example was engaging a health care leadership class in its team project to act as consultants on the Community Supported Agriculture (CSA) program. Another was becoming active in the IHI Open School Chapter case study reviews to enhance student learning outside of just nutrition.

8. **Best practices:** Many times organizations struggle to find new ways to improve. Studer (2009) states that best practices are "over discussed and underused." Yet leaders are reluctant to ask for help. A concerted effort was made by MMC leaders to investigate into what other discipline-specific centers on campus were doing and to meet with their leaders to share information that could be mutually beneficial. Many operational improvements were identified that helped streamline working with the entity on campus which provides accounting services.

New Funding

Most of the improvements identified and implemented enhance operations but do not necessarily help the Center in its quest for sustainability. Cost reduction strategies and pursuit of alternate funding must be found if the long term objective stated is truly to be achieved. It has become increasingly important for health care organizations to understand how to estimate and manage their costs, as discussed in Chapter 10.

Activity Reporting Form

Marilyn Magaram Center for Food Science Nutrition and Dietetics

Marilyn Magaram Center
for [ ] Nutrition & Dietetics

Date of Project Feb 25, 2015   Project Duration 3 Months

Project Name   Healthy Kids Garden Grant

Project Location Northridge, CA   # of Contacts 4514

Event Description

Summarize the event in about 5 sentences.

A program that helps children learn about planting, growing, and harvesting fresh whole foods while at school. Provides education to help prevent and/or curb obesity, and gives children the tools to take what they have learned home in hopes that they start their own gardens.

Attach a flyer as appropriate

Speaker John Doe

Community Partners Acme Food Products, Ace Global Foods, Salad-To-Go.

Total number of volunteers including yourself		Total Number of PEPs		MMC Staff	
Total number of volunteer hours		Total Number of PEP Hours		MMC Staff Hours	

Please list ALL of the volunteers present on the back side of this page

Signature _____

Please turn in this evaluation to the MMC SQ 120
magaram.center@csun.edu
818/677-3102

FIGURE 18-5 Tracking Form

Modified from: Marilyn Magaram Center for Food Science Nutrition and Dietetics.

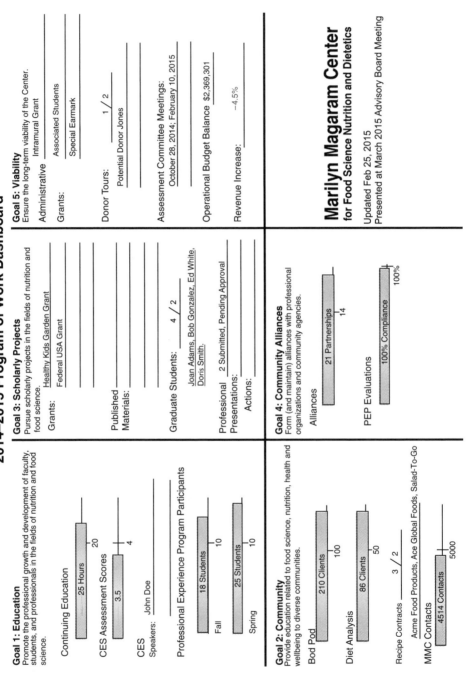

FIGURE 18-6 Marilyn Magaram Center 2014–2015 Program of Work Dashboard

Modified from: Marilyn Magaram Center for Food Science Nutrition and Dietetics.

Evaluation of costs was conducted and procedures set into place which would assure the purchases being made are truly essential to continued operations. Funds that were invested but not receiving interest were examined and the determination was made to move some of the principal to interest-bearing accounts to take advantage of the increase in investment income. In addition, several other innovative strategies to obtain new sources of revenue were pursued.

1. The MMC created a partnership with the University Athletics Department to provide Health Assess services (body composition, diet analysis, and nutrition counseling) to CSUN student athletes. A contractual agreement, which provides these services as a package at a reduced rate for each student athlete, has provided a regular revenue stream for the Center, as well as given the athletes the opportunity to improve their physical health and performance.

2. The Center developed a business plan to reach out to retail food service operators, as well as the health care, food science, and environmental health industries, to market its food safety manager certification services. Initially, the course was offered only in English but instructors have been recruited to provide the course in both in Spanish and Korean to meet the needs of the local area. A profit sharing model has been developed that encourages instructors to market the classes to the populations that they teach and new, multi-lingual marketing materials have been developed that describe the Center's services, including the option of having classes held onsite at their facilities. These are being distributed to restaurants, health care facilities, and food manufacturing facilities through the Center's extensive channels of industry and community contacts. The food safety manager certification program has also been added to the local county Department of Environmental Health Approved Provider list, significantly raising the visibility of the program throughout the county.

3. The MMC connects faculty and students to relevant research experiences in a variety of community health projects. One such project is the Canoga Park Health Improvement Zone (CPHIZ), which provides education aimed at nutrition and physical activity; chronic disease self-management; parent engagement in children's academics; and case management services to families through four local schools. Funded by a larger private foundation, the project is overseen by a local hospital-based, community health agency and the actual services are subcontracted out to a number of other community agencies, each specializing in one of the particular services. As an example, MMC faculty members engage their students in offering the nutrition and physical activity education component. However, in an effort to generate revenue directly to the Center, the MMC also contracted for the evaluation component of the overall project. This entails MMC staff gathering reports from each of the partner agencies on

the project and tracking progress towards stated goals. This is a direct fee-for-service activity, which provides sustaining revenue to the Center.

4. The continued reliance of the MMC on small government grants to fund its programs has not been a positive financial strategy as there are more agencies competing for fewer dollars. The MMC must focus on seeking contracts to provide services to the private food industry sector rather than relying on government grants. With its existing laboratories, the MMC is able to provide sensory analysis services (food taste testing) to companies developing new food products. The MMC also has the capability to offer shelf stability and basic nutrient (sodium, fat, sugar, protein) analysis for food products. To this end, members from the local food industry have been added to the Advisory Board, who give insight into industry needs and help market services. These new Advisory Board members also can help identify potential future donors who may assist with the upkeep of existing facilities and develop new facilities as technology demands.

5. The management of large government grants has proven to be cumbersome for this small center, with very little financial gain from an operational standpoint. Thus, rather than trying to manage these large grants, the MCC focuses on subcontracting for specific services when these large grants are landed by other community partners. Examples include the evaluation services for the CPHIZ project described above. Additionally, the MMC is a subcontractor on two different large grant projects managed by outside community partners (one a county-wide obesity intervention and the other a faith-based nutrition education project). In short, the Center is focusing its efforts on maintaining high quality on numerous small projects that generate operating revenue, rather than one or two large-scale projects that supersede the limitations of its infrastructure.

Conclusion

My nine months are up and my last task was to shepherd a task force to choose a new permanent Director. Having two great internal candidates made it easier on me to feel I was leaving the Center in good hands. The Advisory Board Search Committee had representatives from faculty (both current and retired) and the professional community. Helping them design and implement a criteria-based selection process guaranteed an objective decision as to who will lead MMC in the future. Looking back on my interim director role, I think I made a difference at the time, but how can these improvements be sustained under the new leader? The changes made and the plans for the future can be easily discarded by someone new coming in and wanting to set into motion their own agenda. This gets even more complicated for MMC since the Associate Director has recently decided to move to a new position outside of academia which will provide her much more growth potential. What I have decided, though, is that as long as the policies and procedures are hardwired into the system, the quality improvements are standardized, and there is assurance that the Advisory Board is actively upholding the mission, vision and goals, then I should not be concerned. It is not only money that sustains a Center, it is also processes. We like to sometimes feel it is people who make the difference, and they do; but the truth is no one is irreplaceable. The good work of the Center must be maintained no matter who is in charge.

DISCUSSION QUESTIONS

1. Who would be a better Interim Director of an Academic Center: someone who is outside the specialty area but has administrative experience or someone within the area of specialization but does not have administrative experience? Also answer for someone who has good management competencies or someone who has good leadership qualities?

2. Who are the internal stakeholders for this Center? Who are the external stakeholders? Which stakeholders should the Interim Director primarily focus on while serving in the leadership role?

3. Which leadership theory might be best for the Interim Director to use as a framework? Which leadership style might he/she use? Why?

4. Develop the criteria to select the permanent Executive Director position using the leadership competencies and protocols listed in the chapter.

5. What unique barriers and challenges might the interim leader have when taking over for this short-term period?

6. What additional management processes or systems can the new Executive Director put into place which will help the Center achieve its goals considering today's health care environment?

REFERENCES

McAlearney, A., & Kovner, A. (2013). *Health services management: Cases, readings and commentary* (10th ed.). Chicago, IL: Health Administration Press.

Studer, Q. (2009). *Straight A leadership: Alignment, action, accountability*. Gulf Breeze, FL: Fire Starter Publishing.

Giving Feedback—Empathy or Attributions?—Case for Chapter 4

Sheila K. McGinnis

Feedback is a critical management skill that pervades everything we do in organizations. Feedback is information about the effect we have on others. It is used to tell employees how well their actions have their intended effect and how well job performance meets expectations. Feedback helps employees see how others see them and their performance, find out about their blind spots, and learn how to improve performance. Giving feedback means a manager has the difficult task of making judgments and delivering corrections or negative feedback. Clearly, giving feedback requires sensitivity and empathy. One complicating factor in giving feedback is our tendency to make attributions about an employee's motivations; we often make the mistake of trying to read others' intentions and motivations.

Scenario[2]

Eileen, an instructor in an interpersonal skills workshop, is troubled by the behavior of one of the workshop participants named Geoffrey. She feels that Geoffrey—a manager who is technically competent but seems unable to keep his staff team together for more than three months at a time—needs to see himself as his team members see him. Over the three meetings the course has had so far, Eileen notices that Geoffrey lounges in his chair with a bored expression on his face without contributing to any of the discussions. At times he has taken out a newspaper and read the sports pages while Eileen is speaking. To Eileen, this indicates an arrogance and hostility that will be severely dysfunctional for Geoffrey as he moves about the organization.

---

[2] Scenario used with permission of Dr. Stephen D. Brookfield (2015); retrieved 3/31/15 from http://stephenbrookfield.com/Dr._Stephen_D._Brookfield/Workshop_Materials_files/Developing_Critical_Thinkers.pdf

Eileen decides to write a memo to Geoffrey pointing out the effect his nonparticipation is having on the group. In the memo she picks out the specific behaviors of Geoffrey's that bother her and points out their negative effect. She asks him to work on reducing these behaviors over the next two meetings and points out that, if he can eliminate these tendencies, his power and prestige in the organization will grow.

DISCUSSION QUESTIONS

1. What are the behaviors that seem to bother Eileen?

2. What assumptions—explicit and implicit—do you think Eileen is operating under in this situation? Include as many as you can think of.

3. Of the assumptions you've identified, which ones could Eileen check by simple research and inquiry? How could she do this?

4. What judgments and attributions is Eileen making?

5. What are some possible explanations for how Geoffrey sees this situation?

6. What feedback would you recommend Eileen give Geoffrey?

7. Give an alternative interpretation of this scenario that offers a version of what's happening that is consistent with the events described, but that you think Eileen would disagree with.

Socio-Emotional Intelligence Exercise: Understanding and Anticipating Major Change—Case for Chapter 4

Sheila K.McGinnis

Using social motivation to plan a lay-off from the employee's viewpoint

You have learned some management lessons by examining social motivations in the workplace. Review social motivations (Textbox 18-1) and prepare to participate as part of your hospital's management team in the following scenario to address an impending lay-off. Based on what you have learned about social motivation, you can now make deliberate choices that reduce employees' stressful and negative feelings, and recommend actions that affirm employees' sense of belonging and connection.

TEXTBOX 18-1. MOTIVATIONS THAT INFLUENCE MODES OF SOCIAL COGNITION

Motives ("Needs")	Social Goal or Benefit
Belonging	Being accepted by other people, being valued by one's group
Understanding	Sharing understanding, knowledge, and viewpoints with members of one's group
Controlling	Influencing one's own outcomes that depend on other people
Enhancing self	Seeing one's self positively or at least sympathetically; "saving face" in others' eyes
Trusting in-group	Believing others (e.g., organization managers and colleagues) will not act in ways that will harm our own interests

Modified from Fiske, S. T., & Taylor, S. E. (2008). *Social cognition: From brains to culture.* Boston, MA: McGraw-Hill Higher Education, ISBN 978-0073405520, p. 48.

Given what you have learned, formulate lay-off recommendations for the hospital. Do not simply outline the lay-off procedure. Recommend key principles, actions, and behaviors to guide planning and implementation of this lay-off in a way that softens or reduces potential negative consequences.

Scenario

You are an office supervisor at the local hospital, with a staff of 12 under your supervision. Your hospital has experienced falling patient admissions, declining government and insurance reimbursements, and increased competition. Leadership has taken several measures to improve its financial position in a difficult market: introducing Lean quality methods to improve work processes and increase efficiency, retooling service lines, and partnering with physician groups.

For some time there have been rumors of possible lay-offs. Today your boss told you the lay-offs will take place, and she asked you to participate in the planning process. Planning is getting underway to evaluate the size of the lay-off, including numbers of positions affected and which job classes and departments will be affected. The hospital is committed to transparency in the planning process and one of the key planning tasks will be to develop a communication approach to support all employees and keep them informed.

As you prepare for the first planning meeting, you collect your thoughts about the information needs of all staff as they wait to learn whether or not their position will be eliminated. What will be their concerns and their resulting socio-emotional needs during this difficult time? What are the foremost employee concerns that you and other hospital managers must address through personal conversations and written communications as you break the news and develop the details? How can your organization handle this major change with many potential negative consequences in the most positive way possible?

Either individually or in a group, develop three to five recommendations for handling lay-offs at the hospital. Provide a short explanation of possible effects on employees' social motivations and how each of your recommendations contributes to minimizing potential negative consequences for employees.

REFERENCES

Fiske, S. T., & Taylor, S. E. (2008). *Social cognition: From brains to culture*. Boston, MA: McGraw-Hill Higher Education.

Madison Community Hospital Addresses Infection Prevention—Case for Chapters 7 and 13

Michael Moran

The Quality Issue

Hospitals across the country have seen an increase in *Methicillin-resistant Staphylococcus Aureus* (MRSA), a bacterial infection that is highly resistant to some antibiotics. Patients who contract this infection can develop serious complications, sometimes leading to death. Area hospitals with MRSA outbreaks have been featured in recent media programs, resulting in a loss of public confidence and declining admissions. As the director of an inpatient unit at Madison Community Hospital (MCH), you understand the potential for an increase of MRSA at your hospital. Your infectious disease physicians are concerned about the potential for an outbreak at your hospital. Infection prevention studies have reported that only 40% of health care workers sanitize their hands before treating patients. Hand washing and other hand-sanitizing methods have been proven to reduce the transmission of dangerous infections from one patient to another.

Preliminary Actions at MCH

The MCH products committee has evaluated several hand-sanitizing products and selected an alcohol-based product that effectively eliminates the majority of bacterial microorganisms that can be transmitted by contact. The hand hygiene policy at MCH requires staff members, physicians, and volunteers to apply the hand sanitizer before entering and after leaving a patient's room. The Infection Prevention staff estimates an average of 15–20 individuals enter a patient's room each day.

You have been appointed to serve on a task force charged with improving hand hygiene compliance. The Infection Prevention personnel have gathered preliminary data from various inpatient nursing units (see Table 18-1). Staff on these units were observed in order to assess whether they sanitized their hands prior to entering and upon leaving a

TABLE 18-1 Madison Community Hospital Hand Hygiene Compliance Observation Data

	Number of Staff Observed	Number Sanitizing Hands	Percentage Sanitizing Hands
2 North	15	8	53%
2 South	18	12	67%
2 East	16	6	38%
3 North	19	10	53%
3 South	13	7	54%
3 East	15	6	40%
4 North	18	9	50%
4 South	17	7	41%
4 East	14	6	43%
Total	145	71	49%

patient's room. The Infection Prevention staff observing the inpatient unit personnel are routinely seen on these units as part of their surveillance activities. Staff members were not aware their hand hygiene practices were being observed. At first glance, the data indicates hand hygiene is not practiced, as required by the policy, in more than half the observations.

MCH has adopted the FOCUS-PDCA improvement model and utilizes various tools for collecting data and analyzing processes. The hand hygiene task force will be applying these methods to address the hand hygiene concern.

DISCUSSION QUESTIONS

1. How would your task force use the FOCUS model and the data collection, process mapping, and process analysis tools to plan for a process change?

2. What are some of the issues associated with caregivers sanitizing their hands? Why do you suppose only 40% of caregivers sanitize their hands? What other department personnel, besides nursing, may need to enter a patient's room during their stay?

3. Who should be on this task force to represent which hospital functions and why? To whom should the task force report their results and why?

4. What are the possible causes for noncompliance? Are there other factors contributing to the issue? (Hint: Develop a flowchart to lay out the sequence of events for staff members entering and leaving patient rooms, develop a workflow diagram to identify barriers, and use these to construct a fishbone diagram.)

5. What data are needed to determine the factors involved in the noncompliance?

6. How would the problem look different if it turned out only a handful of personnel were noncompliant? How would this affect the improvement process?

7. Do you have enough data to complete the analysis? What data are needed to determine the factors involved in the noncompliance?

8. What process should be selected for improvement?

9. What aspects of the FOCUS model would be most useful to target the improvement efforts?

10. How can MCH motivate its staff to be more compliant? Do you think posters and recognition awards for units with the best results would help move the numbers in the right direction? Why or why not?

11. What do you think about the idea of installing a *poka-yoke*, that is, an engineering approach to prevent an error before it occurs?

Trouble with the Pharmacy—Case for Chapter 7

Patricia A. Patrician, Grant T. Savage, and Eric S. Williams

Part One

"Darn! I have to call Pharmacy again," Lisa, staff nurse on 6 East, muttered under her breath. "This is the third time today and it's not even noon!" She left the Omni-Cell Cart in the medication room and proceeded to the phone at the nurses' station. She dialed the familiar number—she had it memorized of course—and thought, "There has to be a better way." For the past few days, she had noticed an increase in the number of medications missing from the medication carts. Two days in a row, she was able to get a vitamin from another patient's medication drawer and administer it to her patient, but she knew this did not solve the problem. She was just trying to make it through her shift and get the patients what they needed.

In the meantime, on 6 West across the hall, Deirdre had a similar issue. The morning dose of her patient's oral antibiotic was not in the drawer, so she gave the dose that was labeled "evening dose." The evening shift nurse then had no evening antibiotic dose in the drawer and had to call the pharmacy to get a replacement. Numerous calls were being placed to the pharmacy. The pharmacy technicians were so busy fielding phone calls that none of them were available to deliver medications, so the staff nurses had to leave their units and patients and go to the pharmacy in the basement to retrieve their missing doses. The pharmacy technicians began complaining to their supervisors that those 6th floor nurses call so frequently that they do not have time to do their work. Nurses complained to each other that pharmacy was not stocking the medication carts correctly.

DISCUSSION QUESTION

1. In an organization that espouses a good patient safety culture, what should happen next?

Part Two

Lisa notified her nurse manager, Katie, that there was an increase in the number of medication doses that were unavailable at the time of their scheduled administration. Likewise, Marcus, the nurse manager on 6 West, heard from his night shift nurses that they had to "run to pharmacy" many times during the night to get medications that were not in the medication cart. That same morning, Katie was on the way to a Nurse Manager Meeting when she ran into her colleague on 6 West, Marcus. After exchanging greetings, Katie asked Marcus how it was going. Marcus explained that several of his nurses complained about pharmacy not stocking the medication carts appropriately, but he had no time yet to verify this or to talk to the pharmacist. It was on his "to do" list though. Katie explained that one of her staff nurses made this same complaint earlier that day. They both decided to raise this as an issue to be discussed at the Nurse Manager Meeting.

"Is anyone else having trouble with Pharmacy?" Marcus asked at the end of the meeting. "My staff nurses are complaining that the med carts are not stocked correctly." Many hands went up, and others chimed in that they thought it was an issue only for their specific units, but now they realized how widespread this problem was.

Because the Nurse Managers practice shared governance, they appointed Katie and Marcus to lead a Performance Improvement (PI) Team to figure out what the problem was and to take action. Three other Nurse Managers volunteered and joined the team; after a short meeting, the team agreed upon a plan.

DISCUSSION QUESTION

1. At this point, what should the PI Team's plan entail?

Part Three

The PI Team members queried their respective staffs to better understand the problem. The staff nurses' main complaint was that the 10:00 a.m. medications for patients were not in the medication carts. The pharmacy techs' main complaints were the massive number of phone calls and that the carts were being returned with unused medications that were being thrown away.

The nurse managers and pharmacy representatives on the team met together to develop a process flow diagram of the medication order and administration process. Figure 18-7 depicts their process flow diagram. The PI Team also agreed to maintain a 24-hour record of missed doses and calls to pharmacy during the next work day.

The team met again in two days and determined the numbers of missed doses and calls to pharmacy over a 24-hour period in the five units that were participating in the PI Team. Figure 18-8 contains this information depicted in a run chart format with time on the horizontal axis (hours of the day) and missed medication dosages on the vertical axis.

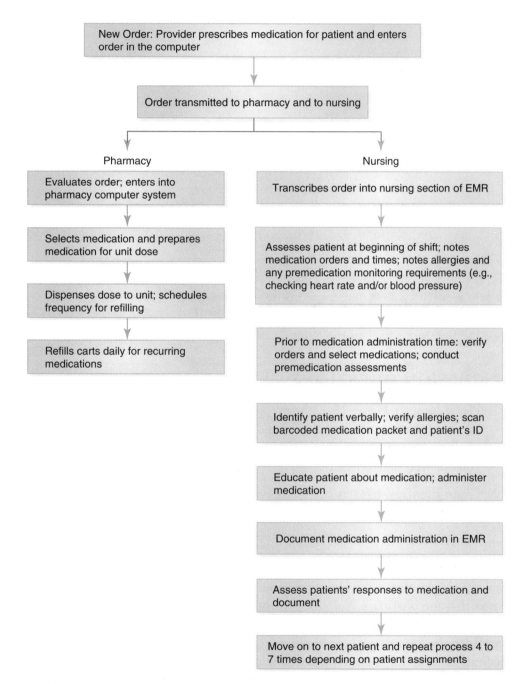

FIGURE 18-7 Process Flow Diagram of Medication Administration Process

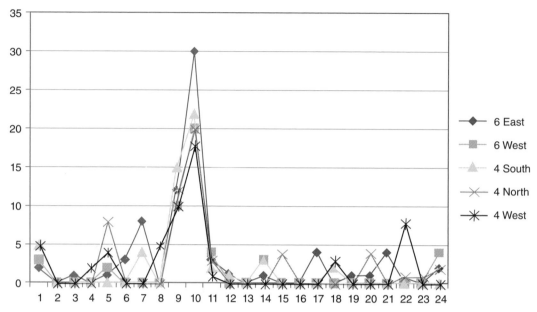

FIGURE 18-8 Run Chart of the Number of Missed Doses and Calls to Pharmacy

---

DISCUSSION QUESTIONS

1. Please compare Figure 18-7, the process flow diagram of the medication process, and Figure 18-8, the run chart of missed doses and calls to pharmacy. What is missing in the flow diagram (Figure 18-7) that is evident in the run chart (Figure 18-8)? Explain your answer.

2. Given the data that has been collected and analyzed (see Figures 18-7 and 18-8), what is still missing from the quality improvement analysis?

Part Four

After examining the flow chart and the run chart, the PI Team discussed why medications were missing during administration around 10:00 a.m. The pharmacy representatives shared that the pharmacy had changed their policy on cart restocking based upon what the new Pharmacy Director was accustomed to in his last job—carts changed out at 9:00 a.m. What the Pharmacy Director did not understand (and did not bother to ask) was that medication times for routine (once) daily medications were set by the hospital for 10:00 a.m. Based on the hospital's once-daily schedule, the nursing staff scheduled twice-daily medications for 10:00 a.m. and 10:00 p.m. As a result of the change by the Pharmacy Director, medications that were supposed to be given at 10:00 a.m. were being returned to pharmacy as unused.

DISCUSSION QUESTION

1. What solution should the nurse managers and the pharmacy director implement?

Part Five

A simple change in the cart turnover time to 11:00 a.m. quickly rectified the problem, thus increasing the doses available for morning and twice-daily medications, decreasing the phone calls to pharmacy, decreasing wasted medications, and eliminating the workarounds that were potentially hazardous to patient safety.

DISCUSSION QUESTION

1. Given the solution, is there a need for any additional quality improvement in the medication administration process?

Emotional Intelligence in Labor and Delivery—Case for Chapters 2, 12, and 13

Louis Rubino and Brenda Freshman

It is Sunday night in Labor and Delivery. An obviously pregnant full-term mother, Mrs. Ford, presents herself, saying her doctor, Dr. Jones, told her to come to the hospital to deliver her baby. The mother tells Ms. Smith, the nurse manager of L&D that the doctor has informed her that the baby has anencephaly, and she understands that the baby will not be expected to live very long after delivery. Ms. Smith is very concerned, since the unit did not receive any prior word about Mrs. Ford coming to the hospital, nor did the unit receive the prenatal record, which is required to be submitted by the 36th week of pregnancy per hospital policy.

Ms. Smith proceeds to call Dr. Jones to ask for orders and to get more information regarding Mrs. Ford's condition. Dr. Jones gets very upset with the phone call, says that he just completed a delivery and was trying to get a couple hours of sleep before he came to the hospital to deliver Mrs. Ford's anencephalic baby. He yells that he will be there shortly now that she has woken him and tells her to start prepping for a C-section and hangs up. Ms. Smith realizes the survivability of the baby is not possible and that no measure will be able to save the life of the baby once delivered. Ms. Smith understands that in these cases, it is the nurses' job to use whatever measures necessary to make the baby and mother as comfortable as possible so the baby can have a dignified death.

Ms. Smith is agitated at Dr. Jones's response. First, he was obviously in the wrong in not notifying the hospital about Mrs. Ford coming in, let alone not sending in the prenatal record. When Dr. Jones enters the unit, he is obviously upset but gets even more upset when Ms. Smith questions why he intends to do a C-section. Ms. Smith could tell that Mrs. Ford was not expecting a C-section based on her comments to her. Dr. Jones dismisses Ms. Smith's comments about doing a vaginal delivery and begrudgingly he does do a vaginal birth, complaining during it about how he will now have to reschedule his whole day, since it will take much longer than a C-section.

The baby is delivered. It is clear that the baby is anencephalic and has very poor circulation. The nurses wrap the baby in blankets and hand the baby to Mrs. Ford for her to view. Dr. Jones says there is no reason to call in a neonatologist and that this baby will obviously only live a few hours at most. Mrs. Ford requests to have her baby fed. Dr. Jones says it is okay to do that and requests the baby be put on a cardio-respiratory monitor with an IV tube for feeding. Ms. Smith is concerned about this, since she knows it will prolong the life of the child, and this would be considered futile care. She wonders how to handle this concern since she realizes Dr. Jones will probably yell at her if she is to question his orders again.

DISCUSSION QUESTIONS

1. What is your opinion of Dr. Jones's emotional intelligence (EI)? Based on a scale of 1–10, with 1 being lowest, how would you rate Dr. Jones? Why?

2. Repeat this process for Ms. Smith, the nurse manager.

3. Do you think there should be any consequences for Dr. Jones as a result of his behavior? What can be done?

4. Should Ms. Smith question Dr. Jones's orders for feeding the terminal baby? How would she do this?

5. What about the patient, Mrs. Ford? What is her stake in all this? Should she get involved in the obvious conflict occurring around her?

6. What should the hospital do to try to educate the staff about emotional intelligence? Explain your answer.

7. How could teamwork training help this Neonatal ICU team? Explain your answer.

Communication of Patient Information During Transitions in Care—Case for Chapters 7 and 12

Sharon Saracino and Sharon B. Buchbinder

Margaret Burns is a 63-year-old woman who has suffered a left occipital hemorrhagic infarct, a cerebrovascular event. In addition to this recent stroke, Margaret has a history of rheumatoid arthritis, which limits her mobility; hypertension, which has been controlled with diet and medication; osteoporosis; gastroesophageal reflux; and depression. She is alert and oriented, and has been identified at risk for falls. She requires moderate assistance with transfers and minimal assistance with ambulation using a rolling walker. Her scheduled medications include: pantoprazole for gastroesophageal reflux disorder (GERD); alendronic acid for osteoporosis; prednisone, a steroid; metoprolol for hypertension and heart disease; and calcium with vitamin D.

Following her acute care hospitalization, she is transferred to a skilled nursing and rehabilitation facility to continue her recovery. Margaret lives alone and must be independent to return home. One week after her admission to the skilled nursing facility, Margaret develops pain and swelling in her right leg and a low grade temperature. Her blood work indicates an elevated white blood cell count. The attending physician orders a venous Doppler ultrasound of the right leg and the results are positive for an acute deep vein thrombosis (DVT). Plans are made to transfer Margaret back to the acute care hospital for possible placement of a filter as she is not a candidate for anticoagulation due to her hemorrhagic stroke.

Carol Stevens, the secretary on Margaret's unit, had a flat tire on the way to work. After calling the auto club and waiting for them to come and change the tire, she arrives late, already behind before her day has even started. After she punches in and hurries to the unit, she learns two patients are being discharged, two patients are scheduled to arrive for admission, and Mrs. Burns is scheduled to be transferred to the acute care setting. She immediately sets to work faxing the histories, current lab results, consults, diagnostics, physician progress notes, nurses' notes, and medication administration records to the physicians of the patients to be discharged and making copies of those items to send to the hospital with Mrs. Burns per protocol for continuity of care, keeping each set of patient records in a separate pile.

Carol's son then calls to say that he missed the school bus. Carol sets the papers aside while she calls a neighbor to arrange transportation for her son. As she hangs up the phone, the ambulance arrives to transport Margaret to the hospital. Carol gathers the copies of Margaret's records together and places them in an envelope. The hospital process is for a nurse to double check the records to ensure they are correct prior to the patient leaving the building, but another ambulance crew arrives simultaneously with a patient for admission, handing that patient's paperwork to Carol. Carol hands the envelope with Margaret's records to the first crew and directs them to Margaret's room.

A week later, the patient care coordinator at the skilled nursing and rehabilitation facility receives a call from the acute care hospital and is informed the medication administration record sent with Margaret Burns was that of another patient. The acute care hospital failed to notice this discrepancy on admission, and the wrong medications were ordered and administered to Margaret for three days. Margaret suffered an extension of her hemorrhagic stroke and was transferred to the ICU.

DISCUSSION QUESTIONS

1. What are the facts of this case?

2. Review the quality improvement tools in Chapter 7 and select the appropriate one to analyze this problem.

3. What are the top three management issues in this case?

4. What are the legal and ethical obligations a health care organization has to its patients and families, and how do they apply to this case?

5. Who should be held responsible for addressing these problems?

6. Which health care facility is responsible for the medication errors? What obligations does the facility have to Margaret? To her family?

Multidrug-Resistant Organism (MDRO) in a Transitional Care Unit—Case for Chapters 7 and 12

Sharon Saracino and Sharon B. Buchbinder

Roger Young is a 43-year-old male hospitalized following a motor vehicle accident in which he was an unrestrained driver. Roger sustained a left femur fracture which required an open reduction and internal fixation. Roger is alert and oriented and requires minimal assistance with transfers and ambulation using a rolling walker secondary to a 50% weight bearing restriction on the left lower extremity. His surgical incision has 27 intact staples with scant serosanguinous drainage, is well approximated, and is open to air. His roommate is Joe Garrett, an 82-year-old male hospitalized following a right hemispheric CVA. Joe is a bit forgetful, and Roger often reminds Joe not to get up on his own, helps him adjust his bedding, or hands him personal items to discourage him from crawling out of bed unassisted.

Joe had an indwelling urinary catheter, inserted in the Emergency Department upon admission, which was removed on Monday, two days ago. Since then, Joe has been voiding frequent, small amounts with occasional incontinent episodes. The physician was made aware and ordered a urine culture and sensitivity, which was collected and sent to the lab for processing on Wednesday evening.

On Friday evening, the culture report was received via print from the lab just as the RN was leaving the unit for her dinner break. The RN quickly reviewed the report and called the physician with a result of >100,000 _E. coli_. Orders for antibiotic therapy were obtained and the medication was initiated. The culture report also indicated in the comment section that the specimen was positive for extended spectrum beta-lactamase (ESBL), a multidrug resistant organism. The nurse failed to note the comment and no contact or isolation precautions were implemented.

The physician assistant (PA-C) reviewed and signed off on the report on Saturday morning and also overlooked the comment. Roger, with his fresh surgical incision, remained in the room coming into close contact with Joe, his bedding, and his personal items, all contaminated with ESBL. Staff continued to care for Joe utilizing standard precautions, but no additional personal protective equipment (PPE) beyond gloves. On Monday morning, the Infection Preventionist noted the results during routine surveillance. Contact precautions were implemented and Joe was moved to a private room.

Roger's day of discharge finally arrived. Roger's girlfriend, Donna, came to take him home. Donna was a frequent visitor during Roger's hospitalization, and was extremely supportive. She has even applied for Family Medical Leave (FMLA) in order to function as his primary caregiver during his convalescence. Unbeknownst to the staff, Donna and Roger have also been taking advantage of the privacy and alone time since Joe was moved into isolation, and they have resumed intimate behaviors.

While they wait for the nurse to come in and review Roger's discharge instructions, Donna excuses herself to use the bathroom three times. Upon their return home, the frequency continues, along with occasional bladder spasms and burning with urination. Roger encourages Donna to see her primary care physician, where she is diagnosed with a urinary tract infection and started on antibiotics. Three days later, Donna receives a call from her physician informing her that her urine culture has come back positive for ESBL.

DISCUSSION QUESTIONS

1. What are the facts of this case?

2. Review the quality improvement tools and select the appropriate one to analyze this problem.

3. What are the top three management issues in this case?

4. What are the legal and ethical obligations a health care organization has to its patients and families and how do they apply to this case?

5. Who should be held responsible for addressing these problems?

6. Is the health care facility responsible for Roger's infection? If no, why not? If yes, what obligations does the facility have to Roger?

7. Is the health care facility responsible for Donna's infection? If no, why not? If yes, what obligations does the facility have to Donna?

Are We Culturally Aware or Not?—Case for Chapters 14 and 5

Nancy K. Sayre

A growing, profitable internal medicine practice of 10 physicians, 2 physician assistants, a physical therapist, and a massage therapist is located in a city of 150,000 people. The clinical personnel are mostly from the majority group in the area and consider themselves open-minded, altruistic, and culturally aware. The administrative support staff is representative of the makeup of the patient population—mostly minority groups in the local community. The patient population is growing and becoming more diverse from those newly arrived in the city. The practice is currently facing several challenges.

DISCUSSION QUESTIONS

1. The practice manager wants to have the local hospital expert on cultural competency come talk to the staff. The administrative support staff does not feel that they need training. How should the practice manager proceed?

2. The practice needs to hire a new administrative assistant to work with the front desk staff. The practice wishes to hire someone from the local minority community rather than an equally qualified individual from another state. How should the practice manager proceed? Justify the rationale for this recommendation.

3. With the recent growth, the practice is considering relocating its office to another, larger office facility. Several options are being discussed. Should they relocate to a more affluent area of the city that is less diverse? Or should they stay in the same neighborhood, even if it is less profitable? What are the pros and cons of staying in this neighborhood versus moving to another area? If the rent is higher in the more diverse area, is that enough to justify not moving there? Or is diversity responsiveness a "cost of doing business?" How should the practice manager proceed?

4. The practice wants to maintain its good standing in the community. What initiatives could it undertake to remain connected to its local patient population?

5. The practice manager wants to complete a strategic plan as a guiding framework for the organization for the next five years. From whom should she get input to help shape this plan? Should cultural competency initiatives be included in this plan?

Patients "Like" Social Media—Case for Chapters 6 and 5

Nancy K. Sayre

A long-term care facility (50 beds) in the Midwestern U.S. has just been acquired by a larger acute care hospital/health care system in the nearby city because they want to offer services across the continuum of care. Last year, they also acquired a provider of hospice services (25 beds). The hospital has relied mainly on television advertising and a strong web presence (landing pages, banner ads), whereas the two smaller organizations used word-of-mouth, physician referrals, networking, and print materials to recruit new patients. Marketers know that social media is changing the way consumers and health organizations interact. The strategic plan indicates that priorities for the new combined health system include enhancing patient safety and the patient experience, expanding into the growing senior market, competing on outcomes, minimizing the total cost of care, expanding geographic reach, extending partnerships with employers, and maintaining or improving the margin of 5.28%. As the newly appointed director of marketing for this combined new health system, you believe there are multiple points of discussion for your team regarding a marketing strategy using social media.

DISCUSSION QUESTIONS

1. What information is needed to create a marketing strategy?

2. How do you create a unified message for potential clients and their families about the new combined system? How will you determine the promotional messages?

3. What marketing tactics will you use? Will you create a new web site? Can you use social media (e.g., Facebook, Twitter) to create a sense of community? Explain how this will work.

4. Will you eliminate all print publications? What about billboard, radio, or television ads?

5. How do you ensure that processes are set up to respond to Internet information requests in a timely fashion?

6. What are the HIPAA-related issues surrounding the use of social media?

7. Map the steps in your new marketing plan and include the use of social media.

8. How will you analyze and document the success of your proposed initiatives?

Where Do You Live? Health Disparities Across the United States—Case for Chapter 14

Nancy K. Sayre

Highly variable health care and patient outcomes occur in different regions of the U.S. According to a report from the American Cancer Society, deaths from colon cancer have declined in all but three regions of the country: eastern Virginia/North Carolina, lower Mississippi delta, and west-central Appalachia. The U.S. colon cancer death rate has declined by half over the past decades, partly due to screening, but there are large differences between states (Preidt, 2015a). Another study showed that 36% of counties in the U.S. are more than 50 miles from the nearest doctor specializing in ovarian, uterine, and cervical cancers, putting many women at a disadvantage for quality care and positive outcomes (Preidt, 2015b). Lastly, kidney dialysis rates in the U.S. are higher in poor neighborhoods (Preidt, 2015c). Possible reasons for these differences include less access to care, greater exposure to environmental toxins, and lifestyle habits.

DISCUSSION QUESTIONS

1. What can or should be done when populations are disproportionately unhealthy or at higher risk for certain health conditions?

2. You are a health educator working for the state Department of Public Health. How do you prioritize on what health conditions or concerns your Department focuses?

3. What data sources will you rely on?

4. How do you help hospitals in the geographic region address these health disparities?

REFERENCES

Preidt, R. (2015a, July 8). Colon cancer deaths falling, but 3 U.S. regions lag behind. *HealthDay*. Retrieved from http://consumer.healthday.com/cancer-information-5/colon-cancer-news-96/colon-cancer-deaths-falling-except-in-3-u-s-regions-701056.html

Preidt, R. (2015b, June 15). Many U.S. women live far from gynecologic cancer care: Long distances may impede evaluation, treatment, researcher says. *HealthDay*. Retrieved from http://consumer.healthday.com/cancer-information-5/cervical-cancer-news-95/many-u-s-live-miles-from-gynecologic-care-700352.html

Preidt, R. (2015c, June 24). U.S. dialysis patients increasingly live in poor areas: One-third with kidney failure come from low-income neighborhoods, study finds. *HealthDay*. Retrieved from http://consumer.healthday.com/diseases-and-conditions-information-37/misc-kidney-problem-news-432/dialysis-patients-in-u-s-increasingly-live-in-poor-areas-700497.html

My Parents Are Turning 65 and Need Help Signing Up for Medicare—Case for Chapter 9

Nancy H. Shanks

I'm in a pickle. My Baby Boomer parents are on the verge of turning 65. They just received their copy of *Medicare & You* in the mail from the Centers for Medicare and Medicaid Services at the Department of Health & Human Services. It's time for them to think about a bunch of new things that happen when you turn 65, like signing up for Medicare and starting to collect Social Security. The latter seems like a relatively easy straight-forward decision. Since both of them have worked throughout their lives and recently retired, all that is needed is to decide at what age they will start taking those retirement benefits.

Medicare is a whole different story. I do know that they paid Medicare taxes while they were employed, so they should be eligible. Also, since they have recently retired, they will not have health care coverage once their COBRA benefits run out. They are currently paying $1,300 per month to retain their medical coverage. Now that I think about it, it may make sense for them to enroll in Medicare before COBRA runs out.

My parents have had their health insurance with Anthem Blue Cross/Blue Shield through my dad's employer and have stayed with this under COBRA for the last 6 months; they have 12 months left on that coverage. They have each used the same primary care physicians for many years, but their doctors are also Baby Boomers and are on the verge of retiring as well. Dad has diabetes and needs regular care and good coverage for his medications. Mom is in pretty good health, but needs annual check-ups, mammograms and the like, and is also on a couple of medications for cholesterol and other things. Plus, you never know when something will go wrong and they'll need more care. My siblings and I want to make sure they have good coverage, so I am thinking that this may be a perfect time for them to change their coverage. But, I am at a loss about what to do. Unfortunately, I don't know anything about health insurance beyond my own family's policy and benefits, and I know absolutely nothing about Medicare. And, unfortunately, my parents seem to be in shock that they have reached this point in their lives and aren't really paying attention to these issues.

You are a health care management student. I understand that you have some knowledge in this area. Can you help me by answering the following questions and making a recommendation about which way my parents should go? And, can you make sure to explain your rationale of making your recommendation, so that my siblings and I can discuss this with our parents and help them make the decision that will be best for them?

DISCUSSION QUESTIONS

1. What is Medicare all about? Who is eligible to be covered?

2. What are these different Parts (A, B, C, and D) of Medicare all about? What are the differences between the parts? What services are covered? Does everyone automatically get coverage under these? What is the cost to the individual enrollee?

3. Given my parents' medical conditions, do they need Parts A, B, and D?

4. What about Part C? Do you think a Medicare Advantage plan might be a good option for my parents? What type do your think would be good?

5. What are the cost considerations for the various Medicare options?

6. How does the cost of Medicare compare to what my parents are currently spending for their COBRA coverage? Will going on Medicare sooner rather than later save them money?

7. What is your recommendation to us for my parents' coverage?

Newby Health Systems Needs Health Insurance—Case for Chapter 9

Nancy H. Shanks

A young entrepreneur, Ima Newby, has been working in the health information technology field for a number of years, both as a developer and user of electronic health records (EHRs) for dental practices. In her spare time she has begun working on a new idea that is innovative and provides a new software option that integrates various functions for the practice, including patient records, billing, HR, etc. It addresses the many complaints from dentists, other practice employees, insurers, and patients, and is user friendly. Ima has taken a giant leap, quit her job, and launched Newby Health Systems as a brand new start-up. She has worked with a lawyer to set up the privately held corporation, and through her various contacts has lined up a number of backers and a few "angel investors" who are providing the needed capital to launch the business. Several of these folks have agreed to become members of the Board of Directors. It is now time to begin setting up the business, acquire office space, hire staff, and begin operations.

A few young hot-shot software developers, engineers, and programmers have jumped on board and embraced Ima's ideas and strategic plan. Given the financial resources at her disposal, Ima has attracted many other staff members with other technical expertise. While these folks are clearly well-versed in developing the EHR package and have the IT aspects of the business well covered, they aren't schooled in management, and Ima needs help putting the pieces in place in terms of financial, HR, marketing, and other aspects of management.

This is where you come in. You have been hired to oversee the HR area and have numerous HR activities on your plate. One of the reasons you were hired is because of your health care management background. In addition to the typical HR functions, however, one of your first tasks is to develop a health insurance package for the company. You have a little time because the new employees have used COBRA policies to maintain coverage or have coverage through a parent or spouse. That coverage, at least under COBRA, is very expensive, making attention to this a priority.

582

Ima has laid out the following parameters and assumptions for this assignment:

- Plan on coverage for 25–50 employees;
- Make sure that the private health insurance coverage is good and will meet the needs of current and future employees; and
- Be thorough in assessing all options for coverage.

Ima wants you to prepare a written, but concise, proposal for her and the other Newby leadership to consider. This should include a recommendation on the type of coverage and justification for that recommendation versus others. Specifically, she wants the following questions addressed.

DISCUSSION QUESTIONS

1. How will you go about figuring out what the employees need in terms of coverage? What data do you have in the HR records that will help you in this regard? What other steps might you need to take?
2. What specific types of benefits do you think the coverage should provide? Is a comprehensive policy the best option, or might a more limited policy, such as a major medical or catastrophic policy, suffice?
3. What specific health plan seems to make the most sense for this group?

   - Should you cover just employees or provide coverage for families?
   - Explain why you would or would not select each type of plan, i.e., conventional indemnity plan, HMO, PPO, POS, or HDHP. Be sure to address all plans.
   - What characteristics of the plan are most important?

4. An option is for Newby to self-insure. Explain why this is a good or a poor option.
5. Cost is always an issue. What do you recommend in terms of having employees share in the cost of coverage? Will there be deductibles, copays, coinsurance?
6. How much do you anticipate this costing the employees and the company on an annual basis?

To Partner or Not to Partner with a Retail Company—Case for Chapters 17, 5, and 6

Nancy H. Shanks

University Healthcare System (UHS) has been a major player and been successful for over 100 years in a large west coast metropolitan area. It operates an EMS system, is a Level 1 trauma facility, is affiliated with a major medical school, has associations with feeder hospitals around the state, maintains centers of excellence in many areas of medicine (including cardiac, cancer, and women's and children's care), is known for conducting cutting-edge research, and is viewed as one of the preeminent leaders of medical care in the community, as well as the state. That said, the UHS leadership team has begun to recognize that they may be out of sync and that the world of health care is rapidly changing.

Consumerism is becoming one of the waves of the future. After reading several recent articles and reports about disruptive innovation and how other large health systems around the country are beginning to work with retailers to provide services, to connect with consumers, and to potentially channel patients to other services within their health care systems, the UHS leadership team thinks that it may be time to consider moving in this direction. In particular, the team recently noted that Kaiser Permanente, one of its major competitors, had begun partnering with Target, had set up walk-in clinics in several Target stores, and was staffing the clinics with Kaiser employees. Kaiser had also hired a Director of Consumerism who was spear-heading its ventures into consumer directed health care.

UHS has always operated from a volume-oriented mindset, but now knows that this too is changing. The Centers for Medicare and Medicaid Services (CMS) is moving toward a value-based approach in reimbursing for Medicare patients. CMS does not want patients to have surgery, be discharged quickly, sent home, and then readmitted with complications. CMS also doesn't want to pay for a second admission and wants better quality and outcomes for patients. That is, CMS wants patients to be sent home, have their care coordinated, not experience complications, not have to struggle through multiple hospital stays, and not be exposed to nosocomial infections.

While the leadership always thought UHS was providing the best health care, the institution now realizes that it has focused on providing mainly medical care in an inpatient setting and has done little to keep people out of the hospital and to promote health and wellness. It's time to start thinking outside the box and to change the organizational mindset. UHS has, however, never done anything like this and really doesn't have the expertise to do it. This is going to force the leaders to make some significant changes in many different areas and to involve several different departments in brainstorming how to approach partnering with a retail organization to deliver care at different sites.

DISCUSSION QUESTIONS

1. Should a team be put together to specifically work on this? Who should be included in this group? What type of team should be used?

2. What should the charge to this group be? What are the goals of this effort given the changes in consumer expectations?

3. From a strategic perspective, where does UHS stand? What are its internal strengths and weaknesses? What are its opportunities and threats?

4. Does UHS need someone whose job is to lead this effort? Would it make sense to hire from outside the organization or from within? What skills are needed?

5. What other types of staffing will be needed for this type of venture?

6. Can these new consumers be linked into the existing EHR system? How might that work?

7. What information will be helpful to learn about and understand these new users? How can this information be obtained? Should this become part of the EHR?

8. What are the estimated costs of setting up a clinic in a retail setting? What are the potential rewards to be gained? When will UHS start seeing a return on its investment?

9. What are the pros and cons of undertaking this type of venture?

10. Are there other types of approaches that UHS should also be considering? What expertise does it have that could be used in different ways? What needs to be done to change the organizational culture?

Wellness Tourism: An Option for Your Organization?—Case for Chapters 17 and 5

Nancy H. Shanks

Annie is the manager of a Health and Wellness Center at Tippy Canoe University Medical Center (TCUMC), a facility that has been known regionally in the mid-west for its research and cutting-edge services in the fields of nutrition, in-patient weight loss programs, and other wellness efforts. She's having lunch with her colleague, Maggie, and they have been commiserating about the recent influx of many new and different types of entities providing these types of services on an outpatient basis. While they were once the only game in town and the region, it now seems like overnight there are many other players and to their astonishment they have lots of competition.

Bill Jones, the CEO of TCUMC, is out of town and attending the annual Congress of the American College of Healthcare Executives (ACHE). As he has listened to a number of presentations on the many changes that are taking place in the health care industry across the country, he has become concerned. The recent trends in medical and wellness tourism have caught his attention. After ignoring the many changes that several futurists have been predicting for a couple of years, he has come to the realization that other organizations and institutions around the country have already begun capitalizing on many new opportunities by developing innovative programs in promoting health and wellness, that his organization is a bit behind the curve, and that TCUMC needs to hustle to not be left in the dust. It's clear to Bill that his boat is being rocked.

While enjoying the end of their lunch break, Annie's cellphone beeps, indicating that she has a text message from Bill. Uh-oh! Something must be up because Bill has never texted before and hasn't paid much attention to the Health and Wellness Center in the past. Annie reads the message aloud to Maggie.

Think we've had our heads in the sand!!! Need to urgently begin investigating medical and wellness tourism asap. Can you and your staff pull some information about what's going on in these areas, as well as put your heads together and come up with ideas about how we can revamp TCUMC's health and wellness offerings? Please call my office and get on my calendar for Monday, when I'm back from Chicago.

Annie and Maggie think it must be ESP because they had just been talking about some of these same issues. It's Thursday afternoon and they need to move quickly to take advantage of this opportunity. Thinking that TCUMC's competition is now almost any organization in the country, they agree that they need to think broadly about this and explore almost any option. Knowing Bill will want solid justification, and they can't do the legwork themselves in this short amount of time, they have asked the health care management intern to help them by responding to the following questions.

DISCUSSION QUESTIONS

1. What exactly is wellness tourism? What do wellness tourists look like?
2. What are the different types of tourists (outbound, inbound, and intrabound)? Which of these should TCUMC be focusing on?
3. Should the focus be only on wellness tourism or include medical tourism as well?
4. How much is spent on wellness in the U.S. and on wellness tourism in particular?
5. Who are their local competitors and what types of programming do they offer?
6. What is the current state-of-the-art in terms of wellness programs around the country? What specific types of services are being offered to tourists?
7. What is the current state-of-the-art in terms of nutrition and weight-loss programs around the country? What specific types of services are being offered?
8. What is your recommendation for Bill? What areas of nutrition, weight-management, and wellness seem like the best fit for TCUMC to undertake?

(Hint: There's a citation in Chapter 17 that may be helpful with some of this.)

Conflict in the Capital Budgeting Process at University Medical Center: Let's All Just Get Along—Case for Chapter 10

Windsor Westbrook Sherrill and Callie E. Heyne

Introduction: The Challenge of Limited Resources

In health care organizations, the business interests of clinicians and management are intricately tied to one another. This is particularly the case in the process of making capital purchase decisions. A good capital budgeting process ensures optimal allocation of resources and helps management and physicians work toward improved services. If clinicians and health services managers are to be partners in creating programs and services that are responsive to a competitive health care environment, capital budgeting and capital acquisition decisions must be managed in a way that minimizes conflict and maximizes organizational resources.

Long-term investment decisions should provide a level of unity within the organization. An effective capital budgeting process must manage the interests of the numerous constituencies in the health care organization, while coming to an agreeable way to allocate scarce resources. The process can be inherently filled with conflict. Clinicians expect participation in decision making from the health care organization, especially in areas of clinical equipment purchases (White & Griffith, 2010). To achieve optimal outcomes, physicians and managers must be allies in making capital decisions.

Different interest groups in the organization have different objectives. Primary care physicians might favor increased funding for ambulatory care, while surgeons might desire more operating or diagnostic tools. Various departments apply for and compete among themselves for scarce organizational resources, particularly funding for capital purchases. In an environment of scarce resources, units of the organization compete for funding. If the interests of various groups are not managed in the capital budgeting process, conflict will inevitably result.

An Example: The Budget Hearing Process

University Medical Center (UMC) has faced reduced resources for capital purchases each year. As reimbursements decrease and third-party payers negotiate ever more stringent contracts, funds are limited, yet requests for purchases seem to be limitless. Such an environment inevitably produces potential for conflict among units of the organization as they compete for limited resources.

One approach to the assessment of capital equipment proposals that has been used effectively at UMC is the budget hearing process. A review process provides structure to capital decisions and reduces associated conflict. Capital proposals are presented before a review panel by the stakeholders who are advocating for their purchase. This provides an opportunity for accountability in feedback on proposals as well as transparency in evaluation of each proposal. Panel members have an opportunity to ask questions concerning each proposal. A consistent set of questions is asked by the review committee. Evaluation focuses on financial impact as well as how well the proposed purchase supports the overall strategy of UMC. The hearing process reduces conflict by providing each requester an opportunity to present their "case" for a capital purchase. The proposal is then considered based on a set of evaluation criteria that are consistently applied across all projects under review.

The Budget Review Panel

Capital planning is designed to be a team process at UMC. The budget review team consists of management representation, clinical representation, and financial services staff. Members of clinical staff are partners in both preparation and evaluation of capital requests. Participation of individuals such as the CEO, CFO, clinical staff leaders, and middle managers reduces conflict in the process, ensures broad representation in assessment of project proposals, and increases commitment to decisions concerning which projects will be funded.

Organizations that wish to establish and maintain strong physician relationships often have physicians heavily involved in the capital allocation and budget process. There are 440 physicians on staff at UMC. Including appropriate physicians in representation and communication of the capital budgeting process assures that they are empowered to influence decisions that affect clinical practice. Medical staff organization bylaws provide a basis for representation of physicians and specify the roles of each committee of the medical staff. This organizational structure is used to identify appropriate representation of each clinical department in the capital budgeting process. For example, the clinical chiefs of service are always asked to sit on the budget review panel for their respective units.

Physicians are also involved in the capital budgeting process for clinical areas because they are typically in the best position to assess patient preferences concerning services.

Proposals for new capital equipment include medical review of scientific merit as well as benefits and risks to patients, and this is facilitated by clinical staff at UMC. The process facilitates the belief that physicians have had fair opportunity to be heard on issues, and that final capital decisions take their perspectives into account and optimize market opportunities for both the organization and its medical staff. The involvement of the physician organization in the budgeting process often identifies potential conflicts in advance and responds in a way that is constructive.

Consistent Timeline

To reduce conflict, the process of generating and evaluating capital purchase proposals is consistent from year to year at UMC. So that the process for making capital decisions can be shared across the organization, all units are provided with a schedule of deadlines and structures for the submission of a capital budgeting request. Although the capital purchasing and evaluation cycle is a continuous process, the request and approval process occurs on a regular and consistent schedule. Consistency in calendars facilitates improved evaluation of capital investment requests and minimizes conflict. Once set, the organization rigorously adheres to the established timeline. The schedule is shared across the organization so that any potential requestors have an opportunity for development and evaluation of their desired purchases. These processes should be familiar to all stakeholders who are interested in proposing capital projects. UMC leadership is cognizant of the importance of all stakeholders having an opportunity to submit capital budget requests; the perception of an "insiders' game" is carefully avoided. Failure to do so can be detrimental to buy-in of final capital purchase decisions.

Consistent Evaluation of Alignment to Organizational Mission

An effective capital budgeting process reduces conflict by making capital decisions that clearly support the mission and strategic objectives of an organization. The best capital management decisions should align with an organization's long-range strategic, financial, and related operating plans while also ensuring the decisions are financially sound (Sussman, 2007). Many projects might have merit or financial viability, but an environment of limited resources dictates that selected projects integrate with the long-term strategy of the institution. Potential proposers are required to demonstrate that funding of capital projects will support the University's strategic plans. To facilitate proposals that are consistent with organizational mission, University leaders ensure that mission and vision for the organization are clearly articulated, and strategic direction is understood throughout the organization. As such, physicians and managers appreciate and accept the capital decisions that emerge through the budgeting process and understand how the selected projects support long-term plans of the organization.

Consistent Data Requirements and Analysis

UMC places a priority on consistency in the type of information required in each capital equipment proposal, as well as its approach to evaluating them. Project justification is required following a very specific set of guidelines developed by the organization. Using consistent methodologies to evaluate capital proposals establishes a "level playing field" between competing groups within the organization (Healthcare Financial Management Association [HFMA], 2005).

Consistency enhances the perception of equity in the process. If one proposer is required to produce a more detailed justification than another, then conflict and perceived inequity result. Examples of the types of required data are market share, assessment of market needs, physician staff and employees to support a project, competitive costs and charges, payer mix, and operating impact of a project (Grube & Wareham, 2005). The University provides guidelines for documentation for a capital project request, and conflict is reduced in the final selection of projects. Consistency in format facilitates better evaluation of capital investment opportunities. Due to the large potential for conflict, successful budget allocation processes should be largely data-driven processes (Sussman, 2007).

Who Facilitates: A Team Approach

To evaluate proposals, credible utilization and financial projections are required for each project request. Capital purchase proposals must include sufficient information, including identifying and forecasting of cash flows, applying capital budgeting tools, and market analysis. In most cases, proposers are assisted in the development of such data. Clinical leaders are involved in developing project requests at the University, but they typically do not have the skills to prepare requests according to organizational requirements. The financial staff in the organization shares responsibility for analysis and data preparation with clinical users of equipment. Planning and finance personnel provide important information related to patient population, revenue and expense projections, and markets. As such, finance staff and managers are partners with clinicians in the preparation of capital equipment proposals.

Conclusion

Viability of UMC depends on wise capital investment decisions; it is important that such decisions be reached without conflict that disrupts organizational processes and relationships. Improved capital budgeting processes can reduce conflict as well as increase accountability for project success. A process that is effective generates detailed and consistent capital project proposals and uses objective data in a fair and consistent process to analyze and select proposals.

The process at UMC involves the participation of key clinical and management stakeholders, uses a consistent timeline, uses consistent evaluation methods, has consistent data requirements for project proposals, and facilitates the buy-in of key constituencies. Effective alliances between managers and clinicians empower a more competitive organization. Capital decision procedures that reduce conflict provide for an organization that integrates goals of physicians and managers, aligning the interests of both at UMC.

DISCUSSION QUESTIONS

1. Does the capital budgeting process used at UMC support the "majority rule" approach to conflict management? How might the process be improved, particularly in regard to due process and ensuring the involvement of appropriate clinical stakeholders?

2. An environment of limited financial resources infers that there will be winners and losers. No matter how standardized the evaluation process for capital proposals, some requests will not be funded. How should the process of communicating funding decisions be handled to reduce conflict, minimize destructive behaviors, and maintain morale?

3. What conflict resolution guidelines are appropriate for UMC in the capital budgeting process?

4. How should a circumstance be handled in which clinical leaders from different areas disagree with the funding decisions of the committee?

5. Is there a process for review of grievance or are committee decisions final?

REFERENCES

Bujak, J. S. (2008). *Inside the physician mind: Finding common ground with doctors*. Chicago, IL: Health Administration Press.

Grube, M. E., & Wareham, T. L. (2005). What's your game plan? Advice from the capital markets. *Healthcare Financial Management, 59*(11), 62–66, 68, 70 passim.

Healthcare Financial Management Association (HFMA). (2005). *Financing the future II report 3: Essentials of integrated strategic financial planning and capital allocation*. Westchester, IL: Author.

Sussman, J. H. (2007). *The healthcare executive's guide to allocating capital*. Chicago, IL: Health Administration Press.

White, K. R., & Griffith, J. R. (2010). *The well-managed healthcare organization*. Chicago, IL: Health Administration Press.

The New Toy at City Medical Center—Case for Chapters 11 and 13

Windsor Westbrook Sherrill and Dale Buchbinder

Capsule endoscopy is used to examine parts of the gastrointestinal tract that cannot be seen with other types of endoscopy. The process uses a very small camera attached to a long flexible tube to view the intestinal tract. The technology is particularly useful when disease is suspected in the small intestine and can sometimes diagnose sources of bleeding or causes of abdominal pain such as Crohn's disease or peptic ulcers.

A group of gastroenterologists at the City Medical Center proposed the purchase of capsule endoscopy equipment through the Capital Equipment Purchasing process. After the equipment was approved and the purchase initiated, providers began the process of applying for specific privileges to use it. Three gastroenterologists, Drs. Smith, Sams, and Amalfi, applied for credentials and were approved by the department of gastroenterology and, ultimately, the Medical Center Board of Directors to use capsule endoscopy.

After the three gastroenterologists began to use the new equipment, they discovered that a surgeon, Dr. Jones, intended to use the capsule endoscopy equipment for procedures, too. Having done this procedure at another competing hospital on numerous occasions, Dr. Jones had also been privileged through the department of surgery and, ultimately, the City Medical Center Board of Directors. When Dr. Jones put his first case on the schedule for the gastroenterology suite where the capsule endoscopy was to be performed, Nurse Tattler called the gastroenterology department and alerted them to this potential intrusion.

Drs. Sams, Smith, and Amalfi were outraged. They had advocated for the equipment, and this poacher was attempting to enter their domain. While each of them told Dr. Jones that they liked him "as a person," they were *not* willing to share their new toy with him or the surgery department. They felt strongly that they "owned" the equipment and the suite. He would just have to go elsewhere.

Dr. Jones pointed out to the trio that the *hospital* purchased the equipment with capital equipment dollars; the Department of Gastroenterology did not pay for it. In addition, the suite and the nurses who staffed the suite were employees of City Medical Center, not of the Department of Gastroenterology. And, he had been privileged by his department and the City Medical Board of Directors.

Tempers flared, and the chairs of the two departments were informed of this escalating conflict. Since Dr. Jones had scheduled the procedure and the patient was expecting to have it the next morning, the chairs called an emergency meeting with all the involved parties.

DISCUSSION QUESTIONS

1. What questions do you think the chairs of each department should ask?

2. Dr. Jones has a busy practice and is the second-highest revenue producer from general surgery. City Medical Center is dependent on revenue from the surgical service. How might this impact how the situation should be handled? What specific steps should be taken to avoid this situation in the future?

3. The goal of physician privileging is to ensure that providers practicing in an organization have appropriate credentials to provide safe and effective treatment. What are three challenges illustrated by this case?

4. Who are the stakeholders in the privileging process at City Medical Center?

5. Who is responsible for communicating about specific privileges?

6. Would these physician behaviors be considered "patient-centric"?

7. Are these physicians "team players"? Explain your response.

8. Reread this case. Using Figure 18-3, the Confidential Teammate Evaluation Form at the start of this chapter, compare the behavior of these physicians with the expected behaviors of teammates. Score each physician as if he or she were your teammate. What scores did they earn?

Recruitment Challenge for the Middle Manager—Case for Chapters 2 and 12

Jon M. Thompson

You are the director of strategic planning and marketing in a large, multihospital-based health system. The office includes 10 professional positions (including yours), and you currently have five professional staff members and one support staff member who report directly to you. Your office has responsibility for managing and updating the organization's annual strategic planning process, including managing external (e.g., competitor and market information) and internal databases (e.g., service volumes and projections, patient origin data, and payer data), as well as managing all public relations and marketing activities. You are engaged in the process of filling a newly approved position that reports to you, called senior planning analyst, which will have a leadership role in managing the planning process. Currently, there are two planning analysts who report to you and will work with this senior analyst. Of all the candidates you are considering, one has the appropriate education and significant experiences in planning in other health care settings and is the best fit for the job. However, her salary demand for the job is $9,000 more than the salary range for the position allows.

Use your knowledge of human resources management, the role of the line manager in recruitment and supervision of staff, and the role of the human resources department staff to effectively address this situation and to respond to the following questions.

DISCUSSION QUESTIONS

1. How do you convince your boss and the human resources department that this is the candidate you want to fill the job?

2. What steps would you undertake to get the salary approved?

3. What problems does this situation present for you, and how can you effectively address each problem?

4. What options do you have if the salary remains a "sticking point"?

I Want to Be a Medical Coder—Case for Chapter 10

Kevin D. Zeiler

Bob Biller is an aspiring health care student who is fascinated by the complex world of medical billing and coding. Since his childhood, Bob has been excited about working in the world of finance, accounting, billing, and coding. Today, he finally has that opportunity. However, Bob needs your help, as he does not completely understand how the process works. Are you willing to help? I thought you were.

First, Bob has a couple of questions that he needs answered.

1. Are coding and billing the same thing?
2. Can Bob be a coder as well as a biller?

Okay, thank you for your help with the above. Bob is ready to roll. Now that Bob is finally on the job, he is hopeful that he has the appropriate background to undertake the task of being a coder. It is essential that Bob has a background in anatomy, medical terminology, financial concepts, and insurance plans; he must also understand the various compliance issues surrounding the profession. Medical coder education exists in many forms, so it depends on where an individual lives when it comes to requirements and opportunities. Some individuals learn on the job and others have degrees in the coding field. Furthermore, numerous certification programs exist to provide individuals the background and skills they need to become medical coders. Now that Bob has a thorough understanding of the skills necessary, he once again requests your help with the actual process.

Bob knows that you are an expert in this area and wants to know:

1. What are ICD codes? Please explain where these codes come from and how they are used.
2. Are there codes other than ICD? If so, what might they be and what are they used for?

Thank you, your answers are a big help. Bob feels like he is ready to undertake his new position. He has a list of questions that he thinks will be helpful to him as he continues his career and he is hopeful that you will be able to answer them for him.

Bob thanks you in advance for researching this topic.

DISCUSSION QUESTIONS

1. Who needs to understand the billing and coding process in health care and why?

2. Are there opportunities for fraud and abuse in the billing and coding professions? Explain.

3. What professional organizations certify coders? What are the requirements?

4. Explain how efficient billing and coding practices can reduce costs and allow an organization to receive payments in a timely manner.

5. Discuss some of the federal laws that mandate and control the medical billing and coding professions.

Managing Costs and Revenues at Feel Better Pharmacy—Case for Chapter 10

Kevin D. Zeiler

Part One

You have been working as an assistant to the financial manager at Feel Better Pharmacy for the past three and a half years, and there is finally an opportunity for you to advance to a lead position within the finance department. You are excited about this new position, but first, you must be able to accomplish a task that the current CFO is assigning to you. He is going to evaluate you on your ability to understand a cash budget and provide the pharmacy with the necessary information to obtain the operating loans that they will need for the next calendar year. This process is more important than ever before because new federal legislation is putting a pinch on lending institutions by restricting their lending practices, and, therefore, the new legislation will impact most. It is your goal to use sound financial management principles, utilize the department employees as time allows, fully calculate third-party reimbursement, and ultimately determine Feel Better Pharmacy's borrowing requirements.

DISCUSSION QUESTIONS

1. Describe the department or clinic personnel that you might utilize to help you with this process. Why would you choose these people?

2. What is a third-party payer, and why do you care about their forecasted reimbursement?

Part Two

You feel prepared because of the experience you have within the finance department, but you also know that cash budgets are never certain, and that financial forecasting can help the organization to be prepared. First, you fully understand that you need to budget for the next 12-month period, so you decide to look at the historical data from the last several years.

Also, you determine that you must also look at what cash is on hand today and what needs to be paid. Finally, you must consider each and every inflow and outflow that may affect your budget and, ultimately, your organization.

DISCUSSION QUESTIONS

1. Define a cash budget as you understand it.

2. What type of historical data will you consider? How far back should you look?

3. Explain what is meant by outflows and provide examples.

4. Explain what is meant by inflows and provide examples.

Part Three

After looking at the available data, you realize that the pharmacy is in an enviable position because the patient revenues are extremely consistent throughout the year. This makes preparing your budget very easy, as you will be able to more readily break down the numbers and manage them on a monthly basis. As you continue your research, you find that more than 40% of your collections are from third-party payers. This is also something that is beneficial to you, as you will be able to compute the amount of income that the pharmacy will make on a per-prescription basis. Also, you have found that about 10% of your collections come from private pay and the final 50% comes from other sources such as government programs, local charities, and so on. It is in this arena that you find numerous inconsistencies, so you are uncertain how this may affect your final financial forecast. To fully understand and present this data, you will develop a revenue budget.

DISCUSSION QUESTIONS

1. Previously, you comprised a list of outflows and inflows, and now you need to better understand how they are costing or benefitting the organization. For instance, let's say that you have established your budget and you feel it is in tune with the current needs of the organization. What outflows and inflows could change to implode your current budget? How might you prepare for these types of circumstances? Think both about third-party payers (inflows) and lending organizations, medical supply companies, real property, and so on (outflows).

2. How would a minimum balance on a term loan affect your organization? What techniques might you employ to ensure that the minimum balances are always met?

Part Four

Through your coursework, you understand that finance by definition is forecasting, and as such, it is not going to provide 100% accuracy all the time. You must consider this when you are preparing a cash budget, especially a cash budget that is 12 months in duration. As you know, there are several factors that you and your organization cannot control, and that makes this type of forecasting all the more difficult. Also, you will have to ensure that you consider loans to the organization that may be paid off during the term of the cash budget. Both inflows and outflows must be carefully considered to allow for consistent and accurate accounting practices. Taxes, both local and federal, and other items such as insurance, licenses, and so on, must also be in the mix. It is key to fully account for all items that affect your organization.

We can now return to the opening paragraph and look at your goals for this project. As you look at the issues presented by your CFO, you will need to ensure that you have accomplished what you set out to do. Were you thorough? Did you consider all inflows and outflows? By understanding the limits of finance, you are in a great position to complete what is required to benefit the organization and its cash needs.

DISCUSSION QUESTIONS

1. How do local and federal legislation, policy, and the economy affect your cash budget decisions? How do you think health care organizations plan for these changes?

2. If you followed the steps outlined previously, would you accomplish the goals of the organization? What might you add or delete to streamline the process as you understand it?

3. Once you are finished putting the above information together, is the process complete? Do you believe that budgeting is something that is used on a daily, weekly, monthly, or annual basis? Explain your answer.

4. Finally, are there standards and/or policy considerations that must be adhered to? If so, list them and explain how they apply.

Who You Gonna Call?—Case for Chapter 16

Kevin D. Zeiler

Working in the billing department for a large, for-profit health care organization has been a dream come true for Nicki Knowitall and she is excited about her future opportunities. Nicki has been with the company for two and a half years and was just promoted to senior Medicare Billing Specialist. Since Nicki has been dealing with Medicare for over two years, she jumps right in and continues with the same billing practices she has been using and trains her staff with these techniques.

Because Nicki's new position allows her to view information that she was not previously privy to, she has started to notice some discrepancies surrounding the way many of the Medicare invoices are coded. She pulls several of these invoices and shows them to her supervisor. The supervisor informs her that this is how they will continue to code these documents and that Ms. Knowitall should focus solely on training and monitoring her staff. Nicki finds the response she received to be very strange, but nevertheless, she goes back to her work.

Six months pass and Nicki has grown more distraught as she has collected literally thousands of invoices that are coded incorrectly, but there is nothing she can do to change them at her level. She does not feel comfortable approaching her supervisor again, and she is concerned that going higher up the chain of command may make it even worse. To compound the problem, Nicki reads in the local paper that another facility in the system that she works in is being investigated for Medicare fraud.

DISCUSSION QUESTIONS

1. Should Nicki quit her job, speak to her supervisor, and/or go over her head to others in the chain of command? Explain your answers.

2. What if Nicki quits her job and moves away?

3. Nicki has kept thousands of documents that she believes are fraudulent in nature. What should she do with these? Should she provide them to her supervisor? The media? Why or why not?

4. What laws, if any, are you familiar with that may help to protect Nicki? Explain your answer and detail the provisions of these laws.

5. In your mind, does this case present an issue of fraud, abuse, or both? Explain.

6. Pretend that you are Nicki. You want to do the right thing, but you aren't sure what that is. Where do you start? Outline a path for Nicki to follow.

7. Think about your own experiences, no matter the working environment: Have you had to deal with issues of dishonesty? How have you handled it? What resources were or were not available to you?

8. Depending on your decision, i.e., do you leave, do you stay, do you do nothing, etc., are you liable if legal action is taken? Why or why not? Explain any actions that may be taken.

You Will Do What You Are Told—Case for Chapter 15

Kevin D. Zeiler

Helping others has always been your passion and the fact that you are working in a cancer care center, as a medical assistant, is a dream come true. You are also completing your undergraduate degree in health care management and are hopeful that there will be a position for you with the center as an entry-level manager. Each day you continually work to prove yourself to the physician, Dr. Bully, who is the owner of the center. You feel like you have done everything you can to prove that you can manage the center once you have completed your degree.

Life is never easy at the center, as extremely sick patients are the norm. Today, however, a young patient comes in after being in remission for the last six months. She states she is often tired and has trouble sleeping at night. She also states she read about an experimental drug called ZX12 that is being touted as a post-cancer treatment medication that will get you on your feet quicker, restore your energy, and prevent cancer from returning. She indicates to you that she would like to try this new medication. Being the student of health care that you are, you explain to her that the medication is not approved by the FDA, and that since her condition is improving, she does not qualify under the current state laws surrounding experimental drugs. You complete your preliminary work up and provide Dr. Bully with her chart.

As the day draws to a close and the last patient leaves the center, Dr. Bully provides you with a form that he asks you to fill out and return to him for a signature. You have done this many times and don't think much about it until you read the form. Dr. Bully is putting in a request for the experimental drug ZX12 for the young female patient you visited with earlier today. Because you feel this is an inappropriate treatment modality based on your understanding of current laws, you decide that you will discuss this with Dr. Bully.

Dr. Bully is in his office when you ask if you can speak with him. After making your case, Dr. Bully becomes enraged and asks you who you think you are to question the decision of an MD. Furthermore, he tells you that the management job that you desire will not be available unless the paperwork is completed and on his desk in the next 30 minutes. He then tells you to leave his office, get back to work, and do what you are told!

DISCUSSION QUESTIONS

1. Outline the major issues in this case that need to be addressed.

2. Assume that you live and work in a state that has adopted one of the "Right to Try Laws." What does your research tell you about how they work? Does this patient fall under the protections of these laws? Why or why not?

3. Assume that you live and work in a state that has not adopted one of the "Right to Try Laws." Is there precedent for Dr. Bully's actions?

4. What do you make of Dr. Bully's comments about the management job opportunity? Is this a threat concerning your future with the company?

5. What is your best option to remedy this situation at this point? Should you fill out the paperwork?

6. You know that there are few jobs in the health care sector where you live, this one pays well, and you are happy working for the center. You mull over the issues and believe that by filling out the form, you carry no legal responsibility. Is this true? Use your knowledge of law and ethics to provide the rationale for this type of thinking.

7. Are there legal actions that can be taken concerning this situation? Explain what actions you might consider.

8. Looking back at the totality of the circumstances that have occurred, was there a better way to handle this from the beginning? What if you were unaware of current "Right to Try Laws" when the patient spoke with you? Where does the issue of education surrounding these types of legislative actions begin and end in the workplace?

360-degree performance appraisal A multi-source feedback approach to assessing the job performance of an individual employee, using input from a manager, subordinates, peers, and internal and external customers.

ABC inventory method In supply chain, ABC analysis is an inventory categorization method which consists of dividing items into three categories, A, B, and C, with A being the most valuable items and C being the least valuable ones.

Abuse Improper acts that are unintentional (not willful) but inconsistent with standard practices.

Access to vs. restrictions on care This pertains to whether access to care is limited or controlled for the insured individual. Under some insurance policies, there is unlimited access, while under others, access is restricted by a gatekeeper.

Accountable care organizations (ACOs) Based on the idea that groups of providers come together and take responsibility for delivering care to a defined patient population. This approach uses a Primary Care Physician (PCP) to orchestrate the care delivered. The ACO is encouraged to deliver efficient and appropriate care and to keep patients healthy.

Accounts receivable, aka, patient accounts Money owed by customers (individuals or corporations) to another entity in exchange for goods or services that have been delivered or used, but not yet paid for. Receivables usually come in the form of operating lines of credit and are usually due within a relatively short time period, ranging from a few days to a year.

Accreditation Council for Continuing Medical Education (ACCME) The organization that establishes criteria for determining which educational providers are quality CME providers.

Activities of daily living (ADLs) Bathing, dressing, feeding, and toileting.

Activity-based costing An accounting method that identifies the activities that a firm performs, and then assigns indirect costs to products. An activity-based costing (ABC) system recognizes the relationship among costs, activities, and products, and through this relationship assigns indirect costs to products less arbitrarily than traditional methods.

Adams' Equity Theory Motivation theory that proposes that individuals are motivated when they perceive that they are treated equitably in comparison to others within the organization.

Adaptive leadership Creating flexible organizations able to meet the relentless succession of challenges.

Adjourning The work of the team is over and the team members realize they enjoyed working with each other. There is often a reluctance to let go and move on to the next task because they have become comfortable working with each other.

Administrative agencies Those entities which establish the necessary rules and regulations to carry out statutes.

Advanced practice clinicians (APCs) Physician Assistants (PAs) and Nurse Practitioners (NPs).

Advertising Various methods used by the HSO to market services and recruit and identify candidates for open positions and generate interest in the open positions, including print and electronic media.

Affinity bias Favoring others because we like them.

Affordable Care Act (ACA) A shortened name for the Patient Protection and Affordable Care Act legislation passed in 2010, which had the goals of bringing uninsured individuals into health insurance coverage, increasing the quality of care, and reducing the cost of care.

Alderfer's ERG Theory Motivation theory that suggests that individuals are motivated to move forward and backward through three levels: existence, relatedness, and growth.

Allied health professionals Refers to individuals trained in more than 2,000 programs in 28 health science occupations.

Ambulatory surgery centers (ASCs) Health care facilities focused on providing same-day surgical care, including diagnostic and preventive procedures.

Amenities of care Part of Donabedian's definition of quality, focusing on characteristics of the setting in which care is delivered.

Analytics/Big Data The process of inspecting aggregated data, looking for patterns and statistics to help improve processes, and creating information, ultimately leading to new knowledge that helps improve efficiency and effectiveness in health care, along with other goals of health and public health. Sometimes referred to as "data mining."

Anti-kickback Act aka Medicare and Medicaid Anti-Kickback Act A criminal statute that prohibits the exchange (or offer to exchange) of anything of value in an effort to induce (or reward) the referral of federal health care program business.

Antitrust Improvement Acts of 1976 (Hart-Scott-Rodino) A U.S. law that requires large companies to file a report with the Federal Trade Commission and Department of Justice before completing a merger, acquisition, or tender offer so that government regulators can determine whether the transaction would violate antitrust laws.

Assault A deliberate threat that intentionally puts another person in reasonable apprehension of an imminent harmful or offensive contact.

At-risk behavior A behavioral choice that increases risk, or where risk is not recognized or is mistakenly believed to be justified.

Attention process The automatic cognitive process of noticing and focusing attention on a stimulus.

Attribution Making an inference about what causes something to happen.

Attribution theory The brain's innate tendency to explain the causes of behavior and outcomes.

Authentic leadership Focused on self-knowledge, defined values, and leadership principles; understanding what motivates the leader; building a strong support team; and staying grounded by integrating all aspects of leaders' lives.

Automatic system Thinking processes that are fast, unconscious, effortless, and use intuition.

Autonomy Independence in one's thoughts or actions.

Availability heuristic Judging the importance of information because it is easy to recall.

Avoidance learning In Skinner's Reinforcement Theory, this refers to actions taken to avoid undesirable or negative behaviors. This is sometimes referred to as negative reinforcement.

Baby Boomers Individuals born between 1946 and 1964.

Bad debt The health care organization bills for services but receives no payment. These operating expenses are based on charges, not costs, and are written off by the organization. This term is usually used with for-profit organizations.

Baldrige Award National award for quality that uses a structure, process, and results framework.

Bargaining When someone says, "If you go along with me this time, I'll back you up next time." If the choices are equally good, then bargaining can be a good tool; if the choices aren't equal, then it may not be a good tool.

Base compensation The wages or salary for a specific position commensurate with fulfilling the basic expectations for the position.

Baseline scenario A starting point for a forecast.

Basic, major medical, or hospital-surgical policies Referred to by several different names, the benefits provided by these policies are limited to types of illnesses that require hospitalization. Benefits include inpatient hospital stays, surgery, associated tests and treatments, related physician services, and other expenses incurred during an illness. There usually are limits on hospital stays and caps on expenditures.

Battery A criminal offense involving actual unlawful physical contact, distinct from assault, which is the act of creating apprehension of such contact.

Behavioral-based interview questions Interview questions that address previous and likely future attitudes and behaviors of candidates, based on responses to different scenarios (e.g., "Tell me about a time when you demonstrated leader decision-making in your prior position").

Belonging needs One of the five levels in Maslow's hierarchy, including the desire for social contact and interaction, friendship, affection, and various types of support.

Benchmarking Comparative market analysis of wages used to adjust salary ranges for positions as appropriate to remain competitive.

Beneficence A positive duty to care. Requires doing the best one can for the recipient of one's services.

Benefits Any type of compensation provided in a form other than salary or direct wages including health insurance; vacation leave, sick leave, or paid time off (PTO); life insurance; retirement plan; and other benefits such as tuition assistance or discounted child care. These are considered to be extrinsic rewards.

Best practices Any practice which is shown to result in the best outcomes.

Bias blind spot We believe others are more influenced by biases than we are.

Biases Systematic errors in thinking and judgment.

Big data Massive, complex information which can be integrated and analyzed to make decisions.

Billing cycle The interval of time during which bills are prepared for goods and services that a company has sold. A billing cycle is recurring and is most often set to repeat on a monthly basis.

Binding policies The principles and regulations established in a community by some authority and applicable to its people, whether in the form of legislation or of custom and policies recognized and enforced by judicial decision. Policy is a requirement that an organization, group, or government agency adopts to make its organization run more smoothly. Therefore, a binding policy means that the policy is final and must be followed when it applies.

Biomedical ethics The actions a leader needs to consider as he or she relates to a patient.

Bioterrorism The use of agents of contagious diseases (bacteria, viruses, etc.) as weapons against humans, animals, or plants.

Board certification Voluntary demonstration of competency within a specialty; serves as a proxy for quality.

Board eligible When a physician is preparing to sit for his or her specialty exams but has not yet taken them.

Bonus, gain-sharing, or goal sharing programs See *Incentive compensation.*

Breach notification rules and enforcement A risk assessment of any PHI breach must now be carried out and must consider the nature and extent of PHI involved, to whom the

PHI may have been disclosed, whether that PHI was actually acquired or viewed, and the extent to which the risk to the PHI has been mitigated.

Breach of duty Failure to meet the standard of care.

Break even analysis The method of determining at what level of volume the production of a good or service will equal the revenues created. It is used by health care managers for the purpose of determining profit or loss.

Break even point The volume of production in units and sale of goods or services where total costs equal total revenue.

Budgeting The process of converting the goals and objectives of the organization's operating plan into financial terms: expenses, revenues, and cash flow projections.

Bundled payments Based on the idea of providing a single payment for a specific episode of care or a specific procedure. Instead of paying multiple providers to perform their specific tasks in, for example, a surgery such as a knee replacement, a single payment is made.

Business associate agreements All groups that hospitals or other covered entities do business with, as well as the subcontractors with whom those associates do business.

Business market All organizations, both non-profit and for-profit, that acquire goods and services.

Business-to-business (B2B) marketing Marketing that concentrates on organizational buyers.

Buy-downs This is a situation that occurs with individual health insurance policies where increases in premiums are mitigated by using policies that are less costly, e.g. a high deductible health plan.

Capital budget The process in which a business determines whether projects such as building a new plant or investing in a long-term venture are worth pursuing. Oftentimes, a prospective project's lifetime cash inflows and outflows are assessed in order to determine whether the returns generated meet a sufficient target benchmark.

Capital budgeting The process of selecting long-term assets, whose useful life is greater than one year, according to financial decision rules.

Capitation Agreement under which a health care provider is paid a fixed amount per member per month (PMPM) by a health plan in exchange for a contractually specified set of medical services in the future. Monthly payment is calculated one year in advance and remains fixed for that year, regardless of how often the patient needs services.

Case mix, aka, patient mix The mix of patients served by an organization based on the severity of illnesses.

Cash budget An estimation of the cash inflows and outflows for a business or individual for a specific period of time. Cash budgets are often used to assess whether the entity has sufficient cash to fulfill regular operations and/or whether too much cash is being left in unproductive capacities.

Cash flow A revenue or expense stream that changes a cash account over a given period.

Cash inflow Funds received by a company due to sales, financing, or investments. Cash inflows are used to gauge the overall financial health of a business, and a company with a large and stable cash inflow can be considered to be in a good financial position.

Cash outflow The total outgoing funds from a company in a given period of time. Cash outflows include expenses such as salaries, supplies, and maintenance, as well as paying dividends or servicing any debt held by the company. A company may be required to seek additional financing if cash outflows exceed cash inflows.

Catastrophic coverage policies Benefits under these health insurance policies are intended to cover extraordinary types of illness; policies typically carry very sizable deductibles ($15,000 or higher) and lifetime limits on coverage.

Categorize The cognitive process of making distinctions by grouping new information with similar concepts or knowledge based upon common features.

Causation The causal relationship between conduct and result from which the specific injury or effect arose. A breach of duty must be directly connected to the harm that occurred.

Cause-and-effect diagram A structured format (often resembling a fish) for identifying and organizing the possible causes for a process problem (special cause variation).

Cause-related marketing A marketing approach that links a for-profit company and its offerings to a societal issue with the goal of building brand equity and increasing profits.

Center for Medical Innovation (CMI) Federal agency tasked with testing innovative payment and service delivery models.

Certified nurse midwives (CNMs) RNs who deliver babies and provide prenatal care. They are licensed as independent practitioners in all 50 states, the District of Columbia, American Samoa, Guam, and Puerto Rico. CNMs are defined as primary care providers under federal law.

Certified nurse's assistants (CNAs) CNAs are often trained on the job in 75 hours of mandatory training and are required to pass a competency examination. CNAs assist RNs and LPNs in the care of patients, particularly in long-term care settings.

Certified registered nurse anesthetists (CRNAs) APNs who specialize in providing anesthesia.

CHAMPVA A fee-for-service program patterned after the TRICARE fee-for-service option with an annual deductible and 25% copay. Unlike TRICARE, CHAMPVA is operated completely by the VA and not through contractors.

Change management A structured management approach to improving the organization and its performance, based on managerial assessment of operational activities and performance and making adjustments in the work structure and processes to improve performance.

Charges The amount of money a provider would charge absent discounts. Charges do not reflect costs, are often published simply for reporting purposes, and do not reflect what the consumer will pay or the true value of the services.

Charges minus a discount or percentage of charges Health care organizations offer discounted charges to third parties in return for large numbers of patients.

Charity care The not-for-profit organization provides care to a patient who it knows will be unable to pay.

Chart abstractions/audits Collection of information from a patient's chart or electronic medical record.

Check sheet A simple data collection form in which occurrence of some event or behavior is tallied.

Chief executive officer (CEO) Hired and delegated authority by the Board and serves as chief administrator of the operations of the entire organization.

Chief financial officer (CFO) May also serve as a vice president; is responsible for the entire financial management function of the organization, including the accounting function and management of financial assets.

Chief information officer (CIO) The corporate officer responsible for all information and data processing systems, including medical records, data processing, medical information systems, and admitting.

Chief operating officer (COO) Often the senior vice president, responsible for the day-to-day operations of the organization.

Children's Health Insurance Program (CHIP) Provides increased access to health care coverage for low-income children who do not qualify for Medicaid; this became Title XXI of the Social Security Act.

Choice phase of decision making Involves assessing options and choosing, implementing, and evaluating the chosen solution.

Civil law Concerned with wrongs against a particular person or organization and regulates ordinary private matters, as distinct from criminal, political, or military matters.

Clayton Act An amendment to the Sherman Antitrust Act of 1890 that attempts to prohibit certain actions that lead to anti-competitiveness.

Clinical Nurse Specialists RNs with educational qualifications as an NP in their area of focus.

Closed community When no one can enter or leave a community.

Closed-panel HMO Physicians practice only with the HMO, frequently in an HMO-owned health center.

Coaching leadership style Recommended for top leadership in an organization, where the leader focuses on personal development, rather than on tasks.

Code of ethics Guidelines for appropriate behaviors for professionals.

Coercive leadership style A directive approach to managing that should be reserved for emergency situations or problem employees.

Cognition The mental processes involved in thinking and reasoning, including perceiving and attending to information, processing information, and ordering information to create meaning.

Cognitive consistency The principle used to integrate new information by comparing it to prior knowledge and deciding how well it fits existing knowledge and beliefs.

Cognitive empathy Knowing and understanding another's perspective.

Cognitive evaluation The categorizing of new information by grouping it with similar concepts or knowledge based upon common characteristics.

Cognitive psychology The study of human thinking.

Coinsurance Under a fee-for-service policy, insured individuals pay a portion of the cost of their care, while the insurer is responsible for the remaining costs.

Collective bargaining Refers to the negotiation of salary, benefits, and working conditions of an HSO's employees who are represented by a labor union.

Committee Comprised of individuals from many departments who are called upon to review ongoing organizational issues.

Committee of Sponsoring Organizations (COSO) A joint initiative of five private sector organizations, established in the United States, dedicated to providing thought leadership to executive management and governance entities on critical aspects of governance, business ethics, internal control, risk management, fraud, and financial reporting.

Common Law or Judge-made Law A form of law that depends on judicial decisions as opposed to legislative acts and is based on custom and precedent, unwritten in statute or code, that constitutes the basis of the English and U.S. legal systems, except in Louisiana.

Common Procedural Terminology (CPT) Updated every year, CPTs describe medical procedures and other services.

Common-cause variation Variation in the process due to natural influences which are typically difficult to control.

Community engagement The process of working collaboratively towards well-being with and through groups of people affiliated by geography, special interest, or a common cause.

Community needs The collective needs of a specific community of people or market.

Competence Speaks to an individual's ability to make decisions or perform tasks and are of sound mind and legal age to do so. Competent also means that a professional is educated, trained, and has the skills to perform a task.

Competencies Knowledge, skills, and behaviors that can be assessed to determine an individual's achievement in key domains of leadership.

Competency A state in which an individual has the requisite or adequate ability or qualities to perform certain functions.

Competitive positioning The identification of targets and the definition of differential advantage constitute the creation of the competitive positioning of the organization and its offerings.

Competitive rivalry Represents the power that local and other competitors may have on an organization's strategy.

Comprehensive policies Provide benefits that typically include physician and other types of outpatient visits, inpatient hospitals stays, outpatient surgery, medical testing and ancillary services, medical equipment, therapies, and other types of services.

Conceptual skills Managerial skills that involve the ability to critically analyze and solve complex problems.

Confidentiality Requires keeping information about others involved in the health care interaction private.

Confirmation bias Noticing and placing more emphasis on information that agrees with existing beliefs.

Conflict of interest A term used to describe when an individual can be influenced by money or other considerations to act in a way that is contrary to the good of the organization for whom he or she works or the patient for whom he or she should be advocating in their best interests.

Consent To fully understand and voluntarily agree to an act or proposal of another.

Consumer behavior The totality of consumers' decisions with respect to the acquisition, consumption, and disposition of goods, services, time, and ideas by humans over time.

Consumer-directed health care The growing trend in health care purchases made in the same manner in which one might purchase other goods or services, e.g., using reviews, cost comparisons, and other indicators of value and quality, and selecting providers based on personal preferences.

Consumers The end-users of health care services.

Contingency leadership Concept with a focus on both the leader's style as well as the situation in which the leader works.

Continuing medical education (CME) Education and training programs for physicians to maintain currency and, in many states, licensure.

Continuous Quality Improvement (CQI) The quality improvement philosophy articulated by Deming that encourages worker participation in process change, focuses on data-based decision making, and embraces a standardized approach to quality improvement.

Contract In order for a contract to exist, there must be four key elements: (1) the agreement must be between two or more parties, (2) the parties must both be competent to consent to such an agreement, (3) the agreement must be for something of value, and (4) the agreement must be lawful.

Contractual allowance The difference between what a hospital charges for one day of an adult hospital bed and the payment the hospital has agreed to accept from an insurance company.

Controllable costs These are variable costs such as raw materials, labor, and other overheads deemed controllable by management.

Controller (also called the comptroller) The chief accounting officer responsible for the accounting and reporting functions, including financial record keeping

Controlling Management function that refers to monitoring organizational performance and taking necessary corrective actions to improve overall performance.

Coordination of benefits (COB) When someone has two insurance plans, each company seeks to ensure that it pays only that which it is obligated to pay.

Copayments Costs borne by the insured individual at the time of service.

Core privileges Covers a multitude of activities a physician is permitted to perform in a facility.

Core strategy The process of developing a detailed and creative assessment of both the company's capabilities—its strengths and weaknesses relative to the competition—and the opportunities and threats posed by the environment.

Cost The total money, time, and resources associated with a purchase or activity.

Cost reimbursement The organization is reimbursed for the projected cost, expressed as a percentage of charges.

Cost allocation The process of identifying, aggregating, and assigning costs to a cost object, any activity or item for which you want to separately measure costs.

Cost driver A cost driver triggers a change in the cost of an activity.

Cost plus a percentage for growth Health care institutions receive the cost for care provided, plus a small percentage to develop new services and products.

Cost sharing Potential risk for losses that might be experienced is pooled and the cost is shared among the many in the group.

Crew resource management Borrowed from the aviation industry, this approach to teamwork and quality improvement has been developed to address attitudes, change behavior, and improve performance. Anyone can speak up if they have safety concerns.

Criminal Disclosure Provision of the Social Security Act (SSA) The portion of the SSA that makes it a felony for a health care provider or beneficiary to knowingly and fraudulently secure payment for any event, benefit, or payment from a federal health care program.

Criminal law The portion of the law concerned with wrongs against society as a whole, even if only a particular individual is harmed.

Critical thinking Identifying and testing assumptions from multiple perspectives.

Cross-functional teams (CFTs) Teams that cut across organizational divisions and departments to address specific organizational needs.

Cultural competence A set of congruent behaviors, attitudes, and policies that come together in a system or agency or among professionals and enable the system, agency, or professions to work effectively in cross-cultural situations.

Cultural proficiency The development of skills and abilities to become culturally competent to work with and/or care for individuals from differing cultural backgrounds.

Culturally competent organization The ability and willingness of an organization's staff to respond respectfully and effectively to people of all cultures, classes, races, ages, sexual orientations, geographic regions, ethnic backgrounds, and religions in a manner that recognizes and values the dignity and worth of all.

Current assets A balance sheet account that represents the value of all assets that are reasonably expected to be converted into cash within one year in the normal course of business.

Current liabilities A company's debts or obligations that are due within one year.

Customer The purchaser of products, services, and ideas.

Customer value The difference between the benefits a consumer perceives from the purchase of a product, service, or idea and the cost to acquire those benefits.

Cybersecurity The discipline that ensures electronic data are housed in secure locations and encrypted to prevent illegal intrusions.

Damages Monetary compensation that is awarded by a court in a civil action to an individual who has been injured through the wrongful conduct of another party.

Dashboard A visual reference used to monitor an organization's performance against targets over time.

Data integrity Assuring that data has been collected, coded, and entered correctly.

Data mining Drawing on large datasets, data miners develop analytical frameworks that help them to understand patterns in the data to predict treatment outcomes or forecast future medical costs and utilization.

Decision making, choice phase of Choosing a course of action by assessing options and choosing, implementing, and evaluating the chosen solution.

Decision making, recognition phase of Recognizing the need for a decision, identifying the decision or problem and its causes, setting goals, and generating options.

Decision-making Management function that addresses making effective decisions based on considerations of benefits and drawbacks of alternatives.

Deductibles Required levels of payments that the insured individual/family must meet before the insurer begins making its payments for care in a fee-for-service plan.

Defamation of character A legal claim you can bring in order to sue someone for making false, damaging statements about you as either slander or libel—oral or written false representations of a person's character that will hold that person up to shame or ridicule.

Defects Medical mistakes or delays in treatment in Lean.

Deliberate system Thinking processes that are slow, conscious, controlled, effortful, and use reasoning.

Deming Cycle The continuous cycle of planning a change, doing the change, checking to see if the change improves the process, and acting on the gains (PDCA Model).

Department of Justice (DOJ) The U.S. federal department responsible for enforcing federal laws.

Derived demand The fact that an organization's goods, services, and ideas are produced in response to consumer demand.

Diagnosis codes In health care, diagnosis codes are used as a tool to group and identify diseases, disorders, symptoms, poisonings, adverse effects of drugs and chemicals, injuries, and other reasons for patient encounters.

Diagnosis-related groups (DRGs) A patient classification system adopted on the basis of diagnosis consisting of distinct groupings. It is a scheme that provides a means for relating the type of patients a hospital treats with the costs incurred by the hospital.

Direct care settings Organizations that provide care directly to a patient, resident or client who seeks services from the organization.

Direct costs Prices that can be completely attributed to the production of specific goods or services that include costs of materials, labor, and expenses related to the production of a product.

Directing Management function that focuses on initiating action in the HSO through effective leadership and motivation of, and communication with subordinates.

Direct-to-the-consumer advertising (DTCA) The marketing of health care products and services directly to the end user.

Discrimination Behaving differently towards or treating differently members of a group.

Disease-specific policies In these health insurance policies, the benefits cover only the specific disease(s) covered (e.g., a cancer care policy).

Disruptive innovation The phenomenon by which an innovation transforms an existing market or sector by introducing simplicity, convenience, accessibility, and affordability where complication and high cost are the status quo.

Diversity leadership Focused on cultural competence, embracing diversity, and enhancing organizational strategies to promote inclusion of all populations.

DMAIC Counterpart of the PDCA used in Six Sigma consisting of Define, Measure, Analyze, Improve, and Control.

Documentation capture Emphasizes the importance of the quality of the written record of patient care by all health care professionals.

Drive theory Motivation theory that proposes all behaviors to be connected to hunger, thirst, sex, and the avoidance of pain.

Dual mode processing The idea that thinking occurs along a continuum of two modes or speeds: the automatic or the deliberate mode.

Duty The responsibility of health care professionals to others to act according to the law.

Ebola virus A disease that can only be transmitted through direct contact with body fluids that contain the virus.

Effectiveness Providing services based on scientific knowledge to all who could benefit and refraining from providing services to those not likely to benefit (avoiding underuse and overuse).

Efficiency Avoiding waste, in particular waste of equipment, supplies, ideas, and energy.

E-health The transfer of health resources and health care by electronic means.

Electronic Health Records (EHRs) Data collection with a focus on the total health of the patient which goes beyond standard clinical data collected in the provider's office and includes a broader view of a patient's care.

Electronic Medical Record Analytical Model (EMRAM) A conceptual model that tracks the advancement of health care organizations into the age of digital record keeping and networking.

Electronic Medical Records (EMRs) An application environment composed of the clinical data repository, clinical decision support, controlled medical vocabulary, order entry, computerized provider order entry, pharmacy, and clinical documentation applications.

Electronic performance monitoring and control systems (EMPCS) Observation tools that enable an employer to keep an eye on its employees to ensure they remain productive.

Emergency Medical Treatment and Active Labor Act (EMTALA) A federal law that requires anyone coming to an emergency department to be stabilized and treated, regardless of their insurance status or ability to pay.

Emerging leader A leader who evolves over time, applying strategies to help build and grow their careers.

Emotion One's feelings towards people, things, or events.

Emotion Contagion (EC) scale A tool that assesses one's ability to read others' emotions.

Emotional empathy Sharing another's feelings.

Emotional intelligence A set of five domains of skills that can be assessed and learned, including self-awareness, self-regulation, motivation, empathy, and social skills.

Emotional social competencies (ESC) Those emotional abilities, social skills, personality traits, motivations, interests, goals, values, attachment styles, and life narratives that can contribute to (or detract from) effective performance across a variety of positions.

Empathic perspective-taking Cognitively understanding and emotionally sharing the feelings of another.

Empathy Sensitivity to the emotional state of others.

Employee Assistance Program (EAP) An HSO-sponsored program made available to employees, and often times their dependents, to assist with personal or family problems that affect the employee's job performance.

Employee engagement The motivation and commitment of staff to contribute to the success of the organization.

Employee retention One of the key functions of human resources management that addresses the care and development of the workforce, and carrying out tasks such as employee relations, training and development, managing compensation and benefits, and providing employee assistance programs.

Employee Retirement and Income Security Act (ERISA) Protects the interests of participants and beneficiaries in private-sector employee benefit plans that are either pension plans (which provide retirement benefits) or welfare benefit plans (which provide health, disability and other benefits).

Employee Suggestion Program (ESP) A formal program to solicit employee suggestions for change, and where the HSO rewards and implements those suggestions that have the most promise to improve the HSO.

EMTALA See *Emergency Medical Treatment and Active Labor Act.*

Ending cash The sum of net change in cash and net cash.

Environment The external space beyond the organization's boundary that contains other organizations and influences.

ERG theory Suggests people are motivated to move forward and backward through the levels of motivators: existence, relatedness, and growth.

Esteem needs In Maslow's motivation hierarchy of needs theory, these needs include status, recognition, and positive regard.

Ethical behavior The ability to tell the difference between right and wrong.

Ethical principles Part of Donabedian's definition of quality focusing on the provider's ethical conduct in delivering care and his/her interest in furthering societal and organizational well-being (or effectiveness).

Ethics The body of moral principles or values governing or distinctive of a particular culture or group.

Event schema Mental representations of how certain events should occur.

Evidenced-based management Effective business practices for supervising subordinates which are supported by research.

Executive orders A policy directive or interpretation of a federal statue, a constitutional provision or a treaty that the President makes of individuals or organizations under the jurisdiction of the executive branch of government.

Existence In Alderfer's theory of motivation this pertains to the physiological and safety needs.

Expense budget Limit to the amount anticipated as an expense to be incurred in a future period.

Expenses The economic costs, i.e., money spent, that a business incurs through its operations to earn revenue.

Explicit bias Overt prejudice in which the actor is consciously aware of stereotyping or discriminating.

Extinction In Skinner's Reinforcement Theory this represents the removal of positive rewards for undesirable behaviors.

Extrinsic rewards Rewards that are external to the individual and are tangible, such money, benefits, flexible schedules, job responsibilities and duties, promotions, etc.

False Claims Act (FCA) aka Lincoln Law A federal law of the U.S. that permits people who do not have a government affiliation to file legal actions against federal contractors to claim acts of fraud against the government, which is known as whistleblowing claim.

False imprisonment An intentional tort which consists of illegal confinement of one individual against his or her will by another individual in such a manner as to violate the confined individual's right to be free from restraint of movement.

Familiarity heuristic Judging an unknown quality of something simply because we are familiar with that thing.

Federal Trade Commission (FTC)   An independent federal agency whose main goals are to protect consumers and to ensure a strong competitive market by enforcing a variety of consumer protection and antitrust laws.

Federal Trade Commission Act   This empowers the FTC to, among other things, (1) prevent unfair methods of competition, and unfair or deceptive acts or practices in or affecting commerce; (2) seek monetary redress and other relief for conduct injurious to consumers; (3) prescribe trade regulation rules defining with specificity acts or practices that are unfair or deceptive, and establishing requirements designed to prevent such acts or practices; (4) conduct investigations relating to the organization, business, practices, and management of entities engaged in commerce; and (5) make reports and legislative recommendations to Congress.

Fee-for-service   Based on the idea of an insured individual purchasing coverage of a set of benefits, utilizing individual medical services, and paying the health care provider for the services rendered, the provider is paid either by the insurer or out of pocket by the insured, who, in turn, is reimbursed by the insurer.

Fee schedule by CPT (Current Procedural Terminology) code, or procedure code   The most common method for reimbursement of specialty physicians; in general, the more complex and time-consuming the procedure, the higher the rate of reimbursement.

Fidelity   Faithfulness to obligations, duties, or observances, which requires keeping one's word.

Fiduciary duty   A legal duty to act solely in another party's interests.

Finance   Generally includes borrowing and investing funds, and analyzing accounting information to evaluate past decisions and make sound decisions that will affect the future of the organization.

Financial accounting   The process of recording, summarizing, and reporting the myriad of transactions from a business, so as to provide an accurate picture of its financial position and performance.

First In, First Out (FIFO)   An asset-management and valuation method that assumes that assets produced or acquired first are the ones that are use, sold, or disposed of first.

Fishbone diagram   See *Cause-and-effect diagram.*

Five pillars of health outcomes priorities   Improve quality, safety, efficiency, and reduce health disparities; engage patients and families in their health; improve care coordination; improve population and public health; and ensure adequate privacy and security for patient health information.

Five Forces Model   A competitive analysis model that looks at five market or industry forces that, when combined, determine the attractiveness of competing in a particular market.

Fixed costs A cost that does not change with an increase or decrease in the amount of goods or services produced.

Fixed mindset The belief that intelligence and abilities are fixed traits that cannot be cultivated or increased.

Flowchart aka Process Mapping Visual representation of the steps in a process using geometric shapes to denote steps, information flows, and decision points.

FOCUS-PDCA Adaptation of the Deming Cycle (PDCA) which specifies the steps (FOCUS) needed prior to implementation of any process change.

Foreign-educated nurses Nurses who have completed a program of nursing study outside the U.S.

Forming Team organizes, becomes oriented to team goals, and finds out what the tasks are, and who they will be working with.

For-profit, investor-owned health care organizations Organizations owned by investors or others who have an interest in making a profit from the services that are provided.

Fraud The act of intentionally (willfully) misleading or deceiving another person by any means so as to cause him or her legal injury, usually the loss of something valuable or the surrender of a legal right resulting from the action of that person on the misrepresentation.

Frustration–regression principle Motivation theory that postulates that individuals would move in and out of the various levels, depending upon the extent to which their needs were being met.

Full costs Both direct costs and indirect costs.

Functional responsibilities Specific areas within an organization overseen by various leaders, e.g., Chief Nursing Officer, Physician Director, Chief Information Officer.

Functional structure An organizational design which identifies the functions carried out within the HSO in a division of labor, where positons are arranged in a hierarchy, managers are assigned authority and responsibilities by function, and a clear chain of command exists.

Fundamental attribution error Erroneously attributing another's behavior to their internal disposition or factors they can control, rather than external circumstances they cannot control.

Gainsharing or goal sharing program A type of incentive compensation program where all staff share in receiving additional compensation in the form of a bonus as a result of meeting annual performance targets.

Generally accepted accounting principles (GAAP) The common set of accounting principles, standards, and procedures that companies use to compile their financial statements.

Generation A group of individuals born and living contemporaneously who have common knowledge and experiences that affect their thoughts, attitudes, values, beliefs, and behaviors.

Generation X Individuals born between 1965 and 1978.

Generation Y Individuals born between 1979 and 1995.

Generation Z Individuals born after 1995.

Generational signpost An experience, event, or cultural phenomenon specific to one generation.

Geographic mapping Pictorial check sheet in which an event or problem is plotted on a map.

Global leader One who recognizes the impact of globalization on their industry.

Governing bodies Groups of individuals who oversee organizations, such as boards of trustees or directors, who have ultimate legal responsibility for the organization's actions and performance.

Great man theory The idea that leaders are born with innate leadership characteristics.

Group model HMO HMO contracts with a multispecialty group practice to care for its enrollees.

Group purchasing organizations (GPOs) Entities that work with multiple health care organizations to buy in large volumes to decrease costs.

Growth In Alderfer's theory of motivation this focuses on the needs of esteem and self-actualization.

Growth mindset The belief that intelligence and abilities are malleable and can be developed through learning, practice, and hard work.

Halo effect Positive or negative information about others on one dimension colors our judgment about them on a different dimension.

Health analytics Systematic use of data and related business insights developed through applied analytical disciplines (e.g. statistical, contextual, quantitative, predictive, cognitive, other models) to drive fact-based decision making for planning, management, measurement, and learning.

Health care and process effectiveness The result of the interaction of structural and process variables.

Health care financial management The process of providing oversight for the health care organization's day-to-day financial operations as well as planning the organization's long-range financial direction.

Health Care Fraud Prevention and Enforcement Action Team (HEAT) A federal program created to fight against Medicare fraud.

Health care management The profession that provides leadership and direction to organizations that deliver personal health services, and to divisions, departments, units, or services within those organizations.

Health care marketing The kinds of activities a firm uses to satisfy customer needs; the approaches managers pursue to create, communicate, and deliver value in selected markets; and the means of capturing value in return.

Health care marketing management The art and science of selecting target markets and creating, communicating, and delivering value to selected customers in a manner that is both sustainable and differentiated from the competition.

Health care quality Degree to which health services for individuals or populations increase the likelihood of desired health outcomes and are consistent with the current professional knowledge.

Health care recruitment or job fairs Events sponsored by hiring organizations to attract and recruit job candidates.

Health disparity Differences in the incidence, prevalence, mortality, and burden of diseases and other adverse health conditions that exist among specific population groups in the U.S.

Health inequality The difference in health outcomes resulting from care provided to individuals in various racial, ethnic, socioeconomic, and other minority groups.

Health inequity The outcome of health care delivered to individuals in various racial, ethnic, socioeconomic, and other minority groups that results from unequal treatment and is deemed to be unjust.

Health informatics The use of information systems and technology to redesign, improve, and create the ways disciplines such as the practice of medicine, nursing, medical imaging, and public health do their work.

Health information systems (HIS) All computer systems (including hardware, software, operating systems, and end-user devices connecting people to the systems), networks (the electronic connectivity between systems, people, and organizations), and the data those systems create and capture through the use of software.

Health Insurance Portability and Accountability Act (HIPAA) Federal legislation passed with the intent of developing standards for health care data and its exchange and regulations on privacy protections.

Health maintenance organizations (HMOs) Individuals become members of the organization by paying a fixed prepayment amount and receive care from providers and facilities aligned with the HMO.

Health savings account (HSA) The savings portion of the HDHP/SO; HSAs serve as a way to bank pretax dollars with an employer up to a certain amount to be used for medical expenses.

Healthcare Common Procedure Coding System (HCPCS) Often pronounced by its acronym as "hick picks," this is a set of health care procedure codes based on the American Medical Association's Current Procedural Terminology (CPT).

Healthcare Effectiveness Data and Information Set (HEDIS) Metrics utilized to assess the effectiveness of health care organizations.

Healthcare Information and Management Systems Society (HIMSS) A professional organization made up of members committed to leveraging information technology to better serve the health care industry.

Herd immunity aka community immunity or indirect immunity Occurs when sufficient numbers of a population have acquired antibodies to a disease such that no new cases are likely to occur and those who are not immunized are protected by the fact that the community is immunized.

Heuristics Mental or cognitive shortcuts that simplify thinking and can cause bias.

High performing health care organization As defined by researchers, a high performing health care organization is a successful health care organization that has achieved high levels of organizational performance due to its adoption of several human resources best practices.

High-deductible health plan with savings option (HDHP/SO) A form of consumer-driven health plan that offers the enrollee catastrophic coverage for a relatively low premium that is coupled with a high deductible.

HITECH Health Information Technology for Economic and Clinical Health Act is a subsection of the American Recovery and Reinvestment Act (ARRA) that funneled billions of dollars into the development of HIS and incentivized providers to adopt meaningful use information systems.

Home health agencies (HHA) Organizations that provide part-time and intermittent skilled nursing and other therapeutic services on a visiting basis to persons in their homes.

Home health aides Individuals who assist patients in their homes.

Home health resource groups (HHRGS) A case-mix classification in which patient characteristics and health status information are obtained from an OASIS assessment in conjunction with projected therapy use during a 60-day episode and used to determine Medicare reimbursement.

Human error An inadvertent slip, lapse, or mistake.

Human resources management Management practices to ensure that an adequate number of qualified and motivated personnel are available to staff the business units operated by the HSO.

Human trafficking The recruitment, transportation, transfer, harboring, or receipt of persons by means of the threat or use of force or other forms of coercion, abduction, fraud, deception, abuse of power or a position of vulnerability, or of the giving or receiving of payments or benefits to achieve the consent of a person having control over another person, for the purpose of exploitation in the form of prostitution, other forms of sexual exploitation, forced labor or services, slavery or practices similar to slavery, servitude, or the removal of organs.

Hygienes A part of Herzberg's Two-Factor Theory of motivation that is characterized as lower-level motivators, such as supervision or working conditions.

Immunization Stimulation of the body with vaccines or a mild case of a disease to create antibodies that fight the infection.

Implementation of marketing strategy Putting the strategy into practice and determining the optimal marketing mix.

Implicit Unconscious thoughts and ideas that are hidden from our awareness.

Implicit bias Subtle and unconscious prejudice towards others, hidden from the actor's direct awareness.

Implicit theories Unconscious preconceptions about how people behave and how the world works.

Implied consent Consent which is not expressly granted by a person, but rather inferred from a person's actions and the facts and circumstances of a particular situation.

Implied contract An agreement created by actions of the parties involved, but it is not written or spoken.

Incentive Something that serves to motivate.

Incentive compensation Monetary rewards tied to initiatives to improve organizational performance, by motivating staff to achieve higher levels of performance that benefit the overall HSO.

Indemnity insurance Insurance products that are based on the fee-for-service model, whereby insured individuals utilize health care services, pay for those services and seek reimbursement from the insurer.

Independent auditor A certified public accountant who examines the financial records and business transactions of a company that he/she is not affiliated with and is used to avoid conflicts of interest and to ensure the integrity of the auditing process.

Independent practice association or IPA model HMO contracts with an association of physicians practicing independently in their own offices.

Indirect costs Costs, such as depreciation or administrative expenses, that are more difficult to assign to a specific product, patient, or service.

Infliction of mental distress Occurs when one intentionally or recklessly causes severe emotional damage to another through extreme and outrageous conduct.

In-group bias Making positive judgments about others who belong to the same social group we belong to.

Innovations in technology Represents the threat of substitute products, as new technologies often replace standard operations and services.

Integrity agreement A written commitment to follow ethical behavior.

Intellectual property laws Laws that constrain the use of other people's copyrighted materials, patents, trademarks, and proprietary secrets, such as the secret ingredients in a recipe.

Intentional tort A category of torts that describes a civil wrong resulting from an intentional (deliberate) act on the part of the tortfeasor.

Internal auditor An employee of a company charged with providing independent and objective evaluations of the company's financial and operational business activities, including its corporate governance.

Internal domain Areas of focus that managers need to address on a daily basis, such as ensuring the appropriate number and types of staff, financial performance, and quality of care.

International Classification of Diseases (ICD) The standard diagnostic tool for epidemiology, health management, and clinical purposes.

International medical graduates (IMGs) Physicians who have attended medical school outside the U.S.

Interoperability The ability of different information technology systems and software applications to communicate, exchange data, and use the information that has been exchanged.

Interpersonal skills Managerial skills that enable a manager to communicate with and work well with others, including peers, supervisors, or subordinates.

Interpretative justice aka judicial authority An academic approach to defining the justice system so that legal standards can be better understood—for example, defining what the U.S. Constitution means and how it applies to specific cases.

Interpretive schema (frames) Mental representations that guide our interpretation of social information by focusing our attention and organizing our understanding.

Intimidating and disruptive behaviors Overt actions such as verbal outbursts and physical threats as well as passive activities such as refusing to perform assigned tasks or quietly exhibiting uncooperative attitudes during routine activities.

Intrinsic or endogenous thought process theories Theories that focus on internal thought processes and perceptions about motivation.

Intrinsic rewards Rewards that are internal to the individual and less tangible.

Invasion of privacy A violation of the right to privacy implicit in the U.S. Constitution, including violation of confidentiality of patient records.

Inventory management aka supply chain management The overseeing and controlling of the ordering, storage, and use of components that a company will use in the production of the items it will sell, as well as the overseeing and controlling of quantities of finished products for sale.

Ishikawa diagram See *Cause-and-effect diagram.*

Job analysis A human resources task that involves identifying unique responsibilities, duties, and activities specific to every position.

Job burnout A prolonged response to chronic emotional and interpersonal stressors on the job.

Job pricing Compensation based on the consideration of a number of factors, including the specialized knowledge and skills associated with the position, the experience required for the position, the relative availability of skilled individuals to fill the position, and average wages that are specific to the local labor market.

Job satisfaction A pleasurable or positive emotional state resulting from the appraisal of one's job or job experiences.

Just culture A problem solving approach that puts the emphasis on what went wrong, not who caused the problem.

Just In Time (JIT) Inventory method An inventory strategy companies employ to increase efficiency and decrease waste by receiving goods only as they are needed in the production process, thereby reducing inventory costs.

Justice Tied to philosophy and implies fairness, this is the process or result of using laws to fairly judge and punish crimes and criminals.

Labor relations A general term that addresses the relationships between staff (labor) and management.

Last In, First Out (LIFO) An asset-management and valuation method that assumes that assets produced or acquired last are the ones that are used, sold, or disposed of first.

Law A binding custom or practice of a community; a rule of conduct or action prescribed or formally recognized as binding or enforced by a controlling authority that govern the relationships between private individuals and organizations and between both of these parties and government.

Leader A person who takes an external focus and spends the majority of time communicating and aligning with outside groups that can benefit their organizations (partners, community, vendors) or influence them (government, public agencies, media).

Leader development Working one on one with a coach or manager to develop an individual.

Leader–Member Exchange Theory Theory that leaders could be more effective if they developed better relationships with their subordinates through high-quality exchanges.

Leadership development Educational interventions and skill building activities designed to improve the leadership capabilities of managers and other individuals.

Leadership protocols Key ways in which a person in a leadership role should act, including: professionalism; reciprocal trust and respect; and demonstrating confidence, optimism, and passion, among others.

Lean Quality improvement system based on the Toyota Production System characterized by its rigorous definition of value and its relentless pursuit of the elimination of non-value added activities (waste) in a process.

Legislature A deliberative body of persons, usually elective, who are empowered to make, change, or repeal the laws of a country or state; the branch of government having the power to make laws, as distinguished from the executive and judicial branches of government.

Licensed Practical Nurses (LPNs) or Licensed Vocational Nurses (LVNs) Individuals trained to perform nursing functions such as checking vital signs, observing patients, and assisting patients with activities of daily living (ADLs), such as bathing, dressing, feeding and toileting.

Licensure Granted by the state, required for physicians, nurses, and other healthcare professionals, licensure establishes the minimum qualifications for a health care professional to be able to practice within a state.

Lifetime limit The maximum amount that the policy will pay out over the lifetime of the insured individual.

Lincoln Law See *False Claims Act (FCA).*

Line manager A manager who has supervisory authority of staff who directly report to the manager.

Linguistic competency The ability to effectively communicate and convey information in an easily understood manner to a diverse audience, including people of limited or no English proficiency, those who are illiterate or disabled, and those who are deaf or hard of hearing.

Liquidity The degree to which an asset or security can be bought or sold in the market without affecting the asset's price and converted to cash quickly.

Locke's Goal-Setting Theory Motivation theory that hypothesizes that individuals are motivated to take action by establishing and achieving goals.

Long-term care insurance Coverage under these policies typically includes various types of assistance for in-home care, assisted living, skilled nursing home care, and other specialized care, such as in an Alzheimer's unit.

Maintenance of certification (MOC) Requirement by the American Board of Medical Specialties that a board certified physician re-certify every 10 years to ensure the physician remains up-to-date in his or her field.

Majority-minority nation A situation where minorities comprise the majority of the population.

Maleficence An act of harm.

Malfeasance Performing an unlawful act.

Malpractice A professional's improper or immoral conduct in the performance of duties, done either intentionally or through carelessness or ignorance.

Managed care plans Health plans that seek to manage cost, quality, and access to health services through control mechanisms on both patients and providers.

Management The process, comprised of social and technical functions and activities, occurring within organizations for the purpose of accomplishing predetermined objectives through human and other resources.

Management innovation Changes to management practices and routines that determine how the work of management gets conducted on a daily basis.

Management of interpersonal relationships Part of Donabedian's definition of quality focusing on the coproduction of care by both providers and patients.

Manager A person who takes an internal focus, maintains current operations, and aligns the organization's functions with strategic objectives.

Managerial accounting The process of identifying, measuring, analyzing, interpreting, and communicating information for the pursuit of an organization's goals.

Managerial ethics Involves business practices and doing things for the right reasons.

Market A diverse group of organizations or individuals who have disparate needs for products and services.

Market assessment An assessment of the organization's operating market(s) to determine (future) implications for the organization.

Market segmentation The process of dividing the total market into groups or segments that have relatively similar needs for products and services.

Marketing The activity, set of institutions, and processes for creating, communicating, delivering, and exchanging offerings that have value for customers, clients, partners, and society at large.

Marketing concept A plan to create, communicate, and deliver customer value to selected target markets more effectively than one's competition to achieve one's goals and objectives.

Marketing plan A written document that serves to guide marketing initiatives across the organization.

Maslow's Hierarchy of Needs A motivation theory that defines a progression from the lowest, subsistence-level needs to the highest level of self-awareness and actualization.

Master leadership A systems-thinking leader who balances being a motivator, vision-setter, analyzer, and task-master.

Matrix model An organization design which arranges staff in a team-based structure, where functional staff from several functions are assigned to program or service managers.

Maximum out-of-pocket expenditure This is an amount where the insured individual's cost sharing is capped.

McClelland's Acquired Needs Theory A motivation theory that postulates that needs are acquired throughout life and thus are learned or developed as a result of one's life experiences.

McGregor's Theory X A motivation theory where managers view employees as unmotivated and disliking work and focus on controlling and directing employees and providing safety.

McGregor's Theory Y A motivation theory in which managers view employees as motivated and focus on assisting them in achieving higher levels.

Meaningful use Rests on the five pillars of health outcomes priorities and the timeframes to produce them. The federal government has incentivized health care providers with payments to achieve faster results.

Measles A highly contagious virus that and can be transmitted via aerosolization, i.e., breathing the droplets of the virus in the same air as someone who has measles, and that can live in a room for up to two hours after an infected person has coughed or sneezed.

Measurement Translation of observable events into quantitative terms.

Measurement reliability If a measure is taken at several points over time or by various people, the measure will generally be consistent, not vary too much.

Medicaid A federal program that provides health care coverage to the medically indigent (those below certain poverty-level determinations) and is jointly funded by state and federal governments.

Medicaid Fraud Control Units (MFCUs) Units that investigate and prosecute Medicaid fraud as well as patient abuse and neglect in health care facilities.

Medical coder A person who assigns numeric codes to represent diagnoses and procedures, describe patient treatment, and delineate fees for health services, based on an official classification system (e.g., CPT-4, ICD-9/10, HCPC).

Medical home, aka, the patient-centered medical home (PCMH) A model that focuses on connecting patients to primary care, linking them to all types of services, and developing a system that encourages and assures quality of care.

Medical screening exam (MSE) An MSE is the initial exam received in the ED to determine if a patient's need is emergent or nonemergent, is done before any financial information is requested from the patient (such as insurance) and is intended to prevent patient dumping and refusal to treat patients without insurance.

Medical tourism Term that relates to patients traveling to seek and receive medical care.

Medicare A federal program providing access to health care for the elderly over 65 years of age, for permanently disabled younger adults, and for those suffering from end-stage renal disease (ESRD), as well as end-of-life "palliative" care for terminally ill enrollees in their last six months of life.

Medicare Access and CHIP Reauthorization Act of 2015 (MACRA) aka Medicare "Doc Fix" Federal legislation that changed the formula for reimbursing physicians and prevented reductions in physician payments, reauthorized the Children's Health Insurance Program, authorized spending cuts to Medicare for supplemental Medigap plans, and changed premium payments for enrollees.

Medicare and Medicaid Anti-Kickback Act See *Anti-Kickback Act*.

Medicare Audit Improvement Act of 2015 This amendment to the Social Security Act to require that any records or documentation of an orthotist or prosthetist who furnished an orthotic, prosthetic, or prosthetic device to an individual shall be considered part of the individual's medical record in determining whether the item is reasonable and necessary.

Medicare Part A—Hospital Insurance (HI) Allows 90 days of inpatient hospital coverage per benefit period (with a 60-day lifetime inpatient hospital reserve), inpatient skilled nursing facility (SNF) coverage of up to 100 days per episode (with a 90-day lifetime SNF reserve), currently prequalified home health care services, and hospice care for the terminally ill.

Medicare Part B—Supplemental Medical Insurance (SMI) Provides coverage for visits to physicians, outpatient treatments, and preventive services, including flu and hepatitis B vaccines, mammography, and Pap smears.

Medicare Part C—Medicare Advantage Plans (MAs) Allows beneficiaries to enroll in a variety of capitated health insurance plans, which are required to provide the same types of services covered under traditional Medicare plans and may offer the option of additional benefits, such as prescription drugs.

Medicare Part D—The Prescription Drug Benefit Drug coverage available through prescription drug plans (PDPs), Medicare Advantage drug plans (MADPs), or other Medicare-approved prescription plans.

Medicare Prescription Drug, Improvement, and Modernization Act of 2003 Federal legislation that made major changes to Medicare, in particular adding the prescription drug benefit under Part D of Medicare.

MediGap policies Insurance policies that provide supplemental coverage of certain benefits that are excluded from other types of policies (e.g., prescription drugs).

Mental models Mental representations of reality that define what we expect or perceive in a situation, and how we interpret it.

Mental representation Structures or templates that organize our information and experience and underlie our knowledge, beliefs, and assumptions.

Metrics The means used to record observable (measurable) events.

mHealth Use of mobile technologies for the purposes of health care, public health, and health-related activities at the individual level.

Midlevel practitioners Physician assistants (PAs) and advanced practice nurses (APNs) who have advanced training and work midway between the level of an RN and an MD.

Mind-sets Implicit assumptions about personal abilities and characteristics.

Misfeasance Performing the correct action incorrectly and causing injury.

Mission The fundamental purpose, or what the organization seeks to achieve.

Mission statement An organization's enduring statement of purpose.

Misuse The right service is provided badly and an avoidable complication reduces the benefit the patient receives.

Monopoly A competitive market where one provider dominates the provision of a particular service.

Moral hazard This concept refers to the idea that existence of insurance coverage provides an incentive for insured individuals to secure and use coverage.

Motion The wasted movement of patients and resources in Lean.

Motivation The act or process of motivating.

Motivators In Herzberg's Two-Factor Theory of motivation these are higher-level factors that impact aspects of work, such as achievement.

Motive A need or desire that causes a person to act.

Myers-Briggs Type Indicator (MBTI) A tool that assesses four domains and four subsets within those domains on a four-by-four grid, assessing whether a person is an Introvert-Extrovert, Sensing-Intuitive, Perceiving-Judging, and Thinking-Feeling.

National Labor Relations Board (NLRB) The federal body that has the authority to oversee and certify the results of union elections, as well as intervene if needed.

National Practitioner Data Bank (NPDB) aka "the Data Bank" The national entity that tracks all disciplinary actions and law suits against physicians.

Need for achievement In McClelland's Acquired Needs Theory of motivation this emphasizes the desires for success, for mastering tasks, and for attaining goals.

Need for affiliation In McClelland's Acquired Needs Theory of motivation this focuses on the desire for relationships and associations with others.

Need for power In McClelland's Acquired Needs Theory of motivation this relates to the desires for responsibility for, control of, and authority over others.

Negative reinforcement See *Avoidance learning.*

Negligence The unintentional commission or omission of an act that a reasonably prudent person would or would not do under the same circumstances.

Network leader A leader who connects people across disciplines, organizational departments, and regions.

Network model HMO HMO contracts with several groups of physicians, individual physicians, or multispecialty medical clinics (physicians and hospitals) to provide a full range of medical services.

Networks Include intranets, which are internal to an organization, or extranets, which are external and allow users to share information. Networks also can include local area networks (LANs), wireless LANs (WLANs), wide area networks (WANs), wireless WANs (WWANs), and storage area networks (SANs).

Niche market An example of a concentration strategy approach that targets a single market in order to specialize with the objective of gaining a large share of the market.

Non-direct care settings Organizations that support the care of individuals through products and services made available to direct care settings.

Nonfeasance The failure to act where there is a duty that a reasonably prudent person would have fulfilled, willfully or in neglect.

Nonmaleficence Do no harm or at least don't make it worse.

Non-rational thinking Thinking without engaging the brain in active, conscious deliberation.

Norming When the team expectations and roles become codified, either formally or informally, and peace breaks out.

Not-covered care See *Uncompensated care.*

Not-for-profit organizations An organization that does not earn profits for its owners and are granted tax-exempt status.

Notice of privacy practice (NOPP) Mandated informed consent which tells the patient how their PHI is used.

Nurse practitioners (NPs) RNs who are prepared for advanced practice in a NP MSN, a post-master's certificate, or a doctoral program.

Obamacare A commonly used name for the Patient Protection and Affordable Care Act or the Affordable Care Act (ACA), which was enacted during President Obama's first term in office.

Offer of employment A written statement offering a candidate employment in a specific position that specifies the position start date, compensation and benefits, line of reporting, and other key information related to the position.

Office of Inspector General (OIG) Federal office that seeks to improve the efficiency and effectiveness of the Department of Commerce's programs and operations, and to detect and deter waste, fraud, and abuse.

Office of the National Coordinator for Health Information Technology (ONC) The principal federal entity charged with coordination of nationwide efforts to implement and use the most advanced health information technology and the electronic exchange of health information.

Oligopoly A competitive market where multiple providers dominate the provision of a particular service.

Open Payments, aka, the Sunshine Act Created as part of the Affordable Care Act, this requires medical device manufacturers and group purchasing organizations (GPOs) to report any payments and "transfers of value" to physicians or teaching hospitals, as well as any ownership of investment interest physicians or immediate family members have in a company.

Open-panel HMO Physicians practice within and outside the HMO.

Operating budget A detailed projection of all estimated income and expenses based on forecasted sales revenue during a given period (usually one year).

Operation Restore Trust (ORT) A program with partnerships within the federal government that fosters cooperation with states and ways of targeting, investigating, preventing, and stopping fraud in the Medicare and Medicaid programs.

Operational innovation Changes to the organization's business processes and service delivery, including such processes as customer service, procurement of supplies and supply chain changes, care coordination across staff and functions, and development and use of clinical procedures and practices.

Operational leader A leader who has functional oversight responsibilities.

Opportunity costs Proceeds lost by rejecting alternatives.

Organizational assessment An analysis of an organization's internal strengths and weaknesses in relation to market trends.

Organizational behavior The study of how people act in organizations.

Organizational culture The character, personality, and experience of organizational life, i.e., what the organization really "is," prescribes the way things are done, and is manifested in staff attitudes and behaviors.

Organizational schema A common viewpoint shared by organization members that serves as a form of organizational thinking.

Organizing Management function that addresses the internal design of the organization or a specific division, unit, or service for which a manager is responsible, and includes designating reporting relationships and intentional patterns of interaction.

Orientation program A formal program coordinated by the human resources staff, which includes the participation of senior managers, that assists new employees with information about the HSO and helps the transition of the new employee.

Ouchi's Theory Z Motivation theory that proposes that employees who are involved in and committed to the organization will be motivated to increase productivity.

Outcomes element of quality Health status of patients resulting from the application of structural and process elements of quality.

Out-of-pocket payments (OOP) Payments by individuals who buy individual insurance policies, pay for services themselves, and/or pay for part of those services through copayments and/or deductibles.

Overconfidence bias Overestimating the accuracy of one's own judgments.

Overprocessing Results when the product provided to the customer is complex or confusing in Lean.

Overproduction Excess, early, or faster creation of products or services than is needed in Lean.

Overuse Providing a health service when its risk outweighs its benefits.

Pace setting leadership style When a leader sets high performance standards for his or her followers.

Pareto chart Frequency chart used to identify the frequency of occurrence of process problems.

Pareto principle The economic concept that important quality problems that are attributable to a small number of factors (e.g., the 80/20 rule, that 80% of quality problems result from 20% of the possible factors).

Participative leadership style Where the leader invites input from employees and gives them a voice for decision making.

Path–Goal Theory of Leadership Theory that places attention on the leader's style and the work situation (subordinate characteristics and work task structure), but also recognizes the importance of setting goals for employees and removal of obstacles in order to provide the support necessary for them to achieve those goals.

Patient advocate Those who work with patients when they get care from the health system, helping them through the complicated processes.

Patient mix The distribution of demographic variables in a patient population, often represented by the percentage of a given race, age, sex, or ethnic derivation, or the distribution of indications by type of admission in a patient population.

Patient Protection and Affordable Care Act, the Affordable Care Act, or ACA Legislation that was intended to expand access to care by providing increased health insurance coverage and bringing the uninsured into coverage, as well as reducing costs, and improving quality.

Patient self-determination A law that requires health care organizations to inform patients of their rights as they pertain to their ability to determine their own health care.

Patient-centered care model Emphasizes caring for patients as well as 360-degree feedback for caregivers for continuous quality improvement.

Patient-centric model of care A health care delivery model where the patient is the central focus of customer service, access, and quality.

Patient–family centeredness A partnership formed in which providers empower patients and their family members to become fully engaged in the patient's care.

People analytics The use of people-related data to optimize business outcomes (and solve business problems) at the individual, team, or organizational levels.

Per diagnosis A payment method in which a set dollar amount is paid for each diagnosis.

Per diem A method in which a defined dollar amount per day for care is provided.

Perception The automatic cognitive process of acquiring information.

Perception, selective The automatic cognitive process of focusing on a subset of available informational cues.

Performance appraisal A method for assessing the job performance of an employee, which is used to evaluate how well an employee performs and to identify ways to strengthen the employee's performance in the future.

Performing When the team gets on with the work at hand and cooperates with open dialogue and collaboration to achieve team goals.

Person schema Mental representations of a certain person's traits and actions.

Pertussis A highly contagious respiratory disease caused by the bacterium *Bordetella pertussis* that can be transmitted via aerosolization, i.e., breathing the droplets of the virus in the same air as someone who has pertussis.

Physician assistants (PA) Mid-level practitioners who must graduate from a master's program, are prepared to work in teams with physicians, and can prescribe medications.

Physician credentialing The process by which a physician is vetted by a health care organization prior to the physician being able to practice within that organization.

Physicians Graduates of osteopathic or allopathic medical schools.

Physiological needs One of the five levels in Maslow's hierarchy, including food, water, sexual drive, and other subsistence-related needs.

Place One of the 4 Ps of marketing that focuses on the offering delivery route.

Plan-Do-Check-Act (PDCA) A cycle model for improving production processes.

Planning Management function that requires a manager to set a direction and determine what needs to be done to realize that direction by establishing a strategy.

Point-of-service plans (POS) These plans provide some flexibility to the HMO model and are sometimes referred to as open-ended plans.

Polio virus A highly infectious disease that spreads through contact with the stool of an infected person and droplets from a sneeze or cough.

Population health The study of health outcomes for a certain group of people for the purpose of looking for patterns and possible interventions.

Position descriptions (job descriptions) Statements that define the required knowledge, skills, responsibilities, training, experience, line of reporting, and any special certification or licensure for a specific position or job.

Positioning The process whereby an organization determines which portion of the larger market to serve and with whom it will compete.

Positive reinforcement In Skinner's Reinforcement Theory this relates to taking action that rewards positive behaviors.

Power of consumers and payers Represents the influence of end-users and funding organizations on the access, quality and delivery of health care.

Power of payers The influence individuals and collective health care insurers have on health care providers and consumers.

Power of the health care workforce An analysis of the availability of all subsets of health care providers who are critical to an organization's success.

Precedent The term refers to legal cases (at common law) that were decided by judges.

Predictive analytics (human resources analytics) The capture and use of a variety of employee and organizational data that identifies employee needs, factors that affect employee satisfaction, factors related to optimal staffing, and factors related to staff turnover to help increase satisfaction and engagement and reduce turnover.

Preemption A doctrine based on the Supremacy Clause of the U.S. Constitution that holds that certain matters are of such a national, as opposed to local, character that federal laws preempt or take precedence over state laws.

Pre-existing conditions Medical conditions that make a person a risk to an insurer, as the pre-existing condition may result in high expenditures.

Preferred provider organization (PPO) Plans that reflect a combination of indemnity insurance and managed care options, where insured individuals purchase coverage on a fee-for-service basis, with deductibles, copays, and coinsurances to be met.

Prejudice Holding certain emotional attitudes (positive or negative) toward members of a social group.

Prepayment An insured individual pays a fixed, prespecified amount in exchange for services.

Price One of the 4 Ps of marketing that involves the value placed on the product. Price involves opportunity costs, what consumers or third-party payers give up in order to acquire medical goods or services.

Priority populations Groups needing to be addressed ahead of others in terms of research, policy, support, and funding, which include: women, children, racial and ethnic minorities, the elderly, low-income, inner-city, rural, and those with special health care needs.

Private health insurance Payments made by individuals and/or their employers for health insurance premiums, which in turn cover the costs of payments made by various health plans.

Private recruitment or "headhunter" firms Employment agencies that engage in general staff recruiting or firms that specialize in health services organization staffing by recruiting nurses, technicians, financial analysts, or office personnel for a fee.

Probationary period Usually a 90-day period post-employment within which an employee may be evaluated for satisfactory performance and may be terminated if it is determined the employee is not a good fit with the organization.

Problem solving Taking time to answer the "what if" scenarios of each alternative.

Procedure codes Numbers or alphanumeric codes used to identify specific health interventions taken by medical professionals.

Process elements of quality Quality of the actual delivery of care as well as its management (treatments, feeding, keeping patients safe from falls and errors).

Process mapping See *Flowchart*.

Process variation The range of values that a quality metric can take as a result of different causes within the process.

Product One of the 4 Ps of marketing that focuses on goods, services, or ideas.

Product costs A cost incurred by a business when manufacturing a good or producing a service.

Promotion One of the 4 Ps of marketing that focuses on activities used to communicate to the target market.

Prospective reimbursement A method of payment to an agency for health care services to be delivered that is based on predictions of what the agency's costs will be for the coming year.

Protected health information (PHI) Information, including demographic data, that relates to the individual's past, present, or future physical or mental health or condition; the provision of health care to the individual; or the past, present, or future payment for the provision of health care to the individual; and that identifies the individual or for which there is a reasonable basis to believe it can be used to identify the individual.

Public health insurance Funding for health care coverage from federal, state, and local government programs.

Published prices A rate of charges a business holds for a service rendered, which is public information and therefore largely indisputable.

Punishment In Skinner's Reinforcement Theory this includes actions designed to reduce undesirable behaviors by creating negative consequences for the individual.

Quantified-self movement Those who use various electronic health IT gadgets and devices to monitor their own health status and link them to other consumer information.

Qui tam **provisions** A type of civil lawsuit that whistleblowers or relators bring under the False Claims Act and rewards them if the case recovers funds for the government.

Ratio method of determining needs Estimating need for staff based on patient volumes or amount of work to be accomplished in non-clinical areas, such as accounting or medical records.

RBRVS See *Resource-based relative value system.*

Reckless behavior A behavioral choice to consciously disregard a substantial and unjustifiable risk.

Recognition phase of decision making Involves recognizing and identifying the decision or problem and its causes, setting goals, and generating options.

Recovery audit contractors (RAC) Workers who protect Medicare by identifying improper payments and referring potential fraud to the Centers for Medicare & Medicaid Services (CMS).

Registered nurse (RN) A person who has completed a program of nursing and successfully passed the National Council Licensure Examination (NCLEX), the nursing licensure examination.

Regulatory environment Represents the collective effects of legislative issues on local, state, and federal levels on an organization's strategy.

Reimbursement modified on the basis of performance The provider is reimbursed based on quality measures, patient satisfaction measures, and so on.

Relatedness In Alderfer's theory of motivation this pertains to the need to belong.

Reliability Consistency of a measure taken at multiple points.

Research Additional study to find out if others have created a solution to the problem or if there are factors that have been overlooked by the team.

Resilient leader A leader who perseveres through using inner strength–building practices.

Resource utilization groups (RUGS) Any number of groups into which a nursing home resident is categorized, based on functional status and anticipated use of services and resources for reimbursement purposes.

Resource-based relative value system (RBRVS) Payments determined by the cost of resources needed to provide each service, including physician work, practice expenses, and professional liability insurance.

Respiratory therapists (RTs) Allied health professionals who evaluate, treat, and care for patients with respiratory disorders, such as asthma, emphysema, pneumonia, and heart disease.

Respondeat superior A legal doctrine which states that, in many circumstances, an employer is responsible for the actions of employees performed within the course of their employment, making the organization liable for harm caused by employees or agents.

Retrospective reimbursement The amount of reimbursement is determined after the delivery of services, providing little financial risk to providers in most cases.

Revenue budget The amount of money allocated to the maintenance and growth of a business.

Revenues The amount of money that a company actually receives during a specific period, including discounts and deductions.

Right to Try Laws Legislation that enables patients to have an opportunity to try experimental drugs that would otherwise not be available to them.

Risk The money that might be lost due to insuring people who utilize health care services.

Role schema Mental representations of appropriate behaviors and expectations for a social category.

Rounding Making visits to various parts of an organization to ensure the leader is visible, approachable, and present.

Safe harbor Regulations that describe various payment and business practices that, although they potentially implicate the federal anti-kickback statute, are not treated as offenses under the statute.

Safety needs In Maslow's hierarchy of needs theory this includes shelter, a safe home environment, employment, a healthy and safe work environment, access to health care, money, and other basic necessities.

Sarbanes-Oxley Act of 2002 Federal legislation that mandates transparency and full disclosure to prevent fraud, conflicts of interest, and other inappropriate actions in organizations.

Satisfaction progression The movement from one level to the next in Maslow's hierarchy of needs theory.

Schema Mental representations of general knowledge and expectations about a concept.

Scientific Management Theory A motivation theory that focuses on studying job processes, determining the most efficient means of performing them, and in turn rewarding employees for continually being more productive and working harder.

Second victim programs Interventions designed to work with clinicians who commit errors, acknowledging the significant emotional impact that errors can have on the clinicians involved.

Selective perception When what we see is guided by our expectations, beliefs, existing knowledge, or striking cues in the situation itself.

Self-actualization needs In Maslow's hierarchy theory of motivation this refers to the desire for achievement, personal growth and development, and autonomy.

Self-talk The internal dialogue that can be a coach or critic.

Semi-variable costs A cost composed of a mixture of fixed and variable components, where costs are fixed for a set level of production or consumption and become variable after the level is exceeded.

Sentinel event An unexpected occurrence involving death or serious physical or psychological injury, or the risk thereof.

Servant leadership A style that focuses on helping others, particularly well-suited to non-profit organizations and charitable missions that seek to meet the community's needs.

Service line management structure An organizational design where a manager heads a specific clinical service line and has supervisory responsibility for all functional staff assigned to the services line, as well as responsibility for resources acquisition, budgets and financial control of all diagnostic and treatment services provided under that service line.

Sherman Antitrust Act Anti-monopoly legislation which attempted to increase economic competitiveness and made it illegal for companies to seek a monopoly on a product or service, or form cartels.

Shewhart cycle See *Deming cycle* and *Plan-Do-Check-Act (PDCA) cycle*.

Shrinkage Inventory loss due to theft.

Similar-to-me bias Favoring those we see as being like us.

Situational leadership The theory that the leader changes or should change his or her behavior in certain situations in order to meet the needs of subordinates.

Six Sigma The quality improvement philosophy and methodology which features the heavy use of data to eliminate variation from a process.

Skinner's Reinforcement Theory Postulates that individuals are motivated when their behaviors are reinforced through positive reinforcement, avoidance learning, punishment, or extinction.

Social awareness Primal empathy (feeling with others, sensing nonverbal emotional signals), attunement (listening with full receptivity, attuning to a person), and empathic accuracy (understanding another person's thoughts, feelings, and intentions).

Social categorization The cognitive process of grouping people into social categories.

Social cognition The study of how people make sense of other people and themselves.

Social determinants Things outside the health care system, such as living or working conditions, geographic isolation, income and socioeconomic status, education, and access to insurance.

Social facility Synchrony (interacting smoothly at the nonverbal level), self-presentation (presenting ourselves effectively), influence (shaping the outcome of social interactions), and concern (caring about others' needs and acting accordingly).

Social loafer, aka, free rider A member of a team who does little to no work, yet obtains credit for the work done by others.

Social marketing The application of commercial marketing principles and techniques, used to influence behavioral change, focus on a specific target audience, promote public health, and benefit society as a whole.

Social Security Act A law that created a system of transfer payments in which younger, working people support older, retired people.

Social Security Act of 1965 Amendments to the Social Security Act of 1935 that established the two largest government-sponsored health insurance programs in the U.S., Medicare and Medicaid.

Socio-emotional intelligence The ability to sense, understand, and effectively respond to others' emotions.

Socio-emotional skills Interpersonal relations, teamwork, communication, empathy, self-awareness, and self-discipline.

Soft skills Thinking and socio-emotional skills, which are central to organizational behavior.

Special-cause variation Variation in processes which is due to easily controllable influences.

Specific identification The actual cost of each item is included in valuing inventory.

Specific privileges Those activities above and beyond core privileges for which a physician must document and demonstrate additional competency in order to be permitted to perform them within a health care organization.

Spiritual leadership A focus that encourages employees to find meaning in their work and embraces strategies to create a shared vision.

Staff manager A manager who does not have any direct reports.

Staff model HMO Groups of physicians are either salaried employees of the HMO or salaried employees of a professional group practice contracting exclusively with the HMO.

Staffing Management function that refers to acquiring and retaining human resources.

Stalking A course of conduct directed at a specific person that would cause a reasonable person to feel fear.

Standard of care The only degree of prudence and caution required of an individual who is under a duty of care.

Standards of behavior The codes of conduct that define expectations of behaviors of all staff members of an HSO.

Stark Laws, aka Stark I and Stark II These prohibit physician referrals of designated health services for Medicare and Medicaid patients if the physician (or an immediate family member) has a financial relationship with that entity.

State constitution Document that delineates state level laws and provides the basis for state level legal decisions.

Statistical process control (SPC) Method by which process variation (due to both common- and special-cause) is measured, tracked, and controlled in an effort to improve the quality of the process.

Statistics budget Statistical budgets determine financial amounts based on one expected activity level.

Statutes A written law passed by a legislative body.

Stereotype Generalized cognitive beliefs about expected attributes of individuals who belong to a group.

Stock-outs Not having enough of a product tha may result in unnecessary deaths or poor outcomes.

Storming Intragroup conflict including attempts at dominance, passive-aggressive behaviors, withholding of information, and other forms of resistance to team tasks and goals.

Strategic direction The goal that the organization desires to accomplish within the planning time frame.

Strategic leader A leader who defines purpose and vision and aligns people, processes, and values.

Strategic planning The process of identifying a desired future state for an organization and a means to achieve it.

Strategic planning process The process consists mainly of two interrelated activities: the development of the strategic plan and execution of the organization's strategy.

Strategy A carefully designed plan to accomplish the desired outcomes.

Strategy execution Ongoing implementation and monitoring of the strategic plan.

Structural elements of quality Quality of personnel and facilities.

Structure, process, outcomes of quality A model depicting three elements of quality.

Structured interviews A script with clearly defined questions to assess job candidates.

Style approach to leadership Task-oriented versus relationship-oriented leaders, with those leaders who attend to both being the best.

Succession planning Organizational actions taken to ensure that staff can move up in management roles within the organization, in order to replace those managers who retire or move to other opportunities in other organizations.

Sunk costs Expenses that have already been incurred and cannot be influenced further.

SWOT analysis An analysis of an organization's Strengths, Weaknesses, Opportunities, and Threats.

Tactical plans Plans that answer the who, what, when, where, and how questions of strategy implementation.

Talent management Another term for defining human resources management, based on the perspective that organizations should view their employees as strategic assets ("talent") who can create a competitive advantage.

Tame problems Issues that can be defined, and while not easy, can be solved.

Target market A more narrowly defined group of individuals or organizations with relatively similar wants and needs.

Task force Group convened to address a specific agenda, have a limited term of tenure, and disband when the agenda is completed.

Tax Equity and Fiscal Responsibility Act (TEFRA) of 1982 Legislation that mandated a prospective payment system (PPS) for hospital reimbursement, using Diagnosis-Related Groups (DRGs); provided managed care plans to Medicare beneficiaries; and made Medicare the secondary payer when a beneficiary had other insurance.

Team A group of people working together to achieve a common goal.

TeamSTEPPS A teamwork system designed for health care professionals that is evidence-based and intended to improve communication and teamwork skills among health care professionals.

Technical management Part of Donabedian's definition of quality focusing on the clinical performance of health care providers.

Technical skills Managerial skills that reflect expertise or ability to perform a specific managerial work task, such as developing and maintaining a budget.

Telehealth The remote delivery of health-related information from one site to another via electronic communications to improve a person's health awareness and access to health-related information.

Telemedicine The use of technology to deliver clinical care to outlying and inaccessible areas.

Thinking skills Critical thinking, reasoning, problem-solving, decision making, and flexibility.

Third-party mediation Sometimes teams cannot decide which solution is the best. The team presents the list of alternatives along with pros and cons of each and the boss makes the final decision.

Tort law In common law jurisdictions, a civil wrong that unfairly causes someone else to suffer loss or harm resulting in legal liability for the person who commits the tortious act.

Tortfeasor A person who causes a tortious act.

Torts Under civil law, a category of "wrongful acts" committed against another person without a preexisting contract, for which courts seek to determine and apply remedies.

Total Quality Management See *Continuous Quality Improvement*.

Toyota Production System (TPS) See *Lean*.

Traditionalist Individuals born before 1945.

Transformational leader A person who could significantly change an organization through its people by raising their consciousness, empowering them, and then providing the nurturing needed as they produce the results desired.

Treasurer An individual charged with the stewardship of the organization's financial assets.

TRICARE The military health program that covers active duty military personnel, retired military personnel, and their family members.

Triple Aim A health care initiative that focuses on enhancing the individual experience of care; improving the health of populations; and minimizing the per capita costs of care for populations.

Truth-telling Implies those involved in health care are to be honest with patients/clients as much as possible.

Turnover The proportion of job exits or quits from a facility in a year.

U.S. Constitution The supreme law of the land that provides the basis for federal legal decisions.

Uncompensated care A measure of total hospital care provided without payment from the patient or an insurer.

Uncontrollable costs Expenditures that cannot be controlled by the manager.

Underserved populations A group with economic, cultural, and/or linguistic barriers to primary medical care services.

Underuse The failure to provide a service whose benefit is greater than its risk.

Underutilization of staff Not using staff time efficiently in Lean.

Vaccines Injections or inhalations that imitate a disease to stimulate the body's immune system to respond as if it were a real infection.

Validity The extent to which the measure used actually measures the concept.

Value stream mapping Used in Toyota Production System/Lean QI efforts to identify waste in a process.

Value-based purchasing Linking payment systems to providing incentives for quality improvements and good outcomes.

Values Principles that the organization believes in and stands for, which shape the organization's purpose, goals, and day-to-day behaviors.

Values statement An organizational statement that should help define the organization's culture—what characteristics it wants employees to convey to customers.

Variable costs Costs that vary depending on a company's production volume; they rise as production increases and fall as production decreases.

Veterans Health Administration (VHA) The organization that manages the nation's largest health care delivery system and provides care to all eligible veterans.

Vision The desired future state for the organization, which reflects what the organization wants to be known and recognized for in the future.

Vision statement An organizational statement that strives to identify a specific future state of the organization, usually an inspiring goal for many years down the road.

Volume forecast The prediction of future market volumes for particular services, usually derived from historic use rates.

Voting Democratic approach to team problem-solving that also bears the weight of potentially taking a team to the incorrect choice.

Vroom's Expectancy Theory Motivation theory that addresses the expectations of individuals and hypothesizes that they are motivated by performance and the expected outcomes of their own behaviors.

Vulnerable populations Those with a disproportionate burden of illness and injury and who experience worse health outcomes.

Weighted average The average cost of inventory items is multiplied by the number of units in inventory.

Wicked problems Issues and concerns that are difficult to define, not easily resolvable, and sometimes never solved due to multiple layers of issues.

Workflow diagram A combination of geographic and process mapping showing the movements of people, materials, documents, or information in a process.

Workforce planning and recruitment A function of human resources management that involves determining needed positions and carrying out tasks to identify, hire, and orient staff.

Working capital A measure of both a company's efficiency and its short-term financial health that is calculated as current assets minus current liabilities.

Workplace violence Violent acts (including physical assaults and threats of assaults) directed toward persons at work or duty.

Worldview How one sees the world.

Note: Page numbers followed by *b, f,* or *t* indicate material in boxes, figures, or tables, respectively.